THE LAW AND PRACTICE IN SPECIAL PROCEEDINGS,

AND IN

SPECIAL CASES,

INCLUDING THE PROVISIONAL REMEDIES OF "ARREST AND BAIL," "ATTACHMENTS OF PROPERTY," AND "CLAIM AND DELIVERY," UNDER THE CODE OF CIVIL PROCEDURE.

WITHIN THE COURTS, ETC.,

OF THE

STATE OF NEW YORK.

WITH AN

APPENDIX OF FORMS,

IN TWO VOLUMES.

BY

CHARLES CRARY,

COUNSELOR AT LAW.

VOLUME II.

FIFTH EDITION.

ALBANY:
W. C. LITTLE & CO., LAW BOOK PUBLISHERS.
1877.

PREFACE

TO THE FIFTH EDITION.

THE several previous editions of this work have been exhausted some time; and another edition is called for.

Since the second edition was published, in 1866, important amendments have been made by the Legislature to several of the Special Proceedings considered in the work. In addition, the Code of Civil Procedure, recently enacted, has revised the whole law on the subjects of Arrest and Bail, Attachments of Property, and Redemption of Real Estate from Sales on Execution. These statutory revisions, as well as the amendments referred to, are stated in full in their proper places, in the Supplements at the end of the chapters.

In the Supplements, also, may be found a digest of the numerous decisions, made by the Courts of this State, since the second edition was published.

The text of the two editions is substantially the same; the difference in the editions being mainly in the Supplements; in which are noted all the recent decisions and alterations in the practice, including those made by the new Code of Civil Procedure.

NEW YORK, *October* 1, 1877.

TABLE OF CONTENTS.

VOLUME SECOND.

CHAPTER XVIII.

PROCEEDINGS IN RESPECT TO IDIOTS, LUNATICS, AND HABITUAL DRUNKARDS.

CHAPTER XIX.

THE WRITS OF MANDAMUS AND PROHIBITION.

CHAPTER XX.

THE PARTITION OF REAL ESTATE.

CHAPTER XXI.

PROCEEDINGS TO OBTAIN LEAVE TO PROSECUTE AS A POOR PERSON.

CHAPTER XXII.

PROCEEDINGS TO DISCOVER THE DEATH OF PERSONS UPON WHOSE LIVES ANY PARTICULAR ESTATE MAY DEPEND.

CHAPTER XXIII.

PROCEEDINGS BY PERSONS TO CHANGE THEIR NAMES.

CHAPTER XXIV.

PROCEEDINGS TO PROVE WILLS IN A FOREIGN STATE

CHAPTER XXV.

PROCEEDINGS BY ACTION TO RECOVER POSSESSION OF DEMISED PREMISES FOR NON-PAYMENT OF RENT.

CHAPTER XXVI.

QUO WARRANTO AND INFORMATIONS IN THE NATURE OF QUO WARRANTO; AND COMPELLING DELIVERY OF BOOKS AND PAPERS.

CHAPTER XXVII.

PROCEEDINGS TO ACQUIRE TITLE TO REAL ESTATE FOR RAILROAD PURPOSES.

CHAPTER XXVIII.

REDEMPTION OF REAL ESTATE.

CHAPTER XXIX.

SALE OF THE REAL ESTATE OF RELIGIOUS CORPORATIONS.

CHAPTER XXX.

SUMMARY PROCEEDINGS TO RECOVER POSSESSION OF LAND.

THE LAW AND PRACTICE IN SPECIAL PROCEEDINGS, AND IN SPECIAL CASES.

CHAPTER XVIII.

PROCEEDINGS IN RESPECT TO IDIOTS, LUNATICS, AND HABITUAL DRUNKARDS.

SECTION I.

APPOINTMENT OF COMMITTEE, AND PROCEEDINGS THEREUPON.

By the Revised Statutes the care and custody of idiots, lunatics, persons of unsound mind, and persons who are incapable of conducting their own affairs in consequence of habitual drunkenness, and of their real and personal estates, were vested in the chancellor. And he was required, to provide for their safe keeping and maintenance and for the maintenance of their families, and the education of their children, out of their personal estates, and the rents and profits of their real estates respectively; and to see that their estates were not wasted or destroyed. 2 *Rev. Stat.* 52, *sec.* 1. The vice-chancellors also, in their respective circuits, had concurrent jurisdiction with the chancellor in these proceedings, subject to his appellate jurisdiction. *Ib.* 168. But now, the powers of the chancellor are vested by the constitution of 1846, and the judiciary act, in the Supreme Court. And the county courts of the respective counties also have concurrent jurisdiction with the Supreme Court, in respect to the care and custody of the person and estate of a lunatic, or person of unsound mind, or an habitual drunkard, residing within their respective counties; and also in respect to the sale, mortgage, or other disposition of the real property of such person, situated within the county. *Code of Pro.* § 30. The same authority is also given to the Court of Common Pleas of the city and county of New York, where the lunatic, &c., resides in that city, or the property is situated therein. *Laws of* 1854, *p.* 464, *sec.* 6; 1 *Abb.* 114, 115. And the like authority is also given to the Superior Court of the city of Buffalo, where the lunatic resides in that city, or the property is situated therein. *Laws of* 1854, *p.* 224, *secs.* 9 and 11

In respect to the Superior Court of the city of New York, although jurisdiction in these proceedings was conferred upon it, in part, by sec. 21, of chapter 470, of the Laws of 1847 (*p.* 641), and which has not in terms been repealed, yet, it seems, the question of jurisdiction is so doubtful that that court will not entertain jurisdiction to issue a commission in lunacy. 1 *Abb.* 108, 115. (*a*)

In addition to the general power and authority of the courts, already stated, the Supreme Court may appoint a committee for a non-resident lunatic, to enable the committee to obtain the control of property in this State. And the court may issue a commission to inquire as to the lunacy of such person; but it cannot be executed beyond the limits of the State. In such case, the court will direct it to be executed in such county as will be most convenient. 2 *Paige*, 174; 9 *Id.* 416; 2 *Barb. Ch. R.* 305; 2 *Johns. Ch. R.* 124. And where a lunatic, after becoming deranged, left his place of residence in this State, leaving personal property here, and went to some place unknown; it was

(*a*) See this case, where the nature and extent of the power to take the persons and property of lunatics and habitual drunkards into custody, and the statutory provisions on the subject, are considered and reviewed by Hoffman, J., of the Superior Court, special term, of the city of New York.

held that for the purpose of an application to the Court of Chancery (now the Supreme Court), for a commission of lunacy, the lunatic must still be considered as a citizen of this State, where he was domiciled at the time he was deprived of his reason. *Ib*

Overseers of the poor and habitual drunkards.] In respect to habitual drunkards, jurisdiction over their persons and estates was first given to the Court of Chancery, by the laws of 1821 (*chap.* 109, *p.* 99); and in the revision of the laws of 1830, that statute was retained, with some modifications.

The statute directs the overseers of the poor, of any city or town, who shall discover any person resident therein to be an habitual drunkard, having property to the amount of two hundred and fifty dollars, which may be endangered by means of such drunkenness, to make application to the Supreme Court for the exercise of its powers and jurisdiction. 2 *Rev. Stat.* 52, *sec.* 2. The overseers of the poor may also make such application to the Court of Common Pleas (now the county court), of the county where the drunkard resides, whatever amount of property the drunkard may have. And that court, upon the application by the overseers, is vested with the same powers in relation to the person and property of the drunkard, as are conferred on the Supreme Court, and is in all respects to proceed in the like manner, subject to an appeal to the Supreme Court. *Ib. sec.* 3; *Code of Pro.* § 30; 24 *New York*, 386, *overruling* 16 *How.* 567; and see *Laws of* 1854, *p.* 464; *Will. Eq. Jur.* 683.

The Revised Statutes further provide, in reference to the jurisdiction of that court in cases of habitual drunkards, that the application by the overseers of the poor for a commission may be made, in vacation, to the first judge of the county; who is authorized to award the same to one or more proper persons, to inquire into the fact of such alleged habitual drunkenness; and the inquisition taken thereon shall be returned to the next term of the court, who shall confirm or set the same aside. *Id. ibid.*; 2 *Rev. Stat.* 52, *sec.* 4.

If the party proceeded against traverses the inquisition on its return, an issue shall be directed by the court, as in other cases, which shall be tried in the same court; and the verdict thereon shall have the same effect as if rendered upon an issue awarded by the Supreme Court. *Ib.* 53, *sec.* 5.

Appeals from any order, judgment, or decree of any county court, made pursuant to the above provisions, shall be filed and entered within three months after the making of such order, judgment, or decree; and shall be accompanied by a bond, with such sureties as the court shall approve, to the opposite party, in the penalty of one hundred dollars, conditioned for the payment of such costs as shall be awarded against the appellant, in case of the order, judgment, or decree being affirmed. *Ib. sec.* 6; and see *Code of Pro.* § 30; *Laws of* 1854, *p.* 464; 16 *How.* 567, *supra.*

The expenses of the overseers of the poor, in conducting the proceedings, are required to be audited and allowed in the same manner as other expenses of the city or town. 2 *Rev. Stat.* 53, *sec.* 7.

Who are idiots, lunatics, &c.] An idiot is a person who has been without understanding from his nativity, and whom the law, therefore, presumes never likely to attain any. A person is not an idiot if he has any glimmering of reason, so that he can tell his parents, his age, or the like common matters. And so, it is said that a person who has understanding enough to measure a yard of cloth, number twenty correctly, tell the days of the week, &c., is not an idiot in the eye of the law. But a man who is born deaf, dumb, and blind is looked upon by the law as in the same state with an idiot; and he is supposed incapable of any understanding, and as wanting in all those senses which furnish the human mind with ideas. 1 *Bl. Com.* 316, 317; and see *Will. Eq. Jur.* 673.

A lunatic, or non compos mentis, is one who has had understanding, which he has lost by disease, grief, or other accident. And under the general name of non compos mentis, which is the most legal term for all defects of the mind which the law notices, are comprised not only lunatics, but persons under frenzies; or who lose their intellect by disease; and those who are deaf, dumb, and blind, not being born so. 1 *Bl. Com.* 317; 26 *Wend.* 299; *Will. Eq. Jur.* 673.

But a person born deaf and dumb is not necessarily an idiot, or non compos mentis; though such, perhaps, may be the legal presumption until his mental capacity is proved, on an inquiry and examination for that purpose. 4 *Johns. Ch. R.* 441.

Persons of unsound mind, consist of lunatics; those under frenzy or temporary derangement, from disease or other cause; those who become deaf, dumb and blind; and such as the court adjudges incapable of managing their own affairs, by reason of old age, sickness or other cause. 1 *Bl. Com.* 317; 26 *Wend.* 299; 2 *Johns. Ch. R.* 233; 1 *Coll. on Lun.* 4.

It is not every case, however, of mental weakness or imbecility or unsoundness, which will authorize the court to exercise the power of appointing a committee over the person and estate; though it is generally sufficient to justify the interference of the court, that the party is mentally incapable of governing himself, or of managing his affairs. 1 *Barb. S. C. R.* 437; and see 7 *Paige*, 236; 3 *Ed. Ch. R.* 380; 2 *Johns. Ch. R.* 233; *Will. Eq. Jur.* 673 to 677; 26 *Wend.* 302, 309.

In respect to an habitual drunkard, and as to who is to be considered such, within the statute, it was observed by Walworth, Ch. (*In the matter of Tracy*, 1 *Paige*, 582), that "a very erroneous impression appears to have gone abroad on this subject. It is supposed by many that the prosecutor in such cases is bound to prove affirmatively that an habitual drunkard is incapable of managing his affairs. On the contrary, the fact that a person is for any considerable part of his time intoxicated to such a degree as to deprive him of his ordinary reasoning faculties, is prima-facie evidence at least, that he is incapacitated to have the control and management of his property."

Who may apply for a commission.] The application for a commission is usually made by the near relatives of the lunatic, &c. Thus, it may be made by a husband against his wife, or by a father or mother, against a child, and *vice versa;* or by brothers, sisters, uncles, aunts, nephews, nieces, and cousins, against each other. And so, also, an executor under a will, may apply for a commission against a legatee under the same will; and a trustee under a deed, against his *cestui que trust;* and creditors against their debtor. And a commission may also issue upon the petition of the tenant of the party. *Shelf. on Lun.* 93; 1 *Coll.* 126.

And so, the commission may be applied for even by strangers; and that, too, in opposition to the members of the family—where the lunacy seems indisputable. 1 *Russ.* 348; 1 *Moll.* 439. The carriage of the commission, however, will be given to relations, in preference to strangers, if there is no valid objection to it. 1 *Ves. & Bea.* 57.

In respect to an habitual drunkard having property in this State, which may be endangered by reason of his drunkenness, the statute makes it the duty of the overseers of the poor of the town or city in which the drunkard resides, to make an application for the commission. 2 *Rev. Stat.* 52, *secs.* 2, 3. But the application may also be made by the friends of the drunkard, notwithstanding this provision of the statute. See 5 *Paige*, 122.

Where the petition is presented by the wife of the supposed lunatic, it must be in the name of her next friend; who will be answerable for the costs of the application, in case the court shall think proper to impose them upon the petitioner. 2 *Barb. Ch. Pr.* 228.

Application for a commission.] The first step to be taken towards the appointment of a committee of a lunatic, or idiot, or habitual drunkard, is to apply for a commission in the nature of a writ *de lunatico inquirendo.* And the court has no jurisdiction to appoint a committee, or to order a sale of the lunatic's property, before such commission has been issued and returned, 8 *How.* 220; but see the remarks of Harris, J., in 1 *Barb. S. C. R.* 441, *post, p.* 13.

The application is founded upon petition, which should be accompanied by affidavits setting forth the unsound state of the mind of the party, and stating such facts in respect to his conduct or language as may show that he is a proper subject for the protection of the court. And in England, as well as in this country, the courts have been scrupulous about granting a commission, without strong preliminary proofs, amounting at least to a probability of insanity. In *Ex Parte Persse* (1 *Moll.* 219), the Lord Chancellor remarked that "the mere issuing of a commission may produce consequences highly detrimental, and it is not to issue without great circumspection;" and he interposed to give directions personally to physicians to visit the supposed lunatic, and afterwards consulted with them apart. And Mr. Shelford remarks (*Shelf. on Lun. p.* 82), that where the lunacy is not apparent, the affidavits of two physicians will be required, swearing to their opinion of the lunacy, and their reasons for that opinion, before granting a commission. And such has, in general, been the practice of our courts. See per C. L. Allen, J., 8 *How.* 223. For form of petition and affidavit, see *Appendix*, Nos. 393 to 397.

Where the lunatic is a non-resident of the State, the petitioner must also show that he is the owner of property situated in this State; and it is not sufficient to state that fact in the affidavits annexed to the petition. 2 *Barb. Ch. R.* 305. A committee of a lunatic, appointed under the laws of another State, where the lunatic resides, will not be recognized by our courts, on an application by the committee for property belonging to the lunatic in this State. 26 *How.* 402.

The application for a commission is ex parte, and should be made to the court at special term, see 17 *Barb.* 348; though in respect to the county court, the application may be made at any term, or even out of term, that court being always open for such business. *Code of Pro.* § 31. If the petition and accompanying affidavits make out a prima-facie case of lunacy, idiocy, drunkenness, &c., the court will, in general, grant the order; though it is not bound to do so. 1 *Ves. & Bea.* 58; 19 *Ves.* 286. For form of order, see *Appendix*, No. 398.

The commission.] Upon the order for a commission being granted, and entered with the clerk of the court, the commission will issue. It is usually prepared by the attorney for the petitioner, and is then endorsed and sealed by the clerk.

The commission is generally directed to three persons, to be appointed by the court; though the court may appoint a larger or smaller number, in its discretion. One of the commissioners should be an attorney of the court; and in cases of idiocy or lunacy, it is usual to name one or more respectable physicians as commissioners.

The commission should direct an inquiry as to the value of the real and personal estate of the lunatic, &c.; the annual value of the rents and profits of such real estate; and also as to who are the next of kin of the lunatic, &c. For form, see *Appendix*, No. 399.

Effect of issuing commission.] After a commission has been issued, persons purchasing property or otherwise dealing with the alleged lunatic, with a knowledge that the same has been issued, will do so at the risk of having their whole proceedings declared illegal and void. And accordingly, where a person purchased real estate and took a conveyance thereof, with full knowledge that a commission had been issued against the grantor as an habitual drunkard, to inquire as to his incapacity to manage his affairs, and that the sheriff was then proceeding to summon a a jury to try the inquisition, the court, in an action commenced by the committee of the habitual drunkard, set aside the conveyance with costs. 15 *Barb.* 520.

Authority of the court pending the proceedings.] Although the court cannot permanently assume the custody and control of the person and estate of the alleged lunatic, without the verdict of a jury, yet after a commission has been allowed, the court may temporarily interfere, for the purpose of protecting and taking care of the alleged lunatic until the jury have passed upon the case. 2 *Wils. & Shaw*, 515.

And the court may interfere to restrain the removal of the supposed lunatic out of the country, even before a commission is issued. See *Shelf. on Lun.* 100. But it will not make an order for that purpose except upon affidavits showing satisfactorily that the party is a fit subject for a commission of lunacy, and that there is cause for reasonable apprehension of his removal. *Ib.*

The court may also permit access to be had to a person supposed to be a lunatic, for the purpose of enabling him and his friends to oppose the commission. Thus, in a case where a commission had been issued against a person who was imprisoned, and access to him had been denied; on the petition of his daughter and her husband, stating that they believed they could produce competent witnesses to prove that the party was of sound mind, and able to manage his own affairs, and that they disapproved of the issuing of the commission, the court ordered that the petitioners, and their solicitors, and such medical advisers as they might think fit to appoint, should have access to and be at liberty to visit the supposed lunatic, at all reasonable times prior to and during the execution of the commission, for the purpose of ascertaining the actual state of his mind and his competency to manage his affairs. *Ib.* 98.

Notice of the execution of the commission.] The party proceeded against as a lunatic, &c., is entitled to reasonable notice of the time and place of executing the commission, and a reasonable time to produce his witnesses before the jury, 1 *Barb. Ch. R.* 38; and he is entitled to such notice, although he resides out of the State. 2 *Paige*, 174. For form, see *Appendix*, No. 401.

But it is not necessary that a lunatic should be served personally with notice where it is evident that he keeps out of the way to avoid such service. 1 *Barb. Ch. R.* 38, *supra.* And in cases of confirmed and dangerous madness, no notice whatever is necessary. *Ib.* Nor is notice necessary where there are peculiar circumstances, rendering it improper or unsafe to give such notice; though in such case they should be stated in the petition to the court, so that a special provision may be inserted in the commission dispensing with notice. 1 *Paige*, 580.

Place of executing the commission.] The order for the commission usually directs the commission to be executed in or near the place of residence of the supposed lunatic, and a jury of the county and of the neighborhood where he resides, to be returned, to inquire of the lunacy, &c. 2 *Barb. Ch. Pr.* 230. But where the alleged lunatic is not a resident of the State, the usual order directing the commission to be executed at or near the residence of the lunatic must be dispensed with; and in such case, it may be executed in such county as will be most convenient, and nearest to the lunatic's residence. 2 *Paige*, 174.

And though the general rule is, where the party resides within the jurisdiction of the court, not to direct the commission to be executed at any other place than his residence, yet there are exceptions to the rule; and it may be departed from where satisfactory reasons are shown to warrant it. Thus, where the supposed lunatic had a town and country residence, both in the county of Middlesex, the commission was directed to be executed at or near either of such places of abode, as the commissioners should direct. *Matter of Jervis, cited in Shelf. on Lun.* 96. In another case, the court took into consideration the convenience and attendance of witnesses upon the inquiry, and directed the supposed lunatic to be conveyed from London, where he had been some time, to the place of his former residence, where the commission was directed to be executed. *Matter of Green, Id ibid.*

Witnesses.] The commissioners may issue subpœnas for witnesses, as incidental to their office; and if the witnesses refuse or neglect to attend, the court will make an order to compel them to do so. 1 *Coll.* 138; *Shelf.* 103. For form of subpœna, see *Appendix*, No. 404.

Precept for a jury.] The commissioners are also authorized to issue a precept to the sheriff of the county in which the commission is to be executed, commanding him to cause a jury of good and lawful men of his county, to come before them at a certain time, and in a certain place, to inquire upon their oaths of the matters and things which shall be given them in charge by virtue of the commission. *Shelf. on Lun.* 95. For form, see *Appendix*, No. 400. The commissioners have no right to dictate to the sheriff what jurors should be summoned. And where they selected and made out a list of jurors, whom they directed the sheriff to summon, it was held to be irregular, and the proceedings were set aside. 6 *Paige*, 11.

The jurors who are sworn upon the inquest, are each entitled to twelve and a half cents. 2 *Rev. Stat.* 644. *sec.* 37.

Duty of Sheriff.] Upon receiving the warrant or precept of the commissioners, it will be the duty of the sheriff to select and summon the jurors. The commissioners have no right to interfere with the sheriff in the exercise of that duty. 6 *Paige*, 11.

The sheriff will summon not less than twelve, nor more than twenty-four jurors, whose names he will write in a panel annexed to the precept; and to which panel he will refer in making his return. No inquest can be taken upon the oaths of less than twelve jurors.

It is the duty of the sheriff, also, to attend on the execution of the commission, if desired to do so by the commissioners, for the purpose of guarding the passage to the room where the jury are deliberating, and preventing them from being intruded upon by others. 1 *Paige*, 498. But it is improper for the sheriff to be in the room with the jury, or to converse with them on the subject of their deliberations. *Ib.* And in a case where the sheriff improperly interfered with the deliberations of the jury in this respect, the inquisition was, for that reason, set aside, and a new commission issued, in which it was ordered that the warrant of the commissioners to summon the jury be directed to the coroners. *Ib.*

The sheriff is entitled for summoning the jury, one dollar; and for attending such jury, when required, fifty cents. 2 *Rev. Stat.* 646.

Proceedings before the commissioners.] The party proceeded against is entitled to be present at the execution of the commission; and he may have counsel, also, to assist him. The friends of the party may also attend before the commissioners in his behalf; thus, where the wife of the supposed lunatic opposed the issuing of the commission, the court made an order that she should be at liberty to attend the execution of the commission, by counsel, if she thought proper. See *Shelf. on Lun.* 99. And the court, also, will see that ample means for resisting the commission, are furnished to those who act on the inquiry, in behalf of the lunatic. 4 *Russ.* 182.

Before entering upon the examination, the commissioners should require due proof of the service of notice of the proceedings upon the lunatic, or party proceeded against. For affidavit of service, see *Appendix*, No. 402.

In conducting the proceedings before the jury of inquiry, one of the commissioners (usually the one first named in the commission), must administer an oath to the jurors, and must also swear the witnesses, previous to their being examined. For forms, see *Appendix*, Nos. 405, 406. He must also read to the jury the commission, and explain the object of their meeting and their duties. The witnesses are then to be examined both as to the fact of lunacy, &c., of the party proceeded against, and as to who are his next of kin, and the nature, extent, and value of his real and personal estate.

And to aid the jury in their inquiries, upon the execution of the commission, they have the right to inspect and examine the lunatic; and they should do so in every case of doubt where such examination can be had. 1 *Barb. Ch. R.* 38. In such cases, the commissioners should direct the person in whose custody the lunatic is, to produce him, or to permit him to attend before them. *Ib.* For form of order or notice, see *Appendix*, No. 403. In case of the refusal of such person to do so, the court will commit him for a contempt. *Ib.;* and see 1 *Coll. on Lun.* 144; 1 *P. Wms.* 702; *Shelf. on Lun.* 99.

After the testimony, &c., is closed, the commissioners should submit the question to the jury in the form of a charge, stating the law applicable to the case, and recapitulating the facts, if necessary, but without arguments of counsel on either side. And the jury are to be instructed if twelve or more of them find that the party is not incompetent, they are to deliver their verdict accordingly; or if the same number decide against his competency, that they then find and determine the other facts directed to be inquired of; and that if twelve of them cannot agree either way, they report the fact to the commissioners, that their return may be made accordingly. 1 *Paige*, 499.

In relation to legal questions which arise in the execution of the commission, a majority of the commissioners must decide. *Ib.*

And the commissioners may also determine upon the validity of challenges to jurors. 6 *Paige*, 11.

If more jurors are sworn on the execution of the commission than are necessary, and the proceeding is commenced before all, it would be irregular to continue it before a part only. 11 *Abb.* 211.

Inquisition.] The jury having deliberated upon the matter of inquiry, and agreed upon a verdict, are to return the same to the commissioners. The blanks in the inquisition (which is a response to the commission, in relation to the fact of lunacy, drunkenness, &c.), are then filled up, and the inquisition is signed and sealed by the commissioners, and by the jury. See 1 *Grant*, 296; 1 *Coll.* 140; 2 *Barb. Ch. Pr.* 233. The inquisition is then delivered to the commissioners, and is annexed by them to the commission. For form, see *Appendix*, No. 407.

With respect to the *form* of the inquisition, the jury should adhere substantially to the technical form of finding in the language of the statute itself; as, that the party is an "idiot," or "lunatic," or of "unsound mind and incapable of the government of himself or the management of his estate;" or that the party is "incapable of conducting his own affairs in consequence of habitual drunkenness." See 1 *Barb. S. C. R.* 437; 3 *Edw. Ch. R.* 380; 7 *Paige*, 236; *Shelf. on Lun.* 108, 109; *Will. Eq.*

Jur. 675 to 680. It seems, however, it is sufficient to give the court jurisdiction, if the jury find that the party is mentally incapable of governing himself, or managing his affairs. 1 *Barb. S. C. R.* 437. "The form of the return to the inquisition," says Harris, J., in the case last cited (p. 441), "is only important so far as it is necessary to satisfy the conscience of the court. If, upon the coming in of the inquisition, enough appears to enable the court to adjudge the party to be within some one of the classes of persons over whom the statute has given it jurisdiction, it is sufficient. A discreet exercise of the power vested in the court undoubtedly requires that before a citizen shall be deprived of his liberty, and the control of his own property, evidence of the most conclusive character should be produced, showing him to be a person for whose benefit the law has benignly provided this delicate and important trust. But I am not prepared to say that a case might not be presented to the court in which the evidence would be so clear and satisfactory as to justify the exercise of its summary power, for the protection of a party, without the intervention of a jury. Whether this be so or not, I cannot doubt that under the law of this State, it is enough to vest the court with jurisdiction of the case, when, as in the case under consideration, the jury find that the party is mentally incapable of governing himself, or managing his affairs." See also, *Will. Eq. Jur.* 675 to 680, where the English and American authorities are stated at large.

Where the return is, that the party is a "lunatic," it is usual, also, to state whether with or without lucid intervals; though, where it omits to do so, it is not therefore bad; as the return, in that case, negatives their existence by implication. 3 *Atk.* 168; 5 *Ves.* 450.

In cases where the party is found a lunatic, it is also usual to state for how long a time he has been so. For the principle on which the court extends its protection to lunatics requires an examination into the circumstances of competence or incompetence, under which the lunatic has performed acts affecting his property. It is usual, therefore, in all such cases, when it appears that the lunacy has been of some duration, to inquire from what period it commenced. *Shelf. on Lun.* 97; and see *Stock's Law of Non Comp.* 101. And inquisitions have sometimes been quashed, on the ground that the commencement of the lunacy was not carried back as far as was warranted by the evidence. *Id. ibid.*

In the case of an idiot, the return is sufficient if it finds the party to be so, without the addition of any other words. 3 *Mod* 43; 2 *Ves. sen.* 408.

The inquisition should also find who are the next of kin of the party proceeded against, the value of his real and personal estate, and generally all the particulars directed to be inquired of in the commission. For form, see *Appendix*, No. 407.

Return of commission.] After the inquisition has been duly signed and sealed by the commissioners and the jury, the commissioners should annex it to the commission, and having endorsed upon the commission their return in these words: "The execution of this commission appears in the schedule hereunto annexed," (1 *Grant*, 296; 1 *Coll. on Lun.* 140,) they should file the commission, and the inquisition annexed, with the clerk of the court.

Fees of commissioners.] On the execution of the commission, the commissioners are each entitled to two dollars for every day they are necessarily employed in hearing the testimony, and taking the inquisition. *Sup. Court Rules*, No. 85; 2 *Rev. Stat.* 643, *sec.* 35. And for drawing the inquisition and process, and serving notices, when no attorney is employed, they are entitled to the fees to which an attorney would be entitled for the same services. *Rule* 85, *supra.* The fees of an attorney are the same as those allowed to a solicitor in the late Court of Chancery; and are regulated by the fee bill in existence prior to the code. *Code of Pro.* § 471; and see 16 *Barb.* 592.

New commission may issue.] In case of the death or incapacity of the commissioners, the commission will be suspended, and a new one directed to be issued. *Shelf. on Lun.* 83.

The court may also direct the issuing of a new commission where, from the evidence before the jury, or otherwise, there is no doubt that the jury erred in finding that the party proceeded against was not of unsound mind. 2 *Barb. Ch. R.* 97; and see *post*, "Setting aside inquisition; new commission, &c."

Proceedings upon the return of the commission.] Upon the filing of the return of the commissioners, &c., a motion should be made to the court to confirm the finding of the jury; which motion is founded upon the commission, inquisition, and return.

Notice of the motion should be given to the party proceeded against, where he appeared either in person or by counsel, and contested the proceedings before the jury. For form, see *Appendix*, No. 408.

The motion to confirm the finding of the jury, is also usually accompanied by an application for the appointment of a committee of the person and estate. This application is founded upon petition and notice, copies of which, where the finding has been contested, should be served upon the party or his attorney. See *post.* For forms, see *Appendix*, Nos. 408, 409.

The alleged lunatic, &c., may also apply at the same time for an order to set aside the inquisition, or for leave to traverse it, or for an issue, and the court will hear the several motions together, when convenient. 5 *Paige*, 242; and see *post, p.* 18.

The alleged lunatic will be entitled to a new trial of the writ, if it appear that the findings against him were induced by any bias or previously formed opinion. 9 *Abb.* 211.

After the jury has passed upon the question, and found the alleged lunatic of unsound mind, the court, upon confirming the inquisition, acquires complete jurisdiction over the lunatic and his property, and the costs of the proceedings. 20 *How.* 385.

Who may be appointed committee.] It is usual, if the lunatic has a son of proper age, and no particular objection exists, to appoint him the committee of the estate. 1 *Moll.* 439. But it is not a matter of course to commit the guardianship of the estate to those who are presumptively entitled to it upon his death, as his heirs or next of kin. They will, however, be appointed the committee where it satisfactorily appears to the court that they are the persons who are the most likely to protect his property from loss. 9 *Paige*, 611.

Other things being equal, persons whose place of residence admits of their frequently visiting the lunatic, and inspecting the management of his concerns, are to be preferred as committees. See *Ex. Parte Fenner*, *Jac.* 404. It is no objection to the appointment of a person who is a resident of the State and with in its jurisdiction, that he does not reside in the county, in the county court of which the proceeding is had. 11 *Abb.* 274, *s. c.* 32 *Barb.* 122; § 19 *How.* 375.

In the appointment of the committee of the person of a lunatic, the court will attend as far as possible to the wishes and inclinations of the lunatic. *Loyd and Goold* (*Temp. Plunk.*), 498. In general, the custody of a lunatic wife will be committed to the husband, and of a lunatic husband to the wife; though otherwise where strong reasons exist against it. In the case of a lunatic husband, the court seems disposed to unite some other person as committee with the wife. 1 *P. Wms.* 701; 18 *Ves.* 22. The custody of an unmarried woman will be given to one of her own sex, in preference to the other. And in the case of a lunatic mother, Chancellor Kent committed the guardianship of the person to the daughter; and observed that the presumption, if one must be indulged, would be in favor of kinder treatment and more patient fortitude from her, than from the collateral kindred. 1 *Johns. Ch. R.* 436.

If the next of kin unite in the petition and name a proper person as committee, or give their consent in writing to the appointment of a particular person, such person will usually be selected as committee. But if they do not do so, there should be an order of reference, and then the next of kin are entitled to notice of the proceedings, and may propose themselves as the committee. 19 *How.* 375, *s. c.* 11 *Abb.* 274; 32 *Barb.* 122.

In general, but one person should be appointed committee of the person. 2 *P. Wms.* 635.

Appointment of committee.] If the party proceeded against has been found a lunatic upon the execution of the commission, an application should then be made to the court for the appointment of a committee of the person and estate. The court may appoint the same person committee of the person and of the estate; though it is usual, where the estate is large, to have a separate committee for each. But the court have no jurisdiction to appoint such committee, without the issuing and return of a commission. 8 *How.* 220; but see, *per* Harris, J., 1 *Barb. S. C. R.* 441, *ante, p.* 13. The motion, as we have seen, is founded upon petition and notice, copies of which, when the finding has been contested, should be served upon the party or his attorney.

Where the next of kin, who are adults, join in the petition, and name a proper person as committee, or give their consent, in writing, to the appointment of the person named by the petitioner, the court usually directs an order to be entered appointing such person, without the expense of a reference, upon his giving the usual security to be approved of by a judge of the court. 19 *How.* 375, *s. c.* 11 *Abb.* 274; 32 *Barb.* 122.

But where the next of kin have not had notice of the application for the appointment of a committee, nor assented to the appointment of the person named as committee, the court usually orders a reference to inquire and report who is a suitable and proper person to be appointed such committee, and to approve of the sureties, and that the next of kin have notice of the proceedings upon the reference. *Ib.* The court, however, may appoint a committee, in such case, without a reference for that purpose. See 2 *Barb. Ch. Pr.* 236; 1 *Barb. S. C. R.* 441. For form of order, see *Appendix*, No. 410.

Upon the proceedings upon the reference, the heirs or next of kin, have the right to propose themselves to the referee, as the committee. 1 *Moll.* 439; 19 *How.* 375, *supra.* And where the order of reference directs notice of the proceedings to be served upon them, notice should be served accordingly; and the heirs may attend upon such reference, though no direction or notice is given.

A state of facts, and proposal of committee and sureties, being presented and delivered to the referee, if he approves of the committee and sureties, and the amount and form of the bond, he reports the same to the court. For form of report, see *Appendix*, No. 411. And upon the coming in of his report, if it is approved by the court, an order is entered for confirming the same, and for the appointment of the committee, upon his executing a bond in the amount and with the sureties reported, conditioned for the faithful execution of his trust, in the usual form, and duly acknowledged or approved according to the rules of the court. For form, see *Appendix*, No. 412.

Bond of committee, &c.] Before entering upon the trust committed to him, the committee must execute a bond with two sufficient sureties to be approved of by a judge of the court, and conditioned for the faithful performance of the trust reposed in him as such committee; and that he will render an account whenever required, in conformity to the rules and practice of the court; and that he will observe the orders and directions of the court in relation to such trust. 2 *Barb. Ch. Pr.* 237. For form, see *Appendix*, No. 413.

The court, however, in a proper case, may dispense altogether with security from the committee; as, where the referee reports that no person can be found to act as committee who will give security. 2 *Russ.* 450; and see 1 *Con. & Lawson*, 309. But the court will not dispense with security merely because the committee is the eldest son and heir at law of the lunatic. 2 *Russ.* 450, *supra.*

The penalty of the bond is usually fixed by the order of the court appointing the committee, and should be in double the value of the real and personal estate of the lunatic, &c., as found by the inquisition; though it is sufficient in the first instance, if the penalty is in double the value of the personal estate alone.

The bond should be made payable to the people of the State, or to the clerk of the court. 1 *Barb. Ch. R.* 43.

And after it has been duly executed by the committee and his sureties, and proved or acknowledged, and the sureties have justified, and the judge's certificate of approval has been indorsed upon it, it should be filed with the clerk of the court. See *Sup. Court Rules*, No. 6.

Traverse of inquisition.] In England, a party who has been adjudged a lunatic, &c., may traverse the inquisition, and proceed to trial thereon, with the like effect, in all respects, as in other cases of traverse. And the traverse, in such case, is considered a matter of right, over which the court has no discretion, except so far as to ascertain that the party in whose name the application is made, wishes to traverse. 1 *Paige*, 582; 1 *Barb. S. C. R.* 436; *Will. Eq. Jur.* 682.

In this State, however, instead of permitting the formal traverse, the practice is to award a feigned issue, in all cases where a jury trial is proper. The court having the whole jurisdiction, and the object being to inform the conscience of the court, and to arrive at the truth, the directing an issue to be made up and tried, under its direction, has been thought preferable to a traverse. *Id. ibid.*; 1 *Johns. Ch. R.* 599.

It is not, however, a matter of course to award an issue; but the same rests in the sound discretion of the court. 1 *Paige*, 580; 1 *Barb. S. C. R.* 436; 1 *Barb. Ch. R.* 38; 20 *How.* 385. But the court will award an issue whenever it entertains a reasonable doubt as to the justice of the finding of the jury upon the execution of the commission; especially under the act respecting habitual drunkards. *Id. ibid;* 1 *Paige*, 582, *supra.*

The application for an issue may be made by the lunatic himself, by a member of his family, or by a relative, or by a purchaser from him, or by any person having an interest in his land, or a party who has entered into a contract with him, or who supposes his interests to be affected by the acts of the lunatic. 9 *Ves.* 478; 2 *Wils. & Shaw*, 520; 5 *Paige*, 242; 11 *Id.* 243.

But the court will not grant an application for an issue in the name of a lunatic, unless it is satisfied upon a private examination of the lunatic, or by the report of a referee, that such is the wish of the lunatic, and that he is capable of understanding the nature and object of the application. 5 *Paige*, 242. It is otherwise, however, where the conveyance of a purchaser is overreached by the inquisition. In such case, the court, upon probable cause shown, will award such issue upon the purchaser's stipulating to be bound by the final decision thereon. *Ib.* And where, in such case, an issue was awarded, and subsequently the counsel for the several parties to the proceedings, without the sanction of the court, stipulated to abandon the trial thereof; it was held that they had no right to do so, and the court set aside the stipulation, and directed the committee of the lunatic to proceed to the trial of the issue. 11 *Id.* 243.

If an issue is awarded, the court will, if necessary, make a provisional order for the care of the lunatic's estate, until the question of lunacy is determined. 1 *Johns. Ch. R.* 599; 3 *Atk.* 634; 1 *Barb. Ch. R.* 42.

In respect to an issue in proceedings commenced by overseers of the poor, against an habitual drunkard, see 2 *Rev. Stat.* 53, *sec.* 5, *ante*, *p.* 3.

Proceedings thereon.] The application for an issue to try the question of lunacy, is founded upon petition and notice; and is also generally accompanied by affidavits of persons setting forth their belief, &c., of the sanity of the alleged lunatic. Copies of the papers on which the motion is founded should be duly served upon the committee, if one has been appointed; or, if not, upon the party instituting the proceeding, or his attorney. For forms, see *Appendix*, Nos. 414 to 417.

If the application is made in the name of the alleged lunatic, and the petition is sworn to by him, the officer before whom the same is sworn should state in the jurat that he has examined the petitioner for the purpose of ascertaining the state of his mind, and that he was apparently of sound mind, and capable of understanding the nature and contents of the petition. 5 *Paige*, 242. For form, see *Appendix*, No. 425.

If an issue is granted it is made up and tried in the usual manner. For form of order directing an issue, see *Appendix*, No. 418.

The issue may be tried before a jury at the Circuit, or in the County Court, the same as issues in actions. And the issue may be referred to referees for trial. Thus, in one case, after the issue had been sent to the circuit for trial, the issue was referred, by stipulation of the parties, to referees, and was tried by them. 20 *How*. 385.

If the inquisition is allowed to be traversed by the lunatic, it will be the duty of the committee appointed under the inquisition, to oppose the traverse, and to see that the issue is properly tried, and not suffered to go by default. *Ib.*

The court may, in a proper case, direct the issue to be tried in a different county from that in which the subject of the inquiry had been found a lunatic. See 2 *Moll.* 517.

In respect to the form of the verdict of the jury on the trial of the issue, see *ante*, *p.* 12, title "Inquisition."

Effect of inquisition.] An inquisition, by which a person is found to be a lunatic, or of unsound mind, and incapable of the management of his affairs, is conclusive evidence of the incapacity of such person.

Accordingly, a contract for the sale of real estate, executed by a person who has been found, upon inquisition, to be a lunatic, and of whose person and estate a committee has been duly appointed, is absolutely void. And the committee cannot, by any act of his, without the authority and direction of the court, make such a contract valid. 12 *Barb*. 235. And so, where an action was brought against the endorser of a bill of exchange, who, after the making and endorsing of the bill, had been found to be an habitual drunkard, upon a commission issued for that purpose; it was held, that after the finding of the inquisition, the defendant was not competent to waive notice of non-payment and protest. 14 *Id.* 169, aff. 4 *Selden*, 388; 4 *How.* 34.

Nor can one who, by inquisition, has been found to be a lunatic, or an habitual drunkard, make a valid will, 2 *Barb. Ch. R.* 208; 4 *How.* 34; nor can he, even in his lucid or sober intervals, make a contract to bind himself or his property. See 4 *Selden*, 388, *supra.*

But the court has the power to suspend the operation of an inquisition, so far as to allow the subject of it to make a testamentary disposition of his property, without discharging the proceedings entirely, or restoring him to the full control of his property for every purpose. 2 *Barb. Ch. R.* 208; 4 *How.* 34; and see 4 *Selden*, 396. And an application for that purpose is addressed to the discretion of the court, and may be made ex parte, or on notice to the committee, and next of kin, as the court may direct. 4 *How.* 34, *supra.*

Upon the confirmation of the inquisition, the court acquires complete jurisdiction over the lunatic and his property, and the costs of the proceedings. 20 *Id.* 385.

The inquisition is analogous to a proceeding *in rem*, and is presumed to be known to all who subsequently deal with the lunatic. 4 *Selden*, 388, 392; 15 *Barb.* 523; 6 *Wend.* 498.

With respect to acts done by a lunatic or drunkard before the issuing of a commission, and which are over-reached by the finding of the jury, the inquisition is presumptive, but not conclusive, evidence of their invalidity. 2 *Paige*, 422; 4 *How.* 34; 2 *Barb. Ch. R.* 208; 11 *Abb.* 252; *s. c.* 19 *How.* 140.

And a judgment recovered in a court of law against a person who has been found a lunatic, or an habitual drunkard, and whose person and property have been placed in the custody of a committee, will not for that reason be held void, or even erronous. 2 *Barb. S. C. R.* 153; 13 *Id.* 424; 14 *Id.* 488. The remedy of the lunatic, or of his committee, in such case, is to apply to the court appointing the committee, to restrain the prosecution of the suit, and to punish the plaintiff for a contempt. If judgment has been obtained, the court will also restrain the further proceedings to enforce its collection. *Id. ibid;* and see 5 *Paige*, 489; 2 *Id.* 423; 3 *Id.* 199. And will set the judgment aside, either on motion, or by action commenced for that purpose. 11 *Abb.* 252, *s. c.* 19 *How.* 140.

Setting aside inquisition; new commission, &c.] The inquisition may be set aside by the court, for irregularity; or where it does not conform to the requirements of the statute; or where the facts do not justify the finding of the jury.

Thus, the inquisition will be set aside, and a new commission issued, where the alleged lunatic or habitual drunkard did not have notice of the execution of the commission, 1 *Paige*, 581; or where a stranger is appointed committee without the request of the relatives and next of kin of the lunatic, and without a reference and without notice to persons prospectively interested in the estate. 11 *Abb.* 274, *s. c.* 32 *Barb.* 122; 19 *How.* 375. So, also, where the commissioners interfered with the sheriff, in the execution of his duties, by making out a list of jurors, and directing him to summon them. 6 *Paige*, 11. So, where the sheriff, having charge of the jury, improperly enters the room and converses with them on the subject of their deliberations. 1 *Paige*, 497.

And where the inquisition does not conform to the requirements of the statute, by failing to find the party an idiot, or a lunatic, or a person of unsound mind, as the case may be; but is argumentative, or in other respects deficient, the court will set it aside and order a new commission to issue. 7 *Id.* 236; 1 *Barb. S. C. R.* 436.

The court may also set aside an inquisition upon the mere examination of the supposed lunatic, in connection with the evidence produced before the jury, where upon such examination and proof it is evident that the jury erred in finding him to be a lunatic. 1 *Barb. Ch. R.* 38. But the court will not dispose of the case thus summarily, where there has been no change in the situation of the alleged lunatic subsequent to the finding of the inquisition, unless there is a very clear case of mistake or undue prejudice on the part of the jury. *Ib.* Nor will the court discharge the inquisition upon ex parte affidavits contradicting the finding of the jury; where there is no reasonable excuse given for neglecting to produce the deponents as witnesses before the commissioners. *Ib.* Nor where there is no room whatever for doubt of the lunacy of the person concerned, although the proceedings were not entirely free from irregularity. 11 *Abb.* 274, *per* Brown, J., *s. c.* 32 *Barb.* 122; 19 *How.* 375.

Suspending or superseding commission.] The statute provides, that in case any lunatic, person of unsound mind, or habitual drunkard, shall be restored to his right mind, and become capable of conducting his affairs, his real and personal estate shall be restored to him. 2 *Rev. Stat.* 55, *sec.* 24.

The practice, in such cases, is, upon the recovery of the lunatic, to apply to the court, upon petition and affidavits, to supersede or suspend the commission. Notice of the motion should be given to the committee, accompanied with copies of the papers on which the same is founded. For forms, see *Appendix*, Nos. 419, 420.

Upon the hearing of the application the attendance of the lunatic is usually required; and strong affidavits should be furnished to the court, made by medical men, or other competent persons, showing the restoration of a sound state of mind. 1 *Coll. on Lun.* 324. Persons who are in the habit of associating with, or watching the lunatic, are competent to give evidence as to his sanity. *Ib.* 328.

And the court may, itself, upon inspection of the lunatic, and the examination of the petition and other papers, suspend or supersede the commission; or it may refer the matter to a referee to take proof of the facts, and to examine the lunatic if he thinks proper, and to report the proof, and his opinion thereon,—and on the coming in of his report, then decide the matter. 3 *Johns. Ch. R.* 567; 2 *Coll. on Lun.* 746. Or, the court may allow an issue to be made up and tried by a jury. 6 *Johns. Ch. R.* 440. For forms of order superseding commission, order of reference, referee's report and order thereon, see *Appendix*, Nos. 421 to 424. And in a case where the lunacy was satisfactorily established in the first instance, and the opinion of the court, after repeated applications of the party for a discharge of his committee, remained unchanged, the trial of the question was directed to be at the expense of the lunatic or his friends, and not at the charge of his estate, which consisted of personal property only, acquired by the industry and skill of his wife, and barely sufficient for the maintenance of herself and children and of her husband. *Ib*; and see *Will. Eq. Jur.* 689.

Where a party has been found an habitual drunkard, the court will not discharge his committee and restore the property to him upon mere proof of the fact that he is competent to manage his affairs, without evidence of a permanent reformation. And the late Court of Chancery required, as a general rule, as evidence of a perfect reformation, satisfactory proof that the habitual drunkard has voluntarily refrained from the use of intoxicating liquors for at least one year immediately preceding the application for the restoration of his property. 7 *Paige*, 312.

The commission may also be superseded if it has remained unexecuted for several years, with costs to be paid by the person guilty of the laches. 1 *Coll. on Lun.* 329; 2 *Atk.* 52.

And so, where a feigned issue has been awarded to a party, who has been found by inquisition to be a lunatic, and upon the trial of such issue, the party is found not to be of unsound mind, the proceedings upon the commission will be discharged, and he will be restored to the full control of his property. 11 *Paige*, 638.

But the court, instead of superseding the commission, in the first instance, may suspend its operation, in whole or in part, either indefinitely or for a limited time, where there is reason to believe that the party has not fully recovered, or there is danger of a relapse. 2 *Barb. Ch. R.* 210; *Mose.* 332; *Jacob*, 404. In such cases, the party will be permitted to have the control of his estate; the powers of the committee being suspended. *Id. ibid.* For form of order, see *Appendix*, No. 421.

And the court may suspend the operation of the commission for a particular purpose only; as, to enable the individual found to be a lunatic to make a testamentary disposition of his property, where he has sufficiently recovered his reason to be able to do so with sense and judgment. 2 *Barb. Ch. R.* 208. And an application for that purpose is addressed to the discretion of the court, and may be made ex parte, or on notice to the committee and next of kin, as the court may direct. 4 *How.* 34.

But the commission, it seems, cannot be *superseded* as to the person, and retained as to the estate. So held, where the party found to be a lunatic, applied to have the committee of his person discharged, alleging that he was so far restored to reason as to be able to govern himself; where it did not appear that he was competent to manage his estate, and no application was made for the discharge of the committee of the estate. *Matter of Burr*, 17 *Barb.* 9; and see 2 *Phil.* 242. The commission, however, may be *suspended* as to the person, and retained in force as to the estate. *Matter of Burr*, before Harris, J., 1854; see *Will. Eq. Jur.* 690. And it may be suspended in part both as to the estate and the person. Thus, in the case of Burr, above referred to, the Supreme Court so far suspended the commission both of the person and the estate, as to allow the lunatic, from time to time, to receive portions of the income of his estate, and finally the whole income, and to invest or expend it in such manner as he should judge best, leaving the committee of the estate, in other respects, in the full control of the property. *MS.* before Willard, J., Saratoga Sp. T., *Will. Eq. Jur.* 690.

Affidavit of lunatic, &c., how certified.] If a petition or affidavit in the proceedings, is sworn to by one who has been found by inquisition to be a lunatic or an habitual drunkard, or a person of unsound mind, the officer before whom it is sworn should state in the jurat that he had examined the petitioner or deponent, for the purpose of ascertaining the state of his mind, and whether he was capable of understanding the nature and object of the petition or affidavit, and that he was apparently of sound mind and capable of understanding the same. See 5 *Paige*, 242. And if the party is blind, the officer should also certify that the petition or affidavit was carefully and correctly read over to him in the presence of such officer, before it was sworn to. *Ib.* 243. For form of certificates, see *Appendix*, No. 425.

Removing or discharging committee.] The committee may, at any time, be removed for any misconduct, upon petition and sufficient affidavits, or on inquiry before a referee. *Shelf. on Lun.* 193; 8 *Paige*, 150. And where the committee has been guilty of gross negligence, he will be charged with the costs of the proceedings against him, to obtain his removal, and the settlement of his accounts. 3 *Paige*, 146.

The committee may also be discharged on his own application. But where he has voluntarily accepted the appointment, he cannot be discharged without showing some valid excuse for resigning the trust. And the fact that his situation is rendered unpleasant, in consequence of controversies existing between different members of the lunatic's family, is not sufficient for that purpose. *Ib.* 251.

Upon the removal or discharge of the committee, it will be referred to a referee, if necessary, to take and state an account between the committee and the estate of the lunatic. And where the court designates a referee for that purpose, it will be irregular and improper for the parties to substitute another referee in his place, without the sanction of the court. *Ib.* 146.

Remedy of persons having claims against lunatic's estate.] After a person is declared, by inquisition, to be a lunatic, it is a contempt of court for a creditor, or other person, who is informed of the proceedings, to sue the lunatic, or to levy an execution upon his property, or otherwise to interfere with it, without the permission of the court. 2 *Paige*, 422; 3 *Id.* 199; 5 *Id.* 489; 26 *Barb.* 172. And such creditor, or other person, upon a proper application by the committee, will be restrained from such interference. *Id. ibid*; 13 *Barb.* 424.

The court will see, however, that the legal and equitable rights of creditors and others are protected and enforced. And the proper course for the creditor whose claim is disputed or refused to be paid by the committee, is to apply to the court, by petition, for the payment of his debt out of the lunatic's estate; or for leave to establish his claim by action, or by reference. For form of petition, and notice of motion, see *Appendix*, Nos. 426, 427. If the court is satisfied that the debt is justly due, the committee will be ordered to pay it out of the estate; or if the claim is doubtful, the court will either have it settled by a referee, on a reference for that purpose, or will permit the party to establish his claim by action, as may be proper, under the particular circumstances of the case. 2 *Paige*, 422; 3 *Id.* 199; 5 *Id.* 489; 5 *How.* 109. For form of order, see *Appendix*, No. 428. But in general, the court will direct a reference under the control of the court, unless some particular advantage is to accrue from an action. 26 *Barb.* 172. Thus, where property was purchased by the lunatic, which he afterwards purposely injured and destroyed, before the same had been paid for, on an application by the vendors for leave to sue the committee of the lunatic for damages, the court denied the application, and directed the appointment of a referee to take proof as to the facts and circumstances, and to report the same to the court, with his opinion thereon. *Ib.*

If a reference is ordered, the referee will proceed in the usual manner, and after having taken testimony, and other proofs presented, will make his report to the court. And upon the coming in of his report, the same must be filed, and a note of the day of filing entered by the clerk in the proper book, under the title of the proceeding; and such report will become absolute, and stand as in all things confirmed, unless exceptions thereto are filed and served within eight days after service of notice of the filing of the same. If exceptions are filed and served within such time, the same may be brought to a hearing at any special term thereafter, on the notice of any party interested therein. *Supreme Court Rules*, No. 32.

Where the court, upon the application of a creditor, settles and adjusts the amount due, and directs the committee to pay the same out of the lunatic's estate, together with the costs of the application, and the committee does not comply with the order, the remedy of the creditor is to compel a compliance by summary proceedings against him. See 8 *Paige*, 146. And it is erroneous for the court, upon the settlement of the claim, to direct an action to be brought by the creditor, in case the committee neglects or refuses to pay it. *Ib.*

If an action to establish a claim is directed by the court to be brought against the committee, it is proper, it seems, to make the lunatic or drunkard also a party defendant in the suit; so as to make the proceedings binding upon him in case the commission should be superseded before the suit is terminated. *Ib.* and see 6 *Paige*, 237.

Duty and authority of the committee.] The first and paramount rule in lunacy, &c., is to provide for the personal ease and comfort of the lunatic. 1 *Beat.* 268; 2 *Ves. jun.* 72. And it is the duty of the committee of the person to administer to the lunatic all the comfort and amusement that the nature of the case will admit, or his funds will afford. He is to be treated with great kindness, and all reasonable means of restoration employed.

Shelf. on Lun. 142, 154; 17 *Barb.* 14. And the committee is responsible for the consequences of any neglect to take proper care of him. See 5 *Paige*, 120.

In the management of his estate, the interest of the lunatic is more to be regarded than the contingent interest of the real and personal representatives. 3 *Johns. Ch. R.* 347; 1 *Ves. jun.* 296; 8 *Ves.* 8. And though the committee ought not, in general, to vary the nature of the property, so as to affect the right of succession, yet he may do this under the direction of the court, where it is necessary for the benefit of the lunatic. *Id. ibid*; 1 *Beat.* 268. Thus, the court may direct real estate to be converted into personal, or personal into real, when the interest of the lunatic requires it. 3 *Johns. Ch. R.* 347, *supra*; 9 *Paige*, 440. And may order the letting for a term of years, or the sale or other disposition of the lunatic's real estate, whenever it is necessary and proper, either for the payment of the debts of the lunatic, or for his support and maintenance, or for his education, or whenever the interest of the lunatic requires or will be substantially promoted by such disposition, by reason of any part of the property being exposed to waste or dilapidation, or on account of its being wholly unproductive, or for any other peculiar reasons or circumstances. *Laws of* 1864, *p.* 999, *post*; 2 *Rev. Stat.* 53, *sec.* 11. Though, formerly, the court could not direct the sale or other disposition of the real estate of the lunatic, except where it was necessary for his maintenance, or the maintenance of his family, or the education of his children, or the payment of his debts; nor in any of these cases if the personal property was sufficient for the purpose. 2 *Rev. Stat.* 53, *secs.* 11, 16; 2 *Paige*, 596; 7 *Id.* 312. The court, however, might direct the committee to apply the surplus income to the improvement of unproductive real estate; and also to apply a portion of the capital of the personal estate in building upon vacant lots, so as to produce an income from the improvements. 9 *Paige*, 441.

Nor is the maintenance of the lunatic limited to the amount of income. 3 *Moll.* 94. But the whole estate, real and personal, may be expended in his support; after which, on the application of the committee, and upon report of a referee, the court will order the lunatic to be delivered over to the overseers of the poor. 2 *Johns. Ch. R.* 440.

Where the lunatic resides in another State, and has property in the hands of his committee appointed at the place of his residence, that property is the primary fund for his support, and should be first applied for that purpose by the committee who has the control of his person. 9 *Paige*, 611.

The committee, under the direction of the court, has also the entire control of the person of the lunatic, and the right to confine him if necessary. 2 *Hoff. Ch. Pr.* 262.

And where the lunatic becomes furiously mad, or so far disordered in his senses, as to endanger his own person, or the person or property of others, if permitted to go at large, if he is possessed of sufficient property to maintain himself, it is the duty of the committee to provide a suitable place for his confinement, and to confine and maintain him in such manner as shall be approved by the overseers of the poor of the city or town. 2 *Rev. Stat.* 634.

In respect to an habitual drunkard, the committee has the right, also, subject only to the superintending control of the court, to decide as to the proper residence of the drunkard; and he is responsible for any neglect to take proper care of the person of such drunkard. And the court will aid and protect the committee in the exercise of that right; and give him directions on the subject when necessary. 5 *Paige*, 120. And where a third person, against the wishes of the committee, has the custody of or harbors the habitual drunkard, it is the duty of the committee to apply to the court, in the first instance for an order that the drunkard be delivered up to the committee, or that such person cease from harboring him; and if such order is disobeyed, the party will be punished for a contempt of court. *Ib.*

And so, where vendors of intoxicating drinks furnish the same to a drunkard against the wishes of his committee, the court will make an order prohibiting them from doing so, upon pain of being held liable for a criminal contempt. And if the order is disobeyed, it is the duty of the committee to apply to the court to punish the offender. 7 *Paige*, 312; 3 *Id.* 200.

If necessary for the reformation of an habitual drunkard, the court, it seems, will direct the committee to confine him in the lunatic asylum; and his real estate may be sold for the purpose of paying the expenses of his support there. 7 *Paige*, 312.

In respect to the property of a lunatic, as a general rule, the committee cannot enter into any transaction or contract, without the authority of the court. Nor can he institute suits in behalf of the estate, without such authority. When authorized to bring any action for any debt, claim, or demand transferred to him, or to the possession and control of which he is entitled as such committee, he may sue for the same in his own name. *Laws of* 1845, *p.* 90; 12 *How.* 287. In all other cases the action must be brought in the name of the lunatic. 8 *Barb.* 552; but see 14 *Id.* 488; *Code*, § 113.

If the lunatic's estate is large, and its interests require the employment of an agent or clerk, the court, upon the petition of the committee, will allow him to employ such agent or clerk, and to pay him a reasonable compensation for his services, out of the income of the estate. 9 *Paige*, 440. But the committee himself cannot receive a compensation for services as such clerk beyond his allowance for commissions as the committee. *Ib.*

If waste is committed upon the lands of the lunatic, it is the duty of the committee to apply to the court for an order to restrain it; and the court may make such order without an action commenced for that purpose. See 7 *Johns. Ch. R.* 24; 1 *Ball and Beatty*, 108. And if there is a breach of the order, the committee may move for an attachment. *Id. ibid.*

In the case of the death of the lunatic, &c., the power of the committee ceases; and his real estate will thereupon descend to his heirs, and his personal estate be distributed according to law, the same as if he had been of sound mind and memory, and capable of conducting his affairs; though without affecting the provisions of any last will and testament duly made, and which shall be duly admitted to probate. 2 *Rev. Stat.* 55, *sec.* 25; as amended *Laws of* 1865, *p.* 1445.

Committee to file inventory and account.] It is also made the duty of the committee, within six months after his appointment, to file with the clerk in whose office the appointment of the committee is entered, a just and true inventory of the whole real and personal estate of such lunatic, &c.; stating the income and profits thereof, and the debts, credits, and effects, so far as the same have come to the knowledge of such committee. And whenever any property belonging to such estate shall be discovered after the filing of any inventory, it is also the duty of the committee to file a just and true account of the same from time to time as the same shall be discovered. 2 *Rev. Stat.* 53, *sec.* 8.

And the committee is also annually, after the first inventory is filed, so long as any part of the estate, or of the income or proceeds thereof, remains in his hands, or under his care or control, to file in the same office an inventory and account, under oath, of his trust, and of any other property belonging to the estate which he has since discovered, and of the amount remaining in his hands, or invested by him, and of the manner in which the same is secured or invested; stating the balance due from or to him at the time of rendering his last account, and his receipts and expenditures since that time, in the form of debtor and creditor. *Rules of the late Court of Chancery*, No. 154; *Laws of* 1848, *p.* 407, *sec.* 8; 2 *Barb. Ch. Pr.* 238. For forms of inventory and account, see *Appendix*, No. 429.

If the committee neglects to file an inventory, or to render his accounts regularly under oath, in the settlement of his accounts every presumption will be taken most strongly against him. 3 *Paige*, 146; and see 2 *Id.* 409. And the court appointing the committee may compel the filing of the inventory, by the order and process usual in such cases. 2 *Rev. Stat.* 53, *sec.* 10.

Before filing the inventories, they must be verified by the oath of the committee, to be taken before a judge of a court of record. 2 *Rev. Stat.* 53, *sec.* 9.

Compensation of the committee.] The committee will be allowed for his services, the same compensation as that fixed by the Revised Statutes for the allowance to be made to executors and administrators. 9 *Paige*, 440; and see 6 *Id.* 213. And for their services they are allowed:

1. For receiving and paying out all sums of money not exceeding one thousand dollars, at the rate of five dollars per cent;

2. For receiving and paying any sums exceeding one thousand dollars, and not amounting to ten thousand dollars, at the rate of two dollars and fifty cents per cent; and,

3. For all sums above ten thousand dollars, at the rate of one dollar per cent.

And in all cases such allowance shall be made for their actual and necessary expenses as shall appear just and reasonable. 2 *Rev.*

Stat. 93, *sec.* 58, as amended *Laws of* 1863, *p.* 608. For previous amendment, see *Laws of* 1849, *p.* 218.

If more than one person is appointed committee, the compensation will be apportioned among them in the manner prescribed by the statute; as to which see *Laws of* 1863, *p.* 608, § 8.

The commissions above provided by statute are intended to be a full compensation for the personal services of the committee; and he cannot be allowed any greater or other compensation. 9 *Paige*, 440; 6 *Id.* 213; and see 2 *Id.* 287; 8 *Id.* 412.

But although the committee cannot be allowed for his services, any greater or different compensation than is allowed by way of commissions to executors and administrators, yet where the interests of the estate require it, the committee, under the direction of the court, may employ an agent or clerk, and pay him a reasonable compensation for his services out of the income of the estate. 9 *Paige*, 440. And in the matter of Burr, before referred to, the court allowed the committee of the estate to employ a clerk at an annual salary; and a salary was also allowed to the committee of the person. The necessity for such an allowance will depend on the amount of property to be managed, and various other circumstances. In Burr's case, the property amounted to about two hundred and fifty thousand dollars, and the lunatic, in addition to the committee of the person, was furnished with a companion, who attended him on his journeys and elsewhere, and to whom a salary was also paid. *Will. Eq. Jur.* 691; and see 2 *Barb. Ch. R.* 208; 17 *Barb.* 10.

Authority of the court over the lunatic's estate.] With respect to the control which the court has over the estate of the lunatic, it has been decided that the court may, out of the surplus income of such estate, provide for the support of persons not his next of kin, and whom the lunatic is under no legal obligation to support, where it appears satisfactorily to the court that the lunatic himself would have provided for the support of such persons had he been of sound mind. 2 *Barb. Ch. R.* 326; 11 *Paige*, 256. And the court may also make an allowance out of the income of a lunatic's estate for the education of persons adopted by him as children before his derangement. *Id. ibid.*

And so, where the lunatic's estate is more than sufficient for his support and for the support of those of his relatives for whom he is legally bound to provide, the court may direct an allowance to be made out of such estate to his near relatives who are in need of assistance. And it seems this is done almost as a matter of course, in reference to the children of the lunatic, or other descendants, who are presumptively entitled to his estate in case of his death; and where there is but little or no hope of his recovery. 11 *Paige*, 259, *per* Walworth, Ch.; *Shelf. on Lun.* 161. In all such cases, the court acts in reference to the lunatic's estate, as it supposes the lunatic himself would have acted, if he had been of sound mind. *Id. ibid.*

In reference to the practice of the courts on applications for allowances, and in explanation thereof, Lord Eldon on one occasion remarked: "When the court is called upon to make an allowance, it has nothing to consider but the situation of the lunatic himself, always looking to the probability of his recovery, and never regarding the interest of the next of kin. With this view, only, in case where the estate is considerable, and the persons who will be entitled to it hereafter are otherwise provided for, the court, looking at what is likely the lunatic himself would do, if he were in a capacity to act, will make some provision out of the estate for those persons. So, where a large property devolves upon an elder son who is a lunatic, as heir-at-law, and his brothers and sisters are slenderly or not at all provided for, the court will make an allowance to the latter for the sake of the former, upon the principle that it would naturally be more agreeable to the lunatic, and more for his advantage, that they should receive an education, and maintenance suitable to his condition, than that they should be sent into the world to disgrace him as beggars. So, also, where the father of a family becomes a lunatic, the court does not look at the mere legal demand which his wife and children may have upon him, and which amounts, perhaps, to no more than may keep them from being a burden on the parish; but considering what the lunatic would probably do, and what it would be beneficial to him should be done, makes an allowance for them proportioned to his circumstances. But the court does not do this because they would be entitled, if the lunatic were to die to-morrow, to the entire distribution of his estate; nor necessarily to the extent of giving them the whole surplus beyond the allowance made for the personal use of the lunatic. The court does nothing wantonly, or unnecessarily, to alter his property; but on the contrary, takes care, for his sake, that if he recovers, he shall find his estate as nearly as possible in the same condition as he left it, applying the property, in the meantime, in such manner as the court think it would have been wise and prudent in the lunatic himself to apply it in case he had been capable." *Ex parte Whitbread*, 2 *Meriv*. 102.

But it seems, in cases of an allowance to the children of the lunatic, that adults in whose favor it is made, will be required to stipulate that the amounts advanced to them respectively shall be brought into hotchpot in the disposition of the lunatic's estate, upon his death, if any part of such estate shall come to them under the statute of distributions. 11 *Paige*, 257. Though it would be otherwise in respect to children of the lunatic who are sickly, or decrepit, so as to give them a special claim upon the estate for support. *Ib*. 259.

The court also, may authorize the committee of the lunatic to provide for keeping up the lunatic's family establishment, to the same extent as before the lunacy; and to place at the lunatic's disposal, so long as he is competent to judge of the claims of applicants, small sums of money for purposes of charity; and to pay for the support of the institutions of religion in the church where the lunatic and his family have been accustomed to worship, such sums as the lunatic may desire, not exceeding the amount which the lunatic had been in the habit of paying annually, before his faculties became impaired. *Ib.;* and see 2 *Barb. Ch. R.* 326.

But the committee will not be allowed personally to expend any part of the estate of the lunatic for general charity, or for objects of benevolence, or piety, for which the lunatic himself had not been in the habit of contributing specifically and regularly while he was competent to manage his own affairs. *Id. ibid.* And see further on this subject, *Will. Eq. Jur*. 685; *Shelf. on Lun*. 160.

Costs of the proceedings.] The person who petitions for and prosecutes a commission of lunacy, is entitled to be repaid the costs and expenses properly incurred by him. 1 *Coll*. 461. And the committee of a lunatic, &c., may pay to such petitioner, or to his attorney, the costs and expenses of the application and of the subsequent proceedings thereon, including the appointment of the committee, and without an order of the court for the payment thereof, when the bill of such costs and expenses has een duly taxed and filed with the clerk in whose office the appointment of the committee is entered; provided the whole amount of such costs and expenses does not exceed fifty dollars. But where the costs and expenses exceed that amount, the committee is not at liberty to pay the same out of the estate in his hands, without a special order of the court directing such payment. *Sup. Court Rules*, No. 85; 20 *How.* 385.

If the petitioner fails to establish the lunacy, he must bear his own costs. And in such case, also, he will be charged with costs in favor of the alleged lunatic upon evidence showing bad faith, or a want of probable cause for the commencement of the proceedings. It would be otherwise, however, where he proceeds in good faith. And in a case where a jury, legally impanneled, found the party proceeded against a lunatic, such finding is presumptive evidence that the petitioner acted in good faith, and upon probable cause, although another jury upon the trial of a feigned issue have found the other way. 11 *Paige*, 638; and see 1 *Id.* 498. And the committee in such a case will be entitled to the legal expenses incurred in the proceedings on the inquisition, and in opposing the traverse of it, including the bills of the attorneys of the committee, and a reasonable counsel fee upon the trial of the traverse, and all disbursements properly made, to be paid out of the funds of the estate in his hands. *Id. ibid.*; 20 *How.* 385.

The court may also, in its discretion, allow to the attorney of the party proceeded against the costs of opposing the commission; though as a general rule, it seems the court will not allow the costs of an unsuccessful opposition, for the reason that a party who is really a lunatic is not benefited thereby. 8 *Paige*, 451, *per* Walworth, Ch. Nor has the attorney in such case, where the jury also find the party to have been a lunatic at the time of the alleged retainer, any legal claim against the estate on the ground of contract; he is not a creditor of the lunatic, who was incompetent to make a valid agreement to pay him for opposing the commission. *Ib.* The taxable costs, however, will be allowed in such cases, in the discretion of the court, where the fact of the lunacy is so much a matter of doubt, that the court, if it has been applied to for that purpose, would have directed or sanctioned such opposition. *Ib.*

The allowance of costs out of the estate to pay the expenses of an issue and trial, to test the question whether the party proceeded against is a lunatic, is discretionary, and depends upon the character of the application, and the conduct of the party. 4 *Johns. Ch. R.* 170. Where the party applying is the alleged lunatic, and the estate is large, or able to defray the expenses of the trial, the court will generally make a suitable allowance. In one case, the sum of twenty-five dollars was allowed. 1 *Paige*, 583. In another, the allowance was not fixed by the court; but the committee was directed to pay such reasonable sums as should be requisite to procure the attendance of witnesses upon the trial, and for the employment of proper counsel before the court and jury. 1 *Barb. Ch. R.* 42. And in another case, where the lunacy was satisfactorily established in the first instance, and the opinion of the court, after repeated applications of the party for a discharge of his committee, remained unchanged, the trial was directed to be at the expense of the lunatic, or his friends, and not at the charge of his estate, which consisted of personal property only, acquired by the industry and skill of the wife, and barely sufficient for the support of the lunatic and his family. 6 *Johns. Ch. R.* 440. "In every case of this kind," says Chancellor Walworth, "the court must exercise a sound discretion, regulated by the particular circumstances, so that while the party proceeded against is not deprived of the means of protecting his legal rights, the property, which is necessary for the support of himself and his family, shall not be unnecessarily wasted in useless litigation." 1 *Paige*, 583.

Where the issue is awarded for the benefit of a third person, and it is found against him, the court will not allow costs out of the estate to the attorney who conducts the proceedings. *Ib.* 489 On the contrary, the party for whose benefit the issue is awarded, in such case, will be required to pay costs to the committee. 4 *Johns. Ch. R.* 489.

When costs are allowed, to be taxed, they are to be regulated by the rates prescribed in such cases, in the late Court of Chancery, in force immediately previous to the 1st of July, 1848. *Code*, § 471; and see *ante, p.* 14, *note b.*

SECTION II.

PROCEEDINGS FOR THE SALE OF THEIR REAL ESTATE.

INDEPENDENT of the statute, the courts have no authority to order the sale of the real estate of a lunatic, person of unsound mind, or habitual drunkard, even for the payment of his debts; and this, too, although the heir at law and the next of kin consent to such sale. 5 *Ves.* 556; 2 *Paige*, 598; 7 *Id.* 312.

Under the statute, the court is authorized to order the letting for a term of years, or the sale or other disposition of the lunatic's real estate, whenever it is necessary or proper either for the payment of the debts of the lunatic, or for his support and maintenance, or for his education, or whenever the interest of the lunatic requires or will be substantially promoted by such disposition by reason of any part of the property being exposed to waste and dilapidation, or on account of its being wholly unproductive, or for any other peculiar reasons or circumstances. *Laws of* 1864, *p.* 999; 2 *Rev. Stat.* 53, *sec.* 11. Formerly, however, the court would not order a sale or other disposition of the lunatic's real estate, except where it was necessary for the payment of his debts, or the maintenance of the lunatic or his family, or for the education of his children; nor in any of those cases, if there was personal property sufficient for that purpose. 2 *Paige*, 596; 7 *Id.* 312; 2 *Rev. Stat.* 53, *secs.* 11, 16.

Before the application for leave to sell is made, if there is no committee of the estate, a commission of lunacy, &c., should be issued and returned, and a committee of the estate duly appointed; and until then, the court has no jurisdiction to direct a sale. 8 *How.* 220.

Nor will an inquisition taken abroad, justify an application for the sale of a lunatic's real estate lying within this State. 2 *Johns. Ch. R.* 124; and see 26 *How.* 402.

I. APPLICATION FOR A SALE, &c., UNDER THE REVISED STATUTES (a).

When sale &c., will be ordered.] The statute provides, that whenever the personal estate of any idiot, lunatic, person of unsound mind, or habitual drunkard, shall not be sufficient for the discharge of his debts, it shall be the duty of the committee of his estate to apply by petition to the court by which the committee was appointed, praying for authority to mortgage, lease or sell so much of the real estate of such idiot, &c., as shall be necessary for the payment of such debts. 2 *Rev. Stat.* 53, *sec.* 11.

And where the personal property, and the rents, profits, and income of the real estate of any such idiot, lunatic, person of unsound mind, or habitual drunkard, is insufficient for his maintenance, or that of his family, or for the education of his children, the committee of his estate may apply by petition to the Supreme Court, or to the county court of the county where the premises are situated, or, in the city of New York, to the Court of Common Pleas of that city, when the premises are situated therein, or to the Superior Court of the city of Buffalo, if the premises are situated in that city,—for authority to mortgage or sell the whole, or so much of the real estate as shall be necessary for that purpose. 2 *Rev. Stat.* 54, *sec.* 16; 2 *Paige*, 596; 7 *Id.* 312. *Code of Pro.* § 30; *Laws of* 1854, *p.* 464; *Ib. p.* 224, *secs.* 9, 11.

If the application is to dispose of the real estate for the purpose of paying debts, and the court, instead of ordering the estate to be sold or mortgaged, directs it to be leased, the lease cannot be given for a longer term than five years (b). 2 *Rev. Stat.* 55, *sec.* 23; *Ib.* 53, *secs.* 11, 16.

If the committee neglects or refuses to apply for leave to sell the real estate, where the personal estate is insufficient for the payment of debts, the creditors may institute proceedings, by action, for that purpose. 2 *Johns. Ch. R.* 400; *Ib.* 242. But in such case, if a sale is ordered, it will be conducted by a refe-

(a) The provisions of the Revised Statutes are not in terms repealed by the act passed April 30, 1864 (*Laws of* 1864, *p.* 999, *post*); nor are they inconsistent with, or repugnant to, that act. As originally passed the act applied only to lunatics, while the Revised Statutes apply to idiots, lunatics, persons of unsound mind, and habitual drunkards. 2 *Rev. Stat.* 53, *secs.* 11, 16. Now, however, under a recent amendment of the act of 1864, it is also to apply to the estates of idiots and persons of unsound mind, and to proceedings for the sale of their real estate. *Laws of* 1869, *ch.* 627.

(b) See *post*, *p.* 43 and note, in proceedings under the statute of 1864.

ree and the committee of the estate, under the directions of the court, and the terms of sale, &c., must be reported to the court for its approval before a conveyance is executed. *Id. ibid.*

Petition for leave to sell, &c.] The application is founded upon petition, which should be addressed to the court to which the application is to be made.

If the application is to sell real estate for the payment of debts, the petition should set forth the particulars and amount of the estate, real and personal, of such idiot, lunatic, or other person, the application which may have been made of any personal estate, and an account of the debts and demands existing against such estate. *Ib.* For form, see *Appendix*, No. 430.

Where application to be made.] The courts having jurisdiction to order the sale of the real estate of a lunatic, &c., are the Supreme Court, the county court of the county where the real estate is situated, and the Court of Common Pleas of the city and county of New York, when the real estate is situated within the limits of that city. 2 *Rev. Stat.* 52, *secs.* 1, 11; *Laws of* 1847, *p.* 323, *sec.* 16; *Code of Pro.* § 30, *sub.* 6; *Laws of* 1854, *p.* 464, *sec.* 6. The like authority is also given to the Superior Court of the city of Buffalo, in respect to real estate situated therein. *Laws of* 1854, *p.* 224, *secs.* 9 and 11.

The application for leave to sell, however, cannot be made to any one of those courts, but only to the court by which the committee was appointed, 2 *Rev. Stat.* 53, *secs.* 11, 16; except that where the application is to dispose of real estate for the maintenance of the lunatic, &c., or his family, or for the education of his children, it may be made to the Supreme Court, notwithstanding that the committee was appointed by another court. (*a*) *Ib. sec.* 16; *Laws of* 1847, *p.* 323, *sec.* 16.

The application is *ex parte*, and should be made to the court at special term. See 21 *Barb.* 348. In respect, however, to the county court, no notice being required, the application may be made at any term of the court, or even out of term, that court being always open for the transaction of such business. *Code of*

(*a*) In proceedings under the statute of 1864, *post*, *p.* 41, the application must, in all cases, be made to the Supreme Court.

Pro. § 31. But whether the application, in such case, is made in court or out, the papers should recite the proceedings to have been in court.

Reference, and proceedings thereon.] On the presentation of the petition, the court will order a reference to some suitable and proper person, to inquire into and report upon the matters contained in the petition. 2 *Rev. Stat.* 54, *sec.* 12. For forms, see *Appendix*, No. 431.

The referee thus appointed is required to examine into the truth of the representations made, to hear all parties interested in such real estate, and to report thereon with all convenient speed. *Ib.*

Notice of the reference should be served upon the next of kin of the lunatic, &c., a reasonable time before proceeding thereon. For form, see *Appendix*, No. 432.

Referee's report, and proceedings thereon.] The statute provides that if, upon the coming in of the report, and an examination of the matter, it shall appear to the court that the personal estate of the lunatic, &c., is not sufficient for the payment of his debts, and that the same has been applied to that purpose as far as the circumstances of the case rendered proper, an order will be entered, directing the mortgage, leasing, or sale of the whole or such part of the said real estate as may be necessary to discharge the said debts. 2 *Rev. Stat.* 54, *sec.* 13.

The order will also contain such directions respecting the time and manner of the sale as the court may deem proper; and should direct, also, that the sale be made subject to the approbation of the court. *Ib. sec.* 18.

In addition thereto, if the application is made for leave to dispose of real estate for the maintenance of the lunatic, &c., or of his family, or for the education of his children, the court will direct the manner in which the proceeds of the sale shall be secured, and the income or produce thereof appropriated. *Ib. sec.* 17.

For form of report and order thereon, see *Appendix*, No. 433.

Sale, by whom conducted.] If a sale is ordered by the court, it must be conducted by the committee, and not by a referee,

2 *Rev. Stat.* 53, *secs.* 11 to 18; though in a case where a sale was ordered upon proceedings instituted by bill in the Court of Chancery, the court directed the sale to be conducted by a master in conjunction with the committee. 2 *Johns. ch.* 400; and see *Ib.* 242.

Report of sale, and confirmation thereof.] The committee, having contracted for the sale of the premises, should report the the terms and conditions thereof to the court, upon oath. For form, see *Appendix*, No. 435. If the sale is approved, an order confirming the same will be entered. For form, see *Appendix*, No. 436. And until such report and confirmation, no conveyance can be executed. 2 *Rev. Stat.* 54, *sec.* 18.

Effect of conveyance.] Every conveyance, mortgage, lease, and assurance, made under the order of the court, pursuant to the statute, is as valid and effectual as if the same had been executed by such lunatic, &c., when of sound memory and understanding. 2 *Rev. Stat.* 55, *sec.* 21. For form of conveyance, see *Appendix*, No. 438.

Additional security from committee.] The court may require any additional security to be given by any such committee, for the faithful application and accounting for the proceeds of such mortgage, lease, or sale; and may require an account thereof to be rendered, from time to time. 2 *Rev. Stat.* 54, *sec.* 14. For form of bond, see *Appendix*, No. 437.

How debts to be paid.] In the application of the moneys raised by any such mortgage, lease, or sale, the committee must pay all the debts in an equal proportion, without giving any preference to such as are founded on sealed instruments. 2 *Rev. Stat.* 54, *sec.* 15.

II. Applications for a Sale, &c., under the Act of 1864. (*a*).

In what cases.] The statute provides that any lunatic seized

(*a*) This act was passed on the 30th of April, 1864. *Laws of* 1864, *p.* 999. It does not in terms repeal any of the provisions of the Revised Statutes on the same subject: and it is doubtful whether it can be held to be a substitute for those provisions. As originally passed, the act applied only to lunatics, but under a recent amendment it is made to apply also to idiots and persons of unsound mind. *Laws of* 1869, *ch.* 627.

of any real estate, or entitled to any term for years in lands, or having any tenancy by the curtesy, or any tenancy by the curtesy initiate, may by committee duly appointed; or if such lunatic is a married woman, having any real estate held by her as her separate estate, or having any dower admeasured, or right of dower or inchoate right of dower in any real estate, she may by committee duly appointed, or by her husband, apply to the Supreme Court for the sale or disposition of the same in the manner prescribed by the statute. *Laws of* 1864, *p.* 999, *sec.* 1.

But no real estate or term for years, or any interest in real estate, as aforesaid, can be sold, leased, or disposed of in any manner against the provisions of any last will, or of any conveyance by which such estate, or term, or interest, was devised or granted to such lunatic. *Ib. sec.* 6; and see 10 *Barb.* 553; 38 *Id.* 473. And a sale of any real estate contrary to any such will or conveyance would be void. See 6 *Hill*, 415; 2 *Paige*, 297; 7 *Id.* 312.

To what court applications to be made.] Applications for the disposition of the real estate of a lunatic under the act of 1864, can be made only to the Supreme Court. *Laws of* 1864, *p.* 999. *sec.* 1.

The application is *ex parte*, and should be made at the special term. See 21 *Barb.* 348. For forms in this proceeding, see *Appendix*, Nos. 439 to 442.

What must be made to appear to the court.] Whenever it appears satisfactorily that a disposition of any part of the real estate of such lunatic, or of an interest in any term for years, or of a tenancy by the curtesy or tenancy by the curtesy initiate in any real estate, or a disposition of any real estate, or of her interest in a term of years of a married woman who is a lunatic, held by her as her separate estate, or of any dower admeasured, or right of dower, or inchoate right of dower of a married woman who is a lunatic, is necessary and proper either for the support and maintenance of such lunatic, or for his education, or that the interest of such lunatic requires, or will be substantially promoted by such disposition on account of any part of such property being exposed to waste and dilapidation, or on account of its being wholly unproductive, or when the same has been contracted to be sold, and a conveyance thereof cannot be made by reason of such lunacy, or for any other peculiar reasons or circumstances, the court may order the letting for a term of years, (*a*) or the sale or other disposition of such real estate or interest to be made by such committee, in such manner and with such restrictions as shall be deemed expedient, or may order the fulfillment of said contract by conveyance by such committee according to the terms of the contract. *Laws of* 1864, *p.* 999, § 5.

Bond to the lunatic.] On the application to the court, the committee or the husband, is required to give bond to the lunatic (in addition to the bond given on the appointment as such committee), to be filed with the clerk of the Supreme Court, in such penalty, with such sureties, and in such form as the court shall direct, conditioned for the faithful performance of the trust reposed, for the paying over, investing, and accounting for all moneys that shall be received by the committee, according to the order of any court having authority to give directions in the premises, and for the observance of the orders and directions of the court in relation to the trust. *Laws of* 1864, *p.* 999, § 2. For form of bond, see *Appendix*, No. 441.

If the bond is forfeited, the court will direct it to be prosecuted for the benefit of the party injured. *Ib.* § 3.

Upon the filing of the bond, the court is authorized to proceed in a summary manner, by reference to a referee, to inquire into the merits of the application. *Ib.* § 4.

Contract to be reported and confirmed by the court.] Upon an agreement for the sale, leasing, or other disposition of the property being made, or upon any conveyance in fulfillment of a contract being executed in pursuance of such order, the same shall be reported to the court on the oath of the committee making or executing the same, and (except in the case of a conveyance to fulfill a contract), if the report be confirmed, a

(*a*) Under the Revised Statutes (*ante*, *p.* 38), if the court authorizes the real estate to be leased, the lease cannot be given for a longer period than five years. This provision is not in terms repealed by the act of 1864; and as the two statutes are not inconsistent with each other, it is questionable at least, whether a lease for a longer period than five years is not still prohibited by law. *See Sedg. Stat. Law.* 124; 9 *Barb.* 260; *Ib.* 302; 16 *Id.* 15; 26 *Id.* 657; 4 *E. D. Smith*, 258; 1 *Hilton*, 271, *s. c.* 13 *How.* 441; 5 *Hill*, 221.

conveyance is required to be executed under the directions of the court. *Laws of* 1864, *p.* 999, § 7.

When sales valid.] All sales, leases, dispositions, and conveyances, made in good faith by the committee in pursuance of the orders of the court, will be valid and effectual, as if made by the lunatic when of sound mind. *Laws of* 1864, *p.* 999, § 8.

Disposition of proceeds.] The court is required to make order for the application and disposition of the proceeds of the property, and for the investment of the surplus belonging to the lunatic, so as to secure the same for the benefit of the lunatic, and to direct the ascertainment of the value of any such tenancy by the curtesy, or tenancy by the curtesy initiate, or dower, or right of dower, or inchoate right of dower, and to direct a return of such investment and disposition to be made on oath, as soon as may be, and to require accounts to be rendered periodically by any committee or other person who may be entrusted with the disposition of the income of such proceeds. *Laws of* 1864, *p.* 999, § 9.

Effect of sale.] The statute provides that no sale made as aforesaid of the real estate or interest therein of any lunatic, shall give to such lunatic any other or greater interest or estate in the proceeds of the sale than the lunatic had in the estate so sold; but the proceeds shall be deemed real estate of the same nature as the property sold, or the interest therein of the said lunatic, and the court shall make order for the preservation of the same. *Laws of* 1864, *p.* 999, § 10; see 1 *Kern.* 544; 3 *Sand. Ch. R.* 456, 464; 1 *Duer*, 286.

Proceedings in case of dower, or other life interest.] If the real estate of any lunatic, or any part of it, shall be subject to dower or other life estate, and the person entitled thereto shall consent in writing to accept a gross sum in lieu of such dower or other life estate, or the permanent investment of a reasonable sum, in such manner as that the interest thereof be made payable to the person entitled to such dower or life estate during life, the court may direct the payment of such sum in gross, or the investment of such sum as shall be deemed reasonable and shall be acceptable to the person entitled to the said dower or other life estate or right therein actual or contingent in manner aforesaid. *Laws of* 1864, *p.* 999, § 11.

And before any such sum shall be paid, or such investment made, the court must be satisfied that an effectual release of the right of dower or other life estate actual or contingent has been executed. *Ib.* § 12

SECTION III.

MISCELLANEOUS MATTERS.

I. Applications for Conveyance where Real Estate is held in Trust, &c.

In what cases.] It is provided by the statute, that whenever any idiot, lunatic, person of unsound mind, or habitual drunkard, shall be seized or possessed of any real estate by way of mortgage, or as trustee for others in any manner, his committee may apply to the Supreme Court for authority to convey and assure such real estate to any other person or persons entitled to such conveyance or assurance, in such manner as the court shall direct. 2 *Rev. Stat.* 55, *sec.* 19; *Laws of* 1847, *p.* 323, *sec.* 16.

And the court may, also, on the application of any person entitled to such conveyance or assurance, compel the committee, on a hearing of all parties interested, to execute such conveyance or assurance. 2 *Rev. Stat.* 55, *sec.* 20.

The Supreme Court has the power, under the above statutory provisions, to direct a specific performance by a lunatic heir of a contract for the sale of lands, made by a party who shall have died before the performance thereof.

Thus, where such a contract was made, and the party died without performing it, leaving an only child as his heir at law, who was a lunatic, it was held that a court of equity might decree a specific performance of the contract, and direct the committee of the lunatic to execute all necessary conveyances for the purpose. 1 *Barb. S. C. R.* 495; *Will. Eq. Jur.* 270. And see, also, the practice in respect to the performance by infant heirs of the contract of their ancestor, *ante*, Chapter xiii.

Application, where and how made.] The application must be made to the Supreme Court, at special term. 2 *Rev. Stat.* 55, *secs.* 19, 20; *Laws of* 1847, *p.* 323, *sec.* 16; 21 *Barb.* 348. It is founded upon petition (*a*) addressed "To the Supreme Court of the State of New York," *Ib.; 2 Rev. Stat.* 55. *sec.* 20, *supra;* and should set forth clearly the facts on which the title to relief is founded; and should be verified in the usual form.

Notice of the application should be served upon the parties interested, in the usual manner, accompanied with copies of the papers on which the motion is founded. See *Ib. secs.* 19, 20.

Reference, and proceedings thereon.] The court, upon the presentation of the petition, will direct a reference to some suitable person, to inquire into the truth of the representations made, to hear the parties interested, and to report thereon with all convenient speed. 2 *Rev. Stat.* 54, *secs.* 12, 19.

Notice of the hearing before the referee should be given to the parties interested in the usual manner.

Upon the coming in of the referee's report and confirmation thereof, the court will, if it is a proper case for it, make an order directing the committee to execute a conveyance of the premises. *Ib. secs.* 19, 20.

If either party wishes to except to the report of the referee, the practice prescribed by Rule 32 of the Supreme Court, must be pursued.

Effect of conveyance.] Every conveyance or assurance made in pursuance of the order of the court on such application, will be as valid and effectual as if the same had been executed by such lunatic, &c., when of sound mind and memory. 2 *Rev. Stat.* 54, *sec.* 21.

Costs of the application.] If the application is made for a specific performance of a contract by the heir of the party who

(*a*) Proceedings may also be instituted, by action under the Code of Civil Pro, to compel the committee to execute a conveyance. 2 *Rev. Stat.* 55, *sec.* 20; 1 *Barb. S. C. R.* 495.

made the contract, and such heir is a lunatic, neither the lunatic nor his estate will be charged with the costs of the proceedings. 1 *Barb. S. C. R.* 495; and see 9 *Paige*, 280, 283; 2 *Ed. Ch R.* 415.

Appeals from order.] The order made upon the report of a referee, is an order in a special proceeding; and an appeal may be taken therefrom to the general term. *Laws of* 1854, *p.* 592; *ante, p.* 19, *note;* and see 1 *Kern.* 52.

The practice upon the appeal is regulated substantially by the Code of Procedure; sections 327, 329, 330, and 332, of which are made applicable in such cases (*a*). *Laws of* 1854, *p.* 592, *supra;* and see 9 *How.* 304; *s. c.* 3 *Duer*, 616.

From the decision of the court, at general term, an appeal may be taken to the Court of Appeals. *Code of Pro.* § 11; and see 1 *Kern.* 52; *Ib.* 276; 2 *Id.* 409.

The costs upon appeals, when allowed, are in the discretion of the court; and are regulated by the Code of Procedure. See *Laws of* 1854, *p.* 592, *sec.* 3; *ante, p.* 14, *note b*; 9 *How.* 304; *s. c.* 3 *Duer*, 616.

II. Specific Performance of Contract may be directed.

In what cases.] The statute provides that the court shall have authority to decree and compel the specific performance of any bargain, contract, or agreement, which may have been made by any lunatic, person of unsound mind, or habitual drunkard, while such lunatic, &c., was capable of contracting; and to direct the committee of such person to do and execute all necessary conveyances and acts for that purpose. 2 *Rev. Stat.* 55, *sec.* 22; *Laws of* 1864, *p.* 999, § 5, *ante, p.* 42.

Proceedings thereon.] The application should be made to the Supreme Court. 2 *Rev. Stat.* 55, *sec.* 22; *Laws of* 1864, *p.* 999; and to the special term of that court. 21 *Barb.* 348. It is founded upon petition, upon the presentation of which the usual reference will be ordered. And upon the coming in of the referee's report, an order may be made directing a specific performance, according to the circumstances of the case.

(*a*) The practice is now regulated by the new Code of Civil Procedure; *ante*, vol. 1, p. 20.

In general, in respect to the proceedings subsequent to the application to the court, the practice is the same, substantially, as upon an application to compel a conveyance of real estate held in trust by the lunatic. See, in such case, *ante*, *p*. 45.

III. Other General Matters.

Limitation of authority over lunatic's real estate.] The real estate of any idiot, lunatic, person of unsound mind, or person incapable of conducting his affairs in consequence of habitual drunkenness, shall not be leased for more than five years, or mortgaged, or aliened, or disposed of, otherwise than is directed by the statute. 2 *Rev. Stat.* 55, *sec.* 23; 2 *Johns. Ch. R.* 403; and see *ante*, *p*. 43, *note*.

Partition of lunatic's estate.] The Supreme Court, on the application of the committee of any lunatic, &c., may authorize such committee to agree to the partition of any real estate owned by such lunatic as a joint tenant or tenant in common with others, and to execute releases of the right of such lunatic in and to the share falling to the other owners. 2 *Rev. Stat.* 331, *secs.* 89 to 91. For the practice, in such case, see Chapter xx. *post*, relating to the partition of real estate.

Estate, how disposed of, on death of lunatic, &c.] The statute provides, that in case of the death of any idiot, lunatic, person of unsound mind, or person incapable of conducting his affairs, during such state of incapacity, the power of any trustees appointed under the provisions of the statute, shall cease, and his real estate shall descend to his heirs, and his personal estate be distributed according to law, the same as if he had been of sound mind and memory, and capable of conducting his affairs; but nothing contained in the statute will be held to affect the provisions of any last will and testament, duly made, and which shall be duly admitted to probate. 2 *Rev. Stat.* 55, *sec.* 25, as amended *Laws of* 1865, *p*. 1445.

SUPPLEMENT TO CHAPTER XVIII.

The new Code of Civil Procedure. By the new Code of Civil Procedure, jurisdiction in the proceedings under this chapter is given to the Supreme Court, generally (§ 217); to the Superior City Courts of cities, and the Court of Common Pleas of the City of New York, in respect to the custody of the person and the care of the property of a person residing in the city, or residing without the State and sojourning in the city, who is incompetent to manage his affairs, by reason of lunacy, idiocy, or habitual drunkenness, and for the appointment of a committee of the person or of the property of such an incompetent person; or for the sale or other disposition of the real property, situated within the city, of a person, wherever resident, who is so incompetent (§§ 263, 286); and to each County Court, generally, in respect to the care of the property of a resident of the county who is incompetent as aforesaid, and for the appointment of a committee of his person and estate; or for the sale or other disposition of the real property situated within the county of a person, wherever resident, who is so incompetent (§ 340). General jurisdiction is also given to the Superior Court of the City of Buffalo in respect to any matter which arises, or the subject whereof is situated, within that city, (§ 293).

Proceedings instituted in the late Court of Chancery, prior to 1846, for the appointment of a committee, etc., and pending when the constitution of 1846 went into effect, became vested in the Supreme Court. 44 *Barb.*, 431.

The will of an habitual drunkard, who is subject to a commission, is not, for that reason, absolutely void. Such a person may make a valid will, notwithstanding the commission. The existence of the commission is only *prima facie* evidence of incapacity, which may be rebutted by proof. 50 *Barb.*, 645.

Contract with lunatic, when sustained. The law implies a contract on the part of the lunatic to pay for necessaries furnished for the support of himself and family. 3 *Hun*, 443.

Effect of the inquisition. An inquisition which finds that the alleged lunatic was of unsound mind, and had been in such condition for twenty.four months, is not conclusive evidence of the incapacity of the alleged lunatic to make a will during that period. 6 *Hun*, 658, citing 8 *N. Y.*, 388; 31 *Id.*, 379; 3 *Lans.*, 173.

Power of the committee. The committee who has invested a portion of the estate in a mortgage, may release a portion of the premises covered thereby, without applying to the court for leave to do so. 5 *Hun*, 170.

An appeal will not lie to the general term from an order removing the committee of a lunatic, and appointing another person in his stead. 5 *Abb.*, *N. S.*, 96.

Costs. In the proceedings against a person as a lunatic, or to traverse or supersede the commission, the costs rest in the sound discretion of the court, and will not be granted unless the proceedings are prosecuted fairly and in good faith, and for the benefit of the lunatic. 3 *Hun*, 443.

The compensation of the commissioners is to be determined by an allowance, fixed by the court. *Supreme Court Rules* (1871), *No.* 86. The clause in the old rule giving the commissioners the same fees for drawing the inquisition, etc., when no attorney is employed, to which an attorney would be entitled, is repealed. *Ib.*

Statutory amendments. By *ch.* 446 of the *Laws of* 1874, *p.* 571 (*as amended*, *Laws of* 1875, *ch.* 574; 1876, *ch.* 267), the statutes relating to the care and custody of persons of unsound mind, and the management of their estates, were revised and consolidated. The following are the several sections of the statute in full:

§ 1. *The court having the custody of lunatics, etc.* The Supreme Court shall have the care and custody of all idiots, lunatics, persons of unsound mind, and persons who shall be incapable of conducting their own affairs in consequence of habitual drunkenness, and of their real and personal estates, so that the same shall not be wasted or destroyed, and shall provide for their safe-keeping and maintenance, and for the maintenance of their families and the education of their children out of their personal estates and the rents and profits of their real estate respectively. And the County Court shall have a similar jurisdiction in the care and custody of the person and estate of a lunatic or person of unsound mind or an habitual drunkard resident within the county.

§ 2. *Commission of lunacy; issue therein; evidence.* In every commission of lunacy appointed to inquire into the mental sanity of any party, the inquiry or issue shall be confined to the question, whether or not the person who is the subject of the inquiry is at the time of such inquiry of unsound mind and incompetent to manage himself or his affairs; and no evidence as to anything said or done by such person, or as to his demeanor or state of mind at any time, being more than two years before the time of such commission or inquiry, shall be receivable in proof of insanity, on any such inquiry unless the court shall otherwise direct.

§ 3. *Committee to file inventory and account, etc.* Every committee or guardian of the estate of any idiot, lunatic, or other person of unsound mind, as hereinbefore specified, shall, within six months after their appointment, file in the office of the clerk of the court which appointed such committee or guardian a just and true inventory of the whole real and personal estate of such idiot, lunatic or other person; stating the income and profits thereof, and the debts, credits, and effects, so far as the same shall have come to the knowledge of such committee or guardian. He shall also file in the office of the clerk of the court aforesaid a semi-annual account, thereafter, under oath, and of the disposition made of the income of such estate; and whenever any property belonging to such estate shall be discovered after the filing of any inventory, it shall be the duty of such committee or guardian to file as aforesaid a just and true account of the same, from time to time, as the same shall be discovered.

§ 4. *Verification of inventory. Filing thereof, how compelled.* Such inventories shall be verified by the oath of the committee or guardian, to be taken before a judge of any court of record. And the filing of such inventories may be compelled by the order and process usual in such cases of the court which appointed the committee or guardian.

§ 5. *Committees may sue, etc., in their own names.* Receivers and committees of lunatics and habitual drunkards appointed by any order or decree of any court of competent jurisdiction may sue in their own names for any debt, claim or demand transferred to them, or to the possession or control of which they are entitled as such receiver or committee; and when ordered or authorized to sell such demands the purchaser thereof may sue and recover therefor in his own name, but shall give such security for costs to the defendant as the court in which such suit is brought may direct.

§ 6. *Sale of real estate.* Any idiot, lunatic, or person of unsound mind, seized of any real estate, or of any interest in any real estate or entitled to dower therein, or to any term for years in lands, may, by committee duly appointed, apply to the Supreme Court or County Court for the sale or disposition of the same in the manner hereinafter directed.

§ 7. *Additional bond to be given.* On such application said committee shall give a bond to such idiot, lunatic, or person of unsound mind, in addition to the bond given on appointment as such committee, to be filed with the clerk of said court, in such penalty, with such sureties and in such form as the court shall direct, conditioned for the faithful performance of the trust reposed, for the paying over, investing and accounting for all moneys that shall be received by such committee, according to the order of any court having authority to give directions in the premises, and for the observance of the orders and directions of the court in relation to the trust.

§ 8. *Mode of proceeding.* Upon the filing of such bond, the court may proceed in a summary manner by reference to a referee, to inquire into the merits of such application; and if such bond be forfeited, the court shall direct it to be prosecuted for the benefit of the party injured.

§ 9. *Grounds for leasing or sale of real estate.* Whenever it shall appear satisfactorily that a disposition of any part of the real estate of such idiot, lunatic, or person of unsound mind, or of any interest in any term for years, is necessary and proper either for the support and maintenance of such idiot, lunatic, or person of unsound mind, or for his or her education, or that the interest of such idiot, lunatic, or person of unsound mind, requires or will be substantially promoted by such disposition, on account of any part of such property being exposed to waste and dilapidation, or on account of its being wholly unproductive, or when the same has been contracted to be sold and a conveyance thereof cannot be made by reason of such lunacy or unsoundness of mind, or for any other peculiar reason or circumstances, the court may order the letting for a term of years, or the sale or other disposition of such real estate or interest, to be made by such committee or guardian, in such manner and with such restrictions as shall be deemed expedient, or may order the fulfilment of said contract by conveyance by such committee or guardian, according to the terms of the contract.

§ 10. *No sale can be made contrary to the provisions of a will, etc.* But no real estate, or term for years, or any interest in real estate hereinbefore named, shall be sold, leased, or disposed of in any manner against the provisions of any last will, or of any conveyance by which such estate, or term, or interest, was devised or granted to such idiot, lunatic, or person of unsound mind.

§ 11. *Report and confirmation of same.* Upon an agreement for the sale, leasing, or other disposition of such property, being made, or upon any conveyance in fulfilment of a contract being executed, in pursuance of such order, the same shall be reported to the court on the oath of the committee making or executing the same, and except in the case of a conveyance to fill a contract, if the report be confirmed, a conveyance shall be executed under the directions of the court.

§ 12. *Validity of sales, etc.* All sales, leases, dispositions, and conveyances made in good faith by such committee, in pursuance of such orders, shall be as valid and effectual as if made by such lunatic when of sound mind.

§ 13. *Disposition of proceeds, return, etc.* The court shall make order for the application and disposition of the proceeds of such property, and for the investment of the surplus belonging to such idiot, lunatic, or person of unsound mind, and shall ascertain the value of any dower, or right of dower, or inchoate right of dower, and shall direct a return of such investment and disposition to be made on oath as soon as may be, and shall require accounts to be rendered periodically by any committee or other person who may be intrusted with the disposition of the income of such proceeds.

§ 14. *Proceeds of sale to be deemed real estate.* No sale made, as aforesaid, of the real estate or interest therein of any idiot, lunatic, or person of unsound mind, shall give to such persons aforesaid any other or greater interest or estate in the proceeds of such sale than such idiot, lunatic, or person of unsound mind had in the estate so sold; but the said proceeds shall be deemed real estate of the same nature as the property sold, or the interest therein of the said idiot, lunatic, or person of unsound mind, and the court shall make order for the preservation of the same.

§ 15. *Dower or other life estate.* If the real estate of any idiot, lunatic, or person of an unsound mind, or any part of it, shall be subject to dower or other life estate, and the person entitled thereto shall consent in writing to accept a gross sum in lieu of such dower or other life estate or the permanent investment of a reasonable sum, in such manner as that the interest thereof be made payable to the person entitled to such dower or life estate during life, the court may direct the payment of such sum in gross or the investment of such sum as shall be deemed reasonable, and shall be acceptable to the person entitled to the said dower or other life estate or right therein, actual or contingent, in manner aforesaid.

§ 16. *Release.* Before any such sum shall be paid or such investment made, the court shall be satisfied that an effectual release of such right of dower or other life estate, actual or contingent, has been executed.

§ 17. *When it is the duty of committee to apply for leave to mortgage, etc.* Whenever the personal estate of any such idiot, lunatic, or person of unsound mind, shall not be sufficient for the discharge of his debts, it shall be the duty of the committee of his estate to apply by petition to the court by which they were appointed for authority to mortgage, lease or sell so much of the real estate of such idiot, lunatic, or person of unsound mind, as shall be necessary for the payment of such debts. The said petition shall set forth the particulars and amount of the estate, real and personal, of such idiot, lunatic, or person of unsound mind, the application which may have been made of any personal estate, and an account of the debts and demands existing against such estate.

§ 18. *Reference.* On the presenting of such petition it shall be referred to a referee or to the clerk of the court, to inquire into and report upon the matters therein contained; whose duty it shall be to examine into the truth of the representations made, to hear all parties interested in such real estate, and to report thereon with all convenient speed.

§ 19. *Report and order thereon.* If, upon the coming in of the report and an examination of the matter, it shall appear to the court that the personal estate of the idiot, lunatic, or person of unsound mind, is not sufficient for the payment of his debts, and that the same has been applied to that purpose, as far as the circumstances of the case rendered proper, an order shall be entered directing the mortgage, leasing or sale of the whole or such part of the said real estate as may be necessary to discharge the said debts.

§ 20. *Additional security may be required.* The court may require any additional security to be given by such committee as may seem necessary to secure a more faithful application of, and accounting for, the proceeds of such mortgage, lease, or sale, and shall require an account thereof, to be rendered from time to time.

§ 21. *Debt, how paid.* In the application of any moneys raised by any such mortgage, lease or sale, the committee shall pay all debts in an equal proportion without giving any preference to such as have a legal priority.

§ 22. *Conveyance, when to be made.* The court shall give such orders respecting the time and manner of any sale herein authorized, as shall be deemed proper; and no conveyance in pursuance of any such sale shall be executed until the sale shall have been reported on the oath of the committee, and confirmed by the court directing the same.

§ 23. *Conveyance of property held in trust.* Whenever any idiot, lunatic, or person of unsound mind, shall be seized or possessed of any real estate by way of mortgage, or as a trustee for others in any manner, his committee may apply to the Supreme Court or to the County Court for authority to convey and assure such real estate to any other person or persons entitled to such conveyance or assurance, in such manner as the said court shall direct, upon which a reference and the like proceedings shall be had, as in the case of an application to sell real estate as aforesaid, and the court upon hearing all parties interested, may order such conveyance or assurance to be made.

§ 24. *Committee may be compelled to convey.* On the application of any person entitled to such conveyance or assurance by action or petition, the committe may be compelled by the Supreme Court, or County Court, on a hearing of all parties interested, to execute such conveyance or assurance.

§ 25. *Validity of conveyance, etc.* Every conveyance, mortgage, lease, and assurance made under the order of the Supreme Court, or of any court, pursuant to the provisions of this act, shall be as valid and effectual as if the same had been executed by such idiot, lunatic, or person of unsound mind, when of sound memory and understanding.

§ 26. *Specific performance.* The Supreme Court shall have authority to decree and compel the specific performance of any bargain, contract, or agreement which may have been made by any lunatic or person of unsound mind while such person aforesaid was of sound memory and understanding, and to direct the committee of such person to do and execute all necessary conveyances and acts for that purpose.

§ 27. *Lease.* The real estate of any idiot, lunatic, or person of unsound mind, shall not be leased for more than five years, or mortgaged or aliened, or disposed of otherwise than is hereinbefore directed.

§ 28. *Restoration of estate.* In case any lunatic or person of unsound mind shall be restored to his right mind, and become capable of conducting his own affairs, his real and personal estate shall be restored to him.

§ 29. *Effect of the death of the lunatic.* In case of the death of any idiot, lunatic, or person of unsound mind, or person incapable of conducting his own affairs during such state of incapacity, the power of any committee appointed under this act shall cease, and the real estate of such idiot, lunatic, or person of unsound mind, or person incapable of conducting his own affairs, shall descend to his heirs, and his personal estate be distributed according to law, in the same way as if he had been of sound mind and memory, and capable of conducting his own affairs. But nothing herein contained shall be held to affect the provisions of any last will and testament duly made, and which shall be duly admitted to probate.

Duty of the committee to maintain the lunatic and confine him, if necessary. Duties of overseers of the poor, etc. In addition to the statutory provisions above quoted, it is provided by a recent statute that whenever any person who is possessed of sufficient property to maintain himself, becomes by lunacy or otherwise so far disordered in his senses as to endanger his own person, or the person or property of others, it shall be the duty of the committee of his person and estate to provide a suitable place for his confinement, and to confine and maintain him in such manner as shall be approved by the proper legal authority; and in every case of lunacy hereafter occurring the lunatic shall be sent within ten days to some State lunatic asylum, or to such public or private asylum as may be approved by a standing order or resolution of the supervisors of the county. The superintendents and overseers of the poor are severally enjoined to see that this provision be carried into effect in the most humane and speedy manner, as well in case the lunatic or his relatives are of sufficient ability to defray the expenses, as in case of a pauper. *Laws* 1874, *sec.* 37, *p.* 571.

And when the personal property and the rents, profits and income of the real estate of any idiot, lunatic or person of unsound mind shall be insufficient for his maintenance, or that of his family, or for the education of his children, it shall be the duty of the committee of his estate to apply, by petition, to the Supreme Court, or to the court having jurisdiction, for authority to mortgage or sell the whole, or so much of the real estate as shall be necessary for that purpose, upon which the same reference and proceedings shall be had, and a like order shall be entered, as directed in section nine of title second of this act, and the court shall direct the manner in which the proceeds of such sale shall be secured, and the income or produce thereof appropriated. *Ib., sec.* 38.

Amendment of Act of April 30, 1864. The provisions of that act (*ante, p.* 41 to 45), as far as applicable, are made to apply to the estates of idiots and persons of unsound mind, and to proceedings for the sale and conveyance of any interest in real estate belonging to them. *Laws of* 1869, *ch.* 627; 1870, *p.* 113.

CHAPTER XIX.

THE WRITS OF MANDAMUS AND PROHIBITION.

Section I. The Writ of Mandamus.
II. The Writ of Prohibition.

SECTION I.

THE WRIT OF MANDAMUS.

The writ of mandamus is described by Sir William Blackstone, as a high prerogative writ issuing in the king's name out of the Court of King's Bench, and directed to any person, corporation, or inferior court of judicature, within the king's dominions, requiring them to do some particular thing therein specified and which appertains to their office and duty, and which such court has previously determined, or at least supposes, to be consonant to right and justice. 3 *Bl. Com.* 110; and see *Bac. Abr.*, *Mandamus;* 12 *Wheat.* 561; 2 *Johns. Cas.* 2*d ed.* 217, *note.*

In this State the writ is issued by our Supreme Court, which, in its judicial relation to the sovereign power of the State, the people, possesses the same authority as the King's Bench. The office of the writ is the same here as in England. *Id.* (*a*).

I. When, and in what Cases it lies.

1. *Generally.*] The writ of mandamus issues in all cases where the party has a right to have anything done, and has no

(*a*) For the origin and history of the Writ of Mandamus, and the proceedings therein, see the elaborate notes in 2 *Johns. Cas.* 2*d. ed.*, 217–1 to 81, where the authorities are collected and stated at large.

other appropriate legal means of compelling its performance. 3 *Bl. Com.* 110; 2 *Barb. S. C. R.* 417; 13 *Id.* 440; 25 *Id.* 73.

But the writ will not issue in cases of doubtful right. The remedy by mandamus is a legal remedy; and a party will not entitle himself to it unless he has a clear legal right to demand what is asked for in his writ. 1 *Kern.* 563; 13 *Barb.* 444; 12 *Id.* 217; 26 *Id.* 240; 21 *How.* 335, aff. 22 *Id.* 276; 18 *Abb.* 8; 1 *Wend.* 324; 10 *Id.* 366; 14 *Johns.* 416; 8 *Peters*, 291; 11 *How. U. S. R.* 272.

And there must be no other specific *legal* remedy to which the party can resort for the enforcement of his right. *Id. ibid;* and see *post.* By legal remedy, is meant a remedy at law; and it is no objection to the granting of the writ that the party may resort to a court of equity for redress; nor that his adversary may be punished criminally for omitting to do the act to compel the performance of which the writ is sought. 10 *Wend.* 395, 397.

The writ, therefore, will not be awarded where the party has an adequate remedy by *action;* as, to compel a *corporation* to transfer stock on its books, 6 *Hill*, 243; 10 *Johns.* 484; 10 *How.* 544; to compel a *county treasurer* to pay money, where he withholds such payment without sufficient cause, 2 *Cowen*, 444; and see 6 *Hill*, 244; to compel the *corporation* of the *city of New York* to pay the salary of one of the associate judges of the Court of General Sessions of that city, 25 *Wend.* 680; and see 2 *Hill*, 45; and 25 *Barb.* 73; to compel the *supervisors of a county*, to allow to a person wrongfully assessed the amount of the tax collected from him on such assessment; his remedy being against the assessors personally, 1 *Kern.* 563; or the like. 1 *Wend.* 318; 19 *Id.* 73; 2 *Johns. Cas. 2d ed., note*, 217–9; 13 *Abb.* 374, *s. c.* 35 *Barb.* 653.

Nor will the writ be awarded where the party has a remedy by *writ of error* or *appeal;* as, to compel a *subordinate court* to vacate a rule arresting judgment, 1 *Cowen*, 143; or to enter the satisfaction of a judgment, 10 *Wend.* 546; or to vacate a rule setting aside a report of referees. 21 *Id.* 20; 2 *Johns. Cas. 2d ed., note*, 217–6. Nor where the party has *any other specific legal remedy;* as, to compel the delivery of the books and papers belonging to an office, where the relator's title to such office is clear and free from reasonable doubt; his remedy, in such case, being by summary process under the statute, 5 *Hill*, 616, 631, *note;* 7 *How.* 124*;* and see 14 *Id.* 315; or, to restore a party to the possession of an office where the right to such office is in dispute; the remedy being by action under the Code of Procedure. 20 *Barb.* 302; 5 *Hill*, and 7 *How. supra;* and see *post*, Chapter xxvii. *of this work.*

But where a specific duty is imposed by a statute upon public officers or bodies, they may be compelled to execute it by mandamus, although an action for damages might also lie. 12 *How.* 224, and cases there cited; and see 20 *Barb.* 294. And, it seems, in order to deprive a party of his remedy by mandamus, the remedy by action must not only be adequate, but it must be specific. 1 *Barb. S. C. R.* 34; but see 6 *Hill*, 243, *per* Bronson, J.

It has been said that the general rule that mandamus will not lie where there is an adequate remedy by action, does not apply where the writ is directed to corporations and ministerial officers. 23 *Wend.* 458; 2 *Barb. S. C. R.* 398; and see 2 *Hill*, 45. But this is denied by Parker, J., in *The People* v. *The Supervisors of Chenango County*, 1 *Kern.* 573–4. "If such an exception exists," he observes, "it can extend no further than was expressly recognized in *McCullough* v. *The Mayor of Brooklyn* (23 *Wend. supra*), viz.: if there be a refusal to perform a duty expressly devolved on the corporation, though an action on the case would *perhaps* lie, a mandamus may be awarded; and that is hardly more than saying, 'If the remedy by action be doubtful, a mandamus will lie.'" *Ib.;* and see, also, 2 *Johns. Cas. 2d ed.* 217–11, *note.*

But although a mandamus will not be awarded where the party has another adequate legal remedy, yet the converse of that proposition does not hold true. And there are many cases where, although the party has no other remedy, a mandamus will not lie. Motions for new trials, on the weight of evidence, on the ground of surprise, or to let in newly discovered evidence, and applications for amendments, for relief against defaults, and the like, are among the number. Such questions are addressed to the sound discretion of the court of original jurisdiction; and their decision is final. 20 *Wend.* 662, *per* Bronson, J.; and see 18 *Id.* 98, *per* Tracy, Senator; and 1 *Denio*, 679.

The mandamus is a prerogative writ which the court will issue or withhold, according to its *discretion*, 4 *Hill*, 583; 13

Barb. 450; 1 *Cowen*, 502; 2 *Johns. Cas. 2d ed.* 217–4, *note;* as, where it is manifest that the writ could not accomplish the object designed, 12 *Barb.* 217; 15 *Id.* 608; 29 *Id.* 96, *s. c.* 17 *How.* 142; 20 *Wend.* 108; or where the end of it is merely to try a private right, 2 *Johns. Cas. 2d ed.* 217–5 *note;* or where the granting of it would be attended with manifest hardships and difficulties, 15 *Barb.* 617; 1 *Cowen*, 502; or where the issuing of it would give rise to greater difficulties than would arise from its refusal. 21 *How.* 335, aff. 22 *Id.* 276.

But although the court may grant or refuse the writ in its discre tion, yet this discretion is not merely arbitrary and capricious, but is regulated by well-settled rules and principles of law, which have been incorporated into our system of judicature; and they will be uniformly regarded in determining the question whether the writ shall be awarded or not. See 2 *Johns. Cas. 2d ed.* 217–4, *note.*

It may also be stated, generally, that the writ of mandamus is never granted except for *public purposes*, and to compel the performance of *public* duties. *Bac. Abr., title Mandamus;* 3 *Bl. Com.* 110; 2 *Johns. Cas. 2d ed.* 217–5, 6, *note.*

And so, it will not be granted unless the application has been preceded by a distinct demand of the specific thing the performance of which is the object of the mandamus, and by a refusal of performance, or conduct equivalent to it. *Q. B. Hil. T.* 1843; 7 *Lond. Jur.* 233; 8 *Id.* 496; 3 *A. & E.* 477. But it is not necessary that the party should actually *refuse* to do the thing required; it is sufficient if it appear that the defendant withholds compliance and distinctly determines not to do what is required. As, where a claim is presented to a board of supervisors for allowance, and they permit their session to expire without taking any action upon it. 20 *New York*, 253; and see 3 *A. & E.* 217.

2. *To inferior courts, &c.*] The writ is frequently resorted to for the purpose of compelling inferior judicial tribunals to do some act belonging to their duty. 2 *Johns. Cas. 2d ed.* 217–15 to 31 *notes.* Thus it has been allowed to compel a court of sessions to enter judgment on a verdict where that court had no power to grant a new trial; 1 *Johns. Cas.* 179; and see 2 *Johns.* 371; to compel a court or judicial officer to seal or amend a bill

of exceptions, 1 *Cai. R.* 511; 2 *Johns.* 279; 2 *Johns. Cas.* 118; 5 *Wend.* 132, *note*, or to settle a case and exceptions, and to settle it correctly, 35 *Barb.* 105; to compel a subordinate court to give judgment in order that a writ of error may be brought, 2 *Johns. Cas.* 215; 19 *Johns.* 247; 1 *Cowen*, 143; 9 *Wend.* 182; to allow an appeal to be placed on the calendar and to hear the argument thereof, and to give judgment thereon, where it had been dismissed without authority, 13 *How.* 279; and see *Id.* 398, 401; 36 *Barb.* 164; to settle a case after the denial of a motion to set aside the report of referees, so as to enable the party to appeal, see 20 *Wend.* 663; 35 *Barb.* 105; to approve a new appeal bond on an appeal from a judgment of a justice of the peace, 1 *How.* 196; and the approval of official bonds, in order to enable the appointee to bring an action to try the title to the office, 11 *Abb.* 17; to vacate its rules and orders in certain cases, 1 *How.* 109, 111, 200; 18 *Wend.* 534; but see *Id.* 79; 2 *Denio*, 192; to compel a justice of the peace to issue an execution upon a judgment rendered by him, 2 *How.* 109; and see 22 *Barb.* 502; and a warrant in summary proceedings to recover the possession of land, 5 *Abb.* 206; and a county judge to file his decision after it is completed. 5 *How.* 47; 2 *Johns. Cas. 2d ed.* 217–15 to 31, *note.*

But the writ of mandamus will not be granted to be directed to a court acting under a special commission which has expired by its own limitation previous to the application for the writ, 20 *Wend.* 108; nor to compel a court of common pleas to permit a cause pending there to be removed to the Circuit Court of the United States, 2 *Denio*, 197; nor to vacate a rule arresting judgment, 1 *Cowen*, 143; nor to compel obedience to an order made by another court, 11 *How.* 563; nor to compel an inferior court to punish for a contempt, where the civil rights of an individual are not implicated in the proceeding, 4 *Cowen*, 49; nor to compel a ministerial officer to disobey an injunction, unless it appears to be plainly void for want of jurisdiction, 4 *Hill*, 581; nor to compel a justice to proceed in a suit before him in which he has given judgment of nonsuit, which subsequently was reversed in the common pleas, 9 *Wend.* 503; nor for the purpose of controlling the mere chamber business of a judge of a subordinate court, 5 *Cowen*, 31; nor the practice of other courts, 2 *How.* 59, and see also 2 *Johns. Cas. 2d ed.* 217–15 to 31, *note;* especially that portion of the practice which does not depend upon established principles, or is not regulated by fixed rules. 15 *How.* 392; and see 16 *Id.* 200.

And so, where the court or officer has *acted judicially* in making a decision or order, whether the decision or order be right or wrong, the party will not be permitted to have the same reviewed or corrected by mandamus. The writ will be awarded to set an inferior court in motion when it has refused to act; but not for the purpose of requiring the court to come to any particular decision, or to retrace its steps when it has already acted. 2 *Denio*, 192; 18 *Wend.* 79; 20 *Id.* 658; 3 *How.* 30; 13 *Id.* 277; 35 *Barb.* 105. Thus, the writ has been denied to compel an inferior court to grant a new trial in a cause before it, where it was alleged injustice had been done to one of the parties, 2 *Chitty*, 250; to reinstate an appeal which the court had dismissed, 3 *Binney*, 273; and see 20 *Wend.* 658; 1 *Denio*, 679; to vacate a rule setting aside a report of referees, although the court clearly erred in the decision made, 21 *Wend.* 20; to compel a judge to issue his warrant on a complaint for an intrusion and settlement upon Indian lands, where he had refused to do so, after hearing evidence on the subject, 1 *Denio*, 617; 1 *How.* 186; to compel an inferior court to vacate an order authorizing a defendant to enter a judgment *nunc pro tunc*, in a case where the Supreme Court would have denied the application for such order on account of delay in making it, 1 *Denio*, 644; to vacate an order opening a judgment to enable the defendant to plead a bankrupt discharge, though it was urged that the order interfered with vested rights, 2 *Id.* 191; to vacate a rule setting aside an execution issued by a justice of the peace, on a judgment rendered before him, and docketed in the county clerk's office. 1 *Id.* 646, *note.* Beardsley, J., in denying the motion, said, "The common pleas have acted and decided, and whether right or wrong will not be determined on an application for a mandamus. If the court had no jurisdiction, the order is void; if it had, it is strictly a judicial decision." *Ib.*; and see the cases cited by Tracy, Senator, 18 *Wend.* 89, and by Bronson, J., 20 *Id.* 659.

It is also a rule applicable to this writ, that where inferior tribunals have a *discretion*, and proceed to exercise it, the court has no jurisdiction to control that discretion by mandamus. 2

Johns. Cas. 2d ed. 217–19, *note.* The writ, therefore, will not be allowed to compel a subordinate court to grant a new trial upon the merits, 2 *Cowen*, 479; nor to vacate a rule setting aside a report of referees on the ground that it is founded on insufficient evidence, *Ib.* 458; and see 19 *Wend.* 68; nor to vacate a rule setting aside a regular default and permitting the defendant to plead on payment of costs, 6 *Cowen*, 392; nor to vacate an order allowing rules for interlocutory judgment and assessment of damages to be entered *nunc pro tunc*, 7 *Id.* 523; nor to vacate the condition of a rule setting aside a *ca. sa.*, for irregularity, 3 *Id.* 59; nor to vacate a rule to quash an appeal taken by default in the absence of the relator's attorney, 7 *Id.* 363; nor a rule granting an amendment without the payment of costs, 8 *Wend.* 509; nor, it seems, to vacate a rule granting an amendment in any case within the power of the court, see 16 *Wend.* 617; 20 *Id.* 658; nor to retax a bill of costs, 19 *Id.* 113; nor for the purpose of controlling the mere chamber business of a judge of an inferior court, 5 *Cowen*, 31—or, the practice in other courts, 16 *How.* 200; 15 *Id.* 392, and cases *supra;* or the like. See 1 *Id.* 417; *Ib.* 371; 1 *Wend.* 73; 18 *Id.* 92.

But, although the Supreme Court will not interfere where the subordinate court has a discretion and proceeds to exercise it, yet if the subordinate court refuses to act or to entertain the question for its discretion, the court will interfere so far as to set the inferior jurisdiction in motion, by directing it to proceed and exercise the discretion and powers conferred upon it. 14 *East*, 395; and see 19 *Johns.* 260; 18 *Wend.* 92, 95, *per* Tracy, Senator; 2 *Johns. Cas.* 2d *ed.* 217–23, *note;* 12 *Barb.* 446.

3. *To corporations and ministerial officers.*] The writ of mandamus is also an appropriate remedy to compel corporations and inferior officers, besides those occupying judicial stations, to perform the duties which the law imposes upon them.

With respect to subordinate judicial tribunals and officers, the operation of the writ, as we have seen, has been confined simply to a mandate that they proceed; but as to corporations and ministerial officers, the authority of the writ is recognized to be not only to compel them to act, but to direct the mode and manner in which they shall act. 20 *Wend.* 658; 2 *Barb. S. C. R.* 418; 19 *Johns.* 263; 12 *How.* 224; 13 *Id.* 277. The writ has been allowed, in such cases, to compel the *supervisors of a county* to allow the account of a county clerk for expenses incurred and services performed by him according to law, 18 *Johns.* 242; and see 2 *Cowen*, 530; 1 *How.* 163; to compel them to restore the names of certain banks which they had struck off from the assessment roll as made by the assessors, 4 *Hill*, 20; to compel them to levy and collect the amount of a deficiency on the sale of lands foreclosed on loan-office mortgages, 10 *Wend.* 363; to levy and collect the amount of damages sustained by owners of lands taken for the improvement of a public highway, 4 *Barb.* 64; to compel them to audit and allow the claims of county officers for expenditures paid or incurred by them in the discharge of their official duties. 32 *New York*, 473; and see, also, in like cases, 19 *Johns.* 272; 5 *Cowen*, 292; 3 *Barb. S. C. R.* 332; 20 *Id.* 294; 35 *Id.* 408; 12 *How.* 50; 11 *Abb.* 114; 32 *New York*, 473. And so, where the supervisors of a county, have neglected to perform any duty required of them at their annual meeting,—*e. g.*, to issue warrants for the military commutation, they may be compelled by mandamus to meet again and perform that duty. 4 *Selden*, 318. And where a creditor has an account against a county, and no discretion is vested in the board of supervisors in relation to it, and there is a clear legal duty resting upon them to cause the whole amount of the account to be collected and paid, which they refuse to perform, it seems the only remedy of the creditor is by an application to the court for a mandamus to compel them to perform that duty. 20 *Barb.* 294, 297; denying the authority in 14 *Barb.* 52, and other cases there cited.

In like manner the writ has been issued to compel *commissioners of highways* to open and work a road which has been laid out by commissioners appointed by an act of the legislature, 19 *Wend.* 56; and to open a road where they had refused to do so, and their decision had been reversed on appeal, and the appellate tribunal had proceeded to lay out the road. 16 *Johns.* 61; 12 *Barb.* 194, 6; 4 *Selden*, 476; 1 *Cowen*, 23; 4 *Id.* 544. And the writ will be granted, in such case, without regard to the near approach of the expiration of their offices; if their term of office expires, it will devolve upon their successors to obey the writ. 19 *Wend.* 56; and see 16 *Johns.* 65; 3 *How.* 56. But this remedy should not be resorted to, where its necessary effect would be to subject the commissioners to an action for trespass. 27 *Barb.* 94.

The writ has been issued, also, to compel a *town clerk* to record the survey of a road, 7 *Johns.* 550; a *county clerk* to record a deed properly acknowledged and certified, 14 *Johns.* 325; the *clerk* of the *Marine Court* of the city of New York, to issue an execution upon a judgment rendered by that court, 13 *How.* 5; 22 *Barb.* 502, aff. 13 *How.* 260; 3 *Abb.* 309; the commissioners of jurors to strike the name of the relator from the list of jurors, *MSS. The People Ex. Rel. Livingston* v. *Taylor, Gen. Term,* 1*st. Dist. Nov.* 1865; the *mayor of a city* to grant a license, where the party was entitled to such license as a matter of legal right, 13 *Barb.* 206; the mayor of a city to administer the oaths of office to persons returned by the inspectors of election, as assessors of a ward, 3 *Hill,* 43; and see 4 *Abb.* 36; and to compel him to countersign a warrant for the payment of money, where his signature is necessary to obtain the same; 40 *Barb.* 306; and see 8 *Abb.* 360, *s. c.* 30 *Barb.* 193; 22 *How.* 286; to compel *the trustees of a school district* to issue their warrant for the collection of a tax, 8 *How.* 358; *Id.* 125; to compel a *sheriff* to execute and give a deed of lands, 1 *Cowen,* 502; 18 *Wend.* 598; 1 *Barb. S. C. R.* 379; 4 *Denio,* 138, aff. 2 *Coms.* 485; to compel *canal appraisers* to appraise damages occasioned by a canal, 6 *Cowen,* 518; and the *canal commissioners* to pay the amount of the damages appraised, 7 *Id.* 526; to compel a jury to complete their assessment of damages for the opening of a street in a village, 1 *Barb. S. C. R.* 34; to compel a *county treasurer* to pay the amount of an account which had been legally audited and allowed by the board of supervisors, 15 *Barb.* 529; 19 *Id.* 468; and see 23 *Id.* 338; 1 *Selden,* 65; 6 *Hill,* 244; to compel the *auditor* of the canal department to pay a draft drawn upon him by a canal commissioner, 13 *Barb.* 86; to compel *commissioners for loaning moneys* of the United States, to pay over surplus moneys in their hands, 1 *How.* 160; and see 24 *New York,* 114; to compel the *comptroller* to issue his warrant to pay certain tolls collected by him for the State, 18 *Wend.* 659; to compel the *comptroller* of the *city of New York,* to draw his warrants upon the chamberlain of the city, for certain moneys ordered to be paid by the corporation, 16 *Barb.* 503; and see 34 *Id.* 69; 39 *Id.* 522; 12 *Abb.* 70; 17 *New York,* 585; but not until the claim has been audited by the finance department, 18 *Abb.* 100; to compel the *common council of Brooklyn* to proceed in the matter of widening a public street, 22 *Barb.* 404; to compel the *trustees of non-resident debtors* to appoint referees in pursuance of the statute, in order to contest the validity of the debts presented and claimed by attaching creditors, 1 *How.* 80; 2 *Id.* 200; to compel a *corporation* to exhibit its books and papers to a director or corporator, he having a right at all reasonable times to examine them, 1 *How.* 247; 12 *Wend.* 183; and the like. 2 *Cowen*, 485; 23 *Wend.* 458; 2 *Johns. Cas. 2d. ed.* 217–32 to 61, *notes.*

But the writ will not be allowed in cases where corporations, and ministerial and other officers have acted *judicially;* nor where they have a *discretion* with regard to the performance of an act, and have exercised the discretion conferred upon them; but if they refuse to act when required by law, the court will compel them by mandamus. And the operation of the writ is the same in these respects as when directed to subordinate judicial tribunals. 19 *Wend.* 56; 12 *Barb.* 446; 39 *Id.* 651; 2 *Johns. Cas. 2d ed.* 217–12, 32, 37, *notes.* Thus, the writ will not be allowed to compel a *board of supervisors* to audit and allow an account for services as marshal, where they have adjudicated upon the account, and allowed part and rejected part, 12 *How.* 204; and see to the same effect, 12 *Johns.* 414; 19 *Id.* 260; 9 *Wend.* 508; 1 *Hill*, 362; 14 *Barb.* 52; 26 *Id.* 118; 1 *How.* 116; 12 *Id.* 224; nor to compel *assessors* to reduce their assessments, where the affidavits produced before them are not in conformity with the statute, *see* 15 *Barb.* 608; nor to compel the *attorney general* to prosecute an action to establish the right of a party to an office, 22 *Barb* 114; *s. c.* 13 *How.* 179 and 3 *Abb.* 131; nor to compel a board of *school trustees* to reinstate a person in his position as teacher, 18 *Id.* 165; or pupil, *Ib. note.*

And so the writ will not be allowed to compel a *county treasurer* to pay an account audited by a board of supervisors, where the subject-matter of the account is not within the jurisdiction of the board, 6 *Hill*, 244; 23 *Barb.* 350; *s. c.* 13 *How.* 314; where there are no moneys applicable to such payment, 15 *Abb.* 115; nor to compel a *board of supervisors* to correct an assessment roll after the same has been finally acted upon by them, and a warrant for the collection of the taxes issued to the collector of the town, 15 *Barb.* 608; 24 *Id.* 166; and see 1 *Hill*, 195;

though it is otherwise, it seems, where the mandamus is directed to the *supervisors* of the county of *New York*, 12 *How.* 224, 230; but see 13 *Id.* 305; *s. c.* 4 *Abb.* 84; 24 *Barb.* 166; nor to compel the *canal board* to approve or disapprove of a contract for the performance of work on the canal, made by the canal commissioners and other state officers, with the relator, 13 *Barb.* 432; nor to compel them to confirm the award of a contract to the lowest bidder therefor, 27 *New York*, 378; 26 *Barb.* 241; 33 *Id.* 510; 11 *Abb.* 289, 12 *Id.* 133, nor to compel the *commissioners of excise*, under the act of 1857, to grant a license, 7 *Abb.* 34; nor to compel the supervisors of a county acting as *county canvassers*, to reorganize for the purpose of correcting the estimate of the votes of the county, or otherwise, after they have acted upon the matter and adjourned, 12 *Barb.* 218; and see 7 *Abb.* 34; nor to compel *commissioners of highways* to lay out a highway where they had refused to do so, and the referees, on appeal, had simply reversed their decision without having made any order laying out the road, 4 *Selden*, 476; or to erect a bridge upon a site selected by them at a different place from that contemplated by the statute under which they were acting, 24 *Barb.* 241; nor to compel a *corporation* to make transfers of stock on the books of the company, 10 *How.* 544; *s. c.* 1 *Abb.* 128; nor to compel the performance of public duties on the part of a corporation of another State, *Ib.;* nor to compel obedience to an order made by another court, when that court possesses the authority to enforce its own orders, 11 *How.* 563; *s. c.* 2 *Abb.* 90; nor to afford relief against an illegal tax, which is about to be collected, 1 *Hill*, 195; *and see* 15 *Barb.* 608; but see as to the city of New York, 12 *How.* 224; 13 *Id.* 305; nor in other like cases. 2 *Johns. Cas. 2d ed.* 217–32 to 61, *notes.*

The writ of mandamus is also frequently resorted to for the purpose of *restoring one to an office*, where he is illegally deprived of the possession thereof. The writ, however, confers no title upon the person thus restored; its sole operation being to put him in a situation to enforce his former title, if sufficient in law. 2 *Johns. Cas. 2d ed.* 217—10, 56, *notes.* The only mode of trying the *title* to an office in dispute, is by an information in the nature of a quo warranto; or, now, by action under the Code of Procedure, 3 *Id.* 79; 5 *Hill*, 616; 12 *Barb.* 222; *post*, Chapter xxvi., of this work; though, if quo warranto, or an action, will not lie, a mandamus will be granted, upon the principle that the party shall not be without a remedy. 6 *East*, 356; 5 *Hill*, 629; 2 *Johns. Cas. 2d ed.* 217–11, *note.*

The writ has been allowed to compel the proper officers to admit to the possession of his office or place one elected to the office of mayor, 2 *Roll. Ab. Restitution*, *pl.* 4; recorder, *Id. pl.* 6; sergeant, *Id. pl.* 71; alderman, 2 *Bulst.* 122; policeman, 26 *New York*, 316; 35 *Barb.* 527; *Id.* 644; and brigadier-general, 20 *Barb.* 302; *s. c.* 12 *How.* 126; and see 25 *Barb.* 216; and 2 *Johns. Cas. 2d ed.* 217–52, *note;* 18 *Abb.* 271.

The writ has also been granted to compel an insurance company to swear in a director, the company having been created by charter from the crown, 1 *Stra.* 696; to restore the directors of a banking company, who were refused the exercise of their rights as directors by a majority of the Board, 7 *Loui. R.* 509; as, where the cashier of a bank refused to permit a director to inspect the discount book, and his conduct had been approved by a resolution of the board, 12 *Wend.* 183; and see 1 *How.* 247; and to compel a medical society to restore a party to membership, where such party had been illegally expelled, 24 *Barb.* 570; 32 *New York*, 187; 2 *Johns. Cas. 2d ed.* 217–56, 57, *notes*, and cases there cited; and so, also, to compel the trustees of a meeting-house to admit a dissenting minister, who was duly elected, 3 *Burr.* 1265; and, it seems, the writ of mandamus is the only proper remedy to put a minister of any religious denomination in possession of the pulpit to which he is entitled, 2 *Barb. S. C. R.* 398, 417, 419; and this, too, notwithstanding such pulpit is occupied by another person, *Ib.;* but see the observations on this case in 7 *How.* 129, *per* S. B. Strong, J.; and see *post.*

But the court will not grant a mandamus to admit a person to an office, where the office is already filled by another person who has been admitted and sworn, and is in by color of right, 3 *Johns. Cas.* 79; 20 *Barb.* 302; *s. c.* 12 *How.* 126; nor where there is an appropriate remedy by quo warranto or the action substituted in its place by the Code. *Id. ibid.;* and see 5 *Hill*, 616; 20 *Barb.* 302, *supra;* nor where there is a real and substantial dispute as to the title to the office, *Id. ibid.;* 7 *How.* 124; nor where there is good cause of removal of the relator from the office. 9 *Abb.* 258. The principles which control in affording relief in these cases, are stated by S. B. Strong, J., as follows: "1st. That a mandamus is inappropriate and should not be issued where there is a real and substantial dispute as to the title to an office. 2d. That where the right of the applicant is clear and unquestionable, and the possession of the official books and papers is all that is necessary to enable him to perform fully and satisfactorily the duties of the office, a resort should be had to the summary process given by the statute to obtain such books and papers, and a mandamus being unnecessary, should not be awarded. But, 3d, That when the title of an applicant to an office is beyond a substantial dispute, so that the objection to it is wholly frivolous, and the possession of the books and papers would not give him the entire control of the office, the remedy by the proceedings substituted by our new Code for the writ of quo warranto, would in many cases be so dilatory as to amount to a failure of justice; and the writ of mandamus would be proper, and should be awarded." 7 *How.* 128; and see 20 *Barb.* 302, *supra;* 2 *Johns. Cas.* 2*d ed.* 217–52 to 59, *notes.*

II. How the Writ is Obtained, and Proceedings Thereon.

Having thus considered the nature of the writ of mandamus, and stated most of the cases in this State, as well where the writ has been allowed as refused, we shall now consider the practice in obtaining the same, and the proceedings thereon.

Who may have the Writ.] In a matter of public right, any citizen may prosecute a mandamus, where the object is to enforce the execution of the common law, or of an act of the legislature. 19 *Wend.* 56; 1 *How.* 186. It has been denied, however, that any citizen can have the writ to compel the performance of public duties on the part of State officers. 13 *Barb.* 449, 450, *per* Cady. J.

Where the matter relates to private or corporate rights, the party interested in the same, is entitled to the writ. As, where a municipal corporation purchased lands, and directed its financial officer to pay the purchase money thereof, on his refusal to do so, a mandamus may be applied for by the vendor or party beneficially interested in enforcing the contract, if the application is assented to by the corporation. 39 *Barb.* 522. So, where parties whose duty it was to open a street, neglected to do so, a mandamus may issue against them on the relation of any person interested in the proposed improvement, or in the damages awarded. 20 *How* 491. And the title to relief, at the suit of the relator, should appear; otherwise, a mere stranger might obtain a mandamus officiously, and for purposes not desirable to the real party. 19 *Wend.* 56; and 1 *How.* 186, *supra;* and see 10 *Wend.* 30.

Where the mandamus is applied for in behalf of a particular class, and the legislature has provided that they should be represented by a particular officer, such officer is the proper person to prosecute the writ, and to be named as relator therein. 1 *Denio,* 617; 1 *How.* 186.

Within what time it should be applied for.] There is no statutory limitation of the time within which the writ may be obtained in this State. *See* 12 *Barb.* 449. The writ, however, will not be granted where the party has slept upon his rights. Thus, the court denied a motion for the mandamus to compel the common pleas to quash an appeal after the lapse of five years from the final decision of the cause. 2 *Wend.* 256. In another case a mandamus to the common pleas, requiring them to compel a justice of the peace to amend his return, was denied, because there had been a delay of a year after the happening of the errors complained of. *Id.* 264; and see 2 *Johns. Cas. 2d ed.* 217-14, *note;* 1 *M. & Sel.* 32; 1 *B. & Ad.* 378, 380.

But it seems where the object is to enforce a substantial right by means of a mandamus, the party should be allowed the time given by statute to obtain a remedy for injuries essentially of a similar character, in the ordinary way, if that could be pursued. 12 *Barb.* 446.

The affidavits.] The application for the writ of mandamus is founded upon affidavits, stating the facts upon which the party relies, and which show that he is entitled to the relief demanded. 1 *Johns. Cas.* 134; 3 *Term R.* 575. The facts should be set forth with precision; and where the allegations in the affidavits are not so positive, that an indictment for perjury could be maintained upon them if false, the affidavits will be insufficient. 5 *Term R.* 466, 469; 2 *Johns. Cas. 2d ed.* 217-62, *note.* "The affidavits should also anticipate and answer every possible objection or argument in fact which it may be expected will be urged against the claim, * * * and where any strong evidence is expected, any disputable or material facts should be corroborated by one or more respectable and experienced individuals." 1 *Chit. Gen. Pr.* 808, 809; and see 2 *Johns. Cas.* 2*d ed.* 217–62, *note.*

The affidavits should not be *entitled;* as, for example: "Supreme Court, Andrew Roddy *v.* Thomas W. Hill," 1 *Wend.* 291; or, "Reuben Turner *adv.* James Haight," 2 *Johns.* 371; and see 2 *How.* 60; and the practice is still the same, in this respect, notwithstanding the Code. 7 *How.* 124. But where the affidavit was entitled: "Supreme Court. In the matter of John La Farge *against* The Judges of the Court of Common Pleas of Jefferson County," it was held, that this was not such an entitling of the affidavit as to bring it within the rule that an affidavit entitled cannot be read. 6 *Cowen,* 61. For form of affidavit, see *Appendix,* No. 443.

How and where applied for.] The necessary affidavits having been prepared, the next step is to apply to the court for the mandamus. The application should be made to the Supreme Court (*a*) at special term. *Sup. Court, Rules* No. 40; and see 12 *Barb.* 219.

The application is either that a peremptory mandamus issue at once, or that an alternative mandamus issue, or for an order to show cause in the nature of an alternative mandamus, why the particular act sought to be commanded should not be performed. 10 *Wend.* 30; 3 *How.* 164.

A peremptory mandamus will seldom be granted in the first instance; although, where both parties are heard on the application, and there is no dispute about the facts, and the law is with the application, the court will permit the peremptory writ to issue at once. 7 *Cowen,* 526; 4 *Abb.* 36; 39 *Barb.* 522. And so, it will be permitted to issue at once, where it is apparent that no excuse can be given for the non-performance of the act, and the party's rights might be endangered by delay, see 14 *Johns.* 325;

(*a*) In the city of Buffalo, the application may also be made to the Superior Court of that city, that court having, within that city, concurrent jurisdiction with the Supreme Court, in proceedings by mandamus. *Laws of* 1857, *vol.* 1, *p* 752.

and, also, where on an order to show cause, the defendant shows cause, but not satisfactory. 12 *Wend.* 183; 6 *Cowen*, 518; 27 *New York*, 378. And see further on the subject of the peremptory mandamus, *post, pp.* 78, 80.

The alternative mandamus issues in all cases where the facts on which the party relies are in dispute, or where the parties wish to review the case on appeal. The usual practice, however, is to grant an order to show cause, instead of issuing the alternative writ, 10 *Wend.* 30; especially where the application is to compel the performance of an act by a subordinate court. 9 *Wend.* 472; 2 *Johns. Cas.* 68.

The difference between the order to show cause, and an alternative mandamus, is stated by Harris, J., thus: "In the one case, the questions arising upon the application are discussed upon affidavits; and in the other, the questions come before the court upon the alternative mandamus, setting forth the facts upon which the application for relief is founded and the defendant's return thereto. In the former case, the questions between the parties, being heard upon affidavits merely, no formal judgment is given, and of course no writ of error can be brought. In the latter case a record is made up, and a writ of error lies as upon other judgments. The only practical difference between the two modes of proceeding is, that in the one case the decision of the court upon the application is final, while in the other case such decision may be reviewed upon error." (*a*) 3 *How.* 165; and see *per* Walworth, Ch., 10 *Wend.* 30, *supra;* 2 *Johns. Cas. 2d ed.* 217–63 *note.* For form of order to show cause, see *Appendix* No. 446.

Whether the writ has been granted or denied, on a motion for a peremptory mandamus, or on the return of an order to show cause, the court, on the suggestion of either party, will permit the alternative mandamus to issue to enable the question to be carried further. 20 *Barb.* 86; 13 *How.* 305, 309; 10 *Wend.* 31; 12 *Id.* 183; 6 *Cowen*, 518.

The court will not determine doubtful questions on the motion

---

(*a*) But now the writ of error is abolished, and either party may appeal from the decision of the court made on the order to show cause. See *post*, under the head of "Appeals, and the proceedings therein"; and see, also *Laws of* 1854, *p.* 592, *ante*, *p.* 14, *note b.*; 19 *Barb.* 657; *s. c. on appeal*, 3 *Kern.* 239, 241.

or application for the writ, but will grant the mandamus that the matter may come before them on the return. See *per* Edmonds, J., 7 *How.* 293; and see 1 *Id.* 163.

The application for the writ is either *ex parte*, or upon notice to the defendant. For form of notice, see *Appendix*, No. 444. It was stated by Sutherland, J. (12 *Wend.* 292), that the court would not, in future, entertain motions for a mandamus, or a rule to show cause, unless upon notice to the parties to be affected by the proceedings. But the rule, thus laid down, has not been generally followed by the courts; and the usual practice now is, to apply *ex parte* for the alternative mandamus, or the rule to show cause. See 3 *How.* 165. Where the application, however, is for a peremptory mandamus, in the first instance, the usual notice of motion for a special term must be served at least eight days before the first day of the court, together with copies of the papers on which the same is founded; and the motion should then be brought on in the usual way. See 2 *Burr. Pr.* 176; and 3 *How.* 166: *Ib.* 379; 2 *Johns. Cas. 2d ed.*, 217–63, *note.*

Where a mandamus was sought against the contracting board of the State, and the notice of motion was served on a majority of its members, including the chairman of the board; it was held that the service was sufficient. 20 *How.* 206.

On the return of the order to show cause, or on the motion for the peremptory writ, if the opposite party appears, the relator will hold the affirmative,—thus, the relator will move for the mandamus, and after the opposite party has been heard in opposition to the motion, the relator will be at liberty to reply. 12 *Wend.* 184, *note.*

Alternative mandamus.] If the alternative mandamus is granted, an order authorizing it should be entered with the clerk of the court. For form, see *Appendix*, No. 445. Although, as we have seen, it would be irregular to entitle the affidavits on which the writ is allowed, yet it is otherwise with the rule granting the writ, which may properly be entitled in the cause. 2 *How.* 60.

The alternative writ should be *directed* to the person, body, or tribunal, who is obliged by law to execute it, or whose duty it is to do the thing required. But where it was prosecuted to compel commissioners of highways to do a certain act; it was held that it need not, in the first instance, be directed to the commissioners by their individual names, and that it was only in case of disobedience to the writ, that they were liable to be proceeded against personally. 16 *Johns.* 61. (*a*) And where it was issued to compel a cashier of a bank to submit a book to one of the directors for inspection, where he had refused to do so, and such refusal had been approved by the board of directors; it was held that the writ might properly be directed to the cashier alone; and, it seems, it would not have been improper to have directed it, also, to the directors, especially as they had had notice of the application for the writ, and several of them had shown cause against it. 12 *Wend.* 187.

If the writ is wrongly directed, as, for example, to the mayor, aldermen, and commonalty of Ripon, and the return shows that they were incorporated by the name of "the mayor, *burgesses*, and commonalty," &c., the proceedings will be irregular, and the writ will be quashed. 2 *Salk.* 443. And so the writ was quashed where it was directed to the mayor and aldermen of Hereford, to compel the admission of a person to an office, and it appeared that in fact, the mayor only was to admit. *Id.* 701; and see *Id.* 699. If the writ is wrongly directed, such misdirection may be specially returned, *Id.* 434; or it may be superseded on motion, *Id.* 701; 1 *Stra.* 55; see further on the subject of direction, 2 *Johns. C.* *2d ed.* 217–64, 65, *note, and the cases there cited.* But amendments of the writ may now be allowed the same as process in ordinary actions. *Code*, § 471, *post*, "Amendments."

An alternative mandamus is in the nature of a rule to show cause. 10 *Wend.* 25, 30; 3 *How.* 165. In it the relator sets forth his title, or the facts upon which he relies for the relief sought, and the defendant is required by it to do the particular act asked for, or to show cause.

The title of the relator must be clearly and distinctly stated in the writ, and in such form, that the facts alleged may be admitted or denied; and so that the defendant may at any time after a return, and before a peremptory mandamus is awarded, object a want of sufficient title in the relator to the relief sought,

---

(*a*) Whether, when the object sought is the enforcement of a duty resting upon a board of officers in their collective capacity, the alternative mandamus is defective merely because, though addressed to all the members of the board, it is addressed to them individually, instead of collectively, *quære?* 5 *Abb.* 241.

or show any other defect in substance. *Id. ibid.*; 2 *Coms.* 490; 15 *Barb.* 607; 3 *How.* 30; 7 *Id.* 81. And it is not enough to refer, in the writ, to the affidavits and other papers on file, on which the order for the mandamus was made; though, it seems, such reference will be permitted to show the amount of a sum of money claimed; but not the right of the relator thereto. 10 *Wend.* 25, *supra.* Thus, where the writ was directed to the canal commissioners, requiring them to pay to the relator certain moneys, "according to the order and certificate of the canal board and assignment, &c., mentioned in the affidavits on file, in our Supreme Court of judicature," &c.; it was held defective, and that the affidavits referred to formed no part of the record, and could not, therefore, be considered by the court. 10 *Wend.* 25; and see 7 *Id.* 476; 15 *Barb.* 607. And so, where the writ commanded the defendants to correct an assessment, or show cause, &c., and asserted generally that injustice had been done to the relators in assessing their property, and that they had been unjustly assessed, and that the defendants had refused to correct the erroneous assessment—it was held that those allegations were not sufficient, of themselves, to entitle the relators to relief. "They should have gone beyond that," said the court; "and stated the particulars, in order that it might be seen from them that the charge was well founded, and that the defendants might be enabled specifically to answer the complaint." 15 *Barb.* 613, *supra;* and see 2 *Johns. Cas. 2d ed.*, 217–66, *note.* So, where the writ is sought to compel a referee to settle a case and exceptions, according to the evidence on the trial, it should contain appropriate recitals from which it will be seen that the case and exceptions, when settled in the manner required by the writ, will give a true history of the trial, especially in the particulars therein specified. 35 *Barb.* 105.

But where the writ is issued to compel a subordinate court to seal a bill of exceptions, it need not set forth the bill. 4 *Cowen,* 73. And if the production of records be the object of the writ, they need not be specifically described; a general description is sufficient. 1 *Sid.* 31; 3 *Steph. N. P.* 2321.

The writ should also set forth, with sufficient certainty, the duty to be performed, 2 *Stra.* 897, 857; 6 *Mod.* 310; 2 *Id.* 316; especially as the peremptory writ is required to correspond with it in this respect. 1 *Hill,* 50; 12 *Barb.* 446. And it should not demand too much; otherwise, judgment will be given for the defendants. 1 *Hill*, 55; and see 39 *Barb.* 523; 35 *Id.* 105.

The writ should be made returnable at a special term. See *Sup. Court Rules*, No. 40; 12 *Barb.* 219. But an objection that it is not made returnable at the special term will not be allowed after the return has been made. 11 *How.* 89. And though the writ should be made returnable at the special term, yet the court, in one case, entertained the motion for the mandamus at the general term, where the questions involved were important, and the writ had been made returnable at that term, and no objection had been made. 12 *Barb.* 219, *supra;* and see 1 *Code R.* 135. In the case last cited, the motion was heard in the first instance at the general term, notwithstanding objection was made thereto; but the rules of the Supreme Court, which then authorized such motion, have since been abrogated in that respect. See *Sup. Court Rules*, No. 40, and *Rule* 57, *of* 1847.

The alternative mandamus should be tested, signed, and sealed, in the usual manner. 1 *Burr Pr.* 95, 97; 2 *Ib.* 177. It is not process, however, within the meaning of the statute regulating the test and return of process. 13 *Wend.* 649, 655, *note;* 3 *How.* 164. For form of alternative mandamus, see *Appendix*, No. 447.

When and how served.] The alternative mandamus should be served at least eight days before the day specified in the writ for showing cause. 3 *How.* 164.

The service is made by showing the original writ and delivering a copy thereof. 4 *Cowen*, 73, 403; 1 *Johns.* 64. When directed to the judges of an inferior court, service may be made in term time or in vacation, *Ib. ibid.;* 7 *Wend.* 536; though where the application is to compel an inferior court to try a cause, service should be made in term. 1 *How.* 114. When directed to a county court, service upon such of the judges as are sitting in open court, is sufficient. 1 *Call.* 562.

Amendment of writ.] If there are any irregularities in the writ, it may be amended at any time before it is returnable. *Bac. Abr.*, *Mandamus, B.;* 6 *Mod.* 133; *Doug.* 135; 5 *Abb.* 241. But an amendment will not be permitted after the return, especially if the return has been traversed. 4 *Term*, 690; but see *contra*, 35 *Barb.* 114, *per* Bockes, J. See also on the subject of amendments, 2 *Rev. Stat.* 424, *title* 5, and *Code of Procedure*, §§ 169 to 177, the provisions of which are made applicable to writs of mandamus. 2 *Rev. Stat.* 424, *sec.* 10; *Laws of* 1863, *p.* 664, amending § 471 of the *Code;* (a) 35 *Barb.* 114.

Under the English practice, the amendment is made by a judge's order. 2 *Johns. Cas.* 2*d ed.* 217–67, *note*, citing 1 *Gude Cr. Pr.* 193; 3 *Steph. N. P.* 2325. If there is a mistake in the writ, the prosecutor may quash it, and have a new one before it is returned. *Id.*

Motion to quash or to set aside the writ.] After the alternative writ is served, the defendant may move the court to quash or to set the same aside. 4 *Cowen*, 73. The motion is founded upon some irregularity in the issuing of the writ, 19 *Wend.* 67; or upon defects in the form or substance of the writ. 10 *Id.* 25; 1 *How.* 186; 1 *Stra.* 55; 2 *Salk.* 699; *Id.* 701.

The motion should be made before the return to the writ, except in cases of defects of substance, which may be taken advantage of at any time before the peremptory mandamus is awarded. 10 *Wend.* 31, *and cases there cited;* and see 2 *Coms.* 492; 14 *Barb.* 52; 11 *How.* 89; 2 *Johns. Cas.* 2*d ed.* 217–67, 68, *notes.*

The motion to quash is in the nature of a demurrer, and admits the facts recited in the writ. 7 *How.* 290.

Proceedings if return is not made.] The party to whom the alternative writ is directed, is required to make return thereto, and for a neglect so to do, such party may be proceeded against by attachment, as for a contempt, in the manner prescribed in the thirteenth title (2 *Rev. Stat.* 534) of chapter eight of part third of the Revised Statutes. 2 *Rev. Stat.* 586, *sec.* 54. See those proceedings in Chapter vii. of this work.

Where the mandamus is directed to a corporation, to do a corporate act, and no return is made, the attachment is granted only

---

(a) It is provided by this amendment to § 471, that "in actions or proceedings by mandamus, amendments of any mistakes in the process, pleadings, or proceedings therein may be allowed, and shall be made in conformity to the provisions of chapter six, title six (§§ 169 to 177) of the second part of the Code of Procedure."

against those particular persons who refuse to pay obedience tc it; but where it is directed to several persons in their natural capacity, the attachment must issue against all, though when they are before the court the punishment will be proportioned to their offense. 2 *Johns. Cas.* 2*d ed.* 217–69, *note*, citing *Hil.* 8 *Geo. II.; Bul. N. P.* 201; 1 *Gude Cr. Pr.* 189; 2 *Salk.* 429

If the writ be directed to a "town council," and they adjourn the corporate assembly in order to prevent the return being made, the members will be punishable for contempt. *Id. ibid.;* 10 *Mod.* 56.

Further time to make return.] If the defendant desires further time in which to make a return, he may apply to the Supreme Court, or to a justice thereof, for an order enlarging the time, the same as in personal actions. 2 *Rev. Stat.* 587, *sec.* 59; 1 *Johns.* 64; 4 *Cowen*, 73, 403; 1 *Barb. S. C. R.* 558; *Sup. Court Rules*, No. 22.

The return.] The person, body, or tribunal to whom the alternative mandamus is directed and delivered, is required to make return thereto, 2 *Rev. Stat.* 586, *sec.* 54; 2 *Johns. Cas.* 2*d ed.* 217–69, *note, and cases there cited:* and he cannot demur to the writ. 6 *Abb.* 30. But no return is necessary where the writ has been quashed; nor where the defendant concludes to put an end to the controversy by performing the act required. 10 *Wend* 31.

The return should be made within the time mentioned in the writ, or within the time allowed by the order enlarging the time, if such order be obtained. 2 *Rev. Stat.* 586, *sec.* 59. And it is no excuse for not making the return that the writ has not been returned and filed. 4 *Cowen*, 73, 76, 403.

The return should deny the facts stated in the writ, on which the claim of the relator is founded, or show other facts in law sufficient to defeat the relator's claim. 10 *Wend.* 25; 14 *Barb.* 52; 11 *How.* 89; 32 *Barb.* 473. Facts should be alleged in it, and not the evidence from which those facts are inferred. 10 *Wend.* 32; 2 *Coms.* 496; 35 *Barb.* 105. It should be positive and certain, 2 *Coms.* 496; 1 *Ld. Raymond*, 559; and not argumentative, *Id.; Doug.* 158; 5 *Term. R.* 66; 6 *Mod.* 309; 18 *How.* 152; *s. c.* 10 *Abb.* 233; nor evasive, 1 *Barb. S. C. R.* 34.

Several matters may be returned, but they should be consistent; for if they are inconsistent, the whole will be quashed, because the court will not know which to believe. 2 *Salk.* 436. But if the return consists of several independent matters not inconsistent with each other, some of which are good, in law, and some bad, the court may quash the return as to such as are bad, and put the relator to plead to or traverse the rest. 2 *Term R.* 456; 5 *Id.* 66; 6 *Id.* 493. But certainty to a common intent will, in general, be sufficient; and the court will not intend inconsistent facts, for the purpose of making it bad. *Doug.* 159; 2 *Salk.* 431.

The return should state all the material steps taken by the defendant, precisely as they occurred; and should, in itself, or by express adoption of the allegations in the writ, either in whole or in part, state the case which makes out the defendant's justification. It may set up any number of facts constituting good reasons for not performing the act which the writ seeks to compel, if they exist in point of fact. 32 *Barb.* 473.

The return must be good, tested by the ordinary rules of pleading, both in form and substance. And the relator may demur or plead to all or any of the material facts contained therein. 35 *Id.* 105; *per* Bockes, J.

An allegation in a return that the law under which the relief is claimed is unconstitutional and void, is not a fact, but an averment of a principle of law, which will be struck out on motion. 11 *How.* 89. And so, if the return contains anything more than a full answer to the substantial averments in the writ, it will be rejected as surplusage, or struck out on motion. 2 *Coms.* 496.

If the defendant makes a false return, he will be liable to the relator for the damages occasioned thereby. Thus, where the supervisors made a false return to a mandamus sued out by an individual whose land had been taken for a highway, and the relator had been kept out of the damages to which he was entitled from the town, it was held that the defendants were properly liable in damages to the extent of the interest upon the damages assessed. 28 *New York*, 112; and see 2 *Rev. Stat.* 587, *secs.* 57, 58.

The court may receive a return without a verification, 1 *Sid.* 227; or they may require such verification. *Pol.* 455; *Ld.*

Raym. 365. The return need not be signed by or on behalf of the party making it; and if it be made by a corporation, it need not be signed nor sealed. 2 *Johns. Cas. 2d ed.* 217–74, *note*, citing 1 *Salk.* 192; *Skin.* 368; *Com. Dig. Man.* 2; and see 1 *Ld. Raym.* 223.

See, further, on the subject of returns to writs of mandamus, 2 *Johns. Cas. 2d ed.* 217–69 to 74, *notes;* and for form of return, see *Appendix*, No. 448.

Amendment of return.] The defendant having made and filed a return, may desire to amend it. But amendments will be allowed with caution. (*a*) In one case, the court, after a verdict on the traverse to a return, refused to allow the defendants to amend the return by setting forth a different constitution of the corporation. 7 *Term R.* 699; and see 2 *Johns. Cas. 2d ed.* 217–74. Clerical mistakes may be amended after the return is filed. *Id.; Doug.* 135.

Motion for a further return.] If the return made by the defendant is thought by the relator to be evasive, or otherwise insufficient, he may apply to the court for a further or supplementary return. 9 *Wend.* 429, 430; 7 *Id.* 475. But where a motion is made for a further return of additional facts, the motion will be denied, unless such additional facts are set forth in the alternative writ. 3 *How.* 30.

Motion to quash and to strike out return.] If the return be defective upon its face, as, if several matters be returned which are inconsistent, the relator may apply to the court to quash it, 2 *Salk.* 436; 4 *Burr.* 2041; *Cowp.* 413; and it may be quashed as to part. 2 *Term R.* 456; 5 *Id.* 56; 6 *Id.* 493.

And so, if the return contain anything more than a full answer to the substantial averments in the writ, the improper matter will be rejected as surplusage, or struck out on motion. 2 *Coms.* 496. And in like manner if a portion of the return is alleged to be immaterial or argumentative, it will be struck out.

(*a*) By an amendment to § 471 of the Code of Procedure (*Laws of* 1863, *p.* 664), the provisions of the Code, §§ 169 to 177, are to apply to proceedings upon mandamus, See *ante*, *p.* 69, *note*.

11 *How.* 89; 8 *Id.* 358. A demurrer in such cases, would be improper. *Id. ibid.*; 4 *Coms.* 496.

So, the return will be quashed if it is evasive; as where a mandamus required the inspectors of election to return whether the relators did not receive the greatest number of votes, and whether they did not declare them duly elected, a return that they were not elected by the greatest number of votes, was held to be evasive, and was quashed. 11 *Abb.* 168.

The motion to strike out parts of a return may be made on the motion for a peremptory mandamus notwithstanding the return. 9 *Id.* 258.

Notice requiring relator to demur or plead to return.] The return to the writ of mandamus having been filed, the party making such return may serve a notice upon the relator requiring him to demur or plead thereto within twenty days after such service. (*a*) *Sup. Court Rules*, No. 51. For form of notice, see *Appendix*, No. 449.

Proceedings if relator does not demur or plead.] If no plea or demurrer to the return is interposed, within the time required, either party may notice the matter for a hearing at the next or any subsequent special term; at which the same may, according to the practice of the court, be heard as a non-enumerated motion; and the same shall be heard and disposed of on the said return. *Sup. Court Rules*, No. 51, *supra.* For form of notice of hearing, see *Appendix*, No. 450.

The relator having failed to demur or plead to the return within the time required, the facts alleged in the return are thereby

---

(*a*) The rule adopted by the Supreme Court in 1858, in respect to proceedings upon mandamus and prohibition, materially altered the practice in such cases. The former rules provided that "the return to a writ of mandamus or of prohibition, where such return shall be adopted by the party, having been filed, a rule may be entered requiring the relator to demur or plead thereto in twenty days after notice of the rule, or to move at the next special term thereafter, for such rule as he may require; and in case of default, on filing an affidavit showing such default, a rule may be entered dismissing such writ and all subsequent proceedings, with costs." *Sup. Court Rules*, 1856, No. 43; and see *Rules of* 1847, No. 75; 10 *Wend.* 632.

The pleadings in mandamus are the same as under the former system of pleading; and the rules prescribed by the Code of Procedure have no application to them. *Code*, § 471; 16 *How.* 4; *s. c.* 5 *Abb.* 372; and see 6 *How.* 179; *Ib.* 319; 32 *Barb.* 473.

admitted to be true, and the case will be determined by the court the same as if he had formally demurred to such return. See 6 *Wend.* 559, 560; 7 *Id.* 475; 10 *Id.* 632; 1 *Barb, S. C. R.* 379, 384.

Demurrer, plea, &c.] At the common law, the relator was not permitted to traverse the return, notwithstanding that it might be false in fact; but the remedy was either by an action on the case for a false return, or if the matter concerned the public, by indictment against the person making the return. 2 *Johns. Cas. 2d ed.* 217-75, *note.*

But the statute has changed the common law in this respect, and it is now provided that whenever a return shall be made to any writ of mandamus, the party prosecuting such writ may demur or plead to all or any of the material facts contained in the return, to which the person making such return, shall reply, take issue or demur; and the like proceedings shall be had therein for the determination thereof, as might have been had, if the person prosecuting such writ had brought his action on the case for a false return. 2 *Rev. Stat.* 586, *sec.* 55; 10 *Wend.* 32; 3 *How.* 380. A similar statutory provision also existed previous to the Revised Statutes. 1 *R. L.* 107, *sec.* 2; 14 *Johns. R.* 61.

The practice under the above provision of the Revised Statutes is stated by Sutherland, J., thus: "Although these statutes contemplate formal written pleadings in the ordinary mode of conducting suits, the practice of the court is virtually to allow pleadings *ore tenus;* that is, the relator is permitted to discuss the return, and to ask for a peremptory mandamus, and whilst he does not put in a *formal demurrer*, the case is considered as embraced in the description of *non-enumerated* business, and is heard as such; but if a formal demurrer is interposed, it becomes *enumerated* business, and can be heard only at the stated terms. It is optional with a relator whether it shall be considered *enumerated* or *non-enumerated* business, unless the court specially direct formal pleadings to be interposed. No injury can result to the defendant in consequence of this privilege allowed the relator, for if he wishes to carry up the cause for review, the court permits him, after its decision, to made up and file formal pleadings, so that a record may be made up; which privilege, however, is not granted to the relator, who has chosen to ask for a peremptory mandamus, without formally demurring; if dissatisfied with the decision of the court, *he* cannot carry up the cause for review." (*a*) 6 *Wend.* 559, 560; 10 *Id.* 632; and see, also, to the same effect, *per* Nelson, J., 7 *Id.* 475; and *per* Welles, J., 1 *Barb. S. C. R.* 379, 384.

But although the relator may demur or plead to the return, yet he cannot do both. 1 *Wend.* 38. The court will not permit him to dissect the return into as many parts as he sees fit, plead to some portions and demur to the residue. *Ib.* And where the return alleges several material facts, the relator, in pleading to it, need not deny all of the facts; but he may deny any one or more of them, and omit to plead to the others, in which case the facts not denied will be taken as true. 3 *How.* 381; 16 *Mod.* 174.

If a demurrer is interposed, the question will be upon the sufficiency of the pleadings, the same as in an ordinary action, and the party must fail who commits the first error in matter of substance. 35 *Barb.* 105; *Ib.* 110, *per* Bockes, J.

Where portions of the return are alleged to be immaterial or argumentative, the relator's remedy is not by demurrer, but by motion to strike out. 2 *Coms.* 496; 11 *How.* 89; 8 *Id.* 358.

Nor will the relator be permitted to demur specially to the return; so held where the mandamus was directed to a subordinate court, to compel them to sign and seal a bill of exceptions, and the judges returned that they refused to seal the bill unless the same should contain all the evidence relating to the matters of law therein excepted to, and which they alleged the bill did not contain, and to which return the relator demurred, specially, that it was not alleged in the return that the bill did not contain all the evidence material and necessary to present the question of law raised by the bill. 9 *Wend.* 429. And *per* Sutherland, J., in that case: "This court will not permit subordinate tribunals to be harrassed with special demurrers to returns made by them. If the relator is dissatisfied with a return made, conceiving it to be evasive, or the construction of any matters alleged in it to be of doubtful character, upon sug-

(*a*) But the practice is no doubt changed, with respect to the right of the relator to have the case reviewed, notwithstanding he has not formally demurred to the return. Such review may now be had by appeal. *Laws of* 1854, *p.* 592, *ante*, *p.* 14, *note b*; 19 *Barb.* 657; 28 *How.* 167; *Code of Pro*, § 11, *sub.* 3; *First Rep. of Com. on Code*, *p.* 11 to 20; and see *post*, under the head of "Appeals, and the proceedings therein."

gestion of its insufficiency, a further or supplementary return will be ordered, and thus the rights of a party as effectually protected as if permitted to demur specially." *Ib.* 430.

If the relator takes issue on the return to the alternative writ, instead of demurring, he cannot afterwards question its legal sufficiency; and if the verdict is against him, the peremptory writ will be refused. 26 *New York*, 316.

If the parties desire further time in which to demur, plead, &c., it may be obtained on application to the court or to a justice thereof, the same as in personal actions. 2 *Rev. Stat.* 587, *sec.* 59.

Issue of law, and proceedings thereon.] If the relator demurs to the return, or the defendant demurs to the plea put in to the return, the facts alleged in such return, or such plea, are thereby admitted to be true; and the question becomes one of law, and should be put upon the calendar and brought on for argument as in personal actions. And so, it is substantially an issue of law where the relator, without formally demurring to the return, applies to the court for a peremptory mandamus, notwithstanding the return. In such case, also, the facts set forth in the return are admitted to be true, and the question is one of law, whether, from the facts admitted, a mandamus should be awarded. 7 *Wend.* 475; and see also, 6 *Id.* 559; 10 *Id.* 632: and 1 *Barb. S. C. R.* 379; *Sup. Court Rules*, No. 51.

Issue of fact and proceedings thereon.] If the facts in the return are denied, or an issue of fact exists in any other way, on the pleadings, the case must go down to the circuit for trial. 7 *Wend.* 475, *supra.*

The case is prepared and brought on for trial, the same as in personal actions.

Allegations in the return, which are denied by the relator, in his plea, and not proved, are not to be taken as true on the trial. 12 *How.* 51. Though where the relator, instead of demurring to the return, put in a plea, taking issue upon all the material allegations in the return—it was held that he thereby admitted that, upon its face, the return was a sufficient answer to the case made by the alternative writ. 24 *Barb.* 341. The relator holding the affirmative of the issue, the return is to be taken as true, until it is falsified upon the trial. *Ib.* 348.

Where the issues are submitted to a jury, the jury may render a general verdict, instead of finding upon each separate issue; and the court will give effect to the verdict, if necessary, by applying it to the issues separately. 35 *Barb.* 644, *s. c.;* 14 *Abb.* 151; *Ib.* 158, *s. c.* 35 *Barb.* 651.

The court will, in a proper case, direct the jury what verdict to render. Thus, where there is no evidence, or the weight of evidence is so decidedly in favor of one side, that the court would set aside the verdict as against the evidence, if rendered, it is the duty of the court to direct the jury what verdict to render. *Ib.*

On the trial of the issue, the relator, sueing in the name of the people, is a competent witness in behalf of the plaintiffs under § 471 of the Code. 14 *Abb.* 305, *s. c.* 23 *How.* 306.

Issues of fact are to be tried in the county within which the material facts contained in the mandamus shall be alleged to have taken place. 2 *Rev. Stat.* 586, *sec.* 56.

Damages.] In case a verdict be found for the relator, or judgment be given for him upon demurrer, or by default, he shall recover damages and costs, in like manner as he might have done if he had brought his action on the case for a false return. 2 *Rev. Stat.* 587, *sec.* 57.

Thus, where a mandamus was issued against supervisors, in favor of an individual whose land had been taken for a highway, and who had been kept out of the damages to which he was entitled from the town, and the supervisors made a false return to the writ; it was held that they were properly made liable in damages, to the extent of the interest upon the damages assessed. 28 *New York*, 112.

The damages are either assessed by the jury on the trial of the issues of fact joined, or if the judgment be by default, or on demurrer, they are assessed on a writ of inquiry, as in personal actions. See 2 *Burr. Pr.* 179.

A recovery of damages under the statutory provision last cited, against any party who shall have made a return, is a bar to any other action against such party, for making such return. 2 *Rev. Stat.* 587, *sec.* 58.

Judgment and execution.] Judgment is entered on the decision of the court, or the verdict of the jury, as in personal actions.

But, it seems, a peremptory mandamus will not be awarded after verdict or judgment by default, without notice to the defendant, and motion to the court for that purpose. 3 *How.* 379, 382, *per* Barculo, J. Nor can judgment for costs, in such case, be entered, except by the special order of the court. *Ib.;* and see *post, p.* 81, "Costs."

The judgment must conform to the verdict of the jury; and there is no judgment *non obstante veredicto*, in these proceedings. 26 *New York*, 316.

If a party has judgment for costs, or for damages and costs, execution issues for the same, as in personal actions. For form of judgment record, see *Appendix*, No. 451.

Peremptory mandamus, and how obtained.] If a verdict, on the trial of an issue of fact, be found for the relator, or judgment be rendered for him upon demurrer or by default, a peremptory mandamus is directed by the statute to be granted to him without delay. 2 *Rev Stat.* 587, *sec.* 57. This language of the statute would seem to authorize the peremptory writ to issue immediately on default, or on the decision by verdict or upon demurrer. But see 3 *How.* 380, 382, where the practice in cases of mandamus on issue and verdict, or judgment by default, is stated by Barculo, J., thus: "After the facts of the case are settled, either by an issue and verdict, or by default of one of the parties, the relator, to obtain a peremptory mandamus, must move the court on notice to the opposite party, upon the return, pleadings, verdict, &c.; when the court can, in view of the whole case, pronounce upon the rights of the respective parties."

The relator may, also, on the coming in of the return without formally demurring or pleading to the same, apply to the court, on notice, for the peremptory mandamus. In such case, the facts alleged in the return are admitted to be true; and the question is one of law, whether upon the facts admitted, the relator is entitled to the peremptory mandamus. 6 *Wend.* 559; 7 *Id.* 475; 10 *Id.* 632; 1 *Barb. S. C. R.* 379; *Sup. Court Rules*, No. 51. If the court determine, on such motion, that the return is insufficient, and the relator is otherwise entitled to the relief sought, a peremptory mandamus will be awarded. *Id. ibid.* The papers on which the alternative mandamus is granted, should be presented to the court on the hearing of the motion, for the purpose of apprising the court of the purport and intent of the proceedings, but not to affect the matters contained in the return. 7 *Wend.* 476; 10 *Id.* 30, 31. And the relator should state in writing the points relied upon in support of the application. 2 *Id.* 255.

Where both the parties are heard on the application for the alternative writ, and there is no dispute about the facts, and the law is with the application, the peremptory mandamus will issue in the first instance. 7 *Cowen*, 526; 4 *Abb.* 36; 39 *Barb.* 522. And it will issue in the first instance where it is apparent that no excuse can be given for the non-performance of the act complained of, and the relator's rights might be endangered by delay. See 14 *Johns.* 325. And so where the defendant on the application for the alternative writ, shows cause against it, but not satisfactory, the peremptory writ will be granted. 12 *Wend.* 183; 6 *Cowen*, 518. But in such case, on suggestion that the defendant wishes to bring error, the court will change the rule into one for an alternative mandamus, so that the facts may be put on record by a return. *Id. ibid.;* but see *ante, p.* 64, *note.*

And where the alternative writ has been regularly served, the court may in their discretion, upon due proof of such service, order a peremptory mandamus, without compelling a return. 1 *Johns.* 64. If, however, the defendants have not had time to prepare a return, the court will extend the time for that purpose, before permitting the peremptory writ to issue. 4 *Cowen*, 73; *Ib.* 403.

And so the peremptory writ will be awarded where the return is insufficient. 7 *Johns.* 549; 6 *Cowen*, 579. So if it is evasive. 1 *Barb. S. C. R.* 34. So, where the court has sustained the return on a motion to quash it, a peremptory mandamus may issue, although the issues raised by the return are found in favor of the defendant. 14 *Abb.* 151; *s. c.* 35 *Barb.* 644.

The peremptory mandamus must correspond with the alternative writ in respect to the thing required to be performed. 1 *Hill*, 50; 12 *Barb.* 446; 10 *Abb.* 233; *s. c.* 18 *How.* 152. And if the relator is not entitled to the relief demanded in the alternative writ. his motion for a peremptory mandamus will be denied, although it appears he is entitled to a portion of the relief. *Ib.*

If the peremptory writ is awarded, an order to that effect should be entered with the clerk. And if costs are granted, their allowance should be inserted in the order awarding the peremptory mandamus. See *post*, "Costs."

After the court has awarded the peremptory mandamus, there is no power to stay the proceedings upon it, 2 *Barb. S. C. R.* 555; though it would be otherwise upon appeal from the order granting it. *Laws of* 1854, *p.* 592, *ante*, *p.* 19.

See further on the subject of the peremptory mandamus, 2 *Johns. Cas. 2d ed.* 217–78, *note; Bac. Abr.*, *Mandamus*, *M;* and for form of peremptory writ, see *Appendix*, No. 452.

Where and how motion for peremptory writ brought on.] The motion for the peremptory mandamus, where it is founded upon the return, and the relator has not formally demurred, is a non-enumerated motion, and is brought on the same as other non-enumerated motions. 6 *Wend.* 559; 7 *Id.* 474; 10 *Id.* 632; 1 *Barb. S. C. R.* 379; *Sup. Court Rules*, No. 51. If there is a demurrer to the return, or an issue of law upon the pleadings, the case is put upon the calendar as an enumerated motion, and brought on for argument in the usual manner. *Id. ibid.* In either case it should be noticed for the special term, *Sup. Court Rules*, 1849, No. 31; *Ib.* 1858, No. 40; 10 *How.* 353; 1 *Abb.* 460; 1 *Code R.*, *N. S.* 338; and in the city of New York, at special term at chambers; though formerly, upon demurrer to the return, or on issue of law upon the pleadings, the argument was brought on at the general term. 1 *Barb. S. C. R.* 384; 2 *Id.* 557; 6 *Wend.* 559, 560; 7 *Id.* 475.

It is optional with the relator whether the motion shall be considered enumerated or non-enumerated business, unless the court specially direct formal pleadings to be interposed; if he elect to have it considered non-enumerated, the court, on the application of the defendant, after its decision of the question, will permit formal pleadings to be made up and filed, and the defendant may thereupon have the judgment reviewed on appeal, the same as in actions, *Ib. ibid.;* or either party may now appeal from the decision of the court as from a final order, without making up a formal record of judgment. *Laws of* 1854, *p.* 592, *ante, p.* 14, *note b;* 19 *Barb.* 657; 28 *How.* 167; *Code of Pro. sec.* 11, *sub.* 3; *First Rep. of Com. on Code, p.* 11 *to* 20; though formerly, the relator, by moving upon the return, lost the right to have the decision reviewed, if adverse to him. 13 *Wend.* 130; 23 *Id.* 648, and see *post,* "Appeals and the proceedings therein."

Disobedience of mandamus, and proceedings thereon.] The mode of enforcing obedience to the peremptory writ of mandamus, is by attachment, founded upon affidavits showing that the peremptory writ has not been obeyed, and that it was duly served upon the proper parties. 2 *Caines,* 97. Where the affidavit showed that the defendant had kept out of the way, so that personal service of the peremptory writ could not be made upon him, and that the writ had been left at his house, the court ordered him to show cause why an attachment should not issue. 12 *Mod.* 312; *and see* 2 *Johns. Cas. 2d ed.* 217–79, *note.*

Whenever the peremptory writ shall be directed to any public officer, body, or board, commanding them to perform any public duty specially enjoined upon them by any provisions of law, if it shall appear to the court that such officer, or any member of such body or board, has, without just excuse, refused or neglected to perform the duty so enjoined, the court may impose a fine not exceeding two hundred and fifty dollars, upon every such officer or member of such body or board; and such fine, when collected, shall be paid into the treasury. And the payment of such fine shall be a bar to any action for any penalty incurred by such officer or member of such body or board, by reason of his refusal or neglect to perform the duty so enjoined. 2 *Rev. Stat.* 587, *sec.* 60.

Costs.] In suits and proceedings upon writs of mandamus, and on appeals therein, the court may, in its discretion, award or refuse costs to any party therein. *Laws of* 1833, *p.* 395, *sec.* 6; *Laws of* 1854, *p.* 592, *sec.* 3, *ante, p.* 14, *note b;* 19 *Barb.* 657; 6 *Abb.* 30; 14 *Id.* 305; *s. c.* 23 *How.* 306; 20 *Id.* 278.

Under the authority here given, the court will award or refuse costs, as the equity and justice of each particular case may require. 1 *Barb. S. C. R.* 557. And costs will not be allowed to be entered against a party unless by the special order of the court. *Ib.*; 3 *How.* 380. Where a rule for a peremptory mandamus is obtained by default, and such a rule is silent as to costs, and there is no evidence to show that the court intended to grant costs to the relator, such rule will not be amended so as to provide for the payment of costs. 1 *Barb supra.*

In addition to the above statutory provisions, it is also provided by statute, that upon refusing an alternative or a peremptory mandamus, the court may award costs to be paid by the party applying for such mandamus. 2 *Rev. Stat.* 619, *sec.* 40. And whenever a peremptory mandamus shall be granted upon the coming in of a return to a previous mandamus, without any issue of fact or of law being joined upon such return, the court shall award costs to the relator in the same manner as if such peremptory mandamus had been awarded upon a judgment on demurrer to such return, unless it shall appear on such return hat there was some reasonable excuse for not having done the act required. *Ib. sec.* 41.

The statutory provisions, last cited, do not authorize costs to be awarded to the relator, except in those cases where a peremptory mandamus shall be ordered *upon the coming in of a return to a previous writ*, 10 *Wend.* 598; 1 *Barb S. C. R.* 559; nor do those provisions affect the rule above laid down, that costs are in all cases to be granted or refused in the discretion of the court. Costs may be granted, therefore, notwithstanding that no return has been made, and there has been no appearance on the part of the defendant. *Id. ibid.*

In awarding a peremptory mandamus against judges or other public officers entrusted with the discharge of judicial duties, the practice of the court is not to grant costs against them, *Anon.* 19 *Wend.* 157; 2 *Id.* 301, 303; 5 *Abb.* 232; though where the judges, instead of obeying the alternative writ, make a return thereto, and on the coming in of the return, the peremptory mandamus is awarded, the relator will be entitled to the costs of the proceedings. 18 *Wend.* 534; "The judges," says Bronson, J., "may always protect themselves against costs, by obeying the alternative writ. Where they omit to do so and make return, it may be presumed that they are indemnified against costs by the party in interest." *Ib.* 537; and see 10 *Id.* 598.

And where a party who is not the defendant in the writ,

though the real party in interest, resists a mandamus by requiring the relators to plead or demur, and subsequently joins in demurrer, he is liable for the costs on judgment being rendered in favor of the relators. 3 *Wend.* 304. But it would be otherwise, if he had not appeared in the proceedings, or done some other affirmative act, substantially bringing him in as a party to the suit. And it would not be sufficient to make him liable for the costs that the return was made at his request, and that he opposed the issuing of the peremptory mandamus. 2 *Id.* 301, 303; and see 2 *Johns. Cas. 2d. ed.* 217–80, *note.*

The costs of the motion on the original application for the mandamus, will also be awarded or not in the discretion of the court. See *Rev. Notes*, 3 *Rev. Stat. 2d ed.* 779; 1 *Barb. S. C. R.* 557; 23 *How.* 306; *s. c.* 14 *Abb.* 305. Where the notice of motion asked for costs, and the motion was denied, costs were given against the relator for that reason. 1 *How.* 222. And although the court may grant costs against the relator, if the motion is denied (2 *Rev. Stat.* 619, *sec.* 40, *supra*), yet the general practice on denying motions for the mandamus, has been not to give costs, especially where the motion is ex parte. 4 *Cowen*, 548. But where notice of the motion is given to the defendant, which he opposes, and the law is plainly against the relator, the motion will be denied, with costs. *Ib.:* and see 2 *Johns. Cas. 2d ed.* 217–80, *note.*

If the relator removes from the State intermediate the issuing of the alternative and peremptory writ, the defendant will be entitled to security for costs, and the proceedings will be stayed until such security be filed. 18 *Wend.* 652.

When costs are granted, they are to be at the rate allowed for similar services in civil actions under the Code, *Laws of* 1854, *ante, p.* 19, *sec.* 3; 19 *Barb.* 657; 28 *How.* 167, 172; unless an alternative writ was issued and there has been a return to the same, and pleadings have been put in, and a trial had therein, in which case, the proceeding becomes an action under the Code, and the costs are taxed under the fee bill contained under the Revised Statutes. 8 *Abb.* 359, *note;* 28 *How.* 159; *Ib.* 471; and see 20 *Id.* 380.

If proceedings are commenced against a public officer, and he succeeds in the proceeding, he will be entitled to double costs. 20 *How.* 378.

Motion to set aside the proceedings.] If the peremptory mandamus has been unfairly or improperly obtained, the defendant may apply on motion at the special term to set the same aside. 1 *Caines*, 8; 2 *Barb. S. C. R.* 557. So, it may be set aside for irregularity where it is issued after an appeal has been duly perfected to the Court of Appeals. 25 *How.* 257.

Appeals, and the proceedings therein.] The proceeding to obtain a review of a decision granting or refusing a mandamus, was formerly had by writ of error. And the writ of error was allowed only upon final judgment rendered after issue joined upon plea or demurrer, interposed on the coming in of the alternative mandamus (*a*). Thus, on a motion for a peremptory mandamus in the first instance, or for a peremptory mandamus on the return of an order to show cause, the decision on such application was not the subject of review. 3 *How.* 165; 10 *Wend.* 30; 2 *Johns. Cas. 2d ed.* 217–63, *note.* Though, to enable the question to be carried further, the court, on the suggestion of either party, permitted the alternative mandamus to issue, and a formal record to be made up, on which the party dissatisfied with the decision might have the case reviewed by a writ of error. 12 *Wend.* 183; 10 *Id.* 31; 6 *Cowen*, 518; 20 *Barb.* 86; 13 *How.* 305, 309.

Again, where the relator moved, on the return to an alternative mandamus, for the peremptory writ, notwithstanding the return, the facts alleged in such return were thereby admitted to be true, and the case was to be determined by the court the same as if the relator had formally demurred to the return. 6 *Wend.* 559, 560; 7 *Id.* 475; 10 *Id.* 632; 1 *Barb. S. C. R.* 379, 384. In such case, neither party was at liberty to have the decision of the court reviewed; though the practice was, where the decision was adverse to the defendant, to permit him to make up a formal record of judgment, on which the decision of the court could be reviewed by writ of error. *Id. ibid;* 13 *Wend.* 130; 23 *Id.* 648. But this privilege was not allowed to the relator; if the

(*a*) The only exception to this was in the case of a contest between the State and individuals, relating to water privileges, &c., on the canal, where, by the statute, a writ of error was allowed to be brought from the decision of the court, notwithstanding no pleadings were had or issue joined in the cause, 1 *Rev. Stat.* 235, *sec.* 97, 10 *Wend.* 30.

decision was adverse to him, it was final. He chose to ask for the peremptory mandamus, without formally demurring, and, by doing so, deprived himself of the right to have the case reviewed. *Id. ibid.*

But the practice has been essentially changed. Now, the only mode by which the decision of the court can be reviewed, is by appeal. And either party may now have the order of the court, granting or refusing a mandamus, reviewed on appeal, in all cases, whether the order is made on the original application for the peremptory mandamus in the first instance, or on the application for the peremptory writ on the return of an order to show cause, or on the application for the peremptory writ, after a return has been put in to the alternative mandamus, without formally demurring or pleading to such return. *Laws of* 1854, *p.* 592, *ante*, *p.* 19; 19 *Barb.* 657; *Code of Pro.* §§ 8, 11, 127, 333, 471; 9 *How.* 304, *per* Duer, J.; *s. c.* 3 *Duer*, 616; 28 *How.* 159; *Ib.* 470; *Laws of* 1859, *p.* 421; 18 *New York*, 487; 20 *Id.* 529. And an appeal may also be taken from the final judgment, after issue joined upon plea or demurrer, interposed on the return of the alternative mandamus. See *Id. ibid.*; 20 *Barb.* 81; 13 *How.* 305, 309; 1 *Kern.* 563; 3 *Id.* 239.

From the order or judgment of the court at the special term, the appeal is to be taken to the general term. *Id. ibid*; *Laws of* 1854, *p.* 592, *ante*, *p.* 19; 19 *Barb.* 657. The practice, in such case, is regulated in part by the Code of Procedure; sections three hundred and twenty-seven, three hundred and twenty-nine, three hundred and thirty, and three hundred and thirty-two, of which, apply to the proceedings on such appeal. *Ib.* (*a*) In other respects, the usual practice on appeals from orders and judgments in civil actions, is to apply, so far as the same is applicable.

The appeal to the general term does not stay the proceedings unless the court or a justice thereof so order. If an order staying the proceedings is obtained, it may be upon such terms as to security or otherwise, as may be just; such security not to exceed the amount required on an appeal to the Court of Appeals. *Laws of* 1854, *ante*, vol. I., p. 19 (*a*). But see *ante*, vol. I., p. 20.

An appeal may also be taken to the Court of Appeals from

(*a*) But see the new Code of Civil Procedure (§§ 1356 to 1361, *ante*, vol. I., p. 20), on the subject of appeals in special proceedings.

the order or judgment of the general term. *Laws of* 1859, *p.* 421; 20 *New York*, 529; and see 18 *Id.* 487; *Code of Pro.* § 11; *First Rep. of Com. on the Code*, *p.* 11 to 20; *Laws of* 1857, *vol.* 1, *p.* 753. The practice, in such cases, is regulated by the Code of Procedure, and is the same as in appeals from judgments in civil actions. *Id. ibid.*

The perfecting of the appeal by complying with the provisions of the Code, stays all further proceedings in the court below. 25 *How.* 257.

Where a verdict was rendered for the relator for the amount of damages assessed for opening a highway, and the interest thereon as damages; on appeal to the Court of Appeals from the judgment rendered, the facts being before the court; it was held that the court might modify the judgment by reversing it as to the sum assessed as damages, and affirming it as to the interest allowed as damages, and directing that the judgment be so amended as to grant to the relator the writ of mandamus without delay. 28 *New York*, 112.

SECTION II.

THE WRIT OF PROHIBITION.

The writ of *Mandamus*, as we have seen, is issued to *compel* the *performance* of public duties on the part of subordinate *courts* and *corporations* and *ministerial officers*. The writ of *Prohibition*, on the contrary, is issued to *forbid* or *prohibit* a *court* and *party* to whom it is directed *from proceeding* in a suit or matter depending before such court, upon the suggestion that the cognizance of such suit or matter does not belong to it. 2 *Rev. Stat.* 587; 3 *Steph. Com.* 685; *Bac. Abr.*, *Prohibition.*

The Supreme Court is the only court having authority to issue the writ of prohibition in this State. (*a*) 2 *Rev. Stat.* 587, *sec.*

(*a*) In the city of Buffalo, however, the application may also be made to the Superior Court of that city, that court having, within that city, concurrent jurisdiction with the Supreme Court, to issue the writ. *Laws of* 1857, *vol.* 1, *p.* 752.

61; 18 *Abb.* 438, *s. c.* 28 *How.* 477. In England, however, it issues in some cases out of the Court of Chancery, the Common Pleas, and the Exchequer, though usually out of the Court of King's (or Queen's) Bench. 3 *Bl. Com.* 112; *Bac. Abr., Prohibition, A.*

The writ is directed to *inferior courts of judicature*, whether such courts be temporal, ecclesiastical, maritime, military, &c.; and to the *party* whose suit or proceeding is sought to be restrained. *Id. ibid.*

When the writ issues.] The office of the writ of prohibition is to prevent *courts* from going beyond their *jurisdiction* in the exercise of *judicial* power, 2 *Hill*, 367; 1 *Id.* 201; 7 *Wend.* 518; 36 *Barb.* 341; *s. c.* 14 *Abb.* 266; 23 *How.* 446; 18 *Abb.* 438, *s. c.* 28 *How.* 477; 27 *Id.* 14; and it stays both the *court* and the *party* from proceeding in the matter. *Ib.* Thus, it has been issued to prohibit a court of sessions from proceeding with an appeal in a bastardy case, where they had no jurisdiction to entertain such appeal. 19 *Wend.* 154. And it lies to prevent the exercise of unauthorized power in a cause or proceeding of which the inferior tribunal has jurisdiction, no less than when the entire cause is without its jurisdiction. 20 *New York*, 531. But the writ does not issue to deprive an inferior court of a jurisdiction which the law in its wisdom has thought proper to give it. 18 *Abb.* 438, *s. c.* 28 *How.* 477.

The court may grant or deny the writ in its *discretion;* and it ought not to issue where the party has a complete and adequate remedy in some other and more ordinary form. 2 *Hill*, 367; 36 *Barb.* 341; *s. c.* 23 *How.* 446; 14 *Abb.* 266; 29 *How.* 176; *s. c.* 19 *Abb.* 137.

Nor will the writ issue to restrain a *ministerial officer* (*e. g.*—a collector of taxes) from the execution of process in his hands, 1 *Hill*, 196; nor to prevent an inferior court from issuing an execution; for this is a ministerial act, 2 *Id.* 367; nor to stay a corporation in the execution of a naked statute power, ministerial in its nature, *Ib.* 15; nor to bring under review the proceedings of an inferior court on the ground of their being erroneous merely. *Ib.* 363; 7 *Wend.* 518. Nor will the writ be awarded in reference to a mere point of practice, where the court has jurisdiction of the general subject of the cause. 12 *Ad. & El.* 201; 3 *Steph.*

Com. 686, *note;* 36 *Barb.* 341; *s. c.* 23 *How.* 446; 14 *Abb.* 266; 27 *How.* 14.

Application for the writ.] The writ should be applied for upon affidavits, by motion, at the special term, in the same manner as writs of mandamus. 2 *Rev. Stat.* 587, *sec.* 61. As to the practice in cases of mandamus, see *ante, p.* 61. For form of notice and affidavit, see *Appendix*, Nos. 453, 454.

The affidavits should set forth, plainly and distinctly, the facts upon which the party relies to show that he is entitled to the relief demanded. If the facts alleged in the affidavits appear to the court to be sufficient, the writ will be directed to be issued, 2 *Rev. Stat.* 587, *sec.* 61; and the rule authorizing it should be entered with the clerk of the court. For form of rule, see *Appendix*, No. 455.

The writ, and how directed.] The writ should be directed to the *court*, and also to the *party* whose proceedings are sought to be stayed; and after reciting or suggesting the facts and proceedings on which it is founded, should command them to desist and refrain from any further proceedings in the suit or matter specified therein, until the next term of the court, and the further order of such court thereon, and then to show cause why they should not be absolutely restrained from any further proceedings in such suit or matter. 2 *Rev. Stat.* 587, *sec.* 61.

It should be tested, signed, and sealed, as in cases of mandamus. Like mandamus, also, it should be made returnable at the special term. (*a*) For form of writ, see *Appendix*, No. 456.

Service of the writ.] The writ must be served upon the court and party to whom it is directed, in the same manner as a writ of mandamus. (*b*) 2 *Rev. Stat.* 587, *sec.* 62.

Return.] The statute also requires a return to be made by the court, in the same manner as returns in mandamus. (*c*) For any neglect to make such return, such court may be proceeded against by attachment as for a contempt, in the manner prescribed in the thirteenth title (2 *Rev. Stat.* 534) of chapter eight of part third of the Revised Statutes. 2 *Rev. Stat.* 587, *sec.* 62. For form, see *Appendix*, No. 457.

(*a*) See *ante, p.* 68. (*b*) See *ante, p.* 68. (*c*) See *ante, p.* 70.

Notice requiring relator to demur or plead to the return.] The return to the writ of prohibition having been filed, the party making such return may serve a notice upon the relator, requiring him to demur or plead thereto within twenty days after such service. (*a*) *Sup. Court Rules*, No. 51. For form of notice, see *Appendix*, No. 458.

Proceedings if relator does not demur or plead.] If no plea or demurrer to the return is interposed, within the time required, either party may notice the matter for a hearing at the next or any subsequent special term, at which the same may, according to the practice of the court, be heard as a non-enumerated motion, and the same shall be heard and disposed of on the said return. (*a*) *Sup. Court Rules*, No. 51, *supra*. For form of notice of hearing, see *Appendix*, No. 459.

Proceedings if party adopts the return.] If the party to whom the writ of prohibition is directed shall, by an instrument in writing to be signed by him, and annexed to the return, adopt the same return, and rely upon the matters therein contained, as sufficient cause why such court should not be restrained as mentioned in the said writ, such party shall thenceforth be deemed the defendant in such matter; and the person prosecuting such writ may reply, take issue, or demur to the matters so relied upon by such defendant; and the like proceeding shall be had for the trial of issues of law or fact, joined between the parties, and for the rendering of judgment thereupon, as in personal actions. 2 *Rev. Stat.* 587, *sec.* 63. For form of writing, adopting return, see *Appendix*, No. 457.

If, in such case, judgment shall be rendered for the party prosecuting such writ, a prohibition absolute shall be issued; but if judgment be given against such party, a writ of consultation shall be awarded, authorizing the court and party to proceed in the suit or matter in question. *Ib.*, *sec.* 65; 3 *Bl. Com.* 114. For form of writ of consultation, see *Appendix*, No. 462.

Proceedings if the return is not adopted.] If the party to whom the writ of prohibition is directed, shall not adopt such return as above provided, the party prosecuting such writ shall

(*a*) See the former practice, in such case, *ante*, *p.* 73, *note*.

bring on the argument of such return, as upon rules to show cause; and he may, by his own affidavit, and other proofs, controvert the matters set forth in such return. And the court, after hearing the proofs and allegations of the parties, shall render judgment, either that a prohibition absolute, restraining the said court and party from proceeding in such suit or matter, do issue, or a writ of consultation, authorizing the court and party to proceed in the suit or matter in question. 2 *Rev. Stat.* 588, *sec.* 64; 3 *Bl. Com.* 114; *Bac. Ab. Prohibition.* For form of prohibition absolute, see *Appendix*, No. 461.

Motion to quash the writ.] If the writ is defective, or was issued irregularly, it may be set aside or quashed on motion at the special term. And a writ, allowed by a justice out of court, even if returnable at a general term, may be quashed at a special term on motion. 29 *How.* 176, *s. c.* 19 *Abb.* 137.

Amendments.] Either party may apply to the court for leave to amend the writ of prohibition, pleadings, &c. 2 *Rev Stat.* 425, *sec.* 10.

Costs.] Costs, in these proceedings, may be awarded or not, in the discretion of the court, *Laws of* 1854, *sec.* 3, *ante*, *p.* 19; and see 19 *Barb.* 658; and when awarded, are to be at the rate allowed for similar services in civil actions. *Id. ibid;* and see 28 *How.* 167. If, however, there has been a return to the writ, and pleadings have been put in and a trial had thereon, the proceeding will be treated as an action, excepted from the operation of the second part of the Code; and costs therein will be taxed under the fee bill contained in the Revised Statutes. See *Code*, § 471; 28 *How.* 159; *Ib.* 471; 20 *Id.* 380.

Appeals and writs of error.] From the decision of the court at the special term, an appeal lies to the general term, the same as in mandamus. See *Laws of* 1854, *p.* 592, *ante*, *p.* 19; 19 *Barb.* 658; 28 *How.* 167; and see *ante*, *p.* 14, *note b.*

The decision of the general term, also, may be reviewed by the Court of Appeals; but such review must be had by writ of error, under the old practice, the provisions of the second part of the Code on the subject of appeals to the Court of Appeals, not applying to proceedings upon prohibition ([a]). *Code*, § 471; 18 *N. Y.*, 487; and see 20 Id., 529; Id., 531; Laws 1859, *p.* 421; *ante, vol.* 1., *p.* 14, *note b.*

(*a*) But see the new Code of Civil Procedure on the subject of appeals to the Supreme Court, or to a Superior City Court, in Special Proceedings; *ante*, vol. 1, p. 20; and see Code of Civil Pro. (§§ 190, 191) on the subject of appeals to the Court of Appeals.

SUPPLEMENT TO CHAPTER XIX.

I. THE WRIT OF MANDAMUS.

The writ of mandamus, generally. To entitle a party to the writ there must be a clear legal right, not merely to a decision in respect to the thing, but to the thing itself. 49 *Barb.*, 31. The remedy is of an exceptionable character, appropriate only to that class of cases where a clear legal right may be made to appear without any other adequate legal means to redress and maintain it. 1 *Hun*, 1; 7 *Id.*, 608; 62 *Barb.*, 570. And although a party may be remediless except by that writ, yet it will issue or not in the sound discretion of the court; and the court will grant or refuse it according as the issuing or withholding it will best promote the ends of justice. 49 *Barb.*, 259; *Ib.*, 31, 55; *Id.*, 197.

In this proceeding, when dealing with a corporation which is required to do a particular thing, the manner being discretionary with it, if the corporation elects a manner which proves ineffectual, and yet claims to have performed its duty, the court has power to and should point out in the writ in what the corporation has failed, and direct particularly what must be done, so that it may not fail again. 58 *N. Y.*, 153.

When the writ will issue. A mandamus will lie to compel the commissioner of jurors to strike the relator's name from the list of jurors, 45 *Barb.*, 129; *S. C.*, 1 *Abb.*, *N. S.*, 200; to compel an incorporated company to allow one of its stockholders to inspect its stock ledger, 3 *Id.*, 364; to compel the comptroller of the city of New York to provide for the payment of a claim adjusted by him under authority of the statute, 4 *Id.*, 375; and the State Comptroller to pay money appropriated by act of the Legislature, 1 *Lansing*, 248; to compel a gas light company to furnish gas to persons who have a right to receive it, 45 *Barb.*, 136; to compel assessors to strike an assessment from their rolls, 44 *Barb.*, 148; 2 *Abb.*, *N. S.*, 233; to compel the clerk of a municipal corporation to execute a contract under the seal of the corporation, 2 *Abb.*, *N. S.*, 315; to compel a county treasurer to issue his warrant for the collection of a tax, 37 *N. Y.*, 344; and the board of supervisors of a county to audit an account, 45 *Id.*, 196; to compel a corporation to restore a person to membership from which he has been improperly expelled, 3 *Hun*, 361; but see 53 *N. Y.*, 103; and the trustees of a village to raise and collect a tax required by a statute of the State. 54 *Barb.*, 481.

When the writ will not issue. The writ will not issue to compel the comptroller of the city of New York to pay money where no appropriation has been made for such payment, 1 *Abb.*, *N. S.*, 184; and see 2 *Id.*, 315; nor where he denies the validity of the contract upon which payment is sought, charges that it was illegally made, and that the prices charged are excessive, 66 *Barb.*, 630; nor to test the relator's claim to the office of president of a board of public officers, 2 *Abb.*, *N. S.*, 348; and see 55 *N. Y.*, 217; nor to reinstate a member of a religious society who has been expelled for a moral delinquency, 53 *New York*, 103, affirming 3 *Lansing*, 434, and reversing 6 *Id.*, 172; and see 3 *Hun*, 361; nor, as a general rule, in cases where the right of the relator depends upon holding an act of the legislature unconstitutional, 2 *Abb.*, *N. S.*, 348; nor where the act sought to be enforced is discretionary, 1 *Abb.*, *N. S.*, 230; *S. C.*, 46 *Barb.*, 27; 49 *Id.*, 259; 55 *Id.*, 197; nor to compel a justice to change his decision in settling a case, 1 *Hun*, 252. The writ will issue to set an inferior tribunal in motion, but not for the purpose of requiring it to come to any particular decision, 2 *Abb.*, *N. S.*, 78, and see *ante, p.* 54; nor will the writ issue where the end sought is only a private right, and when the granting of it would be attended with manifest hardships and difficulties, 49 *Barb.*, 259, and see *Ib.* 31; nor to compel assessors to make oath to their assessment roll, as prescribed by the statute, when to make such oath would compel them to swear to what was not true, 55 *N. Y.*, 252. Nor will a mandanus be granted where the applicant asks for more than he is entitled to, although he may be right in other respects. 2 *Hun*, 224; 64 *Barb.*, 162. But the mandamus will not be denied merely because the relator may have a remedy by action for damages, 1 *Abb.*, *N. S.*, 201; *S. C.*, 45 *Barb.*, 129; nor will this remedy be denied a party by reason of delay occasioned by the adverse party, if the relator's right to relief had not expired at the time the writ was ordered 46 *Barb.*, 255.

Who may have the writ. The rule that the relator must show an individual right to the thing asked, does not apply to cases where the interest is common to the whole community. And therefore any citizen having a common interest in the collection of a tax may apply for a mandamus to compel a county treasurer to issue a warrant for the collection of the same. 37 *N. Y.*, 344, affirming 53 *Barb.*, 547.

Where to be applied for. The application for the writ must be made within the judicial district in which an action resulting from the issue of the writ would be triable, or in a county adjoining the county in which it would be triable. 2 *Abb.*, *N. S.*, 78. If the motion is to compel the Secretary of State to file a certificate of incorporation, it must be made in the third judical district, or in a county adjoining therto. 7 *Hun*, 23.

How directed, etc. A mandamus to compel a municipal corporation to create a stock is properly addressed to the common council, although the corporation is designated in the statute authorizing the issuing of it as the mayor, aldermen, and commonalty of the city. 1 *Abb.*, *N. S.*, 319.

Upon an order to show cause why a peremptory mandamus should not issue —the order containing the usual clause "or for other relief"—the court may grant a peremptory writ for any relief to which the relator is entitled, although not specified in the order. 46 *N. Y.*, 375.

Proceedings on the hearing. Where the application is opposed on affidavit, and material questions of facts are in dispute, such questions must be determined before the court can decide the questions of law and grant a peremptory writ. 2 *Abb.*, *N. S.*, 78. And if the relator elects to rest his case upon affidavits, the answering affidavits which are neither traversed nor confessed and avoided, must be taken as true. 55 *N. Y.*, 180.

The defendant may object to a want of sufficient title in the relator to the relief sought, or show any other defect of substance, at any time after a return and before a peremptory writ is granted, though he cannot, after a return, object to defects in form. 53 *N. Y.*, 128.

The construction of rule 55 (*ante, p.* 73). The purpose of the rule is to enable a defendant to compel a hearing on the return, unless the plaintiff chooses to demur or traverse. If the plaintiff waives this right, and the parties proceed to argument on the return, the court may dispose of the controversy upon its merits. 56 *N. Y.*, 249. In such cases, the court will not consider the affidavits on which the writ was granted, but will determine the case upon the alternative writ, and the return. *Ib.* Mere formal and technical defects in the pleadings will be disregarded; otherwise as to defects of substance. *Ib.*

Peremptory mandamus. The mandatory part of the writ need only to describe the thing to be done with reasonable certainty, so that the defendant will know what is required of him. 46 *N. Y.*, 375. It is not every variation between an alternative and a peremptory writ of mandamus which will cause the latter to be set aside; as, where the substance of the two writs is the same. 58 *N. Y.*, 152. The provision of the Revised Statutes (*ante, p.* 77), providing that in case a verdict shall be found for the relator he shall recover damages and costs in like manner as in an action, etc., and that a peremptory writ shall be granted to him without delay, does not entitle the relator to a peremptory writ where the record shows he has no legal right thereto. 53 *N. Y.*, 128. Where the fact upon which the relator relies is controverted, it must first be tried and determined, before a peremptory writ can issue; and that determination is to be made not upon conflicting affidavits, but upon an issue framed upon the alternative writ, and must be tried by a jury according to the course of the common law. 1 *Hun*, 2. A seal is necessary to the writ. The proper mode of serving a peremptory mandamus, is by showing the original writ under the seal of the court, and delivering a copy. *Ib.*, 464, 468.

Appeals. An order of the general term dismissing an appeal from an order of the special term refusing a mandamus, is not appealable to the Court of Appeals. 36 *N. Y.*, 93. But such order may be reviewed upon an appeal from a judgment in a case in which it was an intermediate order involving the merits and necessarily affecting the judgment. *Ib.*

Appeals in these proceedings are now regulated by the new Code of Civil Procedure. §§ 1356 to 1361 (*ante, vol.* 1, *p.* 20), and §§ 190, 191. And see the next following paragraph in respect to appeals, when the writ is issued to the special term of the Supreme Court, etc.

By ch. 70, *of the Laws of* 1873, *the writ may now issue to the special term of the Supreme Court, or to any justice thereof holding such term, or sitting at chambers.* The following are the provisions of the statute in full, omitting so much of §§ 1, 2, as prescribes a preference of causes on the calendars of the courts (repealed by *ch.* 417 of *Laws of* 1877; a similar provision being substituted therefor by § 792 of the new Code, *post*):

§ 1. The Supreme Court, at a general term, may issue writs of mandamus and of prohibition, directed to any special term of said court, or any justice thereof holding such term or sitting at chambers, and may hear, adjudge and determine the same, and enforce such determination in the same manner and with the same effect, in all respects, as in the like proceedings when the writs are directed to inferior courts and judges thereof. Application for such writ shall be made to the general term of the judicial department in which the subject-matter of the proceeding sought to be enforced or prohibited originated, or in case such general term shall not be in session, then to the general term of an adjoining judicial department, and shall be brought on upon an order to show cause or otherwise, according to the present practice in like cases of writs directed to such inferior courts or officers. The writ or order shall be returnable at such time as the said court shall direct.

§ 2. An appeal may be taken to the Court of Appeals from any order, judgment or final determination of any such general term in any such proceeding; and the practice on such appeal shall be the same in all respects as on appeals to that court in proceedings upon mandamus as now regulated by law or the practice of the court.

§ 3. The proceedings on any application for such writ of mandamus or prohibition shall not be stayed or suspended by any other writ or order of any court or officer, other than that of the general term before which the same is pending; nor shall any appeal from the order, judgment or final determination of such general term, stay the proceedings, unless such general term so order, which order may be upon such terms, as to security or otherwise, as may be just.

§ 4. If the application for the writ shall be made to the general term of an adjoining judicial department, as provided in the first section of this act, such general term, in its discretion, may make the alternative writ or order to show cause returnable before the general term of the department in which the subject matter of the proceeding originated, at the next subsequent term thereof, with the same effect in all respects as if such alternative writ or order had been made by such general term.

By § 792 of the Code of Civil Procedure, it is provided, that where a writ of mandamus or of prohibition has been issued, from the general term, to a special term, or a judge of the same court, the cause may, in the discretion of the court, or, where an appeal is taken therein to the Court of Appeals, in the discretion of that court, be preferred over any of the causes specified in the last section (§ 791 *of Code of Civil Pro.*).

II. THE WRIT OF PROHIBITION.

The office of the writ of prohibition is to prevent the exercise, by a tribunal possessing judicial powers, of jurisdiction over matters not within its cognizance, or to prevent it from exceeding its jurisdiction in matters within its cognizance. 60 *N. Y.*, 31. The character of the writ was not changed by the provision of the Revised Statutes (§ 61 *ante, p.* 86), providing that the party in whose behalf the unauthorized jurisdiction is invoked, may be enjoined with the court from further proceedings in the suit or matters specified. But its operation is only to restrain the party from proceeding with the pending suit or matter. *Ib.*

When the writ issues or not. The writ will not issue of course, but only in the discretion of the court, and should not issue where the party has a complete and adequate remedy at law. It will lie to prevent the exercise of unauthorized power by an inferior tribunal, in cases where it has jurisdiction, as well as where it has not jurisdiction. 51 *Barb.*, 312; 31 *How.*, 237. It will not lie against a board of supervisors to restrain them from imposing and levying a tax assessed upon a national bank. *Id.* Nor will it issue to restrain a magistrate from entertaining proceedings to remove a tenant from premises, merely because the tenant has a clear defence to the proceeding. 3 *Abb.*, *N. S.*, 232; *S. C.*, 49 *Barb.*, 351. It does not lie to restrain a ministerial act, nor can it take the place of a writ of error, or other proceeding to review judicial action, or of a suit in equity to prevent or redress fraud. 60 *N. Y.*, 31.

The writ of prohibition cannot affect the Court of Appeals, or its suitors. 60 *N. Y.*, 37, per ALLEN, J.

If the proceedings have been irregular, the court, on appeal, will reverse the order granting the writ, and set aside the proceedings. 5 *Hun*, 290.

By ch. 70, *of the laws of* 1873, *the writ of prohibition may now issue to the special term of the Supreme Court, or to any justice thereof holding such term, or sitting at chambers.* See the statutory provisions, etc., in full, *ante, p.* 92–1.

Appeals. What is stated *ante, p.* 92–1, on the subject of appeals in proceedings by mandamus, applies, also, to appeals on prohibition.

CHAPTER XX.

THE PARTITION OF REAL ESTATE.

At the common law, although partition could be made in every case by the consent of all the owners, yet it could not be compelled by one cotenant against the will of the others, or of any of them, except in the case of coparceners, until the statute of 31 *Henry* VIII. *ch.* 1; and 32 *Henry* VIII. *ch.* 32, extended the writ of partition to joint tenants and tenants in common. *Co. Litt.* 187; *Bac. Abr., tit. Joint Tenant I. No.* 7; *Will. Eq. Jur.* 699.

The first act on the subject of partition in this State, was passed under the colonial government, on the 30th of October, 1708; and other acts were subsequently passed from time to time, on the same subject. 1 *R. L.* 507, *note.* At the close of the Revolution, on the 16th of March, 1785, the first act was passed for the partition of lands, under the State government. *Ib.;* The latter act, with the amendments and alterations subsequently made, was a substantial re-enactment of the English statutes above mentioned. (*a*) *Ib.;* and see *Will. Eq. Jur.* 699.

The several statutory provisions on the subject were revised by the laws of 1813, 1 *R. L.* 507; and again in 1830, 2 *Rev. Stat.* 317; and the latter revision, with the amendments and alterations since made, constitute the present law of this State. (*b*)

When partition will be made.] The statute provides that where several persons shall hold and be in the possession of any lands, tenements, or hereditaments, as joint tenants, or as tenants

---

(*a*) See the history of the statutory law of this State on the subject of partition, reviewed, by Davies, J., 5 *Abb.* 92 to 106.

(*b*) For the amendments and alterations since the Revised Statutes, see *Laws of* 1830, *p.* 396; 1833, *p.* 311; 1840, *p.* 128; *Ib.* 321; 1846, *p.* 204; 1847, *p.* 556; *Ib.* 640. 1852, *p.* 411; 1863, *p.* 526; 1857, *vol.* 2, *p.* 504; *Pub. Acts, p.* 184; 1863, *p.* 388; *Ib. p.* 804.

in common, in which one or more of them shall have estates of inheritance, or for life or lives, or for years, any one or more of such persons, being of full age, may apply for a division and partition of such premises, according to the respective rights of the parties interested therein; and for a sale of such premises, if it shall appear that a partition thereof cannot be made without great prejudice to the owners. (*a*) 2 *Rev. Stat.* 317, *sec.* 1.

The qualification that the persons applying for partition must be of full age, applies equally to all the plaintiffs; and, therefore, proceedings for the partition of lands cannot be maintained by an *infant*, either separately or jointly, with adult cotenants in common. 4 *Sand. Ch. R.* 508.

The statute, however, has provided, that whenever an infant shall be possessed of real estate, as tenant in common or joint tenant, the Supreme Court (*b*) may authorize proceedings to be instituted on behalf of such infant for a division and partition of said real estate, and for a sale thereof, if it shall appear that such partition cannot be made without great prejudice to the owners. *Laws of* 1852, *p.* 411, *sec.* 1. But such authority will not be given, nor will such partition or sale be directed by the court, unless it is made satisfactorily to appear that the interests of such infant require such partition or sale. *Ib. sec.* 2; 26 *How.* 250; 21 *Id.* 479, *s. c.* 14 *Abb.* 299. And where the question was referred to a referee, and he reported "that in his opinion it would be proper to allow the infant to prosecute an action for the partition or sale of the premises," but without setting forth the facts to warrant such a conclusion,—it was held not sufficient, and the application for leave to prosecute, was denied. See 15 *How.* 383.

And so, the statute provides that whenever it shall appear satisfactorily, by due proof, or on the report of a referee, to the Supreme Court, that any infant holds real estate in joint tenancy, or in common, or in any other manner, which would authorize his being made a party to a suit in partition, and that the

(*a*) A court of equity may also decree a partition of personal property, or a sale thereof where partition is impracticable, and a division of the proceeds, in cases where there is no adequate remedy at the common law. 28 *Barb.* 290, 292.

(*b*) If the premises are situated in the city of Brooklyn, application for leave to institute an action in behalf of infants, may also be made to the city court of that city *Laws of* 1863, *p.* 89.

interest of such infant, or of any other person concerned therein, requires that partition of such estate should be made, such court may direct and authorize the general guardian of such infant to agree to a division thereof, or to a sale thereof, or of such part of the said estate, as in the opinion of the court shall be incapable of partition, or as shall be most for the interest of the infant to be sold. 2 *Rev. Stat.* 330, *sec.* 86, as amended by *sec.* 46 *of ch.* 320 *of Laws of* 1830; *Laws of* 1847, *p.* 323, *sec.* 16; *Ib.* 344, *sec.* 77; and see *post*, "Partition and sale of infant's estate."

By the statute, also, as we have seen, the party applying for partition must hold and be in the *possession* of the premises as joint tenants, or as tenants in common, in which one or more of them shall have estates of inheritance, or for life or lives, or for years. 2 *Rev. Stat.* 317, *sec.* 1, *supra.* Under this provision, it has been held that the party instituting the proceedings must have an estate entitling him to immediate possession. 19 *Wend.* 367. Again, that he must not only have a present estate in the premises, as a joint-tenant, or tenant in common, but that he must be in the actual or constructive possession of his undivided share or interest. 2 *Barb. Ch. R.* 398; 5 *Denio*, 388. And that a party having a mere reversionary interest in the premises, which are in the possession of another having a life estate therein, cannot apply for a partition, not having any possession either actual or constructive. 11 *How.* 489. And again, that a mere reversioner cannot institute proceedings for partition without the concurrence of the owners of the present interest. 2 *Paige*, 387.

In conflict with the above cases, is the case of *Blakeley* agst. *Calder and others* (*a*) (13 *How.* 476), where it is held that although the party applying for partition must be in the possession of the premises, yet it is not necessary that he should be the actual occupant, or should hold an immediate present interest; and, therefore, that an existing admitted life estate, although covering the whole premises, will not prevent the remainderman from being deemed "in possession," within the meaning of the statute. This decision is in accordance with subsequent and

(*a*) See this case in the Court of Appeals, where the decision of the Supreme Court was affirmed, though not on the ground stated in the court below. 15 *New York*, 617. But see to the same effect as stated in the case in the Supreme Court, in the opinion of Denio, Ch. J., concurred in by Judges Comstock, Selden, and Paige *Ib* 623, 629.

other statutory provisions, which seem to contemplate not only a partition, but a sale of the premises, on the application of the remainderman or reversioner, in cases where there is a life estate in the whole or any part of the premises in question. See 2 *Rev. Stat.* 325, *secs.* 50, 51, and *Laws of* 1847, *p.* 557, *sec.* 5; 15 *New York*, 625.

As a general rule, proceedings for partition may be instituted by one tenant in common out of possession against another who is in possession; for the possession of one is the possession of both. 1 *Hoff. R.* 21. And so, where an intestate was seized and possessed of lands which were unoccupied, and which descended to tenants in common in that condition, it was held that one of them, though not in possession, may apply for partition. 4 *Kern.* 235.

So, it is provided by statute, that any heir, claiming lands, tenements, or hereditaments, by descent from an ancestor, who died holding and being in possession of the same (whether the heir is in possession or not), may prosecute for the partition thereof, notwithstanding any apparent devise by such ancestor, or any possession held under the same devise, provided that the heir shall allege and establish in the same action that such apparent devise is void. *Laws of* 1853, *p.* 526, § 2.

Where the party instituting the proceeding is not in the possession of the premises, and there are infant defendants, the court is bound to notice the objection, whether it is taken or not, 11 *How.* 489; though such disability ought regularly to be pleaded, 19 *Wend.* 367; 3 *Paige*, 245; unless it distinctly appears by the complaint itself. 2 *Barb. Ch. R.* 398. If, however, there has been an omission to plead it, it may be taken advantage of at the trial, under the plea of non tenant insimul. 19 *Wend.* 367.

Nor will proceedings for partition be authorized where the defendant is in possession claiming adversely to the plaintiff. *Harp. Eq. R.* 106; 2 *Barb. Ch. R.* 398; 11 *L. O.* 116. Nor in favor of a party who has merely a future contingent interest in an undivided share of the premises. 2 *Paige*, 387. Nor in favor of a widow having only a right of dower in the premises, 1 *Sand. Ch. R.* 199; and see 15 *Johns R.* 319; nor against her where she is the sole defendant in the proceedings. *Id. ibid.* Nor where the title is denied, or is not clearly established, or depends on doubtful facts or questions of law. 1 *Johns. Ch. R.* 111; 1 *Ed. Ch. R.* 266; 5 *Barb.* 52; 4 *Rand.* 493. But where the title is not in dispute, partition is matter of right, 4 *Barb.* 229; 10 *Paige*, 470; 17 *New York*, 213; though where it appeared, on the trial, that the action had been commenced during the pendency of an action brought by the defendant in another court for a dissolution of partnership and an accounting, which involved the premises in question, it was held that the complaint should be dismissed. 14 *Abb.* 206.

And so, where lands are devised subject to the performance of a condition subsequent, and the devisee enters and suffers a breach of the condition, the party entitled to an undivided part of the premises in consequence of the breach of the condition, as tenant in common with the devisee, cannot apply for partition against the devisee. 5 *Denio*, 385. In such case, he must first establish his title by action. *Ib.*; 4 *Paige*, 639; but see *post*. And so, if there has been an actual ouster of the plaintiff by his cotenant, or if the land is held adversely, the party must regain the actual seizin by action before proceedings for partition can be sustained. 3 *Paige*, 245; 9 *Cowen*, 530; 11 *L. O.* 116.

A party, however, may go into a court of equity upon an equitable title. And although the fact that the defendant is in possession of premises, claiming to hold them adversely, is in general a sufficient ground for denying a partition, yet where the question arises upon an equitable title set up by either of the parties, the court will not suspend the proceedings without doing complete justice between the parties. See 5 *Barb.* 52; 4 *Johns. Ch. R.* 271; 1 *Hoff. R.* 21. On the same principle, it has been said, there is no objection, now that the distinction between actions is abolished, and the court has general jurisdiction of both law and equity, to the trial and decision of any litigated question of title, whether equitable or legal, in a suit for partition. 2 *Van Sant. Eq. Pr.* 5; and see *Code of Pro.* § 69; 12 *Abb.* 414, *s. c.* 23 *New York*, 357; 17 *Id.* 270; 3 *Kern.* 493.

Thus, it has also been expressly provided by statute, that a party claiming the premises by descent as heir, in hostility to a devise of the same, may contest the validity of such devise in an action brought for the partition of the premises. *Laws of* 1853, *p.* 526, *supra.*

Where lands leased for a term of years, are owned by several persons as tenants in common both of the rents and the reversion, proceedings for partition may be sustained; and if a sale of the premises is ordered, it must be made subject to the right of the lessees, who, by the sale, will become the tenants to the purchaser of the rents and reversion. 5 *Paige*, 518. But where a lessee of land becomes a purchaser of an undivided moiety of the rent and reversion, the lease and rent thereby become merged and extinguished as to that portion of the premises; and the lessee is not such a tenant of the rent and reversion with the owner of the other half thereof, as to entitle the latter to a partition of the land during the continuance of the lease. 4 *Id.* 639.

Proceedings for partition may also be instituted by parties who are seized of a life estate, in real estate, by virtue of an assignment to them, by one of the tenants in common in trust for the benefit of his creditors. 2 *Barb. S. C. R.* 599. So a tenant by the curtesy initiate, may maintain the proceeding. 4 *Edw. Ch. R.* 668; 26 *How.* 250. So, it was held the action would lie where the grantee's deed conveyed to him, his heirs and assigns forever, all the mines, ores, minerals, and metals, in or upon certain lands described therein, together with the right to raise, work and carry away the same; and the right to put up all buildings, and to use all lands that might be necessary for the purpose specified; and the right of ingress and egress thereto, and therefrom, for the purpose of digging, and working and carrying away said mines, ores, minerals, and metals. 28 *Barb.* 336; 16 *How.* 473.

And so, an action for the partition of real estate among the devisees or heirs at law of a testator or intestate, may be commenced within the three years allowed by law to the creditors to apply to the surrogate for an order of sale. 7 *Paige*, 550; 7 *How.* 307; 10 *Id.* 189; 1 *Barb. S. C. R.* 76; 3 *Abb.* 249; 5 *Id.* 53; 7 *Id.* 473, 478; but see 1 *Edw. Ch. R.* 565, 568, 570. And a purchaser under the judgment will be compelled to take the title if there are no debts against the estate, or the personal property is sufficient to pay all claims against the estate of the deceased; though otherwise if there are debts, and the personal property is not sufficient to pay them. *Id. ibid.*

Where several tracts or parcels of land lying within this State are owned by the same persons in common, no separate proceedings for a partition of a part thereof only, can be brought without the consent of all the parties interested therein; and if brought without such consent, the share of the plaintiff may be charged with the whole costs of the proceedings. *Sup. Court Rules*, No. 77; *Eq. Rules*, 1847, No. 122.

Provisions of the Code.] It is provided by § 448 of the Code of Procedure, that the provisions of the Revised Statutes relating to the partition of lands, tenements, and hereditaments, held or possessed by joint tenants or tenants in common, shall apply to actions for such partition, brought under the Code, so far as the same can be so applied to the substance and subject-matter of the action, without regard to its form.

The proper construction applicable to the above section (§ 448), is stated by Hoffman, J., substantially thus: The Code is to regulate the course of proceedings in the action for partition generally, as well as in any other. But those provisions of the statute which are peculiar to the action of partition, and as to which there is no corresponding provision in the Code, must prevail. And again, provisions of the statute which are in addition to, and consistent with, any provision of the Code upon a particular subject-matter, are likewise to govern. 2 *Abb.* 13; and see 3 *Bosw.* 410.

Accordingly, the provisions of the Revised Statutes (2 *Rev. Stat.* 317, *secs.* 2, 3, and 4, *post*) with respect to the appointment of the guardian, ad litem, of infants, and the security to be given, apply to actions for partition, brought under the Code of Procedure, 2 *Abb.* 6, 11; 2 *Duer*, 635; 3 *Bosw.* 410; though they are inapplicable so far as they relate to the parties to apply for a guardian, and the time and mode of applying. 2 *Abb.* 15, *per* Hoffman, J.,; and see 11 *Id.* 440, 455; 20 *How.* 222; *s. c.* 11 *Abb.* 473; 25 *How.* 266. The Code (§ 116), will regulate the form of applying, and the parties to apply. *Id. ibid.;* and see *post*, "Guardian ad litem for infants."

And so, the service of the summons in an action for partition, is made the same as in other actions, 2 *Abb.* 15; 2 *Duer*, 635; and if the plaintiff is obliged to make "unknown owners" defendants, he is entitled to proceed against them by publication of the summons under § 135 of the Code. 11 *How.* 277.

And so, in actions for partition, the system of pleading prescribed by the Code is to be observed; though with respect to the complaint, it should no doubt contain the same matters required by the statute, to be stated in the petition. These are in addition to, or in compliance with, the requisitions of § 142 of the Code. 8 *How.* 458; 2 *Abb.* 14, 15.

And so, where the defendants in an action for partition omit to answer the complaint, the plaintiff must exhibit proof of his title, &c., on a reference for that purpose, the same as where the proceedings are commenced by petition under the revised statutes. 8 *How.* 456; 6 *Id.* 491; 2 *Abb.* 15, *supra.*

What courts have jurisdiction of the action.] The action may be brought in the Supreme Court; which court, succeeding to the equitable powers of the Court of Chancery, has general jurisdiction of the action; and every intendment will be made in support of a judgment rendered therein, unless the contrary appear on the face of the record, or be affirmatively shown *aliunde. Hill & Denio,* 438; 15 *New York,* 617.

And so, the action may be brought in the county court of the county where the premises are situated, *Code,* § 30; 16 *New York,* 80; and in the Superior Court of the city of New York, the Court of Common Pleas of the city and county of New York, and the mayor's courts, and recorder's courts of cities, where the premises are situated within those cities respectively. *Ib.* §§ 33, 123. And those courts have such jurisdiction without reference to the residence of the parties. 2 *Duer,* 635; and see 13 *How.* 254; *s. c.* 4 *Duer,* 682; 4 *Abb.* 43.

So, the action may be brought in the Superior Court of the city of Buffalo, *Laws of* 1854, *p.* 222, § 9; 1857, *vol.* 1, *p.* 752; and in the City Court of Brooklyn, *Laws of* 1849, *p.* 170; 21 *Barb.* 225; where the premises are situated within the limits of those cities respectively.

The application for leave to institute proceedings on behalf of infants, can be made only to the Supreme Court. (*a*) *Laws of* 1852, *p.* 411; 13 *How.* 106, 107. Whether the proceedings for the partition in such case, must also be brought in that court, is not clear by the statute; though the safer course undoubtedly

(*a*) In the city of Brooklyn, however, in respect to property situated within the limits thereof, the application may also be made to the City Court of that city. *Laws of* 1863, *p.* 89.

would be to institute the proceedings in that court in all cases where there are infant plaintiffs. *Id. ibid;* and see 2 *Abb.* 14.

How proceedings commenced.] The usual, if not the only mode, of commencing proceedings for the partition of real estate, is by summons, or summons and complaint, under the Code of Procedure, *Code*, §§ 127 to 130, 448; though the proceeding could formerly be commenced, and may still be commenced, as is believed, by petition under the Revised Statutes. The proceeding by action, however, is the best and safest mode of procedure, and is more convenient than the proceeding by petition—besides furnishing a perfectly uniform course of practice in all cases similar, in every respect, to the former practice in the Court of Chancery. (*a*) 2 *Van Sant. Eq. Pr.* 2, 3.

(*a*) It is declared by Mr. Justice Pratt, in *Croghan* v. *Livingston*, in the Court of Appeals (6 *Abb.* 350, 355, *s. c.* 17 *New York*, 218, 224), that the provisions of the Revised Statutes in relation to the partition of real estate, by *petition*, are abolished. What is there stated, however, upon that subject, was not necessary to the decision of the case; nor, as I am informed, was the question passed upon by the court, or discussed by the counsel who argued it. Yet upon the authority of that dictum, it has been held, by at least one general term of the Supreme Court, that the remedy for the partition of real estate by petition under the Revised Statutes, is abolished. 14 *Abb.* 258, *s. c.* 37 *Barb.* 22; 23 *How.* 358.

The learned justice bases his conclusions principally upon the changes made in the Code of Procedure, by the amendments of 1849. By § 390 of the Code of 1848, the Code was not to affect the proceedings provided for by titles 2, 3, 4, 5, 6, and 8, of chap. 5, part 3, of the Revised Statutes. Title 3, alluded to, relates to proceedings in partition. In the Code of 1849 that title was omitted; also titles 2, 4, and 5. By the Code of 1849, also, the provisions of the Revised Statutes, relating to the partition of lands, &c., were made to apply to actions for partition brought under the Code of Procedure, so far as the same could be so applied to the substance and subject-matter of the action, without regard to its form. *Code*, § 448. And though the Code of 1848, also clearly authorized proceedings by action for partition (§§ 103, 388, 390), yet the question whether it did in fact authorize such proceedings seemed to be left in doubt by the case of *Traver* v. *Traver* (3 *How.* 351, 354; and see *Id.* 290, *per* Hand, J.; *Id.* 318; 4 *Id.* 83, 84; *Id.* 133). Besides, while it was important that the provisions of the Revised Statutes, relating to proceedings in partition, should be applied to an action for partition brought under the Code, yet the Code of 1848 contained no section in terms making those provisions applicable to such action. Hence the amendments to the Code of 1849; which were no doubt deemed necessary by the legislature, to put at rest the question whether an action for partition was proper under the Code; and for the purpose, also, of making the provisions of the Revised Statutes applicable to such action.

By the amendments of 1849, also, as we have seen, titles 2, 4, and 5, above mentioned, were also omitted from the Code. Title 2 provides for the determination

The remedy by action, therefore, will be the only one considered in this work.

The action is commenced by the service of a summons, or a summons and complaint, as in ordinary actions. *Code*, §§ 127 to 139, 448. For forms, see *Appendix*, Nos. 470 to 473.

In the case of a defendant against whom no personal claim is made, the plaintiff may deliver to such defendant, with the summons, a notice subscribed by the plaintiff or his attorney, setting forth the general object of the action, a brief description of the premises of which partition is sought, and that no personal claim is made against the defendant; in which case no copy of the complaint need be served on the defendant, unless within the time for

---

of claims to real estate; title 4 relates to the writ of nuisance; and title 5 to the action of waste. And the amendments of 1849, in respect to those titles, authorized an action for the proceedings under the Revised Statutes, and in express terms abolished the action of waste and the writ of nuisance. *Code*, §§ 450, 451, 453, 454. But in respect to proceedings for partition, although it authorized an action to be prosecuted for the partition of real estate, and made the provisions of the Revised Statutes applicable to such action, yet it nowhere in terms abolished the proceeding by petition. And as the two proceedings are not inconsistent with each other, the inference is, that the remedy may be taken by action under the Code, or by petition under the Revised Statutes, in like manner as it could formerly be done by bill or petition in the Court of Chancery. See 2 *Rev. Stat.* 329, *sec.* 79; 3 *How.* 351; 4 *Id.* 83; *Id.* 133, *per* Barculo, J.; *Id.* 125.

But it is said that title 3, above mentioned, was not "reserved" by section 471 of the Code of 1849; and, therefore, that it is abolished, unless expressly saved by other provisions of the Code. It is submitted, however, that no such construction can be given to that section. That section, except in respect to statutory provisions inconsistent with the Code, and therefore repealed by § 468, had no effect, either to reserve or to abolish the several proceedings mentioned in it. But its sole object had reference to the application of the Code to them, and to prevent that application, except as therein mentioned; and though it recognized the existence of those proceedings, it did so for that purpose only. And as the proceeding for the partition of real estate by petition is a special statutory remedy, not inconsistent with the Code, the omission to include the title relating to that proceeding among the titles enumerated in § 471 can have no effect upon the question whether that remedy is abolished or not.

It is believed, for the reasons above stated, that title 3 remains unrepealed, and that proceedings for partition may be taken by petition under its provisions, as well as by action under the Code of Procedure. And that such has been the understanding of the profession, will be seen by reference to the following authorities: 3 *How.* 351, 354; 4 *Id.* 83; *Id.* 133; *Id.* 125; 23 *Barb.* 336; 16 *New York*, 82, 83; 2 *Whit. Pr. 2d ed.* 330 to 333; 2 *Mon. Pr.* 254; *Sup. Court Rules*, *Nos.* 77, 78. And see, as evidence of the intention of the legislature to retain the proceeding by petition, *Laws of* 1852, *p.* 411; *Laws of* 1857, *vol.* 2. *p.* 504; *Pub. Acts*, 184.

answering he shall, in writing, demand the same. *Code*, § 131. For form of notice, see *Appendix*, No. 471. If the defendant on whom the notice is served, unreasonably defend the action, he will be required to pay costs to the plaintiff. *Code*, § 131; and see 9 *Paige*, 230.

Parties to the action.] The party applying for the partition, as we have seen, must have an estate in the premises as a joint tenant or a tenant in common, and must be in the possession of his undivided share or interest. 2 *Rev. Stat.* 317, *sec.* 1, *supra.* The party must also be of full age; though on application to the Supreme Court, (*a*) and showing sufficient reasons therefor, authority will be given to commence the proceedings in behalf of an infant; in which case the proceedings must be conducted in the name of such infant by a competent next friend, to be appointed by the court for that purpose. *Laws of* 1852, *p.* 411, *post;* and see 13 *How.* 105; 21 *Id.* 479, *s. c.* 14 *Abb.* 299; 26 *How.* 250.

Several joint tenants, or tenants in common, may unite as parties plaintiffs, but it is usual and more convenient to commence the action in the name of one of them alone, making the others defendants.

A tenant in common of part of the premises, is not debarred from bringing an action for partition individually, merely because he is a trustee as to another part. 1 *Edw. Ch. R.* 629.

If a lessee of land becomes a purchaser of an undivided moiety of the rent and reversion, the lease and rent are merged and extinguished as to that portion of the premises; and he is not such a tenant in common of the rent and reversion, with the owner of the other half thereof, as to entitle the latter to a partition of the land during the continuance of the lease. 4 *Paige*, 639. So, if the owner of an undivided moiety of land is a lessee of the other half thereof, and the lease has become forfeited by the non-performance of a condition subsequent, the landlord must enter for the forfeiture, or must otherwise obtain the possession of his individual half of the premises, before he can sustain an action for partition. *Ib.*

(*a*) In the city of Brooklyn, where the premises are situated therein, the application may also be made to the City Court of that city. *Laws of* 1863, *p.* 89.

If the proceedings are commenced by a wife for the partition of premises owned by her, separately from her husband, it would be improper to join the husband as a party plaintiff, 8 *How.* 389; though in such case, it seems, it would be proper to make him a defendant in the proceedings. See *Ib.* 393; *Laws of* 1862, *p.* 343; 1860, *p.* 157.

Where, however, the suit is instituted by a party whose wife has an inchoate right of dower in the premises sought to be partitioned, the wife in such case, whether an infant or an adult, is a proper and necessary party; and should be joined with her husband as plaintiff in the proceedings. 8 *How.* 456; and see 7 *Paige*, 387.

And so, in proceedings for the partition of the real estate of a lunatic, or of an habitual drunkard, it would be irregular for the committee of such person to institute the proceedings in their name alone; but such lunatic, or habitual drunkard, is a necessary party to the proceedings, and should be joined with the committee as plaintiff therein. 3 *Barb. Ch. R.* 25.

Where the proceedings for partition are commenced by the assignees of a tenant for life, who had assigned the premises for the benefit of his creditors, the legal estate is in the assignees, and the creditors are not necessary parties to the proceedings. 2 *Barb. S. C. R.* 599; and see 8 *Paige*, 513. But where an undivided portion of the premises has been conveyed to trustees, upon a trust not authorized by law, the *cestui que trust* is a necessary party to the proceedings, to make the judgment binding upon his interest in the premises. *Ib.*

With respect to parties *defendants*, it may be stated, generally, that all persons should be made parties to the proceedings, who have any interest whatever in the premises of which partition is sought, or any part thereof.

The statute provides, that every person interested in the premises, whether in possession or otherwise, including those having an interest therein as tenant for years, for life, by the curtesy, or in dower, and the persons entitled to the reversion, remainder, or inheritance after the termination of any particular estate therein, and every person who, by any contingency contained in any devise, grant, or otherwise, may be or become entitled to any beneficial interest in the premises, and every person entitled to dower in the premises if the same has not been admeasured, may be made parties to the proceedings. 2 *Rev. Stat.* 318, *sec.* 6; *Ib. sec.* 5, *sub.* 2; 2 *Paige*, 387; 1 *Barb. S. C. R.* 500; 7 *Id.* 221.

But in an action between tenants in common, for the partition of an interest in real estate, which has been carved out of the fee, the owner of the fee, being the common source of title to all the tenants in common, is not a necessary party. 28 *Barb.* 336.

In respect to making persons entitled to dower parties, the statute authorizes every such person to be made a party to the action, if the dower has not been admeasured. 2 *Rev. Stat.* 318, *sec.* 6.

It was held in Tanner *v.* Niles (1 *Barb. S. C. R.* 560, 564; and see *Ib.* 500), that where the dower interest is in an undivided share of the premises, the person having such interest was a proper party to the action; but that it was not necessary, though generally advisable, to make such person a party, who was entitled to dower which had not been admeasured, and which extended to the whole of the premises of which partition is sought; and that the statute did not, in any case, contemplate an admeasurement of a dower interest, in the proceedings for the partition of the premises. But since the decision in that case, an act has been passed which seems to contemplate an admeasurement of the widow's dower in the premises of which partition is sought, whether the dower extends to the whole or to only a part of the premises in question. *Laws of* 1847, *p.* 557, *sec.* 5, *post.* In view of that act, therefore, and other statutory provisions on the subject, it would undoubtedly be the proper course, in all cases, to make the persons entitled to dower in the premises, parties to the proceedings, whether the dower extends to the whole of the premises, or only to an undivided portion thereof; and even if the same has been admeasured, if a sale of the premises is contemplated. 2 *Rev. Stat.* 318, *secs.* 5, 6; *Ib.* 322, *sec.* 35; *Ib.* 325, *secs.* 50, 51; 15 *New York*, 625; 3 *Paige*, 653; 7 *Id.* 410.

And so, a married woman, having only an inchoate right of dower in the undivided portion of her husband, may be made a party defendant in the action. 7 *Paige*, 386. And if a woman marry one of the parties after the action is commenced, she need not be brought in as a party, unless for the precaution of rendering a purchaser's title more secure; and if so brought in, the proper practice under the old system, was, to enter a simple order that the further proceedings be in the name of herself and her husband, and not by amendment or supplemental bill; and the same practice would probably be held proper now. 2 *Van Sant. Pr.* 13, citing 7 *Paige*, 386; 2 *Barb. Ch. Pr.* 289.

If a married woman has a separate estate as tenant in common with others, she may be made a party defendant alone, without her husband. *Laws of* 1860, *p.* 157; 1862, *p.* 343. And if the action is brought by a married woman having a separate estate, her husband should be made a party defendant, if he has any interest to be affected by the action; otherwise not. *Ib.;* 14 *How.* 456; 31 *Barb.* 314.

Reversioners and remaindermen are proper parties, and necessary in order to bind their interests by the judgment. Thus, a reversioner is a necessary party where the action is brought by a person who is owner of an undivided share of the reversion, as well as of an undivided share of the present interest in the property. 2 *Paige*, 387. And he is also a necessary party where the action is brought by the owner of an undivided share of the premises for life, or of any other particular estate in the same, and some of the other parties own the residue of the premises in fee. *Ib.*

Where an undivided portion of the premises, of which partition is sought, has been conveyed to a trustee upon a trust not authorized by the Revised Statutes, the *cestui que trust* is a necessary party to the action, to make the judgment binding upon his interest in the premises. 8 *Paige*, 513. If, however, the absolute title to such portion is vested in a trustee upon a valid trust, it seems it is not necessary to make the *cestui que trust* a party, but that it is sufficient to bring before the court the trustee who has the whole legal estate. *Ib.*

If persons are interested in the premises who are unknown, they may be made parties to the action generally, without stating their names, by adding to the title of the summons and complaint, "and all persons or owners unknown, having or claiming any interest in the premises sought to be partitioned in this action." 2 *Rev. Stat.* 319, *secs.* 12, 35; *Laws of* 1842, *p.* 363; 2 *Van Sant. Pr.* 7. And in such case, the service of the summons upon them may be made by publication of the same under § 135 of the Code. 11 *How.* 277.

The future contingent interest of persons not *in esse*, such as contingent remaindermen, or persons to take under an executory devise, who may hereafter come into being, are bound by a judgment in partition, they being considered as virtually represented by the parties to the action in whom the present estate is vested. 17 *New York*, 210, affirming 5 *Abb.* 92.

The effect of not making all the persons interested parties to the action, will be to prevent the plaintiff, at the hearing, from obtaining judgment of partition. 2 *Barb. Ch. R.* 398. But where all the parties are adults, and have been personally served with process, the court will not examine the proceedings to ascertain whether all the proper parties are before the court, 8 *Paige*, 513; though it is otherwise if the persons are proceeded against as absentees, or as unknown owners of undivided portions of the premises, or where the rights of infants are concerned. If the parties are adults, and the other necessary parties are not brought in, the defendants who have been served with process should appear, and make the objection. *Ib.;* and see 27 *How.* 289.

If any person interested in the premises, or having any claim by which he may become interested at any future time, has not been made a party to the proceedings, he may, notwithstanding, be admitted to appear and answer as a defendant, on application to the court, or to a judge thereof in vacation, upon his petition accompanied by an affidavit of his interest. 2 *Rev. Stat.* 319, *sec.* 15.

In respect to *creditors*, having liens upon the premises or any part thereof, by judgment, decree, mortgage or otherwise, it had been decided previous to the Revised Statutes, that such persons were not proper parties to an action; and that their rights could not be affected by a sale of the lands. 1 *Paige*, 469; 7 *Johns. Ch. R.* 140; *Hopk.* 501. But the rule has been changed either by the statute or the practice of the court; (*a*) and the court is

(*a*) The statute authorizes creditors having *specific* liens by mortgage, devise, or otherwise, to be made parties to the action, in the discretion of the plaintiff, 2 *Rev Stat.* 318, *sec.* 10; and if a sale of the premises is to be had, they are necessary parties, *Ib. sec.* 42; though if they are not made parties, their liens will not be affected by the sale or conveyance. *Laws of* 1830, *ch.* 320, § 45. In respect, however, to creditors having general liens, by judgment or otherwise, there is no provision of the statute in express terms requiring or authorizing them to be made parties to the action. The statute, indeed, does not seem to contemplate that they shall be made parties, since in case the premises are sold, they may be barred without it, *Laws of* 1830, *supra;* and whether sold or partitioned, their rights seem fully guarded and protected. 2 *Rev. Stat.* 318, *secs.* 8, 9, 42 to 49; *Laws of* 1830, *ch.* 320, § 45.

now authorized to make them parties to the action, and to decree a sale which will give the purchaser a perfect title, discharged from all liens and incumbrances. 1 *Paige*, 470; 7 *How.* 307; 2 *Barb. Ch. Pr.* 288; 2 *Van Sant. Eq. Pr.* 14; *Sup. Court Rules*, No. 79.

It is not necessary, however, in the first instance to make such creditors parties to the proceedings. 2 *Rev. Stat.* 318, *sec.* 8, as altered by amendatory act of 1830, *ch.* 320, *sec.* 40. Though the plaintiff may, at his election, make every creditor a party to the proceedings who has a specific lien upon the undivided interest or estate of any of the parties, by mortgage, devise, or otherwise. *Ib. sec.* 41. And this is the course usually adopted in practice, as it saves the necessity of amending the complaint in case the premises are to be sold. 2 *Rev. Stat.* 324, *sec.* 42; 2 *Barb. Ch. Pr.* 288. And not only are the creditors having specific liens upon the premises, or on any undivided share thereof usually made parties if a sale is to be made, but those, also, having general liens by judgment or otherwise. *Id. ibid.;* and 7 *How.* 307; 1 *Paige*, 470, and see *Sup. Court Rules*, No. 79; 2 *Van Sant. Eq. Pr.* 14; and *ante, p.* 107, *note.*

The effect of omitting to make incumbrancers parties to the action will be that the partition of the premises will not alter, impair, or affect their lien; except that if the lien is on the undivided interest or estate of any of the parties, such lien, if partition is made of the premises, will thereafter be a charge only on the share assigned to such party; and such share will be charged with its just proportion of the costs of the proceedings for partition, in preference to the lien. 2 *Rev. Stat.* 318, *secs.* 8, 9.

The court will allow an amendment of the pleadings or proceedings, so as to make defendant thereto, any person who shall have appeared, in the course of the proceedings, to be interested in the premises, by any will, deed, or grant from any person who is a defendant in such partition, and who might originally have been made defendant, if his interest had then existed or been known. 2 *Rev. Stat.* 320, *sec.* 20. And in respect to amendments generally, and bringing in new parties, the provisions of the Code apply, the same as in ordinary actions. *Code*, §§ 169 to 177, 448.

Notice of lis pendens.] The party instituting the proceedings, on filing the complaint, or at any time afterwards, may file with the clerk of each county in which the property is situated, a notice of the pendency of the action, containing the object thereof, the names of the parties, and the description of the property in that county affected thereby. *Code*, § 132; and see *Eq. Rules*, 1847, No. 121. For form, see *Appendix*, No. 474.

From the time of filing the notice only, will the pendency of the action be constructive notice to a purchaser or incumbrancer of the property affected thereby. *Code*, § 132.

And every person whose conveyance or incumbrance is subsequently executed or subsequently recorded, will be deemed a subsequent purchaser or incumbrancer, and will be bound by all proceedings taken after the filing of such notice to the same extent as if he were made a party to the action. *Ib.*

For the purposes of § 132, an action is deemed to be pending from the time of the filing of the notice; provided, however, that the notice will be of no avail, unless it shall be followed by the first publication of the summons on an order therefor, or by the personal service thereof on a defendant within sixty days after such filing. *Ib.*

And the court in which the action was commenced may, in its discretion, at any time after the action is settled, discontinued or abated, as is provided in section 121, on good cause shown, and on application of any person aggrieved, and on such notice as shall be directed or approved by the court, order the notice of *lis pendens* to be cancelled of record by the clerk of any county in whose office the same may have been filed or recorded. *Ib.*, as amended *Laws of* 1866, *ch.* 824.

Such cancellation shall be made by an endorsement to that effect on the margin of the record, which shall refer to the order, and for which the clerk shall be entitled to a fee of twenty-five cents. *Ib.*

See further on the subject of this notice, *ante*, *vol.* 1, *p.* 285.

Guardian ad litem for infants.] If the proceedings are instituted by an infant *plaintiff*, under the authority of the Supreme Court, a competent next friend or guardian must be appointed by the court to conduct the proceedings; which next friend or guardian is to be appointed upon the like application, and in the like manner, and must give the same security, and will possess the same powers, as are specified and required in sections two, three, and four, of title 3 of chapter 5 of the third part of the Revised Statutes (2 *Rev. Stat.* 317), *Laws of* 1852, *p.* 411, § 2; and see 6 *Abb. Pr.* 350, *s. c.* 17 *New York*, 218; 26 *How.* 250; 21 *Id.* 479, *s. c.* 14 *Abb.* 299.

Those statutes provide, that if it shall be represented to the court by any party intending to make application for partition, that there are any minors who should be parties to the proceedings thereon, and it shall be satisfactorily proved to the court that at least ten days' notice has been served on such minors as shall reside within this State, or upon their general guardians, of an intention to apply to the court for the order therein mentioned, such court shall thereupon appoint a suitable and disinterested person to be guardian for one or more of such minors, whether the said minors shall reside in or out of this State, for the special purpose of taking charge of the interests of such minors in relation to the proceeding for partition. 2 *Rev. Stat.* 317, *sec.* 2.

The statute also prescribes the powers of the guardian, and the security to be given by him on his appointment. *Ib. secs.* 3 and 4. These are the same as in cases of guardians for infant defendants; in respect to which see *post*.

The appointment of a next friend or guardian for an infant plaintiff, must be made by the Supreme Court. (*a*) *Laws of* 1852, *p.* 411. Where it was made by a county judge, the proceedings were declared void for that reason, and were set aside on motion. 13 *How.* 105. Nor can it be made by a judge at chambers; but must be made by the *court*; though in the first judicial district, the order appointing a guardian, when made by a judge at chambers, operates as an order of the court. 5 *Abb.* 53.

It is indispensable that the next friend appointed to institute the action in behalf of infants should give security as required by the statute. 26 *How.* 250; 21 *Id.* 479; *s. c.* 14 *Abb.* 299.

If there are infant *defendants*, a guardian ad litem must be appointed for them. And the provisions of the Revised Statutes are to regulate the appointment and the security to be given by the guardian, 2 *Abb.* 611; 2 *Duer*, 655; 3 *Bosw.* 410; except

(*a*) If the premises, however, are situated in the city of Brooklyn, the appointment may also be made by the city court of that city. *Laws of* 1863, *p.* 89.

in regard to the mere form of applying, and the parties to apply. (a) 2 *Abb.* 15; and see 2 *Duer*, 635; 11 *Abb.* 440, 455; *Id.* 473; *s. c.* 20 *How.* 222; 25 *Id.* 266.

(a) There is some confusion in the authorities on the subject of the proper practice on the appointment of a guardian *ad litem* for an infant defendant in an action for partition.

The Revised Statutes, in respect to the mode of applying for the appointment of a guardian and the parties to apply, provides, that if it shall be represented to the court by any party intending to make application for a partition or sale of real estate, that there are any minors who should be parties to the proceedings thereon, and it shall be satisfactorily proved to the court, that at least ten days' notice has been served on such minors as reside within this State, or upon their general guardians, of an intention to apply to such court for the order therein mentioned, such court shall thereupon appoint a suitable and disinterested person to be guardian for one or more of such minors, whether the said minors shall reside in or out of this State, for the special purpose of taking charge of the interests of such minors in relation to the proceedings for a partition. 2 *Rev. Stat.* 317, *sec.* 2.

In *Jennings* v. *Jennings* (2 *Abb.* 13), Judge Hoffman, in giving a construction to § 448 of the Code, stated substantially, that those provisions of the Revised Statutes which are peculiar to the action of partition, and as to which there were no corresponding provisions in the Code, must prevail. And also, that those provisions of the statute, which are in addition to, and consistent with the Code, must also govern. He accordingly held, that the Revised Statutes were applicable in respect to the appointment of the guardian, and the security to be given; though inapplicable so far as related to the time and mode of applying for the appointment, and the parties to apply.

This construction has been followed in several cases, since decided.

Thus, in *Towsey* v. *Harrison* (25 *How.* 266), decided at General Term in the seventh district, it was held that a guardian *ad litem* for an infant defendant, in an action for partition brought in the Supreme Court, could be appointed by a county judge. This was unlike the practice under the Revised Statutes, as we have seen, which required the appointment to be made by the court; and by the court, too, in which the action was to be brought.

The propriety of proceeding under the Code of Procedure, in respect to the mode of appointing the guardian *ad litem*, is also recognized by Hogeboom, J., in *Van Wyck* v. *Hardy*, 20 *How.* 222, 229, *s. c.* 11 *Abb.* 473; and again in *Rogers* v. *McLean*, 11 *Abb. Pr. R.* 440, 455; and by Ingraham, J., in *Van Wyck* v. *Hardy*, 20 *How. Pr.* 225, *supra.*

In conflict with the above, are the cases of *Disbrow* v. *Folger* (5 *Abb.* 53); *Lyle* v. *Smith* (13 *How.* 104); *Varian* v. *Stevens* (2 *Duer*, 635), and *Althouse* v. *Radde* (3 *Bosw.* 410); but an examination of those cases will show that they were decided upon other grounds, as well as that relating to the application of the Revised Statutes to the practice on the appointment of the guardian, or that what was said was the mere *dicta* of the court, having, in fact, no relation to the question before it.

Thus, in *Disbrow* v. *Folger* (5 *Abb.* 53), where the guardian had been appointed by a Supreme Court judge, at chambers, in the city of New York; the question was upon the regularity of the appointment, the guardian, as it was said, not having been appointed by the *court.* The justice deciding the case, assuming that the

By the Code of Procedure (§ 115), the guardian may be appointed by the court in which the action is prosecuted, or by a judge thereof, or a county judge.

And the guardian is appointed upon the application of the infant, if he is fourteen years of age, and applies within twenty days after the service of the summons. But if he is under the age of fourteen years, or neglects so to apply, then upon the application of any other party to the action, or of a relative or friend of the infant, after notice of the application has been first given to the general or testamentary guardian of the infant, if he has one within this State; if he has none, then to the infant himself, if over fourteen years of age, and within the State, or, if under that age, and within the State, to the person with whom the infant resides. *Code*, § 116.

And where an infant defendant resides out of this State, or is temporarily absent therefrom, the plaintiff may apply to the court in which the action is pending, at any special term thereof, and will be entitled to an order designating some suitable person to be the guardian for the infant defendant for the purposes of the action, unless the infant defendant or some one in his behalf, within a number of days after the service of a copy of the order, which number of days shall be in the said order specified, shall procure to be appointed a guardian for the said infant, and the court shall give special directions in the order for the manner of the service thereof, which may be upon the infant. *Code*, § 116, *as amended* 1865.

---

appointment must have been made by the court, held, nevertheless, that it was regular, because, in that city, the order of a judge at chambers operated as an order of the court. So, in *Lyle* v. *Smith* (13 *How.* 104), the question related to the practice upon the appointment of a guardian for an infant *plaintiff*, under the act of 1852; and what was there said on the subject of infant defendants was not intended to be said, or, at least, was entirely outside of the question before the court. In *Varian* v. *Stevens* (2 *Duer*, 635), what was there said on the subject in question was not necessary to the decision of the case. Besides, it was inconsistent with what was subsequently held in the same opinion (*p.* 638), that the infant might himself apply, under § 116 of the Code, for the appointment of a guardian. And in *Althouse* v. *Radde* (3 *Bosw.* 410), the case was in fact decided upon grounds not relating to the question under consideration.

The practice, therefore, may be stated to be settled, upon the weight of authority, that in the appointment of a guardian for an infant defendant, in an action for partition, the provisions of the Revised Statutes are to apply, except so far as they relate to the time, place, and mode of applying, and the parties to apply; and that in respect to the last-mentioned matters, the Code of Procedure is to apply.

And in case an infant defendant having an interest in the event of the action shall reside in any State with which there shall not be a regular communication by mail, on such fact satisfactorily appearing to the court, the court may appoint a guardian ad litem for such absent infant party, for the purpose of protecting the right of such infant in said action; and on such guardian ad litem, process, pleadings, and notices in the action may be served in the like manner as upon a party residing in this State. *Ib.*

Where a guardian ad litem has been appointed in an action for partition, upon the petition of an infant over the age of fourteen years, the order is valid, although no summons had previously been served upon the infant. 2 *Duer*, 635. And the jurisdiction of the court, therefore, is complete, when the guardian so appointed puts in an answer on behalf of the infant. *Ib.*; and see 3 *Bosw.* 410; 11 *Abb.* 455.

Every person appointed guardian is required, before entering upon the execution of his duties, to execute a bond, in such penalty, and with such surety, as the court shall direct, to the people of this State, conditioned for the faithful discharge of the trust committed to such guardian, and to render a just and true account of his guardianship, in all courts and places, when thereunto required; and before any rule to plead, or any other subsequent rule or order, shall be made, the court is required to be satisfied that such bond has been executed and filed in the office of the clerk. 2 *Rev. Stat.* 317, *sec.* 4; 2 *Abb.* 6; 2 *Duer*, 635; 3 *Bosw.* 410; 26 *How.* 250; 21 *Id.* 479; *s. c.* 14 *Abb.* 299.

When, however, any of the joint tenants or tenants in common, who are defendants, are minors, for whom no suitable or disinterested person shall voluntarily signify his consent in writing to be appointed guardian, and offer to give the security required by the statute, it is the duty of the court, on the petition of the party instituting the proceedings, to appoint the clerk of the court guardian for such minors for the purposes of the partition, and to dispense with the security required by the statute. *Laws of* 1833, *p.* 311; 2 *Duer*, 637. But a copy of the petition, with a notice in writing specifying the time and place when and where the same will be presented, must be served at least ten days before the presentation thereof, upon the general guardian of such minors, in case there be such guardian, or upon the minor, if there be none;

proof of which service must be duly made to the court. *Laws of* 1833, *p.* 311.

The court may also appoint the clerk guardian ad litem of an infant defendant who is an absentee, and without security. 7 *Paige*, 596; and see *Code of Pro.* § 116, *supra.* But no other person can be appointed guardian in such case without giving security. 7 *Paige*, 596.

The bond must be signed by the guardian himself; and if executed by sureties in his behalf, in which he does not join, it is not a compliance with the statute. 2 *Abb.* 6. For form, see *Appendix*, No. 479.

Whenever it appears, in any action for the partition of lands, instituted in any court authorized to decree partition or sale thereof, that any such guardian has entered upon the execution of his duties, and rules or orders have been made, without the filing of the bond above required, or that such bond cannot be found on file, such court, or any judge thereof, may, on application of any party to the suit or proceeding, at any time before judgment or decree, in all cases, or after judgment or decree, in cases of actual partition, authorize and direct the filing of a bond by such guardian, and the penalty and surety thereof to be filed as of the same date with the order appointing the guardian; which bond, when so filed, and all proceedings in the suit subsequent to the date of the order appointing the guardian, shall have the like force and effect, in every respect, as if such bond had been directed by the court, and duly executed and filed by the guardian, at the date of his appointment. *Laws of* 1852, *p.* 411, *sec.* 3; 6 *Abb.* 350; *s. c.* 17 *New York*, 218.

And, in an action for partition, where the guardian, at the time of his appointment, omitted to file the bond, as required by the statute, but, after judgment and sale, an order was made giving him leave to file a bond *nunc pro tunc*, which was done, it was held proper, and that it was a mere irregularity, of which the court, on application, would allow an amendment. 25 *Barb.* 336, aff. 6 *Abb.* 350; *s. c.* 17 *New York*, 218; and see 7 *Abb.* 473.

The guardians thus appointed, who give the bond required by the statute, will represent their respective minors in the proceedings; and their acts in relation thereto will be binding on such minors, and be as valid as if done by such minors after arriving at full age. 2 *Rev. Stat.* 317, *sec.* 3, 3 *Bosw.* 410, 430.

It is unnecessary for the guardian to put in any answer, or to appear in the action, where the only object in doing so is to submit the rights of the infants to the protection of the court. 4 *Bosw.* 410, 435.

For further on the subject of the appointment of a guardian ad litem for an infant defendant, see *ante*, Chapter xiii. of this work.

The summons and notice.] The form of the summons is prescribed by the Code of Procedure. The summons must be subscribed by the plaintiff or his attorney, and directed to the defendant, and shall require him to answer the complaint, and to serve a copy of his answer on the person whose name is subscribed to the summons, at a place within the State, to be therein specified, in which there is a post-office, within twenty days after the service of the summons, exclusive of the day of service, *Code*, § 128; and the summons must contain a notice, also, to the effect that, if the defendant fail to answer the complaint within twenty days after service of the summons, the plaintiff will apply to the court for the relief demanded in the complaint. *Ib.* § 129.

The summons, if served without the complaint, must state where the complaint is, or will be, filed,—that is, the county where it is designed to have the place of trial—which must be the county in which the premises are situated. *Ib.* §§. 123, 130.

In other respects, the summons, also, is the same as in ordinary actions, where the plaintiff is to apply to the court for the relief demanded in the complaint. *Code*, §§ 128, 129, 139; and see *ante*, *vol.* 1, *p.* 281.

In respect to the notice to accompany the summons, it is provided by the Code, that in the case of a defendant against whom no personal claim is made, the plaintiff may deliver to the defendant, with the summons, a notice subscribed by the plaintiff or his attorney, setting forth the general object of the action, a brief description of the premises of which partition is sought, and that no personal claim is made against the defendant, in which case no copy of the complaint need be served on the defendant, unless within the time for answering, he shall, in writing, demand the same. And if the defendant on whom the notice is served, unreasonably defend the action, he will be required to pay costs to the plaintiff. *Code*, § 131; and see 9 *Paige*, and *ante*, *vol.* 1, *p.* 273. For form of notice, see *Appendix*, No. 471.

The complaint.] In actions for partition, the system of pleading prescribed by the Code is to be observed; though, in respect to the complaint, it should, no doubt, contain the same matters required to be stated in the petition for partition under the Revised Statutes. These are in addition to, or in compliance with, the requisitions of § 142 of the Code. 8 *How.* 458; 2 *Abb.* 14, 15; *Code*, § 448.

It is necessary, therefore, by the statute, that the complaint should contain the following matters: It must particularly describe the premises sought to be divided or sold; and must set forth the rights and titles of all persons interested therein, so far as the same are known to the petitioner, including the interest of any tenant for years, for life, by the curtesy, or in dower, and the persons entitled to the reversion, remainder, or inheritance, after the termination of any particular estate therein, and every person who, by any contingency contained in any devise, grant, or otherwise, may be or become entitled to any beneficial interest in the premises. 2 *Rev. Stat.* 318, *sec.* 5; 6 *Paige*, 492.

When infants are interested in the premises, the complaint must also state whether or not the parties own any other lands in common. *Sup. Court Rules*, No. 77; *Equity Rules*, 1847, No. 122.

And where any one or more of the parties to the proceedings, or the share or quantity of interest of such parties, is unknown to the plaintiffs, or is uncertain or contingent, or the ownership of the inheritance depends upon an executory devise, or the remainder is a contingent remainder, so that the parties cannot be named, the same must be set forth in the complaint. 2 *Rev. Stat.* 318, *sec.* 7.

Where the plaintiff shall make creditors having specific liens upon the undivided interests or estates of any of the parties, by mortgage, devise, or otherwise, parties to the proceedings, the complaint must set forth the nature of every such lien or incumbrance. 2 *Rev. Stat.* 318, as amended, *Act of* 1830, *ch.* 320, § 41.

If the complaint alleges that the parties are seized in common, it is not necessary also to allege that the plaintiff is in possession of the premises, as that fact will be presumed from the former allegation. See 3 *Paige*, 242. If the plaintiff is not in possession, this may be set up as a defence to the action. *Ib.*

The complaint may state, in general terms, that each tenant was seized of his part or share in fee, or as the case may be, without setting forth how the seizin was acquired. 8 *Johns.* 558. But if the rights of the defendants, as between themselves, depend upon the validity of a will, or the ownership of the premises is contingent or doubtful, and depends upon the construction of such will, it is proper for the plaintiff to state the fact of the making of the will, and the substance thereof, so far as is necessary to enable the court to understand the rights of the parties. 6 *Paige*, 492.

In respect to the allegation, as to unknown owners required by statute, while the complaint must allege the fact that there are such, yet the averment that there are certain unknown owners, without setting forth their exact interest in the premises, is sufficient to authorize the subsequent proceedings as to them. 23 *Barb.* 285, 303.

Where the complaint alleged, in addition to what was necessary to obtain a partition, that one of the defendants claimed a lien on the premises, and prayed an account of such lien; it was held not to contain an improper joinder of causes of action. 7 *How*, 305. So, the plaintiff, whether in the possession of the premises or not, where he claims the lands by descent from an ancestor who died in the possession of the same, may allege in his complaint that the defendant is in possession, or claims the possession of the premises, under an apparent devise of the same, which is void. *Laws of* 1853, *p.* 526.

The future contingent interests of persons not *in esse* are barred by an actual partition or sale under a judgment in partition. And the complaint, therefore, need not contain allegations in regard to the interest of contingent remaindermen who may hereafter come into being, they being virtually represented by the parties to the action in whom the present estate is vested. 17 *New York*, 210; affirming 5 *Abb.* 92.

The allegations in the complaint may be upon information and belief, as in other actions. And the complaint may be verified or not (according to the form prescribed by the Code), at the option of the plaintiff. *Code*, § 448; 2 *Abb.* 14, 15. For forms of complaint, see *Appendix*, Nos. 472, 473.

Service of summons on the defendant.] The service of the summons on the defendants is made in all respects the same as in ordinary actions, 2 *Abb.* 15; 2 *Duer*, 635; as to which see §§ 133 to 139 of the Code of Procedure, and *ante*, *vol.* 1, *p.* 381.

So, if the plaintiff is obliged to make "unknown owners" parties defendants, he may proceed against them by publication, under § 135 of the Code. 11 *How.* 277.

In case a defendant is an infant, and resides in a State with which there is not a regular communication by mail, and a guardian *ad litem* is appointed for the infant, for the purpose of protecting his rights in the action, the summons may be served upon such guardian. *Code*, § 116, as amended 1863.

And where the defendant is a resident of this State, but cannot be found, or avoids service of the summons, the court or judge may order the same to be served by leaving a copy at his residence, or affixing the same on the outer door thereof, and mailing the same through the post office, &c. *Laws of* 1853, *p.* 974; 1863, *p.* 388.

Proceedings if defendant does not appear, or answer.] If the defendant do not answer or demur to the plaintiff's complaint within the time limited for that purpose, the plaintiff may apply to the court for the relief demanded in the complaint.

And where all the parties are of age, and have been personally served with the summons, the plaintiff will be entitled to judgment of partition, as of course, upon proving title to the premises as required by the statute. 2 *Rev. Stat.* 321, *sec.* 22; 8 *How.* 456. This proof may be made in open court; or a reference may be ordered to take proof of the title and report upon the same with an abstract of the conveyances by which it is held. 2 *Paige*, 27; 2 *Rev. Stat.* 321, *sec.* 22; *Laws of* 1847, *p.* 344, § 77; 2 *Abb.* 16. The proof of title is such as would be required to be made to enable a plaintiff to recover in ejectment. 2 *Paige*, 27; 3 *Wend.* 436; and the title should be traced back to a common source. 7 *Paige*, 39. In those cases, however, where the parties are of age, and have been personally served, the court will not examine the proceedings to ascertain whether all the proper parties are before the court, or whether the referee, if a reference has been ordered, has stated the rights and interests of the parties correctly in his report. 8 *Id.* 513; and see 27 *How.* 289. If the necessary parties are not before the court, so as to make the judgment final and effectual as to all persons interested in the premises, the defendants who are served should appear and make that objection. *Id. ibid.* On the application for judgment in such cases, however, in addition to the usual proof of personal service upon all the defendants, and that no answer or demurrer has been received, the plaintiff should produce an affidavit showing that none of the defendants are infants, or absentees, or unknown. 2 *Van Sant. Pr.* 28. For forms of affidavit, see *Appendix*, Nos. 480 to 483.

Where any of the defendants are infants, or absentees, or where there are unknown owners, a reference is usually ordered by the court, on the application of the plaintiff. The practice in respect to such reference, is regulated by the Rules of the Supreme Court, which provide as follows:

Where the rights and interests of the several parties as stated in the complaint, are not denied or controverted, if any of the defendants are infants or absentees, or unknown, the plaintiff, on an affidavit of the fact and notice to such of the parties as have appeared, may apply at a special term for an order of reference to take proof of the plaintiff's title and interest in the premises and of the several matters set forth in the complaint; and to ascertain and report the rights and interests of the several parties in the premises, and an abstract of the conveyances by which the same are held. *Rule* No. 78.

And where the whole premises of which partition is sought, are so circumstanced that a partition thereof cannot be made without great prejudice to the owners, due regard being had to the power of the court to decree compensation to be made for equality of partition, and to the ability of the respective parties to pay a reasonable compensation to produce such equality, or where any lot or separate parcel of the premises, which will exceed in value the share to which either of the tenants in common may be entitled, is so circumstanced, the plaintiff, upon stating the fact in the affidavit, which is to be filed for the purpose of obtaining an order of reference under the preceding rule (No. 78.), may have a further provision inserted in such order of reference, directing the officer or person to whom it is referred, to inquire and report whether the whole premises, or any lot, or separate parcel thereof, are so circumstanced that an actual partition cannot be made; and that if he arrives at the conclusion that the sale of the whole premises, or of any lot, or separate parcel thereof, will be necessary, that he specify the same in his report, together with the reasons which render a sale necessary; and, in such a case, that he also ascertain and report whether any creditor, not a party to the suit, has a specific lien, by mortgage, devise, or otherwise, upon the undivided share or interest of any of the parties, in that portion of the premises which it is necessary to sell; and if he finds that there is no such specific lien in favor of any person not a party to the suit, that he further inquire and report whether the undivided share or interest of any of the parties in the premises is subject to a general lien or incumbrance, by judgment or decree; and that he ascertain and report the amount due to any party to the suit who has either a general or specific lien on the premises to be sold, or any part thereof, and the amount due to any creditor, not a party, who has a general lien on any undivided share or interest therein, by judgment or decree, and who shall appear and establish his claim on such reference. He shall also, if requested by the parties who appear before him on such reference, ascertain and report the amount due to any creditor, not a party to the suit, which is either a specific or general lien or incumbrance upon all the shares or interests of the parties in the premises to be sold, and which would remain as an incumbrance thereon, in the hands of the purchaser; to the end that such direction may be given in relation to the same, in the decree for the sale of the premises, as shall be most beneficial to all the parties interested in the proceeds thereof, on such sale. *Rule* No. 79.

The proceedings before the referee are governed by the ordinary rules applicable to references in other equity actions.

The referee should require the plaintiff to produce the abstracts of his title, as a tenant in common in the premises, and to trace it back to the common source of title of the several tenants in common; and in his report, the referee should, as far as practicable, give an abstract of the conveyances of the several undivided shares or interests of the parties in the premises from the time they were united in one common source. See 7 *Paige*, 39, and

8 *How.* 456; 6 *Id.* 491. Proof of the plaintiff's title must be exhibited to the referee, *Id. ibid.;* and this proof must be such, as, in an action of ejectment, would establish a *prima facie* right in a plaintiff to recover the premises claimed by him. 3 *Wend.* 436; and see 2 *Paige*, 27.

But the practice does not require the referee in his report of title to annex to his report a search for mortgages or conveyances, affecting the title. It is sufficient if the report states the fact explicitly that he had caused the necessary searches to be made, and certifies what incumbrances, &c., there are. 27 *How.* 289.

Where the parties are proceeded against as unknown owners of undivided portions, or as absentees, or the rights of infants are involved, the court will look into the proceedings to see that all proper persons are made parties, 8 *Paige*, 513; though otherwise if all the parties are adults and have been personally served with the summons. *Ib.;* and see 27 *How.* 289.

If the referee is directed to inquire as to the propriety of a sale of the premises, the true question to be considered by him in determining whether such sale is necessary, is whether the aggregate value of the several parcels into which the whole premises must be divided, will, when distributed among the different parties in severalty, be materially less than the value of the same property, if owned by one person. 6 *Paige*, 541, 547.

The referees' report, with proof of the due service of the summons upon the parties interested, and if the summons has been served by publication, proof of such publication, must be submitted to the court on the application for judgment, and filed with the clerk. See 2 *Rev. Stat.* 321, *sec.* 22.

And where there are infant parties, the application must also be accompanied by the certificate of the clerk, or other proof, showing that the bond required to be given by the guardian ad litem, has been duly executed, and filed in the office of the clerk of the court. *Ib.* 317, *sec.* 4.

Who may defend.] Any person having any interest in the premises, or having any claim by which he may become interested at any future time, in reversion, remainder, or by any executory devise, contingency, or otherwise, and whether such interest be present and vested, or contingent, and whether such parties or their interest be known or unknown, may, within the time prescribed by law, or within such further time as the court may allow for the purpose, appear and answer to the plaintiff's complaint. 2 *Rev. Stat.* 319, *sec.* 15; *Code*, § 448.

And if such person be not named as a party to the action he may be admitted to appear and answer the same, as a defendant, by the court, or by any judge thereof in vacation, upon his petition accompanied by an affidavit of his interest. *Id. ibid.*

Answer of the defendant.] The answer of the defendant in an action for partition, is regulated by the Code of Procedure, the same in all respects as an answer in an ordinary action. *Code*, §§ 149, 448.

It is not necessary or proper for a defendant to put in a general answer merely admitting the matters alleged in the complaint without at the same time setting up new matter constituting a defence. And the plaintiff, instead of treating such an answer as properly put in, may give notice of a motion at special term, to strike it out as irrelevant, accompanied with a notice of application for judgment at the same time. *Ib.* § 247; 2 *Van Sant. Pr.* 24.

And even in the case of an infant defendant for whom a guardian ad litem has been appointed, it is unnecessary for him to put in an answer to the complaint where the facts alleged in the complaint are true, and the answer is put in simply for the purpose of submitting his rights to the protection of the court, in the manner prescribed by the former equity practice *Ib.; and* 3 *Bosw.* 410, 430, 436.

Any party appearing, may answer either separately or jointly, with one or more of his co-defendants, that the plaintiff, or any of them, at the time of the commencement of the action, were not in possession of the premises in question, or any part thereof; (*a*) or that the defendants or any of them, did not hold the premises together with the plaintiffs, at the time of the commencement of the action, as alleged in the complaint; and he may set forth any special matter to sustain such answer, and may give evidence

---

(*a*) It is not necessary, however, for the plaintiff to be in possession of premises claimed by him as heir, by descent, from an ancestor who died in possession, where he seeks in the same action, to invalidate an apparent devise of such premises, by the ancestor, in favor of the defendants or those under whom they claim. *Laws of* 1853, *p.* 526, § 2, *ante*, *p.* 96.

thereof on the trial. 2 *Rev. Stat.* 320, *sec.* 16; *Code*, § 448; 15 *Wend.* 340; 19 *Id.* 367.

And the defendant is not confined in his answer to the two defenses authorized to be pleaded by the above section; but he may allege anything that will abate the action, or bar the plaintiff's right to a judgment; and to the same extent as in other actions. 4 *How.* 125; *s. c.* 2 *Code R.*, 69.

Where the party instituting the action is not in possession of the premises, the disability should regularly be pleaded by the defendant, 19 *Wend.* 367; 3 *Paige*, 242; unless it distinctly appears by the complaint itself. 2 *Barb. Ch. R.* 398. But if there has been an omission to plead it, it may be taken advantage of at the trial under the plea of *non tenant insimul.* 19 *Wend.* 367, *supra.*

The plaintiff's possession of the premises will be presumed from an allegation in the complaint, that the parties are seized as tenants in common. And if the plaintiff has been ousted, or there is an adverse holding, the defendant must allege it in his answer, if he wishes to put the question of possession in issue. 3 *Paige*, 245, 246.

Other and further pleadings may also be had between the parties respectively, according to the practice of the court, as in personal actions under the Code, until an issue or issues in law, or in fact, are joined between the parties, or some of them. 2 *Rev. Stat.* 320, *sec.* 17; *Code*, § 448.

The issues, and trial thereof.] The issues in the action, whether of law or fact, are to be tried by the court, in the same manner as issues in other equity actions. Or the court may award an issue to be tried by a jury; in which case the issues must be settled in conformity to Rule 33 of the Supreme Court.

And whenever the joint tenancy, or tenancy in common, of any defendant shall be denied by a co-defendant, and it shall become necessary to determine the same, in order to effect a complete and final partition, so far as the rights of the parties are concerned, the court may direct an issue to be formed on the record, and may direct the jury to inquire into, try, and determine, as well the tenancy of the defendant so denied, as the other issues joined on such pleadings. 2 *Rev. Stat.* 320, *sec.* 18. And the court may set aside verdicts and grant new trials therein;

and it may, either before or after the trial of such issue, permit the proceedings to be amended, so as to represent truly the rights claimed by any party. *Ib. sec.* 19.

Where there are issues as to one or more, and failure to answer as to the rest of the defendants, the trial of the issue may be brought on in the usual manner, and at the same time, on notice to the defendants who appear, but do not answer; and the proof requisite in case of a default as to them, may be presented to the court, so that the decision of the court upon the issues being rendered, if in favor of the plaintiff, one general order may be made determining such issues, and directing the proper reference as to all the defendants. 2 *Van Sant. Eq. Pr.* 26.

And if there are issues of fact as to some of the defendants, to be tried by a jury, these must be disposed of first before further steps can be taken against those making default. On the coming in of the verdict, if favorable to the plaintiff, a motion may be made, on notice to those who have appeared, for the relief demanded in the complaint, against all the defendants, as well those embraced in the issue tried, as the other defendants who make default. And the proceedings will then be precisely the same as on a simple application for judgment on default. *Ib.* 27.

The place of trial of the action is in the county where the premises, or some part thereof, is situated. *Code*, § 123; *Laws of* 1847, *p.* 332, § 45.

Amendments.] The statute provides that either before or after the trial of any issue, the court may permit the complaint and all subsequent proceedings to be amended so as to represent truly the rights claimed by any party. 2 *Rev. Stat.* 320, *sec.* 19. And the court may also allow any amendment of the pleadings or proceedings, so as to make defendant thereto, any person who shall have appeared, in the course of the proceedings, to be interested in the premises, by any will, deed, or grant from any person who is a defendant in such partition, and who might originally have been made defendant, if his interest had then existed or been known. *Ib. sec.* 20.

After any such amendment, any party whose rights are affected thereby, and who has not had an opportunity to sustain his claim, will be entitled to have an issue made up and tried, to determine such right; and the court may, after an amendment in any other case, where it may be deemed proper, order a trial to be had. *Ib. sec.* 21.

And where the guardian ad litem of an infant has omitted to file the bond required by the statute, he may be allowed to do so *nunc pro tunc*, even after judgment and sale of the premises, 25 *Barb.* 336, aff. 6 *Abb.* 350; 17 *New York*, 218; 7 *Abb.* 473; and so of other like matters. 11 *Id.* 440.

In addition to the above provisions of the Revised Statutes, the one hundred and seventy-third section of the Code of Procedure has been made applicable to these proceedings, by special act of the legislature. (*a*) *Laws of* 1857, *vol.* 2, *p.* 504; *Pub. Acts. p.* 184. That section authorizes the court either before or after judgment, in furtherance of justice, and on such terms as may be proper, to amend any pleading process or proceeding, by adding or striking out the name of any party; or by correcting a mistake in the name of a party, or a mistake in any other respect, or by inserting other allegations material to the case; or, when the amendment does not change substantially the claim or defense, by conforming the pleading or proceeding to the facts proved. See § 173, in *Voorhies' Code and notes;* and see 25 *Barb.* 336, aff. 6 *Abb.* 350; *s. c.* 17 *New York*, 218.

In respect, also, to amendments generally, see the other sections of the Code of Procedure (§§ 169 to 177), which apply to actions for partition. (*a*) *Code*, § 448.

Abatement of the action, and effect thereof.] If one of the defendants, a tenant in common of the premises, dies pending the action, the same must be revived against his heirs. And a sale after his death, and after the bill has been taken as confessed against him, without revivor, is void as against his heirs. 16 *New York*, 193; 26 *Id.* 338.

The heirs, in such a case, are not required to avoid the decree for sale by motion in the original suit, or by writ of error or appeal, but may impeach its validity in an action of ejectment for the land of their ancestor. *Ib.*

So, if one of the tenants in common dies after the appointment

(*a*) This act was unnecessary, so far as related to actions for partition, for the reason that *all* the provisions of the Code (§§ 169 to 177), in reference to amendments, already applied to such actions. *Code*, § 448; 2 *Abb.* 6; 6 *Id.* 350, *s. c.* 17 *New York*, 218; 11 *Abb.* 440.

of commissioners to make the partition, the commissioners cannot proceed with the partition, or make a report that a sale is neces sary until the suit is revived, and the rights of the new parties are ascertained. 5 *Paige*, 161. And in such case, a new reference must be had to ascertain the rights of the new parties. *Ib.*

But where the plaintiff died, while the premises were being advertised for sale, and his share passed to his three children, two of whom were defendants in the original action, and the third was made plaintiff, by order of the court, as successor in interest to his ancestor; it was held, that there was no irregularity in continuing the advertisement in the same form as originally commenced, and selling the premises in pursuance thereof. 18 *How.* 458, *s. c.* 9 *Abb.* 323.

Receiver pending the litigation.] In order to preserve the property from serious loss, the court may appoint a receiver pending the action; as, where a portion of the premises cannot be rented in consequence of the refusal of one of the defendants, a tenant in common with the plaintiff, to unite with the latter; or where the rents cannot be collected by reason of the defendants' interference. 28 *How.* 9.

It is also provided by statute, that where, either by actions or proceedings in partition or division, or for the construction of a last will and testament, an estate has been brought within the possession, direction, or control of the Supreme Court of the State, which shall have acquired jurisdiction over the same, such Supreme Court may, upon the death of the surviving executor of said will and testament, and during the pendency of the action or proceedings, and until they are finally carried into effect, appoint a receiver of said estate upon such terms and conditions, and upon such notice to all parties and persons interested, as said court shall direct, and upon such order as to security or otherwise as to said Supreme Court may seem expedient; and to enable it to carry into effect its orders and decrees in relation to said estate, the receiver, when appointed, shall be the successor in interest of the surviving executor, and shall have like power and authority as administrators with the will annexed, appointed by the surrogate, but subject to the orders of the Supreme Court in the premises. *Laws of* 1863, *p.* 804.

I. Proceedings if Actual Partition is Decreed.

Judgment declaring rights of parties, &c.] The court is required by the statute to ascertain, from the proofs taken upon the reference in case of default; or from the confession, by plea, of the parties if they appeared; or from the verdict of the jury by which any issue of fact shall have been tried; and to declare, the rights, titles, and interests of the parties to such proceedings, plaintiffs as well as defendants, so far as the same shall have appeared; and to determine the rights of the parties in such lands, tenements, or hereditaments, and give judgment that partition be made, between such of them as shall have any right therein, according to such rights. 2 *Rev. Stat.* 321, *sec.* 23; 23 *Barb.* 286, 302.

And where one tenant in common lays out money in improvements on the estate, although the money so expended does not in strictness constitute a lien upon the estate, yet a court of equity will not grant a partition without first directing an account and a suitable compensation; or else, in the partition it will assign to such tenant in common that part of the premises on which the improvements have been made. 1 *Barb. S. C. R.* 505, *per* Paige, J.; and see 3 *Paige,* 546; 3 *Sand. Ch. R.* 64. And see as to other cases of equitable partition, 3 *Paige,* 200; *Ib.* 470.

If the defendants sign a *cognovit,* acknowledging the correctness of the allegations contained in the complaint, and consenting that partition may be made of the premises therein described, the judgment for partition is founded upon the confession, and is limited by it; and the court has no authority to go beyond it. 21 *Barb.* 9.

The court is not restricted to a partition of all the lands, or a sale of the whole. And, therefore, where the interests of the parties require it, part of the lands held in common may be divided, and part of them sold. See 2 *Rev. Stat.* 323, *sec.* 37; *Ib.* 330, *sec.* 81; 4 *Barb.* 228; 9 *Id.* 500. And so, when a portion of the premises may, without prejudice to the interests of any of the parties, be allotted to one of the parties, but the shares of the other parties cannot be allotted to them without prejudice to their interests, the court may allot to the former party his share in the premises, and direct a sale of the interests of the other parties in the residue which cannot be so divided. 4 *Barb.* 228, *supra*

Where the proceedings are instituted in behalf of infants, a partition of the premises will not be directed by the court, unless it is made satisfactorily to appear that the interests of such infants require it. See *Laws of* 1852, *p.* 411, *sec.* 2; 26 *How.* 250.

It is unnecessary to docket the judgment where actual partition is decreed. The rights of the parties are fixed and settled by the final decree, and not by the enrolment thereof. And, therefore, in an action of ejectment by a party claiming title under the decree, in a partition suit, the decree is evidence to show title in the plaintiff, although it was not signed and docketed until after the commencement of the ejectment suit. 42 *Barb.* 591.

Partition in part; setting off shares or proceeds temporarily, &c.] The statute provides, that if, after trial of the issues, or after judgment by default, confession, or otherwise, against those parties who are known, the part or interest of any parties who shall not have pleaded in the cause, whether known or unknown, in and to such premises, shall not have appeared by the evidence in the cause, the court shall give judgment that partition be made, so far as the rights or interests of the parties who are known, and who have appeared in the cause, have been ascertained; and the residue of the premises shall remain for the parties whose interests have not been ascertained, subject to division between them at any future time. 2 *Rev. Stat.* 321, *sec.* 24.

And an actual partition or sale, as the case may require, may be adjudged or decreed, whenever and as often as the court shall have ascertained and declared so many facts concerning the rights, titles, and interests of all or any of the parties to such suit, that a fair and just partition or distribution of the proceeds can be made by assigning to any party or parties, in severalty, and to any set or sets of parties, in common, according to the provisions of this or the next section (*sec.* 2, *post*), the shares in the premises belonging to such parties and sets of parties respectively, or of the proceeds of the sales of the said shares of such parties and sets of parties respectively. *Laws of* 1847, *p.* 556, *sec.* 1.

And whenever a partition or sale shall be so adjudged or decreed, costs may be awarded as shall seem just, and the court may take order to discharge from the suit any party or parties whose interest therein shall have wholly ceased, and for the custody of any lands or shares of proceeds as to which the rights, titles, and interests of the parties shall not have been fully ascertained and declared, and for such further proceedings as may be requisite, until the full ascertainment and declaration of the rights, titles, and interests of all the parties. *Ib.*

And whenever it shall seem proper to the court that a partition or sale should be adjudged, as provided in the preceding section, shares of the premises or proceeds, as to which there are conflicting claims not affecting other shares in the premises or proceeds, may temporarily, and until the determination of such claims upon further proceedings had between the adverse claimants be assigned or set off as in common to such adverse claimants, with a proper reservation of the questions of right between such claimants. *Ib. sec* 2.

Whenever it shall appear on such further proceedings as are mentioned in the last two preceding sections, that any amend ment of the pleadings or proceedings is necessary in respect to any share in controversy, such amendment may be introduced by suggestion to be filed; saving to all parties in interest, the like right to answer such suggestion as in the case of an amendment of the complaint. *Ib. sec.* 3; *Code*, § 448; 2 *Abb.* 17.

Shares may be set off to parties in common.] If it appears to the court that two or more persons interested in the premises, are desirous of enjoying their several shares or interests in common with each other, the court may direct a partition to be made in such manner as to set off to such of the parties as shall desire it, their shares respectively of such premises, and shall permit the respective shares or interests of those who shall desire it to remain without partition or allotment, to be enjoyed by them in common. *Laws of* 1847, *p.* 556, § 4; and see 2 *Wend.* 443.

And for that purpose, where there is no issue formed by the pleadings to prevent it, the court will order a reference to ascertain and report whether the shares of any of the parties can be set off to them in common. 8 *How.* 351. Such reference should be had before the final judgment in partition is entered. *Ib.*

Commissioners to be appointed.] When judgment of partition shall be rendered, the court is required to appoint, by rule, three reputable freeholders, commissioners to make the partition adjudged, according to the respective rights and interests of the parties, as the same were ascertained and determined by such court; and in such rule the court shall designate the part or share which shall remain undivided, for the owners whose interests shall be unknown and not ascertained. 2 *Rev. Stat.* 321, *sec* 25. For form, see *Appendix*, No. 493.

The commissioners are named by the party, to the court, and if approved, are appointed, according to the nomination. 1 *Cai. R.* 121, 122; 4 *Barb.* 228, 232.

If the persons appointed commissioners, or any of them, shall die, resign, or neglect to serve, the court may, from time to time, appoint others in their places. 2 *Rev. Stat.* 321, *sec.* 26.

Oath of commissioners.] The commissioners, before proceeding to the execution of their duties, shall severally be sworn or affirmed, before any officer authorized to take affidavits, honestly and impartially to execute the trust reposed in them, and to make partition as directed by the court; which oath shall be filed with the clerk of the court, at or before the coming in of the report of such commissioners. 2 *Rev. Stat.* 321, *sec.* 27. For form, see *Appendix*, No. 510.

Proceedings of the commissioners.] The commissioners are required to proceed forthwith to make partition, according to the judgment of the court, unless it shall appear to them, or any two of them, that partition cannot be made without great prejudice to the owners thereof; in which case they shall make a return of such fact to the court, in writing, under their hands. 2 *Rev. Stat.* 322, *sec.* 28.

Notice of the proceedings should be given to the parties interested. 9 *How.* 71. The statute does not in terms require such notice, yet the necessity of it is implied; for partition is one of those adjudications of a judicial nature affecting the rights and interests of the parties, in which they have a right to substantial and beneficial notice; and without it the report of the commissioners will be set aside. *Ib.;* but see 4 *How.* 133.

In making partition, the commissioners are required to divide the real estate, and allot the several portions and shares thereof to the respective parties, quality and quantity relatively considered by them, according to the respective rights and interests of the parties so adjudged by the court, designating the several shares and portions by posts, stones, or other permanent monuments; and they may employ a surveyor, with the necessary assistants, to aid them therein. 2 *Rev. Stat.* 322, *sec.* 29.

But if the court directs that the shares of two or more of the parties shall be set off to them in common, the order of the court, in this respect, must be followed by the commissioners; and the partition, in such case, must be made in such manner as to set off to such parties their shares or interests in common, dividing the remainder of the premises between the parties according to their respective rights in the same. See *Laws of* 1847, *p.* 556, *sec.* 4, *supra;* 2 *Wend.* 443; 8 *How.* 351.

The commissioners, in making partition, may assign a portion of the premises, held in common, to one of the parties, charged with a servitude or easement, for the benefit of another party, to whom a distinct portion of the premises is assigned in severalty. 10 *Paige,* 470.

And so, where the premises in question consist of a mill-dam and mill-pond, creating the water-power which supplies the mills held in severalty by the tenants in common of such mill and mill-pond, the commissioners may divide the mill-dam, and the lands under the same, and under the waters of the pond, and may make such provisions for keeping the different portions of the dam, and of the water-gates and flumes in repair, and such regulations for the use of the water-power, which is not capable of actual partition without a destruction of its value, as the parties themselves might make by a partition deed of the same property. *Ib.;* and see 14 *Wend.* 204; 5 *N. Hamp. R.* 134.

If the commissioners do not partition the tract described in the complaint, but extend their action to land consisting partly of a portion of such tract and partly of other property, their proceedings would be without jurisdiction, and the judgment entered upon their report would be void. 21 *Barb.* 9.

Where infants represent a share of the property, their separate proportions of it should be severed and set out to them respectively. And it is not enough merely to set aside for them, collectively, the share of their ancestor. 3 *Edw. Ch. R.* 229.

All the commissioners must meet together in the performance of any of their duties; but the acts of a majority, so met, will be valid. 2 *Rev. Stat.* 322, *sec.* 31.

Compensation for equality of partition.] The statute provides that whenever partition shall be decreed by a court of equity, (*a*) if it shall appear that it cannot be made equal between the parties, without prejudice to the rights and interests of some of them, the court may decree compensation to be made by one party to the other, for equality of partition, according to the equity of the case. 2 *Rev. Stat.* 330, *sec.* 83; 2 *Paige*, 27; 4 *Barb.* 229; *Will. Eq. Jur.* 700, 705.

Partition of interest of tenants for life.] Whenever the estate of any tenant in dower, or by the curtesy, or for life, to the whole or any part or share of the premises in question, has been admitted by the parties, or ascertained by the court to be existing at the time that judgment shall be given that partition be made, and the person entitled to such estate has been made a party to the proceedings, it shall be lawful for the commissioners to allot to such tenant his share thereof, without reference to the duration of such estate; and, also, to make partition of such share, and allot the same to the parties respectively who shall be entitled to the remainder thereof, according to their respective rights therein, whenever in the opinion of the commissioners, it can be done without prejudice to the rights of the parties. *Laws of* 1847, *p.* 556, *sec.* 5; 15 *New York*, 623, 627.

Formerly, in the proceedings for partition, an admeasurement of a dower interest in the premises could not be made, 1 *Barb. S. C. R.* 561; *Ib.* 500; 3 *Sand. S. C. R.* 391; 15 *Johns.* 319; but the statute above cited undoubtedly contemplates an admeasurement of the widow's dower, where she has been made a party to

---

(*a*) In actions for the partition of real estate, all the courts having jurisdiction of such actions, may direct compensation to be made for equality of partition. *Code of Pro.* §§ 8, 30, 33, 123, 448.

the proceedings, whether the dower extends to the whole or to only a part of the premises in question. See *ante*, *p.* 105.

Fees and expenses of commissioners, surveyors, &c.] The expenses of the commissioners, including the expenses of a surveyor and his assistants, when they shall be employed, will be ascertained and allowed by the court; and the amount thereof, together with the fees allowed by law to the commissioners, must be paid by the plaintiffs, and will be allowed to them as part of the costs to be taxed. 2 *Rev. Stat.* 322, *sec.* 32.

The fees allowed by law to commissioners are two dollars to each for every day's actual and necessary service. *Id.* 643, *sec.* 35. And the surveyor, if one is employed, is allowed for actual service in surveying, laying out, marking and mapping the premises of which partition is made, two dollars and fifty cents per day; and for each of his necessary chain and flag bearers, and other necessary assistants, one dollar per day. *Ib. sec.* 34.

The commissioners must look to the plaintiff for their fees, and not to the plaintiff's attorney; and, it seems, the attorney is not liable to the commissioners, though the fees have been collected by him. At any rate, he cannot be attached for not paying them. 4 *How.* 245.

Commissioners' report.] The commissioners are required to make a full and ample report of their proceedings, under the hands of any two of them, specifying therein the manner of executing their trust, and describing the land divided, and the shares alloted to each party, with the quantity, courses, and distances of each share, and a description of the posts, stones, or other monuments thereof, and the items of their charges. 2 *Rev. Stat.* 322, *sec.* 30. For form, see *Appendix*, No. 511.

The report should be signed by all the commissioners; if not, it should state the reason of the omission. And where a sufficient reason is given for its not being signed by all, it should also state that all the commissioners met together and consulted upon the matter of the partition. 1 *Barb. Ch. R.* 73; 2 *Hill*, 625.

The report must also be proved or acknowledged before some officer authorized to take the proof of deeds, in the same manner that deeds are required to be proved or acknowledged to entitle them to be recorded (1 *Rev. Stat.* 756, *sec.* 4); and must be filed in the office of the clerk of the court. 2 *Rev. Stat.* 322, *sec.* 33.

Setting aside report.] On good cause shown, the court may set aside the report, and appoint new commissioners as often as may be necessary, who will proceed in like manner as above directed. 2 *Rev. Stat.* 322, *sec.* 34.

But, it seems, the report will be disturbed or interfered with by the court, only upon grounds similar to those upon which a verdict would be set aside and a new trial granted. 9 *How.* 71; 4 *Ed. Ch. R.* 896. The affidavits of four credible and disinterested persons for, to three against, setting aside such report, does not carry such a weight of evidence as to authorize the court to interfere to disturb the report. 9 *How.* 71, *supra.*

Where one of the parties opposed the confirmation of the report upon the ground that he was not notified of the meeting of the commissioners, and did not attend, it was held that the proceedings were irregular for that reason, and the report was set aside. *Ib.*

Judgment on report.] The party instituting the proceedings should move the court for the confirmation of the report of the commissioners, and that final judgment be rendered upon it. Notice of the motion should be served upon the parties interested, who have appeared in the proceedings, accompanied with copies of the papers on which the motion is founded.

Upon the report of the commissioners being confirmed by the court, judgment will thereupon be given, that such partition be firm and effectual forever. 2 *Rev. Stat.* 322, *sec.* 35.

Effect of judgment of partition.] The statute declares the judgment rendered upon the confirmation of the report of the commissioners, to be binding and conclusive:

1. On all parties named therein, and their legal representatives, who shall, at the time, have any interest in the premises divided, as owners in fee, or as tenants for years, or as entitled to the reversion, remainder, or inheritance of such premises after the termination of any particular estate therein; or who, by any contingency contained in any will or grant, or otherwise, may be or may become entitled to any beneficial interest in the premises;

or who shall have any interest in any undivided share of the premises, as tenant for years, for life, by the curtesy, or in dower;

2. On all persons interested in the premises who may be unknown, and who shall be proceeded against by publication of the summons under § 135 of the Code (11 *How.* 277); and,

3. On all persons claiming from such parties, or persons, or either of them. 2 *Rev. Stat.* 322, *sec.* 35; *Code*, § 448.

But such judgment and partition shall not preclude any person, except those above specified, from claiming any title to the premises in question, or from controverting the title or interest of the parties, between whom such partition shall have been made, 2 *Rev. Stat.* 322, *sec.* 36; nor shall it affect any tenants or persons having claims as tenants, in dower, by the curtesy, or for life, to the whole of the premises which shall be the subject of partition. *Ib.*; *Laws of* 1847, *p.* 556, § 5; 15 *New York*, 625.

An actual sale or partition is effectual, also, to bar the future contingent interests of persons not *in esse*, 17 *New York* 210, aff. 5 *Abb.* 92. And, it seems, independent of the statute, contingent remainder-men, or persons to take under an executory devise, afterwards coming into being, are bound by the judgment as being virtually represented by the parties to the action in whom the present estate is vested. *Ib.*

The judgment is binding upon the parties, in respect to the actual partition of the premises, from the date of the confirmation of the commissioners' report, without regard to the subsequent completion of the record. 9 *Barb.* 500. And it is not necessary that the judgment should be docketed. 42 *Id.* 591.

In respect to the effect of the judgment upon creditors, it is provided by statute, that the partition of the premises shall not alter, affect, or impair the lien of any creditors by judgment, decree, mortgage, or otherwise, except that where the lien is on the undivided interest or estate of any of the parties, such lien, if partition be made of the premises, shall thereafter be a charge only on the share assigned to such party. 2 *Rev. Stat.* 318, *secs.* 8, 9; 12 *Wend.* 270.

And such share shall be first charged with its just proportion of the costs of the proceedings in partition, in preference to any such lien. 2 *Rev. Stat.* 318, *sec.* 9.

Recording the record of judgment.] An exemplification of the judgment record may be recorded in the clerk's office of any county of the State in which any lands described therein may be situated, in the same manner that conveyances of real estate are now authorized to be recorded. *Laws of* 1846, *p.* 204, § 2. And it may, also, in like manner be recorded in the office of the register of the city and county of New York. *Laws of* 1851, *p.* 555.

Such record, or an exemplification thereof, shall be received in evidence, and shall be as effectual in all cases as the original exemplification would be, if produced, and shall be open to the same objèctions. *Laws of* 1846, *p.* 204, *supra.*

II. PROCEEDINGS FOR A SALE OF THE PREMISES.

1. *Proceedings for a sale by commissioners.*] It is provided by the statute, that if it shall appear to the commissioners that the premises of which partition is directed to be made, or any distinct lot, tract, or portion thereof, is so situated that a partition thereof cannot be made without great prejudice to the owners, they are required to report the fact to the court. 2 *Rev. Stat.* 322, *sec.* 28; *Ib.* 323, *sec.* 37. For form, see *Appendix*, No. 494.

If, upon the report of the commissioners being made, the court is satisfied that such report is just and correct, the court will thereupon, by a rule to be entered on the filing of the report, order the commissioners to sell the premises so situated, at public auction, to the highest bidder. 2 *Rev. Stat.* 323, *sec.* 37. For form, see *Appendix*, No. 495. But the court must be satisfied that a necessity for such order exists. The report, therefore, should set forth the facts and circumstances upon which the opinion of the commissioners is founded, so that the court may be enabled to judge as to the propriety of a sale. 19 *Wend.* 226.

And the court is only authorized to direct a sale of the premises where they are so situated that a partition thereof cannot be made without great prejudice to the owners. The statute here refers to comparative prejudice between an actual partition and a sale; and its language will not justify a sale where the aggregate amount of benefits from a sale, instead of a partition, will be small in reference to the value of the property. 10 *Paige,* 470; 2 *Barb. S. C. R.* 599. The prejudice spoken of means a prejudice to all the owners, and not to a part only. And a sale will not be ordered merely because it would be more profitable to one of the parties than a partition. *Ib.*

In determining whether a sale of the premises is necessary, the true question to be considered is, whether the aggregate value of the several parcels into which the whole premises must be divided, will, when distributed among the different parties in severalty, be materially less than the value of the same property, if owned by one person. 6 *Paige*, 541, 547.

Nor is it sufficient to justify the court in directing a sale of the premises, that large arrears of taxes and assessments remain unpaid. 11 *How.* 489.

Where lands leased for a term of years are owned by several persons as tenants in common both of the rents and of the reversion, and the premises, in proceedings for partition, are directed to be sold, the sale must be made subject to the rights of the lessees, who, by the sale, will become the tenants to the purchasers of the rents and reversion. 5 *Paige*, 518.

The court is not restricted to a partition of all the lands, or a sale of the whole; and where the interests of the parties require it, part of the lands held in common may be divided, and part of them sold. 2 *Rev. Stat.* 323, *sec.* 37; *Ib.* 330, *sec.* 81; 4 *Barb.* 228; 9 *Id.* 500. And so, a portion of the premises may be allotted to one of the parties, and the shares of the other parties may be sold, where the interests of the parties require it. 4 *Barb.* 228.

And an actual sale may be adjudged whenever, and as often as the court shall have ascertained and declared so many facts concerning the rights, titles and interests of all or any of the parties to the action, that a fair and just distribution of the proceeds can be made by assigning to any party or parties, in severalty, according to the statute, the proceeds of the sales of the shares of such parties respectively. *Laws of* 1847, *p.* 556; *ante*, *p.* 128. And in such case, costs may be awarded as shall seem just; and the court may discharge from the suit any party or parties whose interest therein has wholly ceased, and for the custody of any shares of the proceeds, as to which the rights and interests of the parties shall not have been fully ascertained and declared, and for such further proceedings as may be requisite, until the full ascertainment and declaration of the rights and interests of all the parties. *Ib. sec.* 1.

And so, shares of the proceeds as to which there are conflicting claims, not affecting other shares, may be temporarily set off to the parties, with a proper reservation of the questions of right between the claimants. *Ib. sec.* 2, *ante, p.* 129.

Where the proceedings are instituted in behalf of infants, a sale of the premises will not be directed unless it also appears satisfactorily to the court that the interests of such infants require it. See *Laws of* 1852, *p.* 411; *sec.* 2; 26 *How.* 250.

2. *Proceedings for sale by a referee.*] The statute provides, that instead of appointing commissioners in the first instance to make partition, if it appears by the report of a referee, or otherwise, that the premises, or any part of them, are so circumstanced that a partition thereof cannot be made without great prejudice to the owners, the court may order a sale of such premises at public auction, by a referee, (*a*) upon the same notice and in the same manner as in sales by commissioners; and on the referee's report being confirmed, he is required to execute conveyances to the purchasers at such sales, which shall have the same effect as if executed by commissioners, as before prescribed. See 2 *R. S.* 330, § 81; *Laws of* 1847, *p.* 344, § 77; 2 *Abb.* 16, 18.

The practice under the above statutory provisions is regulated by Rules 78 and 79 of the Supreme Court.

Under Rule 78, it is provided, that where the rights and interests of the several parties, as stated in the complaint, are not denied or controverted, if any of the defendants are infants, or absentees, or unknown, the plaintiff, on an affidavit of the fact, and notice to such of the parties as have appeared, may apply at special term for an order of reference, to take proof of the plaintiff's title and interest in the premises, and of the several matters set forth in the complaint; and to ascertain and report the rights and interests of the several parties in the premises, and an abstract of the conveyances by which the same are held.

And Rule 79 provides, that where the whole premises of which partition is sought are so circumstanced that a partition

(*a*) The sale may also be directed to be made by the sheriff of the county. 2 *Rev. Stat.* 330, § 81; *Laws of* 1847, *p.* 344, § 77; *Code*, § 287; 2 *Abb.* 18.

Under a recent statute, referees are entitled to receive the same fees and disbursements as are allowed to the sheriff of the city of New York, in sales on mortgage foreclosures, and in addition thereto commissions on all moneys received and paid out by them at the same rate as are allowed by law to executors and administrators,—*provided*, however, that the commissions allowed by the statute cannot in any case exceed five hundred dollars. *Laws of* 1869, *ch.* 569.

thereof cannot be made without great prejudice to the owners, due regard being had to the power of the court to decree compensation to be made for equality of partition, and to the ability of the respective parties to pay a reasonable compensation to produce such equality, or where any lot, or separate parcel of the premises, which will exceed in value the share to which either of the tenants in common may be entitled, is so circumstanced, the plaintiff, upon stating the fact in the affidavit which is to be filed for the purpose of obtaining an order of reference under the preceding rule (Rule 78), may have a further provision inserted in such order of reference, directing the officer or person to whom it is referred to inquire and report whether the whole premises, or any lot or separate parcel thereof, are so circumstanced that an actual partition cannot be made; and that if he arrives at the conclusion that the sale of the whole premises, or of any lot or separate parcel thereof, will be necessary, that he specify the same in his report, together with the reasons which render a sale necessary; and, in such a case, that he also ascertain and report whether any creditor, not a party to the suit, has a specific lien, by mortgage, devise, or otherwise, upon the undivided share or interest of any of the parties in that portion of the premises which it is necessary to sell; and if he finds that there is no such specific lien in favor of any person not a party to the suit, that he further inquire and report whether the undivided share or interest of any of the parties in the premises is subject to a general lien or incumbrance, by judgment or decree; and that he ascertain and report the amount due to any party to the suit, who has either a general or specific lien on the premises to be sold, or any part thereof, and the amount due to any creditor, not a party, who has a general lien on any undivided share or interest therein, by judgment or decree, and who shall appear and establish his claim on such reference. The referee shall, also, if requested by the parties who appear before him on such reference, ascertain and report the amount due to any creditor, not a party to the suit, which is either a specific or general lien or incumbrance upon all the shares or interests of the parties in the premises to be sold, and which would remain as an incumbrance thereon in the hands of the purchaser; to the end that such directions may be given in relation to the same, in the decree for the sale of the premises, as shall be most beneficial to all the parties interested in the proceeds thereof on such sale.

The 79th Rule, so far as it relates to the inquiries before the referee, as to the necessity of a sale, is founded upon the 81st section of the statute (*supra*); and that part of the rule which requires the examination as to liens and incumbrances, is in pursuance of the 42d section of the statute. See 2 *Barb. Ch. Pr.* 305.

The true question to be considered by the referee in determining whether a sale of the premises is necessary, is whether the aggregate value of the several parcels into which the whole premises must be divided, will, when distributed among the different parties in severalty, be materially less than the value of the same property, if owned by one person. 6 *Paige*, 541, 547.

In determining that question, too, the referee is not to be governed by the consideration that it would be for the benefit of infants to have their shares of the estate converted into money intead of remaining in land, producing a less income. If their interest requires the property to be sold for the purpose of a better investment, it may be done afterwards under the general law relative to the sale of infants' estates; and where they will not run the risk of having their interests sacrificed for want of funds to compete with adult tenants in common at the sale. *Ib.* 546.

And the referee is to consider, also, that the words "without great prejudice to the owners," are to be understood to refer to comparative prejudice between an actual partition and a sale. And, therefore, a sale will not be justified where the aggregate amount of benefits from a sale, instead of a partition, will be small, in reference to the value of the property. 2 *Barb. S. C. R.* 599; 10 *Paige*, 470.

The referee should require the plaintiff to produce the abstracts of his title, as a tenant in common in the premises, and to trace it back to the common source of title of the several tenants in common; and in his report, he should, as far as practicable, give an abstract of the conveyances of the several undivided shares or interests of the parties from the time they were united in one common source. 7 *Paige*, 39; 8 *How.* 456; 6 *Id.* 491. The plaintiff must produce proof of his title; and this proof must be such as would enable a plaintiff to succeed in an action of ejectment. 3 *Wend.* 436; and see 2 *Paige*, 27. But it is not necessary for the referee to annex to his report a search for mortgages or conveyances; but it is sufficient if his report states explicitly that he had caused the necessary searches to be made, and certifies what incumbrances, &c., there are. 27 *How.* 289

If the referee comes to the conclusion that the premises are susceptible of actual partition, he need proceed no further, but will report that fact to the court, which will thereupon direct an order for partition, and appoint commissioners. If he finds, however, that a sale is necessary, he will then proceed to execute the further provisions of the order, by inquiring in respect to incumbrances, advertising for liens, &c.

But a reference as to the necessity of a sale, is not absolutely required either by the statute or the rules. And therefore, if it appears either on the pleadings or by the proofs, that the premises are incapable of actual partition, the court may adjudge a sale without a reference, 4 *Paige*, 338, 344; and in such case, the parties, if they choose, may also omit the reference as to liens. 10 *How.* 188. If there are liens in fact, the purchaser will discover them on examining his title, and will decline to take the title until the liens are discharged. *Ib.*

And even if the premises are to be sold, the reference to inquire for liens and incumbrances may be omitted, unless it is asked for by one of the parties to the action. 12 *Wend.* 269; 10 *How.* 188; and see 27 *Id.* 289.

The proceedings in cases of a reference, are substantially the same as in the proceedings before commissioners, in respect to which, see *ante, p.* 136; and see 2 *Barb. Ch. Pr.* 304; and see, also, under the next head, *post.* For forms, see *Appendix*, Nos. 495 to 501.

Upon the coming in of the report of the referee, the same must be filed, and a note of the day of the filing must be entered by the clerk in the proper book, under the title of the cause or proceeding, and the report will thereupon become absolute, and stand as in all things confirmed, unless exceptions thereto are filed and served within eight days after service of notice of the filing of the same. *Sup. Court Rules*, No. 32.

If exceptions are filed and served within such time, the same may be brought to a hearing at any special term thereafter, on the notice of any party interested therein. *Ib.* and see *ante, vol.* 1, *p.* 299, and *note.*

Creditors to be brought in; reference as to liens, &c.] Before the making of any order for the sale of the premises, where the creditors having specific liens shall not have been made parties, the court, on the motion of either party, will direct the plaintiff to amend his complaint, by making every creditor having a specific lien on the undivided interest or estate of any of the parties, by mortgage, devise, or otherwise, a party to the proceedings. 2 *Rev. Stat.* 324, *sec.* 42, as amended by *Laws of* 1830, *ch.* 320.

In such case, also, the court will direct a reference to the clerk, or other suitable person, to ascertain and report whether the shares or interests in the premises of the parties in the suit, or any of them, are subject to any general lien or incumbrance by judgment or decree. *Ib.*; *Laws of* 1847, *p.* 344, §77.

The order directing the clerk to report as to liens, &c., is usually embodied in the order of reference as to the propriety of a sale. See *ante*, *p.* 119. But a reference is not indispensable; and an order for the sale of the premises may be made without such reference, unless it is asked for by one of the parties to the action. 12 *Wend.* 269; 10 *How.* 188; and see 27 *Id.* 289.

It is the duty of the referee, not only to inquire as to liens upon the share of each party in the action, but he should also cause searches of the records to be made in the same manner as if he were examining a title. These are generally furnished by the attorney for the plaintiff. The referee may also, as we have seen, require an abstract of the title to be laid before him. And he should also be furnished with an affidavit as to deaths, descents, intestacy, &c., made by some person acquainted with the facts, to enable him to ascertain in whom any part of the estate is or has been vested. And he should summon before him such persons as he ascertains to be creditors, and get a statement from them. 2 *Van Sant. Pr.* 36, citing 2 *Hoff. Ch. Pr.* 184, 185; *Edw. on Referees*, 457.

The object of the reference is to enable the court to distribute the purchase money in a proper manner; and if the referee reports against the claim of any person having a lien, by judgment or decree, upon the share of any of the parties, the claimant should except to the report within the time prescribed by the rules, to preserve his lien upon the purchase money, which, by the statute, becomes a substitute for the land itself. See 4

Paige, 441, 442. For form of referee's report, see *Appendix*, No. 497.

Upon the coming in of the referee's report, the same should be filed, and a note of the day of filing must be entered by the clerk, in the proper book, under the title of the cause, and the report will stand confirmed, unless excepted to as in other cases. If exceptions are taken, the same are brought to a hearing at a special term; the same, also, as in other cases. *Sup. Court Rules*, No. 32; *ante, vol.* 1, *p.* 299, and *note.*

Advertising for liens, &c.] If a reference is ordered as to liens and incumbrances, the referee is required immediately thereafter to cause a notice to be published once in each week for six weeks successively, in the State paper, and also in a newspaper printed in every county in which any of the lands in question are situated, requiring all persons having any general lien or incumbrance on any undivided interest or share therein, by judgment or decree, to produce to the referee on or before a certain day to be named in such notice, proof of all such liens and incumbrances, together with satisfactory evidence of the amount due thereon; and the referee shall report, with all convenient speed, the names of the creditors, the nature of the incumbrances, the dates thereof, and the several amounts appearing to be due thereon; 2 *Rev. Stat.* 324, *sec.* 43, as amended by *Laws of* 1830, *ch.* 320. For form of notice, see *Appendix*, No. 496.

But it is not necessary to advertise for persons having general liens by judgment or decree to present their claims to the referee, in order to render the sale regular and valid. The reference and the advertisement are only intended as a means of cutting off certain general liens. If there are no such liens, there is no use of the advertisement; and if the parties know there are none, there is no reason why they should be subjected to the expense and delay of a reference and advertisement which must end in nothing. If the advertisement is omitted, and there are in fact such liens, the purchaser on examining the title, would discover them, and decline to take the title until the liens were discharged, and so no one would be injured. 10 *How.* 181, 190, *per* Mitchell, J., and see 27 *Id.* 289; aff. 26 *Barb.* 475; 5 *Abb.* 451.

As, however, judgments and decrees do not cease to be a lien as against heirs-at-law at the end of ten years, the parties to a suit who choose to omit this ordinary advertisement, should produce, at their own costs, regular searches for all judgments and decrees for at least twenty years. 10 *How.* 191, *per* Mitchell, J.

Where the interest of one of the parties in the premises is sold under a judgment against him subsequent to the filing of the complaint and notice of lis pendens, the purchaser must come in before the referee and prove his claim under the order of reference as to general liens; as his interest in the premises will be divested by a sale under the judgment in partition. See 7 *Paige*, 550.

Order directing moneys to be brought into court.] If it appears by the proceedings that there are any existing incumbrances upon the estate or interest in the premises of any party named in the proceedings in the suit, the court will, in the order of sale, direct the commissioners (*a*) to bring into court and pay to the treasurer of the county, or in the city of New York, to the chamberlain of the city, the portion of the moneys arising from the sale of the estate and interest of such party, after deducting the portion of the costs, charges and expenses to which it shall be liable. 2 *Rev. Stat.* 324, *sec.* 44; 1 *Id.* 370, *sec.* 29; *Laws of* 1848, *p.* 404; *Laws of* 1847, *p.* 340, *sec.* 71; *Sup. Court Rules*, No. 81.

Terms of credit.] The court must direct in the order of sale, the terms of credit which may be allowed, for any portions of the purchase money of which it shall think proper to direct the investment, and for such portions of such purchase money as are required, by the provisions herein, to be invested for the benefit of any unknown owners, any infants, any parties out of the State, or any tenants for life, in dower, or by curtesy. 2 *Rev. Stat.* 323, *sec.* 38.

Sale of dower or other life estate in premises.] Whenever the estate of any tenant in dower, or by the curtesy, or for life, to the whole or any part or share of the premises in question, has been admitted by the parties, or ascertained by the court, to be existing at the time of the order for such sale, and the person

---

(*a*) Or the referee, or sheriff, as the case may be. 2 *Rev. Stat.* 330, *sec.* 81; *Laws of* 1847, *p.* 344, § 77; *Code*, § 287; 2 *Abb.* 16, 18.

entitled to such estate has been made a party to the proceedings, the court is required first to consider and determine, under all the circumstances of the case, whether such estate ought to be excepted from such sale, or whether the same should be sold; and in making such determination, they shall have regard to the interests of all the parties. 2 *Rev. Stat.* 325, *sec.* 50; 7 *Paige*, 406; 15 *New York*, 625.

Notice of sale.] The commissioners (*a*) are required by the statute, to give notice of any sale to be made by them, for the same time and in the same manner, as is required by law on sales of real estate by sheriffs on execution. 2 *Rev. Stat.* 326, *sec.* 56.

The time and place of holding any such sale, therefore, must be publicly advertised, previously, for six weeks successively, as follows:

1. A written or printed notice thereof must be fastened up in three public places in the town where the real estate is to be sold; and if such sale be in a town different from that in which the premises to be sold are situated, then such notice must also be fastened up in three public places of the town in which the premises are situated;

2. A copy of such notice must be printed once in each week in a newspaper of such county, if there be one;

3. If there be no newspaper printed in such county, then the notice must be published in the State paper once in each week. *Ib.;* and see 2 *Rev. Stat.* 368, *sec.* 34. For form of notice, see *Appendix*, No. 507.

All the other provisions of the title of the Revised Statutes in relation to the notice of sale by sheriffs on execution (2 *Rev. Stat.* 368, 369, 370), are also made applicable to sales of lands under a judgment in partition. 22 *Barb.* 167. And therefore, the section of the statute which provides that the omission of the sheriff to give notice of sale under an execution, shall not affect the validity of any sale made to a purchaser in good faith, without notice of any such omission, applies to sales under judgments in these proceedings. *Ib.*

In sales in the city of New York, the notice must be for six weeks, the statutory time; and the rule of the Supreme Court (No. 73), providing for a notice of three weeks on the sale of

---

(*a*) See Note *a*, on p. 144, *ante*

lands lying in any of the cities of this State, has no application to sales under a judgment in partition. 5 *How.* 318.

Proceedings on sale.] The commissioners (*a*) should meet at the time and place designated in the notice, and then and there sell the premises, at public auction, to the highest bidder.

If the premises consist of distinct buildings, farms, or lots, they must be sold separately. 2 *Rev. Stat.* 326, *sec.* 57.

Neither of the commissioners, nor any person for the benefit of either of them, shall be interested in the purchase, nor directly, nor indirectly, purchase any of the premises sold; nor shall any guardian of any infant party in such suit purchase, or be interested in the purchase of, any lands being the subject of such suit, except for the benefit or in behalf of such infant; and all sales contrary to the provisions of this section, shall be void. *Ib. sec.* 58; 22 *Barb.* 168. And where the purchase is made by the guardian of an infant, but not for the benefit of such infant or in his behalf, the sale is void, notwithstanding the purchase was not made by such guardian for his own benefit, but as agent for others. *Ib.*

The terms of the sale must be made known at the time. 2 *Rev. Stat.* 326, *sec.* 57. With respect to the terms of credit, these may be determined or ascertained, by reference to the order of the court directing the sale. *Ib.* 323, *sec.* 38.

The portions of the purchase money for which credit shall have been allowed, must always be secured, at interest, by a mortgage of the premises sold, by a bond of the purchaser, and by such other security as the court shall prescribe. *Ib. sec.* 39.

And the commissioners (*a*) may take separate mortgages and other securities, for such convenient shares or portions of the purchase money, as are directed by the court to be invested as aforesaid, in the name of the treasurer of the county in which the premises are situated, or in the city of New York, to the chamberlain of the city, or his successors in office, and for such shares as any known owner of full age shall desire to have so invested, in the names of such owners. *Ib. secs.* 40, 41; 1 *Id.* 370, *sec.* 29; *Laws of* 1848, *p.* 404; *Laws of* 1847, *p.* 341, *sec.* 71.

(*a*) See Note *a*, on p. 144, *ante*.

Upon such sales being confirmed by the court, the commissioners are required to deliver the mortgage or other securities so taken by them, to the treasurer or chamberlain of the county, or to the known owners whose shares were so invested. *Id. ibid.*

No order to stay the sale of the premises can be granted or made by a judge out of court, except upon a notice of at least two days to the plaintiff's attorney. *Sup. Court Rules*, No. 80.

Report of sale.] After completing the sale, the commissioners (*a*) are required to report the same to the court, on oath, with a description of the different parcels of land sold to each purchaser, the name of such purchaser, and the price bid by him; which report must be filed in the office of the clerk of the court in which the action is brought. 2 *Rev. Stat.* 327, *sec.* 59. For form, see *Appendix*, No. 508.

Order thereupon.] If the sale is approved and confirmed by the court, an order must be entered, directing the commissioners, or any two of them, (*a*) to execute a conveyance pursuant to such sale; which they are authorized by statute to do. 2 *Rev. Stat.* 327, *sec.* 60. Such conveyance, when executed, must be recorded in the county where the premises are situated. *Ib. sec.* 61.

Compelling purchaser to complete the purchase.] If the purchaser refuses to take the premises, after having purchased the same, he will be compelled to do so on motion to the court.

But the purchaser will not be compelled to complete the purchase, where there has been unreasonable delay in perfecting the title; and where the delay was ten months, it was held to be unreasonable, and an order to compel the purchaser to take the title, was refused. 22 *Wend.* 498. Nor will the court compel him to take the title where the completion of the sale has been delayed so long, by the fault of the parties, that he cannot have the benefit of his purchase substantially as if the sale had been completed at the time contemplated by the terms of sale. 7 *Paige*, 387. Nor would the purchaser, where the premises are not sold at his risk, be compelled to complete the purchase, in case the premises should be incumbered, or no title should pass by the sale, or there should be difficulty in obtaining possession. 1 *Paige*,

---

(*a*) See note *a*, on *p.* 144, *ante*.

120. Nor if the plaintiff has omitted to file any of the papers necessary to the judgment; though this irregularity may be cured by allowing them to be filed *nunc pro tunc*. 7 *Abb.* 473; 6 *Id.* 350; *s. c.* 17 *New York*, 218. Nor if there is danger of the property being made liable for the debts of a former deceased owner of the premises, where the action for partition is brought by the heirs of such owner. 10 *How.* 189; 7 *Id.* 307; 1 *Barb. S. C. R.* 76; 3 *Abb.* 249; 5 *Id.* 53; 7 *Id.* 473, 478; 7 *Paige*, 550.

The purchaser, however, wonld not be permitted to object to the title merely on the ground that there is a possibility that some person, other than the parties in the suit, has an interest in the premises, where there is no probability that any such interest exists. 4 *Paige*, 441; 3 *Bosw.* 430. And so, where all the necessary parties are joined, it is no excuse for refusing to take the title, that there are errors in stating the interests and shares of the parties, or any omission to state what on motion the plaintiff might have been compelled to insert by way of amendment. 3 *Bosw.* 439; 6 *Abb.* 59. And so, it is immaterial that the plaintiff omitted to allege that there were no incumbrances; or that the referee omitted to annex searches for incumbrances to his report, *Ib.*; 27 *How.* 289; or omitted to advertise for liens or incumbrances, 5 *Abb.* 451; 10 *How.* 188; 27 *Id.* 289, affirming 26 *Barb.* 475; or that the purchaser, not a tenant in common at the commencement of the action, was not made a party to the action—he holding a deed of a portion of the premises purchased *pendente lite* from some of the heirs, defendants in the partition suit; especially where the deed expressed in terms that the conveyance was made subject to the proceedings in partition. 27 *How.* 289, affirming 26 *Barb.* 475. And see, on the same subject, 13 *How.* 476; 15 *New York*, 617; 2 *Abb.* 7; 6 *Id.* 350; *s. c.* 17 *New York*, 218.

Effect of conveyance.] The conveyance so executed by the commissioners, is declared by the statute to be a bar, both in law and equity, against all persons interested in the premises in any way, who shall have been named as parties in the proceedings; and against all such persons and parties as were unknown, if notice shall have been given of the application for partition, by such publication as is before directed; and against all other persons claiming from such parties, or any of them. 2 *Rev. Stat.*

327, *sec.* 61; and see *Ib.* 330, *sec.* 84; 3 *Paige*, 653; 27 *How.* 289; 17 *New York*, 217.

The conveyance will also, under the statute, operate to cure any defect or irregularity in the notice of sale. 22 *Barb.* 167.

And it will also be a bar against all persons having general liens or incumbrances by judgment or decree on any undivided share or interest in the premises sold, in all cases where the notice to such creditors prescribed by the statute, shall have been given; and also against all persons having specific liens on any undivided share or interest therein, who shall have been made parties to the proceedings. *Laws of* 1830, *chap.* 320, § 45, added to 2 *Rev. Stat.* 327; 4 *Paige*, 441.

But no creditor having a specific lien on any undivided share or interest in the premises, will be affected by such sale or conveyance, unless he is made a party to the proceedings. *Id. ibid.*

If a mortgage, however, is given on an undivided share of the premises, pending the proceedings for partition, the lien of the mortgagee will be divested by a sale of the premises under the judgment of the court, and the purchaser will take the estate discharged from the incumbrance. 1 *Paige*, 484. And the same result will follow if a judgment is recovered during the pendency of the proceedings. 8 *Id.* 643. The legal lien, in such cases, is converted into an equitable lien upon the fund produced by the sale; to the same extent as the legal lien. *Ib.*; and see 4 *Id.* 442.

Costs and expenses of the action.] The costs and expenses of the proceedings are required to be deducted from the proceeds of every sale made by the commissioners; and to be paid in the first instance, to the plaintiffs, or their atttorney. 2 *Rev. Stat.* 327, *sec.* 62; 1 *Barb. S. C. R.* 561, 564. And see *post*, *p.* 158, "Costs of the action."

A party entitled to dower in the premises sold, where she has been made a party to the proceedings, is obliged to contribute towards the costs and expenses. 2 *Rev. Stat.* 326, *sec.* 54; 1 *Barb. supra.*

Proceeds of sale.] The statute provides that the proceeds of every sale, after deducting the costs, shall be divided among the parties whose rights and interests shall have been sold, in proportion to their respective rights in the premises; and the shares of such of the parties as are of full age, shall be paid to them or their legal representatives by the commissioners, or shall be brought into court for their use. 2 *Rev. Stat.* 327, *sec.* 63; 16 *Barb.* 531.

If the shares are brought into court, they should be deposited with the treasurer of the county in which the premises sold are situated; or in the city of New York, with the chamberlain of that city. 1 *Rev. Stat.* 370, *sec.* 29; *Laws of* 1848, *p.* 404; *Laws of* 1847, *p.* 340, § 71; *Sup. Court Rules*, No. 81.

The proceeds of the sale are personal property; and upon the death of any of the parties, subsequent to the sale, they will descend to the personal representatives. 16 *Barb.* 531, 534.

Shares of Infants.] Where any of the known parties are infants, the court may, in its discretion, direct the shares of such infants to be paid over to their general guardian, or to be invested in permanent securities, at interest, in the name and for the benefit of such infants. 2 *Rev. Stat.* 327, *sec.* 64; 16 *Barb.* 531; 2 *Barb. Ch. R.* 314. And the shares ought not to be paid to the guardian *ad litem* of such infants. *Ib.*

But such shares, or any part thereof, will not be paid over to the general guardian, except so much thereof, or of the interest or income from time to time, as may be necessary for the support or maintenance of such infants; unless such guardian has previously given sufficient security on unincumbered real estate to account to such infants for the same, in the usual form. *Sup. Court Rules*, No. 70; and see *Code of Pro.* § 420; *Laws of* 1848, *p.* 407, § 8.

And no order shall be made for the payment of any such moneys to any person claiming the same, except upon petition, accompanied by a certified copy of the order in pursuance of which the money was brought into court, together with a statement of the county treasurer, city chamberlain, or other depositary of the money, showing the present state and amount of the funds, separating the principal and interest, and showing the amount of each; and the court may take such proof of the truth of the matters stated in the petition as shall be deemed proper, or may refer the same to a suitable referee, to take proof and report thereon. *Sup. Court Rules*, No. 70, *supra.*

Where the lands of a wife, who is an infant, are sold, the proceeds will not be paid to the husband, but will be directed to be brought into court, and to be secured for her use until she becomes of age. 1 *Paige*, 483; and see *post.*

If the shares of the infants are directed to be invested, they should be brought into court, and paid to the treasurer of the county for that purpose, *Sup. Court Rules*, No. 81; or, by an order of the Supreme Court, such investment may be directed to be made by and in the name of the guardian of such infants. *Laws of* 1848, *p.* 407, *sec.* 8; and see *supra.*

Shares of married women.] When the lands of a married woman are sold, the proceeds will be directed to be paid to her, and not to her husband. See 11 *How.* 176; 8 *Id.* 389; 16 *Barb.* 531, 535; *Laws of* 1860, *p.* 157; 1862, *p.* 343. And where the order of the court directed the share of one of the heirs who was a married woman, to be paid to her husband, in right of his wife, and before actual payment the husband died, leaving his wife surviving,—it was held that the wife became reinstated in her original rights, and entitled to receive her share, not as her husband's widow, or representative, but as the heir of the original owner of the land. 16 *Barb.* 531.

If the wife whose lands are sold, is an infant, the proceeds will be directed to be brought into court, to be invested for her use, until she becomes of age. 1 *Paige*, 483, *supra.*

With respect to the wife's inchoate right of dower in the premises sold, see *post, p.* 157, "Rights of married women and others, having future interests in property."

Shares of unknown and absent owners.] Where any of the parties whose interests have been sold, are absent from the State, without legal representatives in this State, or are not known or named in the proceedings, the court will direct the shares of such parties to be invested in permanent securities at interest, for the benefit of such parties, until claimed by them or their legal representatives. 2 *Rev. Stat.* 327, *sec.* 65; 16 *Barb.* 531.

Shares of tenants for life.] Where the proceeds of a sale, belonging to any tenant in dower, or by the curtesy, or for life, shall be brought into court as directed by the statute, the court shall direct the same to be invested in permanent securities at interest, so that such interest shall annually be paid to the parties entitled to such estates, during their lives respectively. 2 *Rev. Stat.* 327, *sec.* 66; 16 *Barb.* 531; and see *ante, p.* 149, "Proceeds of sale."

And the party entitled to such interest will be charged with the expense of investing such proceeds, and of receiving and paying over the interest or income thereof. *Sup. Court Rules*, No. 84.

But if such party is willing, and consents to accept a gross sum in lieu of such annual interest or income for life, the same is required to be estimated according to the then value of an annuity of six per cent. on the principal sum, during the probable life of such person, according to the Portsmouth or Northampton Tables. *Ib.* See the Northampton Tables in the *Appendix*, No. 527.

Security to refund.] The court may, in its discretion, require all or any of the parties, before they shall receive any share of the moneys arising from such sale, to give security to the satisfaction of the court, to refund the said share with interest thereon, in case it shall thereafter appear that such party was not entitled thereto. 2 *Rev. Stat.* 327, *sec.* 67.

In whose name securities to be taken.] Where any security is directed to be taken by a court, or any investment to be made, or any security shall be taken by commissioners on the sale of any real estate, as directed by the statute, except where provision shall be made for taking the same in the name of any known owner, the bonds, mortgages, or other evidences thereof, shall be taken in the name of the treasurer of the county where the fund belongs, or such other county treasurer as the court shall direct, and his successors in office, who shall hold the same by virtue of their respective offices, and shall deliver them to their successors. 2 *Rev. Stat.* 328, *sec.* 68.

And with respect to the shares or property of infants, the Supreme Court may order any bond, mortgage, or other securities, to be taken by and in the name of the guardian of such infants, to be collected and invested as such court shall direct. *Laws of* 1848, *p.* 407, *sec.* 8.

Treasurer to receive money, and accounts, &c.] The treasurer is required to receive the interest or principal of any sums as they become due, and apply or re-invest the same, according to the circumstances of the case, as the court shall direct. 2 *Rev. Stat.* 328, *sec.* 69; *Laws of* 1848, *p.* 404. And he is required, also, at the first general term of the court, for the district in which he resides, in each year, to render an account to the court in writing, and on oath, of all moneys received by him, and of the application thereof. And any neglect of that duty will subject him to suspension or removal from office. 2 *Rev. Stat.* 328, *sec.* 69; *Sup. Court Rules*, No. 82. (*a*)

How investments to be made.] All investments and re-investments under the provision of the statute, shall be made in the public stocks of the United States, or of this State, or on bond and mortgage upon unincumbered real estate of at least double the value of such investment. 2 *Rev. Stat.* 328, *sec.* 70.

And no such security, bond, mortgage, or other evidence of such investment, shall be discharged, transferred, or impaired, by any act of the officer holding the same, without the order of the court, entered in the minutes thereof. *Ib.;* and 4 *Sand. Ch. R.* 51.

Suits in reference to such investments.] The person interested in such investments or securities, may, with the leave of the court, prosecute the same in the name of the existing treasurer, and no suit shall be abated by the death, removal from office, or resignation of the officer to whom such evidences were executed, or any of his successors. 2 *Rev. Stat.* 328, *sec.* 71; *Laws of* 1847, *p.* 340, *sec.* 71; *Laws of* 1848, *p.* 404.

Application to court for moneys.] Where there are existing incumbrances upon the estate or interest in the premises of any

(*a*) This rule also provides the manner in which the accounts of the treasurer are to be kept, the details of his report to the general term, and the practice in respect to ascertaining the correctness of such report.

party to the proceedings, the court, as we have seen (*ante*, *p.* 144, and *note*), is required, in the order of sale, to direct the commissioners, or referee, or sheriff, to bring into court the portion of the moneys arising from the sale of the interest of such party, after deducting the costs, charges, and expenses to which it shall be liable. 2 *Rev. Stat.* 324, *sec.* 44.

And such party is authorized to apply to the court to order such moneys, or such part thereof as he shall claim, to be paid to him, which application must be accompanied,—

1. By his own affidavit, stating the true amount actually due on each incumbrance, the owner of such incumbrance, and his residence, as far as known to such party;

2. By proof, by affidavit, of the due service of a notice on each owner of any incumbrance, of the intention to make such application, at least fourteen days previously.

If such owner reside in this State, such notice must be served personally, or if he be absent from his residence, by leaving a copy there, with some person of proper age. If such owner reside out of this State, such notice may be served on him personally, twenty days previously, or by publishing the same in the State paper four weeks successively, once in each week. *Ib. sec.* 45.

Upon such application and proof of notice being made, the court will proceed to hear the proofs and allegations of the parties. *Ib., sec.* 46. For forms of affidavit, notice, &c., see *Appendix*, Nos. 524 to 526.

And if any question of fact arises, which, in the opinion of the court, cannot be satisfactorily determined without a trial by jury, the court will award a feigned issue, to be tried as in other cases. The costs of such trial must be paid by the party failing; which payment will be enforced by attachment, as in other cases. 2 *Rev. Stat.* 324, *sec.* 46.

Distribution of moneys; orders for paying out moneys.] When the amount of existing incumbrances is ascertained, the court will proceed to order a distribution of the moneys so brought into and remaining in court, among the several creditors having such incumbrances, according to the priority thereof respectively. 2 *Rev. Stat.* 325, *sec.* 47.

And by Rule 83, it is provided that orders upon banks or other companies for the payment of moneys out of court, shall be made payable to the order of the person entitled thereto, or of his attorney duly authorized, and shall specify in what particular suit, or on what account the money is to be paid out, and the time when the order authorizing such payment was made. And in every draft upon the New York Life Insurance and Trust Company, or the United States Trust Company, by the county treasurer, for moneys deposited with said company, or for the interest or accumulation on such moneys, the title of the cause or matter on account of which the draft is made, and the date of the order authorizing such draft, shall be stated; and the draft shall be made payable to the order of the person or persons entitled to the money, or of his or their attorney, who is named in the order of the court authorizing such draft. And to authorize the payee or indorsee of the draft to receive the money thereon from the Trust Company, the same shall be accompanied by a certified copy of the order of the court authorizing such draft, countersigned by the justice by whom such order was made. But where periodical payments are directed to be made out of a fund deposited with such company, the delivery to the secretary of the company of one copy of the order authorizing the several payments, shall be sufficient to authorize the payment of subsequent drafts in pursuance of such order.

Treasurer to have incumbrances discharged.] The statute makes it the duty of the treasurer, or other officer by whom any such incumbrance shall be paid off, to procure satisfaction thereof to be acknowledged, in the form required by law, and to cause such incumbrance to be duly satisfied or canceled of record, and to defray the expenses thereof out of the portion of the moneys in court belonging to the party by whom such incumbrance was payable. 2 *Rev. Stat.* 325, *sec.* 48; *Laws of* 1848, p. 404.

Other parties not to be delayed.] The proceedings to ascertain and settle the amount of incumbrances, as provided by the statute, are not to affect any other party in the suit for partition, nor delay the paying over or investing of moneys to or for the benefit of any party upon whose estate in the premises there shall not appear to be any existing incumbrances. 2 *Rev. Stat.* 325, *sec.* 49.

Proceedings on sale of dower, or other life estate.] Whenever the estate of any tenant in dower, or by the curtesy, or for life, to the whole or any part or share of the premises in question, has been admitted by the parties, or ascertained by the court, to be existing at the time of the order for the sale of the premises, and the person entitled to such estate has been made a party to the proceedings, the court is required first to consider and determine, under all the circumstances of the case, whether such estate ought to be excepted from the sale, or whether the same should be sold; and in making such determination, they shall have regard to the interests of all the parties. 2 *Rev. Stat.* 325, *sec.* 50; 7 *Paige*, 406; 15 *New York*, 625.

If a sale of the premises including such estate is ordered, the estate and interest of every such tenant or person will pass thereby; and the purchaser, his heirs and assigns, will hold such premises free and discharged from all claims by virtue of any such estate or interest, whether the same be to any undivided share of a joint tenant, or tenant in common, or to the whole or any part of the premises sold. 2 *Rev. Stat.* 325, *sec.* 51.

Upon such sale being made of any such interest or estate, the court will direct the payment of such sum in gross, out of the proceeds thereof, to the person entitled to such estate in dower, tenancy by the curtesy, or tenancy for life, as shall be deemed, upon the principles of law applicable to annuities, a reasonable satisfaction for such estate or interest, and which the person so entitled shall consent to accept in lieu thereof, by an instrument under seal, duly acknowledged or proved in the manner that deeds are required to be proved to entitle them to be recorded. *Ib. sec.* 52. For annuity table, see *Appendix*, No. 527.

In case no such consent be given at or before the coming in of the report of sale by the commissioners, then the court is required to ascertain and determine what proportion of the proceeds of such sale, after deducting all expenses, will be a just and reasonable sum to be invested for the benefit of the person entitled to such estate or interest in dower, by the curtesy, or for life; and to order the same to be brought into court, for that purpose. *Ib. sec.* 53.

The proportions of the proceeds of such sale, are to be ascertained and determined, in the several cases, as follows:—

1. If an estate in dower shall have been included in the order of sale, its proportion shall be one-third of the proceeds of the

sale of the premises, or of the sale of the undivided share in such premises, upon which such claim of dower existed.

2. If an estate by the curtesy, or other estate for life, shall be included in the order of sale, its proportion shall be the whole proceeds of the sale of the premises, or of the sale of the undivided share thereof, in which such estate shall be.

And in all cases, the proportion of the expenses of the proceedings are to be deducted from the proceeds of the sale. *Ib. sec.* 54.

If the persons entitled to any such estate in dower, by the curtesy, or for life, be unknown, the court will take order for the protection of the rights of such persons, in the same manner, as far as may be, as if they were known and had appeared. *Ib. sec.* 55; and see *ante, p.* 151.

Rights of married women and others having future interests in property.] In proceedings for partition, the inchoate right of dower of a married woman, in the undivided share of her husband in the land, where the wife is a party to the proceedings, will be divested by a sale of the premises, under the judgment of the court. 7 *Paige*, 387; 22 *Wend.* 498; 5 *Abb.* 100, 102; *Laws of* 1840, *p.* 128.

And so, also, the interest of those having vested or contingent future rights or estates in the land, will be divested by a sale. *Id. ibid.*; 17 *New York*, 210, aff. 5 *Abb.* 92.

In cases of sales of land in which such inchoate right, or such future right or estate exists, it is the duty of the court under whose judgment such sale is made, to ascertain and settle the proportional value of such inchoate, contingent, or vested right or estate, according to the principles of law applicable to annuities and survivorships, and to direct such proportion of the proceeds of the sale to be invested, secured, or paid over in such manner as shall be judged best to secure and protect the rights and interests of the parties. (*a*) *Laws of* 1840, *supra.*

Formerly, the usual practice where a release could not be

(*a*) For the rule to compute the present value of an inchoate or contingent right of dower, see 7 *Paige*, 408; *M'Kean's Pr. L. Tables*, 25, § 4; *Henry's Ann. Tables*, 87 *Prob.* 4. And of an inchoate tenancy by the curtesy, 11 *How.* 177, 180. And see Annuity Table in *Appendix*, No. 527.

obtained from the wife, of her inchoate right of dower in the premises, was, to pay the money set apart for such right into court. But it seems the practice is now changed; and the money may now be paid directly to the wife. 11 *How.* 176, 178. Such money represents the present worth of her inchoate right in the premises, and is her absolute property. 4 *Sand. Ch. R.* 396.

But the wife may release her right or interest to her husband, and acknowledge the same before any officer authorized to take the acknowledgment of deeds to be recorded in this State, or before the referee or one of the commissioners making the sale, separate and apart from her husband in the manner required by law (1 *Rev. Stat.* 758), in respect to the acknowledgment of deeds by married women. *Laws of* 1840, *p.* 128; *Ib.* 321.

Upon the execution of such release, the share of the proceeds of the sale arising from the wife's contingent interest, is required to be paid to her husband. *Laws of* 1840, *p.* 128, *sec.* 2.

The release, so executed, and also the payment, investment, or otherwise securing the share of such married woman, or of the person having such future right in the proceeds of the sale, as above directed, will be a bar both in law and equity against any such right. *Ib. sec.* 3. And the persons so barred not only include those in being in whom the estate might subsequently vest, but those not in being. 5 *Abb.* 92, 103; aff. 17 *New York*, 210.

With respect to the value of an inchoate tenancy by the curtesy, this depends not only upon the principles applicable to life annuities and survivorships, but upon the fact of issue, and if none, upon the likelihood of issue. 11 *How.* 177, 180.

Costs of the action.] The statute provides that when final judgment for partition is rendered, the court shall direct each of the parties, except the plaintiffs, to pay to the plaintiffs, a proportion of the costs and charges of the proceedings, to be ascertained by the court, according to the respective rights of the parties, and the proportion of such costs assessed upon the unknown owners, to be chargeable on the part remaining undivided; and upon such judgment execution may issue as in personal actions, and may be levied upon the property of the parties respectively charged with such costs, and upon any share or part of the premises allotted on any such division, to any owner unknown or not named, and upon every portion remaining undivided, for the proportion adjudged to be paid by such owners, or chargeable to the part remaining undivided. And a sale of such premises thereupon will be as valid as if such unknown owner had been named in the proceedings and in such execution 2 *Rev. Stat.* 328, *sec.* 72.

But the costs of parties unnecessarily made defendants, in an action for partition, will be directed to be paid by the plaintiff personally; and cannot be charged upon the property unless such parties were so brought into the suit at the request or consent of the other defendants. 7 *L. O.* 127. And so, the plaintiff, where he causes litigation by setting up an unfounded claim, will be charged with the additional costs occasioned thereby. 1 *Sand. Ch. R.* 40.

If an actual partition of the premises is ordered, the aggregate amount of the costs of the several parties, is to be apportioned and charged upon the parties to the proceedings, according to their respective rights and interest in the premises; and the parties whose taxed bills exceed their ratable proportions of the whole costs, are entitled to execution against those whose taxed bills are less. See 7 *Paige*, 204. (*a*)

If the plaintiffs are non-suited, or suffer a discontinuance, or a verdict shall pass against them, or judgment shall be rendered against them on demurrer, they must pay costs, to be recovered and collected as in personal actions. 2 *Rev. Stat.* 329, *sec.* 73.

Where the premises are sold, the costs and expenses of the proceedings are to be deducted from the proceeds of any sale made by the commissioners; and must be by them, in the first instance, paid to the plaintiffs, or their attorney. *Ib.* 327, *sec.* 62.

It is also further provided by statute that on an appeal from the order or judgment of the court, the court may direct the costs to be paid by either of the parties, or by any one or more defendant or plaintiff, to his co-defendant or co-plaintiff. *Ib;* and see 2 *Rev. Stat.* 329, *sec.* 78. And the costs may be allowed or not, in the discretion of the court. *Code*, §§ 306, 448; 16 *How.* 60.

(*a*) See this case, also, for form of judgment with respect to the costs of guardians ad litem of infants, where an actual partition is adjudged.

And they are regulated by the Code of Procedure, the same as in other equity actions. *Code*, §§ 303 to 322.

In addition to the allowances provided by § 307, the plaintiff, upon the recovery of judgment in an action for partition, is entitled to the following percentage to be estimated upon the value of the property of which partition is sought, viz: For any amount not exceeding two hundred dollars, the sum of ten per cent.; for any additional amount not exceeding four hundred dollars, an additional sum of five per cent.; and for any additional amount not exceeding one thousand dollars, an additional sum of two per cent. *Ib.* §§ 308, 309. And the court may also, in its discretion, make a further allowance to any party not exceeding five per cent. *Ib.* § 309.

The value of the property is to be determined by the court, or by the commissioners, in case of actual partition. *Ib.* §§ 308, 309.

If the action shall be settled before judgment therein, like allowances upon the amount paid or secured upon such settlement, at one half the rates above specified. *Ib.* § 308.

In respect to the fees and expenses of commissioners and surveyors, see *ante*, *p.* 133; and of referees, see *ante*, *p.* 138, note *b*.

Appeals.] It is provided by the Revised Statutes, that upon any final judgment rendered that partition be made, or confirming partition, or for the sale of any premises, or confirming such sale, a writ of error may be brought by any of the parties to such judgment, jointly or separately, and without the consent of any co-plaintiff or co-defendant, within the same time and under the like restrictions as in cases of personal actions. 2 *Rev. Stat.* 329, *sec.* 75. And that it shall not be necessary for a plaintiff or defendant bringing such writ of error to summon and sever any co-plaintiff or co-defendant. *Ib. sec.* 76. And, also, that error may be assigned upon such writ for any erroneous adjudication upon the rights of any of the respective defendants or respective plaintiffs, and that the court will direct the person whose interest is affected by the adjudication, to plead to such assignment of errors, and to appear in such cause as a defendant in errror. *Ib. sec.* 77.

But the remedy now, to review the judgment or order of the court, is by appeal, the same as in other actions, the practice in which is regulated by the Code of Procedure. *Code*, §§ 448, 323 to 350.

The appeal is placed upon the calendar, and brought on for argument the same as in other actions. Where the plaintiff's rights are not contested, no copies of the pleadings need be furnished to the court. *Sup. Court Rules*, No. 42.

But an appeal cannot be taken until after the entry of judgment making partition; and, therefore, an appeal will not lie from an order declaring the rights of the parties, and appointing commissioners to make partition. 2 *Selden*, 465. The appeal, in such case, should be delayed until final judgment, when both the intermediate order and the judgment will be open for review. *Ib.*

The court, upon the appeal, may give judgment, either of affirmance or reversal, in whole or in part, and as to any or all the parties, with costs to be paid by either of the parties, or by any one or more defendant or plaintiff to his co-defendant or co-plaintiff. 2 *Rev. Stat.* 329, *sec.* 78; and see *Code of Pro.* §§ 12, 330.

The partition of infants' estates.] With respect to the estates of infants, the statute provides, that whenever it shall appear satisfactorily, by due proof, or on the report of a referee, to the Supreme Court, that any infant holds real estate in joint tenancy, or in common, or in any other manner, which would authorize his being made a party to a suit in partition, and that the interest of such infant, or of any other person concerned therein, requires that partition of such estate should be made, such court may direct and authorize the general guardian of such infant to agree to a division thereof, or to a sale thereof, or of such part of the said estate as in the opinion of the court shall be incapable of partition, or, as shall be most for the interest of the infant to be sold. 2 *Rev. Stat.* 330, *sec.* 86, as amended by *sec.* 46, *of ch.* 320, *of Laws of* 1830; *Laws of* 1847, *p.* 323, *sec.* 16; *Ib.* 344, *sec.* 77.

The object of the statute was not to authorize the guardian of an infant tenant in common to sell to his co-tenants; but only to join with them in a sale of the joint interest in the property. 2 *Paige*, 566. If a co-tenant wishes to purchase the infant's share, at its fair value, the general guardian should apply for liberty to sell, under the article of the Revised Statutes (*ante*,

Chapter xiii. of this work), relative to the sale and disposition of infants' estates. *Ib.*

And it seems, the court will not authorize the guardian to join in a sale, except on the report of a referee, that such sale is necessary and proper. *Ib.*

The guardian must give sufficient security for the faithful performance of his trust on such sale, and to bring the proceeds of the infant's share into court, or to invest and account for the same as the court shall direct. *Ib.;* and see *Sup. Court Rules*, Nos. 62 and 70.

The guardian is required to report to the court, on oath, the partition or sale so made by him; and if the same is approved and confirmed by the court, an order must be entered authorizing the guardian to execute conveyances of the right of the infant to such part of the estate as shall have been sold, to the purchaser thereof, or to execute releases of the right of such infant to such part of the estate as in the division falls to the shares of the other joint tenants, or tenants in common. 2 *Rev. Stat.* 331, *sec.* 87. The conveyance should be by the guardian in the name of the infant: as "A. B., an infant, by C. D., his general guardian," &c., and should be subscribed by the guardian in the same manner. 1 *Kern.* 52. And such deeds will be as valid and effectual to convey the share of the infant as if the same had been executed by him after arriving at full age. 2 *Rev. Stat.* 331, *sec.* 88.

In case of a sale of any part of the estate, the infant is to be deemed a ward of the court; and such order shall be taken as the court may direct, for securing, investing, and applying the proceeds of the sale, and requiring security from the guardian for that purpose. *Ib.*

If the infant is a married woman, the court may, upon petition, appoint her husband as her guardian; and to every husband so appointed, the above provisions of the statute will apply. *Ib. sec.* 97, added by *sec.* 47 *of chap.* 320 *of Laws of* 1830.

Partition of estates of lunatics, &c.] Whenever it is made to appear to the Supreme Court, on the application of any committee of any idiot, lunatic, or person mentally incapable of managing his affairs, holding any real estate in joint tenancy, or in common, or in any other manner, to authorize his being made party to a suit in partition, that the interest of such idiot, lunatic, or other person as aforesaid, or of any of the parties interested in the estate, requires a partition thereof, a reference will be ordered to some suitable person, to inquire into and report upon the circumstances. 2 *Rev. Stat.* 331, *sec.* 89; *Laws of* 1847, *p.* 323, *sec.* 16; *Ib.* 344, *sec.* 77; and see *ante, p.* 48.

Upon the coming in of the report of the referee, and a hearing and examination of the matter, the court may authorize the committee to agree to a partition of such estate, and to execute releases of the right of such lunatic, idiot, or other person, as aforesaid, in and to the share of such estate falling to the other joint tenants, or tenants in common. 2 *Rev. Stat.* 331, *sec.* 90.

Such releases will be as valid and effectual to convey the share of such lunatic, idiot, or other person of unsound mind, as if the same had been executed by them respectively when of sound mind and understanding, and for a valuable consideration. *Ib. sec.* 91.

Partition when State is interested.] Where any lands or tenements shall be held by the people of this State, and by any individuals, as tenants in common, proceedings for the partition thereof may be had against the people of this State, in the Supreme Court, in the same manner as against individuals, and the like orders, decrees, and judgments shall be had therein. 2 *Rev. Stat.* 331, *sec.* 92.

The summons and complaint, and all notices required to be served in other cases, must be served on the attorney general, who is required to appear in behalf of the State, and attend to its interests. *Ib. sec.* 93.

And it is the duty of the attorney general, whenever directed by the commissioners of the Land Office, to cause partition to be made of such tracts of land as are held in joint tenancy, or tenancy in common, in which the people of this State are interested; and for that purpose he is authorized to do all such acts as any joint tenant, or tenant in common, may do by law 1 *Rev. Stat.* 207, *sec.* 65.

Provision as to claims barred by statute of limitations.] The authority given by the statute to proceed for the partition of real estate, will not authorize the revival or prosecution of any claims to lands which would or might be otherwise barred by any statute of limitations, or by the acquiescence of any party having any such claim. 2 *Rev. Stat.* 332, *sec.* 94.

SUPPLEMENT TO CHAPTER XX.

The action of partition under the Code of Civil Procedure. The ordinary proceedings in the action are to be conducted pursuant to the new Code of Civil Procedure. Section 448 of the old Code, however, which makes the provisions of the Revised Statutes relating to partition applicable to actions for partition, so far as the same can be so applied to the substance and subject-matter of the action, without regard to its form, is retained by the general repealing act. *Laws* 1877, *ch.* 417.

The action generally. To maintain the action, the plaintiff must at the time of its commencement have actual or constructive possession in common with the defendants. 46 *N. Y.*, 182; 65 *Barb.*, 237. Thus, where the tenant for life has actual possession, partition is proper between the remainder-men in fee; and this, too, it seems, although the remainder in fee, upon the death of one of them, is liable to be divested for the benefit of the survivors. 7 *Lansing*, 193; and see 4 *Hun*, 198; 1 *Id.*, 589.

A subsisting adverse possession is a bar to the action. The title of the parties must be first established by action before proceedings for partition are proper. 46 *N. Y.*, 182; 59 *Id.*, 426. Even the possession of one of several tenants in common may be adverse, when his acts amount to an exclusion of his co-tenants, and until the excluded parties regain possession, none of them can bring partition. 46 *N. Y.*, 182. But where the fee simple and every equitable title to lands was vested in the parties to an action for its partition, although other equitable questions were involved in the same action, it was held that the action was proper. 6 *Lans.*, 493. So, in an action for a partition, in equity, the court will dispose of all questions arising between the parties in relation to the land and its use, *e. g.*, for the construction of a will upon which the title of the parties depends, for an accounting as to the rents, etc. 60 *Barb.*, 163.

The trustee of an express trust in land, having an absolute power to sell the land and invest the proceeds, may bring an action to partition the lands held by such trustee in common with other persons of adult age. 65 *Barb.*, 583.

It is no objection to the partition of land that one of the tenants in common is an infant or lunatic. 34 *N. Y.*, 536. But he must be made a party to the action before his rights can be passed upon. *Ib.*

A parol partition by tenants in common, followed by exclusive possession, are acts of ownership by each tenant respectively, and are valid and binding upon their heirs. 36 *N. Y.*, 499.

Parties to the action. An administrator of a former owner is a proper party to an action for partition, when an accounting is to be had in the action for the rents, etc. 60 *Barb.*, 164, *aff.* 48 *N. Y.*, 106.

Guardian ad litem. The application for the appointment of a guardian *ad litem* of an infant under the age of fourteen years may be made before service of the summons. 66 *Barb.*, 241. Where it appears that the court had jurisdiction of the subject-matter and of the parties in an action for partition, and that guardians *ad litem* for the infant defendants were appointed, and judgment was entered therein, it will be held that the infants' title was carried by the judgment, and they will not be allowed to question the validity of the proceedings for partition. *Ib.;* and see 7 *Lans.*, 193; 65 *Barb.*, 237.

The guardian *ad litem* is not required by statute to put in an answer in a partition suit, though it is held advisable to do so if he is ignorant of the infant's interest in the property. 45 *Barb.*, 121. But the want of an answer will not affect the regularity of the proceedings. *Ib.*

Unknown owners, in a partition suit, are to be brought in by publication of notice substantially in the form prescribed by the Revised Statutes (2 *R. S.*, 186, § 124, *as amended by chap.* 277, *Laws of* 1842); and the provisions of the Code (§§ 135, 175) are not applicable in such cases. 56 *N. Y.*, 359. But see *contra*, now, § 451 of the new Code of Civil Procedure.

The issues and trial thereof. Where issues of fact are presented by the pleadings, a jury trial is a matter of right. An action for partition is an equitable action, and where it is brought by an heir under the provisions of the act of 1853 (*ch.* 238) relative to disputed wills, the Supreme Court at special term has authority to direct issues of fact to be settled, and that the verdict of the jury thereon be certified to the special term, for further proceedings. 62 *N. Y.*, 75, *affirming S. C.* 3 *Hun*, 736; and see 1 *Hun*, 478. The court may dispose of the case in that way, or may place it upon the circuit calendar, for the purpose of submitting to the jury such questions of fact as are presented by the pleadings. 62 *N. Y.*, 75, *supra.* So the form of the issues is discretionary also, and the order of the court, settling the issues, is not reviewable. *Ib.* On the trial at the circuit, if the issues are imperfect or insufficient, the court, in its discretion, may amend them, or submit such additional issues as the proof warrants. *Ib.*

Amendments of proceedings. If there is any irregularity in bringing an infant or lunatic into court, the same can be cured by subsequent amendment of the proceedings. 34 *N. Y.*, 536. And amendments may be made in such case even on appeal to the general term. 31 *How.*, 279. And the court may direct the modification of a decree, *nunc pro tunc*, to cover subsequent deviations from it, upon proof that the deviations have not been prejudicial to the infants, but desirable for their interests. 6 *Lans.*, 494.

Proceedings upon the partition. If the commissioners, in proceedings for partition among a widow and heirs, determine that the portion assigned to the widow cannot be partitioned without injury to those entitled in remainder, they should so report to the court, and the court should then order a sale of that portion of the premises, subject to the widow's life interest. It would not be proper to leave the land covered by the life estate of the widow, subject to another proceeding to partition it. There can be, regularly, but one judgment in partition, and that should settle all the rights of the parties. 65 *Barb.*, 192.

Where devisees in remainder, with knowledge of the existence of the life estate, and without the consent of other remainder-men, erected buildings upon the premises devised, it was held that they were not entitled to any compensation therefor, and, upon partition, could not exact a reimbursement from, or claim a lien upon, the shares of their co-tenants. 48 *N. Y.*, 107.

The commissioners may require a payment in money from one heir to another to equalize the partition; but cases may arise where it would be unjust to do so, and the court in such a case should refuse to confirm the report, and, if necessary, direct a sale of the whole property. 65 *Barb.*, 192.

Effect of judgment in partition. If the court has jurisdiction of the subject-matter, and of the parties, in an action for partition, the judgment will be conclusive upon the parties. 66 *Barb.*, 242; 65 *Id.*, 237; 7 *Lansing*, 193. And if the court had jurisdiction, the question whether any of the provisions of the judgment are right, *e. g.*, whether the premises should have been sold by a referee, cannot be raised by a purchaser. 55 *Barb.*, 259.

The court may order a sale of lots, reserving a right of way, common to the lot sold, but cannot direct that a public street be opened through the property. 60 *Barb.*, 165.

A sale, instead of actual partition, is a matter in the discretion of the court, and its decision will not be disturbed on appeal except in cases of plain error. 48 *N. Y.*, 107, affirming 60 *Barb.*, 164.

Sales in partition in the city of New York may be made by the sheriff of that city, or by a referee appointed for that purpose by the judgment of the court. *Laws* 1874, *p.* 212, amending § 1 of *Laws* 1869, *ch.* 569.

Fees of the sheriff or referee. In the city of New York the fees and disbursements of the sheriff or referee are limited to the same fees and disbursements as are given to the sheriff of that city on a sale in foreclosure. *Ib.*, and see *ante*, Vol. I., p. 358–1. In the other counties of the State the referee is entitled to receive the same fees and disbursements as are allowed to the sheriff of New York (*ante*, Vol. I., p. 358–1), and in addition thereto commissions on all moneys received and paid out by him, at the same rates as are allowed by law to executors and administrators—provided, however, that the commissions allowed shall not in any case exceed $500. *Laws* 1869, *ch.* 569, *p.* 1377, *sec.* 4; and see *Laws* 1874, *p.* 212.

The proceeds of sale. Where a sale is directed, the question of the distribution of the proceeds arising from any undivided share of the premises between the owner and incumbrancers, is collateral to the main purpose of the action; the court, having jurisdiction of the fund, will adjudge how distribution shall be made. 55 *N. Y.*, 442. And where, in such case, an order of reference is granted directing the referee to ascertain and report the amount due to any party to the action who has any general or specific lien upon the premises, the referee is authorized to take proof and pass upon the question of the validity of a mortgage upon an undivided share, claimed by one of the parties, although the question is not raised by any formal issue in the pleadings. *Ib.*

Amendments to Supreme Court Rules. See the amendments made in 1871, 1874, under the title of "Foreclosure of mortgages by action," in the supplement of notes to Chap. XI. (*ante*, Vol. I., *p.* 358–3); those amendments being applicable, also, to an action for the partition of real estate.

The costs and disbursements in an action for partition are still regulated by the old practice; the provisions of the Code of Procedure on that subject (§§ 303 to 322) being retained by the general repealing act. *Laws* 1877, *ch.* 417.

CHAPTER XXI.

PROCEEDINGS TO OBTAIN LEAVE TO PROSECUTE AS A POOR PERSON.

This proceeding is authorized by title first, of chapter eighth, of part third of the Revised Statutes, entitled "Of the bringing and maintaining of suits by poor persons." 2 *Rev. Stat.* 444.

Applications under the statute are not to be encouraged, 1 *Paige*, 39; *Id.* 588; and the statute will be strictly construed as against the applicant. 2 *Hill*, 412.

The statute applies to actions where the relief claimed is either of a legal or equitable nature. 2 *Rev. Stat.* 445, *sec.* 6; *Code*, *sec.* 69.

Who may petition, and in what cases.] The statute provihes, that every poor person, not being of ability to sue, who shall have a cause of action against any other, (*a*) may petition the court in which such action is depending, or in which it is intended to be brought, for leave to prosecute as a poor person, and to have counsel and attorneys assigned to conduct his suit. 2 *Rev. Stat.* 444, *sec.* 1.

The applicant, to be entitled to prosecute in *forma pauperis*, must be an object of charity, 1 *Paige*, 39; or at least must not be worth twenty dollars, excepting necessary wearing apparel and furniture for himself and his family, and excepting the subject matter of the action when not in possession thereof. 2 *Rev. Stat.* 445, *sec.* 2, *post.*

A party will not be allowed to prosecute a writ of error, as a

---

(*a*) Whether under the statute a party can be admitted in any case, to *defend* an action as a poor person, *quære?* 1 *Paige*, 588. But this doubt is now removed by the provisions of the new Code of Civil Procedure. See the Supplement to this chapter, *post*, p. 168.

poor person, 2 *Hill*, 412; 2 *How.* 35; nor an appeal. 3 *Paige*, 273.

The statute applies to a married woman, who may be allowed to prosecute as a poor person for damages for injuries to her separate property. 18 *How.* 466. And so, a married woman may be permitted to institute an action against her husband for a separation as a poor person. But this will not be allowed until the court has ascertained by the report of a referee that she has probable cause for commencing the action. 3 *Paige*, 387.

Although the statute is general, applying to every person not having the ability to sue, yet it seems it is doubtful whether a non-resident of the State will be allowed to prosecute as a poor person. 6 *Hill*, 257; and see 1 *Duer*, 705.

The application may be made either before or after the action is commenced. 2 *Rev. Stat.* 444, *sec.* 1. Where it was made after the suit had been pending a year, and after it had been referred and noticed for hearing, the application was denied on the ground of delay in making it. 1 *Duer*, 705, *s. c.* 12 *N. Y. Leg. Ob.* 28.

If the applicant has already commenced his suit before making the motion to prosecute as a poor person, he should give notice of the motion to the opposite party. 6 *Hill*, 257; 1 *Paige*, 39. And where, in such case, an order had been obtained without notice, the same was vacated, with costs. *Ib.*

What motion is founded upon.] The motion is founded upon petition, which is required to state: 1. The nature of the suit brought, or intended to be brought; 2. That the applicant is not worth twenty dollars, excepting the wearing apparel and furniture necessary for himself and his family, and excepting the subject-matter of the action, when not in possession thereof.

The petition must be verified by the applicant's own affidavit, and supported by a certificate of a counsellor of the court, that he has examined the claim, and is of opinion that such poor person has a good cause of action. 2 *Rev. Stat.* 445, *sec.* 2. For forms, see *Appendix*, No. 537.

If suit has already been brought by the applicant, notice of the motion, accompanied with a copy of the petition, should be served upon the opposite party eight days before the term at which the application is to be made; or an order to show cause should be obtained in the usual manner. 6 *Hill*, 257; 1 *Paige*, 39; *Sup. Court Rules*, No. 39.

Application to the court and proceedings thereon.] The court to which the petition is presented, if satisfied of the facts alleged, and that the applicant has a meritorious cause of action, is required by rule to admit him to prosecute as a poor person, and to assign to him counsel, solicitors, attorneys, and all other officers requisite for prosecuting his suit, who shall do their duty therein without taking any reward for the same. 2 *Rev. Stat.* 445, *sec.* 3.

If order granted, effect thereof.] The statute provides that every person admitted to sue as a poor person, may prosecute his suit without paying any fees to any officers or ministers of justice; and shall not be prevented from prosecuting the same, by reason of his being liable for the costs of any former suit brought by him against the same defendant (18 *How.* 466); and if he be nonsuited, or a verdict or judgment be given against him, or his bill be dismissed, or a decree be rendered against him, he shall not be liable for any costs in such suit. 2 *Rev. Stat.* 445, *sec.* 4. Nor is he liable to costs for not proceeding to trial, pursuant to notice; nor is he, it seems, liable to costs under any circumstances, until he is dispaupered, 20 *Wend.* 679; though after the order is annulled, he will be liable to costs in the same manner as though it had never been made. *Ib.*

When order may be annulled.] If the person so prosecuting, be guilty of any improper conduct in the prosecution of his suit, or of any willful or unnecessary delay, the court may, in its discretion, annul the order admitting him to prosecute as a poor person; and he shall thereafter be deprived of all the privileges conferred by such order, 2 *Rev. Stat.* 445, *sec.* 5; and will be liable for costs in the same manner as if the order had never been made. 20 *Wend.* 679.

Bringing action.] The action brought or to be brought by the poor person, is to be conducted in all respects in conformity to the Code, the same as actions brought by other persons. *Code*, § 471.

The costs in the action, it seems, are in the discretion of the court. 3 *Johns. Ch. R.* 65. Thus, where the plaintiff sued in *forma pauperis*, and recovered a legacy against executors, the court gave him only the actual expenses of the action, to be paid out of the assets. *Ib.* And so the plaintiff will not be allowed costs of overruling an informal plea, if the defence be finally established. 3 *Paige*, 273. If the plaintiff, however, appeals from the judgment, and succeeds, he will be entitled to the costs of the appeal; for the reason that he cannot prosecute the appeal in *forma pauperis*, but must give security as other persons. *Ib.*

If the party pending the action is permitted to prosecute as a poor person, he will not be excused from the payment of the costs already accrued. 1 *Paige*, 588. He is liable, also, for the costs of any irregular or improper proceedings on his part. *Ib.*, citing *Tothill*, 139.

SUPPLEMENT TO CHAPTER XXI.

The old practice revised. The code of Civil Procedure (§§ 458 to 467) just enacted has revised, and materially amended, the provisions of the Revised Statutes, considered in this chapter. The first five sections of the new Code (§§ 458–462), are a substitute for the provisions of the Revised Statutes; amending the same, by substituting $100 for $20, and omitting the words "when not in possession thereof," in the second subdivision of section 2 of the Revised Statutes (*ante, p.* 166.) The following sections, of the Code of Civil Procedure, are new.

§ 463. *Defendant may apply for leave to defend.* A defendant in an action involving his right, title, or interest, in or to real or personal property, may petition the court, in which the action is pending, for leave to defend the action as a poor person, and to have an attorney and counsel assigned to conduct his defence.

§ 464. *Defendant's petition, and contents thereof.* The petition must contain the same matters, respecting the ability of the petitioner, required to be contained in a petition for leave to prosecute, as a poor person; and it must be supported by a similar certificate, relating to the defence.

§ 465. *Proceedings thereon.* The provisions of this article, relating to the order, to be made upon an application for leave to prosecute as a poor person, and the proceedings subsequent thereto, apply to the order and subsequent proceedings, upon an application for leave to defend as a poor person.

§ 466. *Appeals in these proceedings.* An order made as prescribed in this article, does not authorize the petitioner to take or maintain an appeal, as a poor person; but where an appeal is taken by the adverse party, the order is applicable, in favor of the petitioner, as respondent in the appeal.

§ 467. *Costs, and disposition of the same.* Where costs are awarded in favor of a person, who has been admitted to prosecute or defend as a poor person, as prescribed in this article, they must be paid over to his attorney, when collected from the adverse party, and distributed among the attorney and counsel assigned to the poor person, as the court directs.

CHAPTER XXII.

PROCEEDINGS TO DISCOVER THE DEATH OF PERSONS UPON WHOSE LIVES ANY PARTICULAR ESTATE MAY DEPEND.

This proceeding is authorized by title eighth, of chapter fifth, of part third of the Revised Statutes, entitled "Proceedings to discover the death of persons upon whose lives any particular estate may depend." 2 *Rev. Stat.* 343; and see 1 *R. L.* 104, § 3.

How person may be produced.] It is provided by the statute, that any person entitled to claim any lands or tenements, after the death of any other person having any prior estate in such lands or tenements, may, once a year, apply by petition to the Supreme Court (*a*) for an order, that the person upon whose life such prior estate depends, be produced and shown, as hereinafter provided, by the guardian, husband, trustee, or party who may have the custody of such other person, or of his estate, or who may be entitled to such custody. 2 *Rev. Stat.* 343, *sec.* 1.; 1 *R. L. p.* 104, § 3.

Petition and notice.] The application is founded upon petition duly verified by affidavit, and which must state: 1. The interest of the applicant in the lands or tenements described therein; 2. That he has cause to believe, and does believe, that the person upon whose life such prior estate depends, is dead, and that his death is concealed by the party against whom the application is made. 2 *Rev. Stat.* 343, *secs.* 1, 2, 3. For form, see *Appendix*, No. 541.

(*a*) The *Supreme Court* is substituted in this chapter for the Court of Chancery, and *Referee* for Master in Chancery, under the authority of the Constitution of 1846, and the judiciary act. *Articles* VI. *and* XIV. *of Const., and Laws of* 1847, *p.* 344, § 77.

A copy of the petition is required to be served upon the person against whom the application is intended to be made, with at least fourteen days' notice of the time and place at which the same is intended to be presented. *Ib.*

Order of the court, and service thereof.] If no sufficient cause be shown to the contrary, the Supreme Court, upon due proof of the service of the petition and notice, will make an order requiring the party against whom the application is made, to produce and show the person upon whose life such estate depends, at such time and place, and to such referee or commissioner or commissioners, not exceeding two, as shall be named in such order. 2 *Rev. Stat.* 344, *sec.* 4. For form, see *Appendix*, No. 543.

A certified copy of the order must be served upon the party against whom the application is made, at least fourteen days before the day specified therein, at which any person shall be required to be produced. *Ib. sec.* 5.

Proceedings before the referee or commissioners.] The referee or commissioners are required to attend at the time and place specified in the order, for the purpose of attending to the execution thereof; and power is given to them to take proof, by the examination of witnesses, to be sworn by them, as to the identity of the person upon whose life such estate depends. 2 *Rev. Stat.* 344, *sec.* 5.

Subpœnas to compel the attendance of witnesses before the referee or commissioners, may be issued and served, in the like manner and with the like effect as in any action pending in the Supreme Court. *Ib. sec.* 6; *Laws of* 1847, *p.* 323.

If it appear satisfactorily to the referee or commissioners, on due proof by affidavit, that the person required to be produced is in prison, or is kept or detained by any other, they may allow a writ of habeas corpus to be issued out of the Supreme Court, to bring the body of such person before them; which writ shall be served and executed in the same manner as such writs to inquire into the cause of the detention of any person (See Chapter xii. of this work), and all the provisions of law, in relations to obedience to such writ, shall apply to the writ so allowed by such referee or commissioners. 2 *Rev. Stat.* 344, *sec.* 7.

If the person shall be produced before the referee or commissioners, pursuant to the order of the court, they are required to state the same in their return, and also to state therein, whether they or either of them were personally acquainted with such person, or whether his identity was proved by witnesses examined by them, and shall set forth such proof in their return. If such person shall not be produced before them, they shall so state in their return. *Ib. sec.* 8.

Proceedings if order is complied with.] Upon the filing of the referee's or commissioners' return, if it shall appear that the order has been complied with, the proceedings shall be discharged, and the court shall direct an entry of such return to be made in its minutes; and shall order the costs of the proceedings to be paid by the applicant. 2 *Rev. Stat.* 344, *sec.* 9.

When person presumed to be dead.] If it shall appear, from the return, that the person upon whose life the estate depends, was not produced before the commissioners, as required by the order, and that due service of such order was made as required by the statute, such person shall thereafter be taken to be dead, (*a*) and the party entitled after his death, may forthwith enter upon the said lands or tenements, in the same manner as if such person were actually dead. 2 *Rev. Stat.* 345, *sec.* 10. In like manner, if the person shall not be produced before commissioners residing out of the State, where it is alleged the person is beyond sea, or elsewhere out of the State, he is thereafter presumed to be dead. *Ib. sec.* 14.

Proceedings if person is out of the State.] If it shall be shown to the court, by affidavit on the part of the person against whom any such application shall be made, in any stage of the proceeding, that the person upon whose life such estate depends, is or lately was at some place certain, beyond sea, or elsewhere

---

(*a*) It is also provided by the Revised Statutes, that if any person upon whose life any estate in lands or tenements shall depend, shall remain beyond sea, or shall absent himself, in this State or elsewhere, for seven years together, such person shall be accounted naturally dead, in any action concerning such lands or tenements, in which his death shall come in question, unless sufficient proof be made in such case, of the life of such person. 1 *Rev. Stat.* 749, *sec.* 6.

out of this State, the proceedings shall cease, unless the party prosecuting such order, shall at his own costs and charges, obtain a commission, to be issued out of the Supreme Court, and to be directed to one or more commissioners, to be appointed for that purpose by the court, residing at such place, to obtain a personal view of the person upon whose life such estate depends. 2 *Rev. Stat.* 345, *sec.* 11.

If such party shall elect so to send to such place, he shall give notice, in writing, to the party against whom the original application shall have been made, of the time and place certain at which the commissioners will attend, for the purpose of having such view, as follows:

1. If the place be within any of the United States, or in either of the provinces of Canada, at least two months' notice shall be given.

2. If the place be within either of the West India Islands, at least three months' notice.

3. For all other places, at least four months' notice. *Ib. sec.* 12.

The commissioners possess the same powers, and are to proceed in like manner, as hereinbefore provided, and the like proceedings are to be had, and with the like effect, upon the coming in of their return. *Ib. sec.* 13.

And if it shall appear from their return, that the person upon whose life such estate depends, was produced before them, the application shall be discharged, with the like effect as before provided; but if it shall appear that he was not so produced, he shall thereafter be taken to be dead, and the party entitled after his death, may forthwith enter upon the said lands and tenements, in the same manner as if such person were actually dead. *Ib. sec.* 14.

What the party applied against may show, and order thereon.]
The party against whom any application shall be made, may show by affidavit or otherwise, to the Supreme Court:

1. That the person upon whose life such estate depends, is or was, living, at the time of any return made by any commissioners appointed under the statute.

2. That such party has used his utmost endeavors to procure the person upon whose life such estate depends, to appear before

such commissioners, according to the exigency of the order by which they were appointed; and,

3. That he could not procure or compel such person so to appear. 2 *Rev. Stat.* 345, *sec.* 15.

If the court is satisfied of the truth of such allegations, it shall cause an entry of such proof to be made in its minutes, and shall thereupon declare that there is no reason to presume the death of the person upon whose life such particular estate shall depend; and all further proceedings on such application shall cease. *Ib. sec.* 16.

Copy of orders of court to be evidence.] A copy of any entry made in the minutes of the court, pursuant to the provisions of the statute, duly certified, shall be evidence, in all courts within this State, of the facts therein stated. 2 *Rev. Stat.* 346, *sec.* 17.

Provision for costs.] The statute provides, that when provision is not therein otherwise made for the payment of the costs of the proceedings, the same shall be paid by such party as the court shall direct, 2 *Rev. Stat.* 346, *sec.* 18; and, when allowed, shall be at the rate allowed for similar services in civil actions. *Laws of* 1854, *p.* 592; *ante, vol.* 1, *p.* 19.

Restoration of estates in certain cases.] Any estate, which shall have been recovered upon the presumption of the death of any person, shall be restored to him who shall have been evicted, if, in any subsequent action, the person presumed to be dead shall be proved to have been living at the time of the commencement of such action. 2 *Rev. Stat.* 346, *sec.* 19.

Remedy of person evicted for rents and profits.] Every person so evicted, his executors or administrators, shall recover, in any action to be brought by him or them, the full profits of the estate during the time he shall have been deprived thereof, and during the lifetime of the person on whose life such estate depended, against such as occupied the same, his or their executors or administrators. 2 *Rev. Stat.* 346, *sec.* 20.

CHAPTER XXIII.

PROCEEDINGS BY PERSONS TO CHANGE THEIR NAMES.

The first statute giving jurisdiction to the courts of this State to allow persons to change their names, was passed on the 14th of December, 1847. *Laws of* 1847, *p.* 632. This statute was subsequently amended by an act passed March 17, 1860, by which the powers of the court were materially enlarged, confining the jurisdiction, however, to the county courts, and to the Court of Common Pleas of the city and county of New York. *Laws of* 1860, *p.* 125.

Notwithstanding the general jurisdiction of the court, resort is still frequently had to the legislature by persons desiring to change their names, as will be seen by reference to the session laws of the State.

In what cases.] The statute authorizes any person residing in this State, whether of full age or not, to apply to the court for an order authorizing such person to assume another name. (*a*) *Laws of* 1860, *p.* 125.

Formerly, to give the court jurisdiction, it was necessary to show that the applicant would derive a pecuniary benefit from the change of name (*Laws of* 1847, *p.* 633; 2 *Hilton*, 566); but this is now unnecessary, under the recent amendment of the statute. *Laws of* 1860, *p.* 125.

(*a*) There is no law, it seems, prohibiting a person from assuming another name, if he so desires; nor is there any penalty or punishment for so doing. And a person may enter into a contract by any name he may choose to assume. All that the law looks to is the identity of the individual, and when that is clearly established, the act will be binding upon him and upon others. 2 *Hilton*, 566, 575, *per* Daly, F. J.

The applicant, however, must satisfy the court "that there is no reasonable objection" to his assuming another name. *Ib.* amending § 3 of *Laws of* 1847, *supra.*

If the applicant is a minor, he must apply by guardian or next friend. *Laws of* 1860, *p.* 125.

Where application to be made.] The statute requires the application to be made to the county court of the county where the applicant resides; except that, if his residence is in the city and county of New York, he must apply to the Court of Common Pleas of that city. *Laws of* 1860, *p.* 125.

Petition and what to contain.] The application is founded upon petition, which must set forth the grounds of the application, and must be verified by the affidavit of the applicant annexed thereto, or indorsed thereon. *Laws of* 1847, *p.* 633, § 2.

It should show that the applicant resided in the county where the application was to be made, and should set forth such facts as would satisfy the court that there was no reasonable objection to the applicant's assuming another name. *Laws of* 1860, *p.* 125. For form, see *Appendix*, No. 546.

Order, and publication thereof.] The statute provides that if the court to which the application is made, shall be satisfied by the petition so verified, or by affidavits presented, that there is no reasonable objection that such person should assume another name, the court shall make an order authorizing such applicant to assume such other name from and after some time, not less than thirty days, to be specified in such order. *Laws of* 1860, *p.* 125. For form, see *Appendix*, No. 547.

Within ten days after such order is granted, the applicant is required to cause a copy thereof to be published in a public newspaper printed in the county in which he shall reside at the time of making the application. *Laws of* 1847, *p.* 633, § 4.

Papers to be filed and recorded.] The applicant is required, within twenty days from the granting of the order, to cause the petition, affidavit, or affidavits, order, and an affidavit of the publication of such order to be filed and recorded in the county clerk's office of the county in which the applicant resides at the time of making the application. *Laws of* 1847, *p.* 633, § 5.

When applicant may assume new name.] When the requirements of the statute are complied with, the applicant shall, from and after the day specified for that purpose in the order of the court, be known by the name which, by such order, he shall be authorized to assume, and by no other. *Laws of* 1847, *p.* 633, § 6.

Effect upon legal proceedings subsequently commenced.] The statute provides, that if any suit or legal proceeding shall be commenced by his former name, against any person whose name shall have been changed pursuant to the statute, such suit or proceeding shall not be abated, nor any relief or recovery sought thereby, be prevented by such misnomer, but the plaintiff or party instituting such suit or proceeding may amend in respect to the name of the person against whom it shall be commenced, at any time, and without costs. *Laws of* 1847, *p.* 633, § 7.

Returns to be made by the clerk to the Secretary of State.] It is the duty of the county clerks for the several counties of the State, except the city and county of New York, and of the clerk of the Court of Common Pleas of that city, annually, in the month of December, to make a return to the office of the Secretary of State, of all changes of names of persons made under and by virtue of the statute; and the names of such persons before and after such changes, as the same shall appear in such returns, are required to be published in tabular form with the session laws of each year. *Laws of* 1860, *p.* 125.

SUPPLEMENT TO CHAPTER XXIII.

Applications by incorporated companies to change their names. By the Laws of 1870, ch. 322 (*as amended by Laws of* 1876, *ch.* 280), any incorporation, incorporated company, society or association, organized under the laws of this State, excepting banks, banking associations, trust companies, life, health, accident, marine and fire insurance companies, may apply at any special term of the Supreme Court, sitting in the county in which shall be situated its chief business office, for an order to authorize it to assume another corporate name. The form of the application and the details therof are regulated by the statute. *Laws of* 1870, *ch.* 322, *p.* 750.

CHAPTER XXIV.

PROCEEDINGS TO PROVE WILLS IN A FOREIGN STATE.

This proceeding is authorized by Chapter 329 of the Laws of 1830, and applies to the proof of wills executed according to the laws of this State, as well as the laws of other States. *Laws of* 1830, *p.* 388; 2 *Rev. Stat.* 67; 23 *New York*, 406.

I. Wills executed according to the Laws of this State.

It is provided by statute, that a will duly executed according to the laws of this State, where the witnesses to the same reside without the jurisdiction of this State; or a duly exemplified or authenticated copy thereof, where the original will is in the possession of a court or tribunal of justice in another country or State, whence the same cannot be obtained, may be proved in the Supreme Court, (*a*) upon a commission to be issued for that purpose on application to that court. *Laws of* 1830, *p.* 388; 2 *Rev. Stat.* 67; *Laws of* 1847, *p.* 323, § 16.

It seems that by a sound construction of the statute, a commission may be issued to prove a will, either of real or personal estate, in any case where, from the absence of the will, or the non-residence of witnesses in this State, it cannot be proved before a

(*a*) But the Supreme Court has not exclusive jurisdiction to take proof of a will in a foreign state or country. By the Laws of 1837, p. 537, sec. 77, the surrogate is authorized to issue a commission for the examination of witnesses abroad, in the same manner as courts of record; and thus, it seems, the surrogate is enabled to take proof of wills out of this State, in all cases, without resorting to the aid of the Supreme Court. 1 *Bradf.* 76, 79; *Willard on Ex.* 165; *Dayton on Sur.* 140, 175, 182.

surrogate. 2 *Paige*, 430, *per* Walworth, Ch. And it may be issued, also, although all the subscribing witnesses to the will are dead; though in such case, the proof taken will have no greater effect as evidence, than a will proved before a surrogate without producing any of the subscribing witnesses thereto. *Ib.*

How commission applied for, and who may apply.] The commission may be applied for either by petition, or by summons and complaint in the nature of an action under the Code of Procedure. 2 *Rev. Stat.* 67, *sec.* 64; *Code*, § 69. The former method, however, is the one most usually adopted in practice. 2 *Barb. Ch. Pr.* 315.

The commission can be issued only on the application of some person interested in the establishment of the will. *Laws of* 1830, *p.* 388; 2 *Rev. Stat.* 67, *sec.* 64; 6 *Paige*, 183.

Petition, or complaint.] The statute does not prescribe the form of the petition or complaint.

It has been decided, however, that where the object of the proceeding is to take proof of a will of real estate, the petition should show that the decedent left real property in this State, in which the applicant for the commission has some legal or beneficial interest under the will; and either positively, or upon information and belief, that the instrument sought to be proved, is the last will of the decedent, and was executed in due form of law to pass real property in this State. It should show, also, who are the legal heirs, to whom by the laws of the State such real property would have descended if the decedent had died intestate, and the names and residences of such heirs, so far as the same can be ascertained, to enable the court to determine what notice should be given to them of the proceedings to prove the will; and if the decedent left no heir capable of inheriting lands in this State, that fact should be stated. 6 *Paige*, 183.

If the application is to prove a will of personal property, the petition should show that the decedent at his death left assets in this State, or that assets have come into this State since his death. It should state, also, the necessary facts to show what surrogate has jurisdiction to grant letters testamentary, or of administration; so that the court may be enabled, after the will is proved, to send the mandate to the proper surrogate for that purpose. *Ib.*

And if the instrument is to be proved as a will both of real and personal estate, or as a will of personal estate merely, if the decedent at the time of his death was not domiciled in this State, or if the will was executed out of the State, the domicil of the decedent at the time of his death, should be stated; also the names and residences of his next of kin, or of those who, in case of intestacy, would have been entitled to succeed to his personal estate according to the law of his domicil, so far as the same can be ascertained. *Ib.*

The prayer of the petition should be, that an order may be granted, directing the will to be proved in the Supreme Court upon a commission to be issued for that purpose, under the seal of the court, directed to certain commissioners named therein, to prove such will by the testimony of the subscribing witnesses (if they are living), upon written interrogatories to be annexed to the petition. 2 *Barb. Ch. Pr.* 316. And it is usual to annex to the petition a copy of the will, and of the interrogatories upon which the witnesses are to be examined. *Ib.*

Notice to parties interested.] The statute requires such notice to be given to the parties interested to oppose the validity of the will as the court shall direct; or such notice may be dispensed with, where, from the circumstances of the case, it shall be deemed unnecessary. *Laws of* 1830, *p.* 388; 2 *Rev. Stat.* 67, *sec.* 64.

It seems, if notice is directed to be given, it should be for the same length of time as is required in proving a will before a surrogate, (2 *Rev. Stat.* 56); 2 *Paige*, 214.

Parties authorized to contest the validity of the will, are entitled also to reasonable notice of the time and place of executing the commission. *Ib.*

Commission.] If it appears, upon the hearing of the application, to be a proper case for the exercise of the jurisdiction of the court, and the proceedings have been regular, and notice duly given where it was required, a commission will be directed to be issued according to the prayer of the petition.

The commission is similar, in form, to the commission issued in other cases, to examine witnesses residing out of the State, and is to be executed in a similar manner. 2 *Barb. Ch. Pr.* 316; 1 *Id.* 299, 300; 2 *Rev. Stat.* 180, 181.

Persons authorized to contest the validity of the will may join in the commission, and may be allowed to name a commissioner on their part; and they will be entitled, also, to reasonable notice of the time and place of executing the commission. 2 *Paige*, 214.

Proceedings on the return of the commission.] If the facts necessary to establish the validity of the will shall appear from the proof taken under such commission, the Supreme Court, upon the return of the commission, will direct the will, or the copy thereof, and the proofs or examinations, to be recorded in the office of the clerk of that court. *Laws of* 1830, *p.* 388; 2 *Rev. Stat.* 67, *sec.* 65.

Effect of proof and of record.] It is provided by the statute that every will or copy so proved under a commission shall have a certificate of such proof endorsed thereon, signed by the clerk, and attested by the seal of the Supreme Court, and may then be read in evidence without further proof thereof. *Laws of* 1830, *p.* 388; 2 *Rev. Stat.* 67, *sec.* 66; *Laws of* 1847, *p.* 323, § 16.

If the commission issues in a case where all the subscribing witnesses to the will are dead, the proof taken under it will have no greater effect as evidence, than a will proved before a surrogate without producing any of the subscribing witnesses thereto. 2 *Paige*, 429. The record, in such a case, will be received in evidence only in connection with other proof, that the lands in controversy and devised by the will, have been held under the same for the space of twenty years. 2 *Rev. Stat.* 58, *secs.* 16, 18.

The statute further directs that every record of a will, or copy made in the clerk's office, in pursuance of the statute, or an exemplification thereof, shall be received in evidence, and shall be as effectual in all cases as the original will would be, if produced and proved, and may in like manner be repelled by contrary proof. *Laws of* 1830, *p.* 389; 2 *Rev. Stat.* 67, *sec.* 66.

When will established as a will of personal estate.] The statute makes the several statutory provisions above recited applicable to wills of personal as well as of real property. And where there are assets of the testator within this State, and due notice shall have been given to the parties interested to oppose the will, the court may by decree establish the same as a will of personal estate; and in such case, it is required to transmit the decree to be recorded in the office of the surrogate having jurisdiction, with directions to the surrogate to issue letters testamentary, or of administration with the will annexed thereon, in the same manner as upon wills duly proved before him. *Laws of* 1830, *p.* 389; 2 *Rev. Stat.* 67, *sec.* 67.

But no will of personal property, made out of this State, by a person not being a citizen of this State, can be admitted to probate under any of the above provisions of the statute, unless such will shall have been executed according to the laws of the State or country in which the same was made. *Ib. sec.* 69; 6 *Paige,* 184. This provision of the statute relates only to the case of a person domiciled out of this State at the time of his death. And accordingly, where a citizen of another State executed his will in such manner as to be a valid bequest of personal property according to the law of that State, but not of this State, and subsequently established his domicile and was a citizen of and died in this State; it was held that he died intestate in respect to personal property within our jurisdiction. 23 *New York R.* 394, 408, reversing 26 *Barb.* 252, which aff. 3 *Bradf.* 322. Otherwise, however, it seems, if the person had not been a citizen of this State, though domiciled here. 8 *Paige,* 446; *Id.* 519; 23 *New York,* 407, *per* Denio, J.; and see 1 *Bradf.* 70; 2 *Id.* 105; *Id.* 169.

Proceedings, where to be entered.] The proceedings under the statute were formerly required to be entered in the office of the register of the Court of Chancery at Albany; 2 *Paige,* 429; 2 *Rev. Stat.* 67, *sec.* 65; but that office was abolished by the Constitution of 1846; and by the judiciary act the papers must now be filed in the clerk's office of the county in which the defendants in the proceeding, or some of them, reside; or if they all reside out of this State, in the clerk's office of any other county. *Laws of* 1847, *p.* 333, § 50. And the court may direct the papers to be transferred to any other clerk's office, in its discretion. *Ib.*

II. Wills executed according to the Laws of other States.

The statute provides that wills of personal estate, duly executed by persons residing out of this State, according to the laws of the State or country in which the same were made, may be proved under a commission to be issued by the Supreme Court; and when so proved, may be established and transmitted to the surrogate having jurisdiction, with directions to the surrogate to issue letters testamentary or of administration with the will annexed thereon, in the same manner as upon wills duly proved before him. *Laws of* 1830, *p.* 389; 2 *Rev. Stat.* 67, *secs.* 67, 68.

And where a will, duly executed by a person residing out of this State, according to the laws of the State or country in which the same was made, shall have been duly admitted to probate in such State and country, letters testamentary or of administration, with the will annexed, may also be issued thereon, by the surrogate having jurisdiction, upon the production of a duly exemplified or authenticated copy of such will, under the seal of the court in which the same shall have been proved. *Ib.*

The statute also provides, that no will of personal estate, made out of this State, by a person not being a citizen of this State, shall be admitted to probate under the statute, unless such will shall have been executed according to the laws of the State or country in which the same was made. *Laws of* 1830, *p.* 389; 2 *Rev. Stat.* 67, *sec.* 69, *supra.*

But this prohibition of the statute relates only to the case of a person domiciled out of this State, at the time of his death. And, accordingly, where a citizen of another State executed a will of personal estate according to the laws of that State, but not of this State, and subsequently became a citizen of this State, and domiciled here, and died in this State,—it was held that he died intestate in respect to personal property within our jurisdiction. 23 *New York*, 394, 408, *supra.* It would have been otherwise, however, it seems, if such person had not been a citizen of this State, though domiciled here at the time of his death. 8 *Paige*, 446; *Id.* 519; 23 *New York*, 407, *per* Denio, J.; and see 1 *Bradf.* 70; 2 *Id.* 105; *Id.* 169.

In respect to the manner in which the general law of a foreign State or country is to be made known to the court, in order to enable it to test the validity of the will proposed to be proved, it has been held that where it does not appear that such law exists as statute or written law, and of which an authenticated copy of the record could be produced, it may be proved by parol. 8 *Paige*, 446, *supra.*

The application is founded upon petition, or complaint; which should show the domicile of the decedent at the time of his death; also the names and residences of his next of kin, or of those who, in case of intestacy, would have been entitled to succeed to his personal estate, according to the law of his domicile, so far as the same can be ascertained. And if the will was executed in another State or country by a decedent who was not a citizen and inhabitant of this State, the petition should show, also, that the instrument propounded as a will was duly executed, so as to make a valid testamentary disposition of the decedent's personal property, according to the law of the place where he was domiciled and where such will was made. 6 *Paige*, 183. For further on the subject of the form of the petition, see *ante*, under the head of "Petition or complaint," the proceedings to prove a will executed according to the laws of another State being similar to those to prove a will executed according to the laws of this State.

The commisison, also, is similar in form, and is to be applied for and executed in the same manner as the commission in the other case.

In like manner, the papers must be filed and entered in the office of the county clerk, the same as in proceeding to prove a will executed according to the laws of this State. See *ante*, *p.* 183.

CHAPTER XXV.

PROCEEDINGS BY ACTION TO RECOVER POSSESSION OF DEMISED PREMISES FOR NON-PAYMENT OF RENT.

If a tenant fails to pay rent according to the terms of his lease, the landlord may proceed to recover possession of the demised premises by action. The remedy by action, however, is not allowed, except where a right of re-entry is expressly stipulated for between the parties to the lease. 11 *Johns.* 163; 2 *Coms.* 141; 12 *Barb.* 120.

Formerly, the landlord's mode of proceeding varied, according as there was, or was not, a sufficient distress upon the demised premises to answer the amount of rent due. If there was a sufficient distress, the proceeding was required to be at the common law; if not, it might be under the statute. 7 *T. R.* 117; 2 *Arch. Pr.* 56. Both of these remedies still exist, though, as we shall see, without reference to a sufficiency of distress upon the premises, having been fully recognized by the Court of Appeals in *Van Rensselaer* v. *Jewett*, 2 *Coms.* 141; and see 9 *Barb.* 303; 27 *Id.* 104; 3 *Kern.* 299.

The grantor's interest, in a conveyance in fee, reserving rent, with a right of re-entry, is assignable, and passes to each subsequent assignee of the land, to be enforced by entry for non-payment of rent, or other forfeiture. 27 *Barb.* 104; aff. 19 *New York*, 100.

1. *Proceedings at the common law.*] Before commencing the action, and before the forfeiture can be incurred at the common law, a demand must have been made of the rent; except, however, where by the terms of the lease, a re-entry is authorized

for a default in the payment of rent without a demand of it. 2 *Coms.* 147; and see 12 *Barb.* 120.

In cases where a demand has not been waived, great strictness is required; the landlord must make an actual demand of the exact amount of rent due, on the very day it becomes due, at a convenient time before sunset, and at the particular place where it is made payable, or if no place be specified in the lease, then at the most notorious place on the premises demised. And the demand must be made in fact, and so averred in pleading, although there should be no person on the land ready to pay it. 2 *Arch. Pr.* 56; 2 *Coms.* 141; 17 *Johns.* 71.

If the rent be not paid when thus demanded, the tenant forfeits his term, and the landlord may re-enter for the forfeiture, that is, he may bring an action to recover the possession of the premises. 1 *Vent.* 248; 2 *Ld. Raym.* 750; 1 *Salk.* 258; 1 *Saund.* 287, 319; 3 *Burr.* 1896.

And though a landlord may generally re-enter for non-payment of rent without showing that there was no distress, by making a strict demand, yet this right may be qualified by the terms of the lease so as to depend upon the absence of a distress at the time the rent becomes due. 5 *Denio*, 121.

Where the premises demised are held in separate parcels by different persons under the lessee or grantee, and each is sued separately, the demand of rent, where the re-entry is at the common law, must be for all that is due upon the whole premises included in the demise, and not for the proportionate part due in respect to the defendant's parcel. *Ib. per* McKissock, J. And where the tenant sublets a part of the premises, the sub-tenant, in order to protect his possession, may pay his rent to the original lessor. 3 *Selden*, 528.

The mode of proceeding in the action is the same as in ordinary actions.

But the proceeding, at the common law, is seldom adopted in practice, on account of the great nicety to be observed in the previous demand of the rent, and for the reason, also, that the tenant may obtain an injunction and stay the proceedings upon payment of the rent in arrear. 2 *Arch. Pr.* 57.

2 *Proceedings by statute.*] The statute provides, that whenever any half-year's rent, or more, shall be in arrear from any

tenant to his landlord, and no sufficient distress can be found on the premises to satisfy the rent due, if the landlord has a subsisting right by law to re-enter for the non-payment of such rent, he may bring an action of ejectment for the recovery of the possession of the demised premises; and the service of the declaration therein shall be deemed, and stand instead of, a demand of the rent in arrear, and of a re-entry on the demised premises. 2 *Rev. Stat.* 505, *sec.* 30; 3 *Denio*, 334.

The remedy under the statute is not confined to cases of rent service; but it is applicable to all cases of non-payment of rent, where there is a right to re-enter at common law. 19 *New York*, 100.

Where the lease contains no clause authorizing re-entry for the non-payment of rent, the landlord cannot maintain ejectment under the statute. 11 *Johns.* 163; and see 2 *Coms.* 141; 12 *Barb.* 120.

By an act passed in 1846 (*a*) (*Laws of* 1846, *p*. 369, § 1), distress for rent is abolished; and by section three of the same act, whenever the right of re-entry is reserved, and given to a grantor or lessor in any grant or lease, in default of a sufficiency of goods or chattels whereon to distrain for the satisfaction of any rent due, such re-entry may be made at any time after default in the payment of such rent; provided fifteen days' previous notice of such intention to re-enter, in writing, be given by such grantor or lessor, or his heirs or assigns, to the grantee or lessee, his heirs, executors, administrators or assigns, notwithstanding there may be a sufficiency of goods and chattels on the lands granted or demised, for the satisfaction thereof. This notice may be served personally on the grantee or lessee, or by leaving it at his dwelling-house on the premises.

It has been held that the third section above does not affect the remedy in favor of a landlord under a lease executed prior to the passage of the act; that section provides an additional method for conducting the proceedings, by substituting a fifteen days' notice of the landlord's intention to re-enter in lieu of showing that there was no sufficient distress on the premises. 2 *Barb.*

) In respect to the effect of the passage of this act upon proceedings to recover possession of land for non-payment of rent, at common law, and under the Revised Statutes, see 2 *Barb. S. C. R.*, 316; 9 *Id.* 302; 27 *Id.* 104.

S. C. R. 316, 319, *per* Willard, J.; and see 27 *Id.* 104.; 3 *Kern.* 299. It applies, however, only to those leases in which the right of re-entry, in default of a sufficiency of goods and chattels whereon to distrain, for the satisfaction of any rent due, is reserved in the lease. *Ibid;* 9 *Barb.* 308, *per* Parker, J.

Notice of intention to re-enter, and service thereof.] We have seen, that whenever the lessor has a right to re-enter in default of a sufficiency of goods whereon to distrain for the satisfaction of any rent due, such re-entry may be made at any time after default in the payment of such rent, provided fifteen days' previous notice of such intention to re-enter, in writing, be given by the grantor or lessor, or his heirs or assigns, to the grantee or lessee, his representatives or assigns, notwithstanding there may be a sufficiency of goods and chattels on the lands granted or demised, for the satisfaction thereof. *Laws of* 1846, *p.* 369.

No notice is required to be served, where the lessor proceeds under a lease executed prior to the passage of the above statute. 2 *Barb. S. C. R.* 316. Nor is such notice necessary in any case, except where there is a sufficiency of goods and chattels on the premises for the satisfaction of the rent. 18 *Id.* 156.

In cases, too, where notice is required, it may be waived by the lessee. 2 *Id.* 316, *supra.*

The notice may be served personally on the grantee or lessee, or by leaving it at his dwelling-house on the premises. *Laws of* 1846, *p.* 369. For form of notice, see *Appendix*, No. 550.

The proceedings in the action.] Instead of the service of a declaration as provided by the Revised Statutes, the landlord now proceeds by summons, or summons and complaint; and the action is conducted in conformity to the present practice under the Code of Procedure. *Code*, § 471.

The right of re-entry, with the remedies for enforcing it, being assignable by the lessor, the assignee is authorized to bring the action in his own name. 27 *Barb.* 104; aff. 19 *New York*, 100.

The complaint need not allege a demand of payment of the rent; nor, where it appears on the face of the complaint that there are not goods enough upon the premises to satisfy the rent, as where it is alleged that the premises consist of "a water lot, vacant ground and soil, under water," is it necessary to aver that there is not a sufficiency of goods on the demised premises to satisfy the demand. 18 *Barb.* 156.

If the tenant has been evicted from a portion of the premises, or from any rights therein, by title paramount, he is entitled to an abatement of the rent, and may show such partial eviction by way of counter-claim and equitable defence; and is not driven to a cross action. 18 *New York*, 529.

Judgment and execution therein.] The statute provides that if upon the trial of the cause, it shall be proved, or upon judgment by default, against the defendant, it shall appear to the court by affidavit, that the landlord had a right to commence such action, according to the provisions of the statute, the plaintiff in such action shall have judgment to recover the possession of the demised premises and his costs, and the court shall award execution therefor. 2 *Rev. Stat.* 505, *sec.* 31.

Where a landlord, on a clause of re-entry for the non-payment of rent, obtained judgment by default against the casual ejector, the record of the judgment, without the previous affidavit required by the statute being produced, is a sufficient defence to an ejectment brought by the former tenant for the premises. 3 *Johns. C.* 295.

Staying proceedings.] At any time before judgment in such action, the defendant may either tender to the landlord, or bring into the court where the suit shall be pending, all the rent in arrear, at the time of such payment, and all costs and charges incurred by the lessor; and in such case, all further proceedings in the action shall cease. 2 *Rev. Stat.* 505, *sec.* 32.

The proper practice under the above section of the statute is, to tender to the landlord sufficient to satisfy the rent and costs, and upon an affidavit of this fact, move the court for an order that, upon the defendant's paying the rent, and the costs when taxed, within a certain time, all proceedings in the action be stayed. 2 *Burr. Pr.* 339; 5 *Wend.* 133.

When premises to be restored to tenant.] At any time within six months after possession of the demised premises shall have been taken by the landlord under any execution issued upon a judgment obtained by him in any such action of ejectment, the lessee of such demised premises, his assigns or personal representatives, may pay or tender to the lessor, his personal representatives or attorney, or into the court where the suit shall be pending, all the rent in arrear at the time of such payment, and all costs and charges incurred by the lessor, and in such case, all further proceedings in the cause shall cease, and the premises shall be restored to the lessee, who shall hold and enjoy the demised premises without any new lease thereof, according to the terms of the original demise. 2 *Rev. Stat.* 506, *sec.* 33; 12 *Abb.* 473.

Tenant, when barred.] In case the rent and arrears and full costs remain unpaid for six months after the execution issued upon any judgment in ejectment shall have been executed, the lessee and his assigns, and all other persons, deriving title under the said lease, from such lessee, are barred and foreclosed from all relief or remedy in law or equity (except for any error in the record or proceedings), and the said lessor or landlord shall from thenceforth hold the demised premises free and discharged from such lease or demise. 2 *Rev. Stat.* 506, *sec.* 34.

Mortgagees—how relieved; effect of foreclosure.] A mortgagee of such lease, or of any part thereof, who shall not be in possession of such demised premises, and who shall within six months after such judgment obtained and execution thereon executed, pay all rent in arrear, and all costs and charges as aforesaid, and perform all the agreements which ought to be performed by the first lessee, shall not be affected by such recovery in ejectment. 2 *Rev. Stat.* 506, *sec.* 35.

On the foreclosure and sale of the premises under a mortgage covering the same, the purchaser at the sale is not necessarily to be discharged because the rent is in arrear, and notice has been given of intention to re-enter for non-payment thereof. The officer conducting the sale, in such case, should pay out of the purchase money, the rent due and in arrear, and unpaid at the time of the sale; leaving the rent payable after the sale to be paid by the purchaser himself. 12 *Abb.* 473.

Remedy in equity.] The statute provides that the lessee, or any person claiming any interest in the lease, may within six months after execution executed on such judgment in ejectment, file his bill for relief in a court of equity, but not after that time; and if relieved in such court, he shall hold and enjoy the demised premises, without any new lease thereof, according to the terms of the original demise. 2 *Rev. Stat.* 506, *sec.* 36.

In case of such bill being filed within the time aforesaid, the plaintiff shall not have or continue any injunction against the proceedings at law on such ejectment, unless he shall, at such time as the court shall direct, bring into court such sum of money as the lessor shall in his answer have sworn to be due and in arrear, over and above all just allowances, and also all the costs taxed in the said suit, there to remain until the hearing of the said cause, or to be paid to the lessor on good security, as the court may direct. *Ib. sec.* 37.

The action under the above provisions of the statute, is now brought in the Supreme Court, and is conducted in all respects like other actions in that court, where the plaintiff seeks equitable relief. *Code*, § 69.

Use of premises by lessor.] If the lessor shall have entered into the actual possession of the demised premises, the court may direct that so much, and no more, as he shall really have made of the said premises during his possession thereof, or as he might without wilful neglect, have made of the said premises, be deducted from the amount of the rent in arrear to such lessor, and the costs of such ejectment; and the complainant shall be required to pay the balance, before he shall be restored to the possession of the said premises. 2 *Rev. Stat.* 506, *sec.* 38.

SUPPLEMENT.

The action may be maintained by one of six children, heirs of the owner of a rent charge, to recover the one undivided sixth part of the demised premises. And such action may be brought without a common law demand of the rent, or service of fifteen days' notice of intention to re-enter. 41 *N. Y.*, 219.

The time within which to redeem begins to run after judgment and writ of dispossession have been executed. 2 *Hun*, 55, *affirmed*, 64 *N. Y.*, 27. The time cannot be enlarged by the tenant wrongfully retaking possession of the premises; nor will the right to redeem be revived by a new execution upon the judgment made necessary by such wrongful retaking of possession. 2 *Lans.*, 498; *and see* 64 *N. Y.*, 27.

The statute applies to the so-called Manor Cases; and the relief, in such cases, is not limited at the common law to a right to hold possession of the land for a time sufficient to satisfy the rent in arrears, etc. 2 *Lans.*, 498.

CHAPTER XXVI.

QUO WARRANTO AND INFORMATIONS IN THE NATURE OF QUO WARRANTO; AND COMPELLING DELIVERY OF BOOKS AND PAPERS.

Section I. Quo Warranto, and Informations in the Nature of Quo Warranto.

II. Proceedings to compel the Delivery of Books and Papers by Public Officers to their Successors.

SECTION I.

QUO WARRANTO, AND INFORMATIONS IN THE NATURE OF QUO WARRANTO.

The writ of quo warranto was in the nature of a writ of right for the king, against him who claimed or usurped any office, franchise, or liberty, to inquire by what authority he supported his claim, in order to determine the right. It lay, also, in case of non-user or long neglect of a franchise, or misuser or abuse of it; being a writ commanding the defendant to show by what warrant he exercises such a franchise, having never had any grant of it, or having forfeited it by neglect or abuse. 3 *Bl. Com.* 262.

In this State, the writ of quo warranto, and proceedings by information in the nature of quo warranto, are abolished; and the remedies heretofore obtainable in those forms are now obtained by civil actions under the Code of Procedure. *Code*, § 428; 4 *Seld.* 71.

The action under the Code, although differing in some of the formula of procedure from proceedings by information, or by writ of quo warranto, is nevertheless in substance the same, and is governed by all the rules which regulated the proceedings under the former practice 30 *Barb.* 591.

I. The Different Cases in which Actions may be brought.

1. *Actions to vacate charter by direction of legislature.*] An action may be brought by the attorney-general, in the name of the people of this State, whenever the legislature shall so direct, against a corporation, for the purpose of vacating or annulling the act of incorporation, or an act renewing its corporate existence, on the ground that such act or renewal was procured upon some fraudulent suggestion or concealment of a material fact by the persons incorporated, or by some of them, or with their knowledge and consent. *Code*, § 429; and see 2 *Rev. Stat.* 579, *sec.* 13.

2. *Actions to vacate charter by leave of the Supreme Court.*] An action may be brought by the attorney-general, in the name of the people of this State, on leave granted by the Supreme Court, or a judge thereof, for the purpose of vacating the charter or annulling the existence of a corporation, other than municipal, whenever such corporation shall—

1. Offend against any of the provisions of the act or acts creating, altering, or renewing such corporation; or,

2. Violate the provisions of any law by which such corporation shall have forfeited its charter by abuse of its powers; or,

3. Whenever it shall have forfeited its privileges or franchises by failure to exercise its powers; or,

4. Whenever it shall have done or omitted any act which amounts to a surrender of its corporate rights, privileges and franchises; or,

5. Whenever it shall exercise a franchise or privilege not conferred upon it by law.

And it is the duty of the attorney-general, whenever he shall have reason to believe that any of these acts or omissions can be established by proof, to apply for leave, and upon leave granted, to bring the action in every case of public interest, and also in every other case in which satisfactory security shall be given, to indemnify the people of this State against the costs and expenses to be incurred thereby. *Code*, § 430; and see 2 *Rev. Stat.* 583, *sec.* 39.

Thus, the action will lie against an incorporated company, for carrying on banking operations without authority of the legislature. 15 *Johns.* 358. So, if an incorporated college establish a school in a place not authorized by law, and appoint professors to take charge of the same, this is an usurpation of a franchise, for which an action will lie. 5 *Wend.* 211. So, if an incorporated company fails to comply with the requirements of an act of incorporation, this is *per se* a misuser, and forfeits the privileges and franchises conferred. 23 *Id.* 193. And it is not necessary, to work a forfeiture, that the neglect or refusal to perform the duties enjoined, should proceed from a bad or corrupt motive; but it is sufficient if the duties are neglected or designedly omitted. *Ib.* The duties enjoined upon the corporation are conditions attached to the grant of the franchises conferred; but a substantial compliance is all that is required, whether they are conditions precedent or subsequent. *Ib.;* and see 38 *Barb.* 324.

And so, an action will lie if the ground of action exists at common law, although not embraced by the statute. 23 *Wend.* 222.

It is no answer to the action that parties aggrieved have their remedy by private action, or in some other form, unless the remedy by information is taken away in express terms, or by necessary implication. *Ib.;* and see *Id.* 254.

The statute, as we have seen, does not authorize the attorney-general to institute an action for the purpose of vacating the existence of a *municipal* corporation. But although he cannot do this, yet he may maintain an action in the name of the people to restrain such a corporation from exercising authority not possessed by it under its charter, or by-laws. 32 *Barb.* 35, *s. c.* 10 *Abb.* 144; 19 *How.* 155. Though, it seems, such action can be maintained only for the purpose of restraining it from making a fraudulent or illegal disposition of the corporate property. 28 *Barb.* 65.

Leave to bring an action for the purpose of vacating the charter or annulling the existence of a corporation, may be granted upon the application of the attorney-general; and the court or judge may, at discretion, direct notice of such application to be given to the corporation or its officers, previous to granting such leave, and may hear the corporation in opposition thereto. *Code*, § 431. But leave will not be granted where only private individuals are interested in the controversy; as, in a case where a turnpike company opens a road through the land of a person without making him a compensation pursuant to the requirements of the statute. 2 *Johns.* 190.

In an action by the attorney-general to dissolve a corporation, the court has no power to appoint a receiver, before judgment, except in cases of insolvency; but an injunction may issue in such a case. 18 *Abb.* 382.

3. *Actions against persons usurping public offices, &c.*] An action may be brought by the attorney-general, in the name of the people of this State, upon his own information, or upon the complaint of any private party, against the parties offending in the following cases:

1. When any person shall usurp, intrude into, or unlawfully hold or exercise any public office, civil or military, or any franchise within this State, or any office in a corporation created by the authority of this State; or,

2. When any public officer, civil or military, shall have done or suffered an act which, by the provisions of law, shall make a forfeiture of his office; or,

3. When any association or number of persons shall act within this State as a corporation, without being duly incorporated. *Code*, § 432; and see 2 *Rev. Stat.* 581, *sec.* 28.

Thus, an action lies against one intruding into the office of sheriff in consequence of an unlawful decision of the county board of canvassers in his favor, 4 *Cowen*, 297; and against persons who have usurped, or intruded into the office of directors of an insurance company, or any other corporation, *Ib.* 358, 382, *note;* and against persons who intrude into any offices created for the government of a corporation. *Ib.* 358; and against persons who usurp the right to be a corporation. *Ib.*

So, the action will lie against trustees of a village holding over beyond the term for which they were elected, where they have neglected to notify an election, and by means thereof new trustees have not been chosen, 6 *Wend.* 422; and against a person who has usurped the office of alderman or street commissioner, in a municipal corporation, 4 *Abb. Pr.* 121, 5 *Id.* 171; and against a person usurping the office of brigadier-general, or other military office, 25 *Barb.* 254; and against one claiming to exercise the office of supervisor of a town. 24 *New York*, 86.

And an action to determine the right to the office is the only proper remedy in such cases, and an action for the purpose merely of obtaining an injunction to restrain a party usurping an office, from exercising or discharging its duties, will not lie at the suit of the party rightly entitled to the office. 4 *Abb.* 121; 5 *Id.* 171; 25 *Barb.* 254.

It is in the discretion of the attorney-general to bring an action against a person alleged to have usurped a public office; and the courts will not control him in the exercise of that discretion, nor review his decision upon an application made to him to commence such action. 3 *Abb.* 131, *s. c.* 22 *Barb.* 114.

4. *Actions to vacate letters patent.*] An action may be brought by the attorney-general, in the name of the people of this state, for the purpose of vacating or annulling letters patent granted by the people of this State, in the following cases:

1. When he shall have reason to believe that such letters patent were obtained by means of some fraudulent suggestion or concealment of a material fact, made by the person to whom the same were issued or made, or with his consent or knowledge; or,

2. When he shall have reason to believe that such letters patent were issued through mistake, or in ignorance of a material fact; or,

3. When he shall have reason to believe that the patentee, or those claiming under him, have done or omitted an act, in violation of the terms and conditions on which the letters patent were granted, or have by any other means forfeited the interest acquired under the same. *Code*, § 433; and see 2 *Rev. Stat.* 378, *sec.* 12.

The statute is limited to letters patent granted by the people of this State; and does not extend to letters granted by the king, prior to the revolution. 10 *Barb.* 120; and see 5 *Seld.* 318.

II. PROCEEDINGS IN THE ACTION.

Parties to the action.] When an action is brought by the attorney-general, on the relation or information of a person having an interest in the question, the name of such person is required to be joined with the people as plaintiff. *Code*, § 434.

Thus, where an action is brought in the name of the people, on the relation of an individual, to try the right to an office, the name of the relator should be joined with the people as a party plaintiff. 2 *Kern.* 433; 23 *Barb.* 304. But to entitle the relator to be made a party, in such case, the complaint should state facts showing that he is entitled to the office from which the defendant is sought to be ousted. 2 *Kern.* 433. An omission to join the relator as a party may be cured by amendment, without costs. 23 *Barb.* 304.

If an action is brought on the relation of a person having an interest in the question, the attorney-general may require, as a condition for bringing such action, that satisfactory security shall be given to indemnify the people of the State against the costs and expenses to be incurred thereby. (*a*) *Code*, § 434, as amended *Laws of* 1866, *ch.* 824.

Where several persons claim to be entitled to the same office or franchise, all of them may be joined together as defendants in one action, in order to try their respective rights to such office or franchise. *Code*, § 440; 2 *Rev. Stat.* 584, *sec.* 45.

If the proceeding is against an incorporated company, seeking to deprive it of its franchises on the ground of forfeiture by non-user or otherwise, the action is properly brought against the company in its corporate name. 6 *Cowen*, 217.

Summons and complaint.] The summons is in the same form as in ordinary actions where the plaintiff applies to the court for the relief demanded in the complaint. *Code*, § 129, *sub.* 2; *Ib.* § 428.

The complaint, also, is to be prepared in conformity to the Code; and should contain a statement of the facts constituting the plaintiff's cause of action, and a demand of the relief to which he believes himself entitled. *Ib.* § 142.

If the action is brought against a person for usurping an office, the attorney-general, in addition to the statement of the cause of action, should also set forth in the complaint the name of the person rightfully entitled to the office, with a statement of the facts showing his right thereto. *Ib. sec.* 435; 2 *Kern.* 433.

(*a*) And if security is given, the compensation to be paid to the Attorney General is left to the agreement of the parties. *Laws of* 1867, *p.* 1926.

When defendant may be arrested and held to bail.] It is provided by the Code that whenever an action shall be brought against a person for usurping an office, the attorney-general, in addition to the statement of the cause of action, may also set forth in the complaint the name of the person rightfully entitled to the office, with a statement of his right thereto; and in such case, upon proof by affidavit that the defendant has received fees or emoluments belonging to the office, and by means of his usurpation thereof, an order may be granted by a judge of the Supreme Court, for the arrest of the defendant, and holding him to bail; and thereupon he is required to be arrested and held to bail, in the manner and with the same effect, and subject to the same rights and liabilities as in other civil actions where the defendant is subject to arrest. *Code*, § 435; 2 *Rev. Stat.* 582, *sec.* 30.

Trial, and proceedings thereon.] If an issue of fact is joined upon the pleadings, the cause should be placed upon the calendar for trial the same as in other actions.

The place of trial may properly be laid in any county of the State, the people being the party plaintiffs, their residence extends to every county. 6 *How.* 448.

In an action to try the right to an office, it is competent to look beyond the canvass for the purpose of giving effect to the ballot.

Thus, where justices of the peace of a town had made an appointment of supervisor, supposing there had been a failure to elect one at the preceding town meeting, and on the trial of an information in the nature of a quo warranto against the person so appointed, it appeared that the presiding officers of the town meeting had declared at the close of their canvass that there was a tie vote between the two candidates; it was held that it was proper to prove on the trial that a vote had been given, intended for the relator, in which only the initial letters of his name were inserted, and which if allowed would have elected him. 5 *Denio*, 409. So, in such a case, the parties interested may go back of the ballot-box, and inquire into the legal qualifications of the voters voting at the election, and if it appears that such voters were disqualified for any reason, their votes will be discarded where it will change the result of the election. 25 *How.* 495; 30 *Barb.* 589. And the court will receive hearsay evidence showing such disqualification, as well as the oath of the voter himself. *Id. ibid.* So, the relator may show that in the return of the canvassers of one of the towns of the county, a mistake had occurred in omitting to state the number of votes given for each candidate; and such proof being given, whereby it appeared that the relator and not the defendant had received the greatest number of votes; it was held that the relator was duly elected; and this, too, although the other candidate held the certificate of the county canvassers showing his election to the office. 20 *Wend.* 12.

Upon the trial of the action, the *onus probandi* lies upon the defendant, who is required to prove his title to the office. The mere right to the office is tried, and not the use under color of right, which would be sufficient, ordinarily, to establish the right of the incumbent when collaterally questioned; and the defendant must rely upon the strength of his own title. 30 *Barb.* 591, *per* W. F. Allen, J.

Judgment in the action.] In such cases the judgment may be rendered upon the right of the defendant, and also upon the right of the party so alleged to be entitled; or it may be rendered only upon the right of the defendant, as justice may require. *Code*, § 436; 2 *Rev. Stat.* 582, *sec.* 31.

If the action is in the nature of a quo warranto, and brought against an alleged intruder upon a public office, the judgment of the court, if for the plaintiff, can only be a judgment of ouster, and for costs. And if the plaintiff claims damages to recover the fees collected by the defendant, he must assert such claim in a separate action to be brought for that purpose. 3 *Abb.* 233.

The court, in determining the claims of an individual to an office, may determine, also, the existence of the office itself. The question, therefore, whether a town has been legally erected may be tested in an action in the nature of a quo warranto, against one claiming to exercise the office of supervisor of such town. 24 *New York*, 86; and see 25 *Barb.* 254.

The court is authorized, as we have seen, to render judgment upon the relator's right, or to omit to do so, as justice may require; and where the facts upon which the relator's right depended were obscurely stated, the court declined to render such judgment—

leaving the question to be settled by a direct proceeding. 1 *Denio*, 389

The court will proceed and render judgment notwithstanding that the office has expired at the time when judgment on the right of the parties comes to be pronounced; this, for the reason, that the relators, if successful, are entitled to the costs of the action. 8 *Wend.* 396.

The statute further provides, that when a defendant, whether a natural person or a corporation, against whom the action shall have been brought, shall be adjudged guilty of usurping or intruding into, or unlawfully holding or exercising any office, franchise, or privilege, judgment shall be rendered that such defendant be excluded from such office, franchise, or privilege, and also that the plaintiff recover costs against such defendant. The court may, also, in its discretion, fine such defendant a sum, not exceeding two thousand dollars, which fine, when collected, is required to be paid into the treasury of the State. *Code*, § 441.

If it is adjudged that a corporation against which an action is brought pursuant to the statute, has, by neglect, abuse, or surrender, forfeited its corporate rights, privileges and franchises, judgment will be rendered that the corporation be excluded from such corporate rights, privileges and franchises, and that the corporation be dissolved. *Code*, § 442.

Proceedings if judgment is rendered in favor of party claiming an office.] If judgment is rendered upon the right of the person alleged to be entitled, and the same is in favor of such person, he will be entitled, after taking the oath of office, and executing such official bond as may be required by law, to take upon himself the execution of the office. *Code*, § 437. He becomes, in such a case, upon taking the official oath, and giving bonds *eo instanti*, invested with the office. 6 *Abb.* 220; 7 *How.* 282.

And it is his duty, immediately upon being invested with the office, to demand of the defendant in the action all the books and papers in his custody, or within his power, belonging to the office from which he has been excluded. *Code*, § 437. If the defendant refuses or neglects to deliver over such books or papers, pursuant to the demand, he will be deemed guilty of a misdemeanor, and the same proceedings may be had, and with the same effect, to compel the delivery of such books and papers as are prescribed in article five, title six, chapter five, of the first part of the Revised Statutes, *Code*, § 438; 2 *Rev. Stat.* 582, *secs.* 32, 33; in respect to which see *post*, Section ii. of this chapter, where the practice is considered at large.

If judgment is rendered upon the right of the person so alleged to be entitled, in favor of such person, he may recover, by action, the damages which he shall have sustained by reason of the usurpation by the defendant of the office from which such defendant has been excluded. *Code*, § 439. Thus, if the plaintiff claims damages against the defendant for the fees collected by him while holding the office from which he has been excluded, he must assert such claim in a separate action, to be brought by him for that purpose; and he cannot recover such damages in the action in the nature of a quo warranto, to determine the right to the office. 3 *Abb.* 233.

Costs of the action, and how collected.] The defeated party is liable to the other for the costs of the action, as well as for an extra allowance. 4 *Seld.* 71; 11 *Barb.* 337. The costs are regulated, and are to be taxed, the same as in other actions.

If judgment is rendered against a corporation, or against persons claiming to be a corporation, the court may cause the costs therein to be collected by execution against the persons claiming to be a corporation, or by attachment or process against the directors or other officers of such corporation. *Code*, § 443; 2 *Rev. Stat.* 585, *sec.* 50; 12 *Wend.* 277.

Restraining corporation, and appointment of receiver.] If the judgment is rendered against a corporation, the court has the same power to restrain the corporation, to appoint a receiver of its property and to take an account, and make distribution thereof among its creditors, as are given in article three, title four, chapter eight, of the third part of the Revised Statutes. 2 *Rev. Stat.* 467; and see *ante*, *vol.* 1, *p.* 242; *Code*, § 444.

And it is the duty of the attorney-general, immediately after the rendition of the judgment, to institute proceedings for that purpose. *Ib.*

Copy of judgment roll, where to be filed.] Upon the rendition of judgment against a corporation, or for the vacating or annulling of letters patent, it is the duty of the attorney-general to cause a copy of the judgment roll to be forthwith filed in the office of the Secretary of State. *Code*, § 445; 2 *Rev. Stat.* 580, *sec.* 24.

Entry of judgment relating to letters patent in the records of the commissioners of land office.] The Secretary of State, upon the filing of a copy of the judgment roll in his office, is required, if the record relates to letters patent, to make an entry in the records of the commissioners of the land office of the substance and effect of such judgment, and of the time when the record thereof was docketed; and the real property granted by such letters patent may thereafter be disposed of by such commissioners in the same manner as if such letters patent had never been issued. *Code*, § 446; 2 *Rev. Stat.* 580, *sec.* 25.

Actions for forfeiture of property to the people.] Whenever, by the provisions of law, any property, real or personal, shall be forfeited to the people of this State, or to any officer for their use, an action for the recovery of such property, alleging the grounds of the forfeiture, may be brought by the proper officer, in the Supreme Court. *Code*, § 447.

Appeals.] Appeals may be brought by an aggrieved party, the same as in other actions.

The action is a civil action, and the decisions of the Supreme Court in it are to be reviewed upon the principles applicable to such actions, and not by those which prevail in criminal proceedings. 4 *Seld.* 67.

NOTE. For new matter under the head of "Quo Warranto, etc.," see the Supplement at the end of this chapter, *post*, p. 210.

SECTION II.

PROCEEDINGS TO COMPEL THE DELIVERY OF BOOKS AND PAPERS BY PUBLIC OFFICERS TO THEIR SUCCESSORS.

THE proceedings to compel the delivery of books and papers by public officers to their successors are authorized by the fifth article, title six, chapter five, of the first part of the Revised Statutes. 1 *Rev. Stat.* 124.

To authorize this remedy, the applicant's title to the office must be clear and free from reasonable doubt. 6 *Hill*, 616, 631, *note*. His title cannot be determined in this proceeding. 2 *Barb. S. C.* 514; 5 *Abb.* 73; *Ib.* 282. And if he is not in possession of the office, he must first establish his title to the same by action to be brought for that purpose; and must show a regular judgment of ouster in his favor. 7 *How.* 173; *s. c.* 14 *Barb.* 396; 19 *How.* 323; 24 *Barb.* 588; *Code*, §§ 437, 438.

But it is sufficient if the applicant is in possession of the office under color of title, though if both parties claim to be in possession, and it is doubtful which is the actual occupant, the court will require the parties to have the right to the office determined by action before entertaining the proceeding. 24 *Barb.* 587; and see 15 *How.* 470, *s. c.* 6 *Abb.* 228; and see 5 *Abb.* 74; *Ib.* 282. Where, however, an office becomes vacant, and an individual, with claim and color of title, enters it, and assumes the duties thereof, he will be considered the officer *de facto*, and in possession of the office. And his forcible removal from the rooms occupied for the transaction of the business of the office, and from the presence of the property pertaining to it, will not affect his legal rights. 24 *Barb.* 587.

When books and papers to be delivered to successors.] The statute provides that, whenever any person shall be removed from office, or the term for which he shall have been elected or appointed shall expire, he shall, on demand, deliver over to his successor all the books and papers in his custody as such officer or in any way appertaining to his office. 1 *Rev. Stat.* 124, § 50. Every person violating the above provision of the statute, will be deemed guilty of a misdemeanor. *Ib.*

Proceedings if not delivered.] If any person shall refuse or neglect to deliver over to his successor any books or papers, as required by section 50 of the statute, such successor may make complaint thereof to any justice of the Supreme Court, or county judge of the county where the person so refusing shall reside; and if such officer be satisfied by the oath of the complainant, and such other testimony as shall be offered, that any such books or papers are withheld, he is required to grant an order, directing the person so refusing to show cause before him, within some short and reasonable time, why he should not be compelled to deliver the same. 1 *Rev. Stat.* 125, *sec.* 51.

At the time so appointed, or at any other time to which the matter may be adjourned, upon due proof being made of the service of such order, the officer is required to proceed to inquire into the circumstances. And if the person charged with withholding such books or papers shall make affidavit before such officer, that he has truly delivered over to his successor all such books and papers in his custody or appertaining to his office, within his knowledge, all further proceedings before such officer shall cease, and the person complained against shall be discharged. *Ib. sec.* 52.

Commitment and search warrant.] If the person complained against shall not make affidavit before such officer that he has truly delivered over to his successor, all such books and papers in his custody or appertaining to his office, within his knowledge, and it shall appear that any such books or papers are withheld, the officer, before the proceedings shall be had, shall, by warrant, commit the person so withholding, to the jail of the county, there to remain until he shall deliver such books and papers, or be otherwise discharged according to law. 1 *Rev. Stat.* 125, *sec.* 53.

Thus, where a person appointed to an office under a statute which provided that he should hold it only until the sense of the Governor and Senate should be declared, persisted in holding the office after the Governor and Senate had appointed a successor, who had a clear right. to the office, and the incumbent refused to deliver to his successor the books and papers appertaining to the office; it was held that it was a proper case for the issuing of a warrant to commit the incumbent to jail until he should surrender them. 2 *Barb. S. C.* 513.

In the case stated in section 53, above mentioned, if required by the complainant, the officer will also issue his warrant, directed to any sheriff or constable, commanding them, in the day time, to search such places as shall be designated in the warrant, for such books and papers as belonged to the officer so removed, or whose term of office expired, in his official capacity, and which appertained to such office, and seize and bring them before the officer issuing the warrant. 1 *Rev. Stat.* 125, *sec.* 54. And upon any books and papers being brought before the officer, by virtue of such warrant, he is required to inquire and examine whether the same appertain to the office, from which the person so refusing to deliver, was removed, or of which the term expired, and to cause the same to be delivered to the complainant. *Ib. sec.* 55.

The issuing of the warrant after the officer has decided that the applicant is entitled to the books and papers, is a ministerial and not a judicial act. 24 *Barb.* 636, *s. c.* 26 *Id.* 430.

The warrant should specify with reasonable precision, the books and papers which the party is charged with having in his possession; and the words, "the books and papers appertaining to the Street Commissioners' Department" are, it seems, an insufficient description of the books and papers to be delivered; and a party cannot be held, nor a search made, on a warrant containing no more precise description. 5 *Abb.* 282, 292, 315.

Proceedings when officer dies.] If any person appointed or elected to any office, shall die, or his office shall in any way become vacant, and any books or papers belonging or appertaining to such office shall come to the hands of any person, the successor to such office may, in like manner, as hereinbefore prescribed, demand such books or papers, from the person having the same in his possession; and on the same being withheld, an order may be obtained, and the person charged may, in like manner, make oath of the delivery of all such books and papers that ever came to his possession; and in case of omission to make such oath, and to deliver up the books and papers so demanded, such person may be committed to jail, and a search warrant may be issued, and the property seized by virtue thereof may be delivered to the complainant, as hereinbefore prescribed. 1 *Rev. Stat.* 125, *sec.* 56.

The above section, it seems, is an independent provision, intended to apply to cases of third persons who might come into the possession of books and papers belonging to a public office, and to cases not otherwise provided for. (*a*) 27 *How.* 154, *per* Miller, J.

Certiorari or appeal staying proceedings.] The decision of the officer may be reviewed in the Supreme Court by certiorari. 5 *Abb.* 182, *s. c.* 24 *Barb.* 636; 26 *Id.* 429; 5 *Abb.* 194, *s. c.* 26 *Barb.* 437; 6 *Abb.* 228, *s. c.* 15 *How.* 470; or by appeal under the act of 1854. *Laws of* 1854, *p.* 592, *ante*, vol. 1. pp. 19, 20.

The certiorari—common law—stays the proceedings of the officer. And if it is served after the decision and before the issuing of the warrants, the proceedings of the officer are suspended at that point. 5 *Abb.* 182, and other cases *supra.* An appeal, however, does not stay the proceedings unless the court, or one of the justices thereof, so order, which order may be upon such terms, as to security or otherwise, as may be just; such security not to exceed the amount required on an appeal to the Court of Appeals. *Laws of* 1854, *p.* 592, § 1, *ante*, vol. 1. pp. 19, 20.

Where an action has been brought to determine the right to an office, and judgment of ouster rendered, and an appeal taken from such judgment, such appeal will not operate to stay the proceedings before the officer on the application to compel the delivery of the books. 7 *How.* 282.

(*a*) See, also, 1 *Rev. Stat.* 358, *secs.* 5 to 9, containing special provisions for the delivery of books, papers and records, belonging to the office of supervisor, town clerk, commissioners of highways, commissioners of common schools, and overseers of the poor, of any town.

SUPPLEMENT TO CHAPTER XXVI.

The Code of Civil Procedure does not affect the proceedings by information in the nature of quo warranto; the sections of the Code of Procedure (§§ 428 to 446) are left unrepealed by the general repealing act. *Laws* 1877, *ch.* 417. The action, however, is prosecuted in the manner prescribed by the new Code.

The action in the nature of quo warranto does not lie against the secretary of a railroad company, holding his position as a mere servant thereof, and at the will of its directors. 1 *Lansing*, 202. Nor in favor of an individual, either as corporator or tax-payer, to determine the legality of the election of one claiming to hold a municipal office, or to restrain the exercise of unauthorized powers by the officers of a municipal corporation, or to restrain or avoid the illegal acts of the corporation, unless such individual is thereby affected in his private rights, as distinct from that of other corporators and tax-payers. 63 *N. Y.*, 320. Nor in favor of an individual to compel a municipal officer to cause an election to be held to fill a vacancy. *Ib.* Nor where such individual claims to hold a municipal office, to determine his right thereto, where no other person has claimed such office, and the defendant has not interfered with his legal rights as officer. *Ib.* So the action will not lie in the name of the people of the State for the redress of private wrongs. The people cannot intervene, except a distinct right on the part of the public is alleged in respect to the subject matter litigated. 57 *N. Y.*, 161. Nor will the action lie on behalf of the people to recover from a wrongdoer either money or other property belonging to a public corporation, or for damages for a fraud committed upon such corporation, and especially as against a wrongdoer who occupies no fiduciary or official relation to the corporation injured. 58 *N. Y.*, 1, reversing 13 *Abb.*, *N. S.*, 25. Though otherwise, now, by recent act of the Legislature. *Laws of* 1875, *ch.* 49, *p.* 43.

An intruder into a public office can only be removed by the State; and its decision as to whether or not an action shall be brought for that purpose, is final, and cannot be reviewed by the courts. 8 *Hun*, 334, citing 22 *Barb.*, 114.

The issue in an action to test the title to an office. If the action is brought by the attorney-general on behalf of the people, the issue is with the defendant to show that he has legal title to the office; that his possession is a legal and rightful one. 55 *N. Y.*, 525. Otherwise, however, where the action is brought on the relation of one claiming the office. Upon that issue the plaintiffs have the affirmative, and they must maintain it. *Ib.*; and see 1 *Lansing*, 309.

The issues are legal, and triable by jury. The action to try the title to a corporate office, to which there are several claimants, is one of legal, not equitable cognizance. The issues are strictly legal, and the trial thereof by a jury is the constitutional right of the parties. 57 *N. Y.*, 161; affirming same case, 5 *Lansing*, 251. And if, with such a cause of action, an equitable cause of action is united, both must be tried by a jury, unless a jury trial is waived. *Ib.* But, in such action, where the complaint and the nature of the case call for equitable relief, the cause regularly comes on for trial by the court; and a demand for a jury, made after the parties and witnesses are present, prepared for the trial, and plaintiff has opened the case, read the pleadings and rested, may be refused. 1 *Lansing*, 308.

An injunction is not an appropriate remedy in an action to remove a person from an office into which he has unlawfully intruded. 5 *Hun*, 452.

Judgment of ouster against a corporation. To justify a judgment of ouster against a corporation for the forfeiture of a vested franchise, because of the breach of a condition subsequent, the verdict must show the fact, not merely of the breach of the letter of the subsequent condition, but of its intent and meaning, and must find such facts as the court may adjudge to amount to a substantial breach of the condition. 47 *N. Y.*, 586.

Appointment of receiver. The judgment may direct the appointment of a receiver, although § 444 of the Code (*ante*, *p.* 204) makes it the duty of the attorney-general, immediately after the rendition of the judgment, to institute proceedings for that purpose. 53 *Barb.*, 98, affirmed, 42 *N. Y.*, 217.

Costs in the action. Proceedings in the nature of a quo warranto are a civil action, and the prevailing party is entitled to costs. Judgment for costs against the defendant is properly entered where judgment is rendered ousting him from the office, although the judgment also determines that the relator is not entitled to the office. 52 *N. Y.*, 576. Costs adjudged to the people, in actions prosecuted or defended by the attorney-general, may be applied by him to any of the purposes for which appropriations are made for his office. *Laws* 1874, *p.* 499; 1875, *p.* 420.

Amendment of § 434 *of the Code.* Where an action shall be brought by the attorney-general (*ante, p.* 195), on the relation or information of a person having an interest in the question, the name of such person shall be joined with the people as plaintiff, and in every such case the attorney-general may require as a condition for bringing such action, that satisfactory security shall be given to indemnify the people of this State against the costs and expenses to be incurred thereby; and in every case where such security is given, the measure of the compensation to be paid by such person or persons to the attorney-general, shall be left to the agreement of the parties, express or implied. *Laws of* 1867, *p.* 1926.

CHAPTER XXVII.

PROCEEDINGS TO ACQUIRE TITLE TO REAL ESTATE FOR RAILROAD PURPOSES.

THE first general law authorizing the incorporation of railroad companies, was passed in 1848. *Laws of* 1848, *p.* 221. That act did not give to the companies formed under it, the right to acquire title to real estate, except in those cases where such right was acquired by voluntary gift or purchase by the corporation. It did provide, however, that when the legislature should first declare the public utility of a proposed road, the corporation might thereupon enter upon, take possession of, and use such real estate and property as would be required for the construction and maintenance of their road, and the convenient accommodations of the same, making compensation in the manner provided by the statute, for all such real estate and property. *Ib.* § 20. And thus the law continued for two years, when it was repealed, and the act of April 2d, 1850, substituted in its place. *Laws of* 1850, *p.* 211.

By the last-mentioned act, the restriction upon the right of a company, duly organized under the statute, to acquire title to real estate, where the company was unable to agree for the purchase of the same, was removed, and railroad corporations thereafter, in such cases, were authorized to acquire title to real estate in the manner prescribed by the statute. *Ib.* 215, *sec.* 13. And that act, with the amendments and additions since made to it (*Laws of* 1851, *p.* 20; 1853, *p.* 79; 1854, *p.* 609; 1857, *p.* 94; *Gen. Acts, ch.* 444; 1862, *p.* 811; 1864, *p.* 1335), now constitutes the general railroad law of the State.

The right of the legislature to grant to railroad corporations the power to appropriate private property necessary for their use, on making compensation for the same, is well settled by authority. 1 *Seld.* 439; 5 *Id.* 100; 6 *Id.* 328; 42 *Barb.* 119; 39 *Id.* 494; 18 *Wend.* 9; 3 *Paige*, 45. And such power may be granted by a general act providing for the creation of an indefinite number of corporations, as well as by a special act organizing a particular corporation. 5 *Seld.* 100, 110; 23 *Pick.* 360.

But the power being in derogation of the common law, all the requirements of the statute, authorizing its exercise, must be strictly pursued. 6 *Seld.* 328, 329; and see 4 *Hill*, 76; 2 *Denio*, 323; 1 *Seld.* 439.

The proceeding to acquire the title to real estate is a special proceeding within the meaning of section 3 of the Code of Procedure. 10 *How.* 168; 1 *Kern.* 277.

In what cases application may be made.] The statute provides that in case any company, formed under the general law (*a*), is unable to agree for the purchase of any real estate required for the purposes of its incorporation, it shall have the right to acquire title to the same in the manner, and by the special proceedings prescribed by the statute. (*b*) *Laws of* 1850, *p.* 215, § 13.

But if the company was formed prior to the 25th of March, 1853, either under the act of 1848 or 1850, and has been duly continued in existence, to entitle it to the right to institute proceedings under the statute, at least ten thousand dollars for every mile of its railroad proposed to be constructed in this State, must be in good faith subscribed to its capital stock, and ten per cent. thereof paid in to the company. (*c*) *Laws of* 1853, *p.* 79.

(*a*) By section 49 of the General Law, the provisions of the statute relating to the proceedings to acquire title to real estate, here considered, were made to apply to all the existing railroad corporations within the State, where those provisions were not inconsistent with their charters. *Laws of* 1850, *p.* 235; and see 15 *Barb.* 43; 3 *Sand. S. C. R.* 689.

(*b*) Under a recent amendment of the statute, railroad corporations, after their construction, are authorized to acquire additional lands for switches, turn-outs, or for the flow of water and other purposes, and also the right to take and carry water from any spring, pond, creek or river, and the right of way to and from the same, etc. See *Laws of* 1869, *ch.* 237, amending § 21 of the General Law.

(*c*) A railroad company formed under the General Law, to entitle it to proceed under the statute, is now required to have at least ten thousand dollars for every mile of its proposed road to be constructed in this State, in good faith subscribed to its capital stock, and ten per cent. thereof paid in to the company. *Laws of* 1867, *p.* 1398.

By the statute, also, railroad corporations may institute proceedings to acquire title to real estate, as well where the parties own such real estate in fee simple absolute, as where they have estates in the premises for life, for years, at will, and by sufferance. So, where they have estates in the same, in possession or expectancy, or other estates enumerated in article one, of title two, of chapter one, of the second part of the Revised Statutes. (1 *Rev. Stat.* 722). *Laws of* 1857, *Pub. Acts*, *p.* 94, § 2, *ch.* 444.

A railroad company, as we have seen, is authorized to institute proceedings under the statute, to acquire title to real estate, only where it has been unable to agree for the purchase of the same. *Laws of* 1850, § 13, *supra.* In a somewhat analogous proceeding, where it was sought to acquire title to real estate under the act for supplying the city of New York with water, the statute authorizing the exercise of the power in cases where the water commissioners and owners disagree as to the amount of compensation; it was held to be necesssary, to give the officer jurisdiction, to show that an unsuccessful attempt had been made by the commissioners, to agree with the owners for the purchase of the land. "The legislature," says Foote, J., "manifestly intended to give the owner the benefit and opportunity of a voluntary sale, and required the respondents to make a fair and honest effort to purchase the land of him, before commencing proceedings to take it adversely. Hence the disagreement of the parties as to the amount of compensation was a material requirement of the statute, and an essential pre-requisite, without which, the vice-chancellor had not jurisdiction." 1 *Seld.* 439.

Petition and notice.] The statute provides that for the purpose of acquiring title to real estate, the company may present a petition, praying for the appointment of commissioners of appraisal, to the Supreme Court, at a special or general term thereof, held in the district in which the real estate described in the petition is situated. *Laws of* 1850, *p.* 216, § 14.

The petition must contain a description of the real estate which the company seeks to acquire; and must, in effect, state that the company is duly incorporated, and that it is its intention in good faith to construct and finish a railroad from and to the places named for that purpose in its articles of association; that the whole capital stock of the company has been in good faith subscribed as required by the statute; (*a*) that the company has surveyed the line or route of its proposed road, and made a map or survey thereof, by which such route or line is designated, and that they have located their railroad according to such survey, and filed certificates of such location, signed by a majority of the directors of the company, in the clerk's office of the several counties through or into which the said railroad is to be constructed; that the land described in the petition is required for the purpose of constructing or operating the proposed road; and that the company has not been able to acquire title thereto, and the reason of such inability. *Ib.* The petition must also state the names and places of residence of the parties, so far as the same can by reasonable diligence be ascertained, who own or have, or claim to own or have, estates or interests in the said real estate; and if any of such persons are infants, their ages, as near as may be, must be stated; and if any such persons are idiots, or persons of unsound mind, or are unknown, that fact must be stated, together with such other allegations and statements of liens or incumbrances on said real estate as the company may see fit to make. *Ib.* For form of petition, see *Appendix*, No. 560.

In case of proceedings against parties having future estates, or other estates enumerated in article one, of title two, of chapter one, of part two of the Revised Statutes (1 *Rev. Stat.* 722), the petition should set forth, in addition to the facts above required, the facts in relation to any such estate, and the person, persons, or class of persons, then in being or not in being, who are or may become entitled, in any contingency, to any estate as aforesaid, in such land. *Laws of* 1857, *vol.* 1, *p.* 874.

The petition should be signed and verified according to the rules and practice of the court in like cases. *Laws of* 1850, *p.* 216, § 14.

And it should be accompanied by a notice directed to the persons owning the real estate or interested in it, and stating the time and place, when and where the petition will be presented to the court. *Ib.* For form of notice, see *Appendix*, No. 561.

Petition and notice to be served.] A copy of the petition and

(*a*) Under the statute, as recently amended, a railroad company is entitled to institute the proceedings when at least ten thousand dollars for every mile of its railroad proposed to be constructed in this State shall be in good faith subscribed to its capital stock, and ten per cent. thereof paid in. *Laws of* 1867, *p.* 1398; *and see ante, p.* 212, *and note.*

notice is required to be served on all persons whose interests are to be affected by the proceedings; and this service must be made at least ten days prior to the presentation thereof to the court. *Laws of* 1850, *p*. 216, § 14; 20 *Barb*. 424.

An omission to make such service or a service for a shorter time than required by the statute, will render the proceedings irregular and void, 2 *Kern*. 190; though a voluntary appearance of the parties and contesting the proceedings on the single ground of the inadequacy of the damages awarded, would waive the irregularity. 1 *Seld*. 434. In a like proceeding, however, where the owner appeared before the officer at the time appointed for drawing the jury, and objected to the regularity of the proceedings, without averring the grounds of his objection, and on the day when the jury met to appraise the damages, again appeared and objected to the competency of one of the jurors, who was set aside; it was held that such appearance did not cure the defect as to notice, and that the proceedings were void. 2 *Kern*. 190.

How petition, &c., to be served.] The statute requires the petition and notice to be served as follows:

1. If the person on whom such service is to be made resides in this State, and is not an infant, idiot, or person of unsound mind, service of a copy of the petition and notice must be made on him or his agent or attorney, authorized to contract for the sale of the real estate described in the petition, personally, or by leaving the same at the usual place of residence of the person on whom service must be made, as aforesaid, with some person of suitable age.

2. If the person on whom the service is to be made resides out of the State, and has an agent residing in this State, authorized to contract for the sale of the real estate described in the petition, the service may be made on such agent or on such person personally out of the State; or it may be made by publishing the notice, stating briefly the object of the application, and giving a description of the land to be taken, in the State paper, and in a paper printed in the county in which the land to be taken is situated, once in each week for one month next previous to the presentation of the petition. (For form of notice, see *Appendix*. No. 562.) And if the residence of such person residing

out of this State, but in any of the United States, or any of the British Colonies in North America, is known, or can by reasonable diligence be ascertained, the company must, in addition to such publication as aforesaid, deposit a copy of the petition and notice in the post-office, properly folded and directed to such person at the post-office nearest to his place of residence, at least thirty days before presenting such petition to the court, and pay the postage chargeable thereon in the United States.

3. If any person on whom the service is to be made is under the age of twenty-one years, and resides in this State, such service shall be made as aforesaid on his general guardian; or if he has no such guardian, then on such infant personally, if he is over the age of fourteen years; and if under that age, then on the person who has the care of, or with whom such infant resides.

4. If the person on whom the service is to be made is an idiot, or of unsound mind, and resides in this State, such service may be made on the committee of his person or estate; or if he has no such committee, then on the person who has the care and charge of such idiot or person of unsound mind.

5. If the person on whom the service is to be made is unknown, or his residence is unknown, and cannot by reasonable diligence be ascertained, then such service may be made, under the direction of the court, by publishing a notice, stating the time and place the petition will be presented, the object thereof, with a description of the land to be affected by the proceedings, in the State paper, and in a paper printed in the county where the land is situated, once in each week for one month previous to the presentation of such petition. *Laws of* 1850, *p.* 216, § 14. For form of notice to unknown owners, see *Appendix*, No. 562.

If any of the parties to be affected by the proceedings are infants, idiots or persons of unsound mind, all notices required to be served in the progress of the proceedings may be served on the general or special guardians of such infants, or on the committees of such idiots or persons of unsound mind. *Ib.*

And in all cases not herein otherwise provided for, service of orders, notices and other papers in this proceeding may be made as the Supreme Court shall direct. *Ib.*

Guardian or committee for infants or lunatics.] The statute provides that in case any party to be affected by the proceedings is an infant, idiot, or of unsound mind, and has no general guardian or committee, the court shall appoint a special guardian or committee to attend to the interests of such person in the proceedings; but if a general guardian or committee has been appointed for such person in this State, it shall be the duty of such general guardian or committee to attend to the interests of such infant, idiot, or person of unsound mind; and the court may require such security to be given by such general or special guardian or committee as it may deem necessary to protect the rights of such infant, idiot, or person of unsound mind; and all notices required to be served in the progress of the proceedings may be served on such general or special guardian, or committee. *Laws of* 1850, *p.* 217, § 14, *sub.* 6; and see 36 *Barb.* 600.

A guardian or committee is entitled to such sum for costs, expenses and counsel fees in the proceedings as the commissioners appointed to appraise the land, or a majority of them, shall determine to be proper. *Laws of* 1854, *p.* 609; 1864, *p.* 1337, amending § 16 of General Law.

Attorneys to be appointed for unknown and other owners.] The court is required, by the statute, to appoint some competent attorney to appear for and protect the rights of any party in interest who is unknown, or whose residence is unknown, and who has not appeared in the proceedings by an attorney or agent. *Laws of* 1850, *p.* 220, *sec.* 20.

And so, where there is no attorney appearing in behalf of persons having future estates, or other estates enumerated in article one, title two, chapter one, of part two of the Revised Statutes (1 *Rev. Stat.* 722), the court is required to appoint some competent and disinterested attorney or officer of the court to appear in the proceedings, and represent the rights, interests and estate of the person or class of persons enumerated in said article, in any such land, and to protect the same, on the appraisal and other proceedings. *Laws of* 1857, *vol.* 1, *p.* 871.

The attorney appointed is entitled to such sum for his costs, expenses and counsel fees in the proceeding as the commissioners appointed to appraise the land, or a majority of them, may determine to be proper. *Laws of* 1854, *p.* 609; 1864, *p.* 1337, amending § 16 of General Law

Application to court and proceedings thereon.] The statute provides, that on presenting the petition to the Supreme Court, with proof of the service of a copy thereof and of the notice, as required by the statute, all or any of the persons whose estates or interests are to be affected by the proceedings, may show cause against granting the prayer of the petition, and may disprove any of the facts alleged in it. And the court is required to hear the proofs and allegations of the parties, and if no sufficient cause is shown against granting the prayer of the petition, it shall make an order for the appointment of three disinterested and competent freeholders, who reside in the county or some adjoining county where the premises to be appraised are situated, commissioners to ascertain and appraise the compensation to be made to the owners or persons interested in the real estate proposed to be taken in such county for the purposes of the company, and to fix the time and place for the first meeting of the commissioners. *Laws of* 1854, *p.* 609, amending § 15 of the General Law. For form of order, see *Appendix*, No. 563.

It seems that if the facts alleged in the petition are denied by the owner, upon which an issue is formed, the proof required to be produced by the owner to disprove the facts alleged, must be legal evidence; and that the party's own affidavit, or any other affidavit, will not answer. 6 *How.* 96.

The court may appoint commissioners to appraise all the lands proposed to be taken in a county, though owned by different parties. The sixteenth section of the statute contemplates a succession of appraisals by the same commissioners; and one report may embrace all the cases. And so, it seems, the court may fill more than one commission, where good cause therefor is shown; though this would not be done unless clearly necessary. *Id.* 238.

Objections to the regularity of the proceedings; as, that the petition is not properly verified, or that it does not appear by the petition that the company has been unable to agree for the purchase of the right of way; must be taken at the time of the presentation of the petition. And it is too late to raise such objections on the motion for the confirmation of the commissioners' report. 5 *Id.* 177.

The commissioners and their proceedings.] The commissioners, before proceeding to the discharge of their duties, are each required to take and subscribe an oath to support the constitution of the United States, and the constitution of the State of New York, and faithfully to discharge the duties of his office of commissioner according to the best of his ability. *Laws of* 1854, *p.* 609; 1864, *p.* 1336; amending section 16 of General Law. For form of oath, see *Appendix*, No 564.

Any one of the commissioners may issue subpœnas and administer oaths to witnesses. And a majority of them may adjourn the proceedings before them, from time to time, in their discretion. *Ib.*

Whenever they meet, except by the appointment of the court or pursuant to adjournment, they must cause reasonable notice of their meeting to be given to the parties interested, or their agent, or their attorney. *Ib.* And all parties claiming damages, should attend the meetings of the commissioners and make their objections; otherwise, if the proceedings are regular, they will have no redress unless by leave of the commissioners. 5 *How.* 177.

The statute also provides, that the commissioners shall view the premises described in the petition, and hear the proofs and allegations of the parties, and reduce the testimony taken by them, if any, to writing, and after the testimony in each case is closed, they or a majority of them, all being present, shall, without any unnecessray delay, and before proceeding to the examination of any other claim, ascertain and determine the compensation which ought justly to be made by the company to the owners, or persons interested in the real estate appraised by them. *Ib.*

The commissioners, upon the hearing, have the right to hear the proofs and allegations in such order as they may deem most conducive to justice between the parties, and to decide which party shall open and which shall close the argument. 16 *Barb.* 68.

And in determining the compensation to be made to a party, they are to exercise their own judgment, formed upon a view of the premises, in connection with the testimony of the witnesses before them, and not to the exclusion of it. 6 *How.* 467. They are to be guided in their proceedings by the established rules of evidence; and no testimony should be received which a court of law would reject, and none rejected which a court of law would hold to be admissible. 16 *Barb.* 100. Opinions of witnesses as to the value of the land from which the road is taken, as a whole, and how its value will be affected by severing the portion proposed to be taken for the purposes of the company, are competent as evidence. Though the opinions of witnesses as to how much damage or injury the party whose lands are taken will sustain, otherwise than by diminishing the value of his property, are incompetent. 6 *How.* 467; and see 16 *Barb* 100.

And so, where the question is as to the amount of compensation which ought to be awarded to a turnpike company, for granting to a railroad company an easement, or right of way, across their road, the opinions or conjectures of witnesses as to the effect the use of the railroad will produce in frightening horses traveling upon the turnpike, at a particular place; or as to the necessity for diverting the line of the turnpike, at another place, and the cost of such diversion; or that a bridge ought to be built by the railroad company at a crossing; or as to the amount of damages the turnpike company will sustain by reason of the crossing of their road, are inadmissible in evidence. *Ib.*

In the case last stated, any proof having a legitimate bearing upon the question to be determined, and which, by the established rules of evidence, would be received in a court of law, should be received; and all other proof should be rejected. And it will be assumed, in such a case, that the railroad company will, as required by law, restore the turnpike to such a state as not necessarily to impair its usefulness. And the consideration that the business of the turnpike will be diminished by the construction of the railroad along the same general line of travel, should be disregarded. *Ib.*

In determining the amount of compensation, the rule is, to determine what will be the effect of the proposed change upon the market value of the property remaining. The proper inquiry is, what is the entire property now fairly worth in the market, and what will that part not taken be worth after the improvement is made. 13 *Barb.* 169; and see 16 *Id.* 273.

And in determining such compensation, the commissioners are forbidden by the statute from making any allowance or deduction on account of any real or supposed benefits which the parties interested may derive from the construction of the proposed railroad, or the construction of the proposed improvement connected with the road, for which such real estate may be taken. *Laws of* 1854, *p.* 609; 1864, *p.* 1336, amending § 16 of General Law. The intention of the statute is, to confine the commissioners to an estimate of the price to be paid by the company to the owner of the land, regardless of the benefits or injuries which might result to him as the owner of the adjoining land, in consequence of the contemplated improvement. 16 *Barb.* 68. It is a proper rule, however, for the commissioners to adopt, that they will allow full compensation for the land taken, including therein the damages to the adjacent land by reason of such taking; though they should not allow consequential and prospective damages. *Ib.* And the commissioners are not to be confined in their estimate of the damages, to the actual abstract value of the land to be taken, as though the owner would have no other lands left to be affected by the improvement. They are to consider how the *taking* of the land, not how *the use* of it in any particular mode, will affect the residue of the owner's land, and award compensation accordingly. And, therefore, it is correct for them to reject conjectural evidence, offered for the purpose of showing that the owner might be injuriously affected, should a railroad be constructed and used upon the land to be taken. *Ib.;* and 16 *Barb.* 273.

The commissioners cannot appraise the land taken for a railroad, with a reservation of easements and privileges to the owner; but they must appraise it at its actual value. And, therefore, where the inquisition stated that the award of damages was "based on the supposition and made on the condition and with the understanding" that the owners of the land might open a street across the railroad; it was held that the appraisement was illegal, and that the inquisition should be set aside. 5 *Denio*, 206.

The statute also provides that the commissioners, or a majority of them, shall determine what sum ought to be paid to the general or special guardian of an infant, or committee of an idiot, or person of unsound mind, or to an attorney appointed by the court to attend to the interests of any unknown owner or party in interest not personally served with notice of the proceedings, and who has not appeared, for costs, expenses, and counsel fees. *Laws of* 1854, *p.* 609, § 3; and 1864, *p.* 1336, amending § 16 of General Law.

Where the commissioners have made a report to the court, and by an order are permitted to amend or correct it, so as to conform it to the state of facts which existed, they have no right, at the time of such correction, to hear proofs by claimants as to damages. When they have viewed the premises and decided upon the amount of damages to be paid, their powers under their appointment are exhausted, so far as the amount of damages is concerned, until the further order of the court. 5 *How.* 177.

Commissioners' report, and fees.] The statute requires the commissioners to make a report of their proceedings to the Supreme Court, with the minutes of the testimony taken by them, if any. *Laws of* 1854, *p.* 609; 1864, *p.* 1336, *supra.* And where there has been an appraisal of several different parcels of land, one report may embrace all the cases. 6 *How.* 238.

It is sufficient if the report is signed by a majority of the commissioners, and it is not necessary that all of the commissioners should be present at the signing. 10 *How.* 169. For form of report, see *Appendix*, No. 565.

The commissioners, by the statute, are each entitled to five dollars for services and expenses for every day they are actually engaged in the performance of their duties, to be paid by the company, except where the owners or persons interested in the real estate fail to have awarded them more than the amount of compensation offered them by the company before the appointment of commissioners, then to be paid by the said owners or persons interested, or if not paid by them, to be paid by the company, and deducted from the amount awarded. *Laws of* 1864, *p.* 1336, amending § 16 of General Law.

Motion to set aside report.] The statute does not give the court power to set aside the report of the commissioners, upon motion for that purpose; and the only remedy of the party is by appeal. 7 *How.* 164; and see 5 *Id.* 182; 21 *Id.* 434.

If, however, the report should be untrue in any material respect, or the proceedings of the commissioners have been irregular, and the report fails to state the facts constituting such irregularity, upon a proper application, directly made to the court, on the part of the person opposed to the confirmation, the court will set aside and vacate the report. 10 *How.* 168, 173. On such application either party would have the opportunity of spreading before the court all the facts in their power to furnish, bearing upon the questions of the truth of the report, and the regularity of the proceedings of the commissioners. And in view of such application, the court, or a judge thereof, would, if necessary, order the proceedings on the part of the company to have the report confirmed, stayed, as in the case of other motions, until the motion to set the report aside should be determined. *Ib., per* Welles, J.

Order confirming report.] After the commissioners have made their report, proceedings should be taken to have the same confirmed by the court. Until the report is confirmed, the proceeding is still incomplete, and neither party has any vested right, neither the company, to the lands, nor the owner to the money awarded. 3 *Sand. Sup. C. R.* 689. *Laws of* 1850, *p.* 219, § 18.

It is provided by the statute that on the report being made by the commissioners, the company shall give notice to the parties or their attorneys, to be affected by the proceedings, according to the rules and practice of the court, at a general or special term thereof, for the confirmation of the report. *Laws of* 1850, *p.* 219, § 17. For form of notice, see *Appendix*, No. 566.

The notice should be served, at least eight days before the first day of the term at which the motion is to be made; and should be accompanied with a copy of the commissioners' report. *Code*, §§ 402, 412; *Sup. Court Rules*, No. 49.

At the term specified in the notice, the court is required to confirm the report, and to make an order containing a recital of the substance of the proceedings in the matter of the appraisal, and a description of the real estate appraised, for which compensation is to be made. It will also direct to whom the money is to be paid, or in what bank, and in what manner it shall be deposited by the company. *Laws of* 1850, *p.* 219, § 17. For form of order, see *Appendix*, No. 567.

It is made the duty of the court, also, on or after the confirmation of the report, to ascertain by the report, or by a reference for that purpose, or otherwise, in its discretion, the rights, interest, and estate of persons having future estates or other estates enumerated in article one, of title two, of chapter one, of second part of the Revised Statutes (1 *Rev. Stat.* 722), in the land appraised, and in the compensation awarded therefor, and to make an order determining the amount or share of such compensation, to which such persons or class of persons are or may become entitled on account of such estate, as the same shall arise or become vested in them respectively, and to direct and provide for the payment, investment, or securing thereof, for the benefit of the persons or class of persons aforesaid, who are, or may, in the contingency upon which the estate arises, become entitled thereto. *Laws of* 1857, *vol.* 1, *p.* 871.

If it appears that the commissioners have been regular in their proceedings, and that due notice of the motion for confirmation has been given, it is a matter of course to confirm the report. 5 *How.* 177; 10 *Id.* 168. And no affidavit or other proof will be heard on the application, to contradict or impeach the truth of the matters contained in it. *Ib.* Nor will the court, on such application, review or examine any error of law committed by the commissioners in their decision of the merits, or upon the admission or rejection of evidence. *Ib.* Nor any question in respect to the regularity of the proceedings; as, that the petition is not properly verified, or, that it does not appear by the petition that the company has been unable to agree with the owner for the purchase of the real estate in question. 5 *Id.* 177. Though where neither the report, nor any of the proceedings which precede it, properly designate the lands proposed to be taken, it seems the court will, on the motion to confirm the report, consider the objection, and correct the defect complained of. 21 *How.* 434.

Nor will a commissioner, on application to confirm a report which he has properly signed, be permitted to stultify himself in any case by alleging that he signed the report without reading or hearing it read. 10 *Id.* 169, and see 1 *Barb. S. C. R.* 326; 2 *Id.* 482.

A certified copy of the order confirming the report, is required to be recorded at full length in the clerk's office of the county in which the land described in it is situated. *Laws of* 1850, *p.* 219, § 18.

Effect of the order, &c.] The statute provides that upon recording the order confirming the commissioners' report, and on the payment or deposit by the company of the sums to be paid as compensation for the land, and for the costs, expenses and counsel fees of a guardian, committee or attorney appointed for, or representing, any of the parties in interest, as directed by the order, the company shall be entitled to enter upon, to take possession of and to use the said land for the purposes of its incorporation, during the continuance of its corporate existence, by virtue of this or any other act; and that all persons who have been made parties to the proceedings shall be divested and barred of all right, estate, and interest in such real estate, during the corporate existence of the company. *Laws of* 1850, *p.* 219, § 18. And all real estate acquired by any company under and pursuant to the provisions of the statute, for the purposes of its incorporation, shall be deemed to be acquired for public use. *Ib.*

It is further provided, by statute, in respect to persons having future estates, or other estates enumerated in article one, of title two, of chapter one, of the second part of the Revised Statutes (1 *Rev. Stat.* 722), that upon the company paying or securing the amount or share to which such persons are entitled, in the manner directed by the order of the court, the company shall be deemed to have acquired, and will be vested with, the estate which such persons, or class of persons, have or may be entitled to in said land; and that they shall be barred of and from all right or claim in and to such land. *Laws of* 1857, *vol.* 1, *p.* 871, § 2. (*a*)

The company, however, obtains no greater right or title to the land than the parties possessed, against whom the proceedings are instituted. 9 *How.* 554. Upon recording the order, and paying or depositing the money as required by the statute, the title of the parties proceeded against, to the premises taken, becomes wholly vested in the company. *Id.* 467. And the company is entitled to enter upon and take possession of the land; and the owners become divested and barred of all their interest

---

(*a*) It is also provided in the same section, that any corporation may acquire the title in fee, by proceedings under the statute, to any land which it may require for roadway, and for necessary buildings, depots, and freight grounds.

in the same. They have no longer any legal right to keep the company out of possession; and if they resist the agents of the company, in their attempt to take possession, they will be guilty of an unlawful act. This, however, will not authorize the issuing of a writ of possession, or assistance, upon the application of the company. 16 *Barb.* 270.

But the title which the company acquires is qualified as being taken for public use, and is subject to the exercise by the legis- ture of all the powers to which the franchises of the corporation are subject. 24 *New York*, 345.

It is subject, too, to the duty, on the part of the company, to make and maintain suitable farm crossings, and the right of passage on the part of the former owner over the road at those crossings. 12 *Barb.* 227.

In respect to subsequent transfers of the property after the institution by the company of proceedings to acquire the title to land, the statute provides, that when any such proceedings shall have been commenced, no change of ownership by voluntary conveyance or transfer of the real estate, or any interest therein, or of the subject matter of the appraisal, shall in any manner affect such proceedings; but the same may be carried on and perfected, as if no such conveyance or transfer had been made or attempted to be made. *Laws of* 1854, *p.* 610, § 6.

Power of court, amendments, &c.] The court has the power, at any time, to amend any defect or informality in any of the proceedings authorized by the statute, as may be necessary; or to cause new parties to be added, and to direct such further notices to be given, to any party in interest, as it deems proper, and also to appoint other commissioners in place of any who shall die, or refuse, or neglect to serve, or be incapable of serving. *Laws of* 1850, *p.* 220, § 20.

And where the mode or manner of conducting all or any of the proceedings to the appraisal, and the proceedings consequent thereon, are not expressly provided for by the statute, the court before which the proceedings may be pending, has the power to make all the necessary orders and give the proper directions to carry into effect the object and intent of the statute; and the practice in such cases shall conform as near as may be to the ordinary practice in such courts. *Laws of* 1854, *p.* 610, § 5.

Appeals and proceedings thereon.] The statute provides, that within twenty days after the confirmation of the report of the commissioners, as provided for in the 17th section of the statute (*supra*), either party may appeal, by notice in writing to the other, to the Supreme Court, from the appraisal and report of the commissioners. *Laws of* 1850, *p.* 220, § 18. For form of notice, see *Appendix*, No. 568.

The appeal is required to be heard by the Supreme Court, at a general or special term thereof, on notice thereof being given, according to the rules and practice of the court. *Ib.* For form of notice of hearing, see *Appendix*, No. 569.

If an order is made at the special term, an appeal may be taken to the general term; so held on an appeal from an order confirming the commissioners' report. 10 *How.* 168; *Laws of* 1854, *ch.* 270, *ante*, *vol.* 1, *p.* 19.

But no appeal will lie from the decision of the general term to the Court of Appeals. So held, where the report of the commissioners was confirmed at the special term; from which decision an appeal was taken to the general term, and a new appraisal refused, and the report and proceedings affirmed, from which last decision an appeal was taken to the Court of Appeals. 1 *Kern.* 276.

On the hearing of the appeal, the court may direct a new appraisal before the same or new commissioners in its discretion; the second report to be final and conclusive on all parties interested. If the amount of the compensation to be made by the company is increased by the second report, the difference will be a lien on the land appraised, and shall be paid by the company to the parties entitled to the same, or shall be deposited in the bank, as the court shall direct; and if the amount is diminished, the difference shall be refunded to the company by the party to whom the same may have been paid; the judgment therefor may be rendered by the court, on the filing of the second report, against the party liable to pay the same. *Laws of* 1850, *p.* 220, § 18.

No affidavits can be read on the hearing of the appeal; but the court must act solely upon the report of the commissioners. 6 *How.* 223; 5 *Id.* 177.

The court, on the appeal, will not interfere with the proceedings of the commissioners unless satisfied that some substantial error has been committed. And their award will not be set aside for every technical error, in respect to the admission or rejection of evidence. The error should be of such a character as to show that the commissioners have misapprehended the principles upon which they were to make their appraisal, and that the party appealing may have been injuriously affected by such misapprehension. 16 *Barb.* 100; 13 *Id.* 169. And where evidence has been rejected which the party was entitled to give and have considered, by the commissioners, and which, had it been received, might have led to a more favorable determination for him, the report will be set aside. 6 *How.* 467.

By the statute, as we have seen, on the hearing of the appeal, the court may direct a new appraisal before the same or new commissioners; but this does not entitle a party as a matter of right to a second hearing and appraisal. *Ib.* 223.

The appeal is not to affect the possession by the company of the land appraised; and where the appeal is made by others than the company, it cannot be heard, except on a stipulation of the party appealing, not to disturb such possession. *Laws of* 1850, *p.* 220, § 18.

Proceedings if title proves defective.] The statute provides, that if, at any time after an attempt to acquire title by appraisal of damages or otherwise, it shall be found that the title thereby attempted to be acquired is defective, the company may proceed anew to acquire or perfect such title in the same manner as if no appraisal had been made; and at any stage of such new proceedings, the court may authorize the corporation, if in possession, to continue in possession, and, if not in possession, to take possession, and use such real estate during the pendency and until the final conclusion of such new proceedings; and may stay all actions or proceedings against the company on account thereof, on such company paying into court a sufficient sum, or giving security as the court may direct, to pay the compensation therefor when finally ascertained; and in every such case, the party interested in such real estate may conduct the proceedings to a conclusion, if the company delays or omits to prosecute the same. *Laws of* 1850, *p.* 221, § 21.

The existence of a mortgage which is a lien upon land taken and used by a railroad company for the purpose of constructing and operating its road, is one of the defects contemplated by the above section. And the company need not wait until the mortgaged premises are sold under a decree of foreclosure; but on discovering the existence of the incumbrance, they may proceed immediately, and on complying with all the provisions of the statute, may have the lien extinguished, as to the land occupied by them. 20 *Barb.* 419. The object of the statute was to enable a railroad company to acquire perfect title to real estate upon which their road should be located, unincumbered by any lien of mortgage, judgment or otherwise. *Ib.* 425, *per* C. L. Allen, J.; and see 16 *How.* 575.

Reference, &c., in respect to claimants of money.] If there are adverse and conflicting claimants to the money, or any part of it, to be paid as compensation for the real estate taken, the court may direct the money to be paid into the Supreme Court by the company, and may determine who is entitled to the same, and direct to whom the same shall be paid; and may, in its discretion, order a reference to ascertain the facts on which such determination and order are to be made. *Laws of* 1850, *p.* 220, § 19; 20 *Barb.* 425.

And so, in cases of proceedings to acquire the interest of parties having future estates or other estates enumerated in article one, of title two, of chapter one, of part two of the Revised Statutes (1 *Rev. Stat.* 722), it is the duty of the court, on or after the confirmation of the commissioners' report, to ascertain by the report or by a reference for that purpose, or otherwise in its discretion, the rights, interest and estate of such persons or class of persons in the lands appraised, and in the compensation awarded therefor, and to make an order determining the amount or share of such compensation to which such persons or class of persons are or may become entitled on account of such estate, as the same shall arise or become vested in them respectively, and to direct and provide for the payment, investment, or securing thereof, for the benefit of the persons or class of persons aforesaid, who are, or may in the contingency upon which such estate arises, become entitled thereto. *Laws of* 1857, *vol.* 1, *p.* 871, § 2.

Title, how acquired, when held in trust, or by infants, &c.]

It is provided by the statute that in case any title or interest in real estate required by any railroad company for the purposes of its incorporation, shall be vested in any trustee not authorized tc sell, release, and convey the same, or in any infant, idiot, or person of unsound mind, the Supreme Court shall have the power, by a summary proceeding on petition, to authorize and empower such trustee, or the general guardian or committee of such infant, idiot, or person of unsound mind, to sell and convey the same to such company for the purposes of its incorporation, on such terms as may be just; and in case any such infant, idiot, or person of unsound mind has no general guardian or committee, the court may appoint a special guardian or committee for the purpose of making such sale, release or conveyance, and may require such security from such general or special guardian or committee as the court may deem proper. *Laws of* 1850, *p.* 211, §§ 26, 49; 9 *How.* 554.

But before any conveyance or release authorized by the above section shall be executed, the terms on which the same is to be executed shall be reported to the court, on oath; and if the court is satisfied that such terms are just to the party interested in such real estate, the court shall confirm the report, and direct the proper conveyance or release to be executed, which shall have the same effect as if executed by an owner of said land, having legal power to sell and convey the same. *Laws of* 1850, *p.* 211, § 26.

SUPPLEMENT TO CHAPTER XXVII.

I. DECISIONS OF THE COURTS.

The subject in general. The taking of private property for public uses is in derogation of private right; and the statute authorizing it is not to be extended by inference or implication. 43 *N. Y.*, 137. The proceeding to acquire lands for railroad purposes, is a special proceeding; though it is analogous in its purpose and scope to an action. 55 *Id.*, 145.

In what cases the proceeding is proper. A railroad company cannot take land simply for the purpose of removing gravel therefrom to be used in constructing a distant portion of its road. 1 *Hun*, 496. Nor can it acquire land for speculation or sale, or to prevent interference by competing lines or methods of transportation, or in aid of collateral enterprises remotely connected with the running or operating of the road, although they may increase its revenues and business. 43 *N. Y.*, 146, *per* Andrews, J. Nor can it acquire title to property already dedicated to and held for another public use by authority of law, except in the cases expressly authorized by the statute; and therefore a railroad company cannot take lands held by a municipal corporation in trust for the use of the public, as a public park or common. 53 *N. Y.*, 574. A railroad company may acquire necessary land for its depot, freight, cattle and live stock business; and for the purpose of approaching those structures when erected. 5 *Hun*, 201.

A reasonable necessity for taking the lands must be shown by the company. The question is one of strict practicability; and a reasonable discretion must be allowed to the officers who locate the tracks. 5 *Hun*, 201. But their determination is not conclusive. It is for the court to decide upon the necessity and extent of the lands required. 43 *N. Y.*, 137.

The petition upon which the application is founded. Where a company after the construction of its road seeks to acquire additional lands under the provisions of, chapter 237, of the Laws of 1869 (*ante, p.* 212, note *b*, and Supplement at the end of this chapter) the petition should disclose the specific purpose to which it is intended to apply the land. 5 *Hun*, 86. But it is not necessary to state all the facts which were required to be stated in the original petition; nor is it necessary to make and file the maps which were required when the company first applied to acquire lands for its road. 4 *Hun*, 381.

Restraining the proceedings. An action is not proper for the purpose of restraining a company from proceedings to acquire land on the ground that the statute authorizing them is unconstitutional, when that question can be presented and passed upon in the proceedings themselves. 6 *Hun*, 24.

On the application to the court, the burden is upon the owner of the land to prove, by legal evidence, that the facts alleged in the petition are not true. An affidavit or answer is not sufficient evidence for that purpose. 4 *Hun* 635.

Proceedings of the commissioners. The commissioners need not be controlled by the evidence taken before them as to the value of the property, but must decide according to their own judgment; and if they should decide without evidence, it would be regular. 5 *Lansing*, 298. Evidence may be given before the commissioners of the intended use of the land, as part of the *res gesta*, to show the circumstances under which the land was taken, and its situation when appropriated. *Ib.*

Compensation to owner; appraisal of damages. The compensation is not confined to the value of the land actually taken, nor to the depreciation of the residue by the separation of the other part from it; but the owner is entitled to compensation for all the injury that the taking of the land for the purposes intended, will cause him. 56 *Barb.*, 456. Where only a portion of a lot is taken for the roadway of a railroad, the question is, what will the lot bring as a whole in the market after the road is constructed. And everything which will depreciate the value of that residue is to be taken into the account; *e. g.*, the use to which the land is to be appropriated; and if such use depreciates the value of the residue, the owner is entitled to compensation therefor. *Ib.*, and see 6 *Hun*, 149; but see 53 *Barb.*, 457. Again, the proper inquiry for the commissioners is, what is the fair marketable value of the whole property, and what will be the fair marketable value of the property not taken? The difference will be the sum to be awarded for compensation. 9 *Hun.*, 104. It is not the advantage to the company, but the detriment to the landowner, for which compensation is to be made. Thus, where a railroad company, after expending several thousand dollars in making a rock excavation and embankments, abandoned the route. Another company sought to acquire this land from the owner who had purchased it from the old company. The commissioners allowed him only $525; and their award was sustained, the court holding that the owner was not entitled to receive the amount expended by the old company, but only the fair market value of the land taken. *Ib.*

Discontinuing proceedings. Until the confirmation of the commissioners' report, there is no obligation on the part of the company to take the land which is the subject of the proceeding, and the court may at any time prior to such confirmation, on the application of the company, discontinue the proceeding. 4 *Hun*, 311. Otherwise, however, after the confirmation of the report; which fixes the rights and obligations of both parties, subject only to the right of appeal given by the statute. 8 *Hun*, 34. But see the recent statute authorizing a company to abandon proceedings after confirmation. *Laws of* 1876, p. 203 *post.*

Motion to set aside report. Where it appeared that the commissioners had talked privately with a person from whom they had obtained information discrediting the testimony of the claimant, and that the award to him was greatly inadequate; it appearing also that the neglect to oppose the confirmation of the report arose from the neglect or misbehavior of his attorney, upon whom the notice of motion was served; it was held that the report was properly set aside. 5 *Hun*, 105.

Order confirming report. The order confirming the report of the commissioners is not repugnant to the constitutional provision against private property being taken for public use without just compensation, because, instead of directing the compensation for the land to be paid to the owner, it directs the deposit thereof in bank subject to the order of the court. 60 *N. Y.*, 116. Nor does it affect the validity of the order whether the money is directed to be drawn out on an *ex parte* application, or upon motion. *Ib.*

Effect of the order. When a railroad company is authorized to acquire by legal proceedings only the use of lands for the purpose of operating its road, the fee remains in the owner subject to that use, and on the discontinuance of the use the owner may resume possession. 60 *N. Y.*, 242.

Appeals and proceedings thereon. From the order of the General Term an appeal in these proceedings lies to the Court of Appeals. 43 *Barb.*, 137.

The testimony taken by the commissioners and annexed to their report, is to be considered a part of the report, for the purpose of a review of their proceedings. 5 *Lansing*, 298.

The title, when held in trust, etc. The provision of the statute authorizing the taking of lands when the title is vested in any trustee not authorized to sell, etc. (*ante, p.* 229), has reference only to private and individual, not to public, trusts. 53 *N. Y.*, 575. And it is for the benefit of the trustee and infant or idiot owner, and is not compulsory upon railroad companies. 4 *Hun*, 636.

The court may put a company into the possession of land acquired by it under the proceedings considered in this chapter. 60 *N. Y.*, 116; 8 *Hun*, 35.

Costs in the proceedings. The costs may be allowed or not, in the discretion of the court, and when allowed are regulated by the Code of Procedure. *Laws* 1854, *p.* 592, *ante*, vol. 1, *pp.* 19, 20; 4 *Hun*, 311. But the costs are simply those to which the party is of right entitled, and do not include an extra allowance. 55 *N. Y.*, 145.

II. STATUTORY AMENDMENTS AND ADDITIONS.

By ch. 515 *of the Laws of* 1867 every railroad company, formed under the general law, to entitle it to proceed under the statute, is now required to have at least ten thousand dollars for every mile of its proposed road to be constructed in this State in good faith subscribed to its capital stock, and ten per cent. thereof paid in to the company. *Laws* 1867, *p.* 1398.

By ch. 560 *of the Laws of* 1871, whenever the gauge of a proposed railroad is three feet and six inches or less, but not less than thirty inches within the rails, the company may, whenever six thousand dollars for every mile of its proposed road to be constructed in this State is in good faith subscribed to the capital stock, and ten per cent. thereon paid in good faith, in cash, proceed to acquire title to the lands necessary for its purposes. *Laws of* 1871, *p.* 1184, *sec.* 6.

By ch. 198 *of the Laws of* 1876, section eighteen of the General Law (*ante, pp.* 223 to 225) is amended by requiring the company to pay, in addition to the sum awarded and the costs, etc., *interest upon the same* from the date of the order, to entitle it to enter upon and take possession of the land. The section is also amended by the insertion in it of the following paragraph: "If the company shall neglect to have such order recorded and to make the payment or deposit as herein provided, for the period of ten days after the date of such order, any party to such proceedings and interested therein may at his election cause a certified copy of the said order to be recorded as aforesaid, and thereupon the moneys therein directed to be paid with interest thereon from the date of said order, shall be a debt against the company, and the same shall be a lien on such real estate, and may be enforced and collected by action at law or in equity in the Supreme Court with costs. Except, nevertheless, the company may abandon such proceedings by filing within thirty days, after notice in writing, of such recorded order, in the office of such clerk, a notice of its determination to do so, and paying the reasonable costs and expenses of such party to be ascertained and adjusted, on motion by the court, making such order. But, in case of such abandonment, the company shall not renew proceedings to acquire title to such lands without a tender or deposit in court of the amount of said award and the interest thereon." *Laws of* 1876, *p.* 204, *sec.* 1.

By the same chapter (*Laws* 1876, *ch.* 198) it is provided that whenever any land required by a railroad company for the purpose of its road, is contained in, or forms a part of any street or avenue in any city or village in which the owners of adjoining lands on the line of such street or avenue claim a right of property or the fee thereof, in such case the notice to be given of the application for the appointment of commissioners under the special proceedings under the act to acquire title to such land as well as the notice of hearing before such commissioners shall be served by the publication of the said notice twice each week, for three weeks, in at least two newspapers published in the county in which such city or village is located, to be designated by the court in which the said application is to be made. *Ib. sec.* 2.

By ch. 224 *of the Laws of* 1877, any railroad company, owning, operating, or leasing a railroad, or any mortgagee in possession of the same or receiver, duly appointed and in possession or operating the same, is authorized to acquire additional land for the purposes of the road, or any further right to lands or the use of lands for switches, turnouts, or for the flow of water, or any right to take and convey water from any spring, pond, creek or river, to the railroad for the purposes thereof; and to lay aqueducts and pipes and the right of way to and from the same; provided that nothing in the statute authorizes the taking of any waters used for domestic, agricultural or manufacturing purposes, to such an extent as to injuriously interfere with such use in the future. *Laws* 1877, *ch.* 224, *p.* 242, amending ch. 237 of the Laws of 1869. To entitle a mortgagee or a receiver to take proceedings under the statute he must first obtain leave of the court. *Ib.;* and see the statute for details in the proceedings.

CHAPTER XXVIII.

REDEMPTION OF REAL ESTATE. (*a*)

SECTION I.

REDEMPTION OF REAL ESTATE FROM SALE ON EXECUTION.

The redemption of lands from sale under execution is authorized and regulated wholly by statute, the proceeding being unknown to the common law. The first statute on the subject in this State was passed in 1820 (*Sess. Laws*, 167), prior to which the purchaser of lands upon execution was entitled to a deed on payment of the purchase money; upon receiving which, the title passed absolutely to him. By that statute a system was devised which, in effect, extended a credit of fifteen months to the judgment debtor from the sale; and within which time he, or his representatives, or any assignee of his interest, or any judgment creditor, at the periods designated in the statute, and upon complying with certain conditions therein prescribed, could redeem the premises from the sale. 20 *Wend.* 558. That system was afterwards engrafted into the Revised Statutes; which, with the amendments and additions since made, constitute the present law on the subject in this State. 2 *Rev. Stat.* 370; *Laws of* 1835, *p.* 210; 1836, *p.* 793; 1837, *p.* 540; 1847, *p.* 508; 1857, *vol.* 1, *p* 93; 1862, *p.* 872.

(*a*) For the statutory provisions relating to the redemption of lands sold on mortgages to the State, see 1 *Rev. Stat.* 213; and for the like provisions in reference to the redemption of lands sold for taxes, see 1 *Id.* 402; *Laws of* 1850, *pp.* 344, 641; 1855, *p.* 781; 1860, *p.* 352; 1862, *p.* 481.

The statute was designed for the benefit of the debtor by preventing a sacrifice of his property; and of the junior judgment creditor by giving him a chance to redeem the land sold upon a senior judgment. 1 *Cowen*, 501; 4 *Coms.* 561. The statute, therefore, will be construed liberally as in favor of the debtor and his redeeming creditor; though, in all essential points, care should be taken fully and strictly to follow its provisions. (*a*) *Id. ibid.*; 2 *Hill*, 51; 7 *Id.* 177; 7 *Paige*, 177; 18 *Wend.* 598; 20 *Id.* 555; 25 *New York*, 619. "In relation to the new points which may arise," says Bronson, Ch. J. (4 *Denio*, 144)—"and there is never likely to be an end of them under this very imperfect law—it cannot be very profitable to discuss the abstract question whether the statute should receive a strict or a liberal construction. I think it should receive such a reasonable construction as is best calculated to carry into effect the end which the legislature had in view. That end was, to make the land bring its utmost value, by means of an auction among the creditors, preserving to each one his right, according to the seniority of his lien. The mode of conducting the auction, so far as it has been plainly prescribed, must be followed, whether it be reasonable or unreasonable; unless the party who has the right to insist upon performance, chooses to dispense with it. When the meaning of the statute is doubtful, that construction should be adopted which will secure the rights of all the creditors, according to the seniority of their respective liens, and keep up the auction until the best price has been obtained. And the same great end should be steadily kept in view, in disposing of all questions upon which the statute is silent."

The statute relates to the redemption of real estate, which includes all estates or interests in real property held for life, or some greater estate. See 20 *Wend.* 417. It includes, also, leasehold property, where the lessee, or the assignee of the lessee, is possessed of at least five years' unexpired term of the lease, and also of any building or buildings that may be

(*a*) For the remedy of the purchaser, his heirs or assigns, on failure of title to real estate sold on execution, where such failure arises from irregularity in the proceedings on the sale, or by reason of the judgment being vacated or reversed; and for the remedy to enforce contribution between several owners of lands subject to the same judgment, see 2 *Rev. Stat.* 375.

erected thereon. *Laws of* 1837, *p.* 540; 20 *Wend.* 417. But where the interest of the tenant in a lease given for twenty-one years was sold on execution, but less than five years of the term remained unexpired at the time of the sale, it was held that no right of redemption existed, though the lease contained a covenant for renewal. 7 *Hill*, 150. Nor does the right of redemption exist in respect to sales made upon the foreclosure of a mechanic's lien. 4 *Abb.* 205. It includes, however, a *rent charge*, reserved upon a lease in fee, containing a clause of re-entry and right to distrain; but not a *rent seck.* 7 *Wend.* 464; and see 6 *Hill*, 149.

Certificate of sale; its contents, &c.] The statute provides, that upon the sale of any real estate, by virtue of any execution, the officer making the same shall make out and subscribe duplicate certificates of such sale, containing: 1. A particular description of the premises sold; 2. The price bid for each distinct lot or parcel; 3. The whole consideration money paid; and 4. The time when such sale will become absolute, and the purchaser will be entitled to a conveyance pursuant to law. 2 *Rev. Stat.* 370, *sec.* 42. For form, see *Appendix*, No. 570.

One of the said duplicate certificates is required, within ten days after the sale, to be filed in the office of the clerk of the county, and the other to be delivered to the purchaser. If there are two or more purchasers, a certificate is to be delivered to each. *Ib. sec.* 43. But the omission of the sheriff to file the certificate will not prejudice the purchaser. 5 *Cowen*, 269.

The statute further provides, that whenever the certificate of sale shall be filed in the office of the clerk or register of any county, pursuant to the statute, it shall be the duty of such clerk immediately to record the same in a book to be kept by him for that purpose, and the same shall be properly indexed in the name of the defendant or defendants in the judgment, for which service the clerk or register shall be entitled to the same fees allowed for recording conveyances, to be paid by the sheriff out of the avails of the sale, except in counties where the clerk or register is a salaried office. *Laws of* 1857, *vol.* 1, *p.* 93; *Pub. Acts*, *p.* 8. And a record thereof, or a certified copy of such record, shall be evidence of the facts therein contained, in all courts and places, the same as if the original record were pro duced. *Ib.*

The original certificate, upon being proved or acknowledged in the manner required by law to entitle deeds to be recorded, or a copy of such original, duly certified by the clerk in whose office the original is filed, will be received as presumptive evidence of the facts therein contained. 2 *Rev. Stat.* 370, *sec.* 44; 4 *Barb.* 183.

Within what time redemption may be made.] By the statute, the defendant in the execution, and whose right and title were sold in pursuance thereof, or his grantee, or, if the defendant is dead, his devisee or heir, may redeem the premises any time within one year from the time when the sale was made, 2 *Rev. Stat.* 370, *secs.* 45, 46; and within that time he has the exclusive right of redemption. *Ib.; 1 Cowen*, 443. If an equitable owner of the premises is entitled to redeem, he also must exercise his right within the year, as equity follows the law in such cases. 10 *Paige*, 249

If the defendant, or his grantee, devisee, or heir, omit to redeem the premises within the year allowed to them for that purpose, then the interest vested in the purchaser may be acquired within three months after the expiration of the year, by a judgment or mortgage creditor of the defendant. 2 *Rev. Stat:* 371, *sec.* 50. And the right of the creditors does not attach until after the year has elapsed; from which time, for three months, they have the exclusive right of redeeming. *Ib.;* 1 *Cowen*, 443. The creditor, however, it seems, need not wait until the expiration of a year before presenting the evidence of his right to redeem. 2 *Hill*, 55. The three months commence to run on the day succeeding the expiration of the year, and that day is counted inclusively; thus, if the year expire on the 18th day of a month, the succeeding day is counted as part of the three months. 19 *Wend.* 87. If the last day of the three months falls on Sunday, the redemption should be made on the day previous. 1 *Id.* 42.

By the statute, also, any creditor having a right to redeem, may do so any time within twenty-four hours after any preceding redemption, notwithstanding more than fifteen months have elapsed since the sale was made. *Laws of* 1847, *p.* 509, § 4.

And the sheriff is prohibited from executing any deed upon such sale until after the lapse of twenty-four hours from the last redemption. *Ib.*

The fifteen months allowed by the statute in which the owner and his creditors may redeem, are calendar and not lunar months. 2 *Cowen*, 518. And the creditor is allowed full fifteen months from the day of sale, *Ib.*; the time for redeeming not expiring until the close of the last day allowed for that purpose; business hours not being regarded in that respect. 7 *Hill*, 177.

But the time within which a party may redeem, may be enlarged by agreement between the judgment debtor and the purchaser; and this agreement will be binding upon the creditors of the judgment debtor. Thus, where the purchaser, soon after the sale, agreed with the judgment debtor not to perfect title under the sale within three years, and that at the expiration of that period he would release and discharge all his interest acquired by the sale, on being paid the amount of his bid with interest, and another creditor afterwards, but within fifteen months from the sale, obtained judgment and then redeemed under the statute, receiving the sheriff's deed, after which, but within the three years, the judgment debtor paid up the purchaser according to the agreement; it was held that the redemption by the junior judgment debtor was void, and that he acquired no title by the sheriff's deed. 4 *Coms.* 554; and see 7 *Cowen*, 540.

1. *Redemption by owner, or by his heir, devisee, or grantee.*] The statute provides that within one year from the time when such sale shall have been made, the real estate so sold, or any distinct lot, tract or portion that may have been separately sold, may be redeemed by the payment to the purchaser, his personal representatives or assignees, or to the officer who made such sale, for the use of such purchaser, of the sum of money which was bid on the sale of such lot or tract, together with the interest on that sum from the time of sale, at the rate of ten per cent. a year. 2 *Rev. Stat.* 370, *sec.* 45.

Such redemption may be made, 1. By the person against whom the execution was issued, and whose right and title were sold in pursuance thereof; or 2. If such person be dead, by his devisee of the premises sold, if the same shall have been devised;

and if not devised, by the heirs of such person; or, 3. By any grantee of such person who shall have acquired an absolute title by deed, sale under mortgage, or under an execution, or by any other means, to the premises sold, or to any lot, tract, parcel, or portion which shall have been separately sold. *Ib. sec.* 46.

And trustees, appointed under the absconding, concealed, and non-resident debtor act, are entitled to redeem the lands of the debtor, of whose estate they have charge. Such redemption, however, is only with the same effect as if made by the debtor himself; and it does not, therefore, entitle them to demand a deed of the premises, nor to direct the execution of the deed, to a third person. 15 *Wend.* 248.

The grantee of the judgment debtor, as we have seen, may redeem the premises. But where, after the sale of the premises upon execution, for less than the sum due upon the judgment, the same are redeemed by such grantee, they may be re-sold by the sheriff, upon the same execution, for the balance remaining due thereon. 3 *Barb. S. C. R.* 70. The grantee, to be entitled to redeem, must have acquired the title by deed; and a mere equitable title is not sufficient, even though he was prevented from obtaining the deed by an injunction in an action brought by the judgment debtor. 22 *Wend.* 116.

To entitle the judgment debtor to redeem, he must be the owner of the premises at the time he seeks to redeem them. Thus, a judgment debtor, whose land has been sold on execution, subject to a prior mortgage, upon which his equity of redemption is subsequently foreclosed and sold, cannot redeem the premises under the statute. 17 *Abb.* 137.

Any heir or devisee of the person against whom the execution was issued, and any grantee of such person who has acquired an absolute title to a portion of the estate sold, or to a portion of any lot, tract, or parcel, that has been separately sold, may redeem the lot, tract, or parcel so sold, on the same terms and in the same manner as if he were grantee of the whole lot, tract, or parcel, and shall have the same remedy to enforce contribution from those who shall own the residue of such tract, lot, or parcel, as if the sum required to be paid by him to effect such redemption had been collected by a sale of the portion belonging to the grantee. 2 *Rev. Stat.* 371, *sec.* 47.

If there be several persons having undivided shares, as joint tenants, or as tenants in common, in the premises sold, or in any particular lot or tract sold, each person having such title may redeem the share or interest belonging to him, by paying to the purchaser or to the officer, as directed by the statute, a sum that will bear the same proportion to the whole purchase-money bid for the premises, or for such particular lot or tract, as the share proposed to be redeemed bears to the whole number of shares in the premises or lot or tract, together with the interest on such sum, at the rate of ten per cent. a year. *Ib. sec.* 48.

Where the owner claims that the sale was illegal, and did not confer any title upon the purchaser, he may redeem the same from the effect of the sale, and obtain a temporary injunction, to prevent the sheriff from paying over the money to the purchaser, and may litigate with the purchaser for the money instead of the land. 7 *How.* 329. But the temporary injunction, in such case, cannot be sustained, unless the purchaser is insolvent. *Ib.*

2. *Redemption by judgment creditors.*] In case the judgment debtor, his heir, devisee, or grantee, omits to redeem the premises, or any part of them, within a year from the time when the sale was made, then the interest vested in the purchaser by such sale may be acquired within three months after the expiration of such year by the persons and on the terms hereinafter prescribed. 2 *Rev. Stat.* 371, *sec.* 50.

The statute also provides, that any creditor having in his own name, or as assignee, representative, trustee, or otherwise, a decree in chancery, or a judgment at law, rendered at any time before the expiration of fifteen months from the time of such sale, or having a mortgage duly recorded within the same period, and which shall be a lien and charge upon the premises sold, or upon any parcel which shall have been separately sold, by paying the sum of money which was paid on the sale of such premises, or upon any parcel which shall have been separately sold, together with the interest thereon, at the rate of seven per cent. a year, from the time of such sale, shall thereby acquire all the rights of the original purchaser, subject to be defeated by any other like creditor, in the manner mentioned in the statute. *Ib. sec.* 51, as amended *Laws of* 1847, *p.* 508.

It is no objection that the judgment was confessed for the express purpose of enabling the creditor to redeem, if it was founded upon a sufficient consideration. The debtor may confer the power of redeeming upon as many as he pleases. It keeps up the auction, and is thus directly within the policy of the statute. 2 *Cowen*, 518, 521. And though the judgment be confessed voluntarily, and the creditor at the same time stipulates to stay execution thereon for a year, yet this does not preclude him from redeeming immediately. 1 *Id.* 443; and see 7 *Barb.* 341.

Nor is it any objection to the judgment creditor's right to redeem that he had other security for the debt besides the judgment. 7 *Barb.* 341. Though where a debt for which a junior judgment is confessed is well secured otherwise than by the judgment, it seems equity will interfere to compel the judgment creditor to exhaust his other securities, in favor of a creditor having no other security except a lien upon the premises sold. The sheriff, in such case, however, will be required to give a deed of the premises to the judgment creditor; the remedy of the other creditor being in equity only. 1 *Cowen*, 502.

Nor will the right of a judgment creditor to redeem premises which have been sold upon a prior execution against the property of his debtor, be defeated by the act of the purchaser in paying the judgment under which the creditor claims to redeem, without his consent; especially where such payment is not made until after the redeeming creditor has actually paid to the sheriff the amount of the purchaser's bid, with interest, and has commenced delivering to the sheriff the papers required by the statute to be presented to, and left with him. 1 *Barb. S. C.* 379.

A sale of land on execution, though for only a part of what is due upon it, with the lapse of fifteen months from the time of sale, and a conveyance by the sheriff, destroys the lien of junior judgment creditors, so that they cannot redeem from a purchaser under a judgment older than the one upon which the conveyance is made. 4 *Cowen*, 133; 1 *Denio*, 633. It destroys the lien, too, of the judgment on which the premises are sold even for the balance remaining due, so that the judgment creditor cannot redeem the land from a purchaser under a senior judgment. *Id. ibid.*; and see 10 *Paige*, 249; 5 *Hill*, 228. Nor can lands be redeemed upon a judgment upon which execution has issued and a levy been made upon personal property sufficient to satisfy it. 4 *Cowen*, 417.

The party in whose favor the judgment was obtained, as well

as his assignee, is entitled to redeem under the statute. And it is not necessary that the assignee should have paid the full value of the judgment. Thus, where he purchased the judgment, paying only a small sum down, and agreed to pay a further sum upon a contingency, and took an absolute assignment to himself, it was held sufficient to entitle him as assignee of the judgment, to redeem the premises from the original purchaser. 1 *Denio*, 272.

A senior judgment creditor may redeem from a purchaser at a sale under a junior judgment; and this, too, although the redeeming creditor, also, held the judgment on which the sale was made. 2 *Coms.* 484, aff. 4 *Denio*, 137.

And so, where land is sold under a judgment, a person not being the debtor, but having become the owner of the land which is subject to the lien, may become the purchaser at the sale, and, as such purchaser, acquire a title under the sale. The interest thus acquired is not merged in the title previously held; and therefore, in such a case, another judgment creditor may, under the statute, redeem or acquire the interest of the purchaser, and so become entitled to the sheriff's deed. 19 *New York*, 370.

If there are two judgment creditors having judgments docketed at the same instant, the one first redeeming will be entitled to the sheriff's deed, unless the other redeems from him; and this, though the judgments were docketed under a stipulation that any sums collected thereon should be shared by the creditors in proportion to the amount of their respective judgments. 1 *Hill*, 639.

The right of the judgment creditor to redeem may be affected by an agreement between the purchaser and judgment debtor; as, where the purchaser agrees to enlarge the time beyond the period of fifteen months, in which the judgment debtor may redeem. In such a case, the statute has no application; and the creditor is left to his common-law remedy, by sale or redemption, if the substituted interest is redeemable. 4 *Coms.* 553.

To entitle the creditor to redeem, by virtue of a lien upon a portion of the debtor's property, such property, it seems, should have been sufficiently described in the sheriff's advertisement of sale. 6 *Hill*, 149.

The judgment, too, in virtue of which the right to redeem is claimed, must be against the defendant in the execution under which the sale was made, and, also, a lien on the lands sold. 4 *Id.* 542.

Where the sale of land was made on several judgments, the purchaser takes his title under each; and a judgment creditor, therefore, in order to acquire the rights of the purchaser, must be entitled to do so in respect to *all* of the judgments on which the sale was made. 2 *Coms.* 484.

If the judgment is a lien on any lot, tract, or parcel, that has been separately sold, the creditor having the same, by paying as provided by the statute, the sum which shall have been bid for such lot, tract, or parcel, with interest at seven per cent. per year from the time of the sale, will thereby acquire all the rights of the original purchaser to such lot, tract, or parcel, subject to be defeated as hereinafter provided. 2 *Rev. Stat.* 371, *sec.* 52; 6 *Hill*, 149; 1 *How.* 77.

If the judgment is a lien on a specific portion only of any lot, tract, or parcel, so sold, the creditor having the same, may acquire the title of the purchaser, to the whole of such lot, tract, or parcel, in the same manner as if such lien extended to the whole. 2 *Rev. Stat.* 372, *sec.* 53.

And such creditor having such judgment which is a lien upon any undivided share or interest in any real estate sold under execution, may within the same time, on the same terms and in the same manner, acquire the title of the original purchaser to such share or interest, by paying such part of the whole purchase-money of such real estate as shall be in a just proportion to the amount of such share or interest. *Ib. sec.* 54; *Hill and Denio*, 266.

3. *Redemption by other judgment creditors.*] Whenever any creditor has acquired the title of the original purchaser, pursuant to the statute, any other creditor who might have acquired such title according to the statute, may become a purchaser thereof from the first creditor who acquired the same, upon complying with the conditions of the statute. 2 *Rev. Stat.* 372, *sec.* 55.

And in the same manner, and upon the same terms and conditions, any third or other creditor who might, according to the foregoing provisions, acquire the title of the original purchaser, may become a purchaser thereof from the second, third, or any other creditor who may have become such purchaser from any other creditor. *Ib. sec.* 56.

Where the second creditor, after one creditor had redeemed lands sold under execution, with a view of redeeming the lands, paid unconditionally to the sheriff the requisite amount, but immediately thereafter served an injunction in his own favor restraining the sheriff from paying it over; it was held, nevertheless, that he was entitled to the sheriff's deed. 4 *Hill*, 589.

4. *Redemption by original purchaser, being a creditor.*] If the original purchaser of any premises sold under execution is also a creditor of the defendant against whom the execution issued, and as such might acquire the title of any purchaser, according to the provisions of the statute, he may avail himself of his decree or judgment, in the same manner, and on the same terms prescribed by the statute, to acquire the title which any creditor may have obtained. 2 *Rev. Stat.* 372, *sec.* 57.

5. *Redemption by plaintiff in execution, on which the property is sold.*] By the statute, the plaintiff under whose execution any real estate shall have been sold, shall not be authorized to acquire the title of the original purchaser, or of any creditor to the premises so sold, by virtue of the decree or judgment on which such execution issued. 2 *Rev. Stat.* 373, *sec.* 58; 2 *Coms.* 484.

Thus, where a junior judgment creditor sells the lands of his debtor, and becomes himself the purchaser, and at the expiration of fifteen months from the sale receives the sheriff's deed therefor, and afterwards, the same premises are sold under a prior judgment, such junior judgment creditor being the owner of the lands by his purchase, cannot, after the expiration of the year from the last sale, redeem the premises from such sale; for the lien of his judgment was extinguished by the sale of the premises under it. 10 *Paige*, 249; 5 *Hill*, 228.

And the lien in such case is extinguished, although there remains a balance due upon the judgment beyond the amount bid at the sale; except where the judgment debtor has acquired a subsequent title to the premises which overreaches and divests the title obtained under the sheriff's deed. *Id. ibid.*; and see 4 *Cowen*, 133; 1 *Denio*, 633; 2 *Wend.* 297; 23 *Barb.* 259; 2 *Coms.* 484, aff. 4 *Denio*, 137.

Where, however, lands are sold on execution and are bid in by a third person for less than the sum due upon the judgment, and the judgment debtor subsequently redeems the premises from the sale, the lands may be re-sold on the same execution to pay the balance remaining due. 5 *Hill*, 228.

But if the plaintiff has any judgment which would entitle him to acquire the title to the premises according to the provisions of the statute, other than the judgment upon which the lands were sold, he is entitled to avail himself of the same, in the same manner and on the same terms as any other creditor. 2 *Rev. Stat.* 373, *sec.* 58; 4 *Denio*, 137, aff. 2 *Coms.* 484.

6. *Redemption by mortgage creditors.*] A creditor by mortgage never had the right to redeem, either as grantee or creditor, until it was given him by the act passed May 26, 1836. *Laws of* 1836, *p.* 793; 1 *Barb. S. C.* 379. That act was subsequently modified by Laws of 1847, p. 508, and now, any creditor, by mortgage on real estate, his assignee or representative, having a mortgage duly recorded at any time before the expiration of fifteen months from the time of such sale, and which shall be a lien and charge upon the premises sold, or upon any parcel which shall have been separately sold, by paying the sum of money which was paid on the sale of such premises, or upon any parcel which shall have been separately sold, together with the interest thereon at the rate of seven per cent. a year, from the time of such sale, shall thereby acquire all the rights of the original purchaser, subject to be defeated by any other like creditor, in the manner mentioned in the statute. 2 *Rev. Stat.* 371, *sec.* 51, as amended, *Laws of* 1847, *p.* 508.

The right of the creditor by mortgage, his assignee or representative, to acquire the interest of the purchaser, is the same as is given by the statute to a judgment creditor; and on acquiring such interest, he is subject to all the provisions of the statute in relation to the rights of other creditors, as are applicable to judgment creditors. *Laws of* 1836, *p.* 793; *Laws of* 1847, *p.* 508. Thus, the statute gives the right of redemption of one or more of several lots, or of an undivided share of a single lot or parcel, and defines the time when the title of the judgment debtor may be divested, and how the redeeming creditor may himself be subjected to redemption in favor of some other holder of a like lien, and how the sheriff's deeds are to be given, and when and to whom, &c. 10 *How.* 312, *per* Roosevelt, J.

Formerly, it was held necessary to entitle the holder of a mortgage to acquire the right of a purchaser at a sale, that the mortgage should have been executed by the defendant in the execution (3 *Denio.* 527); but this has been changed by statute, and it is sufficient, now, if the mortgage is a lien upon the premises in question. *Laws of* 1847, *p.* 508, *supra.*

7. *Redemption by superintendents and overseers of the poor.*] By the statute, county superintendents and overseers of the poor in the several counties of the State, except the county of New York, have the same right to redeem the real estate which may have been seized by them pursuant to the statute relating to "the relief and support of indigent persons" (1 *Rev. Stat.* 613) as is possessed by judgment creditors under the statutory provisions here considered. *Laws of* 1862, *p.* 872, § 1.

But no such redemption can be made unless at the time of making the same the seizure of the real estate sought to be redeemed shall have been confirmed by the court of sessions of the county where the premises are situated; nor unless such real estate shall, at the time of making the redemption, be held by the superintendents or overseers under and by virtue of the seizure made by them pursuant to the statute aforesaid. *Ib.* § 2. (*a*).

Where, and how, redemption to be made; duty of sheriff, &c.] If the redemption is made by the defendant in the execution, or by his heir, devisee, or grantee, the payment must be made to the purchaser, his personal representatives or assigns, or to the officer who made the sale. 2 *Rev. Stat.* 370, *secs.* 45, 59.

And so, if the redemption is made by a creditor of the judgment debtor, the payment must be made to the purchaser or prior redeeming creditor, his representatives or assigns, or to the officer making the sale. *Ib. secs.* 50, 59, 60. All redemptions,

---

(*a*) For the manner of effecting redemption by the superintendents and overseers of the poor, and the evidence to be produced by them of their right to redeem, see *Laws of* 1862, *p.* 872.

however, which are made on or after the last day of the fifteen months by any creditor, must be made at the office of the sheriff of the county in which the sale took place; and it is the duty of the officer making the sale to attend at such office during the last day for making such redemptions, and during the time thereafter in which redemptions may be made; and in case of the absence of the officer who made the sale from the sheriff's office at such time, then the redemption may be made to the sheriff; and in his absence, to the under sheriff or any deputy present at such office. *Laws of* 1847, *p.* 508, § 3.

If one creditor has already redeemed from the purchaser, a second or subsequent creditor coming to redeem, must present the evidence of his right, and make payment to the last redeeming creditor, or to the officer who made the sale; and it is irregular in such case to make payment to the original purchaser. 20 *Wend.* 602.

And payment may be made to the officer who made the sale, although the term of office of his principal has expired. *Ib.*

The purchaser is not bound to accept payment from one not authorized to redeem, and may insist that the conveyance be given to him; though, if he accepts the money, even when paid by a stranger, his right to a deed is gone. 15 *Wend.* 248.

The redeeming creditor must deliver the requisite papers to the same party to whom he pays the money. He cannot make payment to the purchaser, and afterward deliver the papers to the sheriff. 4 *Denio*, 145.

Where the purchaser at the sheriff's sale was a banking corporation, and a creditor seeking to redeem, went to the banking house during business hours and tendered the money to the cashier, who accepted the same without objection and gave a receipt, it was held that the creditor acquired the title of the bank, though the affidavit of the amount due on his judgment was invalid. 7 *Hill*, 91.

The officer making the sale may authorize a deposit of the redemption money with another person, as his agent for that purpose; and a payment to such person will be as valid as if paid to the officer himself. 1 *Barb. Ch. R.* 53. So, the officer may authorize another to compute the amount necessary to be paid, and with the like effect. 9 *Barb.* 17.

And no person other than those above mentioned is authorized to receive the money for the sheriff or the party interested; and, therefore, the county clerk of the county cannot, without a special authority for that purpose, act in the sheriff's behalf in receiving money paid for the redemption of real estate, even though the sheriff had no other office than the county clerk's office, and though he, as well as his deputies, is absent from the office. 15 *New York*, 528; 23 *Barb.* 278.

If, however, the sheriff die or be removed from office after having made sale of any real estate, the amount required to be paid on redemption may be paid to his under-sheriff, or to the clerk of the county, in the same manner and with the like effect as if paid to the sheriff. 2 *Rev. Stat.* 374, *sec.* 67.

The statute does not make it the duty of the sheriff to compute the amount to be paid by a party coming to redeem; yet, if he, or one authorized to act for him, voluntarily undertakes to make the computation, and in so doing commits an error, and thereby misleads the party, who does not himself make any computation, in consequence of which he makes a short payment, and the sheriff accepts the same as a payment in full, the redemption will be held valid and effectual, although the sum paid is less than the amount actually due. 9 *Barb.* 17.

Where any redemption is made prior to the last day of the fifteen months allowed for that purpose, the officer before whom the redemption is made, is required, immediately thereafter, to file, in the office of the clerk of the county, a statement of such redemption, containing the title of the cause, or if it is a mortgage, the parties to the mortgage, the amount of the judgment, decree, or mortgage, the assignee, representatives, or trustees thereof, if any, and the amount paid to redeem, the time when such redemption was made, and the sum claimed to be due upon such judgment, decree, or mortgage at the time of such redemption. *Laws of* 1847, *p.* 508, § 3. For form, see *Appendix*, No. 577.

Evidence of creditor's right to redeem.] The creditors by judgment and mortgage, upon the application to redeem the premises from the sale on execution, are required to produce and leave with the purchaser or creditor, or the officer who made the sale, evidence of the existence of the judgment or mortgage, and of all assignments of the same, and the amount actually due thereon.

Thus, it is provided by statute, that to entitle a judgment creditor to acquire the title of the original purchaser, or to become a purchaser from any other creditor, he shall present to, and leave with such purchaser or creditor, or the officer who made the sale, the following evidence of his right:

1. A copy of the docket of the judgment or decree under which he claims the right to purchase, duly certified by the clerk of the court or of the county in which the same is docketed.

2. A true copy of all the assignments of such judgment or decree, which are necessary to establish his claim, verified by his affidavit or by the affidavit of some witness to such assignment.

3. An affidavit by such creditor, or by his attorney or agent, of the true sum due on such judgment or decree, at the time of claiming such right to purchase. 2 *Rev. Stat.* 373, *sec.* 60. For forms, see *Appendix*, Nos. 571 to 574.

And in respect to creditors by *mortgage*, it is also provided by statute, that to entitle such creditor, his assignee or representative, to acquire the title of the original purchaser, or to be substituted as a purchaser from any other creditor, he shall present to and leave with such purchaser or creditor, or the officer who made the sale, the following evidence of his right:

1. A copy of the mortgage under which he claims the right to purchase, duly certified by the clerk of the county where the mortgage is registered or recorded.

2. A copy of the assignment or assignments, where the mortgage has been assigned, verified by his affidavit, or the affidavit of some witness to such assignments.

3. A copy of the letter of administration or letters testamentary where an administrator or executor applies to be substituted as a purchaser.

4. An affidavit by the mortgage creditor, his assignee or representative, or by his attorney or agent, stating the true sum due or to become due on the mortgage at the time of claiming such right to purchase, over and above all payments. *Laws of* 1836, *p.* 793.

A copy of the docket of a judgment rendered in the Supreme Court, and docketed in a county clerk's office, is properly certified by the clerk of the county in which the judgment is docketed. 3 *Barb. S. C.* 301. And a deputy of the county clerk in the absence of the clerk, is authorized to certify a copy of the docket of a judgment; and the certificate is good, although it does not show that the clerk is absent, 4 *Coms.* 554; and though it does not state that the clerk has compared the copy with the original, and that it is a correct transcript therefrom, and of the whole of such original. *Ib.;* and see 4 *Denio*, 145. Nor is it necessary that the clerk's certificate should be under seal. *Ib.* And where the clerk certifies to a mortgage, the certificate is sufficient, though it is neither dated nor sealed. 2 *Hill*, 51.

The statute, as we have seen, requires the judgment or mortgage creditor also to present a true copy of all assignments of the judgment or mortgage necessary to establish his claim, verified by his affidavit, or by the affidavit of some witness to the assignment. See *supra.* But it is sufficient, it seems, if the original assignment is presented; though a mere acknowledgment of it, certified by an officer authorized to take the acknowledgment of deeds, is not a sufficient verification of it for the purpose of redeeming. 4 *Id.* 608.

In a case, however, where the affidavit of the redeeming creditor set forth the assignment at length, and alleged that "the foregoing assignment is a true and correct copy of the original assignment of N. R. and P. G.", it was held to be sufficient. 10 *Barb.* 167. So, it was held sufficient where the affidavit stated "that the following is a true and correct copy of the original assignment of N. R. to P. G.", and then, after giving a literal copy, proceeded further to state, "that the said P. G. sold and assigned said judgment to this deponent, and that the following is a true and correct copy of said original assignment"—also giving a copy thereof. *Ib.* But it is not sufficient evidence of the title of the judgment creditor to leave with the sheriff the judgment creditor's own affidavit that he was the owner and assignee of the judgment, with a paper purporting to be an assignment of the judgment, from the plaintiffs therein, to him, the said paper not being verified by the affidavit of any one, and there being nothing in the affidavit of the judgment creditor by which the paper was identified as the instrument under which he claimed to own and hold the judgment. 27 *Barb.* 55. An assignment of a judgment by an administrator is as effectual as if executed by the plaintiff while living, 4 *Denio*, 137, aff. 2 *Coms*. 484; and the death of the intestate, and the appointment of an administrator, may be shown by an affidavit presented with the other papers. *Ib*.

The statute requiring copies of the assignments to be produced, refers to assignments by deed or writing, and not to assignments by operation of law. And, therefore, where the plaintiff in a judgment died intestate, and the assignee of his administrator sought to redeem premises from the purchaser, it was held that he need not produce the letters of administration. *Ib*.

The copy of assignment, as we have seen, must be verified by the affidavit of the creditor, or of a witness to the assignment. 2 *Rev. Stat.* 373, *sec.* 60, *supra*. And, therefore, the agent of the assignee of the judgment, unless he is also a witness to the assignment, cannot verify it. Though, where there is no subscribing witness, the assignment may be verified by any person who saw it executed and delivered; such person being a witness to the assignment within the meaning of the statute. 2 *Coms*. 485, aff. 4 *Denio*, 137.

The statute also requires, as we have seen, an affidavit by the judgment creditor, or by his attorney or agent, of the true sum due on the judgment, at the time of claiming the right to redeem; or, if the redemption is under a mortgage, an affidavit by the mortgage creditor, his assignee or representative, or by his attorney or agent, stating the true sum due or to become due on the mortgage, at the time of claiming the right to redeem, over and above all payments. See *supra*.

The affidavit should be drawn with care; and, if made by an agent, should state in express terms that the deponent is agent for the creditor. Merely naming him as such, in the affidavit, is not enough. 7 *Hill*, 177; 4 *Denio*, 258. The affidavit, in such case, also, should show that the agent has the means of knowledge, and should state the amount due positively, not according to his belief merely. 7 *Hill*, 177.

The attorney of record, in the judgment, is not authorized, it seems, as such attorney, to make the affidavit; but it must be sworn to by the creditor, or by the attorney or agent employed in making the purchase, under the statute. 4 *Denio*, 258 Though this doctrine, that the affidavit cannot be made by the attorney, in the judgment, is questioned—not without reason—in *The People* v. *Ransom*, 2 *Coms.* 490, 497.

Care should be taken, also, to state correctly the amount due upon the judgment or mortgage; though the affidavit will not be vitiated by an error in stating the amount due, where the creditor acts in good faith, without any intention to deceive, 7 *Barb.* 341, 351; though otherwise, it seems, if the affidavit overstates the amount due. 25 *New York*, 619, 624, *per* Davies, J. And, in the case of a mortgage creditor, the affidavit should state the sum due, or to become due, upon the mortgage positively, or so aver the belief of the affiant as that perjury may be assigned. And an affidavit which states the sum due "as claimed by this deponent," is fatally defective. 20 *Id.* 354; and see 7 *Hill*, 177.

It is not necessary the affidavit should be made on the day the papers are presented to the sheriff; and where it was made five days before they were presented, it was held sufficient. 4 *Id.* 608; and see 2 *Id.* 51.

The sheriff has no power or discretion to dispense with the evidence required to be produced to him on the redemption of real estate. 7 *Paige*, 168, 177; 18 *Wend.* 598; 19 *Id.* 87. And therefore a redemption without that evidence will be held to be invalid. *Id. ibid.* Nor can a creditor waive the production of the evidence required by the statute, so as to affect the rights of other creditors pursuing the same remedy. 2 *Coms.* 490, aff. 4 *Denio*, 145. Though the original, or any subsequent purchaser, may, so far as he himself is concerned, waive the production of the evidence. *Id.*; and see 7 *Hill*, 91.

Amount to be paid or tendered on redemption.] The real estate sold, or any distinct lot, tract, or portion that may have been separately sold, may be redeemed by the defendant in the execution, his heir, devisee, or grantee, by the payment to the purchaser, his personal representatives or assigns, or to the officer who made the sale, for the use of such purchaser, of the sum of money which was bid on the sale of such lot or tract, together with the interest on that sum from the time of sale, at the rate of ten per cent. a year. 2 *Rev. Stat.* 370, *secs.* 45, 46. And those parties are in no case bound to pay more than that sum, with the ten per cent. interest thereon. 1 *Cowen*, 443.

And any heir, devisee, or grantee, owning or having acquired, an absolute title to a portion of the estate sold, or to a portion of any lot, tract, or parcel that shall have been separately sold, may redeem the lot, tract, or parcel so sold, on the same terms, and in the same manner as if he were grantee of the whole lot, tract, or parcel; and may have the same remedy to enforce contribution from those owning the residue of the property, as if the sum required to be paid to effect such redemption had been collected by a sale of the portion belonging to such grantee. 2 *Rev. Stat.* 371, *sec.* 47.

If there are several persons having undivided shares, as joint tenants or tenants in common, in the premises sold, or in any particular lot or tract sold, each of such persons may redeem the share or interest belonging to him, by paying a sum that will bear the same proportion to the whole purchase-money bid for the premises, or for such particular lot or tract as the share proposed to be redeemed bears to the whole number of shares in such premises, or lot or tract, together with the interest on such sum at the rate of ten per cent. a year. *Ib. sec.* 48.

In respect to the creditors of the judgment debtor, whether by mortgage or judgment, they are entitled to redeem the premises sold, by paying to the purchaser, his representatives or assigns, or to the officer who made the sale for the use of the purchaser, the sum of money which was paid on the sale of the premises, or upon any parcel which shall have been separately sold, together with the interest thereon at the rate of seven per cent. a year, from the time of such sale. *Ib. sec.* 51, as amended, *Laws of* 1847, *p.* 508; *Ib. sec.* 59.

If the judgment is a lien on any lot, tract, or parcel that has been separately sold, the creditor having the same, may acquire the rights of the original purchaser, by paying the sum bid for such lot, tract, or parcel, with interest at the rate of seven per cent. a year from the time of the sale. *Ib. sec.* 52. And if the judgment is a lien on a specific portion only of any lot so sold, the creditor having the same may acquire the title of the purchaser to the whole of the lot, in the same manner as if the lien extended to the whole. *Ib. sec.* 53.

Any creditor having a judgment which is a lien upon any undivided share or interest in any real estate sold, may acquire the title of the original purchaser, by paying such part of the whole purchase-money as shall be in a just proportion to the amount of such share or interest. *Ib. sec.* 54.

If a creditor has acquired the title of the original purchaser, any other creditor who is entitled to redeem the premises may become a purchaser thereof from the first creditor who acquired the same, upon the following conditions:

1. By reimbursing to the first creditor, his personal representatives, or assigns, the sum which has been paid by him to acquire such title, together with interest thereon at the rate of seven per cent. a year from the time of such payment to the time of such reimbursement.

2. If the judgment or decree by virtue of which the first creditor acquired the title of the original purchaser is prior to the judgment or decree of the second creditor, then the second creditor must also pay to the first creditor the amount due on his judgment or decree.

3. But if the judgment or decree of the first creditor, at the time of his acquiring the title of the original purchaser, has ceased to be a lien as against the second creditor, it will not be necessary to pay the amount thereof. *Ib. sec.* 55.

And so, any third or other creditor who might, according to the provisions of the statute, acquire the title of the original purchaser, may become a purchaser thereof from the second, third, or any other creditor who may have become such purchaser from any other creditor, upon the same terms and conditions as above stated. *Ib. sec.* 56.

And so, the original purchaser, being also a creditor entitled to acquire the title of any purchaser, may avail himself of his judgment, in the same manner and on the same terms, prescribed for acquiring the title which any creditor may have obtained. *Ib. sec.* 57. The plaintiff, too, though he cannot redeem the premises under or by virtue of the judgment under which they were sold, yet if he have any other judgment which would entitle him to acquire the title according to the provisions aforesaid, may avail himself of such judgment in the same manner and on the same terms as any other creditor. *Ib. sec.* 58; and see 10 *Paige*, 249; and other cases, *ante, p.* 241.

There have been many adjudications of the court under the above-mentioned statutory provisions, giving a construction to the statute, or illustrating its intention or meaning.

Thus, in a case where there were five judgments which were successive liens against the same debtor, and his land was sold under the first, second, and fourth, for a sum sufficient to pay the first two and a part of the fourth, and the respective creditors in the third and fifth judgments, in order to acquire the title of the purchaser, each delivered the proper papers and each paid the amount of the bid, but neither paid the other's judgment; it was held that the creditor in the third judgment was entitled to the conveyance. 2 *Coms.* 484, aff. 4 *Denio*, 137.

So, where a creditor by mortgage became also the purchaser under a senior judgment, furnishing the proper evidence of his right to redeem; it was held that a junior creditor in order to entitle himself to the sheriff's deed, must pay not only the sum bid, but the mortgage also. 2 *Hill*, 51; and see *Hill and D.* 266.

And where a junior judgment creditor complied with the requisites for redeeming from the purchaser, and, on the same day a senior creditor, who had previously become assignee of the original certificate of sale, presented to the sheriff due evidence of that fact, and of his right as creditor; it was held, that he was entitled to the sheriff's deed without the payment of any money. 4 *Hill*, 608; 1 *Denio*, 239.

The several junior creditors do not take precedence according to the time of redemption, but according to the priority of their respective liens. And, therefore, where A redeemed from the purchaser, it was held that B, having a judgment older than A's, could redeem by paying the original purchase-money and interest without also paying A's judgment. 1 *Cowen*, 428; and see 2 *Rev. Stat.* 372, *sec.* 55.

Where a sheriff advertised and sold real estate in separate parcels, on a number of executions, of different dates as to liens; it was held that a prior judgment creditor as to the youngest execution cannot redeem all the pieces sold by paying only the amount of the judgments older than his; but he must pay the amounts bid. 1 *How.* 77; and see 2 *Rev. Stat.* 370, *sec.* 45; *Ib.* 371, *sec.* 51, as amended, *supra.*

So, where one creditor redeemed from another, the judgments of both having been docketed at the same instant; it was held that the creditor seeking to redeem, must pay the amount paid by the other, with the interest thereon; and that a tender of the amount of the original bid only with interest on that was insufficient. 1 *Hill*, 639.

Payment should be made in the legal currency of the country; though a payment in current bank bills, if accepted by the sheriff, without objection, would be sufficient, 9 *Barb.* 17; and the sheriff may receive current bank bills even against the express directions of the creditor. 4 *Cowen*, 420. So, where the judgment creditor paid to the sheriff certain foreign coin, which was received by him at its current value without objection, but which turned out to be legally worth a few cents less; yet it was held to be a valid payment. 4 *Hill*, 613. So, where the payment was made partly in current foreign coin which was not a legal tender. *Ib.* But payment in a check on a bank is not sufficient; the payment must be made in money, or its equivalent. 20 *Wend.* 602.

The purchaser, however, may accept anything he pleases in payment of his bid; the requirement of the statute, in that respect, being for his benefit alone. 2 *Coms.* 490; 2 *How.* 117.

Parties applying to redeem, must be careful also to pay the the amount required for that purpose within the time allowed for redemption. And where one creditor seeking to redeem from another creditor omitted from misapprehension, to pay the whole sum required to be paid; but on discovering his mistake after the fifteen months had expired, immediately paid to the sheriff the deficiency, and obtained a conveyance; it was held that the rights of the parties were fixed at the expiration of the fifteen months, and that a subsequent payment could not change them. 1 *Denio*, 272.

A creditor is not bound to inform another creditor of the amount of moneys to be paid to entitle the latter to redeem. Thus, where, on the last day for redeeming, two judgment creditors came to the sheriff, each accompanied by his counsel, and the junior judgment creditor, intending to purchase from the other, who had acquired the right of the original purchaser, paid to the sheriff a sum less than that required to be paid, it was held that the senior creditor was not bound to give information as to the true sum to be paid, and that his right to a deed was not prejudiced by his omission to do so. The senior creditor, however, if inquired of, could not deceive or mislead, though he might decline to answer. *Ib.*

A creditor, redeeming under a junior judgment, cannot recall the money paid for that purpose, notwithstanding that he has another judgment prior to the one under which the sale took place, and the premises are not worth more than the sum bid by the purchaser. 6 *Hill*, 362.

Who entitled to the money.] The money paid on redemption belongs to the purchaser, his personal representatives, or assigns, or, if the redemption is made from a creditor, who has redeemed the premises, then to such creditor, his personal representatives, or assigns. 2 *Rev. Stat.* 370, *secs.* 45, 59.

And where the purchaser has assigned his interest, and the real estate is subsequently redeemed by a junior judgment creditor, the amount paid by the latter belongs to the assignee of the purchaser, who may maintain an action for the same in his own name. But the action, in such case, must be brought against the sheriff; and his deputy is not liable personally for the money, even though he made the sale and received the money of the redeeming creditor. 3 *Barb. S. C.* 475.

Certificate of redemption.] The statute provides, that whenever any redemption shall have been made of any real estate sold, it shall be the duty of the officer making the sale, or of any other person who may lawfully act in his behalf, to execute to the person making the redemption, his certificate truly stating all such facts transpiring before him at the making of such redemption, as shall be sufficient to show the fact of redemption. *Laws of* 1847, *p.* 508, § 5. For forms, see *Appendix*, Nos. 575, 576.

The certificate may be proved or acknowledged, as deeds are required to be, to entitle them to be recorded, and being duly recorded in the clerk's office of the county where the real estate so sold is situated, shall have the same effect, as against subsequent purchasers and incumbrancers, as deeds and conveyances duly proved and recorded; and such certificate, or the record thereof, or a duly authenticated copy of such record, shall be received in all courts and places as *prima facie* evidence of the facts therein stated. *Ib.* § 6.

But if a redemption is attempted by payment to a person not authorized to receive it, the sheriff's certificate, being wholly unauthorized, is not evidence of the facts contained in it. 23

Barb. 278. Nor is a certificate given by the county clerk, to whom the papers have been given, and the money paid, any evidence, the county clerk having no authority to act in the matter. *Ib.*

The officer making the certificate is entitled to the like compensation as for the certificate of sale. *Laws of* 1847, *p.* 508, § 7.

Effect of redemption.] Upon a redemption by the debtor, his heir, devisee, or grantee, within the year allowed for that purpose, the sale of the premises redeemed and the certificates of such sale become null and void. 2 *Rev. Stat.* 371, *sec.* 49. The same effect follows the redemption of the premises by trustees of the debtor, appointed under the non-resident debtor act. 15 *Wend.* 248.

Such being the effect of a redemption by the debtor or his representatives, a junior judgment under which the premises are sold, though not reached in the application of the proceeds, is restored to the same lien it had before the sale. 18 *New York*, 347. And the same effect follows from the conversion of the land into money by sale under a prior mortgage, and the application of the surplus proceeds, during the time allowed the debtor for redemption, to extinguish the claim of the holder of the sheriff's certificate. *Ib.* So, where the premises are sold on execution for less than the amount due on the judgment, and they are afterward redeemed by the grantee of the judgment debtor, they may be re-sold by the sheriff upon the same execution for the balance remaining due thereon. In such case, the redemption invalidates the sale, the judgment is only satisfied *pro tanto*, and is a lien upon the premises for the unpaid balance. 3 *Barb. S. C. R.* 70.

In respect to a redemption by a creditor from the original purchaser or from another creditor, the statute provides that upon the payment being made of the amount required, the title of the original purchaser shall be thereby transferred to the creditor acquiring the same, and from such creditor to any other creditor becoming a purchaser thereof. 2 *Rev. Stat* 373, *sec.* 59.

The redemption by a junior judgment creditor, is not a satisfaction of the judgment either at law or in equity; and therefore it is no bar to an action upon the judgment, although the value of the lands redeemed far exceeds the amount of the judgment and the money paid on the redemption. 20 *Wend.* 50; 8 *Paige*, 285.

A creditor, redeeming under a junior judgment, cannot recall the money paid for that purpose, even though he has another judgment prior to that under which the sale was had, and the premises are not worth more than the sum bid by the purchaser. 6 *Hill*, 362.

It is no objection to giving the redeeming creditor a deed of the premises, that he has obtained an injunction and restrained the sheriff from paying over the money unconditionally paid by him on the redemption. 4 *Id.* 589.

When the legal estate in lands sold deemed to be vested.] It is provided by statute, that the right and title of the person against whom the execution was issued, to any real estate which shall be sold thereby, shall not be divested by such sale until the expiration of fifteen months from the time of such sale. 2 *Rev. Stat.* 373, *sec.* 61; 1 *Barb. S. C.* 512; 4 *Id.* 159. Nor is the legal estate of the judgment debtor then divested, unless the sale has been consummated, and the title vested in the purchaser, by a deed from the sheriff. Until the sheriff executes a conveyance, the title of the purchaser is inchoate; he acquires no legal estate in the lands, but a right to an estate only, which may be perfected by a conveyance. And until such conveyance, the estate remains in the debtor, who is entitled to the possession, and to the rents and profits, *Id. ibid.*; 17 *Barb.* 157; and which rents and profits may be reached by a creditor of the judgment debtor in a proceeding against him. 10 *Paige*, 598; 15 *Abb.* 373, *note.*

So, if the premises are subject to a mortgage, the purchaser does not become the owner of the equity of redemption until after the expiration of the fifteen months. 4 *Id.* 159.

But if the real estate shall not have been redeemed as provided by the statute, and a deed shall be executed in pursuance of a sale, the grantee shall be deemed vested with the legal estate, from the time of the sale on such execution, for the purpose of maintaining an action for any injury to such real estate. 2 *Rev. Stat.* 373, *sec.* 61. Though the deed will not be held to relate back, so as to give to the purchaser a legal estate which will merge a mortgage previously given to him by the judgment debtor upon the land sold. 1 *Barb. S. C.* 512; and see 4 *Id.* 159; 17 *Id.* 157.

Thus, the purchaser, or redeeming creditor, after receiving the sheriff's deed, may maintain an action for damages against a person who, intermediate the sale and the sheriff's deed, cuts and takes timber from the premises; even though the timber is cut and carried away with the consent of the judgment debtor, who was in possession. 4 *Kern.* 474; and see 3 *Denio*, 79; 2 *Rev. Stat.* 336, *sec.* 20. And see *post*, under the head of "Proceedings if waste is committed on the lands sold."

When, and to whom, conveyances to be executed.] The statute provides that after the expiration of fifteen months from the time of the sale of any real estate, if any part of the premises sold shall remain unredeemed by the person against whom the execution issued, or by any person entitled to redeem the same within one year from the time of such sale, according to the provisions of the statute, then the officer making the sale is required to complete the same, by executing a conveyance of the premises so remaining unredeemed, either to the original purchaser or to the creditor who has acquired the title of the original purchaser, or to the creditor who has purchased such title from any other creditor, as the case may be; which conveyance will be valid and effectual to convey all the right, title, and interest which was sold by such officer. 2 *Rev. Stat.* 373, *sec.* 62. And the holder or owner of the legal title to the judgment under which the redemption is made, is entitled to receive the conveyance of the lands from the sheriff, without reference to the equitable interests of others in such judgment. *Hill and D.* 265.

In case the person who, by the provisions of the statute, would be entitled to a conveyance of any real estate sold by virtue of an execution, shall die previous to the delivery of such conveyance, the officer making the sale shall execute and deliver the conveyance to the executors or administrators of the person so deceased. 2 *Rev. Stat.* 374, *sec.* 63. The real estate so conveyed shall be held in trust for the use of the heirs of such deceased person, subject to the dower of his widow, if there be any; but may be sold for the payment of his debts, by the order of any surrogate or court of equity, in the same manner as lands whereof such deceased person died seized. *Ib. sec.* 64.

The statute further provides, that in all cases where any sale of real estate is made under execution, and a certificate thereof given to the purchaser, but no deed executed pursuant to the statute, it is the duty of the sheriff making the sale, and in case of his death or removal from office, of his under-sheriff, to execute a deed of the estate so sold and remaining unredeemed, to any person or persons to whom the certificate has been duly assigned, or to the executors or administrators of any deceased assignee. (*a*) *Laws of* 1835, *p.* 210.

But before any assignee, or his personal representative, shall be entitled to a deed under the statute, he is required to cause the execution of any and every assignment under which the deed is claimed, to be duly acknowledged or proved, as deeds are required by law to be acknowledged or proved, to entitle them to be recorded, before some officer authorized to take the acknowledgment and proof of deeds; and to cause all such assignments, with their certificates of proof or acknowledgment, to be filed in the office of the clerk of the county in which the real estate so sold is situated *Ib.*

The assignee is not entitled to a conveyance unless he has filed the assignment with the certificate or proof of acknowledgment, 2 *Coms.* 490, aff. 4 *Denio*, 145; and the sheriff, therefore, cannot be compelled to convey real estate sold by him until the assignment has been filed, *Ib.;* though if the sheriff executes a deed where the assignment has not been filed or acknowledged, such deed is nevertheless valid. 7 *Hill*, 91. Nor would the title of a purchaser from a redeeming creditor, who has received a deed from the sheriff, be prejudiced by an omission to prove and file the assignment. 4 *Denio*, 480.

But it is not necessary to file the assignment where it is presented to the officer by a junior judgment creditor for the purpose only of dispensing with the payment by him of the amount paid on the sale. 1 *Id.* 240.

In case any deed shall be executed to executors or administrators of any assignee of the certificate of sale, the estate thereby conveyed, shall be held and may be sold as provided in section sixty-four, *supra. Laws of* 1835, *p.* 210, § 4.

Any officer authorized by law to take the proof of deeds, is

(*a*) This section is repealed, and § 1472 of the Code of Civil Procedure (*post*), is substituted therefor. *Laws of* 1877, *ch.* 417.

authorized and required to take the acknowledgment or proof of such assignments, and to certify the same; which certificate, or a copy certified by the clerk shall have the like force and effect as in case of deeds. *Ib.* § 3.

The sheriff's deed, although executed long after the sale, being founded on the sale, relates back to the time of the sale. 6 *Wend.* 224; 3 *Cowen*, 89; 2 *Coms.* 377. And a deed executed to the purchaser by the deputy of the sheriff in his name and behalf, is good. 10 *Johns.* 223; 12 *Id.* 162. The deputy who has made the sale of the premises, during the term of office of his principal, may, after the expiration of such term, proceed and complete the execution thereof by the giving of a deed. 6 *Wend.* 213.

The conveyance of the sheriff should specify with sufficient certainty, the lands sold, and who was the purchaser. 2 *Johns.* 248. The specification should be so particular, that from the description, the premises can certainly be ascertained. And where lands are conveyed by the sheriff, and two distinct parcels are found equally answering the description contained in the deed, the conveyance will be held inoperative, for the reason that it was intended to pass but one, and it cannot be determined which was intended. 11 *Barb.* 174. The purchaser or redeeming creditor, may direct the deed to be executed to a third party; and the judgment debtor cannot object to its regularity. 1 *Wend.* 46.

Where the rights of several defendants to the premises are sold by the sheriff, and a creditor by mortgage of one of the defendants, redeems the title of such defendant, the deed of the sheriff to such redeeming creditor conveys only the right and title of the defendant which is thus redeemed. 5 *Barb.* 565.

If a deed has been improvidently executed to the purchaser, and afterward the sheriff is directed to execute a deed to a redeeming creditor, the court will not direct the first deed to be canceled, but leave the creditor to enforce his rights as he shall be advised is proper. 7 *Wend.* 463.

Effect of conveyance by sheriff.] By the statute the conveyance of the sheriff is valid and effectual to convey all the right, title, and interest sold by him on the execution. 2 *Rev. Stat.* 373, *sec.* 62. And such conveyance extinguishes a lease given by the judgment debtor between the time of the sheriff's sale and the execution of the sheriff's deed. 5 *Bosw.* 619. It vests, too, in the grantee all the right and title which the debtor had in the land at the time when the judgment first attached as a lien, free from all later incumbrances and unaffected by any subsequent conveyances or acts. 19 *New York*, 373, *per* Comstock, J.

Proceedings if sheriff die, or is removed, &c.] The statute provides, that if any sheriff, to whom an execution shall be delivered, die or be removed from office before such execution be satisfied, his under-sheriff shall proceed thereon in the same manner as the sheriff might have done; and if a sheriff who has sold any real estate, die or be removed before executing any conveyance in pursuance of such sale, such conveyance shall be executed by his under-sheriff, in the same manner, and with the like effect as if done by the sheriff. (*a*) 2 *Rev. Stat.* 374, *sec.* 65; *Laws of* 1835, *p.* 210.

If there be no such under-sheriff, the court from which the execution issued, may, on the application of the plaintiff, appoint some suitable person to proceed on such execution and complete the same, instead of such under-sheriff; and on the application of any person entitled to a conveyance, the court may appoint a proper person to execute the same. The person so appointed shall give such security as the court may require, and shall have the same power in relation to the object of his appointment as the sheriff so dying or removed. 2 *Rev. Stat.* 374, *sec.* 66. But no security will be required, where a deed merely is to be executed, and no money is to be collected or other act done. 10 *Wend.* 562.

If any sheriff shall die, or be removed from office after having made sale of any real estate, the moneys required to be paid to him for the redemption of such estate may be paid to his under-sheriff or to the clerk of the county, in the same manner and with the like effect as if paid to the sheriff. 2 *Rev. Stat.* 374, *sec.* 67.

How possession of premises obtained.] The purchaser or redeeming creditor obtains by the sheriff's deed only the legal title to the land. Actual possession, if the defendant refuses to deliver it, can only be obtained under the statute concerning summary proceedings to obtain possession of land. 2 *Rev. Stat.* 512, *sec.*

(*a*) See note *a*, *ante*, p. 258.

28, *sub.* 4; 13 *Wend.* 31; 17 *Id.* 464; 20 *Id.* 22; and see *post*, Chapter xxx. of this work, where the practice is given at large.

Proceedings where waste is committed on the lands sold.] It is provided by the statute, that whenever any lands or tenements shall be sold by virtue of an execution issued upon any judgment or decree, the person to whom a conveyance may be executed by the sheriff, pursuant to the sale, may maintain an action against any person who may have been in possession of the premises so conveyed, after the sale thereof, for any waste committed on such premises after such sale. 2 *Rev. Stat.* 336, *sec.* 20; *Code*, § 450; 3 *Denio*, 79; 4 *Kern.* 474.

But any person entitled to the possession of lands or tenements sold under execution may, until the expiration of fifteen months from the time of the sale, use and enjoy the same as follows, without being deemed guilty of waste:

1. He may, in all cases, use and enjoy the premises sold in like manner, and for the like purposes in and for which they were used and applied, prior to such sale, doing no permanent injury to the freehold.

2. If the premises sold were buildings, or any other erections, he may make necessary repairs thereto; but he shall make no alterations in the form or structure thereof.

3. If the premises sold were land, he may use and improve the same in the ordinary course of husbandry; but he shall not be entitled to any crops growing thereon, at the expiration of the said fifteen months.

4. He may apply any wood or timber on such land to the necessary reparation of any fences, buildings, or erections, which may have been thereon at the time of the sale.

5. If the land sold is actually occupied by such person, he may take necessary fire-wood therefrom for the use of his family. 2 *Rev. Stat.* 336, *sec.* 22.

And no person lawfully entitled to the possession of the premises so sold, will be liable to such action, for doing any of the acts above mentioned. *Ib. sec.* 21.

If the person against whose property the execution shall have been issued, or any person who may be in possession of the premises sold, shall, at any time after the sale of such premises, and before the time allowed for redeeming the same, do any act of waste thereon, or shall threaten or make preparations to commit waste thereon, the purchaser of such premises, or his authorized agent, may apply by petition to any justice of the Supreme Court, or to the county judge of any county, for an order restraining such wrongdoer from the commission of any further waste upon the premises. *Ib. sec.* 23; *Laws of* 1847, *p.* 323.

If the officer to whom the application shall be so made, shall be satisfied, by due proof, that waste has been actually committed by the person against whom the application is made, or that the same has been threatened, or that preparations for committing it have been made by such person, such officer is required to grant an order restraining such person from the commission of any waste on the premises sold. 2 *Rev. Stat.* 336, *sec.* 24.

If the person against whom any such order shall be made, shall, after the service of a copy thereof, commit any waste in violation of the said order, he shall be liable to be proceeded against and punished in the same manner as for violation of an injunction to stay waste, issued out of the Supreme Court; and for that purpose the officer who may have granted any such order, shall possess the same power and jurisdiction as a justice of the Supreme Court. *Ib. sec.* 25; *Laws of* 1847, *p.* 323.

When complaint shall be made of the violation of any such order to restrain waste, the court or officer may order notice to be given to the person complained of, to show cause why he should not be committed, if from the circumstances of the case they shall judge such order expedient. 2 *Rev. Stat.* 336, *sec.* 26.

Upon satisfactory proof of such violation, such court or officer shall issue a warrant to the sheriff of the county, reciting such order and the proof of the violation thereof, and thereby commanding such officer to commit such defendant to close confinement, for such term of time, not more than one year, as shall be deemed expedient. *Ib. sec.* 27.

The sheriff is required to execute such warrant accordingly, and to commit the person named therein, without allowing him the liberties of the jail. *Ib. sec.* 28.

But such warrant may be superseded, and the person may be discharged by the court or officer committing him, upon receiving a bond in such penalty, and with such sufficient sureties, as the court or officer may approve, to the person applying for the warrant of commitment, conditioned that the prisoner shall not commit any waste on the premises, which bond shall be delivered to the applicant for his use, and to be prosecuted by him for any breach of the condition thereof. *Ib. sec.* 29.

SECTION II.

PROCEEDINGS IN ACTIONS TO REDEEM MORTGAGED PREMISES.

IN equity, a mortgage is a mere security for the debt, and only a chattel interest; and until judgment of foreclosure, the mortgagor is regarded as the real owner of the fee. The equity of redemption is deemed to be the real and beneficial estate, tantamount to the fee at law; and it is accordingly held to be descendible by inheritance, devisable by will, and alienable by deed, precisely as if it were an absolute estate of inheritance at law. 4 *Kent's Com.* 159.

Who may redeem.] The mortgagor, or his grantees, heirs, or devisees, in equity, are the owners of the fee, their equity of redemption being regarded as the real and beneficial estate, and equal to the fee at law. They are entitled, therefore, at any time (within the period of limitation hereafter mentioned), before the equity of redemption is absolutely barred and foreclosed by judgment, to redeem the premises, and thus clear them from the incumbrance upon them. 4 *Kent's Com.* 162. And the equity of redemption is not only a subsisting estate and interest in the land in the hands of the grantees, heirs, and devisees of the mortgagor; but it may also be asserted by any other persons who have acquired any interest in the lands mortgaged, by operation of law, or otherwise, in priority of title; and which interest has not been foreclosed by judgment. *Ib.; 2 Story's Eq.* 291.

Thus, a tenant for life, a tenant by the courtesy, a jointress, a tenant in dower in some cases, a reversioner, a remainder-man, a judgment creditor, and indeed every other person being an incumbrancer, or having a legal or equitable title or lien thereon, may insist upon a redemption of the mortgage, in order to the due enforcement of their respective claims and interests in the land. *Ib.*

And so, a wife, having an inchoate right of dower in the equity of redemption, even where the mortgage is given for a portion of the purchase-money, may, on the death of her husband, redeem the premises by payment of the mortgaged debt. 2 *Bosw.* 524; 10 *Abb.* 152, *s. c.* 20 *New York*, 412. And a foreclosure of the mortgage in the lifetime of her husband, by a suit to which she was not a party, will not cut off her right of redemption. *Id. ibid.*

Thus, also, a subsequent mortgagee may redeem the mortgaged premises as against a prior one, or any person claiming under or through him, such as a purchaser at a sale under the prior mortgage where the subsequent mortgagee has not been made a party to the action. 3 *Johns. Ch. R.* 460.

In respect to judgment creditors, subsequent to the mortgage, and persons claiming under them, the same right exists, if they are not made parties to the foreclosure suit. And a junior judgment creditor, not made a party to the action, may redeem from the purchaser at the sale under the judgment of foreclosure, even though he has not made his lien specific by an execution and sale upon his judgment. 6 *Selden*, 356; 3 *Johns. Ch. R.* 460; 2 *Story's Eq. Jur.* § 1023; 4 *Kent's Com.* 162. So, a junior judgment creditor, not notified of the sale, is not barred by a statutory foreclosure and sale, and may redeem from the purchaser; or, the purchaser may have his action against the creditor for a strict foreclosure. 4 *Paige*, 58.

Redemption by part-owner; leasehold property, &c.] The redemption must be of the entire mortgage, and not by parcels. The mortgagee has the right to insist that the whole of the mortgaged premises shall be redeemed together, and the whole debt paid. 2 *Barb. Ch. Pr.* 194; citing 12 *Ves.* 59; 2 *Root*, 333; 2 *Jac. & W.* 189. Where the land, however, has been sold in parcels, there may be a redemption by the owner of a portion, on payment of his ratable proportion of the mortgage debt. 16 *How.* 571.

If the judgment creditor seeks to redeem against the mortgagee of a leasehold estate, it being only a chattel interest, he must first have issued execution in order to create a lien on the estate. 4 *Johns. Ch. R.* 671; 3 *Atk.* 200.

Within what time action to be commenced.] The party entitled to bring an action to redeem mortgaged premises, must, as a general rule, bring the action within twenty years from the time of the forfeiture, or of actual, quiet, and uninterrupted possession, unless such party has labored under some impediment or disability, such as infancy, or the like; in which case it may be commenced after the period of twenty years and within ten years from the time the impediment is removed; or unless circumstances are proved by the mortgagor, showing an acknowledgment of his title by the mortgagee. 1 *Johns. Ch.* 385, 394; 3 *Id.* 48, 129; 17 *Ves.* 99; 19 *Id.* 327; 1 *Paige*, 48; *Code*, §§ 78, 88.

Thus, proceedings instituted for the foreclosure of a mortgage by advertisement, under the statute, is such an acknowledgment of the right of the mortgagor to redeem, as to repel the presumption arising from the lapse of more than twenty years' possession by the mortgagee. 20 *New York*, 147. So, if the mortgagee, in possession, shows that such possession is under and by virtue of a mortgage; as, by receiving interest upon it, by stating an account, or by treating it as such in a will, deed, or mortgage, a redemption may be adjudged against him, after the time limited for redemption has expired. 2 *Barb. Ch. Pr.* 199, citing *Coop.* 4. And oral evidence, it seems, of such acts, may be received, if clear and unequivocal. 19 *Ves.* 327.

But the statute does not begin to run against the right of a remainder-man to redeem real estate from the mortgagee in possession under the termor, until the determination of the precedent estate. 17 *Abb.* 113. Nor will any length of time bar an action for redemption where there is fraud in the transaction, or where, by the agreement of the parties, at the time, the mortgagee is to enter and keep possession until he is paid out of the profits. 1 *Johns. Ch.* 594.

Parties—1. Plaintiffs.] If the action is brought against a mortgagee, or his assignee, in possession, the mortgagor or his grantee, or other owner of the equity of redemption, is the proper party plaintiff. If the mortgagor be dead, then his heirs, or, if his estate has been devised, his devisee is the proper party plaintiff, if it be a mortgage of a fee; and if a mortgage of a term for years only, then the personal representatives of the mortgagor. *Story's Eq. Pl.* 170; 2 *Rev. Stat.* 82.

If it is claimed that a part of the mortgage has been paid in the lifetime of the mortgagor, the personal representatives of the mortgagor, as well as his heir or devisee, are necessary parties plaintiffs to the action, in order to take the account of what is due on the mortgage, 2 *Barb. Ch. Pr.* 196; or, if they refuse, they may be made defendants, the reason therefor being stated in the complaint. *Ib.*; 2 *Van Sant. Pr.* 112. And where, by law, the personal assets are first to be applied in exoneration of the real estate mortgaged, it seems that in an action by the heir or devisee to redeem, he may properly make the personal representative of the mortgagor a party defendant, in order to have the assets so applied; and thus to relieve himself of the burden of the incumbrance. *Id. ibid.* In this State, however, the heir or devisee must pay the mortgage out of his own property, without resorting to the personal representatives, unless the mortgagor has given express directions in his will that the mortgage be otherwise paid. 1 *Rev. Stat.* 749, *sec.* 4.

If the estate has been assigned by the mortgagor, subject to the mortgage, and the assignee is to pay the mortgage, he may maintain an action to redeem, without making the mortgagor a party. Though, if the assignment be of the whole estate, absolutely free from incumbrances, the mortgagor is a necessary, or at least proper, party defendant, in order to be bound by the judgment, and to assist in taking the account; he being primarily liable to pay the mortgage debt. 2 *Barb. Ch. Pr.* 196.

If the equity of redemption has been conveyed to assignees, or other trustees, for the benefit of creditors, they are the proper parties plaintiffs in the action. And it is unnecessary, in such case, to join the creditors as parties to the action, unless there is collusion between the trustees and mortgagee, or unless the trustees refuse to act, or are insolvent, in which case the creditors, or, if they are numerous, one or more of them, for the benefit of all, may bring the action, making the trustees parties defendants. *Ib.*; *Code*, § 119.

The personal representatives of a judgment creditor, and not his heirs, are the proper parties plaintiffs in an action to redeem; and so in respect to any equity of redemption in a mere chattel interest. But if the judgment creditor has made his lien specific by execution and sale, his heir, and not the personal representative, must bring the action. 2 *Van Sant. Pr.* 112; *Story's Eq. Pl.* 170; 2 *Rev. Stat.* 374, *sec.* 64.

Parties—2. Defendants.] In general, all persons should be made parties defendants who have or claim an interest in the controversy, adverse to the plaintiff, or who are necessary parties to a complete determination or settlement of the questions involved therein. *Code*, § 118.

The mortgagee is the only necessary and proper party in all cases where there is no other outstanding interest under him. And where the mortgagee in possession has made an absolute sale and conveyance of the mortgaged premises, the purchaser must be made a party to the action. 4 *Paige*, 259; 18 *Abb.* 360. But where the mortgage has been assigned absolutely by the mortgagee, without the authority and privity of the mortgagor, it is unnecessary, in an action by the mortgagor to redeem, to make any person but the last assignee a party thereto, however many intervening assignments have been made; for in such a case, the last assignee is understood to have contracted not only to stand in the place of the original mortgagee, and to represent him, but also in the place and as the representative of, all the other mesne assignees, until the title was taken to himself; and he may accordingly be decreed to convey. 2 *Barb. Ch. Pr.* 197.

If the mortgagee has not assigned his entire interest in the property, but retains an interest in part of it, he, as well as the assignee, is a necessary party to the action. 2 *P. Wms.* 643; 5 *Mad.* 475. So, where the mortgagee in possession leases the premises, reserving rent, he or his assignee is a necessary party to an action against the lessee to redeem; so that the lessee may be discharged from his covenant to pay rent, and may also have a judgment for his proportion of the redemption-money, to the extent of the value of the term over and above the rent reserved. 4 *Paige*, 263.

If the entire interest of the mortgagee has been assigned in trust for certain purposes, the trustee and *cestui que trust* are both necessary parties to the action. 2 *Barb. Ch. Pr.* 198, and cases cited.

Terms of redemption.] The mortgagor will not be allowed to redeem without paying what is really due upon the mortgage. This payment is to be made to the mortgagee, or other party occupying his position; and where the mortgagee had bid in the property upon a supposed foreclosure of the mortgage, and afterward had conveyed portions of it to other persons, it was held, in an action to redeem the premises, that the redemption-money should be distributed among the grantees, on the basis of their purchase-money, and in the order of the conveyances. 18 *Abb.* 360.

If the mortgagee has purchased in or discharged a prior mortgage or other incumbrance, the party redeeming must repay this, because the premises are benefited to that amount; and the mortgagee, in such case, as against the mortgagor, will be allowed all that is due upon the incumbrance, although he purchased it for less than its face. 2 *Barb. Ch. Pr.* 198. So, also, a mortgagor, seeking to redeem, will be required to repay taxes, assessments, and reasonable insurance. 13 *Abb. Pr. R.* 33.

But, although a mortgagee in possession may require full payment of the amount due, yet, in an action against him by several plaintiffs, to obtain a redemption of premises, where the right of some of the plaintiffs is barred by the statute of limitations, the plaintiffs not barred are entitled to redeem their share of the land, on payment of their proportion of the debt. 17 *Abb.* 113.

A mortgagor, also, will be required to pay the costs of persons claiming under the mortgagee, who are made defendants in the action, upon the principle that, at law, the mortgage being forfeited, the mortgagee is at liberty to deal with it as his own property. 3 *Mad.* 255. As a general rule, too, a party redeeming will be required to pay costs to the mortgagee, in addition to the amount due upon the mortgage, although he obtains the relief demanded. 4 *Paige*, 58; *Id.* 526; 1 *Id.* 49. Yet if the plaintiff's claim is resisted on a point of law which wholly fails, or is otherwise improperly resisted, or an unconscientious defense is interposed, the defendant will be refused costs, and may be compelled to pay costs to the plaintiff, in the discretion of the court. *Id. ibid.*; 18 *Abb.* 360. So, a junior mortgagee seeking to redeem from a prior mortgagee who is the purchaser under his own judgment of sale, must pay not only the principal and interest due, but the costs of the judgment of foreclosure. 30 *Barb.* 387. But a subsequent mortgagee, it seems, who seeks to redeem from the purchaser under a statute foreclosure of a prior mortgage, is not bound to pay the costs of such foreclosure; which foreclosure, as to his rights, is wholly inoperative. 1 *Paige*, 49; 4 *Id.* 58; *Id.* 526. Nor is a judgment creditor seeking to redeem mortgaged premises after a statute foreclosure, required to pay the costs of the foreclosure. 4 *Paige*, 58. But he must pay the sum actually due upon the mortgage, and not merely the sum bid by the purchaser at the sale. *Ib.*

In respect to improvements and repairs, the general rule is, that upon taking the account in an action for redemption against a mortgagee in possession, or a purchaser, he is to be charged with the rents and profits, and be allowed only for necessary repairs and permanent improvements, made in good faith. He will not be allowed for improvements which were not necessary; such for example, as clearing wild land, &c., made without the acquiescence or consent of the mortgagor. 1 *Johns. Ch. R.* 385. Though where valuable and permanent improvements have been made, in good faith, by a person occupying legally the position of a mortgagee in possession, and who supposed himself to have acquired the absolute title, such mistake having been favored by the omission of the mortgagor for several years to assert any interest in the premises, the mortgagor, in an action to redeem the premises, will be compelled to allow the value of the improvements, though exceeding the rents and profits received. 17 *New York*, 80; and see 14 *How.* 165, *s. c.* 5 *Abb.* 16. And so, where valuable and permanent improvements have been made, in good faith, under the belief of a purchaser that his title is good, and without notice of the existence of the incumbrance under which the redemption is claimed, the enhanced value of the premises arising from the improvements will be required to be paid in addition to the amount due upon the mortgage. 4 *Paige*, 58; 14 *How.* 165, *supra;* 17 *Abb.* 113. All these matters come up on the accounting, where the defendant will be charged with the rents and profits, and credited with his outlays for necessary repairs and improvements, prior incumbrances, taxes, assessments, reasonable insurance paid, &c., 2 *Van Sant. Pr.* 116; though in respect to the rents, he will be charged only with the amount actually received, where there has been no negligence in their collection. *Ib. note;* 13 *Abb.* 33.

But where the lands have been sold in parcels, under a judgment of foreclosure, and a railroad company owning a portion by title subsequent to the mortgage, sought to redeem the premises; it was held entitled to do so on the payment of a ratable proportion of the mortgage debt, which must be the full value by the property (at the time of its appropriation) with interest, if need be, without respect to improvements put thereon by the company. 16 *How.* 571.

What the plaintiff must do before commencing his action.] To entitle the mortgagor, or other party, to commence an action to redeem the mortgaged premises, he must first offer to pay the debt, interest, and costs. 18 *Johns.* 144, *s. c.* 1 *Johns. Ch.* 288.

And if the action is against a mortgagee, or other person, in possession, who has been in the receipt of the rents and profits, and they have been sufficient to pay the principal and interest, it will not be necessary to pay or offer to pay the money, principal or interest; but the party entitled to redeem may demand simply an accounting of such rents and profits, and settlement, which, if refused, will authorize him to bring his action, and if he can show the mortgage paid, he will be entitled to judgment for the possession of the premises. 2 *Van Sant. Pr.* 114, citing 20 *New York*, 147; 6 *Seld.* 356.

The complaint, and other proceedings in the action.] The complaint in an action to redeem mortgaged premises, is drawn according to the principles regulating other equity actions, and there are no special statutory provisions, or other peculiarities, to distinguish it from complaints in ordinary cases. The plaintiff, however, should be careful to allege his offer to pay the amount due for principal and interest, or to come to an accounting for the rents and profits, and the refusal of the defendant; and, also, allege a demand for the delivery of the possession of the premises. 2 *Van Sant. Pr.* 114; 2 *Barb. Ch. Pr.* 199.

The prayer of the complaint is, that an accounting be had in respect to the amount due upon the mortgage; and if the defendants have been in the possession of the premises, receiving the rents and profits, that an accounting also be had in respect to the same; and that the defendant be adjudged to deliver up the possession of the premises on payment of what shall be found due him. *Id. ibid.* For form of a complaint by a junior judgment creditor to redeem premises sold on foreclosure, where he was not a party to the action, see 6 *Seld.* 356; *Van Sant. Prec.* 272.

In respect to the subsequent proceedings in the action, these do not differ materially from those in other equity actions.

Formerly, the practice was to render a decree in the first instance, in which a reference was directed to a master to ascertain and report the amount due; and directing the complainant to pay that amount within a specified time after the confirmation of the report, or that the bill be dismissed. 2 *Barb. Pr.* 199. But now, the practice seems to be, in case of default, to order a reference, if necessary, to take an account of the amount due upon the mortgage, preparatory to final judgment. 2 *Van Sant. Pr.* 114, 115, *note.* And where an account of the rents and profits is part of the relief demanded, a reference is absolutely necessary, whether in case of default, or after trial of the issue. In such case, the reference will embrace both an accounting of the amount due upon the mortgage, and of the amount received by the mortgagee for rents and profits, to the end that upon the coming in of the report, the court may make such judgment as the nature of the case may require. *Ib.; Code,* § 246, *sub.* 2.

The judgment.] The judgment in ordinary cases will be that the plaintiff pay the amount which shall, on the accounting, or if there be no such accounting ordered, on the facts as they shall be proved to the court, appear to be due, and within a specified time, together with the costs, and that upon his doing so, the mortgagee or other person proceeded against, convey to him and deliver up the mortgaged premises; and that upon default of such payment the complaint be dismissed with costs. 2 *Van Sant. Pr.* 115.

The time allowed for redemption rests in the sound discretion of the court, to be regulated by circumstances. And, in general, the time allowed will not be afterward enlarged. 2 *Barb. Ch. Pr.* 200, citing 4 *Johns. Ch.* 140; *Ib.* 65; 17 *Ves.* 417.

Dismissing complaint for failure to redeem.] If the plaintiff fails to redeem within the time fixed by the judgment, the complaint will be dismissed with costs; and such dismissal amounts to a bar of the equity of redemption. 2 *Barb. Ch. Pr.* 199. In case of such omission, the defendant may move, as of course, to dismiss the complaint, upon an affidavit that the time has expired and the money has not been paid. *Ib.*

Effect of redemption.] The party redeeming the premises from a prior mortgage, becomes substituted to the rights and interests of the original mortgagee. The incumbrance is not thereby simply removed, so that he may enforce his own lien, but, as to intermediate incumbrances, he becomes vested with the estate which the person has whose interest he discharges. 2 *Story's Eq.* 291; and see 6 *Seld.* 356.

SUPPLEMENT TO CHAPTER XXVIII.

The practice in proceedings for the redemption of real estate from sales on execution, founded upon the Revised Statutes, has been superseded and a new practice substituted for the same, by art. 3, title 2, of chap. 13 of the Code of Civil Procedure. *Laws of* 1877, *ch.* 417, *p.* 468; *Code of Civil Pro.*, §§ 1430 *to* 1478, *post.* The decisions under the former practice are noted below; and further on, are given in full, the sections of the new Code, as well as the material notes of the Revisers in explanation of the same.

I. DECISIONS OF THE COURTS.

Redemption from sales on execution. The mode of obtaining title to land under execution is wholly a creation of the statute, and its provisions must be strictly followed. 34 *N. Y.*, 235, per Wright, J.

Under the act of 1847 (*ch.* 410, *ante*, *pp.* 243, 244, since repealed by laws of 1877, ch. 417), a redemption by a creditor on the last day of redeeming, to be valid and effectual, must be made at the office of the sheriff of the county in which the sale took place. *Ib.*; and 2 *Hun*, 542.

The right of the judgment debtor to redeem does not depend upon the condition of his title at the time of the sale or redemption. The right follows the person, not the land, and continues for the period prescribed by the statute, although the debtor meanwhile may have parted with his title. 56 *N. Y.*, 507. Co-existent rights of redemption in the judgment debtor and in his grantee, are not inconsistent. *Ib.*

When the sale is made by a deputy sheriff, the payment, on redemption, may be made to him, or to the sheriff. 56 *N. Y.*, 507.

Waiving evidence of creditor's right to redeem, etc. Where a junior judgment creditor applies to redeem to the assignee of the sheriff's certificate of sale, the acceptance of the money and transfer of the certificate by the assignee is a waiver of the production by the junior creditor of evidence of his right to redeem. Such waiver, also, renders the production of such evidence unnecessary to the validity of the sheriff's deed given to the creditor so redeeming. 45 *N. Y.*, 369.

So, the sheriff may waive the recording of the assignment of the certificate of sale, and give a deed to the assignee without requiring it. *Ib.*

Motion to the court for leave to redeem. A subsequent party in interest, whether by way of mortgage, lease, or judgment, cannot on a motion obtain a right to redeem, and have the property conveyed to him by a purchaser. The only remedy in such a case is by action seeking to enforce such right to redeem; and in such an action the rights of all other parties can be protected. 51 *Barb.*, 79.

NEW PRACTICE UNDER THE CODE OF CIVIL PROCEDURE.

The following are the sections of the Code of Civil Procedure on the subject of the redemption of real estate from sales on execution; and also the more material of the Revisers' Notes on the subject:

§ 1430. *To what leasehold property the statute applies.* The expression "real property," as used in this and the succeeding article, includes leasehold property, where the lessee or his assignee is possessed at the time of the sale, of at least five years' unexpired term of the lease, and also of the building or buildings, if any, erected thereupon.

§ 1431. *Real property held in trust when liable to execution.* Real property, held by one person, in trust or for the use of another, is liable to levy and sale by virtue of an execution, issued upon a judgment recovered against the person to whose use it is so held, in a case where it is prescribed by law, that, by reason of the invalidity of the trust, an estate vests in the beneficiary; but special provision is not otherwise made by law for the mode of subjecting it to his debts.

[2 R. S., 368, § 26 (3 R. S., 5th ed., 649; 2 Edm., 381): providing that real property, held in trust, is liable to the debts, judgments, etc., of the cestui que trust, amended so as to conform to the evident intent of the legislature by applying it to cases of invalid trusts, which vest, by law, an estate in the beneficiary; and by omitting the provision relating to "attachment."—*Rev. Notes*, *Laws* 1876, *vol.* 2, *p.* 324.]

§ 1432. *Equity of redemption; when not to be sold.* The judgment debtor's equity of redemption in real property mortgaged, shall not be sold by virtue of an execution issued upon a judgment recovered for the mortgage debt, or any part thereof.

[Substituted for 2 R. S., 368, § 31, *ante*, vol. 1, p. 372.]

§ 1433. *Direction to be endorsed on execution.* Where an execution against property, is issued upon a judgment, specified in the last section, to the county where the mortgaged property is situated, the attorney, or other person who subscribes it, must endorse thereupon a direction to the sheriff, not to levy it upon the mortgaged property, or any part thereof. The direction must briefly describe the mortgaged property, and refer to the book and page, where the mortgage is recorded. If the execution is not collected out of the other property of the judgment debtor, the sheriff must return it wholly or partly unsatisfied, as the case requires.

[2 R. S. 368, § 32, requiring an endorsement on an execution, directing the sheriff not to sell the equity of redemption, in an action for the mortgage debt, confined to an execution issued to the county where the land is situated. *Rev. Notes.*]

§ 1434. *Notice of sale of real property; how given.* The sheriff who sells real property, by virtue of an execution, must previously give public notice of the time and place of the sale, as follows:

1. A written or printed notice thereof must be conspicuously fastened up, at least forty-two days before the sale, in three public places, in the town or city where the sale is to take place, and also in three public places, in the town or city where the property is situated, if the sale is to take place in another town or city.

2. A copy of the notice must be published, at least once in each of the six weeks, immediately preceding the sale, in a newspaper published in the county, if there is one; or, if there is none, in the newspaper printed at Albany, in which legal notices are required to be published.

[2 R. S. 368, § 34, providing for notice of the sale of real property under an execution, amended, in accordance with the authorities, so as to remove obscurity as to the time of posting and publishing the notice; and by requiring publication in the State paper, in all cases, if no paper is published in the county. *Rev. Notes.*]

§ 1435. *Property, how described in notice of sale. Part may be sold.* In each notice, specified in the last section, the real property to be sold must be described with common certainty, by setting forth the name of the township or tract, and the number of the lot, if there is any, or by some other appropriate description. The validity of the sale is not affected by the fact, that the property sold is part only of the property advertised to be sold.

[2 R. S. 369, § 35, amended by adding that a sale of part of the property advertised is valid.]

§ 1436. *Penalty for irregularity in sale.* A sheriff who sells real property, by virtue of an execution, without having given notice thereof, as prescribed in the last two sections, or otherwise than as prescribed in this chapter, forfeits one thousand dollars to the party injured, in addition to the damages which the latter sustains thereby.

§ 1437. *Manner of conducting sale.* Where real property, offered for sale by virtue of an execution, consists of two or more known lots, tracts, or parcels, each lot, tract, or parcel must be separately exposed for sale. If a person who is the owner of, or is entitled by law to redeem, a distinct parcel of the property, of any other description, requires that parcel to be exposed for sale separately, the sheriff must expose it accordingly. No more real property shall be exposed for sale, than it appears to be necessary to sell, in order to satisfy the execution.

[2 R. S. 369, § 38, amended, by introducing the expression, "distinct parcel," which is defined in the Temporary Act (*Laws of* 1876, *ch.* 449) as "a part of the property which is or may be set off by boundary lines, as distinguished from an uncertain or undivided share or interest therein."]

§ 1438. *Sheriff to make duplicate certificates of sale.* The sheriff, who sells real property, by virtue of an execution, must make out, subscribe, and acknowledge before an officer authorized to take the acknowledgment of a deed, duplicate certificates of the sale, containing:

1. The name of each purchaser, and the time when the sale was made.
2. A particular description of the property sold.
3. The price bid for each distinct parcel separately sold.
4. The whole consideration money paid.

§ 1439. *Certificate to be recorded, etc.* The sheriff must, within ten days after the sale, file one of the duplicate certificates, in the office of the clerk of the county, and deliver another to the purchaser. If there are two or more purchasers, a certificate must be delivered to each. The clerk must immediately record the certificate in a book, kept by him, for that purpose, and must index the record, to the name of the judgment debtor. His fees for so doing must be paid by the sheriff, as part of the expenses of the sale.

§ 1440. *Title to real property not divested before deed.* The right and title of the judgment debtor, or of a person holding under him, or deriving title through him, to real property, sold by virtue of an execution, is not divested by the sale, until the expiration of the period, within which it can be redeemed, as prescribed in this article, and the execution of the sheriff's deed. But if the property is not redeemed, and a deed is executed in pursuance of the sale, the grantee in the deed is deemed to have been vested with the legal estate, from the time of the sale, for the purpose of maintaining an action for an injury to the property.

[2 R. S. 369, § 61, enacting when the debtor's title is divested, amended by changing "fifteen months, etc., from the sale," to "after execution of the sheriff's deed;" because this may be postponed longer than fifteen months. *Rev. Notes.*]

§ 1441. *Rights of holder of the property during intermediate period.* The person entitled to the possession of real property, sold by virtue of an execution, as prescribed in the last section, may, during the period therein specified, use and enjoy the same as follows, without being chargeable with committing waste:

1. He may use and enjoy it in like manner, and for the like purposes, as it was used and enjoyed before the sale, doing no permanent injury to the freehold.

2. He may make necessary repairs to a building, or other erection thereupon. But this subdivision does not permit an alteration in the form or structure of the building, or other erection.

3. He may use and improve the land in the ordinary course of husbandry; but he is not entitled to a crop, growing thereon, at the expiration of the period of redemption.

4. He may apply any wood or timber on the land to the necessary reparation of a fence, building, or other erection, which was thereupon at the time of the sale.

5. If he actually occupies the land sold, he may take necessary fire-wood therefrom for use in his household.

§ 1442. *Order to prevent waste.* If, at any time during the period allowed for redemption, the judgment debtor, or any other person in possession of the property sold, commits, or threatens to commit, or makes preparations for committing, waste thereupon, the Supreme Court, or any justice thereof, within the judicial district, or the county judge of the county, in which the property, or any part thereof, is situated, may, upon the application of the purchaser, or his assignee, or the agent or attorney of either, and proof, by affidavit, of the facts, grant, without notice, an order, restraining the wrongdoer from committing waste upon the property.

§ 1443. *Proceedings to punish violation of the order.* If the person, against whom such an order is granted, commits waste in violation thereof, after the service upon him of the order, with a copy of the affidavit upon which it was granted, the court or judge, upon proof, by affidavit, of the facts, may grant an order, requiring him to show cause, at a time and place therein specified, why he should not be punished for a contempt.

§ 1444. *Mode and extent of punishment.* If, upon the return of the order to show cause, it satisfactorily appears that the person, required to show cause, has violated the former order, the court or judge may either punish him, as prescribed by law for the punishment of a contempt of a court of record, other than a criminal contempt; or may grant a warrant, directed to the sheriff of the county, reciting the former order, and the violation thereof, and commanding the sheriff to commit the wrongdoer to close confinement, for a term specified therein, not more than one year. A person thus committed cannot be admitted to the liberties of the jail.

§ 1445. *How warrant, etc., superseded.* The warrant may be superseded, and the prisoner discharged, by an order, in the discretion of the court or judge committing him, upon his executing, to the person who applied for the warrant, an undertaking, in a sum fixed, and with sureties approved, by the court or judge, to the effect that he will pay any judgment, which the applicant, or his assignee, or other representative, may recover against him, by reason of any waste theretofore or thereafter committed on the property; and upon his paying to the applicant, for the costs and expenses of the proceedings, a sum, fixed by the court or judge.

[2 R. S., 338, § 29 (3 R. S., 5th ed., 624; 2 Edm., 348), providing for superseding a warrant against an occupant, who has committed waste upon real property sold under an execution, upon his merely giving security to pay for further waste committed, amended by requiring also security for waste already done, and by making the delinquent pay the costs of the proceedings to commit him. *Rev. Notes.*]

§ 1446. *When and how real property sold may be redeemed.* Within one year after the sale of real property, by virtue of an execution, a person, specified in the next section, may redeem it, by paying to the purchaser, his executor, administrator, or assignee, or to the sheriff who made the sale, for the use of the person so entitled thereto, the sum of money which was paid upon the sale, with interest from the time of the sale, at the rate of ten per centum a year.

§ 1447. *By whom such redemption may be made.* The redemption, specified in the last section, may be made, either by the judgment debtor, whose right and title were sold, or by his heir, devisee, or grantee, who has acquired, by inheritance, devise, deed, sale by virtue of a mortgage or of an execution, or by any other means, an absolute title to the property proposed to be redeemed; or, in a case specified in sections 1458 or 1459 of this act [*post*], to a portion thereof.

§ 1448. *Such redemption avoids the sale.* Upon payment being made, by a person entitled to redeem real property, as prescribed in the last two sections, the sale of the property redeemed, and the certificates of the sale, as far as they relate thereto, become null and void.

§ 1449. *When creditor may redeem.* Real property, sold by virtue of an execution, which remains, at the expiration of one year after the sale, unredeemed by the person or persons entitled to redeem it, as prescribed in the last three sections, may be redeemed, within three months after the expiration of the year, by the creditors specified, and upon the terms and in the manner prescribed, in the following sections of this article.

§ 1450. *What sum to be paid, etc., when creditor redeems.* In a case specified in the last section, a creditor, having in his own name, or as executor, administrator, assignee, trustee, or otherwise, a judgment rendered, or a mortgage duly recorded, at any time before the expiration of fifteen months from the time of the sale, which is a lien upon the real property sold, may redeem that property by paying the sum of money, which was paid upon the sale thereof, with interest at the rate of seven per centum a year from the time of the sale, and executing a certificate of satisfaction, as prescribed in section 1463 of this act.

[2 R. S., 371, § 51, as amended; specifying the mode in which a creditor may redeem real property from a sale under an execution, amended, by requiring him to give a certificate of satisfaction, or of ratable satisfaction, of his judgment or mortgage. *Rev. Notes.*]

§ 1451. *Redemption by another creditor from a redeeming creditor.* Where a creditor has redeemed real property, as prescribed in the last section, any other creditor, who might have redeemed it from the purchaser, as therein prescribed, may redeem it from the first redeeming creditor as follows

1. He must reimburse to the first redeeming creditor, his executor, administrator, or assignee, the sum paid by him to redeem the property, with interest at the rate of seven per centum a year from the time of his redemption.

2. He must execute a certificate of satisfaction, relating to his judgment or mortgage, in like manner as the first redeeming creditor was required to do.

3. If the judgment or mortgage, by virtue of which the first creditor redeemed, is prior to the judgment or mortgage of the second creditor, the second creditor must also pay to the first creditor, the sum specified in the certificate of satisfaction, executed by him upon his redemption, with interest at the rate of seven per centum a year, from the time of his redemption; unless the first redeeming creditor's judgment or mortgage had ceased, when he redeemed, to be a lien as against the second redeeming creditor; in which case, the latter need not pay any part of the sum specified in the certificate.

§ 1452. *Redemption; when second redeeming creditor has the prior lien.* Where the lien of the second redeeming creditor's judgment or mortgage, is prior to that of the first redeeming creditor's judgment or mortgage, so that the former redeems, without paying the sum specified in the latter's certificate of satisfaction, the latter may, without executing another certificate of satisfaction, again redeem from the former, or from any subsequent redeeming creditor, in a case where he would have been entitled to redeem if his first certificate had not been executed; and he has the same rights with respect to any creditor redeeming from him, as if his first certificate had been executed, when he made his second redemption.

[New provision, as to the redemption of real property from a sale under an execution, to the effect that, where the first redeeming creditor is junior to a second redeeming creditor, the former may redeem a second time without executing a second certificate of satisfaction, so as to prevent an injustice, arising from the first certificate being framed with a view to payment of the senior incumbrance. *Rev. Notes.*]

§ 1453. *Subsequent redemption by other creditors.* A third or other creditor, who might have redeemed, as prescribed in the last four sections, may redeem from the second or any other creditor, who has redeemed, in the manner and upon the terms and conditions prescribed in the last two sections.

§ 1454. *When creditor may redeem after fifteen months.* A creditor, who might have redeemed within fifteen months after the sale, as prescribed in the last four sections, may redeem from any other redeeming creditor, although the fifteen months have elapsed; provided, that he thus redeems within twenty-four hours after the last previous redemption.

§ 1455. *When redemption must be made at sheriff's office.* A redemption, made by a creditor, on or after the last day of the fifteen months, must be made at the sheriff's office of the county. The sheriff, or his under-sheriff, or a deputy-sheriff, in his behalf, must attend at the sheriff's office, for that purpose, on the last day of the fifteen months, and on each day thereafter, in which a redemption can be made, during the time when the sheriff's office is required by law to be kept open. In the absence of the sheriff, the redemption may be made, by paying the necessary money, and delivering the necessary papers, to the under-sheriff, or to any deputy-sheriff, present at the sheriff's office. If the term of office of the sheriff, who made the sale, has expired, and he, or his under-sheriff, or a deputy-sheriff authorized in his behalf, to receive the necessary money and the necessary papers, is not present, the money may be paid, and the papers may be delivered to the sheriff then in office, or to the under-sheriff, or a deputy-sheriff of the latter.

[L. 1847, ch. 410, part of § 3 (3 R. S., 5th ed., 656; 4 Edm., 631), prescribing the mode of redemption of real property, from sale under an execution, on or after the last day of the fifteen months, completely remodelled, so as to remove the obscurities of the original, and amended by adding a requirement that such redemption must be made at the sheriff's office. See 34 *N. Y.*, 235; 2 *Hun*, 542. *Rev. Notes.*]

§ 1456. *Original purchaser may redeem, when also a creditor.* If the purchaser, at the execution sale of property, which can be redeemed by a creditor, as prescribed in this article, is also a creditor of the judgment debtor, and as such could redeem from a purchaser, or a redeeming creditor, he may avail himself of his judgment or mortgage, to redeem from any other redeeming creditor.

§ 1457. *Creditor may redeem again under another judgment or mortgage.* The judgment creditor, by virtue of whose execution real property has been sold, cannot avail himself of the judgment upon which the execution was issued, to redeem the property; nor, except as otherwise specially prescribed in this article, can a creditor, who has once redeemed, avail himself of the same judgment or mortgage, to redeem again. But if either has another judgment or mortgage, which would entitle him to redeem, he may avail himself thereof for that purpose, in the same manner and on the same terms, as any other creditor.

[2 R. S., 373, § 53, forbidding the execution creditor to redeem real property under his judgment, extended to a redeeming creditor, who has once redeemed. *Rev. Notes.*]

§ 1458. *Redemption by person entitled to redeem part.* Where a person, who has an absolute title to, or a judgment or mortgage which is a lien upon, a distinct parcel only of the real property, sold by virtue of an execution, would be authorized by this article to redeem the property, if his title or lien extended to the whole, he may redeem from a purchaser the entire property sold, or from a prior redeeming creditor, the entire property redeemed by that creditor; except that if his title or lien extends to a distinct parcel only of one or more parts of the property which were separately sold, he can redeem from a purchaser only the part or parts thus separately sold, in which his distinct parcel is included.

§ 1459. *Redemption by owners of undivided shares.* Where two or more persons own undivided shares, as joint tenants, or as tenants in common, in real property, sold by virtue of an execution, or in a distinct parcel thereof, which has been separately sold; each of them may redeem, from the purchaser, as prescribed in sections 1446 and 1447 of this act, the share or interest belonging to him, by paying a part of the purchase money, bid for the property or for that distinct parcel thereof, bearing the same proportion to the whole, as the share or interest, proposed to be redeemed, bears to the property or distinct parcel separately sold, of which it is a part; together with interest on the sum so paid, from the time of the sale, at the rate of ten per centum a year.

§ 1460. *Redemption by creditors having liens on undivided shares.* Where the judgment or mortgage of a creditor, entitled to redeem, is a lien upon an undivided share, specified in the last section, he may redeem from a purchaser that undivided share, by paying him the same proportion of the purchase money, which the owner must have paid to redeem it, as prescribed in the last section; or he may redeem, from a prior redeeming creditor, the entire property redeemed by the latter, with like effect and in the same manner as if his lien attached to the whole.

[2 R. S., 373, § 54, allowing a redemption of an undivided interest, by a creditor having a lien thereupon, amended so as to allow him to redeem the entire property. *Rev. Notes.*]

§ 1461. *Right to redeem not affected by agreement.* The sheriff, the purchaser, the judgment creditor, or a redeeming creditor, cannot, by his agreement or other act, in any manner impair or prejudice the right of any other person to redeem, as prescribed in this article.

[New provision, changing the rule laid down in 4 *Com.*, 554, *ante*, *p.* 235.]

§ 1462. *To whom money paid upon redemption.* The money required to be paid by a creditor, in order to effect a redemption of real property, as prescribed in this article, may be paid to the purchaser or creditor from whom the property is to be redeemed, his executor, administrator, or assignee; or it may be paid for the use of the person so entitled thereto, to the sheriff who made the sale.

§ 1463. *Certificate of satisfaction required to effect redemption by creditor.* The certificate of satisfaction required to be executed by a creditor, in order to effect a redemption of real property, must be acknowledged or proved, and certified, in like manner as a deed to be recorded in the county; must describe, with reasonable certainty, the judgment or mortgage under which he redeems, and specify the sum due thereupon; and must state that the redemption satisfies the judgment or mortgage in full, or to a specified amount. It must be filed in the county clerk's office at or before the time when the money is paid to effect the redemption, unless the money is paid to the sheriff, in which case the certificate must also be delivered, at the time of the payment, to the sheriff, who must file it in the county clerk's office, as prescribed in section 1467 of this act. The county clerk, immediately after the execution and recording of the deed, must enter, in his docket, the satisfaction, or partial satisfaction, of a judgment, specified in a certificate so filed, as required by law, when a judgment is collected by virtue of an execution. If a mortgage, specified in the certificate, is recorded in his office, he must cancel and discharge the mortgage of record if it is satisfied by the certificate; or, if it is only partially satisfied, he must make a minute of the partial satisfaction upon the record thereof. If the property mortgaged is situated in a county in which there is a register, the county clerk must transmit a certified copy of the certificate to the register, who must in like manner cancel and discharge the mortgage of record, or make a minute of the partial satisfaction thereof. The clerk's and register's fees for performing the services specified in this section must be paid by the sheriff, who may require the person entitled to a deed to pay him the amount thereof before the deed is delivered.

[New provision, regulating the certificate of satisfaction required to be given and filed by a redeeming creditor. *Rev. Notes.*]

§ 1464. *What evidence a redeeming judgment creditor must furnish.* In order to entitle a creditor by judgment to redeem real property, as prescribed in this article, he must, when he redeems, file in the county clerk's office, or deliver to the sheriff, as the case requires, the following evidence of his right:

1. A copy of the docket of the judgment under which he claims the right to redeem, duly certified by the county clerk.

2. Each assignment of the judgment, which is necessary to establish his right. An assignment so filed or delivered must be acknowledged or proved and certified, in like manner as a deed to be recorded, or the execution thereof must be proved by the affidavit of the creditor, or of a witness thereto, unless it has been filed and entered as prescribed in article third of title first of chapter eleventh of this act [*Code of Civil Pro.*, §§ 1245 *to* 1272], in which case a certified copy thereof must be filed or delivered.

3. An affidavit made by him, or his attorney or agent, stating truly the sum remaining unpaid on the judgment at the time of claiming the right to redeem.

[2 R. S., 373, § 60, prescribing the evidence to be furnished by a judgment creditor, of his right to redeem real property, amended so as to require him to produce the evidence of his right at the time when he redeems, and to file it in the county clerk's office, instead of delivering it to the purchaser, etc., because the latter might be interested to destroy it; also by requiring the original, instead of copies of, the assignments under which he claims to be filed, unless they have been already filed. *Rev. Notes.*]

§ 1465. *Evidence to be furnished by mortgage creditor.* In order to entitle a creditor by mortgage to redeem real property, as prescribed in this article, he must, when he redeems, file in the county clerk's office, or deliver to the sheriff, the following evidence of his right:

1. A copy of the mortgage under which he claims the right to redeem, duly certified by the clerk or register of the county.

2. Each assignment of the mortgage, which is necessary to establish his right, acknowledged or proved, and certified, as prescribed in the last section for an assignment of a judgment, unless it has been recorded; in which case a certified copy of the record must be filed or delivered.

3. An affidavit made by him, or by his attorney or agent, stating truly the sum remaining unpaid on the mortgage at the time of claiming the right to redeem.

§ 1466. *Evidence by executor or administrator.* In either of the cases specified in the last two sections, if the person proposing to redeem claims to be entitled so to do by reason of his being an executor or administrator of a person who, if living, would be entitled to redeem, he must file or deliver, with the other papers therein prescribed, a certified copy or a sworn copy of his letters testamentary, or letters of administration.

§ 1467. *Officers to keep papers open to inspection; when to file them.* The sheriff, to whom one or more papers, specified in the last four sections, are delivered, must keep them open, at all reasonable times during the period allowed for redemption, to the inspection of all persons interested. He must have all those papers at the sheriff's office, at the times when he is required to attend thereat, for the purpose of enabling creditors to redeem, as prescribed by law; and he must file them in the county clerk's office within three days after the execution of the deed.

[New provision, requiring evidence of the right to redeem duly filed to be kept open to inspection. *Rev. Notes.*]

§ 1468. *When redemption takes effect.* A redemption by a creditor is effected only when he has paid all the money required to be paid, and filed or delivered all the papers required to be filed or delivered, as prescribed in this article; and a waiver of any of those requirements is void, as against a person who is entitled subsequently to redeem. Where a redemption is thus effected, it vests in the redeeming creditor all the right, title, and interest which the purchaser acquired by the sale.

[New provision, preventing a waiver of the production of the evidence of the right to redeem from affecting a person entitled subsequently to redeem. *Rev. Notes.*]

§ 1469. *Certificate to be given when redemption made.* Where a redemption is made, as prescribed in this article, the officer or other person to whom money is paid, or a paper is delivered, for the purpose of effecting the redemption, must execute and deliver to the person paying the money or delivering the paper, a certificate stating all the facts which transpired before him with respect to the redemption.

§ 1470. *Certificate may be acknowledged and recorded.* Such a certificate may be acknowledged or proved, and certified, in like manner as a deed to be recorded in the county where the property is situated. The recording thereof in the office of the clerk or register of that county, in the book for recording deeds, has the same effect as against subsequent purchasers and incumbrancers as the recording of a conveyance.

§ 1471. *When and by whom conveyance to be executed.* Immediately after the expiration of fifteen months from the time of the sale, except where a redemption has been made on the last day of the fifteen months, and, in that case, immediately after the expiration of twenty-four hours from the last redemption, the sheriff who made the sale must execute the proper deed or deeds, in order to convey to the person or persons entitled thereto, the part or parts of the property sold, which have not been redeemed by the judgment debtor, his heir, devisee, or assignee. The deed conveys to the grantee therein the right, title, and interest which were sold by the sheriff.

§ 1472. *To whom conveyance to be executed.* If any part of the property remains unredeemed by a creditor, it must be conveyed by the sheriff to the purchaser upon the sale; except where the certificate of sale has been assigned; in which case, it must be conveyed to the last assignee. Any part or parts of the property sold, which have been redeemed by a creditor, must be conveyed by the sheriff, to the last redeeming creditor, except where he has assigned the certificate of redemption, or has executed any other assignment of his right, title, and interest in the property redeemed by him; in which case, it must be conveyed to the last assignee.

§ 1473. *When conveyance made to executor or administrator; effect thereof.* Where a person, entitled to a deed, dies before the delivery of the deed, the sheriff must execute and deliver the deed to his executor or administrator. The property so conveyed must be held in trust for the use of the heirs or devisees of the decedent, subject to the dower of his widow, if there is one; but it may be sold, in a proper case, for the payment of his debts, in the same manner as land, whereof he died seized.

§ 1474. *Assignment must be acknowledged and filed.* Before an assignee, or his executor or administrator, is entitled to a deed, as prescribed in the last two sections, each assignment, under which the deed is claimed, must be acknowledged or proved, and certified, in like manner as a deed to be recorded in the county where the property is situated, and must be filed in the office of the clerk of that county.

§ 1475. *Under sheriff or successor to act, if sheriff dies.* Where a sheriff dies, is removed from office, or becomes otherwise disqualified to act, at any time after making a sale of real property, by virtue of an execution, the property, or a distinct parcel thereof, may be redeemed, by paying the necessary money, and delivering the necessary papers to his under-sheriff, who must also execute and deliver the proper deed or deeds of property, not redeemed by the judgment debtor, his heir, devisee, or grantee. If the under-sheriff also dies, is removed from office, or becomes otherwise disqualified to act, the property may be redeemed, by paying the necessary money, and delivering the necessary papers, to the sheriff's successor in office, who must also execute and deliver the proper deed or deeds. The under-sheriff, or the sheriff's successor, as the case requires, possesses all the powers, and is subject to all the duties and liabilities of the sheriff who made the sale, touching the redemption and conveyance of property sold, and the proceedings relating thereto; and each provision of law, regulating those proceedings, and applicable to the sheriff who made the sale, is applicable to his under-sheriff or successor. This section applies where a sale was made, either before or after this act takes effect.

[A provision, reconciling the provisions of the R. S., and of L. 1867, ch. 116, § 1 (7 Edm., 60), as to the devolution of duties, where the sheriff dies, after he has sold real property under an execution, by imposing those duties upon the under-sheriff, or where he is dead, upon the sheriff's successor, so that the parties may have the security of an official bond. *Rev. Notes.*]

§ 1476. *Money may be paid, etc., to under-sheriff, or deputy-sheriff, who sold property.* Where real property is sold, by virtue of an execution, by the under-sheriff or a deputy sheriff, in behalf of the sheriff, money required to be paid, or a paper required to be delivered to the sheriff, in order to effect a redemption, as prescribed in this article, at any time before the last day of the fifteen months from the time of the sale, may be paid or delivered, either to the sheriff, or to the under-sheriff or deputy sheriff, who made the sale.

[New provisions, prescribing to whom money, on the redemption of real property, may be paid (56 *N. Y.*, 507). *Rev. Notes.*]

§ 1477. *Application of this article to sale by coroner, or person specially appointed, etc.* Where real property is sold, by virtue of an execution, by a person specially appointed by the court, as prescribed in section 1362 or section 1388 of this act, it may be redeemed, as prescribed in this article, as if it had been sold by the sheriff, except as follows:

1. Money, required to be paid, or a paper, required to be delivered, to the sheriff, in order to effect a redemption, as prescribed in this article, at any time before the last day of the fifteen months from the time of the sale, must be paid to the officer who made the sale; unless the person entitled to redeem, his agent or attorney, files with the clerk of the county, with the paper or papers required to be filed, or to be delivered to the sheriff, for the purpose of effecting the redemption, his affidavit, to the effect that the officer is dead, or has been removed, or, where he is a coroner, that he is no longer in office; or that after diligent search, the affiant has been unable to find him within the county; in which case, the money may be paid into court, by paying it to the county treasurer, to the credit of the cause, with like effect, as where it is paid to the sheriff after a sale by the latter.

2. The provisions of section 1455 of this act, apply to a redemption, upon a sale made as prescribed in this section; and the officer who sold the property must attend, as the sheriff is therein required to attend. If he is not present, the redemption may be effected, as prescribed in that section for re-

demption in a case where the term of office of the sheriff who made the sale has expired.

§ 1478. *Proceeding where coroner or person appointed dies, etc.* If, when the period for redemption expires, a coroner, or a person specially appointed by the court, who has sold real property, by virtue of an execution, is dead, or has been removed, or, in the case of a coroner, if he is no longer in office, the court must, upon the application of a person entitled to a deed, appoint a person to execute the deed accordingly.

CHAPTER XXIX.

SALE OF THE REAL ESTATE OF RELIGIOUS CORPORATIONS.

At the common law, every corporation aggregate, including religious corporations, had unlimited power over its property. It might alienate the same in fee, or grant any lesser estates therein, without limitation or restriction. *Coke Litt.* 44, *a.* 300; 7 *Paige*, 83; 16 *Barb.* 241; 23 *Id.* 333; 3 *Barb. Ch. R.* 122.

But this common law right, in respect to the disposition of church property, or the property of religious corporations, was taken away, in England, at an early day, by several restraining statutes. See 1 *Evans' Statutes*, 381 to 390. And although those statutes were never re-enacted in this State, yet they were believed to have become a part of the laws of the colony, upon its settlement by emigrants coming hither from the mother country. "For it is a natural presumption," says Chancellor Walworth, "and therefore adopted as a rule of law, that on the settlement of a new territory by a colony from another country and where the colonists continue subject to the government of the mother country, they carry with them the general laws of that country, so far as those laws are applicable to the colonists in their new situation; which thus become the unwritten law of the colony, until altered by common consent or legislative enactment." 3 *Barb. Ch. R.* 122; and see 23 *Barb.* 333; 2 *Kent's Com.* 281, *marg. pag.*

Acting upon that presumption, and deeming it important that provision should be made by which religious corporations might be able to dispose of their real estate, the legislature, in March, 1806, passed an act authorizing the Chancellor, upon the application of a religious corporation, in case he should deem it proper, to make an order for such sale, and for the application of the proceeds thereof to such uses as the corporation, with his consent and approbation, should conceive to be most for the interests of the society to which the real estate so sold belonged. *Id. ibid.; Laws of* 1806, *p.* 90; *Will. Eq. Jur.* 734; 6 *Bosw.* 245. But that provision was not to extend to any of the lands granted by the State for the support of the Gospel. *Id. ibid.* (*a*)

The act thus passed was afterward embodied in the general act for the incorporation of religious societies (2 *R. L.* 218, *sec.* 11), and continues, at this day, the law of the State (3 *Rev. Stat. 3d ed.* 249; 1 *Id. 4th ed.* 1184), except, as we shall see hereafter, the power to consent to the sale of the property, and to direct the application of the proceeds, is now devolved upon other tribunals than the Court of Chancery.

To what courts application to be made.] Formerly, as we have seen, the application was required to be made to the Chancellor; but that office having been abolished by the Constitution of 1846, the powers of the Chancellor were conferred upon the Supreme Court. 3 *Rev. Stat. 3d ed.* 249; 1 *Id. 4th ed.* 1184; *Const. art.* 14, *sec.* 8; 23 *Barb.* 327; *s. c.* 4 *Abb.* 182; *Laws of* 1847, *p.* 323, § 16.

Jurisdiction in this proceeding is also now given to the county court of the county where the premises are situated. *Laws of* 1847, *p.* 643, §. 28; *Code of Pro.* § 30; 18 *New York*, 395. Also, to the Court of Common Pleas of the city and county of New York, when the premises are situated within the limits of that city, *Laws of* 1854, *p.* 464, § 6; and, in the city of Buffalo, to the Superior Court of that city, when the premises are situated therein. *Ib. p.* 224, § 9.

When religious corporations may sell, and the authority of the court.] Religious corporations have an unlimited authority

(*a*) In respect to burying grounds, it is further provided by statute, that it shall not be lawful for any church or religious corporation to mortgage any burying ground used for the interment of human remains, for the use of which they shall have received compensation, without the previous consent in writing of three-fourths in number of the congregation or society of such church or corporation; which consent shall be proved or acknowledged in the same manner as deeds are now required by law to be proved or acknowledged, and shall thereupon be recorded in the office of the register of the city, or clerk of the county, in which such burying ground is situated. *Laws of* 1842, *p.* 259; and see 7 *How.* 477.

to sell or dispose of their real estate; provided, however, that they sell with the consent and approbation of the court. 7 *Paige*, 84. "I have no doubt," observes Chancellor Walworth, in the case cited, "that the intention of the act of March, 1806, was to give to every religious corporation an unlimited power to convey any real property held by them in trust for the corporators; provided, the previous consent of this court to such alienation of the church property and a direction for the proper application of the proceeds thereof for the benefit of the corporators was obtained, in the summary mode which is there prescribed." And see *Will. Eq. Jur.* 735.

The previous assent of the court must, therefore, be obtained to every sale of the real estate of a religious corporation; and, without such assent, it is doubtful whether a subsequent ratification by the court would give validity to it. (*a*) See 7 *Paige*, 84. But the court has power only to ratify or veto a sale made by the corporation. It may withhold its assent to a sale, and thus compel the corporation to retain the property; but it has no power to dictate to the corporation how, or to whom, it shall sell, or to require it to sell against its will, or otherwise to control it in the disposition of its property, or of the proceeds thereof. 16 *Barb.* 237; 23 *Id.* 335; *s. c.* 4 *Abb.* 182; 6 *Bosw.* 246.

But the order of the court is not necessary to give validity to a mortgage executed by a religious corporation for a portion of the consideration money of premises purchased. 18 *Barb.* 36. Nor to give validity to a mortgage executed to secure a debt of the corporation. 27 *Id.* 52; and see 37 *Id.* 582.

Nor is the consent of the court necessary to enable the corporation to sell the pews in its church, 5 *Cowen*, 494; otherwise, however, if an absolute sale is intended. 16 *Barb.* 237; 8 *Id.* 147, aff. 17 *Id.* 104.

The authority of the court to make an order for the sale of the real estate of a religious corporation relates to cases where the absolute right and title to lands belonging to the corporation are to be sold. 5 *Cowen*, *supra*. And Woodworth, J., remarks,

---

(*a*) Nor can a religious corporation submit the question of sale to an arbitrator for decision. And if an arbitrator is chosen, and he decides the property shall be sold, his award is not binding upon any one, and gives no authority to make the sale 23 *Barb.* 327; *s. c.* 4 *Abb.* 182.

in the case cited, that cases of that kind may and do occur. "It is often necessary," he observes, "to sell a portion of the real estate for the advancement of the residue. Sometimes it becomes necessary to sell the church and lot, when a new church is built and located at a different place. In all these cases, the purchasers acquire the absolute inheritance; and to such only, in my opinion, does the statute apply. A sale of real estate *ex vi termini* means an absolute transfer of the property. But the sale of pews in a church is not a sale of real estate, within the meaning of the act. By the grant of a pew, the grantee acquires a limited usufructuary right only. He may use it as a pew in a house of religious worship; but has not an unlimited, absolute right. He cannot use it lawfully for purposes incompatible with its nature. The right, too, is limited as to time. If the house be burnt, or destroyed by time, the right is gone." And see 8 *Barb.* 147; aff. 17 *Id.* 104; 16 *Id.* 237; 18 *New York*, 396.

How, and by whom application to be made.] The application is *ex parte*, and should be made to the court at special term. If the proceeding, however, is instituted in the county court, the application may be made at any term of the court, or even out of term, or to the judge at chambers, that court being always open for the transaction of such business. *Code of Pro.* § 31. But, in such case, whether the application is made in court, or out, the papers should recite the proceedings as in court.

The application must be made by and in the name of the corporation; and the court has no power to grant an order of sale upon the application of the trustees, or otherwise than upon the application of the corporation. *Wyatt* v. *Benson* (a). 23 *Barb.* 327; *s. c.* 4 *Abb.* 182; and see 1 *Kern.* 94; *Id.* 243.

(a) The correctness of the decision in *Wyatt* v. *Benson* is questioned in the *Matter of St. Ann's Church*, 23 *How.* 285; *s. c.* 14 *Abb.* 424. It is there held that the trustees of a religious corporation are its managing agents, and may act for it as fully as the directors or agents of other corporate bodies; and that it is no objection to an application by the trustees for leave to sell real estate that such application is not authorized by an express vote of the corporation, where neither the good faith of the application nor the propriety of the proposed sale is questioned. See also 20 *How.* 325; 18 *New York*, 401. It is usual, however, in such cases, to show that, at a

The corporation consists of every member of the congregation having the privilege of voting; and the acts of a majority are binding upon the whole. 23 *Barb. supra;* and see 16 *Id.* 243, *per* Harris, J.

And where the court made an order giving its consent to the sale of property, on the petition of a majority of the board of trustees, but such petition had not been authorized or sanctioned by a majority of the corporators, and the order was still *in fieri*, and not executed, no rights having been acquired under it—it was held that the order was still under the control of the court, and that it was competent for the court to revoke its consent. 23 *Barb.* 327, *supra.* And it appearing to the court, in that case, that a sale of the property would be in opposition to the views of a large majority of the corporators, the previous order of sale was revoked.

The application is by petition, which should set forth the lands desired to be sold, and the disposition which the corporation proposes to make of the proceeds of the sale. And the petition, or affidavit accompanying it, when presented by the trustees in behalf of the corporation, should allege that the application was authorized by a majority of the corporators thereof, or otherwise show that such application was made in their behalf, and with their assent. *Wyatt* v. *Benson*, (a) 23 *Barb.* 327, *supra.* For form, see *Appendix*, No. 580.

In the city of New York, it is necessary, also, to submit to the court, with the petition, a statement specifying what property had been sold by the corporation under any order of the court at any time within five years next preceding such application, and also showing the object for which sales, if any, were ordered, and the disposition actually made of the proceeds of any sale. Such statement must be verified by one of the officers of the corporation. *Rules of Gen. Term, First District*, March, 1862. For form, see *Appendix*, No. 580.

It is not necessary for the corporation to show that it has found a purchaser for the premises proposed to be sold; but a conditional order can be made, authorizing a sale at a price not

---

meeting of the society called for that purpose, the proposed disposition of their property had been sanctioned. 20 *How.* 325, *per* Harris, J.

(a) See note (a), on page 276, *ante.*

less than a sum fixed by the court, and so that if a purchaser cannot be found at that sum, there will be no sale. 3 *Edw. Ch. R.* 157, *post.*

Reference to ascertain facts.] The court may order a reference to some suitable and proper person to ascertain the facts, and report the same to the court; or it may dispose of the application without such reference, in its discretion. 1 *Barb. Ch. Pr.* 468; *Laws of* 1847, *p.* 344, § 77. But in respect to the propriety and effect of references, in such cases, where the proceedings are contested, see 16 *Barb.* 239, *per* Harris, J.

Order of the court, and disposition of the proceeds.] If the application is approved by the court, an order will be entered directing a sale of the premises in pursuance of the prayer of the petition. The order will direct the sale to be made by the trustees of the corporation; or, it seems, the sale may be directed to be made by a referee, or other officer, appointed or selected for that purpose. 3 *Coms.* 238.

If the persons proposing to purchase the property have not actually agreed to buy, a provisional order may be entered, in the first instance, authorizing a sale generally, at a price not less than a sum fixed by the court. And if a purchaser "be found, and an actual agreement is made, the court, by a subsequent order, can approve or confirm it, and direct the application of the proceeds." See 3 *Edw. Ch. R.* 157.

The order of the court will also direct the uses to which the proceeds of the sale shall be applied.

"In case of a sale, the proceeds are to be applied to such uses as *the corporation*, with the consent and approbation of the court, shall conceive to be most for the interest of the society. The authority of the court is entirely *negative.* It may withhold its assent, and thus prevent the application of the proceeds in any specified manner; but it cannot direct the corporation how to apply the moneys. It is the right of the corporation to designate the object for which the moneys arising from the sale of its real estate shall be used. If the object thus designated meet the approval of the court, the appropriation will be made. If not, the money must be retained by the corporation until it can make such an application of it as will secure the consent and approbation of the court." 16 *Barb.* 237, 242, *per* Harris, J. For form of order, see *Appendix*, No. 581.

The trustees are not authorized to distribute the property of the corporation among the individual members, or any class of them; nor can that authority be conferred by the vote of a majority of the members, and the order of the court. 18 *New York*, 395. Nor can the court approve of any plan for the application of the proceeds, which does not regard the interests of the society as an organization to continue for the purposes of its creation. *Ib.* The court, therefore, has no jurisdiction to direct the proceeds to be distributed among the pew-holders; and its order in that respect would be void. *Ib.;* and see 16 *Barb.* 237.

SUPPLEMENT.

The trustees of a religious corporation are authorized to act in its behalf, in taking the steps necessary to effect a sale of its real estate. And the acts of the trustees are binding upon the corporation, although it does not appear they had the express sanction or authority of a majority of its corporators. 46 *N. Y.*, 131, reversing 3 *Robertson*, 570, *S. C.*, 1 *Abb. N. S.*, 214; and see 30 *How.*, 455; 32 *Id.*, 335; 2 *Abb. N. S.*, 254.

A religious corporation has no common law right to alienate its real estate. There must be a valuable consideration enuring to the corporation as such. An order of the court, therefore, which authorizes a conveyance founded upon a petition showing the only consideration for the proposed transfer to be a benefit to the individual corporators is without jurisdiction, and a deed executed in pursuance thereof is void. 46 *N. Y.*, 131; and see cases, *supra.*

On the application to the court, it seems, it is the better practice to agree upon the terms of the sale first, and then bring the agreement before the court for its sanction. 1 *Abb. N. S.*, 214, *supra.* The order directing the application of the proceeds may be separate from that authorizing the sale. *Ib*

Sales, after dissolution. By ch. 424 of the Laws of 1872 (p. 1013), provision is made for the dissolution of religious corporations (except in the city of New York), and for the sale of their property, and the disposition of the proceeds thereof.

CHAPTER XXX.

SUMMARY PROCEEDINGS TO RECOVER THE POSSESSION OF LAND.

Section I. Summary Proceedings to Remove Tenants and Others.
II. Proceedings to Recover Possession of Premises Deserted.

The proceedings considered in this chapter, giving the landlord a summary remedy in certain cases, were first authorized by statute in 1820. *Laws of* 1820, *p.* 176. Prior to that time, the landlord was obliged, in such cases, to resort to his action, which was dilatory and expensive. The law of 1820 was afterward incorporated, with some material modifications, into the Revised Statutes, the provisions of which have also been altered and amended from time to time. 2 *Rev. Stat.* 512; *Laws of* 1849, *p.* 291; 1851, *p.* 852; 1857, *chap.* 684, *vol.* 2, *p.* 509; 1863, *p.* 328; 1866, *ch.* 754.

These statutory provisions, being in derogation of the common-law rights of tenants, are to be strictly construed; and the proceedings under them must conform in all respects to the requirements of the statute. 6 *Hill*, 314; 22 *How.* 183; 32 *Barb.* 540.

SECTION I.

SUMMARY PROCEEDINGS TO REMOVE TENANTS AND OTHERS.

In what cases.] It is provided by statute that any tenant or lessee at will, or at sufferance, or for any part of a year, or for one or more years, of any houses, land, or tenements, and the assigns, under-tenants, or legal representatives of such tenant or lessee, may be removed from such premises in the following cases:

1. Where such person shall hold over and continue in pos-

session of the demised premises, or any part thereof, after the expiration of his term, without the permission of the landlord;

2. Where such person shall hold over without such permission, as aforesaid, after any default in the payment of rent pursuant to the agreement under which such premises are held; and a demand of such rent shall have been made, or three days' notice in writing requiring the payment of such rent or the possession of the premises shall have been served, by the person entitled to such rent, on the person owing the same, in the manner prescribed for the service of the summons in the thirty-second section of the statute (*post*);

3. Where the tenant or lessee of a term of three years or less shall have taken the benefit of any insolvent act, or been discharged under any act for the relief of his person from imprisonment during such term;

4. Where any person shall hold over and continue in possession of any real estate which shall have been sold by virtue of an execution against such person, after a title under such sale shall have been perfected. *Laws of* 1849, *p.* 291, amending 2 *Rev. Stat.* 512, *sec.* 28. (*a*) (*b*)

To warrant proceedings under the statute (except in the case mentioned in the fourth subdivision above), the conventional relation of landlord and tenant, created by agreement, and not by mere operation of law, must exist between the parties, or between those under whom they hold. 4 *Denio*, 185; 1 *Selden*, 383; 5 *Wend.* 281; 9 *Id.* 227; 10 *How.* 84; 16 *Id.* 454; 28 *New York*, 55; aff'ing. 14 *Abb.* 457; *s. c.* 23 *How.* 481.

Thus, the relation of landlord and tenant exists between the lessee or his assignee, and the assignee or grantee of the lessor, provided there was a conventional relation between the original parties. 17 *Wend.* 473; 2 *Rev. Stat.* 512, *sec.* 28, *supra.* So, it exists where the owner agrees that his creditor may occupy the premises for the term of one year, and until a mortgage held by

(*a*) In the city of Brooklyn, the grantee of lands sold for taxes is entitled to recover the possession of the same by proceedings under the statute, the same as in cases of sales on execution. *Laws of* 1850, *p.* 285, § 40.

(*b*) Under a recent amendment of the statute, keepers of bawdy-houses, or houses of assignation for lewd persons, may be dispossessed on application of the owner or landlord of the premises, or of any neighboring owner or tenant. See *Laws of* 1868, *p.* 1724 (which prescribes the practice in such cases), in the *Appendix of Notes* at the end of this chapter.

the creditor is paid; and on payment of the money, after the first year, and refusal of the creditor to give up possession, the owner may institute proceedings under the statute to obtain possession. 15 *Wend.* 665. So, that relation exists between the owner of the premises and a tenant holding over after the expiration of his term, though in such case the former may, at his option, treat the latter either as a trespasser or a tenant holding upon the terms of the original lease. 1 *Denio*, 113; and see 11 *Wend.* 617; 19 *How.* 29. And where a party enters into possession of premises under an agreement to accept a lease for twenty months, and subsequently refuses to accept the lease, the relation of landlord and tenant exists between the parties; the party in possession being a tenant at will or by sufferance. 23 *Wend.* 616. So, an agreement to construct a wharf, to be occupied, when finished, by the grantee, at a stipulated rent, accompanied by words of present demise, operates as a lease, within the statute. 14 *Abb.* 372; *s. c.* 38 *Barb.* 269.

But the relation of landlord and tenant does not necessarily exist in many cases, where the legal ownership is in one person and the possession in another, although by the express compact of the parties. It can arise only where the one in possession has, by some act or agreement, recognized the other as his lessor, or landlord, and taken upon himself the character of a tenant under him, so that he is not at liberty afterward to dispute his title; and this statutory remedy in favor of a lessor or landlord can properly be resorted to only in cases of a holding over after the expiration of such tenancy. If any other question than such as relates to the tenancy and the holding over is to be litigated between the parties, recourse must be had to an action. 1 *Selden*, 388, *per* McCoun, J.; 28 *New York*, 55, and cases *supra*.

An agreement, therefore, to work a farm on shares does not create the relation of landlord and tenant, so as to entitle a party to avail himself of this statute. 15 *Wend.* 226; and see *Id.* 379; 1 *Hill*, 234; 16 *How.* 454. Nor a conditional agreement, for the sale of real estate, where the purchaser makes default in payment, and, having possession, holds over, after notice and demand. 11 *How.* 84; 16 *Barb.* 622; and see 3 *Id.* 589; 7 *Id.* 75. Nor an agreement of A. with B., a boarding-house keeper, for rooms and board for himself and family for one year from the 1st day of May ensuing, at a certain amount per week for the rooms, and another sum per week for the board. 1 *Denio*, 602. Nor an agreement between H., the owner of a farm, and M., wherein the latter agreed that he and his wife should work for H. one year; M. to labor on the farm, and his wife to perform the duties of a housekeeper; M. and his wife, during the time, to occupy as their home a house upon the farm. 3 *Hill*, 90.

Nor does the relation of landlord and tenant exist where a tenant for the life of another continues in possession without the consent of the owner after the determination of the life estate, 4 *Kern.* 64; reversing *s. c.* 12 *Barb.* 481; and see 4 *Kern.* 430; nor as between the owner of the fee subject to a life estate, and the person to whom he had assumed to rent the premises, 3 *Barb.* 391; nor as between the plaintiff and the defendants who entered upon the premises immediately before the expiration of the term of the plaintiff's tenant, but without the tenant's consent; the defendants entering as the tenant left, and claiming that the premises were theirs, 1 *Hilton*, 399; nor where the affidavit showed that the plaintiff was a grantee claiming under the defendant, and that the defendant had not given up possession, and alleged that the defendant became a tenant at sufferance of the plaintiff, and that such tenancy was terminated by a month's notice to quit. 14 *Abb.* 458; *s. c.* 23 *How.* 481; aff. 28 *New York*, 55; and see 4 *Denio*, 185.

Nor can such proceedings be instituted on the ground of the expiration of the term by forfeiture; the statute meaning expiration by lapse of time, not by forfeiture, 15 *Wend.* 226; and see 5 *Selden*, 35, *post;* nor against a mortgagor to turn him out of possession of the mortgaged premises. 9 *Wend.* 227.

In cases of non-payment of rent, if the tenant at the time of the proceeding is holding under a new agreement with the landlord, he cannot be dispossessed upon the ground that he is in default in the payment of rent, under a former one, 16 *Barb.* 621; nor because he has failed to pay the taxes which he has covenanted to pay as one of the conditions of his lease. 15 *Abb.* 432.

Nor can the tenant be removed where the landlord has done some act which amounts to an acknowledgment of a subsisting tenancy; as, if he receive rent due at a subsequent quarter, or distrain for that in respect of which the forfeiture accrued, &c. 21 *Wend.* 587; 19 *Id.* 391; 5 *Cowen*, 448. And where the lease provided, that in case of the non-performance or violation of any of the lessee's covenants in the lease, the relation of landlord and tenant should cease at the option of the landlord, and that he should be entitled to recover the possession under the statute, for holding over after the expiration of the term, without any notice other than by the usual summons—it was held that the clause in the lease created a condition only, and that the estate was not determined by the breach; and that, therefore, a default in the payment of rent did not constitute a holding over after the expiration of the term, so as to authorize proceedings under the statute, to recover the possession of the premises. The statute not giving jurisdiction to remove a tenant by warrant in such a case, it cannot be given by the agreement of the parties. 5 *Selden*, 35.

In respect to proceedings to remove a person in possession, in cases arising under the fourth subdivision above, where land has been sold on execution, it has been held, that the judgment debtor, who continues in possession after title thereto has been perfected under a sale on execution against him, is a tenant within the meaning of that word, as used in the statute, and is entitled to deny the facts upon which the summons against him was issued, and to have a trial by jury. 16 *New York*, 567. And where the proceedings are before a justice of the peace, and the debtor appeals from the judgment rendered by the justice, he is also entitled to stay the issuing of a warrant to remove him, by giving the undertaking prescribed by section five of chapter one hundred and ninety-three, of the act of 1849 (*post*). *Ib.*

And the remedy given by the statute is not limited to the purchaser at the sale, but the application for process may be made by any person in whom the title is at the time of such application. 13 *Wend.* 29.

The regularity and validity of the judgment on which the execution issued are not to be inquired into in this proceeding; nor whether the sale was fraudulent; nor whether the purchaser was a *bona fide* purchaser. It is sufficient if the judgment and execution are regular upon their face, and the applicant shows a title under them. 13 *Wend.* 29. And the officer does not lose jurisdiction by proof that the person and estate of the defendant were, at the time the proceedings were instituted, in the charge of guardians appointed under the act respecting habitual drunkards. *Ib.* 32. And it is no objection, either, that the person proceeded against is a tenant in common whose interest has been sold; the purchaser acquires all his right and interest, and is entitled to be substituted in his place in the possession. *Ib.* 33.

The proceeding to dispossess a party, where land has been sold on execution, is equally applicable against the judgment debtor, and all who hold under him, under pretense of title acquired subsequent to the judgment. 17 *Wend.* 474. And where a defendant entered under title subsequent to the judgment, that fact must be distinctly alleged or the proceeding will be quashed. 20 *Id.* 22.

Who may institute the proceeding.] If the original landlord or lessor is the owner of the premises, he is the proper party to institute the proceedings. It is further provided by statute that the grantees of any demised lands, tenements, rents, or other hereditaments, or of the reversion thereof, the assignees of the lessor of any demise, and the heirs and personal representatives of the lessor, grantee, or assignee, shall have the same remedies by entry, action, distress, or otherwise, for the non-performance of any agreement contained in the lease so assigned, or for the recovery of any rent, or for the doing of any waste or other cause of forfeiture, as their grantor or lessor had, or might have had, if such reversion had remained in such lessor or grantor. 1 *Rev. Stat.* 747, *sec.* 23 as modified by *ch.* 274, *Laws of* 1846.

And where any lands or tenements shall be occupied by a tenant, a conveyance thereof, or of the rents or profits, or of any other interest therein, by the landlord of such tenant, shall be valid without any attornment of such tenant to the grantee; but the payment of rent to such grantor, by his tenant before notice of the grant, shall be binding upon such grantee; and such tenant shall not be liable to such grantee for any breach of the condition of the demise until he shall have had notice of such grant. 1 *Rev. Stat.* 739, *sec.* 146.

The mortgage by the landlord of his interest in the premises, does not alter his relations to the tenant until the foreclosure of the mortgage; nor will the sale of the landlord's interest under an execution change that relation, until the sale becomes absolute. 2 *Wend.* 507.

The remedy given to remove a person holding over after title to the premises has become perfect under a sale on execution, is not limited to the purchaser at the sale, but the application for the summons may be made by any person in whom the title is at the time of such application. 13 *Id.* 29.

Where a part of the premises were leased by parol to a monthly tenant, and subsequently the landlord leased the whole premises to another tenant, the lease to commence on the 1st day of May thereafter, at the same time giving notice to the first tenant that his term would expire on the 1st May thereafter, the landlord, and not his lessee, is the proper person to institute proceedings, under the statute, to recover possession of the premises, by reason of the monthly tenant holding over after the first of May. 23 *How.* 456.

Where the premises were originally leased by two persons, as landlords, and subsequently one of them becomes the sole owner, as purchaser of the other's interest, he may demand the whole rent, and, if it is not paid, may institute proceedings for the removal of the tenant, in his own name. 33 *Barb.* 46.

Against whom the proceeding may be instituted.] The proceeding may be instituted against any tenant or lessee at will, or at sufferance, or for any part of a year, or for one or more years, of any houses, land, or tenements, or against the assigns, under-tenants, or legal representatives of such tenant or lessee. 2 *Rev. Stat.* 512, *sec.* 28, as amended, *Laws of* 1849, *p.* 291.

Tenants from year to year are included in the terms "tenant at will," or "tenant for one or more years;" and may also be removed under the statute, 5 *How.* 81; 19 *Id.* 29; and see 16 *Id.* 454; *Wood Land. & Ten.* 163.

A wharf or pier, reclaimed from tide water by embankment, or by raising the bottom with stone, earth, or other material, is a "tenement" within the meaning of the statute. 14 *Abb.* 372; *s. c.* 38 *Barb.* 269.

The proceeding, in cases where land has been sold on execution, is equally applicable against the judgment debtor, and all who hold under him, under pretense of title acquired subsequent to the judgment. 17 *Wend.* 474.

Officers having jurisdiction in this proceeding.] The tenant or party in possession may be removed by any judge of the county courts of the county, or by any justice of the peace of the city or town, where the premises are situated, or by any mayor or recorder of the city where such premises are situated, *Laws of* 1849, *p.* 291, § 1; or, in the city of New York, by the mayor, recorder, city judge, any justice of the Marine Court, or any one of the justices of the district courts of that city. *Ib.*; *Laws of* 1852, *p.* 471; 1857, *vol.* 1, *p.* 727; 1850, *p.* 388; 1863, *p.* 328; 5 *Abb.* 208; 6 *Id.* 146; 29 *How.* 176; *s. c.* 19 *Abb.* 137. And also by any justice of the Superior Court of the city of Buffalo, when the premises are situated within that city, *Laws of* 1857, *vol.* 1, *p.* 754, § 25; and by the city judge of the city of Brooklyn, when the premises are situated within the county of Kings. *Laws of* 1849, *p.* 174, § 26.

Where the proceedings are commenced before a justice of the district courts in the city of New York, the application must be made to a justice of the district court in the district in which the premises are situated. *Laws of* 1863, *p.* 328. And in such case, they may be continued before any other justice, having jurisdiction of the subject-matter in that city, the same as if they had been originally commenced before him. *Laws of* 1857, *vol.* 1, *p.* 728, § 78. And so, where they are commenced before a justice of the Superior Court of the city of Buffalo, they may be continued, with the like effect, before any other justice of that court. *Ib.* 754, § 25

Demand of rent, or notice to pay, &c.] We have seen (2 *Rev. Stat.* 512, *sec.* 28, *sub.* 2, *supra*) that in cases where the tenant is proceeded against for default in the payment of rent, the person entitled to the rent, before instituting the proceeding, is required, by the statute, to make a demand of the rent of the person owing the same, or serve him with three days' notice, in writing, requiring the payment of such rent, or the possession of the premises. For form of notice, see *Appendix*, No. 583.

It is not necessary that there should be both a demand and a notice. 14 *Wend.* 172.

The rent must be demanded of the person owing the same; and where it was demanded of an under-tenant, who was described in the affidavit as a person in possession of the demised premises, it was held not sufficient. 43 *Barb.* 116. Where two tenants hold jointly, a demand of the rent of one of them is sufficient. 5 *Selden*, 227. So, where the demise is by joint-owners, either may demand the whole rent, and commence the proceedings for possession in the name of both. 33 *Barb.* 46.

Where the lessees have made an assignment for the benefit of creditors, and the lease is not specified in the assignment, and there is no positive act of the assignee showing that he has accepted a transfer of the lease, the landlord is not obliged to recognize him as the tenant, so as to make it necessary to demand the rent of him. But a demand of the lessee and tenant in possession, in such case, is sufficient. 16 *How.* 461.

It will be seen that the statute does not point out how, or at what time, the demand of rent is to be made—whether it may be made at any time after the rent becomes due, and at any place, or whether, the object of the landlord being a forfeiture of the estate and his claim *stricti juris*, all the niceties of the common law, with respect to the demand, must be complied with. 2 *Hilton*, 217, 229, 232; 16 *How.* 451; and see 16 *Johns.* 222; 17 *Id.* 66; 18 *Id.* 447. But the statute requires only, that "a demand of the rent shall have been made." Substantially the same language is used in the act of 1820. *Laws of* 1820, *p.* 177, § 1. Statutes are not presumed to make any alteration in the common law further or otherwise than the act expressly declares; and, therefore, in all general matters, the law presumes the act did not intend to make any alteration, for, if the legislature had had that design, they would have expressed it in terms. *Per* Trevor, Ch. J., 11 *Mod.* 150; *Bac. Abr. Statutes;* 16 *Barb.* 12. If, then, the statute intended a common law demand of the rent, great particularity and strictness is required in making it. It must be of the precise rent due. It must be made on the very day when the rent is due and payable, and at a convenient time before sunset. It must be made on the land, and at the most notorious place of it, unless a place is appointed where the rent is payable. And a demand must be made in fact, although there should be no person on the land ready to pay it. 17 *Johns.* 71.

Thus, in the case of *Wolcott* v. *Schenk*, the affidavit of the landlord stated, that "the sum of $350 was due and payable on the 24th day of September instant; that deponent on that day demanded said rent at the usual place of business of said Schenk, in the town of Fishkill, of his agent, who informed him that said rent could not be paid;" it was held that the affidavit was radically defective, and wholly insufficient to support the landlord's proceedings. 16 *How.* 450. And, it seems, where there is a personal covenant of the lessee for the payment of the rent, a demand of payment from him personally, either upon the land or elsewhere, would be a good demand within the meaning of the statute. *Ib.* 452, *per* Brown, J.

In the absence of any decisions giving a definite construction to this language of the statute, it would be safer, in all cases where there has not been a strict common law demand, to give the three days' notice in writing, requiring the payment of the rent or the possession of the premises. This notice is required to be served in the same manner prescribed for the service of the summons. 2 *Rev. Stat.* 512, as amended, § 28, *sub.* 2, *supra*); in respect to which, see *post*, *p.* 296, "How summons to be served."

Affidavit of termination of tenancy; demand of possession, &c.] Previous to the issuing of the summons hereinafter mentioned, in the case of a tenancy at will, or at sufferance, the magistrate shall be satisfied, by affidavit, that such tenancy has been terminated by giving notice in the manner prescribed by law. (See *post*, "Notice to quit, and how served.") And if application be made for such summons to be served on any person holding over real estate which shall have been sold on execution, the magistrate shall, in like manner, be satisfied that a demand of the possession of such premises has been made. 2 *Rev. Stat.* 513, *sec.* 31. For forms, see *Appendix*, Nos. 585, 586.

Notice to quit, and how served.] Wherever there is a tenancy at will, or by sufferance, created by the tenant's holding over his term, or otherwise, the same may be terminated by the landlord's giving one month's notice in writing to the tenant, requiring him to remove therefrom. 1 *Rev. Stat.* 745, *sec.* 7. For form, see *Appendix*, No. 584.

Such notice shall be served by delivering the same to such tenant, or to some person of proper age residing on the premises; or, if the tenant cannot be found, and there be no such person residing on the premises, such notice may be served by affixing the same on a conspicuous part of the premises, where it may be conveniently read. *Ib. sec.* 8. At the expiration of one month from the service of such notice, the landlord may proceed in the manner prescribed by the statute, to remove such tenant, without any further or other notice to quit. *Ib. sec.* 9.

Where the notice required the tenant to remove from the premises in "thirty days," and it was served during a calendar month which contained but thirty days; it was held to be a "month's notice," within the meaning of the statute. 2 *Abb.* 28.

A tenant for a year who holds over after the expiration of his term, without the permission of his landlord, is not a tenant *at sufferance*, within the meaning of the statute; and, therefore, he may be removed from the demised premises, without having been served with the month's notice to quit above provided for To entitle such tenant to a month's notice to quit, the holding over must be continued for such length of time, after the expiration of the term, as to authorize the implication of assent on the part of the landlord to such continuance; and where the landlord waited three months and twelve days before instituting proceedings, under the statute, it was held that he was not chargeable with laches, especially as it appeared that he had attempted to obtain possession without recourse to coercive measures. 11 *Wend.* 616.

Tenants from *year* to *year*, at the common law, were entitled to six months' notice to quit, terminating with the year. 4 *Cow.* 349; 1 *Johns.* 325. But now, tenants from year to year, with respect to these proceedings, are included in the term "tenant at will," within the meaning of the statute, and may be summarily removed upon *one month's* notice to quit, terminating with the year. 5 *How.* 81; 16 *Id.* 454; but see 19 *Id.* 29. (*a*) And so of a tenancy from month to month: the notice must terminate with the month. 5 *Id.* 92; see, also, 23 *Wend.* 616.

Where the landlord after service of notice to quit accepted rent, which accrued subsequent to the notice, it was held to be a waiver of the notice. 19 *Wend.* 391. It would have been otherwise, it seems, had the acceptance been stated as conditional, and as saving and reserving all rights under the notice. *Ib.* 394; see, also, 11 *Barb.* 33; 21 *Wend.* 587.

(*a*) In this case (19 *How.* 29), the court held at special term, that a tenancy from *year to year* is, within the meaning of the statute, a tenancy for *one or more years*. And therefore, that such a tenant may be proceeded against at the expiration of each year he holds over the original term, without any notice to quit.

Where the premises on the first of September, 1837, were demised to the defendant "for and during the will and pleasure of the plaintiff," and the plaintiff on the 12th of February, 1852, caused notice to be served on the tenant, requiring him to remove from and quit the premises within one month after the service of such notice—it was held to be strictly a case of tenancy at will, within the meaning of the statute; and that the landlord had a right to give the month's notice to quit at any time, and commence proceedings to remove the tenant after the expiration of the notice. 14 *Barb.* 253.

Under the act of 1820, from which the present statute was taken, where there was proof of a tenancy, and nothing appeared as to the terms of holding, it was presumed to be a tenancy at will. 8 *Cowen*, 13.

Affidavit to remove tenant.] In preparing the affidavit upon which to found an application for a warrant to remove a tenant, or party in possession, great particularity is required, and every fact necessary to give the officer jurisdiction must be distinctly alleged. 20 *Wend.* 22; 22 *How.* 183. And, unless this be done, the proceeding will not only be declared void, but if a warrant be issued and executed, the landlord as well as the officer issuing the same will be a trespasser, and liable in damages to the party injured, 8 *Cowen*, 68; and this, too, it seems, notwithstanding that the person dispossessed came illegally into possession. 5 *Wend.* 281.

The affidavit must not be uncertain, or contradictory; but must make out a plain case. 16 *Barb.* 474; 24 *Id.* 438; 43 *Id.* 168; 6 *Hill*, 314; 5 *How.* 95. The facts, and not the evidence of facts, should be alleged, nor should matter of law be stated, but facts, from which the matter of law arises. 6 *Hill*, 317; *per* Bronson, J. The affidavit is not to be regarded as evidence on the merits, but as a plaint in a cause, and stands for a declaration, or complaint. 20 *Wend.* 103. For forms, see *Appendix*, Nos. 587 to 590.

The provisions of the statute with respect to the requisites of the affidavit to be made are as follows:

Any landlord, or lessor, his legal representatives, agents, or assigns, may make oath in writing of the facts which, according to the preceding section (§ 1, *Laws of* 1849, *supra*), authorize the removal of a tenant, describing therein the premises claimed; and may present the same to one of the officers authorized by law to issue the warrant. 2 *Rev. Stat.* 513, *sec.* 29.

Among other things, it should appear that the relation of landlord and tenant exists between the parties; and the facts to establish that relation should be set out in the affidavit. 3 *Barb S. C. R.* 391; 43 *Barb.* 168; 1 *How.* 213; 14 *Abb.* 457; *s. c* 23 *How.* 481; aff. 28 *New York*, 55. Though it is sufficient, it seems, if these facts are substantially alleged. 2 *Abb.* 29; but see 14 *Abb.* 457, 460, *supra, per* Ingraham, P. J.

Where the proceedings were instituted by S., and the affidavit stated that J. demised the premises, &c.; that he afterward died, leaving S. his widow, that she became legally entitled to receive the accruing rents, and to have possession of the premises, without setting forth any fact explaining how she became entitled—it was held that the affidavit was not sufficient to show her right to proceed. 6 *Hill*, 314. And this is so, even though the affidavit state further that the tenant and those claiming under him "have recognized the widow's right to the premises, by paying rent to her and by other acts." *Ib.* In another case, however, where the landlord described himself "as trustee of the estate of A. B., deceased," that he "now owns said premises and holds said lease, as sole trustee of said estate," the court held it was a sufficient description as landlord of the premises. 2 *How.* 63.

Nor is it necessary to state in the affidavit how the landlord acquired title to the premises. But it is sufficient if the affidavit shows that the relation of landlord and tenant was created between the parties, by an agreement of hiring, and that the tenant has made default in the payment of rent after it was due, and after demand for payment thereof made. 33 *Barb.* 153.

The affidavit should point out, too, the person intended to be removed, by *name*, and should show with reasonable certainty that he is in the possession or occupation of the premises, together with his relation to the landlord. 6 *Hill*, 314; *Lal. Supp. to Hill & Denio*, 236; 24 *Barb.* 438. Where the affidavit stated that W. (the lessee), "or his assigns, or those claiming under him or them," held over, and it appeared that W. was not in possession, but that the premises were occupied by H., it was held that the affidavit was insufficient to give the officer jurisdiction. *Id.*

ibid.; and see 14 *Wend.* 172. And where the proceedings are against several parties, the affidavit should show which of the persons proceeded against are tenants, and which of them are under-tenants. 16 *Barb.* 474; *Lal. Supp. to Hill & Denio,* 236.

If the affidavit is made by the agent of the landlord, it is not sufficient that he describes himself as agent, but that fact must be distinctly sworn to. 4 *Denio,* 71; and see 3 *Coms.* 41.

The affidavit should show that the tenant is holding over "without the permission of his landlord," and where it fails to do this, it is error, for which the proceedings will be reversed, 5 *How.* 81, 95; 22 *Id.* 183; and it is not enough that the affidavit shows probable want of permission. *Id. ibid.;* but see 20 *Wend.* 103.

The affidavit, also, should give a particular description of the premises from which the defendant is sought to be removed; and where it described the premises as being "a certain house and lot situate in the village of Penn Yan, in the town of Milo, and county of Yates;" it was held that the affidavit was too general, and the proceedings were declared void. 22 *How.* 183.

In proceeding under the statute against a tenant for the *non-payment of rent,* it is laid down by Cowen, J. (20 *Wend.* 107), that the affidavit should disclose an agreement by which the lessors were entitled to re-enter. But it is believed that the position there taken is not sustained by the letter or spirit of the statute. It is sufficient if there has been a default in the payment of the rent, pursuant to the agreement under which the premises are held, and that a demand of the rent has been made, or notice served, requiring payment or the possession of the premises. *Laws of* 1849, *p.* 291, § 1, *sub.* 2; 16 *How.* 449; 33 *Barb.* 153.

The affidavit in cases of non-payment of rent should name the person of whom the rent was demanded; but though defective in this particular, if it states that the demand was made upon the premises, it is sufficient to give the officer jurisdiction, and the defect cannot be objected to collaterally: the remedy, if any, is by certiorari or appeal. 14 *Wend.* 172.

In cases where real estate has been *sold on execution,* and the party proceeded against is one who has come into possession of the land under the judgment debtor, under title derived from him subsequently to the lien of the judgment under which the sale was made, the fact that he entered under title so subsequently acquired must be distinctly alleged in the affidavit, or the proceedings will be void. 20 *Wend.* 22.

The affidavit cannot be twice used. Accordingly, where a verdict was found for the tenant under the statute authorizing these proceedings, it was held that the original affidavit could not be used as the foundation of a new proceeding. And the affidavit having been so used, and the tenant turned out of possession, it was further held that the proceedings were void, and that trespass lay against both the landlord and judge. 8 *Cowen*, 68.

In proceedings before a justice of the district courts in the city of New York, the affidavit must be sworn or affirmed to before, and be filed with, the clerk of the district court in the district in which the premises are situated, or his deputy. *Laws of* 1863, *p.* 328. And, if not so sworn to, the proceedings will be void. 26 *How.* 166.

The summons.] On receiving the affidavit, the officer is required to issue his summons, describing the premises of which the possession is claimed, and requiring any person in the possession of said premises, or claiming the possession thereof, forthwith to remove from the same, or to show cause, before the said magistrate, within such time as shall appear reasonable, not less than three nor more than five days, why possession of said premises should not be delivered to such applicant; provided, however, that in the cases where a person continues in possession of the demised premises after the expiration of his term, without permission of his landlord, the magistrate, if the summons be issued on the day the term expires, or on the day next thereafter, may direct such summons to be made returnable on the same day, at any time after twelve o'clock, noon, and before six o'clock in the afternoon. 2 *Rev. Stat.* 513, *sec.* 30, as amended by *Laws of* 1851, *p.* 852; as amended by *Laws of* 1868, *p.* 1930 (see the amendment of 1868, in the *Appendix of Notes* at the end of this volume); and see 24 *Barb.* 438.

If the summons is issued in a case of holding over after the expiration of the term, it may be made returnable on the same day, except as above mentioned, or on any day within the five days, in the discretion of the officer. 30 *How.* 93.

The summons must be directed to the tenant or occupant by name; and, where the direction was left in blank, the proceedings were held to be defective, though service was made upon the proper party. 4 *Denio*, 71; *Ib.* 185; 6 *Hill*, 314; 24 *Barb.* 438. And an appearance by the defendant, for the purpose of objecting to the summons, is not a waiver of the defect. 4 *Denio*, 71. But where the proceeding was instituted against two, both of whom were named in the affidavit, and the summons was directed to one of them, "and any other person in possession of the premises," and both appeared before the officer, made affidavit, and had a trial by jury, without objecting to the summons, it was held that it was sufficient. 4 *Denio*, 185. For form of summons, see *Appendix*, No. 591.

Where the proceedings are before a justice of the district courts of the city of New York, the summons must be made returnable before a justice of the court in the district in which the premises are situated; and be made returnable by the clerk of that court, at the court thereof. *Laws of* 1863, *p.* 328.

Service of summons.] The summons must be served, either, (*a*)

1. By delivering to the tenant, to whom it shall be directed, a true copy thereof, and, at the same time, showing him the original; or,

2. If such tenant be absent from his last or usual place of residence, by leaving a copy thereof at such place, with some person of mature age, residing on the premises, 2 *Rev. Stat.* 514, *sec.* 32; or, if there be no such person residing thereon, then such service may be made by affixing such copy upon a conspicuous part of said demised premises (*a*). *Laws of* 1857, *vol.* 2, *p.* 509, § 1.

The summons may be served by any person competent to testify as a witness, and who is not a party to the proceeding. Due proof of such service is required to be made, 2 *Rev. Stat.* 514, *sec.* 33; and this proof should be by affidavit, except when the service is made by a sheriff or other officer, in which case it may be made by his return or certificate signed by him. *Ib.* 440, *sec.* 77. For form, see *Appendix*, No. 592.

Where the summons was served by copy, and the only proof of such service was that the tenant was absent, and that the

---

(*a*) By a recent statute the practice has been materially changed in respect to the service of the summons. See *Laws of* 1868, *p.* 1930, in the *Appendix of Notes* at the end of this chapter.

copy was left with R., residing on the premises—it was held that the proof was insufficient, as not showing the tenant's absence from "his last or usual place of residence," or that the copy was left with a "person of mature age." 1 *Hill*, 512; and see 43 *Barb.* 168. So, the proof is insufficient where it is alleged that the service was upon an under-tenant on the demised premises, and that the tenant was absent from his last and usual residence, without stating that such residence was upon the demised premises. *Ib.* 116.

If the summons is directed to the original lessee, but served only upon an under-tenant in possession, the service is insufficient; it should be served upon both. 1 *How.* 213.

What the defendant to do in certain cases.] If the defendant holds the premises by lease or agreement from any other party than the plaintiff mentioned in the affidavit or summons, he must forthwith give notice of the service upon him of such summons, to his immediate landlord. And this he is required to do, under a penalty of forfeiting the value of three years' rent of the premises so occupied by him; which may be sued for and recovered by the landlord or person of whom such tenant holds. (*a*) 1 *Rev. Stat.* 748, *sec.* 27.

If the tenant do not defend, warrant to issue.] If, at the time appointed in the summons, no sufficient cause be shown to the contrary, and due proof of the service of the summons be made to such magistrate, he is required thereupon to issue his warrant to the sheriff of the county, or to any constable or marshal of the city or town, where the premises are situated, commanding him to remove all persons from the premises, and to put the applicant into the full possession thereof. 2 *Rev. Stat.* 514, *sec.* 33. For form, see *Appendix*, No. 393.

The officer, to whom the warrant for delivering the possession of the premises shall be directed and delivered, is required to execute the same according to the tenor thereof. *Id.* 515, § 40.

Denial by defendant of landlord's affidavit.] Any person in possession of the demised premises, or any person claiming the possession thereof, may, at the time appointed in such sum-

(*a*) See, also, the recent statute in respect to the duty of the party served, where he is not the real party in interest. *Laws of* 1868, *p.* 1931, *post.*

mons for showing cause, file an affidavit with the magistrate who issued the same, denying the facts upon which the summons was issued, or any of those facts. 2 *Rev. Stat.* 514, *sec.* 34, as amended by *Laws of* 1857, *vol.* 2, *p.* 509, § 2; and for previous amendment, see *Laws of* 1849, *p.* 292. For form of affidavit, see *Appendix*, No. 594.

The denial in the defendant's affidavit should be express and positive, and not circumstantial and argumentative; no possibility of evasion should exist. 25 *Wend.* 284. Allegations in the landlord's affidavit, not denied by the defendant, will be taken as true. 2 *Abb.* 29. A denial in general terms of each and every allegation contained in the landlord's affidavit will be sufficient. 42 *Barb.* 96.

Where the proceeding was against the tenant after default in the payment of rent, and the tenant in his affidavit stated that the landlord had before commenced a similar proceeding for the non-payment of the same rent, and that the parties appeared, and after their proofs and allegations were heard, the magistrate gave judgment for the tenant; it was held that the affidavit was insufficient, as it did not show what issue, or whether any, was joined, or upon what ground the judgment proceeded. 5 *Seld.* 227. And where two tenants were jointly charged in the affidavit of the landlord, an affidavit by one of the defendants, that the rent was not demanded of *him*, is not sufficient to make an issue requiring the summoning of a jury. *Ib.*; see also *post*, *p.* 301, "What the defendant may show in defense."

Adjournments.] Any magistrate, before whom the application may be pending, may, upon the request of either party, adjourn the hearing of such application, for the purpose of enabling such party to procure his witnesses, whenever it shall appear to be necessary; such adjournment, however, shall in no case exceed ten days. 2 *Rev. Stat.* 515, *sec.* 41.

Subpœnas for witnesses.] The magistrate may, also, at the request of either party, issue his subpœna, requiring any person to appear and testify before such magistrate, or before the jury, touching the matters directed by law to be heard by them; and every person who, being served with such subpœna, shall, without reasonable cause, refuse or neglect to appear; or, appearing, shall refuse to answer upon oath, touching the matters aforesaid; shall be subject to the proceedings and penalties provided by law in similar cases. 2 *Rev. Stat.* 515, *sec.* 42.

Trial of the issue, and proceedings thereon.] The statute provides that, if the defendant appears and denies the facts alleged in the landlord's affidavit, or any of them, the matters, thus controverted, may be tried by the magistrate, or by a jury; provided either party to such proceedings shall, at the time designated in the summons for showing cause, demand a jury, and at the time of such demand pay to the magistrate the necessary costs and expenses of obtaining such jury. (*a*) 2 *Rev. Stat.* 514, *sec.* 34, as amended by *Laws of* 1857, *vol.* 2, *p.* 509, § 2; *Pub. Acts*, *p.* 65. For previous amendment, see *Laws of* 1849, *p.* 292, § 2.

The necessary costs and expenses of obtaining the jury are the magistrate's fees for the venire, the sheriff's or constable's fees for the service thereof, and the fees of the jury.

In order to form the jury, the magistrate with whom the affidavit is filed is required to nominate twelve reputable persons, qualified to serve as jurors in courts of record (2 *Rev. Stat.* 411, *sec.* 13), and to issue his precept, directed to the sheriff or to one of the constables of the county, or any constable or marshal of the city or town, commanding him to summon the persons so nominated, to appear before such magistrate at such time and place as he shall therein appoint, not more than three days from the date thereof, for the purpose of trying the said matters in difference. 2 *Rev. Stat.* 514, *sec.* 35, as amended by *Laws of* 1849, *p.* 292. For form of precept, see *Appendix*, No. 595.

Six of the persons so summoned shall be drawn in like manner as jurors in justices' courts (2 *Rev. Stat.* 243, *sec.* 98, &c.), and shall be sworn by such magistrate well and truly to hear, try, and determine, the matters in difference between the parties. 2 *Rev. Stat.* 514, *sec.* 36, as amended, *Laws of* 1849, *p.* 292; 1862, *p.* 621.

(*a*) It was held by M'Coun, J. (1 *Selden*, 385), prior to the amendment of this section in 1857, where the proceedings were before a county judge, and the defendant had appeared and denied the facts alleged in the landlord's affidavit, that the judge had no authority to try the issue, thus joined, without a jury. But it will be seen, by the section as amended, that the power to try, in such case, is now given to him.

And whenever a sufficient number of jurors, duly drawn and summoned, do not appear, or cannot be obtained to form a jury, the magistrate may order any sheriff, constable, or marshal to summon from the bystanders, or from the county at large, so many persons qualified to serve as jurors as shall be sufficient, and return their names to the magistrate. *Ib.*, as amended, 1862, *p.* 621. (*a*)

Every person so summoned is required to attend forthwith and serve as a juror, unless excused by the magistrate, and for every neglect or refusal so to attend he will be subject to fine by the magistrate, in the same manner as is now provided by law in the case of jurors in courts of record. *Ib.*

It would be erroneous for the magistrate to nominate more than twelve jurors, especially if the tenant object to the proceeding. 20 *Wend.* 207. If there be a default of jurors on the return of a venire, the magistrate may renew the venire until a jury appears. 9 *Wend.* 227. And so, also, if some of the jurors are disqualified. 7 *How.* 441.

On the trial before a jury, neither party has any right to a peremptory challenge of any of the jurors. 15 *Abb.* 328.

On the trial of the proceeding, whether tried with or without a jury, the parties may be examined in their own behalf, the same as in actions. *Code*, § 399, as amended, *Laws of* 1860, *p.* 787; 1862, *p.* 858; 1865, *p.* 1290; 23 *How.* 313; *s. c.* 14 *Abb.* 305; though previous to the amendment of the Code this was not allowed. 19 *How.* 34; and see 1 *Park. Cr. R.* 169; 2 *Brad.* 224; 16 *Barb.* 201; 1 *Selden*, 383; 3 *Sand. S. C. R.* 665; 10 *How.* 83; 5 *Abb.* 212.

After the evidence is closed, it is right and proper for the magistrate to charge the jury upon the law of the case. 38 *Barb.* 269; *s. c.* 14 *Abb.* 372.

After hearing the allegations and proofs of the parties, the jury are to be kept together until they agree on their verdict, by the sheriff or one of his deputies, or a constable, or by some proper person appointed by the magistrate for that purpose, who shall be sworn to keep such jury as is usual in like cases in courts of record. 2 *Rev. Stat.* 514, *sec.* 37. If the jury cannot agree,

(*a*) Prior to this amendment, the magistrate had no power to summon talesmen to form a jury. 32 *Barb.* 540, *per* Bonney, J.

after being kept together for such time as the magistrate shall deem reasonable, he may discharge them, and nominate a new jury, and issue a new precept in manner aforesaid. *Ib. sec.* 38.

What the defendant may show in defense.] We have seen (*supra*) that the defendant may answer to the affidavit of the landlord, by filing an affidavit with the magistrate, denying the facts upon which the summons issued, or any of those facts. 2 *Rev. Stat.* 514, *sec.* 34; and see *ante*, *p.* 297, "Denial by defendant of landlord's affidavit." Anything, therefore, which would tend to disprove those facts, or any of them, would be proper for the defendant to show in defense. He would not, however, be permitted to set up title to the premises acquired by him from a third party since the taking of his lease. 11 *Wend.* 616. But though the tenant cannot deny his landlord's title, yet, no doubt, in analogy to the rule which prevails in actions to recover the possession of real estate, he may show that the landlord's title has terminated either by its own limitation, or by conveyance, or by operation of law. 5 *Cowen*, 124; 11 *Wend.* 621; 3 *Barb. S. C. R.* 402; 3 *Sand. S. C. R.* 664, *per* Mason, J.; see, also, 6 *Wend.* 666; 22 *Id.* 121; 1 *Sand. S. C. R.* 517; 15 *New York*, 377; 16 *Id.* 573.

In cases arising under the fourth subdivision of the statute, where land has been sold on execution, the defendant will not be permitted to inquire into the regularity and validity of the judgment on which the execution issued; nor whether the sale was fraudulent; nor whether the purchaser purchased in good faith; but it will be sufficient if the judgment and execution are regular upon their face, and the plaintiff shows a title under them. 13 *Wend.* 29.

Proceedings when before a justice of the peace.] In case of proceedings before a justice of the peace, the justice is required to enter the finding of the jury, or, in case no jury is called, his final decision upon the application for the warrant, in his docket, and render judgment therefor, and include in such judgment costs of such proceedings to the prevailing party, at the same rate of fees now allowed by law in civil actions in courts of justices of the peace, and limited in like manner; and in the warrant for delivery of possession, or by execution, issued by him, the justice shall direct the collection of such costs. *Laws of* 1849, *p.* 292, § 5, *sub.* 1.

Judgment and warrant of possession.] If the decision of the magistrate, or the verdict of the jury, shall be in favor of the lessor, or landlord, or other person, claiming the possession of the premises, the magistrate is required to issue his warrant to the sheriff, or to any constable of the county in which the premises are situated, commanding such officer to put the landlord, lessor, or other person, into the full possession of the premises. 2 *Rev. Stat.* 515, *sec.* 39, as amended by *Laws of* 1857, *ch.* 684, § 3. For form, see *Appendix*, No. 596. And if he refuses thus to issue the warrant after demand duly made upon him for it, he will be compelled to issue it by mandamus. 5 *Abb.* 206, *ante*, *p.* 58.

The officer, to whom the warrant for delivering the possession of the premises shall be directed and delivered, is required to execute the same according to the tenor thereof. 2 *Rev. Stat.* 515, *sec.* 40.

Where the warrant is properly and regularly issued, it will protect all who act under it, unless they act willfully and maliciously. And therefore, where a warrant was issued in favor of an incoming tenant to remove a tenant holding over the term, the former is not liable for assisting, at the request of the constable, to remove the goods, if they are removed carefully, and in a proper manner; and this, too, though the day may be rainy, and the goods are put out in the rain and thereby suffer injury. 28 *How.* 221. The law does not recognize the state of the weather in the execution of the warrant. *Ib.*

Effect of issuing warrant.] The statute provides that, where a warrant shall be issued for the removal of any tenant from any demised premises, the contract or agreement for the use of the premises, if any such exists, and the relation of landlord and tenant between the parties, shall be deemed to be canceled and annulled. 2 *Rev. Stat.* 515, *sec.* 43.

Though the tenant has been removed from the demised premises for non-payment of rent, yet the landlord may recover the same by action. And he may recover all the rent due up to the time of issuing the warrant. 6 *Hill*, 507; 3 *Denio*, 452; 4 *Coms.* 270; 4 *E. D. Smith*, 339; 2 *Hilton*, 218. But it seems that compensation for the use of the premises by the tenant intermediate the default and the time he is dispossessed, cannot be recovered by action on the lease; but the landlord's remedy is by proceeding against the tenant as a trespasser. *Id. ibid.;* and see 1 *Wend.* 134.

Where the rent was payable quarterly, in advance, it was held that an eviction during the quarter, but after the rent became due, did not bar an action for the rent. The most the evicted tenant could equitably claim, in such case, was a deduction for so much of the quarter as elapsed after his eviction. 1 *Duer*, 266; 4 *Coms.* 270; and see 1 *E. D. Smith*, 416; 2 *Id.* 121.

The expenses of the proceedings to dispossess a tenant are recoverable from him by action. 2 *Rev. Stat.* 516, *sec.* 49; 4 *E. D. Smith*, 339; and see 5 *Sand.* 249.

Staying proceedings on payment of rent, &c.] The statute authorizes the proceedings to be stayed before warrant issued, except where the tenant holds over after the expiration of his term.

It provides that the issuing of the warrant of removal shall be stayed in case of *a proceeding for the non-payment of rent*, if the person owing such rent shall, before such warrant be actually issued, pay the rent due, and all the costs and charges of the proceedings; or give such security as shall be satisfactory to the magistrate, to the person entitled to the rent, for the payment thereof and the costs aforesaid, in ten days. But in case the person giving such security shall not within the said ten days produce to the magistrate satisfactory evidence of the payment of the rent and costs, the warrant of removal may at any time thereafter be issued. 2 *Rev. Stat.* 515, *sec.* 44, as amended by *Laws of* 1857, *vol.* 2, *p.* 509, § 4; 16 *How.* 466. For form of security, see *Appendix*, No. 597.

Where the application is founded on the fact that the tenant or lessee has taken the *benefit of any insolvent act*, or been *discharged* under any act for the relief of his person *from imprisonment*, the proceedings will be stayed, if, at any time before issuing the warrant for removal, the tenant or lessee, or his assignee, shall pay the costs of such proceedings as have been had, and give such security to the person entitled to the rent, for the payment thereof as it shall become due, as shall be satisfactory to the magistrate. 2 *Rev. Stat.* 515, *sec.* 45. For form, see *Appendix*, No. 598.

When the application is founded upon an alleged *sale by execution* of the premises occupied by the defendant in such execution, the proceedings shall be stayed, if, at any time before issuing the warrant of removal, the occupant shall,

1. Pay the costs of such proceedings;
2. File with the officer, before whom the application is pending, an affidavit that he claims the possession of such premises by virtue of some title or right acquired after such premises were sold, or as guardian or trustee for any other; and,
3. Execute a bond to the applicant for such warrant, in such penalty and with such sureties as the magistrate shall approve, conditioned to pay the costs which may be recovered against him in any ejectment that may be brought by such applicant within six months, for the recovery of the possession of such premises; and to pay the value of the use and occupation of such premises, from the date of such bond to the time such applicant shall obtain possession of the same by virtue of a recovery in such action of ejectment; and also conditioned not to commit any waste or injury to such premises, during his occupation thereof. *Ib. sec.* 46. For forms of affidavit and bond, see *Appendix*, Nos. 599, 600.

Redeeming the premises in certain cases.] In case of proceed ings against the tenant for default in the payment of rent, if the unexpired term of the lease under which the premises are held exceeds five years, at the time of issuing the warrant upon such proceedings, the lessee, his assigns, or personal representatives, may, at any time within one year after possession of the demised premises shall have been delivered to the landlord, pay or tender to the lessor, his representatives, or attorney, or to the officer who issued the warrant, all rent in arrear to the time of such payment or tender, and all costs and charges incurred by the landlord; and in such case the premises shall be restored to the lessee, who shall hold and enjoy the same without any new lease thereof, according to the terms of the original demise; and any mortgagee of the lease, or of any part thereof, who shall not be in possession of the demised premises, or any judgment creditor of the lessee who shall, within one year after the execution of such warrant, pay all rent in arrear, all costs and charges as aforesaid, and perform all the agreements which ought to be performed by the first lessee, shall not be affected by such recovery; and such judgment creditor may file a suggestion of such payment upon the record, and may issue execution for the amount of the original judgment and of such payment. *Laws of* 1842, *p.* 293.

To entitle the tenant to redeem the premises, the unexpired term of the lease must exceed five years at the time of issuing the warrant; and this, too, although the lease contains a conditional covenant of renewal by the landlord for a further term of five years and upward, after the expiration of the first. 16 *How.* 461, 466.

Appeal to the county court.] If the proceedings are before a justice of the peace, either party may have the same reviewed on appeal to the county court, or a writ of certiorari may be awarded by the Supreme Court, for the purpose of examining any adjudication made in such proceedings; the remedy by appeal and by certiorari, in such case, being concurrent. 11 *How.* 83; and see *post*, "Certiorari to remove proceedings."

But an appeal does not lie from the decision of a justice of one of the district courts of the city of New York, to the Court of Common Pleas of that city. The only mode of review in such case is by certiorari, issuing out of the Supreme Court. 5 *Abb.* 205; 17 *Id.* 326, *note;* 2 *Hilton*, 519; but see *contra*, 5 *Abb.* 61.

In respect to appeals from the decision of a justice of the peace, it is provided by statute, that proceedings before a justice of the peace may be removed by appeal to the county court of the county, in the same manner, and with the like effect, and upon like security, as appeals from the judgment of justices of the peace in civil actions, except that the decision of such county judge shall be an affirmance or reversal of such judgment, and be final. But in addition to the security for such judgment as required by law, in case of such appeal, in order to stay the issuing of such warrant or execution, there shall, in case of appeal by the tenant, be security also given for the payment of all rent accruing or to accrue upon such premises subsequent to the said application to such justice. *Laws of* 1849, *p.* 292, § 5, *sub.* 2.

The statute further provides that no appeal will be allowed unless the security for said judgment shall be given, and approved by the judge at the time of allowing such appeal, and served on the justice with the affidavit for appeal. *Ib. sub.* 3.

The practice on appeals to the county court, in these proceedings, has been somewhat modified by subsequent statutory provisions.

Thus, under the present practice, no affidavit is necessary to be served on the justice in order to perfect the appeal; nor is it necessary that the appeal should be allowed by a judge of the appellate court, or other officer. See 24 *Barb.* 438; 29 *How.* 43.

The appeal is now brought by the service, within twenty days after judgment, of a notice of appeal, stating the grounds upon which the appeal is founded. If the judgment, however, was rendered upon process not personally served, and the defendant did not appear, he has twenty days, after personal notice of the judgment, to serve the notice of appeal. *Ib.; Code of Pro.* § 353. For form of notice, see *Appendix*, No. 601.

The notice of appeal must also, within the same time, be served on the justice personally, if living and within the county, or on his clerk, if there be one, and on the respondent personally, or by leaving it at his residence, with some person of suitable age and discretion, or, in case the respondent is not a resident of such county, or cannot after due diligence be found therein, in the same manner on the attorney or agent, if any, who is a resident of such county, who appeared for the respondent on the trial; and if neither the respondent nor such agent or attorney can be found in the county, the notice may be served on the respondent by leaving it with the clerk of the appellate court, and the appellant must, at the time of the service of the notice of appeal on the justice, or on his clerk, as herein provided, pay to such justice or clerk the costs of the proceeding included in the judgment, together with two dollars costs of the return, which shall be included in the judgment for costs on reversal. *Ib.* § 354; and see 24 *Barb.* 438.

In order to perfect the appeal, security must be given, the same as on appeals in actions in cases where the appellant desires a stay of execution. *Ib.;* and see 10 *How.* 87; 29 *Id.* 43; *Ib.* 201; *s. c.* 19 *Abb.* 324.

The security is a written undertaking, executed by one or more sufficient sureties, to the effect that, if judgment be rendered against the appellant, and execution thereon be returned unsatisfied, in whole or in part, the sureties will pay the amount unsatisfied. *Code*, § 356. For form, see *Appendix*, No. 602.

And it seems, the security must be approved by the county judge, or by a justice of the Supreme Court, 24 *Barb.* 442, *supra;* but see 29 *How.* 46, *per* Balcom, J., where the opinion is expressed that it may also be approved by a justice of the peace.

In addition to the security on the judgment, in case of an appeal by the tenant, in order to stay the issuing of the warrant or execution, security must also be given, as we have seen, for the payment of all rent accruing, or to accrue, upon the premises, subsequent to the application to the justice. *Ib.;* and see *Laws of* 1849, *supra.* For form, see *Appendix*, No. 602.

A judgment debtor, whose land has been sold on execution, and who holds over and continues in possession of the premises after title thereto has been perfected under the sale, is a "tenant" within the meaning of the statute requiring security to be given on appeal. 16 *New York*, 568, 574. And the word "rent" above mentioned, where the proceeding is between such debtor and the purchaser of his land, on execution, means compensation for the use and occupation of the premises, subsequent to the commencement of the proceedings. *Ib.*

No appeal lies from the judgment of the county court to the Supreme Court. The judgment is final, in the sense of being ultimate and conclusive; at least, so far as an appeal to the Supreme Court is concerned. 24 *Barb.* 438, *supra.*

But an appeal may nevertheless be taken to the Supreme Court from an order of the county court dismissing an appeal taken from a judgment of a justice of the peace. 29 *How.* 43.

The proceedings upon the appeal, subsequent to notice of appeal, security, &c., are substantially the same as on appeals in actions. 19 *Abb.* 323; *s. c.* 29 *How.* 201; and see *Ib.* 43; 24 *Barb.* 438, *supra.*

And, therefore, where the appellant in good faith gives due notice of appeal, an omission through mistake to do any other act necessary to perfect the appeal, or to stay proceedings—*e. g.*, the giving of security—is amendable by leave of the court. 19 *Abb.* 323, *supra.*

If the tenant fails to appear, on the return of the summons, before the justice, he will thereby admit the rights of the landlord; and will be precluded, on the appeal, from objecting to irregularity in the proceedings. 2 *Abb.* 28.

Where judgment is rendered against the tenant, and he is turned out of possession of the premises, and, on appeal, the judgment is reversed, the court has no power to restore him to the possession of which he has been deprived by the erroneous judgment. 10 *How.* 83. If the tenant desires to retain possession, in such case, he must give security for the payment of the rent. *Ib.*

Certiorari to review proceedings.] The Supreme Court is authorized to award a certiorari for the purpose of examining any adjudication made on any application authorized by the statute; but the proceedings on any such application shall not be stayed or suspended by such writ of certiorari, or any other writ, or order of any court or officer. 2 *Rev. Stat.* 516, *sec.* 47; 9 *Wend.* 228. For form of writ, see *Appendix*, No. 603.

It was formerly held, that on the return to a certiorari, under the above section, no other questions could be raised than those relating to the *jurisdiction* of the officer before whom the proceedings were had, and to the *regularity* of such proceedings. 17 *Wend.* 464; 19 *Id.* 391; 20 *Id.* 103, 189. But it is now fully settled that the authority of the court is not limited in such case to questions of jurisdiction and regularity; but that the court has power, also, to examine upon the merits every decision of the judge, *a quo*, upon a question of law, and to look into the evidence, and affirm, reverse, or quash the proceedings, as justice should require. And the court will direct the return of such parts of the proceedings as are material to the examination of the case upon its merits. 23 *Wend.* 616; 25 *Id.* 280; 1 *Selden*, 383; 2 *Id.* 309; 3 *Barb. S. C. R.* 391; 7 *How.* 154; 16 *Id.* 461.

In the return to the certiorari, it should affirmatively appear that the statute has been strictly pursued, in the proceedings before the magistrate. 20 *Wend.* 207. But the tenant will be precluded from objecting to irregularity in the proceedings, on certiorari, where he has failed to appear before the magistrate on the return of the summons. 2 *Abb.* 28.

A party who has no interest in the subject-matter of the proceedings cannot have the writ. 12 *Wend.* 234; and see 42 *Barb.* 532.

The court will not reverse the judgment as to part of the

defendants and affirm it as to the rest. See 5 *Selden*, 227. If it is irregular as to one, it is irregular as to all of them, *Ib.;* and see *Lal. Supp. to Hill & Denio*, 236; though where the Supreme Court reversed the proceedings as to part of the defendants and affirmed them as to others, the error was held not available on appeal to the Court of Appeals, brought by those against whom judgment was rightfully pronounced in the Supreme Court. 5 *Selden*, 227, *supra.*

The certiorari may be brought to a hearing by either party upon the usual notice of argument; and is entitled to preference, on the morning of any day during the first week of term. *Sup. Court Rules*, No. 47.

The certiorari does not stay the proceedings.] The statute directs that the proceedings on the application shall not be stayed or suspended by such writ of certiorari, or any other writ or order of any court or officer. 2 *Rev. Stat.* 516, *sec.* 47; and see 20 *Johns.* 80.

But the certiorari, notwithstanding the statute, suspends the effect of the judgment of the magistrate in everything except what remains to be done by the magistrate himself. The magistrate may issue his warrant to dispossess the tenant; but, during the pendency of the writ of certiorari, his judgment is no evidence that the tenancy has ceased, or of a right to re-enter. And after the writ is issued, and while it is pending, the landlord cannot maintain an action for the costs of the proceedings, nor for rent accruing intermediate the forfeiture and the issuing of the warrant. 5 *Sand. S. C. R.* 249.

Injunction staying proceedings, and for other relief by action.] It is provided by the 47th section of the statute, that "the Supreme Court may award a certiorari for the purpose of examining any adjudication made on any application hereby authorized; but the proceedings on any such application shall not be stayed or suspended by such writ of certiorari, or any other writ or order of any court or officer." 2 *Rev. Stat.* 516.

Under the second branch of the above section, forbidding the proceedings to be stayed or suspended, it was held by Edmonds, J. (1 *Barb. S. C.* 65), that that provision operated as a prohibition to a court of equity to stay the landlord's proceedings on the application to remove his tenant. But afterward, the same justice held that the statute, being inconsistent with the provisions of the Code of Procedure (§ 219), which authorizes an injunction in any case where the act complained of would "produce injury to the plaintiff," was repealed (§§ 468, 471); and accordingly he denied a motion to dissolve an injunction restraining the landlord's proceedings, *Cure* v. *Crawford*, 5 *How.* 293; *s. c.* 1 *Code R.*, *N. S.*, 18. See also to the same effect, 3 *Sand. S. C. R.* 662; 1 *Duer*, 624; 16 *How.* 170; *s. c.* 1 *Bosw.* 645.

But see *contra*, 5 *How.* 463; *s. c.* 1 *Code R.*, *N. S.*, 163, *per* Barculo, J., where the decision of Justice Edmonds in *Cure* v. *Crawford* is disapproved; and where it is held that, to authorize the issuing of an injunction under § 219, it must appear that the plaintiff is entitled to the final relief demanded according to other or pre-existing laws, independently of the Code.

To the same effect is *Hyatt* v. *Burr* (8 *How.* 168), in the Supreme Court, first district, at special term, where it was held, that, by the true construction of the Code, an injunction cannot be granted to stay or suspend proceedings under the statute for the recovery, by summary proceedings, of the possession of premises. And, *per* Roosevelt, J., in a note at p. 170, "I have consulted on this subject with two of my colleagues, with the view of establishing a uniformity of practice on a point so important to the community, as well as the profession—and they concur with me in saying that, by the true construction of the Code, an injunction cannot be granted to stay or suspend proceedings under the statute for recovering summary possession of houses or lands." And see, also, 16 *How.* 164; *s. c.* 1 *Bosw.* 645. (*a*)

But it has been held that even if the statute applies to injunctions, issued out of courts of equity, as well as to proceedings at

---

(*a*) The Revisers, in their original note to the 47th section, say it is "conformable to 20 Johnson's R. 82" (3 *Rev. Stat.*, 2*d ed.* 766). That case merely decides, that the writ of certiorari will not lie to remove the proceedings until the magistrate has finally adjudicated upon them; and that, even then, the certiorari will not stay the writ of restitution or possession. Taking the whole of the section together, in connection with the note of the Revisers, it is doubtful whether it was intended by the section to do more than to declare that the proceedings before the magistrate should, in no case whatever, *on account of the certiorari*, be stayed or suspended—thus leaving the court to exercise its equitable power to restrain by injunction in all proper cases, unaffected by the statute.

law, yet it can only affect cases in which the magistrate has jurisdiction, and not where, by the admission of the person assuming to be landlord, he has no jurisdiction. 3 *Sand. S. C. R.* 665, *per* Mason, J.; *s. c.* 1 *Code R., N. S.*, 90. Nor would the statute prevent a court of equity from relieving the tenant in case of fraud or surprise, *James* v. *Stuyvesant*, 3 *Sand.* 665, *note;* 1 *Duer*, 624; 16 *How.* 170; *s. c.* 1 *Bosw.* 645; nor, it seems, where he is without an adequate remedy at the common law, 2 *Abb.* 125, *per* Clerke, J.; nor where he is prevented by means beyond his control from attending before the justice, or setting up his defense. 16 *How.* 461; 28 *Id.* 4; 6 *Duer*, 624; 16 *How.* 170; *s. c.* 1 *Bosw.* 645.

But the injunction will not be allowed to issue where the tenant has a defense to the proceedings before the justice, and does not show that he had no evidence to prove his defense, and there is no fraud or abuse shown, 11 *Abb.* 95; *s. c.* 21 *How.* 224; nor upon any ground as to which the party could have relief in a fixed statutory method, adequate to the purpose, 11 *Abb.* 88, *per* Hoffman, J.; nor on the ground that the tenant has a claim against the landlord for damages for breach of his covenant to repair, exceeding the amount of rent in arrear. 1 *Bosw.* 645; *s. c.* 16 *How.* 164.

Nor will an injunction be issued after the warrant has been executed. 18 *Abb.* 199.

Appeal to the Court of Appeals.] The judgment of the general term is final, unless an appeal is allowed by that court to the Court of Appeals, before the end of the term next after the judgment. The appeal is brought on as a preferred cause on fourteen days' notice of argument. *Laws of* 1868, *p.* 1932. (*a*)

Awarding restitution, &c.] Whenever the proceedings brought before the Supreme Court by certiorari shall be reversed or quashed, the court may award restitution to the party injured, with costs; and may make such orders and rules, and issue such process, as may be necessary to carry their judgment into effect. 2 *Rev. Stat.* 516, *sec.* 48.

And restitution may be awarded although the lease contains

(*a*) See the statute in the Supplement, at the end of this chapter.

a covenant that, upon failure to pay the rent at the time stipulated, the estate of the lessee and his interest in the demised premises should thenceforth cease and be absolutely void. 16 *How.* 450.

But where the proceedings of the landlord are reversed in the Supreme Court, upon certiorari, that court will not award restitution to the tenant, if the term has expired before the judgment of reversal is rendered, 1 *Coms.* 450; nor where the reversal is on the ground of irregularity, and it appears that the landlord would again succeed in regularly conducted proceedings. 15 *Abb.* 328. Nor will restitution be ordered in favor of a person not a party to the proceedings. 42 *Barb.* 530, 532.

If there has been a restitution, and the decision upon which it was had is afterward reversed, a re-restitution will be awarded as of course. 1 *Caines*, 125; 10 *Johns.* 304.

The court may give costs on the reversal of the judgment, whether restitution is awarded or not. 1 *Coms.* 423, *per* Ruggles, J.

In cases of appeal to the county court from the decision of a justice of the peace, the court has no power, upon a reversal of the justice's judgment, to award restitution of the possession of the premises to the tenant. 11 *How.* 83.

Costs and expenses of the proceedings.] In all cases of an application under the statute, the prevailing party is entitled to costs, and may maintain an action for the recovery thereof. 2 *Rev. Stat.* 516, *sec.* 49; 4 *E. D. Smith*, 339.

The costs allowed are merely the fees of officers who are required to perform the services, such as the magistrate, sheriff, constable, &c., and do not embrace any compensation to the attorney or counsel. 5 *How.* 21; 6 *Id.* 178; 4 *Hill*, 541. County judges are not now entitled to fees in these proceedings. *Laws of* 1857, *chap.* 564.

To recover the costs of the proceedings on the application for the warrant, the party is limited to an action, in all cases, except where the proceedings are before a justice of the peace; in which case the justice is authorized to include the costs in his judgment, and to direct their collection in the warrant for delivery of possession, or by execution. *Laws of* 1849, *p.* 292, § 5, *sub.* 1.

If a certiorari is issued before the landlord's action to recover his costs is commenced, the action will be stayed until the writ is disposed of. And, if issued while the action is pending, the certiorari suspends the force of the judgment before the officer, as well as the right to recover the costs. 5 *Sand.* 249.

Where the proceedings are taken by certiorari into the Supreme Court, and reversed or quashed, costs will be awarded to the successful party, 2 *Rev. Stat.* 516, *sec.* 48; and this, too, whether restitution is awarded or not. 1 *Coms.* 420, 423.

In respect to the rate at which costs are to be taxed upon certiorari, this is to be regulated by the statute in existence prior to the adoption of the Code, the second part of the Code not applying to these proceedings. *Code*, § 471; and see *ante, p.* 14, *note b.*

The costs in justices' courts are: for the summons, twenty-five cents; for precept to summon a jury, fifty cents; and for the hearing, fifty cents. *Laws of* 1866, *ch.* 692. In other respects, the costs in proceedings before justices of the peace are to be at the same rate of fees allowed by law in civil actions in justices' courts, and limited in like manner. *Laws of* 1849, *p.* 292, § 5, *sub.* 1; *Laws of* 1866, *ch.* 692.

Damages on reversal of proceedings, &c.] The statute provides that, in case the proceedings on the certiorari shall be reversed or quashed by the Supreme Court, the tenant or lessee may recover, by action, against the person making application for his removal, any damages he may have sustained by reason of such proceedings, with costs. 2 *Rev. Stat.* 516, *sec.* 49.

Saving of rights.] It is also provided by the statute that nothing contained therein shall be construed to impair the rights of any landlord or lessor, or of any tenant in any case not therein provided for. *Ib. sec.* 50.

SECTION II.

RECOVERY OF POSSESSION OF PREMISES DESERTED.

Viewing premises; notice to tenant.] If any tenant, being in arrear for rent, shall desert the demised premises, and leave the same unoccupied and uncultivated, without any goods thereon subject to distress to satisfy the arrears of rent, (*a*) any justice of the peace of the county may, at the request of the landlord, and upon due proof that the premises have been so deserted, leaving such rent in arrear, and no goods thereon subject to distress, go upon and view the said premises; and upon being satisfied, upon such view, that the premises have been so deserted, he shall affix a notice in writing upon a conspicuous part of the premises requiring the tenant to appear and pay the rent due, at some time in the said notice specified, not less than five nor more than twenty days after the date thereof. 2 *Rev. Stat.* 512, *sec.* 24; 2 *Abb.* 123.

The subsequent proceedings.] At the time specified in the notice, the justice is required again to view the premises; and, if the tenant appear and deny that any rent is due to the landlord, all proceedings shall cease. 2 *Rev. Stat.* 512, *sec.* 25.

If, upon such second view, the tenant, or some one for him, shall not appear and pay the rent in arrear, and there shall not be sufficient distress on the premises to satisfy the rent, then such justice may put the landlord into possession of the demised premises; and any demise of the said premises to such tenant shall from thenceforth become void. *Ib.*

But, unless the tenant appears and denies that any rent is due, he will not be entitled to a hearing, and his lease will be annulled. 2 *Abb.* 123.

Fees of the justice.] The justice is entitled to a fee of fifty

(*a*) Distress for rent is now abolished. *Laws of* 1846, *p.* 369; and see *ante*, *p.* 189.

cents for each view of the premises alleged to be deserted. *Laws of* 1866, *ch.* 692.

Appeal by tenant.] An appeal from the proceedings of any justice in such case may be made by the tenant, at any time within three months after such possession delivered, to the county court of the county, or in the city of New York to the Court of Common Pleas, by serving notice in writing thereof upon such justice, and by giving security, to be approved by such justice, to pay to the landlord all costs of such appeal which may be adjudged against such tenant; and thereupon such justice shall return the proceedings had before him to the said court, within ten days after such notice and security given, and shall give notice to the landlord of such appeal. 2 *Rev. Stat.* 512, *sec.* 26.

The appellate court shall examine the proceedings and hear the proofs and allegations of the parties, in a summary way; and may order restitution to be made to such tenant, with costs to be paid by the landlord; or, in case of affirming such proceedings, may award costs against the tenant. *Ib. sec.* 27.

It is thought that the proofs and allegations intended by the statute are not the mere proofs and allegations before the justice, but that they may be new proofs and allegations, substituted or additional. 2 *Abb.* 124, *per* Clerke, J.

SUPPLEMENT TO CHAPTER XXX.

I. DECISIONS OF THE COURTS.

The proceeding is not an action within the meaning of the Code of Procedure. 39 *N. Y.*, 107.

In what cases the proceeding is proper. To warrant proceedings under the statute, the conventional relation of landlord and tenant, created by agreement and not by mere operation of law, must exist between the parties. Thus, proceedings are not warranted where the defendant was hired for a year to work the plaintiff's farm for a specified sum, with house room for himself and family, and a garden and pasture for a cow, 45 *Barb.*, 304; nor where the defendant holds the premises under an agreement to work the same on shares, 32 *How.*, 400; but see otherwise, now, under a recent statute, *Laws of* 1874, *p.* 612, *post.* So, where the plaintiffs, who were entitled to use a pier for loading and unloading canal boats, agreed to pay the defendant, the lessee of the pier, $50 a month for the privilege of placing a derrick, etc., upon a certain portion thereof, it was held that this did not create the relation of landlord and tenant, and that, after the termination of the agreement, they could not be removed under the statute. 1 *Hun*, 73. Where the landlord agreed that, if the tenant should erect certain buildings, he would, at the expiration of the term, pay the appraised value of the buildings or grant a new lease, the tenant being in default for the rent; it was held that the landlord could institute proceedings to dispossess him, and that the agreement to pay the value of the buildings at the expiration of the term did not take the case out of the statute. 7 *Hun*, 89.

If the nature of the hiring was such that the landlord was not entitled to the remedy under the statute, the tenant must set up that defence. 33 *How.*, 238.

In whose name proceedings to be instituted. Where the landlord sold the premises, conditioned upon delivery of possession to the vendee, the legal title not having actually passed from the landlord, it was held that this did not terminate the relation of landlord and tenant, so that proceedings could not be had in the name of the orignal lessor. 44 *N. Y.*, 489.

Demand of rent, or notice, etc. The demand of rent, as distinguished from the notice in writing, means a personal demand. 50 *Barb.*, 231. The notice in writing, required by the statute where no personal demand has been made, should be in the alternative, and should require the payment of the rent *or* the possession of the premises. *Ib.*

Notice to quit is not necessary to determine the tenancy where a parol agreement provided for the renting of the premises for one month from the 1st August, 1866, and for each successive month thereafter, until the landlord should want the premises for his own use, whereupon the tenancy should expire. 48 *Barb.*, 551. So, notice is not necessary where the premises are rented by the month, in such way as, to be continued, the lease must be renewed each month. 64 *Barb.*, 476. But where one enters upon lands by permission of the owner, without any term being prescribed or rent reserved, he is a tenant at will, and is entitled to one month's notice to quit. 60 *N. Y.*, 102. So, where a tenant is in possession under a parol agreement void by the statute of frauds, and has occupied for a year, paying the rent monthly, a tenancy from month to month is created, which can only be terminated by a month's notice to quit, expiring with the end of some month reckoning from the beginning of the tenancy. 47 *N. Y.*, 666.

Where the lease provided that the lessor may "terminate the lease at the end of any year, by giving sixty days' previous notice, in case he should sell or desire to rebuild," it was held that this was not a condition, but a limitation, and that the term expired by force of a sale and notice, in sixty days thereafter, without any further act on the part of the lessor. 44 *N. Y.*, 489.

The notice served upon a tenant at will takes effect in thirty days after the service; and the specification therein of a day on which the time will expire, which will be less than thirty days from the time of service, will not vitiate the notice. 48 *Barb.*, 551.

The affidavit upon which the application is founded should show that the conventional relation of landlord and tenant exists, and that by an agreement between the parties. 32 *How.*, 400; and see 45 *Barb.*, 304. It is not required that the landlord should state in the affidavit the date or duration of the lease. 33 *How.*, 238.

An affidavit of the service of a summons, showing that the summons, returnable Nov. 25th, was served Nov. 23d, is sufficient (under Ch. 828, of Laws of 1868, *post*) to satisfy the requirements of the statute. 5 *Hun*, 218.

The trial and proceedings thereon. On the trial neither party is entitled peremptorily to challenge a juror. 39 *N. Y.*, 107. It is proper to demand interest upon the rent. The landlord is entitled to interest from the time of the default in payment. 58 *N. Y.*, 323, affirming 1 *Hun*, 102.

Effect of issuing warrant of possession. The eviction of the tenant by proceedings under the statute, does not discharge him from the payment of rent or other obligations already accrued; the lease is only annulled as to future rights and liabilities. 55 *N. Y.*, 281.

Injunction restraining proceedings. The court will not grant an injunction restraining the landlord from instituting proceedings against a tenant, on the ground that the landlord has extended the tenant's lease. 1 *Hun*, 716. Nor will it be granted unless it appears that the magistrate has no jurisdiction, or that the proceedings are fraudulent or collusive. 49 *N. Y.*, 228. The injunction can only be granted in favor of the tenant, or of some one who is a party to the proceedings to be enjoined. 4 *Abb. N. S.*, 65.

Appeals in cases instituted before a justice of the peace. The statute of 1849 (*ante*, p. 305) providing for a stay of the issuing of the warrant, pending an appeal, does not apply to proceedings instituted solely on the ground that the tenant is holding over after the expiration of his term. Otherwise, however, as to the other three classes of cases mentioned in the statute. 34 *How.*, 1; *s. c.* 49 *Barb.*, 116. The appeal from the justice's judgment does not of itself stay his proceedings. *Ib.* The fact that an appeal has been taken to another court does not affect the conclusiveness of the judgment as a bar, while the judgment remains unreversed. *Ib.*

An appeal does not lie to the supreme court from the decision of a county court reversing the judgment of a justice of the peace. 4 *Hun*, 416.

Certiorari to review proceedings. The certiorari authorized by the statute requires the court to review any questions of law arising either in the proceedings or upon the trial; also all questions of law arising upon the rulings of the court as to the challenge of jurors, or the admissibility of evidence, or the charge to the jury, 39 *N. Y.*, 107. A person not a party to the proceedings cannot sue out a certiorari. He must be a party in form or in substance, so as to be concluded by the determination thereon. If not, although his rights may have been infringed, he cannot bring up the matter for review. 45 *Barb.*, 164.

Under the Code of Civil Procedure, just enacted, an appeal is now allowed from the judgment in these proceedings; the effect of which will be substantially to supersede the review by certiorari. *Rev. Notes*, *Laws of* 1876, *vol.* 2, *p.* 322, *ante*, *vol.* 1, *pp.* 20, 167.

Effect of the reversal of the judgment. The reversal of the judgment restores the parties to the position occupied before the proceedings were instituted; entitling the plaintiff, however, to his action for damages (*ante*, p. 313); and the ground of the reversal is entirely immaterial. 54 *N. Y.*, 221.

II. STATUTORY AMENDMENTS AND ADDITIONS.

Since the second edition of this work, several important amendments and additions have been made to the statutes in relation to the proceedings considered in this chapter; and the same are given below, in full.

By ch. 828 *of the Laws of* 1868, §§ 1 to 6 (p. 1930), the following amendments were made to the Revised Statutes (2 *R. S.*, 513):

Section 1 amends § 30 of 2 R. S., 513 (*ante*, p. 295), as follows:

§ 30. *Summons, and when returnable, etc.* On receiving such affidavit, such officer shall issue his summons describing the premises of which possession is claimed, and requiring any person in possession of the said premises, or claiming the possession thereof, forthwith to remove from the same, or to show cause before the said magistrate, within such time as shall appear reasonable, not less than three nor more than five days, why possession of the said premises should not be delivered to such applicant; provided, however, that in the cases where a person continues in possession of the demised premises, after the expiration of his term, without the permission of his landlord, the magistrate, if the summons be issued on the day the term expires, or on the day next thereafter, may direct such summons to be made returnable on the same day, at any time after twelve o'clock noon, and before six o'clock in the afternoon.

Section 2 amends § 32, of 2 *R. S.*, 514 (*ante*, *p.* 296), as follows:

§ 32. *Summons and the service thereof.* Such summons shall be served, either—

1. By delivering to the tenant to whom it shall be directed a true copy thereof, and at the same time showing him the original; or,

2. If such tenant be absent from his place of residence, and such place is in the city or town in which the demised premises are situated, by leaving a copy thereof at such place with some person of mature age residing on the premises; or,

3. If no such person can be found at such place, or if such place is not in the same city or town with the demised premises, and the tenant cannot be found upon the demised premises, by leaving a copy thereof at the demised premises with some person of mature age residing thereon; or, if there be no such person residing thereon, with some person of mature age connected with the demised premises by employment in any business for which the premises are used; or, if no person residing or employed on the demised premises can be found thereon, then such service may be made by affixing such copy upon a conspicuous part of said demised premises. If the summons be returnable on the day on which it is issued, it shall be served at least two hours before the hour at which it is made returnable, and if not returnable on the same day, it shall be served at least two days before the day on which it is made returnable. The proof of the service of the summons shall state particularly the exact time, place, and manner of service, including the name of the person on whom the service was made, if it can be ascertained.

Section 3 makes it the duty of every person to whom a copy of a summons shall be delivered, in pursuance of the second or third subdivision of § 32 of 2 R. S., § 514 (above mentioned), to deliver such copy to the tenant to whom the same is directed, or, if such tenant cannot be found, to his agent for the demised premises, without any avoidable delay; and a copy of this section shall be written or printed upon the outside of every such copy. If neither the tenant nor his agent can be found for that purpose, then the person to whom such copy is delivered shall take the same to the magistrate by whom the summons is issued, at the time and place named therein, and inform him that the tenant cannot be found. Every person who shall wilfully violate any of the provisions of this section shall be deemed guilty of a misdemeanor, and upon conviction shall be punished by imprisonment for not less than thirty days nor more than one year.

Section 4 repeals ch. 754 of the Laws of 1866 (*ante*, p. 295).

Section 5 amends § 47 of 2 *R. S.*, 516 (*ante*, pp. 308, 309), as follows:

§ 47. *Certiorari to the Supreme Court.* The Supreme Court may award a certiorari for the purpose of examining any adjudication made, on any application hereby authorized; but the proceedings on any such application shall not be stayed or suspended by such writ of certiorari, or any other writ or order of any court or officer. The judgment of the Supreme Court, at a general term, upon such certiorari, shall be final, unless an appeal shall be allowed by the said court, at a general term, before the end of the term next after that at which the judgment was rendered. The appeal upon any judgment rendered upon any such certiorari may be brought on for argument as a preferred cause at any term of the Court of Appeals, by either party, upon fourteen days' notice.

Section 6 is a proviso in respect to appeals to the Court of Appeals, &c., in judgments theretofore rendered.

By ch. 764 *of the Laws of* 1868 (p. 1724), the following sections were added to the Revised Statutes, relating to the proceedings considered in this chapter (2 R. S., 512), viz.:

§ 55. *Warrant to issue against keepers of bawdy houses.* When any house, or other real property, is used or occupied as a bawdy house, or house of assignation for lewd persons, the owner or landlord thereof may apply to any officer mentioned in section twenty-eight of this title, for a warrant of dispossession, as hereinafter set forth.

§ 56. *Application for warrant, and what to contain.* Such application shall be made upon an affidavit setting forth that the house or premises in question, or some part thereof, is used or occupied as a bawdy house, or house of assignation for lewd persons, describing the premises and naming, if it can be done, the persons occupying the same, or some one of them.

§ 57. *Proceedings on the application.* Upon such application, accompanied by such affidavit, the magistrate shall issue a summons describing the premises, and requiring the persons named or described in the affidavit to remove therefrom forthwith, or show cause before him why they should not do so, in the same time and manner as is prescribed by this article in case of non-payment of rent.

§ 58. *The summons, how served; warrant, etc.* The summons shall be served in the manner prescribed by section thirty-two of this title (*ante*, p. 316-2), and if, at the return day, no cause be shown to the contrary, the magistrate shall, upon due proof of service of the summons, issue his warrant to the proper officer, commanding him to remove from the premises aforesaid the persons on whom the summons was served.

§ 59. *Hearing and proceedings thereon.* The person on whom the summons was served, or any other person in possession of the premises aforesaid, may appear and show cause against the application, in the manner prescribed by section thirty-four of this title, and such proceedings shall, thereupon, be had as are prescribed by sections thirty-four, thirty-five, thirty-six, thirty-seven, thirty-eight, forty-one, and forty-two; and if the decision of the magistrate, or the verdict of the jury, be in favor of the complainant, the magistrate shall issue the warrant mentioned in the last section.

§ 60. *Effect of the issuing of the warrant.* A warrant issued under either of the last two sections shall have the effect prescribed by section forty-three of this title.

§ 61. *Application for warrant by parties residing in neighborhood.* Any owner or tenant of real property in the immediate neighborhood of other real property used or occupied as a bawdy house, or house of assignation for lewd persons, may give written notice to the owner or landlord of the property so used, to make the application hereinbefore mentioned; and if such owner or landlord do not within five days after personal service of such notice upon him or his agent, make such application, or if, having made it, he do not, in good faith, prosecute the same, the owner or tenant giving such notice may apply to any officer, mentioned in section twenty-eight of this title, for a warrant of dispossession, as is hereinafter described.

§ 62. *Proceedings on such application.* Such application shall be accompanied by an affidavit similar to that required by section fifty-five, and further setting forth the facts necessary to bring the case within the provisions of the last section, and thereupon the officer to whom the application is made, shall issue a summons describing the premises, and requiring the defendant to show cause before such officer, in the same time and manner as is prescribed by this article in case of non-payment of rent, why he should not be compelled to remove from such property.

§ 63. *Service of summons; warrant, etc.* Such summons shall be served in the manner prescribed by section thirty-two of this title on the owner or landlord, or his or their duly authorized agent, and also on the tenant, if any, occupying the premises as a bawdy house, or a house of assignation for lewd persons; and if at the return day no cause be shown to the contrary, the magistrate shall upon due proof of service of the summons, issue his warrant to the proper officer, commanding him to remove from the premises the persons on whom the summons was served, within two days from the issue of such warrant.

§ 64. *Hearing and proceedings thereon.* The owner or landlord of the premises, and also any tenant occupying the same, may appear and show cause against the application in the manner prescribed by sections thirty-four, thirty-five, thirty-six, thirty-seven, thirty-eight, forty-one, and forty-two, and if the decision of the magistrate, or the verdict of the jury, be in favor of the complainant, the magistrate shall issue a warrant requiring the defendant to be removed, as is mentioned in the last section.

The above sections affect only leases made after the statute took effect. *Laws of* 1868, p. 1726.

By ch. 583 *of the Laws of* 1873 (p. 895), it is provided that whenever the lessee or occupant other than the owner of any building or premises, shall use or occupy the same, or any part thereof, for any illegal trade, manufacture, or other business, the lease or agreement for the letting or occupancy of such building or premises, shall thereupon become void, and the landlord of such lessee or occupant may enter upon the premises so let or occupied, and shall have the same remedies to recover possession thereof as are given by law in the case of a tenant holding over after the expiration of his lease.

By ch. 208 *of the Laws of* 1874 (p. 229), sub. 4, of § 28, of the Revised Statutes, herein considered (*ante*, p. 282), was amended so as to read as follows:

4. When any person shall hold over, and continue in possession of any real estate, which shall have been sold pursuant to the foreclosure of a mortgage thereon, or by virtue of an execution against such person, after a title under such sale shall have been perfected.

By ch. 471 *of the same Laws* (Laws of 1874, p. 612), there was added to the same section (§ 28, *ante*, p. 282), the following sub-division:

5. When any person shall hold over and continue in possession of any real estate occupied or held by him under an agreement with the owner to occupy and cultivate the same upon shares or for a share of the crops, after the expiration of the time fixed in the agreement for such occupancy, without the permission of the other party to said agreement, his heirs or assigns.

By ch. 356 *of the Laws of* 1876 (p. 333), and *ch.* 187 *of the Laws of* 1877 (p. 200), the following sections were passed in reference to proceedings considered in this chapter, in the district courts of the city of New York.

§ 1. No proceedings shall be taken before any justice of any district court of the city of New York to dispossess any tenant or tenants under the statute in relation to summary proceedings to recover the possession of lands, unless the summons is returnable and all the proceedings are before such justice at the district court-house, or the building designated by the mayor, aldermen, and commonalty of the city of New York as the place where the court of said justice shall be held. *Laws* 1876, p. 333.

§ 2. All costs and fees allowed by law to any such justice in any such proceeding, shall be paid to the clerk of the district court of the justice before whom such proceeding is commenced, and every such clerk shall monthly, on the last day of each month, account for, return, and pay over all such costs and fees therefor paid to the comptroller of the city of New York. *Ib.*

§ 1. No justice of the district courts in the city of New York shall hereafter have jurisdiction under the statutes relative to summary proceedings to recover the possession of lands for non-payment of rent, and for holding over after expiration of term, unless the premises, the possession of which is sought to be recovered, are located in the judicial district, in and for which said justice was elected. Provided, however, that on the first hearing of any such proceeding the justice before whom such proceeding is brought, may, on motion of either party thereto, make an order directing the trial of the issues therein to be held before the justice of an adjoining district. *Laws* 1877, p. 200.

§ 2. The justice elected in each district must hold court at his court room, and at no other place, for the hearing and disposing of proceedings under the statutes referred to in the first section of this act. If he be unable to hear such proceedings by reason of illness or absence from the place where his court is held, or if said justice be a necessary witness in any such proceeding, or if for any reason he be disqualified to try the issues in any such proceeding, all power and jurisdiction by the said statutes conferred on him may be exercised in his stead by a justice of any of the other district courts of the city of New York, acting for him and in his place and stead. *Ib.*

The affidavits used in the proceedings in the district courts of the city of New York, may be taken before any officer authorized by law to take affidavits. *Code of Pro.*, § 66.

APPENDIX OF FORMS.

CHAPTER I.

FORMS IN ADMEASUREMENT OF DOWER.

No. 1.

PETITION FOR ADMEASUREMENT.

See ante, Vol. I., p. 2.

To the Supreme Court of the State of New York [*or other court; or*, To M. F., Esquire, Surrogate of the county of ——].

The petition of A. B., of, *&c.*, respectfully shows, that she is the widow of J. B., late of said town, deceased; that she was lawfully married to the said J. B. in his lifetime, and lived and cohabited with him until his decease, on the —— day of —— 18—; that the said J. B., at the time of his decease and prior thereto, was seized of an estate of inheritance, of and in the following lands and premises situated in said county, viz.: [*here describe the premises*] (*).

And your petitioner further shows, that W. B., an infant child and heir of the said J. B., deceased, and R. B., another son and heir of said deceased, claim to be the owners of said lands and premises, as the heirs at law of the said deceased; and your petitioner believes they are the owners of the said lands and premises, subject to your petitioner's right of dower in the same.

Your petitioner, therefore, prays for an order that admeasurement may be made of the dower of your petitioner in said lands and premises; and that three reputable and disinterested freeholders may be appointed commissioners, for the purpose of making the said admeasurement, pursuant to the statute in such case made and provided.

J. S. C., Attorney for Petitioner. A. B.

County of ——, ss. A. B., the petitioner above named, being duly sworn, says, That she has read the above petition, subscribed by her, and knows the contents thereof, and that the same is true of her own knowledge, except as to the matters which are therein stated on information and belief, and that as to those matters she believes it to be true.

Sworn, *&c.* A. B.

No. 2.

NOTICE OF APPLICATION FOR ADMEASUREMENT.

See ante, Vol. I., p. 3.

To W. B. and R. B., heirs at law of J. B., late of the town of ——, deceased, and to all others claiming a freehold estate in the lands described in the annexed petition.

Take notice, that a petition, of which the annexed is a copy, will be presented to the Supreme Court [*or other court*], at the next special term thereof, to be held at the Court House in the village of ——, on the —— day of ——, 18—, at the opening of the court on that day, or as soon thereafter as counsel can be heard; and that a motion will then and there be made, that the prayer of the said petition be granted.

Dated, *&c.* Yours, &c., A. B.

J. S. C., Attorney for Petitioner.

No. 3.

NOTICE BY HEIRS, ETC., TO WIDOW.

See ante, Vol. I., p. 3.

To A. B., widow of J. B., late of, *&c.*, deceased.

Take notice, that you are required to make demand of your dower in the lands owned by the said J. B. at the time of his decease, within ninety days after the service of this notice. The said lands are bounded and described as follows: [*insert description.*] Dated, *&c.*

Yours, &c., R. B., *&c.*

No. 4.

PETITION BY HEIRS, ETC., FOR ADMEASUREMENT.

See ante, Vol. I., p. 4

[*The petition and notice in Nos.* 1 *and* 2, *ante, may be modified so as to suit this case.*]

No. 5.

PETITION FOR APPOINTMENT OF GUARDIAN.

See ante, Vol. I., p. 4.

[*Same as in No.* 1 *to the* (*), *and then proceed as follows:*]

And your petitioner further shows, that W. B., of, &c., is an infant under the age of twenty-one years, and is one of the owners of the lands and premises aforesaid, as your petitioner believes; that the said W. B. has no guardian; and that your petitioner has a right of dower in the said premises, and is desirous of obtaining an admeasurement thereof.

Your petitioner, therefore, prays that some suitable and proper person may be appointed guardian of the said infant, for the purpose of appearing for, and taking care of, the interest of such infant in the proceedings.

J. S. C., Attorney for Petitioner. A. B.

[*Add verification, as in No.* 1.]

No. 6.

ORDER APPOINTING GUARDIAN.

See ante, Vol. I., p. 3.

At a special term of the Supreme Court [*or other court*], held at the Court House in ——, in and for the county of ——, on the —— day of ——, 18—,
Present, A. B. J., Justice.

In the matter of the application of A. B. for the admeasurement of dower.

On reading and filing the petition of A. B., widow of J. B., late of the town of ——, deceased, dated the —— day of ——, 18—, showing that the said petitioner is desirous of obtaining an admeasurement of her dower interest in the lands and premises described in said petition, and praying that a guardian may be appointed for W. B., an infant, and one of the owners of said premises; It is, on motion of J. S. C., attorney for the petitioner, ordered, that O. F. T., a freeholder of said county, be and he is hereby appointed guardian of the said W. B., for the sole purpose of appearing for and taking care of the interest of the said infant in the proceedings.

No. 7.

ORDER FOR ADMEASUREMENT, AND APPOINTING COMMISSIONERS.

See ante, Vol. I., p. 5.

At, *&c.* [*as in No.* 6].

[*Title as in No.* 6.]

On reading and filing the petition of A. B., widow of J. B., late of the town of ——, in the county of ——, deceased, dated the —— day of ——, 18—, and the notice accompanying the same; and also on reading and filing proof of the due service of the said petition and notice upon O. F. T., special guardian for W. B., an infant, and upon R. B., named in said petition, and after hearing J. S. C., of counsel for said petitioner, and O. F. T., the special guardian aforesaid, in behalf of said infant; It is ordered that admeasurement be made of the dower of the said A. B., in the lands of her husband, the said J. B., deceased, specified in said petition, and which are therein described as follows: [*insert description.*]

And it is further ordered, that J. R. L., J. C. B., and J. H. C., of, *&c.*, three reputable and disinterested freeholders, be and they are hereby appointed commissioners, for the purpose of making such admeasurement.

It is further ordered that the said commissioners report their proceedings to this court on the —— day of —— next.

No. 8.

OATH OF COMMISSIONERS.

See ante, Vol. I., p. 5.

[*Title as in No.* 6.] We, J. R. L., J. C. B., and J. H. C., commissioners appointed by the Supreme Court [*or other court*], to make admeasurement of the dower of A. B., above named, in the premises described in the order of said court, dated the —— day of ——, 18—, being duly sworn, do severally make oath, and each for himself makes oath and says, that he will faithfully, honestly, and impartially discharge the duty, and execute the trust reposed in him by such appointment.

[*Signatures of Commissioners.*]

Subscribed and sworn, *&c.*

No. 9.

REPORT OF COMMISSIONERS.

See ante, Vol. I., p. 8.

[*Title as in No.* 6.]

To the Supreme Court of the State of New York [*or other court, or,* To M. F., Surrogate of the county of ——].

The undersigned, J. R. L., J. C. B. and J. H. C., commissioners appointed by an order of the Supreme Court [*or other court, &c.*] dated the —— day of ——, 18—, to make admeasurement of the dower of A. B., above named, widow of J. B., late of the town of ——, in said county, deceased, in the lands and premises described in said order, and situated in the town of —— aforesaid, do respectfully report, that having first been duly sworn, faithfully, honestly, and impartially to discharge the duty and execute the trust reposed in us by the said appointment, we met on the premises hereinafter described on the —— day of ——, to discharge the duty and exercise the trust aforesaid, and as well the said A. B., and W. B., by his guardian, O. F. T., and R. B., by his attorney L. F., appeared at the time and place aforesaid [*or, if they did not appear, state the fact, and that they had been duly notified to appear at the time and place aforesaid*], whereupon the undersigned, commissioners, caused a survey of the said lands and premises to be made, in the presence of the said parties, a map of which survey is hereunto annexed.

And we do further report, that we have admeasured and allotted to the said A. B., for her dower in the said lands and premises, the one-third part thereof, which part is bounded and described as follows: [*insert description, containing the quantity, courses, and distances of the land admeasured and allotted to the widow, with a description of the posts, stones, and other permanent monuments thereof*] being the part designated on the said map, hereto annexed, by the letter "A."

We do further report that the following are the items of the charges attending said admeasurement, including our fees as commissioners, viz.:

Three days' services for each commissioner, at $2 per day for each, -	$18 00
Cash paid A. F., for two days' services as surveyor, $2 50 per day, - -	5 00
Cash paid for two chain and flag bearers, two days each, at $1 per day, for each - - - -	4 00
	$27 00

In witness whereof, we have hereunto set our hands, this —— day of ——, A. D. 18—.

[*Signatures of Commissioners.*]

No. 10.

NOTICE OF MOTION TO CONFIRM REPORT.

See ante, Vol. I., p. 9.

[*Title as in No.* 6.]

SIR,—Take notice that I shall move the Supreme Court [*or other court*], at the next special term thereof, to be held at the Court House in ——, in the county of ——, on the —— day of —— next, or as soon thereafter as counsel can be heard, for an order confirming the report of the commissioners appointed to make admeasurement of the dower of A. B., in the premises mentioned in said report; and for such further or other order as may be just; which motion will be founded upon the said report, a copy of which is herewith served. Dated, *&c.*

Yours, &c., J. S. C., Atty. for A. B.

To O. F. T., Special Guardian for W. B., and
L. F., Attorney for R. B.

No. 11.

ORDER CONFIRMING COMMISSIONERS' REPORT.

See ante, Vol. I., p. 9.

At, *&c.* [*as in No.* 6.]

[*Title as in No.* 6.] On reading and filing the report of J. R. L., J. C. B., and J. H. C., commissioners appointed to admeasure the dower of A. B., widow of J. B., late of the town of ——, in the county of ——, deceased, which report is dated the —— day of ——, 18—, and by which it appears, among other things, that the said commissioners have admeasured and allotted to the said A. B., for her dower, the one-third part of the lands and premises described in the order appointing said commissioners, a map of which is annexed to said report; which third part, so allotted to the said A. B., is particularly described in said report, as will more fully appear by reference to said report, and to the minutes of the court where said report is entered at large.

Now, on motion of J. S. C., attorney for the said A. B., no one appearing to oppose [*or*, and after hearing O. F. T., special guardian for W. B., and L. F., attorney for R. B.], it is ordered that the said report and admeasurement be, and the same is, in all respects confirmed.

No. 12.

NOTICE OF APPEAL.

See ante, Vol. I., p. 10.

R. B. and O. F. T., Appellants,
against
A. B., Respondent.

To A. B. Take notice,—That the above-named appellants appeal to the Supreme Court, from an order made by the county court of the county of

—— [*or*, by M. F., surrogate of the county of ——], confirming the report and admeasurement of J. R L., J. C. B., and J. H. C., commissioners appointed by the said court [*or*, surrogate] to admeasure and set off to the said A. B. the one-third part of the lands and premises, mentioned in said report. Dated, *&c.*

Yours, &c., L. F., Atty. for Appellants.

To A. B., Respondent.

No. 13.

BOND ON APPEAL.

See ante, Vol. I., p. 11.

Know all men by these presents, That we O. F. T., of, *&c.*, and R. B. of the same place, and S. R. C., of, *&c.*, are held and firmly bound unto A. B., of, *&c.*, in the penal sum of one hundred dollars, to be paid to the said A. B., her executors, administrators, and assigns; for which payment well and truly to be made, we bind ourselves, our heirs, executors, and administrators, firmly by these presents. Sealed with our seals, and dated the —— day of ——, 18—.

Whereas, the above-bounden, O. F. T. and R. B., have this day appealed to the Supreme Court, from the admeasurement of the dower of the above-named A. B., lately made by J. R. L., J. C. B., and J. H. C., commissioners appointed by the county court of said county of —— [*or*, by M. F., surrogate of the county of ——], to admeasure and set off for the dower of the said A. B., one-third part of the lands and premises described in their report to the said court [*or*, surrogate], and from an order confirming the said report and admeasurement.

Now, the condition of this obligation is such, that if the above-bounden, O. F. T. and R. B., shall diligently prosecute the said appeal, and shall pay all costs that may be adjudged by the Supreme Court against the said appellants, then the above obligation to be void, otherwise to remain in full force and virtue.

[*Signatures and Seals.*]

Sealed and delivered, *&c.*

[*Indorse upon the bond the following certificate:* The security in the within bond is approved, Dated, *&c.*; *which certificate is to be signed by the surrogate or a judge of the court by which the order appealed from was made.*]

No. 14.

ORDER OF REVERSAL.

See ante, Vol. I., p. 12.

At a general term of the Supreme Court held at the Court House in ——, in the county of ——, on the —— day of —— 18—.

Present, C. L. A., A. B. J., and E. H. R., Justices.

O. F. T. and R. B., Appellants,
against
A. B., Respondent.

On reading and filing an appeal from the admeasurement of dower made in pursuance of an order of the county court of the county of —— [*or*, in pursuance of an order made by M. F., surrogate of the county of ——], and the affidavits and report of commissioners and other papers accompanying the said appeal; and on hearing L. F., attorney for the appellants, and J. S. C., attorney for the respondent, It is ordered, that the order confirming the said report, and the admeasurement of dower therein made, be, and the same is hereby, vacated and set aside. (*)

And it is further ordered that the commissioners appointed by the said court [*or*, surrogate], proceed to admeasure the dower of the said A. B., as in the order appointing said commissioners they were directed to do.

No. 15.

ANOTHER FORM OF ORDER OF REVERSAL, WHERE THE RIGHT OF DOWER IS IN MINES WHICH HAVE BEEN WORKED.

See ante, Vol. I., p. 12. 1 Cowen, 480.

[*Same substantially as in last form to the* (*), *and then proceed :*]

And it is further ordered, that the commissioners proceed to assign to the said Maria her reasonable dower in the lands and tenements mentioned and described in the order of the said surrogate.

And whereas it appears that, on the premises in which dower is claimed, there is a valuable *iron ore bed*, which J. C., the husband of the said Maria, opened and worked in his lifetime, and that he was the owner and proprietor of the said lands, when the said ore bed was opened and worked, as aforesaid; by reason whereof the said Maria is dowable of, and in, all such ore beds on the same premises as were, in fact, opened and wrought before the death of her said husband, and wherein he had an estate of inheritance during the coverture; It is therefore further ordered, that in making the assignment, the admeasurers estimate the annual value of the ore beds that had been opened as aforesaid, as part of the value of the estate of which the said Maria is dowable; that the admeasurers may, in their discretion, assign the dower of the said Maria, in lands set out by metes and bounds, and containing none of the said ore beds, or they may include any of the said ore beds, so as aforesaid opened, in the said assignment, describing them specifically, if the particular lands in which they lie should not also be assigned; but if those lands should be included in the assignment, the open ore beds within them need not be so described, being part of the land itself assigned; or the said admeasurers may divide the enjoyment or perception of the profits of any of the said open ore beds, by directing a separate alternate enjoyment of the whole, at short periods, proportioned to the share each party had in the subject, or by giving the said Maria a proportion of the profits. In each and every case, however, the said admeasurers are not to take into account, or assign dower of any part or portion of said ore bed opened by said A. C., the appellant, and others, since the death of the said J. C., nor the improvements made on the said premises by the said A. C., and others, since the death of the said J. C.

CHAPTER II.

FORMS IN ARBITRATIONS.

No. 16.

GENERAL SUBMISSION TO ARBITRATION.

See ante, Vol. I., p. 28.

Whereas divers disputes and controversies have existed and arisen, and are now existing and pending, between A. B. of the town of —— in the county of ——, and C. D. of the same place. Now, therefore, we the undersigned, A. B. and C. D. aforesaid, do hereby mutually covenant and agree to and with each other, that E. F., G. H., and K. L., of, *&c.*, or any two of them, shall arbitrate, award, order, adjudge, and determine of and concerning all and all manner of actions, cause and causes of action, suits, bills, bonds, judgments, quarrels, controversies, trespasses, damages, claims, and demands whatsoever, now pending, existing, or held, by and between us the said parties. And we do further mutually covenant and agree, to and with each other, that the award to be made by the said arbitrators, or any two of them, shall in all things by us, and each of us, be well and faithfully kept and observed;—provided that the said award be made in writing and signed by the said E. F., G. H., and K. L., or any two of them, and ready to be delivered to the said parties in difference, or such of them as shall desire the same, on or before the —— day of —— next ensuing the date hereof.

[*If a judgment is intended to be entered on the award, in pursuance of the statute, add the following clause:* And it is hereby further mutually agreed by and between the said parties, that judgment in the Supreme Court of the State of New York [*or*, county court of —— county, *or other court of law and of record*] shall be rendered upon the award to be made pursuant to this submission.]

Witness our hands this —— day of ——, 18—

In presence of A. B.
M. N. C. D.

No. 17.

BOND OF ARBITRATION. (*a*)

See ante, Vol. I., p. 28.

Know all men by these presents: That I, A. B., of the town of —— in the county of ——, am held and firmly bound unto C. D., of the same place [*or as the case may be*], in the sum of five hundred dollars, lawful money of the United States, to be paid to the said C. D., or to his certain attorney, executors, administrators, or assigns, for which payment to be well and faithfully made, I bind myself, my heirs, executors, and administrators firmly by these presents. Sealed with my seal, and dated the ——, day of ——, A. D. 18—. (*)

The condition of this obligation is such, that if the above-bounden A. B. shall well and truly submit to the decision and award of E. F., G. H., and K. L., arbitrators, named, selected, and chosen, as well by and on the part and behalf of the said A. B. as of the said C. D., to arbitrate, award, order, adjudge, and determine of and concerning all and all manner of actions, cause and causes of action, suits, controversies, claims, and demands whatsoever, now depending, existing, or held by and between the said A. B. and the said C. D., so as the said award be made in writing, and signed by the said E. F., G. H. and K. L., or any two of them, and ready to be delivered to the said parties, or such of them as shall desire the same, on or before the —— day of ——, 18—, then this obligation to be void, or else to remain in full force and virtue.

[*If there is no submission in writing, separate from the bond, and it is intended to have a judgment on the award in pursuance of the statute, insert the*

(*a*) The parties should execute bonds to each other. The obligor in one will be the obligee in the other.

following clause: And the above-bounden A. B. hereby agrees that judgment in the Supreme Court of the State of New York, [*or*, county court of —— county, *or other court of record*], shall be rendered upon the award to be made pursuant to this submission].

Signed, sealed, and delivered A. B. [L. S.]
in presence of M. N.

No. 18.

LIKE BOND,—AWARD BY AN UMPIRE.

See ante, Vol. I., p. 28.

[*Proceed as in last form to the asterisk* (*) *and then continue:*]

The condition of the above obligation is such, that if the above-bounden A. B. shall well and truly submit to the decision and award of E. F. and G. H., arbitrators indifferently named, selected, and chosen, as well by and on the part and behalf of the said A. B. as of the said C. D. to arbitrate, award, order, adjudge, and determine of and concerning all and all manner of actions, cause and causes of action, suits, controversies, claims, and demands whatsoever, now depending, existing, or held, by and between the said A. B. and the said C. D., so as the said award be made in writing, signed by the said E. F. and G. H., and ready to be delivered to the said parties, or such of them as shall desire the same, on or before the —— day of ——, 18—, (*); but if the said arbitrators do not make such their award of and concerning the premises by the time aforesaid, then if the said A. B. shall in all things well and truly stand to, obey, perform, fulfill, and keep the award, order, arbitrament, umpirage, and final determination of such person as the said arbitrators shall appoint as an umpire between the said parties, of and concerning the premises aforesaid, so as the said umpire do make his award or umpirage of and concerning the said premises in writing, signed by the said umpire, and ready to be delivered to the said parties or such of them as shall desire the same, on or before the —— day of ——, 18—; then the above obligation to be void, or else to remain in full force and virtue.

[*If a judgment is intended to be entered on the award, in pursuance of the statute, then add the following clause:* And the above-bounden A. B. hereby agrees that judgment in the Supreme Court of the State of New York [*or other court of record*] shall be rendered upon the award to be made pursuant to this submission.]

Signed and sealed A. B. [L. S.]
in presence of M. N.

No. 20.

CONDITION PROVIDING FOR A THIRD ARBITRATOR.

See ante, Vol. I., p. 28.

The condition of this obligation is such, *&c.*, [*as in last form, to the* (*)—*then proceed:*] But if the said arbitrators do not make such their award by the time aforesaid, then if the said A. B. shall in all things well and truly stand to, obey, perform, fulfill, and keep the award, order, arbitrament, and final determination, of and concerning the premises aforesaid, which either of said arbitrators shall make with such person as they shall appoint as an arbitrator to act with them, or one of them, in hearing and determining the said matters in controversy, so as the said award be made in writing, and signed by the said arbitrators, or any two of them, and ready to be delivered to the said parties, or such of them as shall desire the same, on or before the —— day of ——, 18—, then the above obligation to be void, or else to remain in full force and virtue, *&c.*, [*as in last form.*]

No. 21.

ARBITRATOR'S OATH.

See ante, Vol. I., p. 31.

You and each of you do swear that you will faithfully and fairly hear and examine the matters in controversy submitted to you as arbitrators, by and between A. B., of the one part, and C. D., of the other part, and a just award thereof make, according to the best of your understanding.

No. 22.

NOTICE OF HEARING BEFORE ARBITRATORS.

See ante, Vol. I., p. 31.

In the matter of an arbitration, of and concerning certain matters in difference between A. B., of the one part, and C. D., of the other part.

SIR:—Take notice, that the above matter will be brought to a hearing before the arbitrators appointed therein, at the office of ——, in the village of ——, on the —— day of ——, 18—, at —— o'clock, in the —— noon of that day.

Yours, &c.,

To C. D.

A. B.

No. 23.

OATH ON APPLICATION FOR A SUBPŒNA.

See ante, Vol. I., p. 33.

You do swear that you will true answers make to such questions as I shall put to you, touching the necessity and propriety of my issuing a subpœna upon your present application for the same.

No. 24.

SUBPŒNA TO APPEAR BEFORE ARBITRATORS.

See ante, Vol. I., p. 33.

The People of the State of New York: To O. P., Q. R., and S. T.:—You and each of you are commanded personally to appear and attend at the office of ——, in the village of —— in said county, on the —— day of ——, 18—, at —— o'clock, in the —— noon of that day, before E. F., G. H., and K. L., arbitrators, chosen to determine a controversy between A. B., on the one part, and C. D., on the other, then and there to testify as a witness in relation thereto, before the said arbitrators, on the part of the said A. B. Hereof fail not at your peril. Given under my hand, this —— day of ——, 18—.

O. S., Justice of the Peace.

No. 25.

OATH OF WITNESS.

See ante, Vol. I., p. 33.

You do swear that the evidence you shall give to these arbitrators [*or*, this arbitrator, *or*, this umpire], touching or concerning the matters in difference submitted for their [*or*, his] determination and award, by and between A. B., of the one part, and C. D., of the other part, shall be the truth, the whole truth, and nothing but the truth. [*Or, the oath may be varied, as follows:* You do solemnly, sincerely, and truly affirm and declare, that, *&c., as above.*]

No. 26.

REVOCATION.

See ante, Vol. I., p. 50.

To E. F., G. H., and K. L.:—Take notice, that I do hereby revoke your powers as arbitrators, under the submission made to you by C. D. and myself, by our mutual bonds [*or*, agreement in writing], dated, *&c.* Witness my hand and seal, (*a*) this ——, day of ——, 18—. A. B.

No. 27.

NOTICE OF REVOCATION.

See ante, Vol. I., p. 50.

To C. D.:—Take notice, that I have this day revoked the powers of E. F., G. H., and K. L., arbitrators, chosen to settle the matters in controversy

(*a*) The revocation need not be under seal unless the submission was under seal.

between us, by an instrument of revocation, of which see a copy below. Dated —— day of ——, 18—.

Yours, &c., A. B.

[*Here insert copy of revocation.*]

No. 28

AWARD.

See ante, Vol. I., pp. 33 to 40.

To all to whom these presents shall come, or may concern: E. F., G. H., and K. L. send greeting.

Whereas, divers suits, disputes, controversies, and differences have happened and arisen, and are now depending, between A. B., of ——, and C. D., of ——, for pacifying, composing, and ending whereof, the said A. B. and C. D. have entered into a written agreement, dated the —— day of —— last past, to submit the said matters to the award and final determination of the said E. F., G. H., and K. L., arbitrators, selected by the said parties, as by reference to which agreement will more fully appear, [*or*, the said A. B. and C. D. have bound themselves each to the other in the penal sum of $——, by bonds bearing date the —— day of —— last past, with condition thereunder written, to stand to, obey, abide, perform, and keep the award, order, arbitrament, final end and determination of the said E. F., G. H., and K. L., arbitrators, selected by the said parties, as by reference to the said bonds of submission will more fully and at large appear.]

Now, therefore, know ye that the said E. F., G. H., and K. L., having taken upon themselves the charge and burden of the said award, and having deliberately heard the allegations and proofs of the said parties, do by these presents arbitrate, award, order, and adjudge of and concerning the premises in manner and form following, that is to say:

First. They do award, order, and adjudge that the said C. D., or his representatives, shall and do, on or before the —— day of —— next ensuing the date hereof, make and execute a good and sufficient conveyance of his interest as lessee for years of a certain farm in the possession of the said C. D., situate [*describe the premises*], pursuant and according to the true intent and meaning of certain articles of agreement, bearing date on or about the —— day of ——, and made between the said C. D. of the one part and the said A. B. of the other part.

Second. The said arbitrators do further award, order, and adjudge that the said C. D., his executors or administrators, shall and do, on or before the —— day of —— next ensuing the date hereof, pay, or cause to be paid, unto the said A. B., his executors, administrators, or assigns, the sum of —— dollars, in full payment, discharge, and satisfaction of and for all moneys, debts, duties, due or owing unto the said A. B. by the said C. D. upon any account whatsoever, at any time before their entering into the said agreement of submission [*or*, bonds of arbitration] as aforesaid.

Third. The said arbitrators do hereby further award, order, and adjudge that all actions and suits commenced, brought, or depending between the said A. B. and C. D. for any matter, cause, or thing whatsoever, arising or existing at the time of, or before, their entering into the said agreement of submission [*or*, bonds of arbitration], shall from henceforth cease and determine, and be no further prosecuted or proceeded in by them, or either of them, or by their, or either of their, means, consent, or procurement.

And lastly. The said arbitrators do hereby further award, order, and adjudge that the said A. B. and C. D. shall and do, within the space of —— days next ensuing the date of this present award, seal and execute unto each other mutual and general releases of all actions, cause and causes of actions, suits, controversies, trespasses, debts, duties, damages, accounts, and demands whatsoever, for or by reason of any matter, cause, or thing whatsoever, from the beginning of the world to the day of the date of the said agreement of submission [*or*, bonds of arbitration], as aforesaid.

In witness whereof the said arbitrators have hereunto set their hands and seals, this —— day of ——, 18—. [*Signatures and Seals.*]

Signed and sealed, in presence of

A. T.

No. 29.

AFFIDAVIT PROVING THE AWARD.

See ante, Vol. I., p. 41.

County of ——, ss. A. T., of —— in said county, being duly sworn, deposes and says: That he was present and saw E F., G. H., and K. L. sign, publish, and declare their final award and determination in writing between A. B., of, *&c.*, and C. D., of, *&c.*, bearing date the —— day of ——, 18—, and hereunto annexed; that the names E. F., G. H., and K. L., subscribed to the said award, are the proper and genuine signatures of the said E. F., G. H., and K. L., and that they severally acknowledged the execution thereof; and that the said deponent set his name as a subscribing witness to the said award at the time of its execution and publication as aforesaid; and further he says not.

Sworn to, *&c.* A. T.

No. 30.

AFFIDAVIT PROVING THE BOND OF ARBITRATION.

See ante, Vol. I., p. 41.

County of ——, ss. M. N., of ——, in said county, being duly sworn, says: That he was present and saw A. B. sign, seal, acknowledge, and deliver, as and for his act and deed, the within bond of arbitration; that the name

A. B., subscribed to the said bond, is the proper and genuine signature of the said A. B.; and that the said deponent set his name as a subscribing witness to the same, at the time of its execution and delivery by the said A. B. as aforesaid; and further says not. M. N.

Sworn to, *&c.*

No. 31.

AFFIDAVIT PROVING THE AGREEMENT OF SUBMISSION.

See ante, Vol. I., p. 41.

County of ——, ss. M. N., of —— in said county, being duly sworn, deposes and says: That he knew A. B. and C. D., the individuals described in and who executed the within agreement of submission, that he was present and saw them sign, acknowledge, and deliver the same as and for their act and deed, and that he set his name as a subscribing witness to the same, at the time of the execution and delivery of the said agreement, as aforesaid.

Sworn to, *&c.* M. N.

No. 32.

NOTICE OF MOTION TO CONFIRM THE AWARD.

See ante, Vol. I., p. 41.

SUPREME COURT [*or other court*].

In the matter of an Arbitration of and concerning certain matters in difference between A. B. of the one part and C. D. of the other part.

SIR: Take notice that I shall move the Supreme Court, at the next special term thereof, to be held at the Court House in ——, in and for the county of ——, on the —— day of ——, next, at the opening of the court on that day, or as soon thereafter as counsel can be heard, for an order (*) that the award made by the arbitrators in the above matter be confirmed; and that judgment be rendered thereon in favor of the said A. B.; and for such further or other order as the court may think proper to grant,—which motions will be founded upon the agreement of submission [*or*, bond of arbitration], and proof thereof, and the award of said arbitrators, and the proof thereof. Dated the —— day of ——, 18—. Yours, &c.

L. P. C., Atty. for A. B.

To C. D., above mentioned.

No. 33.

NOTICE OF MOTION TO VACATE THE AWARD.

See ante, Vol. I., p. 42.

[*As in last form to the* (*)—*then as follows*:] That the award made by the arbitrators in the above matter be set aside and vacated with costs; and for such further or other order as the court may think proper to grant, —which motions will be founded upon the affidavits, with copies of which you are herewith served, and also upon the agreement [*or*, bond] of submission, and the award of said arbitrators.

The following are the grounds upon which it is sought to vacate said award: [*Here set forth the irregularities complained of.*]

Dated the —— day of ——, 18—. Yours, &c.

J. S. C., Atty. for C. D.

To A. B., above mentioned.

No. 34.

NOTICE OF MOTION TO MODIFY OR CORRECT THE AWARD.

See ante, Vol. I., p. 44.

[*As in No.* 32, *to the asterisk* (*) —— *then as follows*:] That the award made by the arbitrators in the above matter be modified and corrected in the fol lowing particulars: [*Here set forth the particulars as to which the party desires the award to be modified, or corrected; and then continue*:] and for such further or other order as the court may think proper to grant,—which motions will be founded upon the said award, and the agreement [*or*, bond] of submission between the said parties, and also upon an affidavit, with a copy whereof you are herewith served. Dated the —— day of ——, 18—.

Yours, &c.,

L. F., Atty. for A. B.

To C. D., above mentioned.

No. 35.

ORDER CONFIRMING AWARD, AND FOR JUDGMENT.

See ante, Vol. I., p. 45.

At, *&c.* [*as in No.* 6.]

[*Title as in No.* 32.] On reading and filing the award, *&c.* [*recite the papers on which the motion is founded*], and on motion of L. P. C., of counsel for A. B., one of the parties to said arbitration, no one appearing to oppose [*or*, and on hearing J. S. C., of counsel for C. D., the other party to said arbitration, in opposition thereto], it is ordered that the award of the arbitrators in this matter be, and the same hereby is, confirmed. It is further ordered and adjudged that the said A. B. do recover against the said C. D. the sum of —— dollars awarded to the said A. B. in the said award, and also —— dollars and —— cents, for his costs and charges by the court now here adjudged to the said A. B., which said sum so awarded as aforesaid, and said costs and charges, in the whole amount to —— dollars.

And it is further ordered that the said C. D. execute and deliver to the said A. B. a good and sufficient conveyance of his interest as lessee for years, of a certain farm in the possession of the said C. D., situated in the town of, *&c.* [*describe the premises*], in the manner required in and by the said award.

No. 36.

ORDER VACATING AWARD.

See ante, Vol. I., p. 45.

At, *&c.* [*as in No.* 6.]

[*Title as in No.* 32.] On reading and filing affidavits and notice of motion, and the award and the agreement [*or*, bond] of submission in the above matter, and on motion of J. S. C.. of counsel for C. D., one of the parties to said arbitration, no one appearing to oppose [*or*, and on hearing L. P. C., of counsel for A. B., the other party to said arbitration, in opposition thereto], it is ordered that the award of the arbitrators in this matter be, and the same hereby is, vacated, with —— dollars costs, to be paid by the said A. B. to the said C. D.

No. 37.

JUDGMENT RECORD.

See ante, Vol. I., p. 48. Yates' Pl. 813.

Pleas before the Supreme Court of the State of New York, the 21st day of February, in the year of our Lord one thousand eight hundred and fifty-eight. Witness, C. L. A., Justice of the Supreme Court.

County of ——, ss. Be it remembered that at a special term of this court, held at the Court House in the village of ——, on the —— day of February, in the year of our Lord one thousand eight hundred and fifty-eight, A. B., by L. P. C., his attorney, being in the Supreme Court of the State of New York, brings, according to the statute in such case made and provided, a certain submission of matters in difference between the said A. B., of the one part, and C. D., of the other part, to E. F., G. H., and K. L., which submission was made by an agreement in writing executed by the said parties, and is in the words and figures following, that is to say [*copy agreement*], [*or*, which submission was made by bonds of arbitration executed by the said A. B., of the one part, and the said C. D., of the other part, one of which said bonds executed by the said C. D. is in the words and figures following, that is to say [*copy the bond*]. The said agreement [*or*, bond] of submission was duly proved by the affidavit of M. N., a subscribing witness thereto, in the words and figures following, that is to say [*copy affidavit*]. And the said A. B. says, that after the making of the said submission, to wit, on the —— day of January last past, the said arbitrators met at the house kept by ——, in the village of ——, and as well the said C. D. as the said A. B. appeared before the said arbitrators; and the said arbitrators did then and there proceed to the hearing and examination of the matters in controversy, and of the proofs and allegations of the respective parties, and continued such hearing, by adjournment from time to time, until the —— day of February instant, on which day, last aforesaid, the said arbitrators made and signed their award in writing under their hands and seals, in the words and figures following, that is to say [*copy award*]; which award is duly proved by the affidavit of A. T., a subscribing witness thereto.

And hereupon the said A. B. prays that the said award may be in all things confirmed, together with his costs and charges in and about the confirmation of said award. And the said C. D., by J. S. C., his attorney, comes and says nothing in bar or preclusion thereof. Whereupon the matters aforesaid having been seen, and by the court now here fully understood, and mature deliberation thereupon had,

Judgment signed this —— day of ——, A. D. 18——. N. B. M., Clerk.

It is hereby ordered, adjudged and determined that the said award be in all things confirmed, and that the said C. D. do execute and deliver to the said A. B. a good and sufficient conveyance of his interest, as lessee for years, of a certain farm in the possession of the said C. D., situate in the town of, &c. [*describe the premises and the order, the same as it is in the award*].

And it is hereby further ordered, adjudged, and determined, that the said A. B. do recover, against the said C. D., the sum of —— dollars, so awarded to be paid by the said C. D.; and also —— dollars and —— cents for his costs by him about his proceedings in this behalf expended, by the court aforesaid now here adjudged to the said A. B., which damages and costs amount to —— dollars and —— cents.

CHAPTER III.

FORMS ON ARREST AND BAIL.

No. 38.

AFFIDAVIT FOR ARREST; PERSONAL INJURIES TO PLAINTIFF.

See ante, Vol. I., pp. 58, 74.

Title of the cause.]

County of ——, ss. A. B., of said county, being duly sworn, deposes and says (*): That on the —— day of ——, 18—, at the, *&c.*, the said defendant violently assaulted and beat this deponent, by kicking him, and knocking and throwing him upon the ground, whereby deponent was greatly injured, and was made insensible, and has since been dangerously ill; and that this deponent has suffered damages by reason thereof, in the sum of —— dollars.

Sworn, *&c.* A. B.

No. 39.

LIKE AFFIDAVIT—ACTION TO RECOVER POSSESSION OF PERSONAL PROPERTY.

See ante, Vol. I., pp. 64, 74.

[*Title of the cause.*]

County of ——, ss. A. B., of said county, being duly sworn, deposes and says: That on the —— day of ——, 18—, the plaintiff was lawfully possessed of certain goods and chattels, then and ever since the property of this deponent, consisting of [*here describe the property*] of the value of —— dollars.

That on the —— day of ——, 18—, at —— in said county, the defendant wrongfully took the said property from the possession of the plaintiff and still wrongfully detains the same, to the damage of the plaintiff —— dollars.

And deponent further says, that he has commenced an action against the said defendant to recover the possession of the said property. That the said property was in the possession of the defendant at his residence in ——, on the —— day of ——, 18—: That upon that day deponent applied to the defendant for the said property, who refused to deliver it to deponent, informing deponent, that, even if he issued a requisition to the sheriff for it, on claim and delivery under the statute, deponent would not be able to find it.

That, as appears by the sheriff's return annexed hereto, the said defendant has refused to deliver the said property to him; and that the said sheriff has been unable to find the same.

Sworn, *&c.* A. B.

No. 40.

LIKE AFFIDAVIT—DEBT FRAUDULENTLY CONTRACTED (*a*).

See ante, Vol. I., pp. 65, 75.

[*Title of the cause.*]

County of ——, ss. Z. I., of said county, being duly sworn, deposes and says: That on or about the —— day of ——, 18—, the defendant, who was then doing business in ——, applied to deponent to purchase goods on credit; and, for the purpose of inducing deponent to make sales of goods to him on credit, represented to deponent that he, the defendant, had a capital in his business, paid in, amounting to twenty thousand dollars; that he had that amount of capital over and above all liabilities whatever; that he had done a small, but safe business, and mostly with his friends and relatives, and had not lost to exceed five hundred dollars since he commenced business in 18—. That he wanted to purchase goods of the plaintiff on a credit of eight months, and could and would pay for the same when such credit had expired.

Deponent further says, that thereupon, relying upon the representations so made by the said defendant, and solely induced thereby, he sold and delivered to the defendant a bill of goods amounting to —— dollars on a credit of eight months. And that subsequently, relying upon the like representations which were repeated to deponent, this deponent sold to the defendant other goods, as follows:

On the —— day of ——, 18—, upon a credit of eight months, goods of the value of $3,376 50

On the —— day of ——, 18—, upon a like credit, goods of the value of 560 00

[*Continue in same way with the several sales.*]

That the said defendant gave to the plaintiff his notes for the amounts of said purchases as follows:

On the —— day of ——, 18—, note for —— dollars, payable in eight months from date.

On the —— day of ——, 18—, note, *&c.*

[*Continue in same form with the different notes.*]

Deponent further says, that one of said notes, that first above mentioned, has become due and payable, but the same has not been paid nor any part thereof; nor have any of said notes been paid, or any part of them.

And deponent further says, that the representations made as aforesaid by the defendant were, and each and every of them was, as deponent is informed and believes, untrue.

That the defendant, on the —— day of —— last, and since the purchase of said goods, made a general assignment of his property, with preferences. That, after hearing of said assignment, deponent made inquiries in reference to the pecuniary condition of the said defendant at the time of, and before,

(*a*) This form is taken from an actual case.

his failure; and that deponent was informed, and believes, that, at the time of the making of the representations above mentioned, the defendant was in fact insolvent. That the said defendant did not have in the month of —— last, and has not since had, capital invested in his business to an amount exceeding five thousand dollars; and that the defendant owed debts at that time to an amount greater than the said capital; and that said defendant knew that such was his pecuniary condition at the time the said representations were made.

Sworn, *&c.* Z. I.

[NOTE.—The matters stated in the above affidavit on information and belief should be corroborated by the affidavits of persons having knowledge on the subject; or facts and circumstances should be given tending to establish the truth of those matters.]

No. 41

LIKE AFFIDAVIT—MONEY RECEIVED IN A FIDUCIARY CAPACITY.

See ante, Vol. I., pp. 60, 74.

[*Title of the cause.*]

County of ——, ss. G. S., of ——, in said county, being duly sworn, deposes and says: That on or about the —— day of ——, 18—, the defendant called upon him at his store in ——, and stated to deponent that he had heard that deponent desired to borrow some money, and if so, that he, the defendant, could and would procure a loan for him upon his, deponent's, own notes. That deponent, desiring to borrow the sum of one thousand dollars, thereupon entered into an engagement with the defendant, whereby the said defendant was to procure one thousand dollars for deponent upon deponent's note, and was to receive, for his services in effecting such loan, the sum of twenty-five dollars.

That deponent thereupon delivered to the defendant his, deponent's, note for $1,000, dated the —— day of ——, 18—, and payable to deponent's order in three months from date with interest, at the —— bank, and indorsed by deponent. That the defendant received the said note, promising to negotiate the same, if possible, for deponent, and to bring the money to deponent, after deducting his commission, as aforesaid.

And deponent further says, that afterward, and on or about the —— day of ——, 18—, the said defendant negotiated the said note, delivering and transferring it to C. W. B., of ——, who paid to said defendant the full amount thereof.

That deponent, on the —— day of ——, 18—, caused a demand to be made of said defendant for the moneys so received by him on said note; but the said defendant refused to pay the same, or any part thereof. Nor has the defendant ever paid the said moneys or any part thereof to this deponent; but has converted the same to his own use.

Sworn, *&c.* G. S.

No. 44.

UNDERTAKING ON ARREST.

See ante, Vol. I., p. 77.

[*Title of the cause.*]

Whereas, A. B., plaintiff above named, has made application to one of the justices of the Supreme Court [*or as the case may be*] to arrest the above named C. D., in an action for money received by the said C. D., in a fiduciary capacity [*or otherwise as the case may be*].

Now, therefore, we, the above-named A. B., of, *&c.*, and E. F., of, *&c.*, and G. H., of, *&c.*, do hereby, pursuant to the statute in such case made and provided, undertake, that if the defendant in the said action recover judgment therein, the plaintiff in said action will pay all costs which may be awarded to the said defendant and all damages which he may sustain by reason of the arrest in said action, not exceeding the sum of —— hundred dollars.

Dated, *&c.* A. B.

Signed and delivered in E. F.

presence of G. H.

W. B. B.

AFFIDAVIT OF SURETIES.

County of ——, ss. E. F. and G. H., above named, being severally sworn, each for himself, says, that he is a resident of the State of New York, and a householder [*or*, freeholder] therein, and worth double the sum specified in the said undertaking over all his debts and liabilities, and exclusive of property exempt by law from execution.

Sworn, *&c.* E. F.

G. H.

ACKNOWLEDGMENT.

County of ——, ss. On this —— day of ——, 18—, before me personally appeared the above-named A. B., E. F., and G. H., known to me to be the individuals described in and who executed the above undertaking, and severally acknowledged that they executed the same.

W. B. B., Justice of the Peace.

PROOF BY SUBSCRIBING WITNESS.

County of ——, ss. On this —— day of ——, 18—, before me personally came W. B. B., subscribing witness to the above undertaking, to me known, who, being by me duly sworn, did depose and say, that he resided in the town of ——, in said county; that he was acquainted with A. B., E. F., and G. H., above mentioned; that he knew them to be the same persons described in and who executed the above undertaking; that he saw them and each and every of them sign the same; that the said A. B., E. F., and G. H., and each and every of them, acknowledged the execution thereof in his presence; and that he subscribed his name as a witness thereto.

J. L., Justice of the Peace.

No. 46.

ORDER OF ARREST.

See ante, Vol. I., p. 79.

[*Title of the cause.*]

To the Sheriff of the City and County of ——.

It appearing to me by affidavit that the defendant C. D. is liable to arrest under § 179 of the Code of Procedure.

You are therefore required forthwith to arrest the said defendant, and hold him to bail in the sum of —— dollars, and to return this order to A. N. W., Esq., plaintiff's attorney, at his office, No. Street, in the city of ——, on the —— day of ——, 18—.

Dated, *&c.* W. H. L., Justice of the Supreme Court.

A. N. W., Attorney for Plaintiff.

No. 48.

UNDERTAKING BY DEFENDANT ON ARREST.

See ante, Vol. I., p. 81.

[*Title of the cause.*]

The above-named defendant C. D., having been arrested by J. K., the sheriff of the city and county of ——, upon an order of arrest granted by the Hon. W. H. L., one of the justices of the Supreme Court, in an action commenced in said court by the above-named plaintiff against the above-named defendant:

Now, therefore, we, E. D., of ——, in said county, by occupation, grocer, and D. D., of ——, by occupation, physician, do hereby undertake in the sum of —— dollars that C. D., the defendant, shall at all times render himself amenable to the process of the court, during the pendency of the said action, and to such as may be issued to enforce the judgment therein.

Dated, *&c.* E. D.

Signed and delivered in the D. D.
presence of A. S.

[*Add affidavit of sureties, and acknowledgment, as in No.* 44.]

No. 48 (A).

LIKE UNDERTAKING IN AN ACTION FOR CHATTELS.

See ante, Vol. I., p. 81.

[*Title of the cause.*]

The above-named defendant C. D., having been arrested for the cause mentioned in the third subdivision of section 179 of the Code of Procedure:

Now, therefore, we, E. D., of ——, in said county, by occupation, grocer, and D. D., of ——, by occupation, physician, do hereby undertake in the sum of —— dollars [*double the value of the property as stated in the affidavit of the plaintiff*] for the delivery of [*describe the property*] to the plaintiff, if such delivery be adjudged; and for the payment to the plaintiff of such sum as may, for any cause, be recovered against the defendant in this action.

Dated, *&c.*

[*Signatures, &c., as in last form.*]

No. 49.

NOTICE OF EXCEPTION TO BAIL.

See ante, Vol. I., p. 81.

[*Title of the cause.*]

To J. K., Sheriff of the City and County of ——,

Take notice that the plaintiff does not accept the bail offered by the defendant in this action [*and if the undertaking is defective in form, or otherwise, add also*], and, further, he excepts to the form and sufficiency of the undertaking.

Yours, &c., A. N. W., Attorney for Plaintiff.

Dated, *&c.*

No. 50

NOTICE OF JUSTIFICATION OF BAIL.

See ante, Vol. I., p. 81.

[*Title of the cause.*]

To A. N. W., Esq., Attorney for Plaintiff.

Take notice, that the bail in this action will* justify before W. B. B., a justice of this court [*or*, the county judge of —— county, *or*, a justice of the peace of the town of ——, in the county of ——], at the office of said justice [*or*, judge], in ——, on the —— day of ——, 18—, next, at —— o'clock in the ——noon.

Dated, *&c.*, E. B., Attorney for Plaintiff.

No. 51.

NOTICE OF OTHER BAIL.

See ante, Vol. I., pp. 81, 82.

[*Title of the cause.*]

To A. N. W., Esq., Attorney for Plaintiff.

Take notice, that E. B., grocer, of ——, in the county of ——, and D. B., physician, of the same place, are proposed as bail in addition to [*or*, in place of] E. D., and D. D., the bail already put in; and that they will [*conclude as in last form*].

No. 52.

CERTIFICATE OF DEPOSIT WITH SHERIFF.

See ante, Vol. I., p. 84.

[*Title of the cause.*]

I, J. K., sheriff of the county of ——, do hereby certify that I have received from C. D. above-named, the sum of —— dollars, as a deposit instead of bail, being the amount mentioned in the order of arrest in this action.

Dated, *&c.*, J. K., Sheriff.

No. 53.

CERTIFICATE OF CLERK THAT MONEY HAS BEEN PAID INTO COURT.

See ante, Vol. I., p. 84.

[*Title of the cause.*]

I, R. C., clerk of the county of ——, do hereby certify that J. K., sheriff of said county, has paid into court the sum of —— dollars, as having been paid him by C. D., the defendant, in lieu of bail in this action.

Dated, *&c.* R. C., Clerk.

No. 54.

EXAMINATION OF BAIL.

See ante, Vol. I., p. 83.

[*Title of the cause.*]

On this —— day of ——, 18—, before W. B. B., one of the justices of this court [*or*, county judge of the county of ——, *or*, a justice of the peace of the town of ——, in the county of ——], personally appeared E. D. and D. D., the bail given by the defendant C. D., in this action, for the purpose of justifying pursuant to notice; and the said E. D., being duly sworn, says [*take down the testimony, showing the qualifications of bail*].

And the said D. D., also being duly sworn, deposes and says [*as with the other bail*].

[*Signatures of bail.*]

Examination taken, and sworn to before me this —— day of ——, 18—,

W. B. B., Justice, *&c.*

[*Official addition.*]

No. 55.

ALLOWANCE OF BAIL.

See ante, Vol. I., p. 83.

[*Title of the cause.*]

The bail of the defendant C. D., within mentioned, having appeared before me, and justified, I do find the said bail to be sufficient and allow the same.

Dated, *&c.* W. B. B., *&c.*

CHAPTER IV.

FORMS IN ATTACHMENTS UNDER THE CODE.

No. 56.

AFFIDAVIT TO OBTAIN ATTACHMENT (*general form*).

See ante, Vol. I., p. 106.

[*Title of the cause.*]

County of ——, ss. A. B., plaintiff above named, being duly sworn, deposes and says:

That the defendant C. D. is indebted to the plaintiff in the sum of —— dollars, for goods, wares, and merchandise, sold and delivered to said defendant by the plaintiff on or about the —— day of ——, 18— [*or other cause of action upon contract, or for wrongful conversion of property*]. (*)

And deponent further says, That the said defendant does not reside in the State of New York; but resides in ——, in the State of ——, [*or other facts, bringing the case within one of the classes in which an attachment may be issued*].

Sworn, *&c.* A. B.

No. 57.

LIKE AFFIDAVIT AGAINST A FOREIGN CORPORATION.

See ante, Vol. I, pp, 98, 99.

[*Same as in last form to the asterisk* (*) *and then as follows:*]

That the defendant is a foreign corporation created under the laws of the State of ——, having its place of business in —— in that State.

That the plaintiff resides at ——, in the State of New York [*or*, That the cause of action, above mentioned, arose in this State; *or*, That the subject of the action is situated within this State].

No. 60.

UNDERTAKING ON ATTACHMENT.

See ante, Vol. I., pp. 107, 108.

[*Title of the cause.*]

The above-named plaintiff, A. B., having applied to one of the justices of this court [*or*, to J. P., Esq., county judge of the county of ——,] for a warrant of attachment against the property of the defendant, C. D., on the ground that the said defendant is a non-resident of this State [*or other cause*].

Now, therefore, we, ——, of, *&c.*, farmer, and ——, of *&c.*, merchant, do undertake, pursuant to the statute in such case made and provided, in the sum of —— dollars, that if the said defendant recover judgment in this action, or the said attachment be set aside by the order of the court, the plaintiff will pay all costs that may be awarded to the defendant, and all damages which the defendant may sustain by reason of the said attachment, not exceeding the sum above mentioned.

[*Signatures of sureties.*]

[*Add affidavit of sureties and acknowledgment as in No.* 44.]

No. 61.

WARRANT OF ATTACHMENT.

See ante, Vol. I., p. 108.

The People of the State of New York, to the Sheriff of the County of ——

Whereas, an application has been made to the undersigned by A. B., plaintiff, for a warrant of attachment against the property of C. D., defendant; and it appearing by affidavit that a cause of action exists against the said C. D. for the sum of —— dollars, and in which the grounds of said action are stated, and that the said C. D. is a non-resident of the State of New York [*or*, has departed from this State with intent to defraud his creditors; *or as the case may be*]; and the said plaintiff having given the undertaking required by law:

You are hereby required forthwith to attach and safely keep all the property of the said defendant, C. D., within your county, or so much thereof as may be sufficient to satisfy the said plaintiff's demand of —— dollars, together with all costs and expenses, and that you proceed hereon in the manner required of you by law.

Witness, W. H. L., one of the justices of the Supreme Court [*or*, county judge of the county of ——], at the, *&c.*, this —— day of ——, 18—.

S. T. F., Attorney. W. H. L.

No. 61. (A).

SHERIFF'S RETURN,—INDORSED ON ATTACHMENT.

See ante, Vol. I., pp. 109 to 117.

County of ——, ss.: I, J. K., sheriff of said county, do hereby certify and return that, by virtue of the within attachment, I have seized and taken into my possession the property of the defendant within named, specified in the inventory hereto annexed, and have appraised the property therein specified at the sums stated in the said inventory.

Dated, *&c.* J. K.

No. 62.

INVENTORY OF PROPERTY ATTACHED.

See ante, Vol. I., p. 115.

[*Title of the cause.*]

I, J. K., sheriff of the county of ——, and L. F. and G. R., two disinterested freeholders in said county, hereby certify that the following is a just and true inventory of all the property seized by me, the said sheriff, on a warrant of attachment, issued in the above-entitled action, by W. H. L., a justice of the Supreme Court [*or*, county judge of —— county], together with a statement of the books, vouchers, and papers taken into the custody of said sheriff by virtue of said warrant, and the value of each article of personal property—and also a true statement of such articles thereof as are perishable, as the same has been appraised by us, viz.: [*Insert list of property, with the value of each item.*]

We do further certify that the following property mentioned in the said inventory is perishable, viz.: [*state it*].

Dated, *&c.* [*Signatures.*

No. 63.

ORDER DIRECTING SALE OF PERISHABLE PROPERTY.

See ante, Vol. I., p. 116

[*Title of the cause.*]

It appearing to me by the inventory made under the warrant of attachment granted by me in this action, that the following property mentioned in said inventory is perishable, viz.: [*list of property*].

It is, therefore, ordered that the said property be sold by the said sheriff, at public auction, at such time and place as he shall deem advisable, within the city [*or*, town] of——; and that the said sheriff give notice of such sale as on the sale of personal property on execution. It is further ordered that the proceeds of such sale be retained by said sheriff, and disposed of in the same manner as the property, if the same had not been sold.

Dated, *&c.* W. H. L., Justice, &c.

No. 64.

NOTICE OF LEVY ON PROPERTY NOT CAPABLE OF MANUAL DELIVERY.

See ante, Vol. I., p. 114.

[*Title of the cause.*]

To E. F.:—Take notice, that by virtue of a warrant of attachment issued in this action, a certified copy of which is herewith served upon and left with you, I have levied upon and do hereby levy upon, your indebtedness, amounting to —— dollars, or thereabouts, to the defendant above named, &c. [*describing, as particularly as possible, the property levied upon*].

Dated, *&c.*

Yours, &c., J. K., Sheriff.

[*A certificate to be indorsed on copy of warrant as follows:*]

I, J. K., the sheriff within mentioned, do hereby certify that the within is a true copy of the warrant of attachment in my possession, issued in this action, and of the whole thereof.

Dated, *&c.* J. K., Sheriff.

No. 66.

ORDER DIRECTING THIRD PERSON TO APPEAR AND BE EXAMINED.

See ante, Vol. I., p. 117. 2 Abb. Forms, 32.

[*Title of the cause.*]

It appearing to me by the certificate of J. K., sheriff of the county of——, that the said sheriff, with a warrant of attachment against the property of C. D., the defendant in this action, has applied to O. P., for the purpose of levying upon property of said defendant held by said O. P. [*or*, a debt owing to the defendant by said O. P.], and that the said O. P. refuses to furnish the said sheriff with a certificate designating the amount and description of the property held by said O. P. for the benefit of the defendant [*or*, the amount of the debt owing by said O. P. to the defendant], I hereby order and require the said O. P. to attend before me at ——, on the —— day of ——, 18—, at —— o'clock A. M., and be examined on oath concerning the same.

Dated, *&c.* [*Signature of judge.*]

No. 68.

NOTICE OF MOTION TO VACATE ATTACHMENT.

See ante, Vol. I., p. 118.

[*Title of the cause.*]

Take notice, that I shall apply to the next special term of this court, to be held at the Court House in ——, on the —— day of ——, 18—, at 10 o'clock A. M., at the opening of the court on that day, or as soon thereafter as counsel can be heard, for an order vacating and discharging the attachment issued in this action [*if for irregularity, add*], upon the ground that *&c.* [*specifying the irregularity complained of*]; and for such further or other order as may be just, with the costs of the motion—which motion will be founded upon the affidavit, with a copy of which you are herewith served, and upon the pleadings and other papers in this action.

Dated, *&c.* J. W. F., Att'y for Defendant.

To A. N. W., Esq., Att'y for Plaintiff.

No. 69.

NOTICE OF MOTION TO DISCHARGE ATTACHMENT, ON GIVING SECURITY.

See ante, Vol. I., p. 120.

[*Title of the cause.*]

Take notice, that I shall apply to the next special term of this court, to be held at the Court House in —— [*or*, to the Hon. W. H. L., Justice of the Supreme Court, *or as the case may be*], on the —— day of ——, 18—, at 10 o'clock A. M., for an order discharging the attachment in this action, on giving security according to law.

Dated, *&c.* J. W. F., Att'y for Defendant.

To A. N. W., Esq., Att'y for Plaintiff.

No. 70.

UNDERTAKING ON DISCHARGE OF ATTACHMENT.

See ante, Vol. I., p. 120.

[*Title of the cause.*]

Whereas the property of the above-named C. D. has been levied upon by virtue of a warrant of attachment issued in this action; and the defendant desires a discharge of said attachment on giving security according to law.

Now, therefore, we, J. L., of, *&c.*, merchant, and J. K., of, *&c.*, broker, do undertake that, if the said attachment be discharged, we will, on demand, pay to the plaintiff the amount of judgment that may be recovered against C. D., the defendant in the action, not exceeding —— dollars [*at least double the amount claimed by the plaintiff in his complaint*].

Dated, *&c.* J. L.,
In presence of J. K.
R. S.

[*Add affidavit of sureties, acknowledgment, &c., as in No.* 44.]

No. 71.

ORDER VACATING ATTACHMENT ON MOTION.

See ante, Vol. I., p. 118.

At a Special Term of the Supreme Court [*or other court*], held at the Court House in ——, on the —— day of ——, 18—.
Present: W. H. L., Justice, *&c.*

[*Title of the cause.*]

On reading and filing the affidavit of C. D., defendant above mentioned, and notice of motion to vacate the attachment in this action, and after hearing J. W. F., Esq., of counsel for the defendant, and A. N. W., Esq., of counsel for the plaintiff,

It is ordered, that the attachment issued in this action on the —— day of ——, 18—, be and the same is hereby vacated and discharged; and that any and all proceeds of sales and moneys collected by the said sheriff, and all the property attached now in his possession, be paid and delivered to the said defendant or his agent, and he be released from said attachment.

[It is further ordered, that the said plaintiff pay to the defendant —— dollars, costs of this motion.]

No. 72.

ORDER VACATING ATTACHMENT, ON SECURITY BEING GIVEN.

See ante, Vol. I., p. 120.

At, *&c.* [*as in No.* 6].

[*Title of the cause.*]

The defendant having appeared in this action, and applied to the court to discharge the attachment on giving security to pay the judgment obtained by the plaintiff in the action; and the said defendant having delivered to the court an undertaking in the form prescribed by § 241 of the Code of Procedure, and which has been approved by the court,

It is therefore ordered that, *&c.* [*conclude as in last form, omitting the clause as to costs.*]

No. 73.

EXECUTION TO SHERIFF WHO MADE THE LEVY UNDER THE ATTACHMENT, BUT WHO HAS SINCE GONE OUT OF OFFICE.

See ante, Vol. I., p. 124.

The People of the State of New York,

To J. K., late Sheriff of the County of ——.

Whereas, in pursuancce of a warrant of attachment, dated the —— day of ——, 18—, issued out of the Supreme Court [*or other court*] against the property of C. D., in an action pending in said court, wherein A. B. was plaintiff and the said C. D. was defendant, and delivered to J. K., then sheriff of said county, the following property, the property of the said defendant, was, on the —— day of ——, 18—, duly levied upon, and taken into the custody of the said J. K., viz.: [*set forth the several items of property*], which property amounted in value to the sum of —— dollars;

And whereas, judgment was rendered in said action on the —— day of ——, 18—, in favor of the said A. B., against the said C. D., for the sum of —— dollars, as appears to us by the judgment roll filed in the office of the clerk of the county of ——; and whereas, the said judgment was docketed in your county on the —— day of ——, 18—, and the sum of —— dollars is now actually due thereon;

Therefore we command you that you satisfy the said judgment out of the property so attached as aforesaid, by the sale of said property, or so much thereof as shall be sufficient to satisfy the said judgment; and if a sufficient sum be not realized therefrom, then that you satisfy the said judgment out of other personal property of the said judgment debtor within your county, or if sufficient personal property cannot be found, then out of the real property in your county belonging to the defendant on the day when the said judgment was so docketed in your county, or at any time thereafter, in whose hands soever the same may be, and return this execution, within sixty days after its receipt by you, to the clerk of said county.

Witness, C. R. I., one of the justices of the Supreme Court [*or*, county judge of the county of ——], at the city of——, the —— day of ——, 18—.

A. N. W., Att'y for Plaintiff.

CHAPTER V.

FORMS IN CLAIM AND DELIVERY OF PERSONAL PROPERTY.

No. 76.

AFFIDAVIT UNDER § 207 OF THE CODE.

See ante, Vol. I., p. 134.

[*Title of the cause.*]

County of ——, ss. A. B., the above-named plaintiff, being duly sworn, deposes and says:

That the plaintiff is the owner and entitled to the immediate possession of the following described property, now in the possession of the defendant, at ——, viz.: [*describe the property particularly*].

That the said property is wrongfully detained by C. D., the defendant above named. (*)

That the alleged cause of the detention thereof, according to deponent's best knowledge, information, and belief, is as follows: [*state it, as*, That said property was purchased by the defendant of the plaintiff in the city of New York, on the —— day of ——, 18—, and that the defendant is the lawful owner of the same].

That the said property has not been taken for a tax, assessment, or fine, pursuant to a statute; or seized under an execution or attachment against the property of the said plaintiff.

That the actual value of the said property is the sum of —— dollars.

Sworn, *&c.* A. B.

No. 77.

LIKE AFFIDAVIT—PROPERTY CLAIMED TO BE EXEMPT FROM EXECUTION.

See ante, Vol. I., p. 134.

[*Same as in last form to the asterisk* (*) *and then proceed.*]

That the said property has not been taken for a tax, assessment, or fine, pursuant to a statute; or seized under an execution or attachment against the property of the said plaintiff, except as hereinafter mentioned.

That the said C. D. is the sheriff of the county of ——, and as such sheriff claims to have levied upon the said property, under an execution said to have been issued against the property of the plaintiff; which is the alleged cause of the detention of said property, according to deponent's best knowledge, information, and belief.

That the plaintiff is a householder and resides in this State; and the said property is a part of his necessary household furniture, the whole value of which was less in the aggregate than —— dollars, besides the property specifically is exempt from execution under the Revised Statutes, and that the said property, so seized by the said C. D., is exempt by law from levy and sale on execution, as deponent is advised by counsel and verily believes [*or*, That the plaintiff is a householder, residing in this State, and is by occupation a carpenter; and that the property above mentioned are the working tools of the plaintiff, necessary to the carrying on of his said business].

That the actual value of the said property is the sum of —— dollars.

Sworn, *&c.* A. B.

No. 78.

REQUISITION TO BE INDORSED ON AFFIDAVIT.

See ante, Vol. I., p. 135.

To the Sheriff of the County of ——

SIR:—You are hereby required to take the property within mentioned from the defendant, and deliver the same to the plaintiff in this action.

Dated, *&c.* A. N. W., Attorney for Plaintiff.

No. 79.

UNDERTAKING BY PLAINTIFF'S SURETIES.

See ante, Vol. I., p. 135.

[*Title of the cause.*]

Whereas, A. B., the plaintiff in this action, has made an affidavit that the defendant therein wrongfully detains certain personal property in the said affidavit mentioned, of the value of —— dollars; and the plaintiff claims the immediate delivery of such property, as provided for in the second chapter, of the seventh title, of the second part of the Code of Procedure.

Now, therefore, in consideration of the taking of said property, or any part thereof, by the sheriff of the county of ——, by virtue of the said affidavit, and the requisition indorsed thereupon by the plaintiff's attorney, we, the undersigned, E. F., of No. —— Street, in the city of New York, merchant, and G. H., of No. —— Street, in said city, broker, do hereby undertake and become bound to the defendant in the sum of —— dollars [*double the value of the property as stated in the affidavit*] for the prosecution of this action, and for the return to the defendant of the said property, or so much thereof as shall be taken by virtue of the said affidavit and requisition indorsed thereupon, if a return thereof shall be adjudged; and for the payment to him of such sum as may, for any cause, be recovered against the plaintiff in this action. [*Signatures of sureties.*]

Signed and delivered in
presence of
J. K.

[*Add affidavit of sufficiency of sureties, and acknowledgment or proof, as in No.* 44.]

APPROVAL BY SHERIFF, INDORSED ON UNDERTAKING.

I approve of the within undertaking, both as to its form and the sufficiency of the sureties therein.

No. 80.

NOTICE OF EXCEPTION, AND OF JUSTIFICATION OF SURETIES.

See ante, Vol. I., p. 137.

[*Same as ante, Nos.* 49 *and* 50.]

No. 81.

UNDERTAKING BY DEFENDANT TO OBTAIN A RETURN OF PROPERTY.

See ante, Vol. I., p. 138.

[*Title of the cause.*]

Whereas, the plaintiff in this action has claimed a delivery to him of certain personal property, specified in the affidavit made on his behalf for the purpose of obtaining such delivery, which property is alleged to be of the value of —— dollars; and, whereas, the said plaintiff has caused the said property to be taken by the sheriff of the county of ——, pursuant to the second chapter, of the seventh title, of the second part of the Code of Procedure, but the same has not yet been delivered to the plaintiff; and, whereas, the defendant is desirous of having the said property returned to him:

Now, therefore, we, the undersigned, L. M., of No. —— Street, in the city of ——, merchant, and N. O., of No. —— Street, in said city, merchant, for the procuring of such return, and in consideration thereof, do hereby undertake and become bound to the said sheriff in the sum of —— dollars [*double the value of the property as stated in the plaintiff's affidavit*] for a delivery of the said property to the plaintiff, if such delivery shall be adjudged, and for the payment to him of such sum as may, for any cause, be recovered against the defendant in this action.

Signed and delivered in [*Signatures of sureties.*]
presence of
P. R.

[*Add affidavit of sufficiency of sureties, and acknowledgment or proof, as in No.* 44.]

No. 82.

NOTICE REQUIRING RETURN OF PROPERTY TO DEFENDANT.

See ante, Vol. I., p. 138.

To the Sheriff of the County of ——

SIR:—You are hereby required to return to the defendant the personal property taken and held by you in this action.

Dated, *&c.* J. W. F., Att'y for Defendant.

No. 83.

AFFIDAVIT OF CLAIM OF THIRD PERSON.

See ante, Vol. I., p. 140.

[*Title of the cause.*]

County of ——, ss. R. S., of —— in said county, being duly sworn, deposes and says: That he is the sole owner of certain personal property in the possession of the sheriff of the county of ——, and taken by him in this action, which property is described as follows: [*describe the property*]. That deponent purchased the said property of the defendant on the —— day of ——, 18—, paying for the same the sum of —— dollars, and that he has not sold or disposed of the said property, or any part thereof.

Sworn, *&c.* R. S.

No. 84.

NOTICE TO SHERIFF—CLAIM OF THIRD PERSON.

See ante, Vol. I., p. 141.

To the Sheriff of the County of ——.

SIR:—You will please take notice that I claim the personal property mentioned in the within affidavit [*or*, the affidavit annexed hereto], and that you are required to deliver the same to me.

Dated, *&c.* R. S.

No. 85.

SHERIFF'S NOTICE TO PLAINTIFF—CLAIM OF THIRD PERSON.

See ante, Vol. I., p. 141.

[*Title of the cause.*]

To A. N. W., Attorney for Plaintiff.

You will please take notice that R. S. claims the property taken by me in this action, and that, unless the plaintiff indemnifies me against such claim, I shall not keep the property or deliver it to the plaintiff.

Dated, *&c.* J. K., Sheriff.

No. 86.

UNDERTAKING BY PLAINTIFF TO SHERIFF—CLAIM OF THIRD PERSON.

See ante, Vol. I., p. 141.

[*Title of the cause.*]

Whereas, the plaintiff claims to own the following property now in the possession of the sheriff of the county of ——, and taken by him in this action; and one R. S. claims to have title thereto, and the right to the possession of the same:

Now, therefore, we, the undersigned, E. F., of No. —— Street, in the city of ——, merchant, and G. H., of No. —— Street, in said city, broker, undertake to indemnify the said sheriff against the claim of the said R. S. if the said property be delivered to the plaintiff.

Signed and delivered [*Signatures of sureties.*]
in presence of
J. K.

AFFIDAVIT OF SUFFICIENCY.

County of ——, ss. E. F. and G. H., the sureties in the within undertaking, being duly and severally sworn, each for himself, says, that he is worth —— dollars [*double the value of the property as stated in the plaintiff's affidavit*] over all his debts and liabilities, and exclusive of property exempt from levy and sale on execution; and that he is a householder and freeholder in the county of ——.

Sworn, *&c.* [*Signatures.*]

[*Add acknowledgment or proof in the usual form. See No.* 44.]

No. 87.

AFFIDAVIT TO RECOVER POSSESSION OF PERSONAL PROPERTY—ACTION IN JUSTICE'S COURT.

See ante, Vol. I., p. 146

[*Title of the cause.*]

County of ——, ss. A. B., of, *&c.*, plaintiff herein, being duly sworn, deposes and says:

That he is the owner, or entitled to the immediate possession of the following described property now in the possession of C. D., the defendant, viz.: [*describe it particularly*].

That the said property is wrongfully withheld or detained by C. D., the defendant above named.

That the cause of the detention or withholding of said property, according to the best knowledge, information, and belief of deponent, is as follows: [*state it, as,* That the said property was purchased by the said C. D., of deponent, on the —— day of ——, 18—, and that the said C. D. is the lawful owner of the same, *or as the case may be*].

That the said property has not been taken for any tax, fine, or assessment, pursuant to statute, or seized by virtue of an execution or attachment against the property of said plaintiff.

That the actual value of said personal property is the sum of —— dollars.

Sworn, *&c.* A. B.

No. 88.

UNDERTAKING BY PLAINTIFF'S SURETIES—IN JUSTICES' COURTS.

See ante, Vol. I., p. 146.

[*Title of the cause.*]

Whereas, it appears by an affidavit made by A. B., the plaintiff, on the —— day of ——, 18—, that C. D., the defendant, wrongfully withholds and detains from him certain personal property in said affidavit described, of the value of —— dollars; and the said A. B. claims the immediate delivery of such property, as provided for by chapter 131 of the Laws of 1860,

Now, therefore, in consideration of the taking of said property, or any part thereof, by any constable of the county of ——, by virtue of the said affidavit, and the requisition indorsed thereupon, we, the undersigned, N. R., of the town of ——, in said county, farmer, and B. C., of the same place, merchant, do hereby undertake and become bound to the said C. D. in the sum of —— dollars [*double the value of the property as stated in the affidavit*] for the prosecution of the action to recover the possession of said property, and for the return of said property to the said C. D. if return thereof be adjudged; and for the payment to him of such sum as may for any cause be recovered against the said A. B., plaintiff in said action.

Signed and delivered [*Signatures of sureties.*]
in presence of
W. B. B.

[*Add affidavit of sufficiency of sureties, and acknowledgment or proof, as in No. 44, ante.*]

No. 89.

REQUISITION, TO BE INDORSED ON AFFIDAVIT.

See ante, Vol. I., p. 147.

[*Title of the cause.*]

To any Constable of the County of ——.

You are hereby required to take the property within described from the defendant, C. D., and keep the same, to be disposed of according to law.

Dated, *&c.* W. B. B., Justice of the Peace.

No. 90.

SUMMONS—ISSUED BY JUSTICE.

See ante, Vol. I., p. 147.

[*Title of the cause.*]

To C. D., the defendant.

You are hereby required to appear before me, at my office in the village [*or*, town] of ——, in the county of——, on the —— day of ——, 18—, [*not more than twelve days from date*], at nine o'clock A. M., to answer the complaint of A. B., the plaintiff above named. And if you fail to appear at the time and place above mentioned, the plaintiff will have judgment for the possession of the property described in the affidavit hereto annexed, together with the costs and disbursements of the action.

Witness my hand this —— day of ——, 18—,

W. B. B., Justice of the Peace.

No. 91.

NOTICE OF EXCEPTION TO PLAINTIFF'S SURETIES.

See ante, Vol. I., p. 148.

[*Title of the cause.*]

To A. B., plaintiff above named, [*or*, To J. R. L., constable of the town of ——, in the county of ——],

Take notice,—That the defendant excepts to the sureties in the plaintiff's undertaking in this action.

Dated, *&c.* C. D., Defendant.

CHAPTER VI.

FORMS ON CERTIORARI.

No. 92.

AFFIDAVIT TO MOVE FOR CERTIORARI.

See ante, Vol. I., p. 158.

County of ——, ss.: R. O. M., of, *&c.*, being duly sworn, says: He is the district attorney of said county; that on or about the —— day of ——, 18—, a writ of habeas corpus was allowed by —— [*officer issuing the writ*], and returnable before him on the —— day of ——, 18—, at ten o'clock,

A. M., of that day, for the relief of one J. C., and to inquire into the cause of his detention. That, at the time last aforesaid, a return was made to said writ, to which return a traverse was interposed. That, on the said return, deponent was heard before the said justice [*or other officer*], and, on the —— day of —— instant, an order was made by said justice, under which the said J. C., the party named therein, was discharged from custody, and a final adjudication was thereupon made by said justice.

That in and by the said return it appears, that, &c. [*set forth sufficient of the return to show the point desired to be raised*].

That the order of said justice was erroneous, as deponent believes, inasmuch as, &c. [*stating the error*].

Sworn, &c. R. C. M.

No. 94.

CERTIORARI TO REMOVE PROCEEDINGS INTO THE SUPREME COURT.

See ante, Vol. I., p. 160; and 2 Park. Cr. R. 650; and see 3 Id. 533; Id. 600.

The People of the State of New York, to G. D., Esq., one of the Justices of the Supreme Court [*or*, to A. D. W. Esq., County Judge of the County of ——], greeting:

Whereas, we have been informed, by the complaint of R. C. M., [SEAL.] district attorney of the county of ——, that certain proceedings were had before you, on behalf of J. C., lately convicted of a misdemeanor in our Court of Oyer and Terminer [*or*, Court of Sessions], of the county of ——, and imprisoned, pursuant to sentence thereon, in the common jail of said county, whereby an order was made by you, on the —— day of ——, 18—, allowing a writ of habeas corpus, tested of that day, and directed to E. L., sheriff of said county, and keeper of the common jail thereof, commanding him to bring before you the body of the said J. C., together with the cause of his imprisonment, at the ——, in the city [*or*, village] of ——; and whereby a certain other order was made by you in said proceedings, upon the return of said writ, on the —— day of ——, in the year aforesaid, discharging the said J. C. from his imprisonment aforesaid; and we being willing, for certain reasons, to be certified of the said proceedings, writs, and orders, and all things appertaining thereto, do command you that you certify the same, with all things appertaining thereto, unto our justices of our Supreme Court, at the City Hall [*or*, Court House], in——, on the —— day of ——, next [*time and place of the next general term*], under your seal, as fully and amply as the same remain before you, that our said justices may cause to be done further thereupon what of right and according to law ought to be done; and have you then there this writ.

Witness, S. B. S., Esq., Justice of the Supreme Court, at the, &c., the —— day of ——, one thousand eight hundred and ——.

C. A. D., Clerk.

R. C. M., District Attorney of —— County.

[*Indorsed:*] On the application of R. C. M., district attorney of ——

county, upon his affidavit, dated the —— day of ——, 18—, I allow the within writ of certiorari to issue; and let said affidavit be filed in the office of the clerk of —— county.

Dated, *&c.* W. R., Justice of Supreme Court.

No. 95.

CERTIORARI—ANOTHER FORM.

See ante, Vol. I., p. 160.

[*For form of certiorari in summary proceedings to remove tenants, see No.* 603; *and in cases of forcible entries and detainers, see No.* 159.]

No. 97.

ANSWER OR RETURN TO WRIT OF CERTIORARI.

See ante, Vol. I., p. 162, and 2 Park. Cr. R. 652.

The answer or return of G. D., one of the justices of the Supreme Court [*or*, county judge of the county of ——], to the writ of certiorari hereto annexed.

By virtue of, and in obedience to, the writ of certiorari hereto annexed, and to me directed, I do hereby certify and return to the justices of the Supreme Court, that on the —— day of —— last, the petition of J. C. was presented to me, duly verified, which petition is as follows: [*insert petition.*]

That I did thereupon, pursuant to the prayer of said petitioner, order and allow a writ of habeas corpus to issue to E. L., sheriff of said county of ——, commanding him to have before me the body of the said J. C., together with the cause of his imprisonment, at the City Hall [*or*, Court House, *or*, at my office], in the city [*or*, village] of ——, on the —— day of ——, 18—; at which last-mentioned time and place, appeared before me the said sheriff, together with the said J. C., and also the district attorney of said county, on behalf of the people, and the said sheriff did then and there make the following return to the said writ: [*insert sheriff's return*].

And thereupon the said J. C. did traverse under oath the said return of said sheriff, which traverse is as follows: [*insert the prisoner's traverse*].

Whereupon I did then and there proceed to hear the allegations and proofs produced in behalf of said prisoner, and also in behalf of said people; and being satisfied upon such hearing that, *&c.* [*state the conclusions of the judge*], I did thereupon [for the reasons stated in the annexed opinion] make and indorse upon said writ of habeas corpus, an order as follows: [*insert the order or decision made*].

All of which I do hereby certify, and return as within I am commanded.

In testimony whereof I have hereunto set my hand and seal, this —— day of ——, in the year one thousand eight hundred and ——.

G. D. [*seal.*]

No. 98.

ANSWER OR RETURN TO CERTIORARI—ANOTHER FORM.

See ante, Vol. I., p. 162.

[For return in cases of Forcible Entries and Detainers, see *post*, No. 161.]

No. 100.

JUDGMENT RECORD ON CERTIORARI.

See ante, Vol. I., p. 165; Yates Pl. 514.

SUPREME COURT. Pleas before the Justices of the Supreme Court of Judicature of the People of the State of New York, at the Court House in ——, of the term of —— [*term at which judgment is entered*], in the year of our Lord one thousand eight hundred and sixty ——.

Witness, W. B. L., Esq., Presiding Justice.

State of New York, ss.: The People of the State of New York (*) sent to A. D. W., county judge of the county of —— [*or other officer*], their writ of certiorari close in these words, to wit:

The People of the, *&c.* [*insert certiorari in full*].

At which day and place, in the return of the said writ mentioned, before the justices aforesaid, comes the said A. B., by S. D., his attorney, and the said C. D., by O. F. D., his attorney. And the said county judge [*or other officer*], to whom the said writ was directed, now here makes return thereto, as follows: [*insert return*].

And now, at this day, to wit, on the —— day of ——, at the village [*or*, city] of ——, before the justices aforesaid, come the parties aforesaid; and the said court now here, having seen and fully understood all and singular the premises and mature deliberation being thereupon had, it seems to the court now here, that the proceedings and adjudication of the said judge are in all respects irregular, erroneous, and void [*or otherwise, according to the decision*].

Judgment signed this —— day of ——, 18—. N. B. M., Clerk.

Therefore it is considered that the said proceedings and adjudication be, and the same are hereby, reversed and in all things held for naught [*or otherwise, as the decision may be*].

And it is further considered that the said A. B. [*or*, the said C. D.] recover —— dollars, for his costs and charges by him laid out and expended, in and about the prosecution of the said writ of certiorari [*or*, in and about his defense to the said writ of certiorari], adjudged to the said A. B. [*or*, C. D.] by the court now here with his assent, [and that the said C. D. have restitution of the premises aforesaid].

No. 101.

JUDGMENT RECORD ON CERTIORARI—ANOTHER FORM.

See ante, Vol. I., p. 165.

[For form of Judgment Record in Forcible Entries and Detainers, see *post*, No. 163.]

CHAPTER VII.

FORMS IN PROCEEDINGS AS FOR CONTEMPTS.

No. 102.

AFFIDAVIT OF SERVICE OF ORDER TO PAY MONEY, AND OF DEMAND OF PAYMENT.

See ante, Vol. I., p. 171.

SUPREME COURT [*or other court*].

A. B.
against
E. D.

County of ——, ss.: M. T. G., of, *&c.*, being duly sworn, says, that on the —— day of ——, 18—, he served upon C. D. above named, a copy of the order hereto annexed, by delivering the same to, and leaving the same with, the said C. D., at his residence in ——, in said county; and that at the time he so served the said copy, he showed him the said order hereto annexed.

And deponent further says, that at the time of the service of such copy of order, as aforesaid, he personally, on behalf of said A. B., demanded of said C. D. payment of the costs [*or*, moneys] mentioned in said order; but the said C. D. neglected and refused to pay the same, or any part thereof.

And deponent further says, that the said demand was made on behalf of the plaintiff in this action, and that deponent was duly authorized to make such demand, as appears by the power of attorney hereto annexed. And that at the time the said demand was made, deponent stated to the said C. D. the nature of his authority, and showed him the said power of attorney.

Sworn, *&c.* M. T. G.

[*Annex order and power of attorney.*]

No. 103.

ORDER FOR PRECEPT TO COMMIT FOR NON-PAYMENT OF MONEY.

See ante, Vol. I., pp. 171, 206.

[*Title, as in last form.*] At, *&c.* [*as in No.* 6].

On reading and filing the affidavit of M. T. G., dated the —— day of ——, 18—, showing due personal service on the defendant of a copy of the order made in the above action, on the —— day of —— last, and also showing a demand of the payment of the costs [*or*, moneys] mentioned in said order, of the defendant personally, and of his neglect and refusal to pay the same or any part thereof; and the costs of this proceeding to compel such payment having been fixed by the court at —— dollars;

Now, on motion of L. P. C., attorney for the plaintiff, it is ordered that a precept be issued out of, and under the seal of this court, directed to the sheriff of the county of ——, commanding him to take the body of the said C. D., if he shall be found in his bailiwick, and commit him to the common jail of said county of ——, and to keep and detain him therein, under his custody, until he shall pay the sum of —— dollars, as required by said order, and also the further sum of —— dollars for the costs and expenses of the proceeding to compel such payment, together with the sheriff's fees on such precept.

No. 104

PRECEPT TO COMMIT FOR NON-PAYMENT OF MONEY.

See ante, Vol. I., p. 171.

The People of the State of New York, to the Sheriff of the County of ——, greeting:

[SEAL.] Whereas, on the —— day of ——, 18—, by a certain order made in our Supreme Court [*or other court*], in a certain action depending in our said court, wherein A. B. is plaintiff, and C. D. is defendant, it was ordered that the said C. D. pay to the said A. B. the sum of —— dollars, for, *&c.* [*state for what the moneys were ordered, &c.*]. And, whereas, we have been informed in our said court that although the said sum of —— dollars has been personally demanded of the said C. D., by or in behalf of said A. B., yet the said C. D. has hitherto neglected and refused, and still neglects and refuses to pay the same; and whereas the costs and expenses of the proceeding on the part of the said A. B. to compel payment thereof amount to —— dollars:

Now, therefore, we command you to take the body of the said C. D., if he shall be found in your bailiwick, and commit him to the common jail of the county of ——, and keep and detain him therein under your custody, until he shall pay the said sum of —— dollars for the said moneys so ordered to be paid; and also the said sum of —— dollars for the costs and expenses of the proceeding to compel such payment, together with your fees on this writ. And you are to make and return to our said court on the —— day of —— next, at the county clerk's office in the said county of ——, a certificate, under your hand, of the manner in which you shall have executed this our writ; and have you then there this writ.

Witness C. L. A., one of the justices of our said court, at ——, the —— day of ——, one thousand eight hundred and ——.

L. P. C., Attorney. N. B. M., Clerk.

(*Indorsed:*) "By the Court."

N. B. M., Clerk.

No. 105.

NOTICE TO SHERIFF TO RETURN PROCESS, ETC

See ante, Vol. I., p. 189.

[*Title as in No.* 102.] To H. R., Sheriff of the County of ——:

SIR: You are hereby notified to return the execution in the above cause delivered to you on the —— day of —— last, within ten days after the service of this notice, or show cause at a special term of this court, to be held at the village of ——, in the county of ——, on the —— day of —— next [*or*, instant], why an attachment should not issue against you.

Dated, *&c.* L. P. C., Attorney for Plaintiff.

No. 106.

AFFIDAVIT TO OBTAIN ATTACHMENT AGAINST A SHERIFF.

See ante, Vol. I., p. 189.

[*Title as in No.* 102.]

County of ——, ss.: L. P. C., being duly sworn, deposes and says: He is the attorney for the plaintiff in the above-entitled action. That judgment was duly entered against the defendant in this action, for the sum of —— dollars, and the judgment roll therein duly filed with the clerk of said county, on the —— day of ——, 18—. That on the —— day of —— last, he delivered to H. R., Esquire, sheriff of said county of ——, an execution in this action, for —— dollars and interest from the —— day of —— last. directed to the said sheriff, by delivering the same to, and leaving the same with, the said sheriff, at his office in the village of ——, in said county [*or*, with J. R. L., under-sheriff of the said county, at his residence in the village of ——, in said county, *or otherwise, according to the mode of delivery*].

And deponent further says, That on the —— day of —— last [*or*, instant], he served the said sheriff with a true copy of the notice hereto annexed, by delivering the same to, and leaving the same with, the said sheriff, at his office in the village of ——, in said county.

And deponent further says, That he has this day searched in the office of the clerk of said county for the said execution; but the same has not been returned to said office, although sufficient time has elapsed therefor; and that no part of said execution has been paid to deponent or to said plaintiff.

Sworn, *&c.* L. P. C.

No. 107.

WRIT OF ATTACHMENT AGAINST SHERIFF.

See ante, Vol. I., p. 189.

The People of the State of New York, to the Coroners of the County of ——, greeting: We command you that you attach H. R., Esq., sheriff of our said county, so that you may have his body before our Supreme Court, [SEAL.] at a special term thereof, to be held at the Court House in ——, on the —— day of —— next, there to answer unto us, as well touching the contempts which he, as is alleged, hath committed against us, as also such other matters as shall then and there be laid to his charge; and further to perform and abide such order as our said court shall make in this behalf; and have you then and there this writ, and make and return a certificate under your hand, of the manner in which you shall have executed the same.

Witness, A. B. J., one of the justices of our said court, the —— day of ——, one thousand eight hundred and ——.

L. P. C., Attorney. N. B. M., Clerk.

[*Indorsed:*] In Supreme Court: The People of the State of New York, *ex rel.* A. B. *vs.* H. R., sheriff of the county of ——. Attachment; returnable the —— Tuesday of ——, 18—. L. P. C., Attorney.

Let the defendant give security for his appearance, in the sum of —— dollars. A. B. J., Justice of the Supreme Court.

Dated, *&c.*

No. 108.

ORDER FOR A HABEAS CORPUS TO BRING UP THE DEFENDANT.

See ante, Vol. I., p. 193.

At, *&c.* [*as in No.* 6].

[*Title as in No.* 102.] An attachment having issued in the above-entitled action against the defendant therein, for a contempt of court, directed to the sheriff of the county of ——; and the said sheriff having returned to the said writ that, *&c.* [*set forth the return showing the defendant to be already in custody*]. Now, on reading the said attachment, and the return thereon indorsed; and on motion of L. P. C., attorney for the plaintiff; it is ordered, that a writ of habeas corpus do issue, directed to the said sheriff, ordering him to bring the said defendant forthwith before this court, at the village of ——, to answer for the said contempt.

No. 109.

HABEAS CORPUS TO BRING UP THE DEFENDANT.

See ante, Vol. I., p. 193.

The People of the State of New York, to the Sheriff of the County of ——, greeting: We command you that you have the body of C. D., detained [SEAL.] in your custody, by virtue of an execution against his body [*or*, under a commitment for a contempt], under safe and secure conduct, together with the day and cause of his being taken and detained, by whatsoever name he may be called in the same, before the special term of the Supreme Court, at the village of ——, forthwith, to answer A. B. in a proceeding as for a contempt; and further to do and receive all and singular those things which our said court shall then and there consider of him in this behalf; and have you then there this writ. And further, that you detain the said C. D., at the place last aforesaid, until some order is made by our said court for his disposition.

Witness A. B. J., one of the justices of our said court, at ——, the —— day of ——, one thousand eight hundred and ——.

L. P. C., Attorney. N. B. M., Clerk.

[*Indorsed:*] "By the Court."

N. B. M., Clerk.

No. 110.

AFFIDAVITS TO OBTAIN ATTACHMENT OTHER THAN AGAINST SHERIFF, OR FOR NON-PAYMENT OF MONEY.

See ante, Vol. I., pp. 192, 194.

[*Title as in No.* 102.] County of ——, ss. M. T. G., of, *&c.*, being duly sworn, says: That on the —— day of ——, 18—, he served upon C. D., above named, a copy of the original injunction order hereto annexed, by delivering the same to, and leaving the same with, the said C. D., at his residence in the village of ——, in said county; and that at the time of such service he showed the said C. D. the said original order annexed. [*Or*, That on the —— day of ——, 18—, he served upon C. D. above named, a copy of the injunction order hereto annexed, duly certified by the county clerk of said county, by delivering the same to, and leaving the same with, the said C. D., at his residence in the village of ——, in said county].

Sworn, *&c.* M. T. G.

[*Title as in No.* 102.] County of ——, ss. A. B., of ——, in said county, being duly sworn, says: He is the plaintiff in the above-entitled action; that, as he is informed and believes, the injunction order hereto annexed was duly served upon the defendant, on the —— day of ——, 18—; that since that time the defendant has repeatedly violated said order; that he has cut and carried away from the premises described therein, within the last ten days, large quantities of timber, in direct violation of the same; that deponent is the owner of said premises, &c., &c. [*setting forth the facts showing the interest of the plaintiff and the misconduct alleged*].

Sworn, &c. A. B.

[*Title as in No.* 102.] County of ——, ss. J. K., of ——, in said county, being duly sworn, says: He is acquainted with the parties to the above action, and resides within half a mile of the premises described in the injunction order hereto annexed; which premises are owned by the plaintiff, but are now occupied by said defendant; that deponent has seen said defendant, several times within ten days last past, engaged in cutting and removing the timber growing upon the said premises; that the said defendant has cut and carried away twenty or more loads of wood and other timber from said premises, within the time aforesaid, &c., &c. [*setting forth the facts and circumstances showing a breach of the injunction, or other contempt complained of*].

Sworn, &c. J. K.

No. 111.

ORDER TO SHOW CAUSE WHY DEFENDANT SHOULD NOT BE PUNISHED FOR CONTEMPT.

See ante, Vol. I., p. 192.

At, &c. [*as in No.* 6].

[*Title as in No.* 102.] On reading the affidavit of A. B., plaintiff above named, and others, annexed hereto, showing the violation, by the defendant, of the order of injunction issued in the above action, on the —— day of ——, 18— [*or other contempt*], and on motion of L. P. C., attorney for the plaintiff, it is ordered, that the defendant, C. D., show cause at the special term of this court now sitting at the Court House in the village of —— [*or*, at the next special term of this court to be held at the Court House in ——], on the —— day of —— instant, why he should not be punished for cutting and carrying away timber from the premises described in said order of injunction, in violation thereof [*or as the case may be*].

And it is further ordered, that copies of the affidavits and other papers on which this order is made, together with a copy of this order, be served upon the defendant personally, at least —— days previous to the said —— day of ——, 18—.

No. 112.

NOTICE OF MOTION FOR AN ATTACHMENT.

See ante, Vol. I., p. 190.

[*Title as in No.* 102.]

Sir:—Take notice that I shall apply to the next special term of this court, to be held at the Court House in ——, in the county of ——, on the —— day of —— next, at the opening of the court, on that day, or as soon thereafter as counsel can be heard, for an order that an attachment, as for a contempt, be issued against the defendant C. D., for the violation of the order of injunction issued in this action; and for such other or further order or relief as the court may think proper to grant; which motion will be founded upon the affidavits, with copies whereof you are herewith served.

Dated, *&c.* Yours, &c.,

L. P. C., Attorney for Plaintiff.

To H. G., Esq., Attorney for Defendant.

No. 113.

ORDER FOR AN ATTACHMENT.

See ante, Vol. I., pp. 188, 192.

[*Title as in No.* 102.] At, *&c.* [*as in No.* 6.]

On reading and filing the affidavits of A. B., plaintiff above named, and others, showing the violation, by the defendant, of the order of injunction issued in the above action on the —— day of ——, 18—, and on motion of L. P. C., attorney for the plaintiff [after hearing H. G., for the defendant]; It is ordered, that an attachment as for a contempt be issued against the defendant, C. D., returnable at the next special term of this court, to be held at the Court House in ——, on the —— day of ——, 18—. [And it is further ordered, that the said C. D. be held to bail on said attachment in the sum of —— dollars.]

No. 114.

WRIT OF ATTACHMENT; INDORSEMENT AND OFFICER'S RETURN.

See ante, Vol. I., pp. 188, 196.

[SEAL.] The People of the State of New York, to the Sheriff of the County of ——, greeting:

We command you that you attach C. D., so as to have his body before our Supreme Court at the next special term thereof, to be held at the Court House in ——, on the —— day of ——, 18—, there to answer unto us, as well touching the contempt which he, as is alleged, hath committed against us, as also such other matters as shall then and there be laid to his charge, and further to perform and abide such order as our said court shall make in this behalf. And have you then there this writ; and make and return a certificate under your hand of the manner in which you shall have executed the same.

Witness, A. B. J., one of the justices of our said court, at ——, the —— day of ——, 18—,

L. P. C., Attorney. N. B. M., Clerk.

HOW INDORSED.

[*If the attachment is issued by the special order of the court, it is to be indorsed as follows:* "Issued by the special order of the court." N. B. M., Clerk; *or*, "Issued by the special order of the court. Hold the defendant to bail in the sum of —— dollars." N. B. M., Clerk.]

[*If issued of course, without the special order of the court, it may be indorsed thus:* "Let the defendant give security for his appearance by bond, in the penalty of —— dollars." Dated, &c., A. B. J., Justice of Sup. Court.]

SHERIFF'S RETURN TO ATTACHMENT.

If the attachment is served, and bail is given by the defendant, the return is: "I have attached and let the defendant at large on bail; and the bond taken by me is herewith returned. J. R. G., Sheriff.]

[*If the defendant cannot be found, the return is:* "Not found."]

[*If, upon the defendant's arrest, bail is not given, the return is:* "By virtue of the within attachment, I have arrested the defendant, C. D., and for want of bail, have him now here in custody before the court."]

[*If the attachment is placed in the hands of the sheriff at too late a time to enable him to execute it before the return day, the return is:* "The within attachment was not received by me in time to arrest the defendant thereon, and bring him before the court on the return day thereof."]

[*If the defendant is already in custody, the return is:* I have arrested the defendant on the within writ; but he is now, and was, before such arrest, in my custody by virtue of an execution against his body [*or otherwise, as the case may be*], issued out of the Supreme Court, at the suit of S. T."]

No. 115.

BOND ON ATTACHMENT.

See ante, Vol. I., p. 195.

Know all men by these presents, that we, C. D., of the town of ——, and W. M. and J. F., of the same place, farmers, are held and firmly bound unto J. R.

G., sheriff of the county of ——, and his assigns, in the penal sum of —— dollars, to be paid to the said J. R. G., sheriff as aforesaid, and his assigns. For which payment well and truly to be made, we bind ourselves jointly and severally, and our and each of our heirs, executors, and administrators, firmly by these presents. Sealed with our seals, and dated the —— day of ——, 18—.

Whereas the above-named C. D. has been arrested upon an attachment issued out of the Supreme Court of the State of New York [*or other court, according to the fact*], in a proceeding as for a contempt, for disobedience to an order of injunction, issued in a certain action pending in said court, wherein A. B. is plaintiff, and the said C. D. is defendant, and is now in the custody of the said J. R. G., as sheriff, as aforesaid.

Now, therefore, the condition of this obligation is such, that if the above bounden C. D. will appear on the return of said attachment at the next special term of this court, to be held at the Court House in ——, on the —— day —— next, and answer to the said alleged contempt, and abide the order and judgment of the court thereupon, then this obligation to be void, otherwise to remain in full force and virtue

C. D. [L. S.]
Sealed and delivered in presence of } W. M. [L. S.]
J. F. [L. S.]
R. S.

No. 116.

ORDER FOR ALIAS ATTACHMENT WHERE DEFENDANT FAILS TO APPEAR.

See ante, Vol. I., p. 197.

At, *&c.* [*as in No.* 6].

[*Title, as in No.* 102.] The sheriff of the county of ——, having returned the writ of attachment heretofore issued in this action, against the above-named defendant, C. D., by which return it appears that the defendant was arrested, and afterward set at liberty on bail, and that the bond given by the said defendant has been duly returned by the said sheriff; and the said defendant being now called, in open court, and failing to appear, it is, on motion of L. P. C., attorney for the plaintiff, ordered (*) that an alias attachment issue against the said C. D., directed to the said sheriff, returnable before the next special term of this court, to be held at the Court House, in ——, on the —— day of —— next. [And it is further ordered, that the said C. D. be held to bail on the said alias attachment in the sum of —— dollars.]

No. 117.

ORDER FOR ARREST IN PROCEEDINGS SUPPLEMENTARY TO EXECUTION—ON ORDER TO EXAMINE THIRD PARTY.

See ante, Vol. I, p. 206.

IN COMMON PLEAS; City and County of New York.

[*Title of the cause.*]

To the Sheriff of the City and County of New York:

It appearing to me that the plaintiff duly recovered a judgment against the defendant, in the Marine Court of the city of New York, on the —— day of ——, 18—, for the sum of —— dollars; and that a transcript thereof was duly filed on that day, in the clerk's office of said city and county; and that an execution on said judgment against the property of the defendant was duly issued to the sheriff of said city and county, where said defendant resided; and that such execution has been returned unsatisfied; and that subsequent to such return, to wit: on the —— day of ——, 18—, an order was made by Hon. C. P. D., one of the judges of the Court of Common Pleas, for the city of New York, upon sufficient affidavit, requiring E. L. to appear before T. C., Esquire, Referee, at his office No. —— Broadway, New York, on the —— day of ——, 18—, to answer and be examined concerning the property of the defendant, in the possession of the said E. L., and that a copy of said order, and affidavit was duly served upon the said party on the —— day of ——, 18—, and that the said party did not attend before said referee, at the time and place designated in said order, although the said plaintiff attended there in person, and by his counsel; and it also appearing to me, that an order was made by me, on the —— day of ——, 18—, upon proof of the aforesaid facts, requiring the said party to show cause before me at Chambers, at the City Hall, New York, on the —— day of ——, 18—, at 10 o'clock A. M., why an attachment should not be issued against him (the said E. L.) for his alleged contempt, in neglecting to appear before said Referee, as aforesaid; and that said last-mentioned order, with copies of the affidavits and papers upon which it was founded, was personally served upon the said party in the city of New York, on the —— day of ——, 18—, and the said E. L., now, at the time designated for his appearance, to wit: the —— day of ——, 18—, at 10 o'clock A. M., being called in open court, before me, and failing to appear, as required by said last-mentioned order:

Now, therefore, you are hereby required to arrest the said E. L., and to bring his body before me, at the Chambers of the said Court of Common Pleas, at the City Hall, in said city, on or before the —— day of ——, 18—, at ten o'clock A. M., then and there to answer touching the alleged contempt aforesaid, and further to perform and abide such order as shall then be made in this behalf.

And have you then and there this writ, and make and return a certificate, under your hand, of the manner in which you shall have executed the same.

Dated, *&c.* C. P. D., Judge, *&c.*

No. 118.

ORDER DIRECTING PROSECUTION OF BOND.

See ante, Vol. I., p. 197.

[*Same as in No.* 116, *to the asterisk* (*), *and then continue:*] that the bond so given by said defendant be prosecuted; and that the said plaintiff, A. B., be, and he hereby is, authorized to prosecute the same [*or*, and that the same be prosecuted by the district attorney for said county, in the name of such sheriff.]

No. 119.

ORDER ON APPEARANCE OF DEFENDANT, AND DIRECTING INTERROGATORIES TO BE FILED.

See ante, Vol. I., p. 198.

[*Title as in No.* 102] (*a*). At, *&c.*, [*as in No.* 6].

The defendant, C. D., being charged with a contempt of court, in violating an order of injunction, issued in this action, on the —— day of ——, 18—, and a writ of attachment having issued against him for such contempt, directed to the sheriff of the county of ——, returnable on the —— day of —— instant; whereupon the said sheriff has returned that he had attached the said defendant, and had let him at large on bail [*or*, that he had attached the said defendant, and had him in custody before the court], and the said defendant now being, by virtue of such attachment, personally before the court, and denying that he is guilty of the misconduct charged, as aforesaid, against him; it is, on motion of L. P. C., attorney for the plaintiff, ordered that the said plaintiff do forthwith [*or*, within —— days], file, in the office of the clerk of this court, interrogatories, specifying the facts and circumstances alleged against the said defendant; and that he serve a copy thereof upon the said defendant [*or*, the attorney of the said defendant], and that the said defendant put in written answers to such interrogatories, upon oath, and file the same with said clerk, within twenty-four hours after the time when such interrogatories are served on him.

And it is further ordered, that it be referred to J. I. L., Esq., counselor-at-law, residing in the county of ——, to examine the said defendant, on oath, upon the said interrogatories; and to take such further proofs as either party may produce before him, in relation to the misconduct alleged, and that he report such answers and proofs to this court.

And it is further ordered, that the said defendant attend before the said referee, in the custody of said sheriff; and that the said sheriff detain the said defendant in his custody until the further order of the court.

(*a*) If the attachment is issued against a person not a party to the original suit, the order and subsequent proceedings should be entitled thus: "The People of the State of New York, *ex rel.* A. B., *against* G. D." See ante, vol. I., p. 195.

No. 120.

INTERROGATORIES TO BE ADMINISTERED TO DEFENDANT.

See ante, Vol. I., p. 198.

[*Title as in No.* 102.]

Interrogatories to be administered to C. D. above named, touching a contempt alleged against him, for the violation of the order of injunction issued in this action; which interrogatories are hereby exhibited pursuant to an order of this court, dated the —— day of ——, 18—.

First Interrogatory. Were you, or were you not, on or about the —— day of —— last, or at any other and what time, served with a copy of an order of injunction, issued in this cause on the —— day of —— last? Was, or was not, such order served upon you by showing you the original order of injunction, signed by the judge granting the same, and leaving with you a copy thereof? [*or*, by delivering to, and leaving with you, a copy of said order, certified by the county clerk of the county of ——?] When, and by whom was this service made? Answer this interrogatory fully and particularly.

Second Interrogatory. [*Proceed in the form above, with such questions as will show, or tend to show, the defendant guilty of the misconduct charged.*]

No. 121.

INTERROGATORIES TO BE ADMINISTERED TO SHERIFF.

See ante, Vol. I, p. 198.

IN SUPREME COURT.

The People of the State of New York, *ex rel.* A. B.,
against
G. D., Sheriff of the County of ——.

Interrogatories to be administered to G. D., Esq., sheriff of the county of ——, touching a contempt alleged against him, in not returning an execution issued out of this court, in favor of A. B., plaintiff, against C. D., defendant.

First Interrogatory. Did you or not, at any and what time, receive a certain execution, to you directed as the sheriff of the county of ——, between A. B., plaintiff, and C. D., defendant, dated the —— day of ——, 18—, in which you were directed to levy, of the defendant's goods and chattels, the sum of —— dollars, with interest thereon from the —— day of ——, 18—, besides your fees? Declare fully and particularly.

Second Interrogatory. Did you or not execute the said execution? If yea, in what manner, and at what time in particular? If nay, why did you not execute the same? Declare fully.

Third Interrogatory. Did you or not receive from L. P. C., plaintiff's attorney, in the said action of A. B. against C. D., a notice in writing, requiring you to return the said execution within ten days, or show cause why an attachment should not be issued against you? If yea, what was the purport of that notice, and when did you receive it? Answer fully.

Fourth Interrogatory. Have you or not returned the said execution? If yea, when, where, and how in particular? If nay, why have you not returned the same? Declare fully and particularly.

Dated, *&c.* L. P. C., Attorney for Plaintiff.

No. 122.

ANSWER TO INTERROGATORIES.

See ante, Vol. I., pp. 198, 200.

[*Title, as in the Interrogatories.*]

The answer and examination of C. D. [*or*, G. D., sheriff of the county of ——] above named, to the interrogatories exhibited by the plaintiff for his examination, pursuant to an order of this court, dated the —— day of ——, 18—.

First. To the first interrogatory, this examinant answers and says that, *&c.* [*insert the defendant's answer to the questions put to him*].

C. D. [*or*, G. D.]

Sworn and subscribed before me,
this —— day of ——, 18—,

J. I. L., Referee.

No. 123.

ORDER DISCHARGING ATTACHMENT.

See ante, Vol. I., pp. 198 to 202.

[*Title as in No.* 119, *and note.*] At, *&c.* [*as in No.* 6].

On reading and filing the answer of C. D. [*or*, G. D., sheriff of the county of ——] to the interrogatories filed against him in this cause, and on motion of H. G., of counsel for the said C. D. [*or*, said sheriff], it is ordered that the attachment issued in this cause be and the same is hereby discharged.

No. 124.

ORDER CONVICTING DEFENDANT OF CONTEMPT, FOR VIOLATION OF INJUNCTION.

See ante, Vol. I., pp. 202 to 205.

[*Title as in No.* 119, *and note.*] At, *&c.* [*as in No.* 6].

A writ of attachment having heretofore issued out of this court against the defendant C. D., for his contempt in violating the order of injunction issued in this action, on the —— day of ——, 18—; which attachment was directed to the sheriff of the county of ——, and returnable on the —— day of —— instant; and the said sheriff having returned that he had attached the said C. D., and had let him at large on bail [*or*, that he had attached the said defendant, and had him in custody before the court], and the said C. D. having appeared personally before the court; and interrogatories, specifying the facts and circumstances alleged against the said C. D., having, by order of the court, been filed, and a copy thereof having been served on said defendant [*or*, on said defendant's attorney]; and it having been referred to J. I. L., Esq., to examine the said C. D. on oath upon such interrogatories, and take such further proofs as either party might produce before him in relation to said alleged contempt; and the said referee having made his report, and it appearing to the court from such report and the answers and proofs thereto, and the original affidavits on which said attachment issued, that the said C. D. is guilty of the contempt charged against him, and that such misconduct was calculated to, or did actually, defeat, impair, impede, or prejudice the rights of the plaintiff above named;

Now, on motion of L. P. C., attorney for the plaintiff, it is ordered, that a fine of —— dollars be, and the same is hereby, imposed upon the said C. D. for his misconduct. And it is further ordered, that the said C. D. pay to the plaintiff the costs and expenses of these proceedings, amounting to the sum of —— dollars.

It is also further ordered, that the said C. D. be, and he is hereby, directed to stand committed to the common jail of the county of ——, there to remain charged upon said contempt, until the fine imposed as aforesaid, together with the said costs and expenses, shall be fully paid, unless he shall be sooner discharged by the court; and that a warrant issue to carry this order into effect.

No. 125.

ORDER CONVICTING DEFENDANT OF CONTEMPT, FOR VIOLATION OF INJUNCTION—ANOTHER FORM.

See ante, Vol. I., pp. 202 to 205; and 1 Duer, 571, note.

[*Title, see ante, note to No.* 119.] At, *&c.* [*as in No.* 6].

A writ of attachment having heretofore issued out of and under the seal of this court, directed to the sheriff of the city and county of New York, against the above-named O. W. S., for contempt in disobeying an injunction granted in the action, pending in this court, of T. E. D. and C. P., as plaintiffs, against the Mayor, Aldermen, and Commonalty of the city of New York, as defendants; and the said S. having been, by virtue of said attachment, attached by said sheriff, and having personally appeared in court, and interrogatories, specifying the facts and circumstances alleged against said S., having, by order of this court, been filed, and a copy thereof served on said S.; and he having been required to answer, and having answered the same; and several affidavits and papers touching the said contempt having been produced and read; and counsel, as well for the said relators as the said O. W. S., having been heard, and mature deliberation being thereupon had;

It is now here considered and adjudged, that the said O. W. S. has been, and is, guilty of the misconduct alleged against him in the proceedings, and that such misconduct was calculated to, and actually did, defeat, impair, impede, and prejudice the rights and remedies of the said plaintiffs, T. E. D. and C. P., in their said action against the Mayor, Aldermen, and Commonalty of the city of New York, and that the said D. and P. have, by reason of the said misconduct, been put to a large amount of costs and expenses, to wit, the sum of —— dollars.

And it is further considered and adjudged, that the said O. W. S., for his said misconduct, be imprisoned in the common jail of the city and county of New York, for the period of —— days; and further that a fine of —— dollars and —— cents be, and the same is hereby, imposed upon the said O. W. S., for his said misconduct, and that he stand committed to the common jail of the city and county of New York until the said fine be paid.

And it is further considered and adjudged, that the sum of —— dollars and —— cents part, of the said fine, be paid over to the said D. and P., or their attorneys, to satisfy their said costs and expenses in the premises; and that the residue of the said fine be paid to the clerk of this court, to be disposed of according to law, and that a warrant issue to carry this judgment into effect.

No. 126.

ORDER OF COMMITMENT FOR REFUSAL TO TESTIFY, ETC.

See ante, Vol. I., p. 206; 7 Abb. 98.

The People of the State of New York, to the Sheriff of the City and County of New York, greeting:

Whereas, in a certain action pending in the Court of Common Pleas for the city and county of New York, between J. H. M., plaintiff, and J. M., defendant, for the recovery of a certain lot of land in the said city of New York, one J. F. B. had been examined upon the trial thereof, as a witness for the defendant, and, upon such examination, had sworn that he claimed the title to the said land, that the said defendant was his tenant, and that he, the said J. F. B., was defending the said action as the landlord of the said defendant; and being asked whether he had in his possession any old deeds, leases, or assignments relating to the said land, and having answered that he had received from his grantors a certain lease, and other papers, which he had kept in his possession until a few days before the said trial, when he had delivered them to J. W. M., his attorney, and the attorney of the said defendant in the said action; and being asked to produce the said old lease and other papers, answered that he was unable to do so, because they were in the possession of the said J. W. M., who was then in court, acting as the attorney and counsel of the defendant in the said trial. And, whereas, the said J. W. M., who is a counselor of the Supreme Court of the State of New York, and of the Court of Common Pleas of the city and and county of New York, and counsel for the defendant in the said action, pending in the said Court of Common Pleas, between J. H. M., plaintiff, and J. M., defendant, being then placed under examination, as a witness for the plaintiff in the said action, upon the trial thereof before the said Court of Common Pleas, at a special term thereof, held at the City Hall of New York, on the —— day of ——, 18—, was asked a question material and pertinent to the issue, that is to say, whether he had in his possession any deed, lease, or other papers, delivered to him by one J. F. B. And, whereas, the said J. W. M. said he could not state whether there was any such deed, lease, or other papers, without looking at a bundle of papers then being in court, and in his possession, and thereto brought by him. And, whereas, the said J. W. M. was thereupon, during the sitting, and in the presence of the court, and by the direction of the said court, directed to look at said bundle of papers, for the purpose of answering the said question, which he refused to do; and, whereas, after having so declined to make such examination, and pending the consideration by the court of a motion for his commitment, then to the said court made, upon the ground of such refusal, he, the said J. W. M., gave the said lease and other papers to his client, with instructions to take them from the said court to the office of his counsel; and, whereas, the examination of the said J. W. M. being, by regular adjournment of the said trial, continued on the —— day of ——, aforesaid, he was then examined, and admitted that he had in his possession the paper thus received from the said J. F. B., and he was then asked whether he would state what said papers were, and he answered that he could not without examining them; and he was then asked whether he would look at the papers, and state what they were, so far as to identify them, and he answered that he would not; and he was then asked to look at the papers, and state what they were, and he refused to do so, though thereto required by the court; and he was further asked to produce the said papers, and, though required by the court to do so, refused, and gave as his reasons for refusing, that to answer would be a breach of his privilege as attorney for the defendant; and, whereas, all the said questions were material and pertinent to the issue in the said action; and, whereas, it appears that the said J. W. M., before his said examination, was duly served with a subpœna *duces tecum*, requiring him to appear on the days and at the times and places aforesaid, and produce the said papers, and has been paid his fees thereon; and, whereas, the said J. W. M. has thus been guilty of contemptuous behavior in the immediate view and presence of the said Court of Common Pleas, during its sitting, tending directly to interrupt its proceedings, and impair the respect due to its authority; and, whereas, the aforesaid misconduct of the said J. W. M. was calculated to impair or defeat the rights of the plaintiff in the said action; and, whereas, the said J. W. M., for the cause aforesaid, was adjudged to be guilty of contempt of the said court: Now, therefore, you are hereby ordered to take the body of the said J. W. M., and commit him to the common jail of the city and county of New York, and there keep him in prison for the space of ten days, or until he be sooner discharged, according to law.

Witness, J. R. B., judge of the said Court of Common Pleas, at the City Hall, in the city of New York, the —— day of ——, 18—.

N. J., Clerk.

[*Indorsed:*] "Allowed in open court."

N. J., Clerk.

No. 127.

COMMITMENT BY WARRANT.

See ante, Vol. I., p. 206.

The People of the State of New York, to the Sheriff of the County of——, greeting

[SEAL.] Whereas, on the —— day of ——, 18—, by an order made by the Supreme Court [*or other court*], at a special term thereof, held at the Court House in —— on the —— day of ——, 18—, in an action depending therein, wherein A. B. was plaintiff, and C. D. was defendant, it was ordered, that the said C. D. be committed to the common jail of said county, there to remain charged with the contempt mentioned in said order, until he should have paid the fine therein imposed upon him for his misconduct, amounting to —— dollars, together with the costs and expenses of the proceedings for such misconduct, amounting to the sum of —— dollars; and that a warrant issue to carry the said order into effect.

Now, therefore, we command you, that you take the body of the said C. D., and him safely and closely keep in your custody, in the common jail of the county of ——, until he shall have fully paid the fine imposed, as aforesaid, to wit, the sum of —— dollars, and also the costs and expenses aforesaid, amounting to —— dollars, with your fees hereon, or until the said C. D. shall be discharged by the further order of the court. And you are to return this writ, and to make and return to our said court a certificate, under your hand, of the manner in which you shall have executed the same.

Witness, A. B. J., one of the justices of our said court, at ——, the —— day of ——, 18—.

N. B. M., Clerk.

L. P. C., Attorney.

[*Indorsed:*] "By the Court."

N. B. M., Clerk.

CHAPTER VIII.

FORMS IN PROCEEDINGS BY AND AGAINST CORPORATIONS.

No. 128.

PETITION BY JUDGMENT CREDITOR, FOR SEQUESTRATION OF PROPERTY.

See ante, Vol. I., p. 219; 2 Van Sant. Eq. Pr. 721.

[*Title of the cause.*]

To the Supreme Court of the State of New York:

The petition of A. B., of, &c., respectfully shows: That heretofore, to wit, on the —— day of ——, 18—, your petitioner obtained a judgment in the Supreme Court of the State of New York against the —— railroad company (which at the time aforesaid was, and still is, a corporation, duly incorporated under the laws of this State), for the sum of —— dollars damages, and ——dollars costs, which judgment was duly entered and docketed in the office of the clerk of the county of —— on the —— day of ——, 18—.

That on the —— day of ——, 18—, the plaintiff caused to be issued and delivered to the sheriff of the county of ——, in which county was the principal place of business of the said —— railroad company, defendant, an execution in the usual form, directed to the sheriff of said county, by which the said sheriff was commanded to satisfy the said judgment out of the personal property of said —— railroad company, and if sufficient personal property could not be found, then out of the real property of said —— company, belonging to it, on the day when the judgment was so docketed in said last mentioned county, or at any time thereafter. And said execution was, before the delivery thereof, duly indorsed, with a direction to said sheriff to levy for —— dollars damages and costs, with interest thereon from the —— day of ——, 18—, besides sheriff's fees.

That the said sheriff has duly made return of said execution to the office of the clerk of the county of ——, that said defendant, had no goods or chattels, lands, tenements, or real estate within his county, whereon to levy and satisfy the said execution, or any part thereof.

That no part of said judgment has been paid, and that the whole amount is due, with interest from the —— day of ——, 18—, [*or state how much is due*].

Wherefore your petitioner prays, on behalf of himself, and all others similarly situated, who may come in and contribute to the expenses of this proceeding, that the stock, property, things in action, and effects of the said corporation may be sequestrated; that a receiver thereof may be appointed, with the usual powers and duties, and with the usual directions to take into possession and sequestrate such property, things in action, and effects, and convert the same into money, and pay therefrom to your petitioner the amount of his said judgment and interest, with the costs of these proceedings, or for such further or other relief as the court shall think proper to grant.

Dated, *&c.* A. B.

County of ——, ss.: A. B., the petitioner above named, being duly sworn, deposes and says: That he has read [*or*, heard read] the above petition subscribed by him, and knows the contents thereof, and that the same is true to his own knowledge, except as to the matters which are therein stated on information and belief, and that as to those matters he believes it to be true.

Sworn, *&c.* A. B.

No. 129.

NOTICE OF PRESENTATION OF PETITION.

See ante, Vol. I., p. 220; 2 Van Sant. Eq. Pr. 722.

[*Title of the cause.*]

To G. C., Esq., President, *&c.*

Take notice that upon the petition, with a copy of which you are herewith served, a motion will be made at the next special term of the Supreme Court, appointed to be held at the City Hall, in the City of Albany, on the —— day of ——, 18—, on the opening of the court on that day, or as soon thereafter as counsel can be heard, for an order that the prayer of the said petition be granted; that is to say, that the stock, property, *&c.* [*as the prayer of the petition*]. Yours, &c.,

Dated, *&c.* M. C. N., Attorney for Plaintiff.

No. 130.

ORDER SEQUESTRATING PROPERTY OF CORPORATION, ETC.

See ante, Vol. I., p. 220.

[*Title of the cause.*] At a special term, *&c.* [*as in No.* 6].

On reading and filing the petition of A. B., of, *&c.*, a creditor by judgment of the —— railroad company, praying, *&c.* [*state substance of prayer*], and after hearing counsel for the respective parties [*or*, on proof of due service of a copy of said petition, and notice of motion on the defendant, and on motion of J. L. F., of counsel for the petitioner, no one appearing in opposition thereto], it is ordered (*) that the stock, property, things in action, and effects of the said —— company be, and the same are hereby, sequestrated.

And it is further ordered that G. H., Esq., of, *&c.*, be, and he is hereby, appointed receiver of the said stock, property, things in action, and effects of said company, with the usual powers and duties, according to the practice of the court, upon his executing and acknowledging, in the usual form, and filing with the clerk of this court, a bond to the people of this State in the penal sum of —— dollars, with two sufficient sureties, freeholders, or householders of said county of —— (who shall severally justify that they are each worth double the amount of such penalty), conditioned for the faithful discharge of the duties of receiver, and for the due accounting for all moneys received by him as such receiver; which bond is to be approved, as to its form and manner of execution, by a justice of this court, and filed in the office of the clerk of said county of ——; and that upon filing said bond, so approved, said receiver do forthwith proceed to take possession of and sequestrate the said stock, property, things in action, and effects of said corporation, and convert the same into money with all convenient speed.

And that the said receiver do also forthwith proceed and recover, by process of law or otherwise, pursuant to the statute in such case provided, any sum which may remain due upon any share of stock subscribed in said corporation, if the person so indebted be not wholly insolvent. [*A clause may be inserted, if necessary, that he also proceed against directors or others who have improperly disposed of or misapplied the property of the corporation.*]

It is further ordered that the said receiver, in the discharge of the duties of his trust, be vested with all the rights and powers, and be subject to all the duties and liabilities declared by statute in such cases, and proceed in all respects pursuant to article three, title four, chapter eight, part third, of the Revised Statutes (except as herein otherwise provided).

It is further ordered, that, before any distribution of any portion of said funds or assets shall be made, and within —— months from the date of this order, the said receiver report to this court his proceedings under this order, with an exhibit of the accounts and demands for and against said —— company, and all its open and subsisting contracts, and a statement of the amount of money and assets in the hands of said receiver, together with a statement of his expenses and commissions; to the end that such order may be made in regard thereto as the nature of the case may require. And it is further ordered that, until the coming in of said report, and the hearing thereon, the question as to the distribution of said assets and moneys, and of the rights and interests of the respective parties claiming the same, or any portion thereof, and other questions not herein disposed of, including the question of costs, be reserved for further directions.

No. 131.

THE LIKE ORDER, AND DIRECTING REFERENCE AS TO ISSUES, ETC.

See ante, Vol. I., p. 220; 2 Van Sant. Eq. Pr. 723.

[*Same as in the last form to the* (*) *then add:*] that it be referred to R. C. M., Esq., of, &c., to inquire into the truth of the matters set forth in said petition, and report thereon the facts, with his conclusions of law and opinion thereon. It is further ordered that said referee, in case he finds the matters set forth in said petition to be true, report to the court the name of a suitable and proper person to be appointed receiver of the stock, property, things in action, and effects of said —— company, together with the amount of the security to be given by him, and as to the sufficiency of the persons who may be proposed as sureties for such receiver.

And it is further ordered, that in the mean time and until the further order of the court, the said —— company, its officers, directors, attorneys, and agents, be, and they hereby are, restrained and enjoined from selling, assigning, or transferring, receiving, collecting, discharging, or incumbering, or in any manner disposing of or interfering with any portion of the property, real or personal, of the said —— railroad company, or of the debts, accounts, and demands, contracts, bills, bonds, notes, or evidences relating thereto, things in action, or other equitable property or interests and effects of any kind whatever, of said —— railroad company, or in which it has an interest, and from doing or suffering to be done any act or thing to enable any person to obtain any portion of said property; and that all further questions be reserved until the coming in of the report of said referee and the further order of the court.

No. 132.

BOND OF RECEIVER.

See ante, Vol. I., p. 222; 2 Van Sant. Eq. Pr. 556.

Know all men by these presents, that we, G. H., C. D., and E. F., of, *&c.*, are held and firmly bound unto the people of the State of New York, in the sum of —— dollars, lawful money of the United States of America, to be paid to the said the people of the State of New York. For which payment will and truly to be made, we, and each of us, bind ourselves respectively, and our respective heirs, executors, and administrators, jointly and severally, firmly by these presents. Sealed with our seals, dated the —— day of ——, 18—.

Whereas, by an order of the Supreme Court, bearing date the —— day of ——, 18—, made before, *&c.*, wherein A. B. was plaintiff, and the —— railroad company were defendants, it was ordered that G. H., Esq., of, *&c.*, be, and he was thereby, appointed receiver of the stock, property, things in action, and effects of the said —— company, with the usual powers, &c., upon executing and filing a bond, *&c.* [*recite the substance of the order*].

Now, the condition of this obligation is such, that if the said G. H. shall, as required by the rules and practice of this court, duly file an inventory, and annually, or oftener if required by the court, duly account for what he shall receive, or have in charge as receiver in the said cause; and pay and apply what he shall receive or have in charge, as he may from time to time be directed by said court, and obey such orders as the said court may from time to time make in relation to said trust, and in all respects faithfully discharge the duties of said trust, then the above obligation to be void, otherwise to be and remain in full force and virtue.

Sealed and delivered G. H. [L. S.]
in presence of C. D. [L. S.]
N. Y. E. F. [L. S.]

[*Add acknowledgment and affidavit of sureties, as in No.* 44.]

APPROVAL TO BE INDORSED ON BOND.

I approve the within bond as to its form and manner of execution; and as to the sufficiency of the sureties. [*Signature of justice.*]

No. 134.

PETITION BY DIRECTORS FOR VOLUNTARY DISSOLUTION OF CORPORATION.

See ante, Vol. I., p. 243; 2 Van Sant. Eq. Pr. 725.

To the Supreme Court of the State of New York:

The petition of the undersigned, directors [*or*, a majority of the directors] of the —— company, respectfully shows:

That the said —— company is a corporation, duly incorporated under the provisions of an act entitled, *&c.*, [*stating the statute under which the company is incorporated*].

That your petitioners constitute the president and directors [*or*, a majority of the directors] of the said corporation.

That the said company was incorporated on the —— day of ——, 18—, and from that time to the present has transacted business as such corporation, at its principal place of business in the city of ——.

That within the past year the said company has sustained great losses, by reason of, *&c.* [*state the general character of the same.*] And that by reason of such losses its stock, property, and effects have been so far reduced that it will not be able to pay all just demands to which it is liable; and that it cannot afford a reasonable security to those who may deal with the said company [*or state any reason to show that a dissolution will be beneficial to the interests of the stockholders*].

Your petitioners further show that the schedule hereto annexed, marked "A," exhibits a full, just, and true inventory of all the estate, both real and personal, in law and equity, of said corporation, and of all the books, vouchers, and securities relating thereto.

Your petitioners further show, that the schedule annexed, marked "B," is a full, just, and true account of the capital stock of said corporation, specifying the names of the stockholders, their residences, when known, the number of shares belonging to each, the amount paid in upon such shares respectively, and the amount still due thereon.

That the schedule marked "C," hereunto annexed, exhibits a statement of all incumbrances on the property of said corporation, by judgment, mortgage, pledge, or otherwise.

And that schedule marked "D," hereunto annexed, exhibits a full and true account of all the creditors of said corporation, and of all the engagements entered into by said corporation which are not fully satisfied or canceled, specifying the place of residence of each creditor, and of every person to whom such engagements were made, so far as known; the sum owing to each creditor; the nature of each debt or demand; and the true cause and consideration of such indebtedness in each case.

Your petitioners therefore pray, that the said corporation may, by the order or decree of this court, be dissolved, and that a receiver may be appointed, with the powers and duties of receivers in such cases, and under the usual directions, pursuant in all respects to the statute in such case provided, and the rules and practice of the court.

And your petitioners, will ever pray, &c.

Dated, *&c.*, [*Names of petitioners.*]

County of ——, ss.: A. B., C. D., E. F., *&c.* [*stating the names*], being severally duly sworn, each for himself, deposes and says, that the facts stated in the foregoing petition, by him subscribed, and the schedules, accounts, inventories, and statements thereto annexed, are just and true, so far as he knows, or has the means of knowing.

Sworn, *&c.* [*Names of deponents.*]

[*Annex to the petition the schedules therein referred to.*]

No. 135.

ORDER THEREON.

See ante, Vol. I., p. 243; 2 Van Sant. Eq. Pr. 726.

At a special term, *&c.* [*as in No.* 6].

In the matter of the application of the President and Directors of the ——, for a voluntary dissolution.

On reading and filing the petition of the president and [a majority of the] directors of the —— company, and the schedules thereto annexed, duly verified by the petitioners, and bearing date on, *&c.*; and on motion of C. F. T., of counsel for the petitioners, it is ordered that all persons interested in such corporation, or having claims against the same, show cause, if any they have, why such corporation should not be dissolved, before J. B. G., Esq., who is hereby appointed referee for that purpose, at his office, in the city of ——, on the —— day of ——, 18—, at 10 o'clock in the forenoon. And it is further ordered that said referee hear the proofs and allegations of the parties, and take testimony in relation to the matters set forth in said petition, and report the same to the court with all convenient speed, with a statement of the property, effects, debts, credits, and engagements of such corporation, and of all other matters and things pertaining to the affairs of such corporation.

No. 136.

AFFIDAVIT OF PUBLICATION.

See ante, Vol. I., p. 242; 2 Van Sant. Eq. Pr. 727.

SUPREME COURT:
[*Title as in No.* 135.]

County of ——, ss.: C. F. T., of, *&c.*, being duly sworn, says that the order, of which the annexed is a printed copy, has been duly published three weeks successively, once in each week, in the State paper, commencing on the —— day of ——, and also in the ——, a newspaper published in ——, where the principal place of conducting the business of said corporation is, once a week for three weeks successively, commencing on the —— day of ——, 18—, and terminating the —— day of ——, 18—.

Sworn, *&c.* C. F. T.

No. 137.

REPORT OF REFEREE.

See ante, Vol. I., p. 244; 2 Van Sant. Pr. 727.

[*Title as in No.* 135.]

To the Supreme Court of the State of New York:

I, the subscriber, the referee to whom it was referred, by an order heretofore made in this matter, bearing date, *&c.*, to hear the proofs and allegations of the parties interested, and to take testimony upon the matters set forth in said petition, and report the same to the court with a statement, *&c.* [*as in the order* , respectfully report:

That due proof having been made by affidavit (which is hereto annexed) of the publication of said order as required by statute, I proceeded to a hearing of the matters so referred, being attended by C. F. T., Esq., the counsel for the petitioners, and also by —— and ——, *&c.* [*mentioning the names of the parties who appear*]. That I thereupon heard the proofs and allegations of the said parties, and took testimony in relation to the matters set forth in said petition, and also in regard to such other matters and things pertaining to the affairs of said corporation as were brought before me· which testimony, duly subscribed by the respective witnesses and certified by me, is hereto annexed.

I further report that schedules A, B, and C, annexed to said petition, are in all respects just and true, [*or*, that schedule A is just and true with the exception of several items of personal property contained in the additional schedule hereto annexed, marked F, which I find belongs to said corporation, and is to be added to said schedule, *or state otherwise as the facts may be.*]

I further find that schedule D is to be amended and corrected by adding thereto the several debts of said corporation, proved before me and not entered on said schedule, and which are contained in the additional schedule hereto annexed, marked G, which shows the name of each of said creditors, the sum due him, his place of residence, the nature of the debt, and the true cause and consideration of the indebtedness.

All of which is respectfully submitted.

Dated, *&c.* J. B. G., Referee.

No. 138.

ORDER OR DECREE FOR DISSOLUTION AND APPOINTMENT OF RECEIVER.

See ante, Vol. I., p. 244; 2 Van Sant. Eq. Pr. 728.

At a special term, *&c.* [*as in No.* 6].

[*Title as in No.* 135.]

On reading and filing petition in this matter, duly verified, and the report of J. B. G., Esq., referee, with the testimony and schedules thereto annexed, bearing date on, *&c.*, with due proof that notice of the order herein, requiring all persons interested in said corporation to show cause before said referee why said corporation should not be dissolved, had been duly published for the time and in the manner required by statute, and after hearing counsel for the parties interested herein, and the said testimony so reported being duly considered, on motion of C. F. T., of counsel for the petitioners, it is ordered and decreed that the said corporation be and the same hereby is dissolved, and shall from henceforth cease and determine.

And it is further ordered, (*) that G. H., Esq., of, *&c.*, be, and he hereby is, appointed receiver of all the stock, property, things in action, and effects of said corporation, with the usual powers, *&c.* [*proceed as in No.* 130.]

No. 139.

THE LIKE, REFERRING IT TO A REFEREE TO NOMINATE OR APPOINT A RECEIVER.

See ante, Vol. I., p. 244; 2 Van Sant. Eq. Pr. 728.

[*Same as in the foregoing to the* (*), *then add:*] that it be referred back to the said referee, J. B. G., Esq., to inquire and report to the court the name of a suitable and proper person to be appointed receiver, and the amount of the security to be given by such receiver; and also to inquire into the sufficiency of the sureties proposed for such receiver, and report thereon to the court with all convenient speed.

CHAPTER IX.

FORMS IN DETERMINATIONS OF CLAIMS TO REAL ESTATE.

No. 140.

SUMMONS.

See ante, Vol. I., p. 248.

[*Title of the cause.*]

To the above-named defendant:

You are hereby summoned to answer the complaint of A. B., which is hereto annexed [*or*, which will be filed in the office of the clerk of the county of ——], and to serve a copy of your answer on me, at my office, in ——, in said county, within twenty days after the service of this summons, exclusive of the day of service; and if you fail to answer the said complaint, as hereby required, the plaintiff will apply to the Supreme Court [*or other court*] for the relief demanded in the said complaint.

J. T. L., Att'y for Plaintiff.

No. 141.

COMPLAINT FOR DETERMINATION OF CLAIM TO REAL ESTATE.

See ante, Vol. I, p. 248.

[*Title of the cause as in No.* 165,]

The complaint of the above-named plaintiff respectfully shows to the court:

That on the —— day of ——, 18—, one J. J. was lawfully seized, in fee, of the following described premises [*insert particular description*].

That on the day above named, being then in possession of said land, the aforesaid J. J. did sell, grant, and convey the land aforesaid to the plaintiff in this action, by a deed duly executed under his hand and seal, and delivered the same to the plaintiff, and which deed was duly recorded in the clerk's office of the county of ——, on the —— day of ——, 18—, in liber —— of deeds, page ——.

That the plaintiff is now, and has been in the actual possession of the premises above described for the last three years preceding the commencement of this action.

That the defendant in this action unjustly claims title to the lands aforesaid in fee [*or*, to an estate for life in said premises, *or*, to an estate for —— years, in said premises].

Wherefore, the plaintiff demands judgment, that the defendant, and all persons claiming under him by title accruing subsequently to the commencement of this action, be forever barred from all claim to any estate of inheritance or freehold, [or, for any term of years not less than ten, in the said premises, or, that the plaintiff may have such further or other relief as to the court may seem meet.

J. T. L., Attorney for Plaintiff.

[*Add verification or not, as the plaintiff may desire.*]

CHAPTER X.

FORMS IN FORCIBLE ENTRIES AND DETAINERS.

No. 143.

COMPLAINT AND AFFIDAVIT.

See ante, Vol. I., p. 257.

County of ——, ss.: To A. D. W., Esq., County Judge of the County of —— [*or other officer to whom the application is made*].

The complaint of A. B., of ——, in said county, shows: That C. D., of ——, in said county, at the town [*or*, city] aforesaid, on the —— day of ——, 18—, did unlawfully make a forcible entry [*or*, did make entry in a forcible manner, *according to the fact*], into the lands and premises of this complainant, to wit: the, *&c.* [*describe premises particularly*], and that the said C. D. did then and there violently, forcibly, and unlawfully, and with strong hand, eject and expel this complainant from his said lands and premises [*or*, hold this complainant out of possession of his said lands and premises].

And the said complainant further shows: That he had at the time aforesaid an estate of freehold [*or*, for a term of years in the premises then subsisting; *or some other right to the possession thereof, stating the same*] then and still subsisting, in the lands and premises aforesaid; and that the said C. D. still unlawfully and forcibly holds and detains the said lands and premises from the said A. B., against the form of the statute in such case made and provided. Dated this —— day of ——, 18—.

A. B.

County of ——, ss.: A. B., of ——, in said county, being duly sworn, says: He is the complainant above named; that the foregoing complaint is true to his own knowledge, except as to the matters therein stated or information and belief, and as to those matters, he believes it to be true.

Sworn, *&c.* A. B.

No. 144.

PRECEPT FOR JURY.

See ante, Vol. I., p. 258.

The People of the State of New York, to the Sheriff, or any Constable, of the County of ——, greeting:

You are hereby commanded to cause to come before me, at my office, in ——, in said county, on the —— day of ——, 18—, at 10 o'clock in the forenoon, twenty-four inhabitants of the said county, duly qualified by law to serve as jurors, to inquire upon their oaths for the said people, of a certain forcible entry made by C. D., as it is said, into the lands and premises of A. B., in the —— of ——, in said county [*or*, certain forcible holding out of possession of A. B., by one C. D., of the lands and premises of the said A. B., situated in ——, in said county], against the form of the statute in such case made and provided.

Given under my hand, this —— day of ——, 18—.

A. D. W., County Judge
of —— County.

No. 145.

NOTICE TO THE DEFENDANT.

See ante, Vol. I., p. 258.

To C. D., of ——, in the County of ——.

On the complaint of A. B., of ——, in said county, accompanied by an affidavit, duly verifying the same, made to the undersigned, county judge of said county, that you did, on the —— day of ——, 18—, unlawfully make a forcible entry [*or*, did make entry in a forcible manner] into the lands and premises of the said A. B., situate in —— aforesaid, to wit [*describe premises*]: and that you did violently, forcibly, unlawfully, and with strong hand, eject and expel the said A. B. from his said lands and premises [*or*, hold the said A. B. out of possession of his said lands and premises], and that you do still unlawfully and forcibly hold and detain the said lands and premises from the said A. B.; and that, at the time aforesaid, the said A. B. had an estate of freehold [*or other estate*] in the said lands and premises, then and still subsisting in the same.

You will therefore take notice, that I have this day issued my precept, directed to the sheriff, or any constable, of said county, commanding him to cause to come before me, at my office, in ——, in said county, on the —— day of ——, 18—, at ten o'clock in the forenoon, twenty-four inhabitants of the said county, duly qualified by law to serve as jurors, to inquire, upon their oaths, of the forcible entry [*or* forcible holding out] aforesaid.

A. W. D., County Judge
of —— County.

No. 146

AFFIDAVIT OF SERVICE OF LAST NOTICE.

See ante, Vol. I., p. 258.

County of ——, ss.: H. S., of ——, in said county, being duly sworn, says: That on the —— day of ——, 18—, he served upon C. D., of ——, in said county, a notice, of which the annexed is a copy, by delivering the same to him personally [*or*, by delivering the same to W. D., the wife of the said C. D., on the premises described in said notice; and that such service could not be made upon the said C. D., for the reason that, after diligent inquiry, he could not be found; *or*, by affixing the same on the front door of the house on the premises described in said notice, there being no person of proper age on the premises, and that such service could not be made upon the said C. D. for the reason that after diligent inquiry he could not be found.]

Sworn, *&c.* H. S.

No. 147.

OATH TO JURY OF INQUIRY.

See ante, Vol. I., p. 258.

You, and each of you, do swear that you will well and truly inquire into the forcible entry [*or*, forcible holding out], complained of by A. B. against C. D., and a true inquisition thereof to make.

No. 148.

OATH TO WITNESSES.

See ante, Vol. I., p. 258.

You do swear that the evidence you shall give, touching the forcible entry [*or*, forcible holding out], complained of by A. B. against C. D., and now to be here inquired into, shall be the truth, the whole truth, and nothing but the truth.

No. 149.

INQUISITION.

See ante, Vol. I., p. 259.

An inquisition taken before A. D. W., county judge of the county of ——, at his office in the town [*or*, city] of ——, in the county of ——, on the —— day of ——, 18—, by the oaths of E. F., G. H., *&c.* [*insert the names of the jurors who concur in the inquisition*].

The undersigned, inhabitants of the county of ——, aforesaid, qualified to serve as jurors, having been summoned to inquire of the forcible entry [*or*, forcible holding] hereinafter mentioned, and having appeared at the time and place aforesaid, before the said county judge, who then and there administered to the undersigned an oath well and truly to inquire into the forcible entry [*or*, forcible holding out] complained of by A. B., against C. D., and a true inquisition thereof to make. Whereupon the undersigned jury so sworn, having then and there proceeded to make inquiry into the said forcible entry [*or*, said forcible holding out] complained of, and examined witnesses on oath administered by the said judge before him then and there made, now here make this their inquisition as follows, to wit:

The undersigned jury have found and hereby find and present, that A. B., of ——, aforesaid, long since had an estate of freehold [*or other estate, according to the fact*], in that certain piece or parcel of land situate in the town of ——, aforesaid, and which is bounded and described as follows: [*insert description as in complaint*], and that the said A. B. was long since peaceably and lawfully possessed of the same, and that the estate and possession of the said A. B. so subsisted and continued until C. D., of ——, in said county, on the —— day of ——, at —— aforesaid, (*) did forcibly and unlawfully, and with strong hand, enter into the said land and premises and eject and expel him, the said A. B., therefrom; and the said A. B., so expelled from the said land and premises, from the said —— day of —— until the day of the taking of this inquisition, unlawfully and forcibly, and with strong hand, did keep out, and does yet keep out, to the great disturbance of the people of the State of New York, and contrary to the form of the statute in such case made; and that the estate of the said A. B., as aforesaid, still subsists therein.

And the said jurors, whose names are subscribed hereto, do, on the evidence produced before us, find the inquisition aforesaid true.

[*Signatures of jurors.*]

[*If the inquisition finds the entry in a peaceable manner, and that the possession was held by force, then proceed from the asterisk* (*) *as follows:*]—made entry in a peaceable manner into the said lands and premises, and after such entry did then and there violently, forcibly, and unlawfully, and with strong hand, hold the said A. B. out of possession of his said lands and premises; and the said A. B., from the said —— day of —— until the day of the taking of this inquisition, unlawfully and forcibly did keep out, and does yet keep out, of the possession of the land and premises aforesaid, to the great disturbance of the people of the State of New York, and contrary to the form of the statute in such case made; and that the estate of the said A. B., as aforesaid, still subsists therein.

And the said jurors, whose names are subscribed hereto, do, on the evidence produced before us, find the inquisition aforesaid true.

[*Signatures of jurors.*]

No. 150.

AWARD OF RESTITUTION, AFTER INQUISITION.

See ante, Vol. I., p. 259.

The People *ex rel.* A. B.
vs.
C. D.

The jury, summoned and sworn to inquire into the forcible entry [*or*, forcible detainer] complained of by A. B. against C. D., having made their inquisition, by which the said C. D. is found guilty of the said forcible entry [*or*, forcible detainer], and the defendant, not having traversed the said inquisition within the time allowed by law, I, the undersigned, county judge of the county of ——, before whom the said proceeding is pending, do hereby award restitution to the said A. B., of the premises described in the said inquisition; and do also hereby assess the costs and expenses of the said proceedings at the sum of —— dollars.

Dated, *&c.* A. D. W., County Judge.

No. 151.

WRIT OF RESTITUTION.

See ante, Vol. I., p. 259.

The People of the State of New York, to the Sheriff or any Constable of the County of ——, greeting:

Whereas, A. B., of ——, in said county, did, on the —— day of —— last, make complaint in writing, duly verified, to the undersigned A. D. W., county judge of said county, that C. D., of ——, in said county, on the —— day of ——, at —— aforesaid, did, *&c.* [*recite the complaint and the subsequent proceedings, and then add:*]

This is, therefore, to command you, to go to the premises aforesaid, and to cause the said A. B. to be restored and put into full possession of the said lands and premises according as he was seized or possessed thereof before the said entry.

And you are also further commanded to levy and collect the sum of —— dollars of the goods and chattels of the said C. D. (excepting such goods and chattels as are by law exempt from levy and sale on execution), and to bring the money before me within sixty days from the date hereof, to render to the said A. B.

Given under my hand, the —— day of ——, 18—.

A. D. W., County Judge.

No. 152.

TRAVERSE OF INQUISITION.

See ante, Vol. I., p. 259; Yates' Pl. 500; 1 Humph. Pr. 115.

C. D.
ads.
The People *ex rel.* A. B.

And afterward, to wit: on the —— day of ——, at the town [*or*, city] of —— aforesaid, before the said A. D. W., county judge, as aforesaid, comes the said C. D., in his proper person, and having heard the said inquisition read to him, hereby traversing the same (*), denies that he is guilty of the said supposed forcible entry [*or*, forcible holding out] in manner and form as in the said inquisition alleged, and of this, he, the said C. D., puts himself upon the country, and the said people do the like, *&c.* [*or, from the asterisk* (*) *proceed thus:*] alleges that he, the said C. D., or his ancestors, or those whose estate he has in the lands in said inquisition described, have been in quiet possession thereof for the space of three whole years next before the said inquisition found, and that his, the said C. D.'s, interest therein is not ended or determined, and of this, he, the said C. D., puts himself upon the country, and the said people doth the like, *&c.*] C. D.

No. 153.

PRECEPT FOR JURY TO TRY TRAVERSE.

See ante, Vol. I., p. 260.

The People of the State of New York, to the Sheriff or any Constable of the County of ——, greeting:

You are hereby commanded to summon twelve good and lawful men of the town of ——, in said county, duly qualified to serve as jurors, and not exempt from serving on juries in courts of record, and in no wise akin to A. B., of ——, in said county, or to C. D., of the same place, to come before the undersigned, county judge of said county, at his office in ——, on the —— day of —— inst., to make a jury of the county, upon their oaths to try a certain traverse of an inquisition, found upon the complaint of the said A. B. against the said C. D., and now pending before me, for a certain forcible entry [*or*, forcibly holding out of possession], made by the said C. D. into the lands and premises of said A. B., in ——, aforesaid, against the form of the statute in such case made and provided; and that you make a list of the persons summoned, and certify and annex the same to this precept, and make return hereof to me.

Given under my hand, this —— day of ——, 18—.

A. D. W., County Judge.

No. 154.

SUBPŒNA FOR WITNESSES.

See ante, Vol. I., p. 262.

County of ——, ss.: The People of the State of New York, to F. B., R. S., &c., greeting:

We command you, and each of you, that all business and excuses being laid aside, you and each of you be and appear, in your proper persons, before the undersigned, county judge of said county, at his office in said county, on the —— day of ——, to testify before a petit jury [*or*, a jury of inquiry], touching a certain forcible entry alleged to have been made into certain lands and premises of A. B., by C. D., and wherein it is alleged the said A. B. has a freehold estate, on the part of the said A. B. Hereof fail not at your peril.

Witness my hand this —— day of ——, 18—.

A. D. W., County Judge.

No. 155.

OATH OF JURORS.

See ante, Vol. I., p. 262.

You and each ot you do swear that you will well and truly hear, try, and determine, the traverse of an inquisition found upon the complaint of A. B. against C. D., for a certain forcible entry [*or*, forcible detainer], made by the said C. D. into the lands and premises of the said A. B., and a true verdict give according to the evidence.

No. 156.

OATH TO WITNESSES.

See ante, Vol. I., p. 262.

You do swear that the evidence you shall give touching the forcible entry [*or*, forcible detainer] complained of by A. B. against C. D., on the traverse of the inquisition found upon the said complaint, shall be the truth, the whole truth, and nothing but the truth.

No. 157.

AWARD OF RESTITUTION AFTER VERDICT.

See ante, Vol. I., p. 261.

[*Title as in No.* 150.]

The jury summoned and sworn to hear, try, and determine the forcible entry [*or*, forcible detainer] complained of by A. B. against C. D., having rendered their verdict, by which the said C. D. is found guilty of the said forcible entry [*or*, forcible detainer], I, the undersigned, county judge of the county of ——, before whom the said proceeding is pending, do hereby award restitution to the said A. B. of the premises described in the complaint of the said A. B.; and do also hereby assess the costs and expenses of the said proceedings at the sum of —— dollars. Dated, &c.

A. D. W., County Judge.

No. 158.

WRIT OF RESTITUTION AFTER VERDICT.

See ante, Vol. I., p. 262.

[*Same as in No.* 151, *reciting the complaint and all the subsequent proceedings.*]

No. 159

CERTIORARI TO REMOVE PROCEEDINGS.

See ante, Vol. I., p. 263.

The People of the State of New York, to A. D. W., County Judge of the County of ——, greeting:

Whereas, we have understood, on the complaint of C. D., that lately before you a certain inquisition was found against him, for, *&c.* [*state the finding of the jury*]. And we being willing, for certain reasons, that the said inquisition, and all other proceedings concerning the same before you remaining, should be certified and returned by you into our Supreme Court of judicature, before our justices thereof, do command you that you certify and return the same unto our justices of the Supreme Court of judicature, with all the proceedings thereto appertaining, at the next term of this court, to be held at ——, on the —— day of —— next, so that our said justices may further act thereon, as of right and according to law ought to be done; and have then there this writ.

Witness, C. L. A., Justice of the Supreme Court,
at ——, the —— day of ——, 18—.
N. B. M., Clerk.

L. P. C., Attorney.

[*Indorsed:*] "On the application of L. P. C., attorney for C. D., and upon his affidavit, dated the —— day of ——, 18—, I allow the within writ of certiorari to issue."

C. L. A., Justice of the Supreme Court.

No. 160.

BOND ON ALLOWANCE OF CERTIORARI.

See ante, Vol. I., p. 263.

Know all men by these presents, That, *&c.* [*in the usual form; the obligee is the complainant; there must be two sureties, or, in case the defendant is absent, three sureties; penalty, not less than one hundred dollars.*]

The condition of the above obligation is such, that if C. D. shall appear at the return of a certain writ of certiorari, issued out of the Supreme Court of this State, tested on the —— day of ——, 18—, and returnable on the —— day of ——, and directed to A. D. W., county judge of said county, commanding him to certify the inquisition and all other proceedings concerning a certain forcible entry alleged to have been made into certain lands and premises of A. B., the obligee above named, by the said C. D.; and if the said C. D. shall answer to the inquisition found against him, as aforesaid, and abide such order and judgment as the said Supreme Court shall make in the premises, and pay all costs that shall be awarded against him, then the above obligation to be void, otherwise to remain in full force and virtue.

[*Signatures and seals of obligors.*]

Signed, sealed, and delivered in presence of
F. H.

[*Add acknowledgment, and affidavit of sureties, in the usual form, see ante, No.* 44; *also, approval of sureties, as follows:*]

I approve of the sureties in the above bond, and of the sufficiency thereof.

C. L. A.,
Justice of the Supreme Court.

No. 161.

ANSWER OR RETURN TO CERTIORARI.

See ante, Vol. I., p. 263.

The answer or return of A. D. W., County Judge of the County of ——, to the writ of certiorari hereto annexed.

By virtue of, and in obedience to, the writ of certiorari hereto annexed, and to me directed, I do hereby certify and return to the justices of the Supreme Court, that on the —— day of —— last, the complaint of A. B., of ——, in said county, duly verified, was presented to me; which complaint, with the affidavit verifying the same, is as follows: [*insert the complaint, &c.*]

That I did thereupon, *&c.* [*proceed in the same manner, and make return of all the proceedings down to the time of the service of the writ of certiorari.*]

All of which I do hereby certify and return as within I am commanded.

In testimony whereof I have hereunto set my hand and seal, this —— day of ——, in the year one thousand eight hundred and ——.

A. D. W. [*Seal*].

No. 162.

TRAVERSE IN THE SUPREME COURT.

See ante, Vol. I., p. 264.

[*Same substantially as in No.* 152, *ante.*]

No. 163.

JUDGMENT RECORD ON CERTIORARI.

See ante, Vol. I., p. 264.

[*Same substantially as in No.* 451, *to the asterisk* (*), *and then continue*]: sent to A. D. W., county judge of the county of ——, their writ of certiorari close in these words, to wit:]*insert writ*].

At which day and place in the return of the said writ mentioned, before the justices aforesaid, comes the said C. D., by L. P. C., his attorney, and the said A. D. W., county judge, aforesaid, now here, makes return to the said writ in the words and figures following, that is to say: [*insert copy of return in full*].

And the said C. D., not having traversed the inquisition mentioned in said return, day is given to him for that purpose, to wit, the —— day of ——, 18—, at which last-mentioned day, the said C. D. traverses the said inquisition as follows: [*insert the defendant's traverse*].

It is thereupon ordered by the Supreme Court, that the said traverse be tried at the Circuit Court appointed to be held at the Court House in ——, on the —— day of ——, 18—.

Afterward, to wit, on the day and at the place last aforesaid, before C. L. A., Esq., one of the justices of said court, come as well the above-named C. D., as the above-named A. B.; and the jurors summoned to try the said traverse, being called, also come; who, to speak the truth of the matters above contained, being duly sworn, say, upon their oath, that the said C. D. is guilty [*or*, not guilty] of the forcible entry [*or*, forcible detainer] as by the complaint of the said A. B. is alleged.

Whereupon the said A. B. prays judgment of restitution, with costs, and that a writ or warrant may be issued by the said court, restoring to him the possession of the premises aforesaid.

Judgment signed the —— day of ——, A. D. 18—. N. B. M., Clerk.

It is therefore considered that the said A. B. recover against the said C. D. —— dollars, for his costs and charges by him laid out and expended in and about his defense to the said writ of certiorari, adjudged to him by the court now here, with his assent, and that he have execution therefor. And it is further considered that the said A. B. be restored to the possession of the premises described in the proceedings aforesaid.

[*If judgment is for the defendant, proceed thus:*]

It is therefore considered that the inquisition aforesaid be, and the same is, hereby quashed. And it is further considered that the said C. D. recover against the said A. B. —— dollars, for his costs and charges by him laid out and expended in and about the prosecution of the said writ of certiorari, adjudged to him by the court now here, with his assent, and that he have execution therefor, *&c.*

No. 164.

WRIT OF RESTITUTION.

See ante, Vol. I., p. 263.

The People of the State of New York, to the Sheriff of the County of ——, greeting:

Whereas, we lately caused to be removed, by our writ of certiorari, into our Supreme Court of judicature, before our justices therein, certain proceedings had before A. D. W., county judge of said county.

And, thereupon, it was considered, in our said Supreme Court, before our justices aforesaid, that the said A. B. be restored to the possession of the following described lands and premises [*insert description*].

Now, therefore, we command you, that you forthwith restore the said A. B. to the full possession of the said premises; and how you shall have executed this our writ, make appear to our justices of our Supreme Court, at, *&c.*, on, *&c.*; and have you then there this writ.

Witness, *&c.* [*in usual form*]. N. B. M., Clerk.

J. G., Attorney.

CHAPTER XI.

FORMS ON THE FORECLOSURE AND DISCHARGE OF MORTGAGES.

I. FORMS ON FORECLOSURE BY ACTION.

No. 165.

SUMMONS AND NOTICE OF OBJECT OF ACTION.

See ante, Vol. I., p. 273.

IN SUPREME COURT, [*or other court*]; County of —.

G. T., Plaintiff,
against
D. K. &c., [*defendants in full*].

To the defendants D. K., and others, above named:

You are hereby summoned and required to answer the complaint of the plaintiff in this action, which will be filed in the office of the clerk of the county of ——, at —— in said county, and to serve a copy of your answer on me at my office, No. 128 Broadway, in the city of New York, within twenty days after the service of this summons upon you, exclusive of the day of such service; and if you fail to answer the said complaint within the time above mentioned, the plaintiff will apply to the court for the relief demanded in the complaint.

Dated, &c. J. W., Att'y for Plaintiff.

To the defendants D. K., and others, above named:

Take notice, that the summons herewith served on you in the above-entitled action is issued in an action brought for the foreclosure of a mortgage, executed by D. K. to G. T., on the —— day of ——, 18—, recorded in the clerk's office of the county of ——, in book of mortgages No. 11, p. 123, on the —— day of ——, 18 —, at 9 o'clock A. M.; [and which said mortgage was duly assigned by the said G. T. to the plaintiff above named, on the —— day of ——, 18 —.]

The said mortgage was executed to secure the payment of —— dollars, with interest from the —— day of ——, 18—, and covers the following described premises, situated in the town of ——, in the county of ——, viz.: [*insert brief description of mortgaged premises*].

You will further take notice that no personal claim is made against you, or against any defendant except the said D. K.

Dated, &c. J. W., Att'y for Plaintiff.

No. 166.

AFFIDAVIT TO OBTAIN ORDER OF PUBLICATION.

See ante, Vol. I., p. 283.

[*Title as in No.* 165.]

County of ——, ss.: G. T., of ——, in said county, plaintiff above named, being duly sworn, deposes and says, That this action is brought to foreclose a mortgage upon real estate situated in the town of ——, in said county, in which county the place of trial is laid: That the defendant, D. K., is the owner of the equity of redemption of the said mortgaged premises, [*or*, that the defendant, L. S., is a creditor of the mortgagor D. K., by judgment rendered subsequent to the said mortgage, and docketed in the clerk's office of said county of ——, on the —— day of ——, 18 —.] That the said defendant D. K. [*or* L. S.] is not a resident of the State of New York, and as deponent believes is not now to be found therein; but the said defendant resides at ——, in the State of Wisconsin; at which place the said defendant was a few days since, as deponent believes, this deponent having received a letter from the said defendant dated and post-marked at that place, on the —— day of ——, inst. [*or other sources of information, according to the fact*].

No. 167.

ORDER DIRECTING SERVICE BY PUBLICATION.

See ante, Vol. I, p. 283.

[*Title as in No.* 165.]

It appearing satisfactorily to me by the affidavit of G. T., that this action is brought to foreclose a mortgage upon real estate situated within this State, and that the defendant D. K. is a proper party to the action, and that the said defendant cannot be found in this State, I do order that the summons in this action be served on the said defendant by the publication thereof, once a week, for six weeks, in the newspaper printed in the county of ——, called the ——, and also in the newspaper printed in the county of Albany, called the ——.

I do further order and direct that a copy of the summons and complaint in this action, properly folded and enveloped, be forthwith deposited in the post office of ——, directed to the said D. K., at ——, Wisconsin, his place of residence, and the postage prepaid thereon [*omit this paragraph if the defendant's residence is unknown.*]

Dated, &c. W. H. L., Justice of the Sup. Court.

No. 168.

NOTICE OF LIS PENDENS

See ante, Vol. I., p. 285.

[*Title as in No.* 165.]

Notice is hereby given that the above-named plaintiff, G. T., has commenced an action in this court against D. K., R. K., and L. S., for the foreclosure of a mortgage, bearing date the ——, day of —— 18—, executed by D. K. and R. K. his wife, defendants, above named, of the town of ——, in the county of ——, to the said G. T. [*or*, to L. M., who duly assigned the same to the said G. T., plaintiff above named] and recorded in the office of the clerk of the county of ——, on the —— day of ——, 18—, at nine o'clock in the forenoon. That the mortgaged premises in the county of ——, affected by the said action, were at the commencement of this action, and now are, situated in the town of ——, in said county of ——, and are described in the said mortgage as follows, to wit: [*insert description of the premises, following the description in the mortgage*].

Dated, *&c.*, J. W., Attorney for Plaintiff.

No. 169.

COMPLAINT IN ACTION TO FORECLOSE MORTGAGE.

See ante, Vol. I., p. 288.

[*Title in full, as in No.* 165.]

The complaint of the plaintiff above named shows to the court:

That the defendant D. K., for the purpose of securing the payment to the plaintiff of the sum of —— dollars, with the interest thereon, on the —— day of ——, 18—, executed and delivered to the plaintiff a bond, bearing date on that day, sealed with his seal, in the penal sum of —— dollars, and conditioned that the same should be void, if the defendant, D. K., should pay to the plaintiff the said sum of —— dollars, as follows: [*set forth the condition of the mortgage*]; and as collateral security for the payment of the said moneys, the said defendant D. K., and the defendant R. K., his wife, on the same day, duly executed, acknowledged, and delivered to the said plaintiff a mortgage, whereby they granted, bargained, and sold to the plaintiff the premises hereinafter described, with the appurtenances thereto, that is to say: all that piece or parcel of land situated, lying, and being in the town of ——, in the county of ——, and bounded, *&c.* [*insert description of mortgaged premises*]; which said mortgage contained the same condition as the said bond. And in case of default in the payment of the said sum of money, or any part thereof, the said plaintiff was empowered to sell the said premises in due form of law, and from the moneys received from the sale to pay the said sum of money and interest thereon, with the costs and expenses of the proceedings, the surplus to be returned to the mortgagor.

[*If the mortgage has been assigned, and the action is brought by the assignee, insert the assignment as follows:* The plaintiff further shows, that G. T., mortgagee aforesaid, on or about the —— day of ——, 18—, for a valuable consideration, duly assigned, transferred, and set over to the plaintiff above named the said bond and mortgage, and the moneys due thereon and secured thereby, and thereupon delivered the said bond and mortgage to the plaintiff; which assignment was duly recorded in the office of the clerk of the county of ——, on the —— day of ——, 18—, in book —— of mortgages, on pages ——.]

And the plaintiff further shows, that the said mortgage was duly recorded in the office of the clerk of the county of ——, on the —— day of ——, 18—, in book —— of mortgages, on pages ——.

The plaintiff further shows, that the said defendant has not complied with the condition of said bond and mortgage, and has omitted to pay the sum of —— dollars, which became due on the —— day of ——, and that there is now justly due to the plaintiff, upon the said bond and mortgage, the sum of —— dollars, with interest from the —— day of ——, 18—. And that no proceedings have been had at law, or otherwise, for the recovery of the moneys secured by the said bond and mortgage, or any part thereof.

The plaintiff further shows, upon information and belief, that the defendant, L. S., has, or claims to have, some interest in, or lien upon, the said mortgaged premises, or some part thereof, as a judgment creditor of the said mortgagor [*or otherwise, as the case may be*], which interest or lien, if any, has accrued subsequently to the lien of the said mortgage.

Wherefore, the plaintiff demands judgment, that the defendants, and all persons claiming under them subsequent to the commencement of this action, may be barred and foreclosed of all right, claim, lien, and equity of redemption in the said mortgaged premises; that the said premises may be directed to be sold according to law; that, out of the proceeds thereof, the plaintiff may be paid the amount due on the said bond and mortgage, with interest to the time of such payment, and the costs and expenses of this action, so far as the amount of such moneys properly applicable thereto will pay the same; and that the residue of said moneys be brought into court to abide the further order of the court thereon; and that the defendant, D. K., may be adjudged to pay any deficiency which may remain after applying all of said moneys so applicable, as aforesaid, to the payment of said mortgage, and the costs and expenses of the proceedings; and that the plaintiff may have such further or other relief as shall be just and equitable.

J. W., Att'y for Plaintiff.

County of——, ss.: G. T., the plaintiff above named, being duly sworn, deposes and says, that the foregoing complaint is true, to his own knowledge, except as to the matters therein stated on information and belief, and as to those matters, he believes it to be true.

Sworn, *&c.* G. T.

No. 170.

AFFIDAVIT TO OBTAIN JUDGMENT OR ORDER OF REFERENCE ON DEFAULT.

See ante, Vol. I., p. 293.

[*Title of the cause.*]

County of ——, ss.: J. W., attorney for plaintiff, being duly sworn, deposes and says, that this action is brought for the foreclosure of a mortgage upon real estate, situated in the town of ——, in said county; that the whole amount of the said mortgage is due; that none of the defendants have answered or demurred to the complaint; (*) that none of them have appeared in the action; and that none of them are non-residents, or under the age of twenty-one years.

Sworn, *&c.* J. W. F.

No. 171.

ORDER OF REFERENCE—ALL DUE, AND NO INFANTS.

See ante, Vol. I., pp. 293, 294.

[*Title of the cause.*] At, *&c.*, [*as in No.* 6].

On filing proof of the personal service of the summons in this action upon all the defendants therein, on or prior to the —— day of ——, 18—; and that no answer or demurrer to the complaint has been put in by any of the defendants: Now, on motion of J. W., attorney for the plaintiff, it is ordered, that it be referred to L. F., Esq., of the city of New York, to compute and ascertain the amount due to the plaintiff for principal and interest on the bond and mortgage mentioned in the complaint, and report the same to the court. [*If it is desired that the reference shall take place in a county different from that named for the place of trial, insert, also, the following:* It is further ordered that the said referee may proceed with such reference in the county of ——.]

No. 172.

AFFIDAVIT TO OBTAIN ORDER OF REFERENCE, WHERE THERE ARE INFANT OR ABSENT DEFENDANTS.

See ante, Vol. I., p. 293.

[*Same as in No.* 170, *to the asterisk* (*), *and then continue:*] except A. B., who is an infant defendant, and has, by his guardian, put in the usual general answer; that the defendants, C. D. and E. F., are absentees, and service has been made upon them by publication of the summons, as appears by the affidavit of O. G., hereto annexed; and that neither of said last-named defendants has put in an answer or demurrer to the complaint herein.

Sworn, *&c.* J. W., Att'y for Plaintiff.

No. 173.

ORDER OF REFERENCE THEREON—INFANT OR ABSENT DEFENDANTS.

See ante, Vol. I., p. 293.

[*Title of the cause.*] At, *&c.* [*as in No.* 6].

On filing proof of the personal service of the summons in this action upon the defendants, D. K. and R. K., his wife, on or prior to the —— day of ——, 18— [*at least twenty days previously*], and of service of the summons upon the defendants, C. D. and E. F., who are non-residents of this State [*or*, who cannot be found within this State], by the publication thereof, pursuant to the order of this court; and no answer or demurrer having been put in by any of the defendants, except the defendant A. B., who is an infant, and has, by his guardian, put in the usual general answer; and the time for the defendants to answer or demur having expired, on motion of J. W., attorney for plaintiff, it is ordered that it be referred to L. F., Esq., of, *&c.*, as referee, to compute and ascertain the amount due to the plaintiff on the bond and mortgage mentioned in the complaint, and take proof of the facts and circumstances stated in the complaint, and to examine the plaintiff, or his agent, on oath, as to any payments which have been made to him, or for his use, and which ought to be credited on said bond and mortgage, and that he report thereon the facts to the court.

[It is further ordered that the said referee may proceed with such reference in the county of ——.]

No. 174.

AFFIDAVIT, WHOLE SUM NOT DUE—ABSENT OR NON-RESIDENT DEFENDANTS.

See ante, Vol. I., p. 293.

[*Title of the cause.*]

County of ——, ss.: J. W., attorney for the plaintiff, being duly sworn, deposes and says: That this action is brought for the foreclosure of a mortgage upon real estate situated in the town of ——, in said county; that the whole amount secured by said mortgage is not all due, but that —— dollars thereof, with interest on the whole sum secured by said mortgage, is due, and the residue thereof will become due as follows: [*state amounts and times when payable.*]

And deponent further says, that none of the defendants are under the age of twenty-one years, except the defendant A. B., who is an infant, and has by his guardian put in the usual general answer; and that the defendants C. D. and E. F., *&c.* [*conclude as in No.* 172].

No. 175.

ORDER OF REFERENCE—WHOLE SUM NOT DUE—ABSENT DEFENDANTS, ETC.

See ante, Vol. I., p. 293.

[*Title of the cause.*]

On reading and filing affidavits of the personal service of the summons in this action upon all the defendants therein, on, or prior to, the —— day of ——, 18—, and that no answer or demurrer to the complaint has been put in by any of the defendants; that all the defendants are of full age, and residents of this State, except the defendant A. B., who is an infant under the age of twenty-one years, and except the defendants C. D. and E. F., who are non-residents; and that only a part of the sum secured by the bond and mortgage mentioned in the complaint is due and payable.

Now, on motion of J. W., of counsel for the plaintiff, it is ordered that it be referred to L. F., of, *&c.*, as referee, to compute the amount due to the plaintiff on the said bond and mortgage; and also to compute and report the whole amount due and to become due, and remaining unpaid thereon, with interest to the date of such report; and that he ascertain and report the situation of the mortgaged premises, and whether the same can be sold in parcels, without injury to the interest of the parties hereto, or any of them. And if the said referee be of opinion that a sale of the whole of said premises, in one parcel, will be most beneficial to the parties, that he report his reasons therefor.

It is further ordered that the said referee also take proof of the facts and circumstances stated in the complaint; and that he examine the plaintiff or his agent on oath as to any payments which have been made to him or for his use, and which ought to be credited on said bond and mortgage; and that he report thereon the facts to the court.

No. 176.

REFEREE'S REPORT—WHOLE AMOUNT DUE.

See ante, Vol. I., p. 298.

[*Title of the cause.*]

To the Supreme Court of the State of New York [*or other court*].

I, L. F., appointed referee in this action by an order of this court dated the —— day of ——, 18—, by which order it was referred to me to compute and ascertain the amount due to the plaintiff for principal and interest on the bond and mortgage mentioned in the complaint, do respectfully report that I have computed and ascertained the amount due to the plaintiff on said bond and mortgage, and that the amount so due for both principal and interest, up to and including the date hereof, is the sum of —— dollars. (*)

I do further report that the schedule annexed hereto, marked "A," and making a part of this my report, contains a statement and account of the principal and interest due upon said bond and mortgage; the period of the computation thereof, and its rate.

All which is respectfully submitted.

Dated, *&c.* L. F., Referee.

Schedule "A," referred to in the annexed report.

One bond in the penal sum of —— dollars, dated the —— day of ——, 18—, executed by D. K., to G. H., to secure the payment of —— dollars, on the —— day of ——, 18—, with interest; accompanying which is a mortgage, dated the same day, to secure the same moneys, executed by the said D. K., with R. K., his wife, to the said G. T.

Principal sum due..................................	$ ——
Interest thereon from the —— day of ——, 18—, to the —— day of ——, 18—, being —— years and —— months, at seven per cent. per annum, is...........	——
Total amount due plaintiff for principal and interest, is..	$ ——

L. F., Referee.

No. 177.

REFEREE'S REPORT—WHOLE SUM NOT DUE—PROPERTY CANNOT BE SOLD IN PARCELS.

See ante, Vol. I., p. 298.

[*Same as in last form to the asterisk* (*), *and then proceed*:] And I do further report that I have computed and ascertained the amount due and to become due and remaining unpaid thereon, and the same, including interest to the date of this report, is the sum of —— dollars.

I do further report that the schedule annexed hereto, marked "A," and making a part of this my report, contains a statement of the computations of the amounts due and to grow due on said bond and mortgage; also the period of such computations, and the rate of interest.

And I do further report, that I have ascertained the situation of said mortgaged premises; that they consist of a house and lot, the lot being fifty feet front by one hundred and fifty feet deep; that the said premises cannot, on account of the size of the lot, be divided; and for that reason I am of opinion that a sale of the whole premises is necessary [*or other facts showing why a sale of the premises in one parcel will be most beneficial to the parties*].

I do further report that the schedule annexed hereto, marked "B," contains the proofs taken by me on this reference, except such as are documentary, and of those an abstract is set forth in said schedule.

All which is respectfully submitted.

Dated, &c. L. F., Referee.

[*Annex the schedules referred to in the report.*]

No. 178.

REFEREE'S REPORT—INFANT OR ABSENT DEFENDANT.

See ante, Vol. I., p. 298.

[*Same as in No.* 176, *to the end, if whole sum is due; if all not due, then same as in No.* 177. *In either case, add the following clause:*]

And I do further report, that I have taken proof of the facts and circumstances stated in the complaint in this action, and have examined the plaintiff on oath as to any payments which may have been made to him or to any person for his use, on account of the demand mentioned in the complaint, and which ought to be credited thereon; and that such proofs, except such as are documentary, together with such examinations, are annexed hereto; and that I am of the opinion that the facts and circumstances stated in the complaint are true.

No. 179.

PETITION BY PLAINTIFF FOR APPOINTMENT OF GUARDIAN AD LITEM.

See ante, Vol. I., p. 283.

[*Same substantially as in No.* 476.]

No. 180.

LIKE PETITION BY INFANT DEFENDANT UNDER FOURTEEN YEARS OF AGE.

See ante, Vol. I., p. 283.

[*Same substantially as in No.* 475.]

No. 181.

ORDER APPOINTING GUARDIAN AD LITEM.

See ante, Vol. I., p. 283.

[*Same substantially as in No.* 478.]

No. 182.

JUDGMENT ON DEFAULT—WHOLE AMOUNT DU

See ante, Vol. I., p. 283.

At, &c. [*as in No.* 6]

[*Title of the cause—names of all the parties in full.*]

The summons in this action having been served on all the defendants on, or prior to, the —— day of ——, 18—, personally [except on the defendants C. D. and E. F., who were served with the summons by the publication thereof, pursuant to an order of this court], and the time for answering the complaint in this action having expired, and no answer or demurrer having been put in on behalf of any defendant, except the defendant A. B., who is an infant under the age of twenty-one years, and has put in the usual general answer by E. B., Esq., his guardian ad litem, such answer, however, not denying any material facts in the complaint. And an order of reference having been made to compute the amount due to the plaintiff upon the bond and mortgage set forth in the complaint, and to take proof of the facts and circumstances stated in the complaint, and to examine the plaintiff or his agent on oath as to any payments made and which ought to be credited on said bond and mortgage; and on reading and filing proof of the due service of the summons upon the defendants herein, and also proof that the complaint herein, and due notice of the pendency of this action, were duly filed in the office of the clerk of the county of ——, on the —— day of ——, 18—; and on reading and filing the report of the referee named in said order of reference, dated the —— day of ——, 18—, by which report it appears that —— dollars was due upon said bond and mortgage, at the date of said report: (*)

Now, on motion of J. W., attorney for the plaintiff, it is ordered and adjudged that the mortgaged premises described in the complaint in this action, and hereinafter set forth, or so much thereof as may be sufficient to raise the amount due to the plaintiff for principal, interest, and costs, and which may be sold separately without material injury to the parties interested, be sold at public auction at the front door of the Court House in the town of ——, in the county of ——, by or under the direction of B. F. M., who is hereby appointed referee for that purpose [*or*, by or under the direction of the sheriff of the county of ——]; that the said referee [*or*, sheriff] give notice of the time and place of such sale according to law and the practice of the court; that either or any of the parties to this action may purchase at such sale; that the said referee [*or*, sheriff] execute to the purchaser or purchasers a deed or deeds of the premises sold; that out of the moneys arising from such sale, after deducting the amount of his fees and expenses on such sale, and any lien or liens upon the premises sold, at the time of the sale, for taxes or assessments, the said referee [*or*, sheriff] pay to the plaintiff or his attorney the sum of —— dollars and —— cents, adjudged to the plaintiff for his costs and charges in this action, with interest from the date hereof; and also the amount so reported due as aforesaid, together with the interest thereon from the date of the said report, or so much thereof as the purchase-money of the mortgaged premises will pay of the same, and take a receipt therefor, and file it with his report of sale; and that he bring the surplus of said proceeds (if any) into court, and deposit the same with the treasurer of the county of —— [*or other place of deposit*] to the credit of the parties entitled thereto in this action, subject to the further order of the court, and take a receipt for the same, and file it with his report of sale.

It is further ordered and adjudged that the said referee [*or*, sheriff] make a report of such sale, and file it with the clerk of this court with all convenient speed; that if the proceeds of such sale be insufficient to pay the amount reported due to the plaintiff as aforesaid, with the interest and costs, as aforesaid, the said referee [*or*, sheriff] specify the amount of such deficiency in his report of sale, and that the defendant D. K. pay the same to the plaintiff, and that the plaintiff have execution therefor.

It is further ordered and adjudged that the purchaser or purchasers at such sale be let into possession of the premises purchased by them, on production of the referee's [*or*, sheriff's] deed, and a certified copy of the order confirming the report of sale [*or*, and the certificate of the clerk of said county that said report has been filed in his office eight days, and that no exceptions thereto have been filed].

And it is further ordered and adjudged that the defendants and all persons claiming under them, or any or either of them, subsequent to the filing of such notice of the pendency of this action, be forever barred and foreclosed of all right, title, interest, and equity of redemption in the said mortgaged premises so sold, or any part thereof.

The following is a description of the mortgaged premises above referred to: [*insert description*].

No. 183.

JUDGMENT—PART ONLY DUE—PREMISES CANNOT BE SOLD IN PARCELS.

See ante, Vol. I., p. 303.

[*Same as last form to the asterisk,* (*) *and then as follows:*] and that the amount secured by and unpaid upon said bond and mortgage, including interest to the date of said report, is the sum of —— dollars, and that the said premises are so situated that they cannot be sold in parcels without injury to the interests of the parties, for the reasons stated in said report.

Now, on motion of J. W., attorney for the plaintiff, it is ordered and adjudged that the mortgaged premises described in the complaint in this action, and hereinafter set forth, be sold at public auction at the front door of the Court House in the town of ——, in the county of ——, by or under the direction of B. F. M., who is hereby appointed referee for that purpose [*or*, by or under the direction of the sheriff of the county of ——]; that the said referee [*or*, sheriff] give notice of the time and place of such sale, according to law and the practice of the court; that either or any of the parties to this action may purchase at such sale; that the said referee [*or*, sheriff] execute to the purchaser or purchasers a deed or deeds of the premises sold; that out of the moneys arising from such sale, after deducting the amount of his fees and expenses on such sale, and any lien or liens upon the premises sold at the time of the sale; for taxes or assessments, the said referee [*or*, sheriff] pay to the plaintiff, or his attorney, the sum of —— dollars, adjudged to the plaintiff for his costs and charges in this action, with interest from the date hereof, and also the whole amount so reported as secured and unpaid on said bond and mortgage, together with the interest thereon from the date of the said report, or so much thereof as the purchase-money of the mortgaged premises will pay of the same, and take a receipt therefor and file it with his report of sale; and that he bring the surplus of said proceeds (if any) into court, and deposit the same with the treasurer of the county of —— [*or other place of deposit*], to the credit of the parties entitled thereto in this action, subject to the further order of the court.

It is further ordered and adjudged that the said referee [*or*, sheriff] make a report of such sale, and file it with the clerk of this court with all convenient speed; and that if the proceeds of such sale be insufficient to pay the amount so reported due the plaintiff, with the interest and costs as aforesaid, the said referee [*or*, sheriff] specify the amount of such deficiency in his report of sale, and that the defendant D. K. pay the same to the plaintiff, and that the plaintiff have execution therefor.

It is further ordered and adjudged that, in the event that the amount reported as actually due, with interest and the costs of this action, shall be paid before such sale, the said plaintiff be and he is at liberty, at any time hereafter when any principal sum or interest secured by said bond and mortgage shall become due, according to the condition of the said bond, to go before the said referee, who is hereby continued referee for that purpose, or such other referee as the court may hereafter designate, on the foot of this judgment, and procure a report of the amount which shall be then due thereon, to the end that, upon the coming in and confirmation of such report, a judgment may be made for a sale of the said premises to satisfy the amount which shall then be due, with interest, and the costs of such report and sale. And in case the said premises shall be sold under this judgment and shall not produce sufficient to satisfy the amount so reported as secured and unpaid, with interest and the costs of this action and of such sale, it is then further ordered and adjudged that the plaintiff be at liberty, at any time thereafter, whenever any such deficiency of principal or interest shall have become due according to the condition of the said bond, to apply to the court for an execution against the said D. K., to collect the amount which shall then be due thereon.

It is further ordered and adjudged that the purchaser, *or*, *&c.*, [*continue as in last form to the end.*]

No. 184.

NOTICE OF SALE BY REFEREE.

See ante, Vol. I., p. 309.

NOTICE OF SALE.

[*Title of the cause.*]

In pursuance of a judgment of the Supreme Court of the State of New York [*or other court*], rendered in this action on the —— day of ——, 18—, the subscriber, as referee therein, will sell at public auction, at the front door of the Court House, in the town of ——, in the county of ——, on the —— day of ——, 18—, at twelve o'clock at noon, all that piece or parcel of land situated in said town of ——, and described in the complaint in this action as follows: [*insert description*].

Dated, *&c.* L. F., Referee.

No. 185.

CONDITIONS OF SALE.

See ante, Vol. I., p. 309; 2 Van Sant. Pr. 484

TERMS OF SALE.

[*Title of the cause.*]

The premises described in the annexed advertisement of sale will be sold under the direction of L. F., referee, upon the following terms:

1st. Ten per cent. of the purchase-money of said premises will be required to be paid to the said referee, at the time and place of sale, and for which the referee's receipt will be given.

2d. The residue of said purchase-money will be required to be paid to the said referee at his office, No. 128 Broadway, in the city of New York, on the —— day of ——, 18—; when the said referee's deed will be ready for delivery.

3d. All taxes, assessments, and other incumbrances, which, at the time of sale, are liens or incumbrances upon said premises, will be allowed by the referee out of the purchase-money; provided the purchaser shall, previous to the delivery of the deed, produce to the referee proof of such liens, and duplicate receipts for the payment thereof.

4th. The purchaser of the premises, or of any portion thereof, will, at the time and place of sale, sign a memorandum of his purchase.

5th. The biddings will be kept open after the property is struck down; and, in case any purchaser shall fail to comply with any of the above conditions of sale, the premises so struck down to him will be again put up for sale under the direction of said referee, under the same terms of sale, without application to the court, unless the plaintiff's attorney shall elect to make such application; and such purchaser will be held liable for any deficiency there may be between the sum for which said premises shall be struck down upon the sale, and that for which they may be purchased on the re-sale, and also, for any costs or expenses accruing on such re-sale.

[*Insert here, also, as to a portion of the purchase-money remaining on bond and mortgage, or special conditions, according to circumstances*].

L. F., Referee.

[*Annex copy of the advertisement of sale.*]

No. 186.

REFEREE'S DEED.

See ante, Vol. I., p. 317.

This indenture, made the —— day of ——, in the year one thousand eight hundred and ——, between L. F., of, *&c.*, referee in the action hereinafter mentioned, of the first part, and R. D., of the second part.

Whereas, at a special term of the Supreme Court [*or other court*], held at ——, on the —— day of ——, 18—, it was, among other things, adjudged by the said court in an action then pending therein, between G. T., plaintiff, and D. K., R. K., and L. S., defendants, that all and singular the mortgaged premises mentioned in the complaint in the said action, and in said judgment described, or so much thereof as might be sufficient to raise the amount due to the plaintiff for principal, interest, and costs in said action, and which might be sold separately, without material injury to the parties interested, be sold at public auction, according to the course and practice of said court, by or under the direction of the said L. F., who was appointed a referee in said action, and to whom it was referred by the said order and judgment, among other things, to make such sale; that the said sale be made in the county where the said mortgaged premises, or the greater part thereof, were situated; that the referee give public notice of the time and place of such sale, according to the course and practice of said court, and that any of the parties in said action might become purchaser or purchasers on such sale; and that the said referee execute to the purchaser or purchasers of the said mortgaged premises, or such part or parts thereof as should be sold, a good and sufficient deed or deeds of conveyance of the same.

And whereas, the said referee, in pursuance of the judgment of the said court, did, on the —— day of ——, 18—, at ——, sell at public auction the premises in the said judgment mentioned, due notice of the time and place of such sale having been first given, agreeably to the said judgment, at which time the premises hereinafter described were struck off to the said party of the second part, for the sum of —— dollars, that being the highest sum bid for the same.

Now, this indenture witnesseth, that the said referee, the party of the first part to these presents, in pursuance of the said judgment, and in conformity to the statute in such case made and provided, and in consideration of the said sum of money so bid as aforesaid, duly paid by the said party of the second part, the receipt whereof is hereby acknowledged, hath granted, bargained, sold, and conveyed, and by these presents doth grant, bargain, sell, and convey, unto the said party of the second part, all, *&c.* [*insert description of premises, same as in the judgment*].

To have and to hold, all and singular, the premises above mentioned and described and hereby conveyed, or intended so to be, unto the said party of the second part, his heirs and assigns, to his and their only proper use, benefit, and behoof forever.

In witness whereof the party of the first part, referee aforesaid, has hereunto set his hand and seal the day and year first above written.

L. F., Referee. [L. S.]

Sealed and delivered in
presence of S. S.

[*Acknowledgment substantially as in No.* 44.]

No. 187.

REFEREE'S REPORT OF SALE.

See ante, Vol. I., p. 318.

[*Title of the cause.*]

To the Supreme Court of the State of New York [*or other court*].

In pursuance of a judgment in this court, made in the above-entitled action, and dated the —— day of ——, 18—, entered in the office of the clerk of the county of ——, I, the subscriber, referee named in said judgment, do respectfully report, that I advertised the premises described in said judgment to be sold by me at the front door of the Court House in the town of ——, in said county, on the —— day of ——, 18—, that previous to the said sale I caused due notice thereof to be publicly and duly advertised for six weeks successively [*or, if within any city,*for three weeks, successively, twice in each week], which notice contained a brief description of the mortgaged premises.

I do further report, that on the —— day of ——, 18—, the day on which the said premises were so advertised to be sold as aforesaid, I attended at the time and place fixed for the said sale, and exposed the same for sale, at public auction, to the highest bidder; and the said premises were then and there fairly struck off to R. D., at the sum of —— dollars, he being the highest bidder therefor, and that being the highest sum bidden for the same. [*If the premises were sold in separate parcels, state the fact accordingly.*]

And I do further certify and report, that I have executed, acknowledged, and delivered to the said purchaser the usual referee's deed for the said premises; and have paid over or disposed of the purchase-money or proceeds of the said sale, as follows, namely: I have paid to the attorney for the plaintiff the sum of —— dollars, being the amount of his costs, of this action, as adjusted, and have taken a receipt therefor, which is hereto annexed. I have also retained in my hands the sum of —— dollars, being the amount of my fees, commissions, and disbursements on the said sale, as will appear, by reference to the statement of items thereof annexed to this my report, to which I refer. I have paid also to the plaintiff, through J. W., Esq., his attorney, the sum of —— dollars, being the full amount of principal and interest due to the said plaintiff on the judgment in this action, and have taken a receipt therefor, which is also hereto annexed; and have paid the balance in hand, amounting to —— dollars, to the treasurer of the county of —— [*or*, to the chamberlain of the city of New York], and taken his receipt therefor, which is also hereto annexed [*or*, I have also paid to the plaintiff, through J. W., Esq., his attorney, the whole of the residue, amounting to ——, and have taken a receipt therefor, which is hereto annexed. And I also report, that the deficiency due to the plaintiff from the defendant D. K., and for which he is personally liable under the judgment in this action, is the sum of —— dollars, with interest from the date of this report.]

All which is respectfully submitted. B. F. M., Referee.

[*Annex the receipts referred to in the report.*]

No. 188.

ORDER CONFIRMING REPORT.

See ante, Vol. I., p. 318.

At, *&c.*, [*as in No.* 6.]

[*Title of the cause.*]

On reading and filing the report of sale of B. F. M., Esq., the referee mentioned in the judgment in this action, dated the —— day of ——, 18—, and on motion of J. W., Esq., attorney for the plaintiff; it is ordered that the said report be and the same hereby is in all things ratified and confirmed.

II. Forms on Strict Foreclosure of Mortgages.

No. 188(A).

COMPLAINT IN ACTION FOR STRICT FORECLOSURE.

See ante, Vol. I., p. 331; 2 Van Sant. Eq. Pr. 528.

[*Title of the cause as in No.* 165,]

The complaint of the above-named plaintiff shows to the court, upon information and belief, that the defendant, A. B., for the purpose of securing the payment to the plaintiff of the sum of $5,000, with interest thereon, on or about the —— day of ——, 18—, executed and delivered to the plaintiff a bond bearing date on that day, sealed with his seal, in the penalty of $10,000, upon condition that the same should be void if the said defendant should pay to the said plaintiff the said sum of money first above mentioned, as follows: [*setting forth the condition of the bond*]; and, as collateral security for the payment of the said indebtedness, the said defendant, A. B., and the defendant, C. D., his wife, on the same day executed, duly acknowledged, and delivered to the said plaintiff a mortgage, whereby they granted, bargained, and sold to the said plaintiff the following described premises, with the appurtenances thereto, that is to say: [*describing the premises*] with the same condition as the said bond; and in case of default in the payment of the said sum of money, or any part thereof, the said plaintiff was empowered to sell the said mortgaged premises in due form of law, and out of the moneys arising from the sale to pay the said sum of money and interest, with the costs and expenses of the proceedings thereupon, the surplus to be returned to the mortgagor.

And the plaintiff further shows, that the said mortgage was duly recorded in the office of the clerk of the county of ——, on the —— day of ——, 18—.

And the said plaintiff further shows, that the said defendant has failed to comply with the condition of the said bond and mortgage, by omitting to pay the sum of —— dollars which became due on the —— day of —— 18—; and there is now justly due the plaintiff, upon the said bond and mortgage, the sum of —— dollars, with interest from the —— day of ——, 18—. That soon after the said mortgage debt became due, as aforesaid, the said plaintiff entered into the possession of the said mortgaged premises and the receipt of the rents and profits thereof, and has since continued, and still is, in possession.

That the said rents and profits so received by the plaintiff have not been sufficient in amount to equal the annual interest upon the said bond and mortgage [*or, state the fact as it may be*].

That the plaintiff has laid out considerable expenditures for permanent improvements upon said premises, to wit: [*stating the general nature and value of same*], which he claims should be allowed him as an offset against so much of said rents and profits. And has also paid the sum of —— dollars for taxes and assessments; [*or, if any prior lien has been discharged, state the nature of the lien, amount, and time of payment of same*]; all of which sums the said plaintiff also claims should be allowed him, and credited on his account against so much of said rents and profits; which several sums, when so applied and credited to the said plaintiff, charging the plaintiff with the amount of rents and profits so received by him, will leave remaining due him, the said plaintiff, on his said bond and mortgage, as he claims, the sum of —— dollars.

The plaintiff further alleges that the defendant, C. D., has an interest in said mortgaged premises, under and by virtue of a mortgage thereon, from the said defendant, B. F., subsequent to the mortgage of the plaintiff; and the defendant E. H. has an interest therein, &c., [*setting forth generally the interest of the respective parties*].

That the plaintiff has applied to the said defendant, C. D., &c., and requested him [them] to pay him, the said plaintiff, the said sum so due on his, the plaintiff's, said bond and mortgage, or come to an accounting with him thereon for the said rents and profits, permanent improvements, &c., and, after the proper charges and credits, pay the said plaintiff what should appear to be due him on his said bond and mortgage; or, in default thereof, to release his [their] right and equity of redemption in the said mortgaged premises. But the said defendant has hitherto refused, and still refuses so to do, or to comply with any part of said plaintiff's request.

Wherefore the plaintiff demands judgment against the defendants, that an account may be taken of what, if anything, is due and owing to the plaintiff for principal and interest on his said bond and mortgage, and that an account may also be taken of the rents and profits of the said mortgaged premises which have been received by said plaintiff, and also of the expenditures of the said plaintiff for permanent improvements, and for taxes and assessments [*or*, for the amount so paid for prior incumbrances, &c., *as the case may be*], and that the said defendants may be adjudged to pay the plaintiff what may be found due him on taking the said account, together with his costs of this action, by a short day to be appointed by the court for that purpose; or, in default thereof, that the said defendants and all persons claiming under them may be absolutely debarred and foreclosed of and from all right and equity of redemption in and to the said mortgaged premises, and every part thereof, and that said defendants may deliver up to the plaintiff all deeds, papers, or writings in their custody or power relating to or concerning the said mortgaged premises, or any part thereof, or for such further or other relief in the premises as the court shall think proper to grant, with costs of action.

J. L. F., Plaintiff's Attorney.

[*Add usual verification.*]

III. Forms on Foreclosure by Advertisement

No. 189.

NOTICE OF FORECLOSURE BY ADVERTISEMENT.

See ante, Vol. I., p. 338.

MORTGAGE SALE.

Whereas, default has been made in the payment of the money secured by a mortgage dated the —— day of ——, 18—, executed by ——, and ——, his wife, of the town of ——, county of ——, and State of New York, to ——, of the same place [*or as the case may be*], and which mortgage was recorded in the clerk's office of said county in Book No. ——, of mortgages, on page ——, on the —— day of ——, 18—, at —— o'clock — M. [*If the mortgage is foreclosed by an assignee, then say:* And whereas the said mortgage has been duly assigned to ——, of ——, and the same is now owned by him.] And whereas the amount claimed to be due upon said mortgage, at the time of the first publication of this notice, is the sum of —— dollars and —— cents, to wit: $—— of principal, and $—— of interest, and which is the whole amount claimed to be unpaid on said mortgage [*or*, and the whole amount claimed to be unpaid on said mortgage is the sum of —— dollars]

Now, therefore, notice is hereby given, that by virtue of the power of sale contained in said mortgage, and duly recorded as aforesaid, and in pursuance of the statute in such case made and provided, the said mortgage will be foreclosed by a sale of the premises therein described, at public auction, at the front door of the Court House [*or*, hotel, kept by ——], in the town [*or*, city] of ——, in the county of ——, on the —— day of —— next, at ten o'clock in the forenoon of that day.

The said premises are described in said mortgage as follows: [*or*, substantially as follows: *and then give description of premises as stated in the mortgage*].

Dated the —— day of ——, 18—. [*Date of the first publication of the notice.*]

A. B., mortgagee [*or*, assignee].

L. P. C., Attorney.

No. 190.

AFFIDAVIT OF PUBLICATION OF NOTICE OF SALE.

See ante, Vol. I., pp. 348, 349.

State of New York, }
County of ——, } ss.

[*Attach here a printed notice of sale.*]

E. F., of ——, in said county, being duly sworn, says: That he is, and during the whole time hereinafter mentioned has been, the printer, [*or*, foreman, *or*, principal clerk of the printer], of the —— Herald, a newspaper printed in said county of ——, and that the annexed printed notice of sale was published in the said newspaper twelve weeks, successively, at least once in each week; which publication commenced on the —— day of ——, 18—, and terminated on the —— day of ——, 18—.

E. F.

Sworn to, before me, this }
—— day of ——, 18—. }

J. A. M., Justice of the Peace.
[*or other officer authorized to take affidavits*]

No. 191.

AFFIDAVIT OF AFFIXING NOTICE ON COURT HOUSE DOOR.

See ante, Vol. I., pp. 348, 349.

State of New York, }
County of ——, } ss.

[*Attach here a printed notice of sale.*]

C. D., of ——, in said county, being duly sworn, says: That on the —— day of ——, 18—, he affixed a true copy of the annexed printed notice in a conspicuous place, and in a proper and substantial manner, on the outward door of the building where the county courts are directed to be held in the county of ——, to wit, at the Court House [*or as the fact may be*], in the town [*or*, city] of ——, in said county. [*If there be two or more such buildings in the county, then add:* that being the building where such courts are directed to be held, nearest to the premises described in said notice]. C. D.

Sworn, *&c.* [*as in No.* 190].

No. 192.

AFFIDAVIT OF AFFIXING NOTICE IN CLERK'S OFFICE.

See ante, Vol. I., p. 349.

State of New York, }
County of ——, } ss.

[*Attach here a printed notice of sale.*]

C. D., of ——, in said county, being duly sworn, says: He is the clerk of said county. That on the —— day of ——, 18—, he affixed a true copy of the annexed printed notice of sale in the book prepared and kept by him, as such clerk, for that purpose, at the clerk's office in ——, in said county. [*Or, if the affidavit is made by one who saw the notice affixed, say:* L. P. C., of ——, in said county, attorney at law, being duly sworn, says, that he saw a true copy of the annexed printed notice affixed in the book prepared and kept for that purpose by the clerk of said county of ——, at his office in ——, in said county, during the time required, to wit, on the —— day of ——, 18—. *The time stated should be twelve weeks prior to the time of sale.*] C. D.

Sworn, *&c.* [*as in No.* 190].

No. 193.

AFFIDAVIT OF SERVICE OF NOTICE OF SALE.

See ante, Vol. I., pp. 340, 349.

State of New York, }
County of ——, } ss.

L. P. C., of ——, in said county, attorney at law, being duly sworn, says: That on the —— day of ——,

[Attach here a printed notice of sale.] 18—, he served upon A. B., C. D., and E. F., and each and every of them, a copy of the annexed printed notice of sale, by delivering to the said persons, and each and every of them personally, a true copy of the said notice.

[*If the service was by leaving the notice at the dwelling-house, say:*] That on the —— day of ——, 18—, he served upon A. B. a copy of the annexed printed notice of sale, by leaving a true copy thereof at his dwelling-house in charge of the wife [*or* daughter, aged eighteen years or thereabouts] of the said A. B.

[*If the service was by depositing in the post-office, say:*] That on the — day of ——, 18—, he served upon A. B. a copy of the annexed printed notice of sale, by depositing a true copy thereof in the post-office in ——, properly folded and directed to the said A. B. at his place of residence, to wit, at ——, and paying the postage on the same. L. P. O.

Sworn, *&c.* [*as in No.* 190].

No. 194.

AFFIDAVIT OF SALE.

See ante, Vol. I., p. 349.

State of New York, }
county of ——, } ss. L. M., of ——, in said county, being duly sworn, says: That he officiated as auctioneer at the sale of the premises, hereinafter mentioned; and, as such auctioneer, sold the premises described in the annexed printed copy of notice of sale, at public auction, at the time and place of sale therein mentioned, to wit, on the —— day of ——, 18—, at — o'clock in the ——noon, at the front door of the Court House [*or*, hotel, kept by ——], in the town [*or*, city] of ——, in the county of —— aforesaid; and that J. R., of ——, then and there purchased the said premises for the price of —— dollars, he being the highest bidder, and that being the highest sum bidden for the same.

[Attach here a printed copy of the notice of sale.]

And deponent further says, That said sale was in all respects honestly and fairly conducted, as deponent verily believes; and that the said J. R. purchased the said premises fairly and in good faith, as deponent also verily believes. L. M.

Sworn, *&c.* [*as in No.* 190].

No. 195.

BILL OF COSTS ON FORECLOSURE.

See ante, Vol. I., pp. 353, 354.

Dr. notice of sale, 5 fol., at 2s.	$1 25
Copy same to keep, at 1s.	62½

Copy notice for printer, at 1s.	62½
Copy notice for posting on Court House door, at 1s. . .	62½
Expense of posting, ...	1 00
Dr. affidavit of posting, 2 fol. and copy, at 3s. . . .	75
Copy notice annexed, at 1s.	62½
Copy notice for posting in clerk's office, at 1s. . . .	62½
Clerk's fees on same, ...	25
Dr. affidavit of posting in clerk's office, 2 fol. and copy, at 3s. .	75
Copy notice annexed, at 1s.	62½
Printer publishing notice, 13 insertions 5 fol. . . .	21 75
" " two postponements of sale, 1 fol. each, .	1 50
" " two additional insertions of notice of sale, .	5 00
Dr. affidavit of publication, 2 fol. and copy, at 3s. . .	75
Copy notice annexed, at 1s.	62½
Copy notice to serve on mortgagor, at 1s. . . .	62½
Serving notice, ...	1 00
[*Same charges for each and every other notice served, if any,*]	
Dr. affidavit of service, 2 fol. and copy, at 3s. . . .	75
Copy notice annexed, 5 fol. at 1s.	62½
Postages [*to be stated by items*]	
Clerk's fees for searches [*the fees actually paid*]	
Dr. affidavit of circumstances of sale, 4 fol. and copy, at 3s. .	1 50
Copy printed notice annexed, ...	62½
Superintending sale, &c.	10 00
Recording affidavits [*the fees actually paid*]	
Oaths to five affidavits, 10 cts. each, ...	50
[*If a deed has been executed by the mortgagee to the purchaser, then add:*]	
Dr. deed to purchaser, 6 fols. and copy, at 3s. . . .	2 25
Acknowledgment of deed, 2s.	25
Recording same [*the fees actually paid.*]	

No. 196.

NOTICE OF TAXATION OF COSTS.

See ante, Vol. I., p. 354.

[*To be indorsed on copy bill to be served.*]

To C. D. Sir: Take notice that the bill of costs, of which the within is a copy, will be presented for taxation to C. L. A., Esquire, justice of the Supreme Court [*or*, to A. D. W., Esquire, county judge], at his office in ——, in said county, on the —— day of —— next, [*or*, instant], at ten o'clock in the forenoon. Dated the —— day of ——, 18—.

Yours, &c., L. P. C., Att'y for Mortgagee [*or*, Assignee].

No. 197.

AFFIDAVIT OF DISBURSEMENTS.

See ante, Vol. I., p. 355.

State of New York, } ss.
[County of ——, }

L. P. C., of ——, in said county, being duly sworn, says: That he is the attorney for ——, the mortgagee [*or*, assignee] of a mortgage executed by ——, to ——, and which has been duly foreclosed under the statute. That, according to the best of deponent's knowledge and belief, the several disbursements charged in the bill of costs hereto annexed have been actually and necessarily paid or incurred. That the copies of papers charged therein were actually and necessarily used or obtained for use. That such bill of costs contains no charge for any draft or copy of any affidavit, or other paper, which has not been made, or for any other service which has not been performed, except such services as are allowed by law to be taxed prospectively; and that the number of folios contained in the draft, or in the copies of said papers, are not overcharged in such bill.

L. P. C.

Sworn, *&c.* [*as in No.* 190].

No. 198.

PETITION FOR DISCHARGE OF MORTGAGE OF RECORD. (*a*)

See ante, Vol. I., p. 356.

In the matter of the petition of A. B., to have mortgage discharged of record.

To the Supreme Court of the State of New York [*or*, to the Superior Court of the City of New York [*or*, of Buffalo].

The petition of A. B., of ——, in the county of ——, shows to the court: That he is the owner of that piece or parcel of land situated in the city [*or*, county] of ——, in the State of New York, and described as follows: [*insert description*].

Your petitioner further shows, that there is recorded, in the clerk's [*or*, register's] office of said county of ——, a mortgage covering the premises aforesaid; executed by C. D., and S., his wife, mortgagors, to E. F. mortgagee, conditioned to pay to the said mortgagee, in five years from the

(*a*) Under a recent amendment of the statute material alterations are made in the allegations to be inserted in the petition. *Laws of* 1868, *p.* 1787, in *Appendix of Notes* at the end of this volume.

date thereof, the sum of —— dollars, with interest, annually, on the 1st day of April in each year. That the said mortgage is dated the —— day of ——, 18—, and was recorded in said clerk's [*or*, register's] office on the —— day of ——, 18—, in liber "B" of mortgages, pages 213, 214.

Your petitioner further shows, that the said mortgage is paid; that E. F., the mortgagee named in said mortgage, is deceased, having departed this life at the city of New York more than five years since, to wit: on the —— day of ——, 18—; and that the place of residence of the said mortgagee, at the time of his death, was in said city of New York; that no letters testamentary, or of administration, have been taken out in this State upon the estate of said mortgagee; that the heirs of the said mortgagee, so far forth as the same can be ascertained by your petitioner, are R. F. and J. F., both of whom reside in ——, in said county; and that the said mortgage was never assigned or transferred to any other party [*or, if assigned, state to whom, and the facts in regard to the same*].

Your petitioner, therefore, prays that the said mortgage may be discharged of record. A. B.

[*Add verification, as in No.* 1.]

No. 199.

ORDER TO SHOW CAUSE.

See ante, Vol. I., p. 357.

At, *&c.* [*as in No.* 6].

[*Title as in last form.*]

On reading and filing the petition of A. B., dated the —— day of ——, 18—, praying that a mortgage executed by C. D., and S., his wife, to E. F., dated the —— day of ——, 18—, and recorded in the clerk's [*or*, register's] office of the county of ——, in liber "B" of mortgages pages, *&c.*, on the —— day of ——, 18—, and covering premises situated in the city [*or*, county] of ——, may be discharged of record:

It is, on motion of G. H. T., of counsel for the said petitioner, ordered, that all persons interested show cause at the special term of this court, to be held at Chambers, in the City Hall, New York, on the —— day of ——, 18—, at ten o'clock A. M., why the said mortgage should not be discharged of record.

It is further ordered, that this order be published in the ——, a newspaper printed in said city, once in each week for —— weeks, successively; and that a copy of this order be served personally on R. F. and J. F., heirs of the said E. F., —— days before the said —— day of ——.

No. 200.

ORDER OF REFERENCE.

See ante, Vol. I., p. 357.

At, &c. [*as in No.* 6].

[*Title as in No.* 198.]

It appearing to the court that the order made in this matter on the —— day of ——, 18—, was duly published in the ——, a newspaper printed in the city of New York, for —— weeks successively, commencing on the —— day of ——, 18—, and terminating on the —— day of ——, 18—, and that a copy of said order was, on the —— day of ——, 18—, personally served on R. F. and J. F., heirs of E. F., deceased, as required in and by the said order:

It is now, on motion of G. H. T., of counsel for the petitioner, ordered, that it be, and it hereby is, referred to L. F., Esq., as referee, to take and report proofs of the facts stated in the said petition.

No. 201.

REFEREE'S REPORT.

See ante, Vol. I., p. 357.

[*Title as in No.* 198.]

To the Supreme Court of the State of New York:

The undersigned, appointed a referee by an order of this court dated the —— day of ——, 18—, to take and report proofs of the facts stated in the petition in this matter, do hereby certify and report:

That, before entering upon the execution of said order, I caused —— days' notice, in writing, to be given to R. F. and J. F., of the time and place of executing the same, to wit: on the —— day of ——, 18—, at 10 o'clock A. M., at my office, No. 161 Broadway, New York. That, at the time and place aforesaid, I proceeded to execute the said order, in the presence of G. H. T., attorney for the said petitioner, no one appearing for other parties interested herein, and that I have taken proofs of the facts stated in the said petition; and that the said proofs are annexed hereto, marked as schedules "A," "B," and "C."

Dated, &c. L. F., Referee.

No. 202.

ORDER DISCHARGING MORTGAGE OF RECORD.

See ante, Vol. I., p. 358.

At, &c. [*as in No.* 6].

[*Title as in No.* 198.]

On reading and filing the report of L. F., Esq., referee in this matter, to whom it was referred to take and report proofs of the facts stated in the petition herein, by an order dated the —— day of ——, 18—; and it appearing from the proofs so taken that A. B., the petitioner above named, is the owner of the real estate described in the said petition; that, *&c.* [*recite the other matters alleged in the petition*].

Now, on motion of G. H. T., of counsel for the said petitioner, no one appearing in opposition thereto, it is ordered, that the mortgage above referred to be discharged of record; and that the clerk [*or*, register] of the county of —— make the proper entries in his books showing such discharge.

CHAPTER XII.

FORMS ON HABEAS CORPUS AND CERTIORARI.

No. 205.

PETITION FOR HABEAS CORPUS, OR CERTIORARI, TO INQUIRE INTO THE CAUSE OF DETENTION.

See ante, Vol. I., p. 368.

To the Supreme Court of the State of New York [*or*, To Hon. A. B. J., Justice of the Supreme Court; *or other officer to whom application is to be made*].

The petition of A. B., respectfully shows: That he is now a prisoner, confined in the custody of C. D., sheriff of the county of ——, in the county jail in the village [*or*, city] of ——, in said county, for a supposed criminal offense, to wit: [*here state the offense*].

Your petitioner further shows: That such confinement is by virtue of a warrant, a copy of which is hereto annexed [*or*, and your petitioner avers that by reason of his being removed or concealed before this application, a demand of a copy of the warrant, or process by virtue of which he is confined, could not be made. *Or thus:* And your petitioner avers, that, prior to this application, a demand of a copy of the warrant or process by virtue of which he is confined, was made of the said C. D., and the legal fees therefor tendered to him; and that such copy was refused].

And your petitioner further shows: That to his best knowledge and belief he is not committed or detained by virtue of any process issued by any court of the United States, or any judge thereof [in a case where such courts or judges have exclusive jurisdiction under the laws of the United States, or have acquired exclusive jurisdiction by the commencement of a suit in such courts], or by virtue of the final judgment or decree of any competent tribunal of civil or criminal jurisdiction, or by virtue of any execution issued upon such judgment or decree.

And your petitioner states and shows, that he is advised by his counsel, O. F., Esq., residing at ——, and verily believes that his imprisonment is illegal, and that such illegality consists in this [*state in what the alleged illegality consists*].

Wherefore your petitioner prays a writ of habeas corpus [*or*, certiorari]; to the end that he may be bailed or discharged from custody.

Dated, *&c.* A. B.

O. F. Attorney.

County of ——, ss. A. B., the above-named petitioner, being duly sworn, says: That the foregoing petition is true to his own knowledge, except as to the matters which are therein stated on information and belief, and as to those matters he believes it to be true. A. B.

Sworn to, *&c.*

No. 206.

ANOTHER FORM OF PETITION—BY THIRD PARTY.

To the Supreme Court, *&c.* [*as in last form*].

The petition of E. F. respectfully shows: That A. B. [*or if his name is not known, describe him*] is imprisoned, or restrained of his liberty, by —— [*state the name of the officer or person by whom he is restrained, if known, and if not known, describe him*], and that the said A. B. is so confined or restrained, at —— [*state the place where the party is confined*].

And your petitioner further shows, that, according to the best of the knowledge and belief of your petitioner, the cause or pretense of the aforesaid confinement, or restraint, of the said A. B. is as follows: [*state cause of detention*].

And your petitioner further shows, *&c.* [*as in last form, including verification, varying it to suit an application made by a third person on behalf of the person imprisoned*]. E. F., in behalf of A. B.

No. 207.

ANOTHER FORM, IN CASE OF INFANTS.

See ante, Vol. I., pp. 364, 388.

To the Supreme Court of the State of New York:

The petition of A. B., of ——, in the county of ——, and State of New York, respectfully shows:

That, *&c.* [*Here state the matters alleged in the last form, so far as the same are applicable; and also all the facts and circumstances in relation to the ability of both parents; and all the facts and circumstances proper to be considered in determining the custody and disposition of an infant. And make the prayer in the petition according to the relief required.*]

No. 208.

WRIT OF HABEAS CORPUS.

See ante, Vol. I., p. 370.

The People of the State of New York, to C. D., Sheriff of, *&c.* [*or other person in whose custody the party is*].

[SEAL.] We command you that you have the body of A. B., by you imprisoned and detained, as it is said, together with the time and cause of such imprisonment and detention, by whatsoever name the said A. B. shall be called, or charged, before our justices of our Supreme Court, *&c.* [*or*, before A. D. W., county judge, *&c.*, *as the case may be*], at, *&c.*, on, *&c.* [*or*, immediately after the receipt of this writ], to do and receive what shall then and there be considered concerning the said A. B. And have you then there this writ.

Witness, C. L. A., one of the justices of our Supreme Court, at ——, the —— day of ——, 18—.

O. F., Attorney. N. B. M., Clerk.

HOW WRIT INDORSED.

See ante, Vol. I., p. 371.

Allowed the —— day of ——, 18— [*or*, allowed on application of tne attorney-general, *or*, district attorney, this —— day of ——, 18—. *Or, if the writ is directed to any party other than a sheriff, coroner, constable, or marshal, and the charges for bringing up the prisoner are required by the court or judge to be paid by the petitioner, then add to the allowance the following:* And the charges for bringing up such prisoner, amounting to —— dollars, are hereby required to be paid by the petitioner on whose application this writ is issued].

C. L. A., Justice of the Sup. Court.

No. 209.

WRIT OF CERTIORARI.

See ante, Vol. I., p. 370.

The People of the State of New York, to C. D., Sheriff of, *&c.* [*or other person in whose custody the party is*].

[SEAL.] We command you that you certify fully, and at large, to our justices of our Supreme Court [*or*, to A. D. W., county judge, *&c.*, *as the case may be*], at, *&c.*, on, *&c.* [*or*, immediately after the receipt of this writ], the day and cause of the imprisonment of A. B., by you detained, as it is said, by whatsoever name the said A. B. shall be called or charged. And have you then and there this writ.

Witness, *&c.* [*as in last form*].

O. F., Attorney. N. B. M., Clerk.

[*Indorsement as in last form.*]

No. 210.

BOND ON SERVING WRIT.

See ante, Vol. I., p. 373.

Know all men by these presents, That I, E. F., farmer, of the town of ——, in the county of ——, am held and firmly bound unto C. D., sheriff of said county, in the penal sum of —— dollars [*penalty double the amount of the sum for which the prisoner is detained, if detained for any specific sum, and, if not, then for one thousand dollars*], to be paid to the said C. D., or to his certain attorney, executors, administrators, or assigns, for which payment, well and truly to be made, I bind myself, my heirs, executors, and administrators firmly by these presents. Sealed with my seal, and dated the —— day of ——, 18—.

Whereas, A. B. is now confined as a prisoner in the custody of the said C. D., sheriff, as aforesaid, and a writ of habeas corpus has been issued by the Supreme Court [*or*, by A. D. W., Esq., county judge of said county], to inquire into the cause of his detention, directed to the said sheriff.

Now, therefore, the condition of this obligation is such, that if the said E. F. shall pay to the said sheriff the charges for carrying back the said A. B., if he shall be remanded on the said habeas corpus, and if the said A. B. shall not escape by the way, either in going to or returning from the Court House in the village of —— [*or*, the office of said county judge, *or other place where the prisoner is required to be taken*], then this obligation to be void, otherwise to remain in full force and virtue.

Sealed and delivered E. F. [SEAL.]
in presence of
S. T.

No. 211.

PETITION SHOWING THAT PARTY MAY BE CARRIED OUT OF THE STATE, OR MAY SUFFER SOME INJURY BEFORE WRIT CAN ISSUE.

See ante, Vol. I., p. 374.

To the Supreme Court, &c. [*proceed, substantially as in No.* 205, *to the end, and then as follows*]:

And your petitioner further shows, that the said G. H., in whose custody the said A. B. is, has threatened to carry the said A. B. out of this State, and has told several persons, publicly, that such was his intention. That your petitioner had a conversation with said G. H., this morning, in which he informed your petitioner that he should leave immediately with said A. B., for the State of ——, and that your petitioner, or any other person, had no power to prevent him from doing so, &c. [*setting forth the facts showing the illegal confinement or custody, and that the party confined will be carried out of the State, or suffer some irreparable injury before the can be relieved by habeas corpus or certiorari*]. E. F.

O. F., Attorney.

[*Add verification as in No.* 205].

AFFIDAVIT TO ACCOMPANY THE ABOVE PETITION.

County of ——, ss.

R. S., of ——, in said county, being duly sworn, deposes and says: He is acquainted with A. B. and G. H., mentioned in the annexed petition. That, *&c.* [*setting forth facts in corroboration of the facts stated in the petition*].

Sworn to, *&c.* R. S.

No. 212.

WARRANT UNDER THE LAST FORM.

See ante, Vol. I., p. 374.

To C. D., Sheriff of the County of ——, [*or*, to any Constable of the County of ——.]

Whereas, E. F. has applied to me for a warrant to take A. B., alleged to be illegally confined by [*or*, in the custody of] G. H.; and whereas it appears from the proofs before me on such application, that, *&c.* [*recite the facts showing the illegal confinement or custody, and that the party will probably be carried out of the State, or that he will suffer some irreparable injury before he can be relieved*].

From which facts it satisfactorily appears to me that the said A. B. is held in illegal confinement [*or*, custody], by the said G. H., and that there is good reason to believe that he will be carried out of the State [*or*, that he will suffer some irreparable injury], before he can be relieved by the issuing of a habeas corpus or certiorari.

These are, therefore, in the name of the People of the State of New York, to authorize and command you forthwith to take the said A. B. (*a*) and bring him before me, to be dealt with according to law.

Given under my hand and seal, at the village of ——, in said county, this —— day of ——, A. D. 18—.

[*Signature and Seal of Judge.*]

O. F., Attorney.

(*a*) The warrant may also direct the arrest of the party illegally confining the prisoner, where the facts justify it. See 2 *Rev. Stat.* 572, *sec.* 66, *ante*, *p.* 374.

No. 213.

ATTACHMENT FOR DISOBEDIENCE TO WRIT.

See ante, Vol. I., p. 375.

To the Sheriff of the County of ——.

It appearing satisfactorily to me on oath, that G. H., to whom a writ of habeas corpus [*or*, certiorari] was directed and delivered, commanding him to bring before me A. B., in the said writ named, has neglected [*or*, refused] to obey the said writ according to the command thereof, by not producing the said A. B. before me, and also by not making a return [*or*, a full and explicit return] to such writ within the time limited by law; and no sufficient excuse having been shown for such neglect [*or*, refusal];

These are, therefore, to authorize and command you, in the name of the People of the State of New York, forthwith to arrest the said G. H., and to bring him immediately before me at my office in the village of ——, in said county.

Given under my hand and seal, at —— aforesaid, on the —— day of ——, 18—. [*Signature and Seal of Judge*].

O. F., Attorney.

No. 214.

COMMITMENT FOR DISOBEDIENCE TO WRIT.

See ante, Vol. I., p. 375.

To the Sheriff of the County of ——.

Whereas, G. H. has been brought before me on a warrant issued by me, stating that the said G. H., &c. [*recite the warrant, as in last form.*]

And whereas, the said G. H. still refuses to obey the said writ of habeas corpus, by producing the body of the said A. B., as therein required, and by not making a return [*or*, a full and explicit return] to such writ of habeas corpus [*or*, certiorari].

These are therefore to authorize and command you, in the name of the People of the State of New York, forthwith to convey the said G. H. to the jail of said county, and there commit him to close custody in such jail, without being allowed the liberties thereof, there to remain until he shall make return to the writ in such warrant mentioned, and also comply with my order this day made, wherein the said G. H. &c. [*state what the order is in relation to the person for whose relief the writ has been issued*].

Given under my hand and seal, at, &c., the —— day of ——, 18—.

[*Signature and Seal of Judge.*]

O. F., Attorney.

No. 215.

PRECEPT FOR PARTY ILLEGALLY CONFINED OR RESTRAINED.

See ante, Vol. I., p. 376.

To the Sheriff of the County of ——.

Whereas, a writ of habeas corpus has heretofore been issued by me, directed to G. H., in which he was commanded to have the body of A. B., by him imprisoned and detained, as it was said, together with the time and cause of such imprisonment, and which writ has been duly served upon the said G. H.; and, whereas, the said G. H. has neglected [*or*, refused] to produce the body of the said A. B., according to the command of said writ; and for which neglect [*or*, refusal] an attachment has been issued against the said G. H.

These are therefore to command you, in the name of the People of the State of New York, forthwith to bring before me the said A. B., at my office in the village of ——, in said county.

O. F., Attorney. [*Signature and Seal of Judge.*]

No. 216

RETURN TO HABEAS CORPUS.

See ante, Vol. I., p. 376.

The return of C. D., Sheriff of the County of ——, to the writ of habeas corpus hereto annexed.

In obedience to the writ of habeas corpus hereto annexed, I do hereby certify and return to the Supreme Court [*or other court or officer allowing the writ*], (*) that before the coming of the said writ to me, to wit, on the —— day of ——, 18—, at the village [*or*, city] of ——, the said A. B., mentioned in said writ, was placed in my custody by virtue of an execution [*or*, commitment] issued, *&c.* [*state the cause of imprisonment*], a copy of which warrant is hereto annexed; and that the said A. B. is now in my custody under the said execution [*or*, commitment].

All which I certify, and have here the body of the said A. B., as by the said writ I am commanded.

Dated, *&c.* C. D., Sheriff.

ANOTHER FORM—PARTY NOT IN HIS CUSTODY.

[*Same as last form to the asterisk* (*), *and then proceed:*] That neither at the time of the allowance of the said writ, nor at any time since, was the said A. B. in my custody or restrained by me of his liberty; wherefore I cannot have his body before the said court [*or*, officer], as by the said writ I am commanded.

C. D., Sheriff.

[*Unless the person making the return is a sworn public officer, and shall make such return in his official capacity, it must be verified substantially as follows:*]

County of ——, ss. G. H., above named, being duly sworn, says, that the above return, subscribed by him, is true to his own knowledge, except as to the matters therein stated on information and belief, and as to those matters he believes it to be true.

No. 217.

NOTICE TO PARTY INTERESTED, OF THE TIME AND PLACE WRIT IS RETURNABLE.

See ante, Vol. I., p. 377.

To A. G. [*or*, To O. F. D., Esq., Attorney for A. G.].

SIR: You will please take notice that a writ of habeas corpus [*or*, certiorari] has been issued by the Supreme Court [*or other court or officer, as the case may be*], to inquire into the cause of the imprisonment of A. B., now confined in the jail of —— county, under process in which you have, or claim [*or*, the said A. G. has or, claims] some interest; and that the said writ is made returnable before the said court [*or*, officer,] at the Court House, [*or*, at his office], in the village of ——, in said county, on the —— day of —— instant, at 10 o'clock A. M.

Dated, *&c.* Yours, &c.,

L. P. C., Attorney for A. B.

No. 218.

LIKE NOTICE TO DISTRICT ATTORNEY.

See ante, Vol. I., p. 378.

To A. L. M., Esq., District Attorney of the County of ——.

SIR: You will take notice that a writ of habeas corpus [*or*, certiorari] has been issued by the Supreme Court [*or other court, or officer, as the case may be*], to inquire into the cause of the imprisonment of A. B., now confined in the jail of said county under a criminal accusation; and that the said writ is made returnable before the said court [*or*, officer], at the Court House [*or*, at his office], in the village of ——, in said county, forthwith [*or*, on the —— day of —— inst. at 10 o'clock A. M.]

Dated, *&c.*, Yours &c.,

L. P. C., Attorney for A. B.

No. 219.

WRIT OF DISCHARGE.

See ante, Vol. I., p. 379.

To the Sheriff of the County of ——.

It appearing, on the return of the writ of habeas corpus [*or*, certiorari] allowed by me, that A. B. is illegally imprisoned [*or*, detained] by you, I do therefore command you, forthwith to discharge him from your custody.

Given under my hand and seal, this —— day of ——, 18—.

[*Signature and Seal of Officer.*]

No. 220.

ORDER DIRECTING PRISONER TO BE REMANDED.

See ante, Vol. I., p. 381.

Whereas, A. B. has been brought before me on a writ of habeas corpus, directed to you, for the purpose of inquiring into the cause of his imprisonment. And whereas, it appears from the return to said writ that the said A. B. is legally detained in custody, by virtue of an execution issued upon a final judgment rendered in the Supreme Court [*or other court*,] in favor of A. G., as plaintiff, against the said A. B., as defendant, [*or*, by virtue of a commitment for a contempt issued by the —— Court, in which commitment the said contempt is specially and plainly charged, the said court having authority to commit for the contempt so charged *or otherwise, as the case may be.*]

It is therefore ordered that the said A. B. be, and he is hereby, remanded to his former imprisonment under the execution [*or*, commitment] aforesaid.

Dated, *&c.* [*Signature of Judge.*]

No. 221.

TRAVERSE OR DENIAL OF RETURN.

See ante, Vol. I., pp. 383 to 388.

Before Hon. C. L. A., *&c.*

In the matter
of
A. B.

The said A. B., in answer to the return of C. D., sheriff of the county of ——, denies that, *&c.* [*set forth the allegations which the defendant wishes to deny*].

And the said A. B., in further answering said return, shows: That, *&c.* [*allege the facts, to show either that the imprisonment or detention is unlawful, or that the party is entitled to his discharge*].

A. B.

County of ——, ss.: A. B., above named, being duly sworn, says that he has read the above answer, subscribed by him, and knows the contents thereof, and that the same is true to his own knowledge, except as to the matters therein stated on information and belief, and as to those matters he believes it to be true.

Sworn, *&c.* A. B.

No. 222.

BAIL BOND.

See ante, Vol. I., pp. 392, 398.

County of ——, ss.: Be it remembered that, on the —— day of ——, 18—, J. S., of ——, in said county, and J. N., farmer, and S. S., merchant, of the same place, personally appeared before [*name of officer*], and severally and respectively acknowledged themselves to be indebted to the People of the State of New York in the sum of —— dollars, to be levied of their respective goods and chattels, lands and tenements, to the use of the said people, if default shall be made in the condition following:

Whereas, the above-named J. S. is in the custody of the sheriff of said county, under a commitment from ——, a justice of the peace for the town of ——, in said county, from which commitment it appears that the said J. S. is charged with the crime of grand larceny, committed within said county.

Now, therefore, the condition of this recognizance is such, that, if the said J. S. shall personally appear at the next Court of Sessions [*or*, Court of Oyer and Terminer], to be held in and for said county of ——, then and there to answer to an indictment to be preferred against him for the said offense, and to do further and receive what shall, by the said court, be then and there enjoined upon him, and shall not depart the said court without leave; then this recognizance to be void; otherwise to remain in full force and virtue. [*Signatures.*]

Taken, subscribed, and acknowledged before me, by the said J. S., J. N., and S. S., the day and year first above written.

C. L. A., Justice of Sup. Court.

No. 223.

ORDER ON RETURN TO CERTIORARI, THAT THE PRISONER BE BAILED.

See ante, Vol. I., p. 398.

It appearing to me, upon the return to the writ of certiorari issued by me on the —— day of ——, 18—, that A. B., in whose behalf the said writ was issued, is detained in the custody of the sheriff of the county of ——, under a commitment in which the said A. B. is charged with the offense of grand larceny, and that the said A. B. is entitled to bail, it is therefore ordered by me, that the said A. B. be held to bail for his appearance at the next Court of Sessions [*or*, Court of Oyer and Terminer], to be held in and for the county of ——, in the sum of —— dollars.

And it is further ordered by me, that upon such bail being entered into, in conformity to this order and the provisions of law, that the said A. B. be discharged. [*Signature of Judge.*]

No. 224.

RECOGNIZANCE UNDER THE LAST FORM.

See ante, Vol. I., p. 398.

[*Same substantially as in No.* 222; *and for forms of Affidavits of Sureties, see No.* 261.]

No. 226.

AFFIDAVIT FOR HABEAS CORPUS AD TESTIFICANDUM.

See ante, Vol. I., p, 405.

[*Title of the action, or proceeding.*]

County of ——, ss. A. B., the plaintiff [*or*, defendant] above named, being duly sworn, says: That this action is brought upon a promissory note executed by, *&c.* [*describe cause of action*]. That the defense to said action is as follows [*set forth briefly the nature of the defense*].

And deponent further says, that E. F., who is now a prisoner in the custody of the sheriff of the county of ——, under execution upon final judgment in favor of K. L., is and will be a material witness for this deponent on the trial of the said action, as he is advised by J. G., Esq., residing at ——, in said county, his counsel in this action, and verily believes; and that he cannot safely proceed to the trial of this action without the testimony of the said E. F., as he is also advised by his said counsel and verily believes.

And deponent further says: That this action is noticed for trial at a Circuit Court to be held at the Court House in ——, in the county of ——, on the —— day of —— instant.

Sworn, *&c.* A. B.

No. 227.

WRIT OF HABEAS CORPUS AD TESTIFICANDUM.

See ante, Vol. I., p. 406.

[*Seal.*] The People of the State of New York, to the Sheriff of the County of ——, greeting:

We command you that you have the body of E. F., detained in our prison under your custody, as it is said, under safe and secure conduct, before our Supreme Court, at a Circuit Court [*or*, before our county court of the county of ——], to be held at the Court House in ——, on the —— day of —— inst., by ten o'clock A. M. of that day [*or*, forthwith], then and there to testify the truth, according to his knowledge, in a certain action, now depending in the said court, then and there to be tried between A. B., plaintiff, and C. D., defendant, on the part of the plaintiff [*or*, defendant]. And immediately after the said E. F. shall then and there have given his testimony, in the said action, that you return him, the said E. F., to our said prison under safe and secure conduct. And have you then there this writ.

Witness, C. L. A., one of the justices of our said court, the —— day of ——, 18—.

N. B. M., Clerk.

L. P. C., Attorney.

[*Indorsed*:] Allowed this —— day of ——, 18—.

C. L. A., Justice Sup. Court.

No. 228.

BOND ON SERVICE OF WRIT.

See ante, Vol. I., p. 407.

[*Same as in No.* 210, *except in reciting the character of the writ.*]

CHAPTER XIII.

FORMS IN PROCEEDINGS BY AND AGAINST INFANTS.

I. Forms on Appointment of Guardian by Supreme Court.

No. 229.

PETITION FOR APPOINTMENT OF GENERAL GUARDIAN BY SUPREME COURT; INFANT OVER FOURTEEN YEARS OF AGE.

See ante, Vol. I., p. 424.

To the Supreme Court of the State of New York.

The petition of R. H. respectfully shows: That he resides in the town of ——, in the county of ——, is the son of W. H., late of the town of ——, in said county, deceased, and is of the age of about sixteen years. That as heir at law of his said father, your petitioner is seized of, and entitled to an estate in fee in and to a certain piece or parcel of land, containing about —— acres, situated in said town of ——, the gross income of which is about —— dollars per year; also in and to a certain house and lot situated in the village [*or*, city] of —— in the county of ——, the gross income of which is about —— dollars per year. That your petitioner is also the owner of the following personal estate [*describe it generally, giving the value thereof*].

Your petitioner further shows, that he has no other property, real or personal, nor any right or interest in other property than that above mentioned, according to his knowledge or belief. That on account of his inability to protect his rights and interests, he is desirous of having some suitable and proper person appointed by the court to take charge thereof.

Your petitioner, therefore, prays that B. H., of the town of ——, *&c.*, who is the mother of your petitioner, may be appointed the general guardian of his person and estate, upon her giving security for the faithful performance of her trust as such guardian, according to the statute, and in conformity with the rules and practice of the court.

Dated, *&c.*, R. H.

[*Add verification substantially as in No.* 1.]

CONSENT OF PROPOSED GUARDIAN.

I hereby consent to be appointed the general guardian of the above-named R. H., and I offer, as my sureties, T. C. and R. C., both of the town [*or*, city] of ——, in the county of ——.

Dated, *&c.* B. H.

No. 230.

LIKE PETITION—INFANT UNDER THE AGE OF FOURTEEN YEARS.

See ante, Vol. I., p. 424.

To the Supreme Court of the State of New York.

The petition of A. H., of the town of, &c., respectfully shows: That your petitioner is the mother of M. A. H., an infant under the age of fourteen years, and is the widow of W. H., late of said town of ——, deceased. That as the heir at law of her said father, the said W. H., deceased, the said infant is seized of and entitled to an estate in fee in and to a certain house and lot situated in the town of, &c., the gross income of which is about —— dollars per year. That she is also the owner of the following personal property [*describe the personal property generally, giving the value thereof*].

Your petitioner further shows that the said infant has no other property, real or personal, nor any right or interest in other property than that above mentioned, according to your petitioner's best knowledge or belief. That on account of the said infant's inability to protect her own rights and interest, your petitioner is desirous of having some suitable and proper person appointed by the court to take charge thereof.

Your petitioner, therefore, prays that she may be appointed the general guardian of the person and estate of the said infant, upon giving security for the faithful performance of her trust as such guardian, according to the statute, and in conformity with the rules and practice of the court.

Dated, &c. A. H.

[*Add verification, substantially as in No.* 1.]

No. 231.

ORDER OF REFERENCE.

See ante, Vol. I., p. 424.

At a special term, &c. [*as in No.* 6].

SUPREME COURT.

In the matter of the petition of R. H., an infant, for the appointment of a general guardian.

On reading and filing the petition of R. H., an infant over the age of fourteen years, dated the —— day of ——, 18—, praying for the appointment of a general guardian of his person and estate; and on motion of L. P. C., of counsel for the petitioner, it is ordered that it be referred to W. E., Esq., of, &c., to ascertain the truth of the matters stated in said petition, and particularly, by inspection or otherwise, to ascertain the age of the said infant R. H., and if of the age of fourteen years, or upward, to examine him as to his voluntary nomination of a suitable and proper person as guardian. And if the said infan be under the age of fourteen years, the referee shall ascertain who is entitled to the guardianship, and shall name a suitable and proper person as guardian. The said referee is also required to ascertain the amount or value of the personal property, and the gross amount or value of the rents and profits of the real estate of the infant during his minority; and also to ascertain the sufficiency of the security offered by the guardian. And the said referee, in his discretion, may direct notice to be given to such of the relatives of the infant as he may think proper, to appear before him and be heard in relation to the application. The said referee is directed, also, to pass upon the security to be given by the guardian under the 65th Rule of this court; and, in doing so, shall state that each of the persons proposed as sureties for such guardian and for the performance of his duties, is worth the requisite amount over and above all his debts, or that the real estate proposed to be given as security is of the value required by such 65th rule, and that the same is unincumbered.

No. 232.

REFEREE'S REPORT THEREON.

See ante, Vol. I., p. 426.

[*Title, as in last form.*]

To the Supreme Court of the State of New York.

In pursuance of an order of this court in the above-entitled matter, dated the —— day of ——, 18—, whereby it was referred to the undersigned, as referee to, *&c.* [*state the substance of the order of reference*], I, the subscriber, referee aforesaid, do certify and report that, having been attended by the said infant and by his attorney, I proceeded to make such inquiries and examination as the said order required, having previously directed notice to be given to the mother of the said infant with whom he resides, and to, *&c.*, to appear before me if they desired to be heard in relation to the said application, and required the attendance of such witnesses as appeared to me to be necessary to give testimony on the subject of such application.

I do further report that from an inspection of the said infant, as well as from the testimony of B. H., his mother, taken before me, I am satisfied the age of the said infant is about fifteen years; that I examined him as to his nomination of a guardian, and that he voluntarily nominated his mother, the said B. H., to be his general guardian; and that I am of opinion the said B. H. is a suitable and proper person to be appointed such guardian.

I further report that the personal property of the said infant consists of about —— dollars in money, and bonds and mortgages of the amount or value of about —— dollars; and that the gross amount or value of the rents and profits of the real estate of the said infant is about —— dollars per year; and that the aggregate amount of such rents and profits during his minority will be about —— dollars.

And I further report that the said proposed guardian should be required to give security in the sum of —— dollars; and that she has offered T. C. and R. C., of, *&c.*, as her sureties, and having taken from each of them an affidavit as to his sufficiency, and made inquiries relative thereto, I am satisfied that the sureties so offered are sufficient; and I certify that each of said sureties is worth the sum of —— dollars over and above all his debts, and exclusive of property exempt by law from levy and sale on execution.

All which is respectfully submitted.

Dated, *&c.* W. E., Referee.

No. 233.

ORDER APPOINTING GENERAL GUARDIAN.

See ante, Vol. I, p. 426.

At a special term, *&c.* [*as in No.* 6].

[*Title as in No.* 231.]

On reading and filing the report of W. E., Esq., the referee in this matter, appointed by an order of this court, dated the —— day of ——, 18—, and which report is dated the —— day of ——, 18—, from which report it appears to the court that B. H. is a suitable and proper person to be appointed guardian of the person and estate of the above-named R. H., that the said proposed guardian should give security in the sum of —— dollars, and that T. C. and R. C., proposed sureties for the said B. H., are each worth the requisite sum and are sufficient.

Now, on motion of L. P. C., of counsel for the said infant, it is ordered that the said B. H. be and she hereby is appointed general guardian of the person and estate of the said infant upon her executing a bond to the said infant, with the said T. C. and R. C. as her sureties, in the penal sum of —— dollars, conditioned that the said B. H. shall faithfully perform her trust as such guardian, and file an inventory of the estate of the said infant within six months after her appointment, and render the annual inventory or account of her guardianship, required to be rendered and filed by the practice of the court; that she shall observe and obey all the general rules of the court respecting general guardians, and such orders as shall be made by the court from time to time in relation to such trust; and that she shall render a just and true account of all moneys and property of said infant, which shall come to her hands as such general guardian, and of the application thereof, and of her guardianship generally before any court having jurisdiction, whenever she shall be thereunto lawfully required.

It is further ordered that the execution of such bond be acknowledged for proved, and that the sureties therein justify in the usual manner; and that the said bond be approved as to its form and manner of execution by one of the justices of this court, to be signified by his approval indorsed thereon, and be filed in the office of the clerk of this court.

No. 234.

BOND OF GUARDIAN.

See ante, Vol. I., p. 427.

Know all men by these presents, that we, B. H., T. C., and R. C., of, *&c.*, are held and firmly bound unto R. H., an infant, son of the late ——, of, *&c.*, deceased, in the sum of —— dollars, to be paid to the said R. H., his heirs, executors, administrators, or assigns; for which payment, well and truly to be made, we bind ourselves, our heirs, executors, and administrators, jointly and severally, firmly by these presents. Sealed with our seals, and dated the —— day of ——, one thousand eight hundred and ——. (*)

Whereas, by an order of the Supreme Court of the State of New York, made on the —— day of ——, 18—, the above-bounden B. H. was appointed the general guardian of the person and estate of the above-named R. H., an infant under the age of twenty-one years, upon her executing a bond to the said R. H., with the said T. C. and R. C. as her sureties, in the penalty and upon the condition therein mentioned.

Now, therefore, the condition of this obligation is such, that if the above-bounden B. H. shall faithfully perform her trust as such guardian, and shall file an inventory of the estate of the said infant, within six months after her appointment, and render the annual inventory and account of her guardianship required to be rendered and filed by the practice of the said court, and shall observe and obey all the general rules of the said court respecting general guardians, and such orders as shall be made from time to time by the said court in relation to such trust, and if she shall render a just and true account of all moneys and property of said infant which shall come to her hands as such general guardian, and of the application thereof, and of her guardianship generally, before any court having jurisdiction, whenever she shall be thereunto lawfully required, then this obligation to be void; otherwise to be and remain in full force and virtue.

B. H.
Sealed and delivered T. C.
in presence of S. T. R. C.

[*Add acknowledgement, and affidavit of sureties, as in No.* 261.]

APPROVAL [*to be indorsed on bond*].

I approve of the within bond as to its form and manner of execution.

W. H. L., Justice Supreme Court.

Dated, *&c.*

II. Forms on Appointment of Guardian by Surrogate.

No. 235.

PETITION FOR APPOINTMENT OF GENERAL GUARDIAN BY SURROGATE—MINOR OVER FOURTEEN YEARS OF AGE.

See ante, Vol. I., p. 430.

To the Surrogate of the County of Washington.

The petition of R. H. respectfully shows: That your petitioner is a minor over the age of fourteen years, to wit: of the age of sixteen years and three months, as he verily believes. That your petitioner is a resident of the town of Salem, in said county, and is the son of B. H., late of the same place, deceased. That the said B. H. departed this life on the —— day of ——, 18—, without having appointed any guardian for your petitioner, either by deed or will, to his knowledge or belief. That your petitioner is seized of real estate, the rents and profits of which are worth —— dollars per year, and that he is possessed of personal estate of the value of —— dollars, as he is informed and believes.

Your petitioner further shows, that he is desirous that a guardian should be appointed of his person and estate during his minority, and for that purpose nominates L. F., of said town of Salem, an attorney and counselor of the Supreme Court, and aged about —— years, to be such guardian. That the said L. F. is a proper and suitable person to be appointed such guardian; and that he has consented to act in that capacity, if appointed, and to give the requisite security.

Your petitioner, therefore, prays that the said surrogate will inquire into the circumstances above stated, and grant the prayer of the said petition.

Dated, *&c.* R. H.

County of Washington, ss.: J. H., being duly sworn, deposes and says: He is acquainted with the above-named R. H., and was present and saw him subscribe his name to the foregoing petition.

Sworn, *&c.* J. H.

CONSENT OF GUARDIAN.

I hereby consent to act as guardian of the person and estate of R. H., the minor named in the foregoing petition, if I should be appointed for that purpose. L. F.

In the presence of

T. C.

County of Washington, ss.: T. C., being duly sworn, deposes and says: He is acquainted with L. F., named in the foregoing petition, and was present and saw him subscribe his name to the above consent.

Sworn, *&c.* T. C.

No. 236.

LIKE PETITION—INFANT UNDER FOURTEEN YEARS OF AGE.

See ante, Vol. I., p. 430.

To the Surrogate of the County of Washington.

The petition of A. H., of, *&c.*, respectfully shows: That B. H., late of the town of ——, in said county, departed this life on the —— day of ——, 18—, without having appointed, by deed or will, any guardian for his children, to the knowledge or belief of your petitioner. That the said deceased left two children, under the age of fourteen years, to wit: J. H., aged —— years, and S. H., aged —— years, both of whom are now residents of said town of ——. That the said infants are seized in fee-simple as tenants in common of a farm in said town, consisting of about —— acres of land, and worth —— dollars, the annual rents and profits of which are —— dollars. That the said infants are also the owners of considerable personal property, and which is of the value of —— dollars, as your petitioner believes.

Your petitioner further shows, that the relatives of said infants, residing in said county, are your petitioner, who is the paternal uncle of said infants; B. R. H., the mother of said infants, with whom they now reside, in —— aforesaid; and O. H. and S. T., cousins of the said infants, residing in the same place. That the said infants have no other relatives residing in said county to the knowledge or belief of your petitioner.

Your petitioner prays that L. F. may be appointed the guardian of the person and estate of said infants, until they arrive at the age of fourteen years, respectively, and until another guardian shall be appointed; and that a day may be assigned for the hearing of said matter, and that an order may be entered, directing notice to be given of such hearing to the relatives of said infants, residing in said county.

That the said L. F. is a suitable and proper person to be appointed guardian for said infants, and he has consented to act as such, if appointed, and to give the requisite security.

Dated, *&c.* A. H.

County of ——, ss.: A. H., the petitioner above named, being duly sworn, says: That the matters of fact alleged in the foregoing petition are true, according to the best of his knowledge and belief.

Sworn, *&c.* A. H.

[*Annex consent of guardian, as in the last form.*]

No. 242.

AFFIDAVIT OF MINOR'S PROPERTY.

See ante, Vol. I., p. 430.

County of Washington, ss.: T. C., of, *&c.*, being duly sworn, deposes and says: He is acquainted with R. H., the minor named in the annexed petition; that the said R. H. is the son of B. H., late of ——, deceased, and is of the age of sixteen years and three months, as he verily believes.

And this deponent further says, that the said R. H. is a resident of ——, in said county of Washington; that the said R. H. is seized in fee-simple of a certain farm, consisting of —— acres of land, situated in said town of ——, upon which land there is a dwelling-house, several barns, and necessary out-buildings; that the said farm, with its appurtenances, is worth about the sum of —— dollars, and that the rents and profits thereof are about —— dollars per year; that the said R. H. is the owner of personal property of the value of —— dollars, which personal property is composed of the following items, viz.:

Ten shares of stock in the —— Insurance Company, worth	$1,250
A bond and mortgage on real estate in the county of ——, on which is due $——, and which is worth	3,000
Twelve cows, worth	600
One hundred sheep, worth	325
And household furniture, worth	750
Total	$5,925

And deponent further says, that he is acquainted with L. F., the person nominated by the said minor as guardian; that the said L. F. is the uncle of the said R. H., and is a proper and suitable person to act as guardian for the said R. H., as he believes.

Sworn, *&c.* T. C.

No. 243.

ORDER DIRECTING APPOINTMENT OF GUARDIAN.

See ante, Vol. I., p. 431.

In the matter of the guardianship of the person and estate of R. H., a minor.

On reading and filing the petition of R. H., a minor, showing that he is the son of ——, late of ——, deceased, and is aged fifteen years and three months, and is a resident of ——, in said county, and is seized and possessed of certain real and personal property therein mentioned, and nominating

L. F., of, *&c.*, to be appointed guardian of the person and estate of the said minor; and on reading and filing the consent in writing of the said L. F. to act as such guardian, if appointed; and the affidavit of T. C., annexed to the said petition, showing the circumstances of the said minor: It is ordered that the said L. F. be appointed guardian of the person and estate of the said R. H., during his minority, on his entering into a bond to the said minor, with sufficient security, to be approved of by the surrogate, in the penal sum of —— dollars; conditioned that the said L. F. will faithfully, in all things, discharge the duty of a guardian to the said minor, according to law, and that he will render a true and just account of all moneys and property received by him, and of the application thereof, and of his guardianship in all respects, to any court having cognizance thereof, when thereunto required.

No. 244.

BOND OF GUARDIAN.

See ante, Vol. I., p. 433.

[*Same substantially as in No.* 234, *to the* (*), *and then proceed:*]

The condition of this obligation is such that, if the above-bounden L. F. shall faithfully, in all things, discharge the duty of a guardian to the above-named R. H., minor, according to law, and shall render a true and just account of all moneys and property received by him, and of the application thereof, and of his guardianship in all respects, to any court having cognizance thereof, when thereunto required, then this obligation to be void, otherwise to remain in full force and virtue.

Sealed and delivered in presence of [*Signatures.*]

[*Add acknowledgment and affidavit of surety or sureties, as in No.* 261.]

APPROVAL [*to be indorsed on bond*].

I approve of the surety [*or*, sureties] in the within bond.

Dated, *&c.* U. G. P., Surrogate.

No. 245.

ORDER APPOINTING GUARDIAN ON FILING BOND, ETC.

See ante, Vol. I., p. 433.

[*Title, as in No.* 243.]

L. F. having produced the bond required by the former order in this matter, duly executed, with security, approved by the surrogate. Now on filing the said bond, and the affidavit of justification thereto annexed, it is ordered that the same be approved, and that the said L. F. be appointed guardian of the person and estate of the said R. H., during his minority, and that the appointment be made out and recorded forthwith in the book provided for that purpose.

No. 246.

LETTERS OF GUARDIANSHIP.

See ante, Vol. I., p. 433.

The People of the State of New York, by the grace of God, free and independent,

To L. F., of, *&c.*, send greeting:

Whereas, an application in due form of law has been made to our surrogate of our county of ——, to have you, the said L. F., appointed the guardian of the person and estate of R. H., a minor, residing in ——, of the age of fourteen years; and whereas you, the said L. F., have consented to become such guardian, and have duly executed and delivered a bond, pursuant to law, for the faithful discharge of your duty as such guardian; and we being satisfied of the sufficiency of the said bond, and that you, the said L. F., are a good and respectable person, and in every respect competent to have the custody of the person and estate of said minor, do, by these presents, allow, constitute, and appoint you, the said L. F., the general guardian of the person and estate of said minor, during his minority, hereby requiring you, the said guardian, to do and perform all the matters and things required by law of such guardian, and to render an account of all moneys and property received by you, and of the application thereof, and of your guardianship in all respects, to any court having cognizance thereof, when thereunto required.

In testimony whereof, we have caused the seal of office of our [L. S.] said surrogate to be hereunto affixed. Witness, U. G. P., surrogate of our said county, at Sandy Hill, in said county, the —— day of ——, 18—.

U. G. P., Surrogate.

[*Annex to the letters a copy of the* 57*th section of chapter* 460 *of the Laws of* 1837, *which is as follows:*]

"§ 57. Every general guardian appointed by the surrogate shall, annually after such appointment, so long as any part of the estate or the income or proceeds thereof remain in his hands or under his control, file in the office of the surrogate appointing him an inventory and account, under oath, of his guardianship and of the amount of property received by him and remaining in his hands, or invested by him, and the manner and nature of such investment, and his receipts and expenditures in form of debtor and creditor."

III. Forms in Reference to Duties, Accountability, and Removal of Guardians.

No. 247.

GUARDIAN'S INVENTORY AND ACCOUNT CURRENT.

See ante, Vol. I., p. 440; and see also Ch. Court Rules, 1844, p. 169, and Rules of Supreme Court in Eq., 1847, p. 102.

Supreme Court.

In the matter of the guardianship of R. H., an infant.

INVENTORY.

A just and true inventory of the whole real and personal estate of the above-named infant, R. H., committed to the care of B. H., his guardian, showing the manner in which the funds are invested, the income thereof, &c., &c.

A farm of 100 acres of land, situated in the town of ——, in the county of ——, estimated to be worth about $50 per acre	$5,000
This farm is now occupied by J. D., under lease, at the annual rent of	300
A bond and mortgage for $3,000, executed by C. E., and covering lands in the town of —— aforesaid, worth double the amount of the mortgage, and upon which there is no other incumbrance, the annual income from which is	210

B. H., Guardian.

[*Proceed in like manner in respect to other items.*]

ACCOUNT CURRENT.

The Estate of R. H., an infant, to B. H., guardian *Dr.*

1864.		
May 2.	To cash paid M. Low's bill for board and lodging of said infant, from Jan. 1, to this date	$75 00
June 4.	To Dr. Jones' bill for medical attendance	9 17

[*Proceed in like manner with the other items.*]

CONTRA.

1865.		*Cr.*
Jan. 1.	By balance due as by last annual account	$27 32
April 1.	By cash received, six months' rent on farm of J. D.	150 00

[*Continue with the items as before, and foot up the columns, so as to show the balance due the estate, if any.*]

Dated, &c.

B. H., Guardian.

City and county of ——, ss. B. H., the general guardian of the above-named infant, being duly sworn, says: That the above is a just and true inventory of the whole real and personal estate and effects of the above-named infant, so far as the same have come to her knowledge; and a just and true account of all the receipts and disbursements on account of the said estate [since this deponent rendered her last account current in this matter]. [*In the original or first account, the words within the brackets are to be omitted.*]

Sworn, *&c.* B. H.

No. 248.

PETITION CALLING GENERAL GUARDIAN TO ACCOUNT.

See ante, Vol. I., p. 441.

[*Title as in last form.*]

To the Supreme Court of the State of New York.

The petition of A. B., an infant, by his next friend, L. P. C., respectfully shows: That your petitioner is an infant of the age of —— years, and resides with his mother, in the town of ——, *&c.* That by an order of the Supreme Court, dated, *&c.*, and duly entered in the clerk's office of the county of ——, C. D., of, *&c.*, was appointed general guardian of said infant, on his executing and filing with the clerk of said county the security mentioned in said order, duly approved by a justice of this court; which security was so executed and approved, and on the —— day of ——, 18—, the said security was duly filed with the said clerk, and thereupon the said guardian entered upon the duties of his said trust, and took into his possession all the estate, property, and effects, of his said ward. (*)

That shortly after his appointment, and on the —— day of ——, 18—, the said guardian filed in said clerk's office an inventory of the said infant's estate, showing that personal property, to the amount of $ ——, consisting of [*state the kind of property, giving the items thereof*], had come to his possession. That the said guardian has not, since then, filed any inventory or account current, and has not rendered any account of his guardianship,—but, although often requested, refuses so to do.

That the said guardian has received the whole of the income and profits of said infant's estate, amounting in the aggregate up to the present time, as your petitioner believes, to the sum of ——— dollars, that, *&c.*, [*set out the cause of complaint against the guardian, and the facts showing his liability to account*].

Wherefore your petitioner prays, that the said guardian may be required to account with your petitioner for the trust fund and property in his hands, as aforesaid; and that a referee may be appointed to take and state his accounts, according to the practice of the court; and that the said guardian be charged in his accounts with the costs of these proceedings; or for such further or other relief as the court shall think proper to grant.

Dated, *&c.* A. B.

by L. P. C., his next friend.

[*Add verification, substantially as in No.* 1].

No. 249.

NOTICE TO GUARDIAN.

See ante, Vol. I., p. 441.

[*Title as in No.* 247.]

To C. D., Guardian.

Take notice, that upon the petition, with a copy whereof you are herewith served, a motion will be made at, *&c.*, on, *&c.*, that the prayer of the said petition be granted, and also for an order of reference to take an account of the trust fund and property in your hands, as guardian of the said A. B., infant above named; or for such further or other order as the court may think proper to grant. Yours, &c.,

Dated, *&c.* T. C., Att'y for Petitioner.

No. 250.

ORDER OF REFERENCE DIRECTING AN ACCOUNTING.

See ante, Vol. I., p. 442.

At a special term, *&c.* [*as in No.* 6].

[*Title as in No.* 247.]

On reading and filing the petition of A. B., an infant, by L. P. C., his next friend, duly verified, and bearing date the —— day of ——, 18—, and due proof of the service of notice of the presentation thereof, upon C. D., the general guardian of said infant, and on motion of T. C., the attorney for the petitioner, no one appearing in opposition thereto, [*or*, after hearing J. W. F., of counsel for the said C. D.], it is ordered (*) that the said C. D. forthwith account for the trust funds and property in his hands as guardian of said infant; and that it be referred to L. F., Esq., of, *&c*, as referee, to take and state such account, and report thereon to the said court with all convenient speed [and that the said guardian be charged in his accounts with the costs of these proceedings, now here adjusted at —— dollars].

No. 251.

REPORT OF REFEREE.

See ante, Vol. I., p. 443.

[*Title as in No.* 247.]

To the Supreme Court of the State of New York.

The undersigned, referee, to whom it was referred by an order of this court, dated the —— day of ——, 18—, to take and state an account of the trust funds and property remaining in the hands of C. D., as guardian of the said infant A. B., respectfully reports: (*)

That I caused notice to be given to the said guardian to appear before me, and submit his inventory and account of said trust funds and property, duly verified, and his papers and vouchers in support thereof. That the said guardian accordingly appeared before me with said inventory and account, *&c.*, and that the same are hereto annexed, marked schedule A.

I further report, that on such hearing, having examined the said guardian on oath, and witnesses produced by him, touching the said account and the items thereof, and his said papers and vouchers, I proceeded to take and state such account, and to ascertain the balance of such trust fund and property remaining in said guardian's hands; and that the schedule hereto annexed, marked schedule B, is an exhibit of said account so taken and stated by me, making all just allowances to said guardian for his disbursements, fees, and commissions relative to his said trust; and for all payments and expenditures properly chargeable thereon; and that my fees as referee in this matter are —— dollars.

All which is respectfully submitted.

Dated, *&c.* L. F., Referee.

[*Annex the schedule, indorsed by referee.*]

No. 252.

ORDER CONFIRMING REPORT ABSOLUTELY, OR AS MODIFIED.

See ante, Vol. I., p. 443.

At a special term, *&c.* [*as in No.* 6].

[*Title as in No.* 247.]

This matter having been brought to a hearing upon the report of L. F., Esq., the referee herein, to whom it was referred to take and state an account of the trust funds and property remaining in the hands of C. D., as guardian of said infant, A. B., which report is dated the —— day of ——, 18—, and upon the exceptions to said report:

Now, therefore, after hearing counsel for the respective parties, on motion of T. C., of counsel for the petitioner, it is ordered that the said exceptions be and the same are hereby overruled, and the said report is in all things hereby ratified and confirmed. (*) [*Or*, that all of said exceptions but the first be and the same are hereby overruled, and the said first exception allowed, and said report modified and corrected accordingly; and that said report, as so modified, be and the same is hereby ratified and confirmed.]

No. 253.

CLAUSE DIRECTING REMOVAL OF GUARDIAN, AND REFERENCE TO APPOINT ANOTHER GUARDIAN.

See ante, Vol. I., p. 443.

[*Same as in last form to the asterisk* (*), *and then add :*]

And it is further ordered that the said guardian, C. D., for the misconduct aforesaid, be and he hereby is removed from his guardianship and the further execution of said trust. And that it be referred to L. F., Esq., referee aforesaid, to nominate a suitable person for guardian to take the place of the said C. D., and that the said referee report to the court the security proposed by the person so nominated by him and the sufficiency thereof.

No. 254.

PETITION OF GUARDIAN TO BE DISCHARGED FROM HIS TRUST.

See ante, Vol. I., p. 441.

[*Title as in No.* 247.]

To the Supreme Court of the State of New York.

The petition of C. D., of, *&c.*, the general guardian of A. B., an infant, respectfully shows:

That by an order of this court, bearing date the —— day of ——, 18—, and duly entered in the office of the clerk of the county of ——, your petitioner was appointed general guardian of said infant, on executing and filing the security in said order mentioned. That such security was thereupon executed, and, on the —— day of ——, 18—, duly filed in said clerk's office, and thereupon your petitioner entered upon the duties of his trust as such guardian. That, as such guardian, he took possession of the property of his said ward, consisting of, *&c.* [*statement of property*]. That your petitioner has now on hand of said property, *&c.* [*state property on hand*].

Your petitioner further shows that his health is such as to incapacitate him from the discharge of the duties of guardian [*or*, that private business renders it necessary that he should go to Europe, and that he will be compelled to remain out of this country for several months, *or any other proper cause*], and that it is necessary, for the benefit of the estate of the said infant, that another general guardian of the person and estate and effects of the said infant should be immediately appointed in the place and stead of your petitioner; that your petitioner should account and close his guardianship in the premises pursuant to the rules and practice of the court, and pay over all proper amounts and balances (which he is willing and hereby offers to do), and that his sureties may be discharged.

Your petitioner, therefore, prays that an order may be granted, whereby your petitioner may be required forthwith to account before a referee touching the receipts and disbursements of his said guardianship, and pass his accounts before him; that such referee may be directed to make to your petitioner all just allowances; and that your petitioner, on paying over the amount of balance to be found due by a report of such referee, may be discharged from all his duties and responsibilities as such guardian; and that the bond entered into by your petitioner's sureties, —— and ——, may be thereupon considered as canceled, and they be discharged from all responsibility in the premises, and so that a new guardian may be appointed in the place of your petitioner, and that your petitioner may hand over all property, documents, and papers in his possession to his successor in said trust, or such further or other order as the court shall think proper to grant.

And your petitioner will ever pray, &c.

Dated, *&c.* C. D.

No. 255.

THE LIKE, BY NEXT FRIEND, TO REMOVE A GUARDIAN FOR MISCONDUCT.

See ante, Vol. I., p. 443; 2 Van Sant. Eq. Pr. 643

[*Same as in No.* 248, *to the* (*); *then proceed, showing the misconduct charged, e. g.* :]

That said guardian has received the whole of the trust property and funds, amounting, as appears by his inventory on file, to the sum of —— dollars, all of which is personal property, and which, since the filing of said inventory, he has reduced to money. That he neglects to keep them properly invested, but mingles them with his own, and uses them for his own purposes. That said guardian is now in embarrassed circumstances, and, as your petitioner is informed and believes, is insolvent [*or*, has become of intemperate habits, *&c.*, *as the case may be*].

Wherefore, your petitioner prays that said guardian may be removed from his trust, and that another guardian of the persou and estate of said infant, and also, *&c.* [*proceed as in the prayer for relief in No.* 248, *adding the further prayer that said guardian be directed to pay over to such new guardian the balance of the property and funds which shall be ascertained by said report, and found remaining in his hands*].

And your petitioner will ever pray, &c.,

Dated, *&c.* A. B.,

By E. L. B., his next friend.

[*Add verification, &c., as in No.* 248.]

No. 256.

NOTICE TO GUARDIAN THEREON.

See ante, Vol. I., p. 441.

[*Same, substantially, as in No.* 249.

No. 257.

ORDER OF REFERENCE THEREON.

See ante, Vol. I., p. 441; 2 Van Sant. Eq. Pr. 644.

[*Same as in No.* 250, *to the* (*), *then add:*] that it be referred to L. F., of, &c., to take proof of all the material facts set forth in said petition, and to report thereon with his opinion to the court, with all convenient speed.

It is further ordered, that such guardian do forthwith account before said referee for the trust funds and property and the revenue and proceeds thereof which have come to his hands as such guardian, and pass his accounts in full before said referee; and that, on such accounting, said referee make all just allowances to said guardian for his disbursements, expenditures, &c., which are properly chargeable on said trust fund, and report thereon to this court with all convenient speed. [*If proper also, a clause may be added, directing the referee to nominate a proper person to be appointed as substituted guardian, and also to report upon the sufficiency of the proposed sureties, and fixing the amount of the bond.*]

No. 257(A).

REPORT OF REFEREE THEREON.

See ante, Vol. I., p. 443; 2 Van Sant. Eq. Pr. 644.

[*Title as in No.* 247.]

To the Supreme Court of the State of New York.

In pursuance of an order in this matter, bearing date on, *&c.*, by which it was referred to me to [*state substance of order*], I, the subscriber, referee, as aforesaid, do respectfully report that, having been attended by said parties and their counsel, and having heard the proofs and allegations in regard to the matters so referred, find that all the material allegations set forth in said petition are true [*or*, that said guardian, the said C. D., did on, *&c.*, *setting forth specifically the facts so found*]. And I further report that, from the facts so found by me, I am of the opinion that said C. D. has mismanaged [*or*, is incapable, *or*, is an improper person to manage] said trust property and estate, and ought to be removed from such guardianship.

And I further report that, *&c.* [*proceed as in No.* 251, *from the* (*) *to the end. If the order direct an inquiry as to the proposed substituted guardian, insert as follows:*]

And I further report that I have taken proofs and have examined in regard to the person proposed on behalf of the petitioner for substituted guardian, and the sufficiency of his proposed sureties; and that C. F. B., of, *&c.*, the person so proposed, is in all respects a suitable and proper person to be appointed guardian, on his executing and filing with the clerk of ——

county, a duly acknowledged or approved bond, in the penal sum of —— dollars, being double the amount of the balance so remaining in said guardian's hands, with G. T. and L. P. S., of, *&c.*, freeholders, residing in said county, being the persons so proposed as security, who have duly justified before me, and who, in my opinion, are in all respects sufficient.

All which is respectfully submitted.

Dated, *&c.* G. S. C.

No. 258.

ORDER THEREON, REMOVING GUARDIAN, APPOINTING SUCCESSOR, AND DIRECTING PAYMENT OVER TO HIM OF TRUST FUND.

See ante, Vol. I., p. 443; 2 Van Sant. Eq. Pr. 645.

At a special term, *&c.* [*as in No.* 6].

[*Title as in No.* 247].

On reading and filing the report of S. G. C., referee herein, dated, *&c.*; and whereby he reports that, *&c.* [*recite substance of report*]; and on proof that no exceptions have been filed to such report within the time prescribed by the rules; and after hearing A. N. W., Esq., of counsel for and on behalf of the above infant, and J. W. F., Esq., for the said guardian, it is ordered and adjudged that the said C. D. be, and he is hereby discharged from the further performance of his trust as guardian of the person and estate of the said infant A. B.; that the said C. F. B. be, and he is hereby appointed guardian of the said infant, on executing the bond in such amount and with such sureties as so reported by the said referee, for the faithful execution of his trust; and that he be deemed fully appointed after he and his sureties shall have executed such bond, and it shall have been duly acknowledged or proved, and be approved as to its form and execution by the said referee [*or*, by one of the justices of this court], and been filed by the clerk of this court, in the county of ——. And it is further ordered that the said C. D. pay over to the said C. F. B. (*), within —— days after he shall have so given and filed such security, as aforesaid, the balance of property in his hands, according to the said referee's report, and surrender to the said C. F. B. all the property, real and personal, of the said infant in his hands. And in default of his doing so, in whole or in part, the said infant, by his next friend, is at liberty to move for an attachment or to put the bond of the said C. D. in suit, as he may be advised. And, inasmuch as the present reference and appointment of a new guardian has been caused by the misconduct of the said C. D., it is also ordered and adjudged that the said C. D. pay all and every the costs and disbursements of the same, namely, —— dollars, to the attorney of the infant, and to the referee —— dollars; in all, —— dollars; and that execution go therefor. But which sum, in the first instance, may be made good and paid by the said C. F. B., out of the first moneys which shall come to his hands, and in paying the same that he take receipt therefor, and be allowed the amount in his accounts, but if the said amount shall be paid by or made out of the said C. D. by execution, then the amount shall be paid to the said C. F B., to make good the amount paid in the mean time by him.

IV. Forms on Sales of Infants' Estates.

No. 258.(A)

PETITION FOR ORDER TO SELL IN BEHALF OF INFANTS.

See ante, Vol. I., p. 449.

In Supreme Court [*or other court*]:

To the Supreme Court of the State of New York [*or*, To the County Court of the County of ——; *or*, to the Court of Common Pleas of the City and County of New York]:

The petition of A. B., an infant over the age of fourteen years, and of E. B., an infant under the age of fourteen years, by C. B., their mother and next friend, respectfully shows:

That your petitioner, A. B., is an infant of the age of sixteen years and upward, and resides at ——, in the county of ——, and has no general guardian. That your petitioner, E. B., is an infant of the age of twelve years, and resides at ——, aforesaid, and has no general guardian; and that the said infants are two of the children and heirs at law of W. B., late of, *&c.*, deceased; and that as such heirs at law they are each entitled to an undivided fifth part, subject to the right of dower of the said C. B., their mother, of a lot of land situated in the town [*or*, city] of ——, in the county of ——, and State of New York, and bounded and described as follows: [*insert description*]. That the said lot of land is worth about $——; but is wholly unproductive, being wild and unimproved [*or*, that the said lot of land is worth about the sum of $——, and produces an annual income of $——]. That the brothers of your petitioners, R. B., J. B., and S. B., own the other three-fifths of the real estate above described, and threaten to commence proceedings against your petitioners for the partition thereof.

And your petitioners further show that they do not own any other real estate than that above described; and that they have no personal estate of any kind, or to any amount whatever, except their necessary wearing apparel [*or*, that each of them is the owner of an undivided fifth part of another piece or parcel of land, situated, *&c.*, which is worth about $——; but which is entirely unimproved and unproductive; and that your petitioners are each the owner of the following personal property, to wit: The said A. B., is, *&c.*, and the said E. B., is, *&c.* [*state the property, its situation and value*]. And that the property, real and personal, above mentioned, is the only property owned by your petitioners, or in which they have any interest].

And your petitioners further show, that the said C. B., the mother of the said infants, as the widow of the said W. B., deceased, the father of said infants, is entitled to dower in the real estate above described, and that she has no means of support for herself and her said infant children, except what she and they may acquire by their industry; and that it is necessary the said premises, or some part thereof, should be sold, and the proceeds, or some part thereof, be applied toward the necessary education and maintenance of said infants. And the said C. B. hereby offers to unite in the sale of said premises, and to release her right of dower therein, upon condition that one-third of the purchase-money be securely invested, and the annual interest thereof be paid to her during her natural life; or that a gross sum be paid to her in lieu thereof, equal in value to her life estate therein, to be ascertained upon the principle of life annuities.

Your petitioners, therefore, pray, that the said real estate may be sold by and under the direction of this court; and that W. R., of the town [*or*, city] of ——, counselor at law, who is the uncle of [*or*, who is in no way related to] the said infants, may be appointed their special guardian for the purpose of selling the interests of said infants in said real estate. And J. N. D. and T. L., of, *&c.*, gentlemen, are proposed as sureties for the said W. R. as such special guardian, to join with him in a bond, in such penalty, and upon such condition, as shall be required.

C. B.
A. B.

State of New York, }
County of ——, } ss.

On this —— day of ——, 18—, before me personally appeared C. B. and A. B., above named, and being severally sworn, each for herself deposes and says that she has read [*or*, heard read] the above petition subscribed by her, and knows the contents thereof, and that the same is true of her own knowledge, except as to the matters which are therein stated on information or belief; and that as to those matters, she believes it to be true.

J. H. F., Justice of the Peace.

CONSENT OF GUARDIAN.

I hereby consent to be appointed the special guardian of the above petitioners, for the purposes mentioned in the above petition.

Dated, *&c.* W. R.

Witness, L. P. C.

No. 259.

AFFIDAVIT OF DISINTERESTED PERSONS.

See ante, Vol. I., p. 449.

State of New York, }
County of ——, } ss.

E. F., farmer, of the town [*or*, city] of ——, in said county, and G. H., of the same place, being severally sworn, each for himself, deposes and says, that he is acquainted with A. B. and E. B., the petitioners named in the annexed petition, and also with their property, and the situation and value thereof. That he has read [*or*, heard read] the said petition, and knows the contents thereof, and that the facts and circumstances therein stated are true, according to his best knowledge and belief. [*Or*, that he is acquainted with A. B. and E. B., infant children of W. B., late of, *&c.*, deceased; that they reside in the town [*or*, city] of ——, in said county; that the said A. B. is an infant over the age of fourteen years, and has no general guardian, and the said E. B. is an infant under the age of fourteen years and has no general guardian. That he is also acquainted with the real estate described in the petition of said infants, hereto annexed, and with the situation and value thereof. That the said real estate is worth about —— dollars, but is wild and unimproved, and wholly unproductive. That in the opinion of deponent a sale of said real estate would be for the benefit of said infants, and that his reasons for that opinion are the same as those stated in said petition.] E. F

Sworn, *&c.* G H.

No. 260.

ORDER OF REFERENCE, AND FOR APPOINTMENT OF GUARDIAN.

See ante, Vol. I., p. 453.

At a special term, *&c.* [*as in No.* 6].

In the matter of the application of A. B. and E. B., infants, for leave to sell their real estate.

On reading and filing the petition of A. B., of, *&c.*, an infant over the age of fourteen years, who has no general guardian, and of E. B., an infant under the age of fourteen, who has no general guardian, by C. B., their mother and next friend, dated the —— day of ——, 18—, praying that the real estate therein described may be sold, by and under the direction of this court; and that W. R., of, *&c.*, be appointed special guardian, for the purpose of conducting the sale; and on reading and filing the affidavits of E. F. and G. H., verifying the material facts and circumstances alleged in said petition; and it appearing satisfactorily to the court that there is reasonable ground for the application, it is, on motion of L. P. C., attorney for the said petitioners, ordered, that the said W. R. be, and he hereby is, appointed the special guardian of the said infants for the purposes of the application, upon executing and filing with the clerk of the county of —— the bond of the said W. R., and of J. N. D., and T. L., to each of the said infants, in the penalty of $——, conditioned for the faithful performance, by the said W. R., of the trust reposed in him as such guardian, and for paying over, investing, and accounting for all moneys that shall be received by such guardian, according to the order of any court having authority to give directions in the premises· and that he will observe the orders and directions of the court in relation to such trust; which bond shall be approved of, as to its form and manner of execution, by a justice of this court, signified by his approbation indorsed thereon. And it is further ordered that it be referred to L. F., Esq., of, *&c.*, to ascertain the truth of the matters stated in said petition, and whether a sale of the premises therein described, or any and what part thereof, would be beneficial to the infant, and the particular reasons therefor; and to ascertain the value of the said premises, and of each separate lot or parcel thereof, and the terms and conditions upon which it should be sold; and whether the said infants, or either of them, is in absolute need of any and what part of the proceeds of the sale for his support and maintenance, over and above the income thereof, and his other property, together with what he might earn by his own exertions; and also to ascertain the value of the life estate of C. B., the mother and next friend of said infants, in the said premises, on the principle of life annuities, by reason of her right of dower in said premises.

And it is further ordered, that no proceedings be had before said referee until the special guardian produces a certificate of the clerk, in due form, that the security herein required has been duly proved, or acknowledged and filed, agreeably to this order.

No. 261.

BOND OF SPECIAL GUARDIAN.

See ante, Vol. I., p. 452.

Know all men by these presents, that we, W. R., counselor at law, of the town [*or*, city] of ——, in the county of ——, and State of New York, and J. N. D. and T. L., gentlemen, of the same place, are held and firmly bound unto A. B., in the penal sum of $——, to be paid to the said A. B., his heirs, executors, administrators, or assigns; for which payment, well and truly to be made, we bind ourselves, our heirs, executors, and administrators, jointly and severally, firmly by these presents. Sealed with our seals, and dated the —— day of ——, 18—.

Whereas, by an order of the Supreme Court of the State of New York [*or other court*], made on the —— day of ——, the above-bounden W. R. was appointed the special guardian of A. B., an infant, over the age of fourteen years, for the purpose of selling the real estate of said infant, mentioned in said order, upon the execution of the bond therein required: Now, therefore, the condition of the above obligation is such, that if the above-bounden W. R. shall faithfully perform the trust reposed in him as such special guardian, and shall pay over, invest, and account for all moneys that shall be received by him, according to the order of any court having authority to give directions in the premises; and shall observe the orders and directions of the court in relation to such trust, then the above obligation to be void, otherwise to remain in full force and effect.

Sealed and delivered in presence of G. D.

W. R. [SEAL.]
J. N. D. [SEAL.]
T. L. [SEAL.]

ACKNOWLEDGMENT OF BOND.

State of New York, County of ——, } ss.

On this —— day of ——, 18—, before me personally came the above-named W. R., J. N. D., and T. L., to me known to be the individuals described in and who executed the above instrument, and severally acknowledged that they executed the same.

J. H. F., Justice of the Peace.

AFFIDAVIT OF SURETIES.

State of New York, County of ——, } ss.

J. N. D., of the town [*or*, city] of ——, in said county, and T. L., of the same place, the sureties named in the foregoing bond, being severally sworn, each for himself, deposes and says, that he is a resident and householder [*or*, freeholder] within the State of New York, and is worth the sum of $—— over and above all debts and responsibilities which he owes or has incurred, and exclusive of property exempt from execution.

Sworn, *&c.*

J. N. D.
T. L.

CERTIFICATE OF APPROVAL [*to be indorsed on bond*].

I approve of the within bond, as to its form and manner of execution, and as to the sufficiency of the sureties. Dated this —— day of ——, 18—.

A. B., Justice of the Supreme Court.

No. 262.

CERTIFICATE OF CLERK. (*a*)

See ante, Vol. I., p. 453.

[*Title as in No.* 260.]

I do hereby certify that the bond required by the order of this court, made on the —— day of ——, 18—, to be given by W. R., the special guardian appointed by the court in this matter, has been duly proved [*or*,

(*a*) This certificate, when obtained, is to be annexed to the referee's report. *Sup. Court Rules, No.* 67.

acknowledged], and filed in my office, agreeably to the said order. And I further certify that the said bond was approved as to its form and manner of execution, and the sufficiency of the sureties, by A. B., Esq., justice of the Supreme Court. Dated this —— day of ——, 18—.

H. S., Clerk of —— County.

No. 263.

REFEREE'S REPORT.

See ante, Vol. I., p. 454.

[*Title as in No.* 260.]

To the Supreme Court of the State of New York [*or other proper court*]. In pursuance of an order made in this matter on the —— day of ——, 18—, by which it was referred to me to ascertain the truth of the facts stated in the petition in this matter, and to examine and report thereon, agreeably to the said order, and to ascertain the value of the life estate of C. B. in the said premises, on the principle of life annuities,

I, the subscriber, the referee aforesaid, do respectfully report, that I have been attended by L. P. C., the attorney for the petitioners, who, before proceeding with said reference, produced before me the certificate of the clerk of this court, that the bond required to be given by W. R., the special guardian appointed in this matter, had been duly proved [*or*, acknowledged] and filed in his office agreeably to the said order, and that the said bond had been approved by A. B., Esq., justice of the Supreme Court, which certificate is hereto annexed.

And I further report that in my opinion a sale of the whole of the real estate belonging to said infants, and described in said petition, would be for the benefit of said infants, and that the reasons for my opinion are as follows: [*state the particular reasons which in the opinion of the referee render a sale of the premises necessary or proper*].

And I do further report, that I have taken testimony and examined into the matters alleged in said petition, and from the testimony so taken, and such examination, I am satisfied, *&c.* [*state all the facts in detail, required to be ascertained and reported, and substantially as follows:*] that the said real estate, described in said petition, is worth —— dollars [*if there is more than one lot, state the value of each separately*]; that it is exceedingly unproductive, and yields only an annual income to said infants of about —— dollars; that in my opinion it will be for the interest of the said infants to have the said real estate sold upon the following terms and conditions, viz.: That so much of the proceeds of their shares or interests in the said premises as may be necessary to pay their respective proportions of the gross value of the right of dower of their mother, C. B., therein, and the costs of these proceedings be paid by the purchaser on the delivery of the deed; and that the payment of the residue of the purchase-money of the interests of said infants be secured by the bond of the purchaser and a mortgage upon the said premises, to be given to the treasurer of the county of —— [*or*, to W. R., the special guardian aforesaid], in trust for the said infants, conditioned to pay the interest thereon, semi-annually, at the rate of seven per cent. per annum, and the principal in two equal installments, one of which shall be paid when the said A. B. shall arrive at the age of twenty-one years, and the other on the day when the said E. B. shall arrive at full age.

I do further report that the said infants are not in absolute need of any part of the proceeds of said sale for their support and maintenance, over and above the interest or income thereof, and their other property, together with what they may earn by their own exertions.

And I do further report that C. B., the mother of the said infants, who is entitled to a right of dower in said premises, is willing to join in the said sale; and that I have ascertained the value of her life estate in the premises, on the principle of life annuities; and that the present value of the same is —— dollars.

All of which is respectfully submitted.

Dated, *&c.* L. F., Referee.

No. 264.

ORDER AUTHORIZING GUARDIAN TO CONTRACT.

See ante, Vol. I., p. 454.

[*Title as in No.* 260.] At a special term, *&c.* [*as in No.* 6].

On reading and filing the report of L. F., Esq., the referee in this matter, appointed by an order of this court, dated the —— day of ——, 18—, and which report is dated the —— day of ——, 18—, from which report it appears satisfactorily to this court that the interests of the said infants will be promoted by a sale of their shares of the real estate described in the petition in this matter;

Now, on motion of L. P. C., attorney for said infants, it is ordered that the said report be, and the same is hereby, confirmed. And it is further ordered that W. R., the special guardian of said infants, be, and he is hereby, authorized and empowered to contract for the sale and conveyance of all the right, title, and interest of the said infants in and to such real estate, at a price not less than the sum specified by said referee in his report as the value thereof, and upon the terms and conditions therein specified. And it is also further ordered, that before executing any deed or instrument of conveyance of the said premises to the purchaser or purchasers thereof, the said guardian report to this court, upon oath, the terms and conditions of the agreement made by him for the sale of said premises.

No. 265.

REPORT OF SPECIAL GUARDIAN, OF AGREEMENT TO SELL.

See ante, Vol. I, p. 455.

[*Title as in No.* 260.]

To the Supreme Court of the State of New York [*or other proper court*].

In pursuance of an order of this court, made in the above matter, on the —— day of ——, 18—, authorizing and empowering me, as the special guardian of the infants above named, to contract for the sale and conveyance of all the right, title, and interest of the said infants in and to the real estate mentioned and described in the petition of the said infants in this matter, dated the —— day of ——, 18—; and to report upon oath the terms and conditions of the agreement made by me with the purchaser or purchasers, before executing any deed or instrument of conveyance of the said premises;

I, the said special guardian, do certify and report, that I have entered into a written agreement (subject to the approval of the court), with B. P., of, *&c.*, for the sale of all the right, title, and interest of the said infants in and to the said real estate, upon the following terms and conditions: The said B. P. to pay therefor the sum of $——, as follows: So much of the said purchase-money as may be necessary to pay the respective proportions of such infants, of the gross value of the right of dower of their mother, C. B., therein, together with the costs of these proceedings, on the delivery of the deed; and the payment of the residue of the said purchase-money to be secured by the bond of the purchaser, and a mortgage upon the said premises, to be given by him to the treasurer of the county of ——, or to such other person as the court may direct, in trust for the said infants, conditioned to pay the interest thereon, semi-annually, at the rate of seven per cent. per annum, and the principal in two equal installments, one of which shall be payable on the day when the said A. B. shall arrive at the age of twenty-one years, and the other on the day when the said E. B. shall arrive at that age.

I do further report that the said C. B. has executed a release of all her right of dower in and to the undivided two fifth parts of said premises owned by said infants, which release is hereto annexed; and that the gross value of such right of dower in the premises owned by said infants is —— dollars; and the costs and expenses of these proceedings amount to —— dollars; after deducting which sums from the amount of the purchase-money, as aforesaid, there will remain the sum of —— dollars due the said infants collectively, to be secured as aforesaid, or —— dollars to each.

And I further report that the above are the best terms upon which I could sell the said property; and that, in my opinion, the premises are an ample security for the payment of the residue of the purchase-money aforesaid, and the interest thereon, as aforesaid.

All which is respectfully submitted.

W. R.

Dated this —— day of ——, 18—.

County of ——, ss. W. R., the special guardian above named, being duly sworn, says, that he has read the above report, subscribed by him, and knows the contents thereof, and that the matters therein stated are true.

Sworn, *&c.* W. R.

No. 266.

ORDER CONFIRMING REPORT OF GUARDIAN, AND DIRECTING A CONVEYANCE.

See ante, Vol. I., p. 455.

At a special term, *&c.* [*as in No.* 6].

[*Title as in No.* 260.]

On reading and filing the report of W. R., the special guardian of the infants above named, made in pursuance of the order of this court, dated the —— day of ——, 18—, stating that he had entered into a written agreement, subject to the approval of this court, with B. P., for the sale of all the right, title, and interest of the said infants in and to the real estate mentioned in said order, upon the terms and conditions specified in the said report; and that C. B., the mother of said infants, had executed an effectual release of her right of dower in said premises.

Now, on motion of L. P. C., attorney for the said petitioners, it is ordered that the said report, and the agreement therein mentioned, be and the same are hereby ratified and confirmed.

It is further ordered, that the said special guardian, in the name of said infants, execute, acknowledge, and deliver to the said B. P. a good and sufficient conveyance of all the estate, right, title, and interest of the said infants in and to the premises aforesaid, upon his complying with the terms and conditions upon which, by the said agreement, the deed was to be delivered; and that the bond and mortgage to be executed by said purchaser, be executed to the treasurer of the county of —— [*or*, to the said special guardian]; and that the said mortgage be duly recorded in the clerk's [*or*, register's] office of said county, and the fees for recording paid thereon.

And it is further ordered, that out of the purchase-money paid by the said B. P., upon the delivery of the deed, the said special guardian pay the sum of —— dollars to C. B. for her right of dower in the shares of the said infants in the premises, and take her receipt therefor; and that he pay to the attorney for the petitioners the sum of —— dollars for the costs and expenses of these proceedings.

And it is further ordered, that the moneys which shall be received by the treasurer of the county of ——, from time to time, for interest upon the bond and mortgage given by the purchaser, be paid over by him to the special guardian aforesaid, to be applied by such special guardian to the maintenance and education of said infants [*or, if the bond and mortgage are taken in the name of the special guardian, then:* that the moneys which shall be received by such special guardian, from time to time, for interest upon the bond and mortgage given by the purchaser, be applied by him to the maintenance and education of said infants.]

No. 267

DEED BY SPECIAL GUARDIAN.

See ante, Vol. I., p. 455.

This indenture, made the —— day of ——, 18—, between A. B. and E. B., of, *&c.*, infant children of W. B., late of, *&c.*, deceased, by W. R., their special guardian, parties of the first part, and B. P., of, *&c.*, party of the second part. Whereas a petition was heretofore presented to the Supreme Court of the State of New York [*or other proper court*], by the said A. B., an infant over the age of fourteen years, and having no general guardian, and said E. B., an infant under the age of fourteen years, and having no general guardian, by C. B., their mother and next friend, praying for a sale of the right, title, and interest, of the said infants in the real estate therein mentioned; and whereas such proceedings were afterward had in the said court, upon the said petition, that by an order of said court, made on the —— day of ——, 18—, the said W. R. was appointed the special guardian of the said infants, for the purposes of the said application, upon his giving the security therein required; and whereas such security, duly acknowledged and approved, was subsequently filed by the said guardian, in the proper office; and whereas, by another order of the said court, made on the —— day of ——, 18—, the said W. R. was authorized and empowered to contract for the sale and conveyance of the right, title, and interest of the said infants in such real estate, at a price not less than that specified in the referee's report referred to in said order, and upon the terms and conditions therein mentioned. And whereas, in pursuance of the last-mentioned order, the said special guardian afterward made his report to the said court, dated the —— day of ——, 18—, stating that he had entered into an agreement, subject to the approval of said court, with B. P., of, *&c.*, for the sale of all the right, title, and interest of the said infants, in and to the said real estate, upon the terms and conditions therein mentioned; and whereas, by another order of said court, made on the —— day of ——, 18—, it was ordered that the said report of such special guardian, and the agreement therein mentioned, be and the same were thereby ratified and confirmed, and that the said special guardian, in the name of said infants, execute, acknowledge, and deliver to the said B. P. a good and sufficient conveyance of all the estate, right, title, and interest of the said infants in and to the said premises, upon his complying with the terms and conditions upon which, by the said agreement, such deed was to be delivered. And whereas, the said B. P., the purchaser aforesaid has complied with the said terms and conditions;

Now, therefore, this indenture witnesseth, that the said parties of the first part, by their special guardian aforesaid, in virtue of the several orders aforesaid, and in pursuance of the statute in such case made and provided, for and in consideration of the sum of —— dollars to him in hand paid, at or before the ensealing and delivery of these presents, by the party of the second part, the receipt whereof is hereby acknowledged, hath granted, bargained, sold, remised, released, and conveyed, unto the said party of the second part, his heirs and assigns forever, all the right, title, and interest of the said infants, parties of the first part, of, in, and to the following described real estate and premises, situated in the town [*or*, city] of ——, in said county of ——, viz.: The undivided two-fifths of all that certain piece or parcel, *&c.* [*insert description*], to have and to hold the said premises with the appurtenances unto the said party of the second part, and his heirs and assigns forever.

In witness whereof, the parties of the first part, by their special guardian, aforesaid, have hereunto set their hands and seals, the day and year first above written.

Sealed and delivered
in presence of
L. P. C.

A. B. [L. S.]
E. B. [L. S.]
by W. R., their Special Guardian.

No. 268.

RELEASE OF WIDOW'S DOWER, ANNEXED.

See ante, Vol. I., p. 461.

Know all men, by these presents: That I, C. B., of, *&c.*, widow of W. B., deceased, for and in consideration of the sum of —— dollars to me in hand paid, at or before the ensealing and delivery hereof, by B. P., of, *&c.*, the receipt whereof is hereby acknowledged, have granted, bargained, and sold, remised and released and quit-claimed, and by these presents do grant, bargain, sell, remise, release, and quit-claim unto the said B. P., his heirs and assigns, all that, *&c.* [*insert description*]. To have and to hold the said premises, with the appurtenances, unto the said B. P., his heirs and assigns, to and for the use and behoof of him and his heirs and assigns forever. And the said C. B., for herself, her heirs, executors, and administrators, doth covenant and agree to and with the said B. P., his heirs and assigns, that she hath not done any act whereby, or by means whereof, the said above-described premises now are, or at any time have been, charged, incumbered, or affected in any manner whatever.

In witness whereof, the said C. B. has hereunto set her hand and seal this the —— day of ——, 18—.

Sealed and delivered in
presence of
A. B.

C. B. [L. S.]

[*Add acknowledgment or proof, as in No.* 44.]

No. 269.

GUARDIAN'S FINAL REPORT.

See ante, Vol. I., p. 462.

[*Title as in No.* 260.]

To the Supreme Court of the State of New York [*or other court*].

I, W. R., the special guardian of the above-named infants, having been directed by an order of this court, dated the —— day of ——, 18—, to execute, acknowledge, and deliver, in the name of said infants, to B. P. of, *&c.* [*recite substance of order*], do respectfully report:

That I have executed, acknowledged, and delivered, in the name of said infants, to the said B. P., a good and sufficient deed of said premises, he having complied with the terms and conditions of the said agreement; that I have paid the said sum of —— dollars for the dower right of C. B. and have taken a receipt therefor; and that I have paid the said sum of —— dollars to L. P. C., attorney for the petitioners herein, and have taken a receipt therefor.

I do further report that I have taken the bond and mortgage of the said B.P. for the sum of —— dollars, covering the said premises, which bond and mortgage is executed to the treasurer of the county of —— [*or as the case may be*], and that the same has been left by me in the clerk's [*or*, register's] office of said county, to be recorded, and the fees for recording paid thereon.

All which is respectfully submitted.

Dated, *&c.* W. R., Special Guardian.

[*Add verification as in No.* 265.]

No. 270.

ORDER CONFIRMING FINAL REPORT.

See ante, Vol. I., p. 462.

At a special term, *&c.* [*as in No.* 6].

[*Title as in No.* 260.]

On reading and filing the report of W. R., special guardian of, *&c.*, bearing date the —— day of ——, 18—, and on motion of L. P. C., attorney for said guardian, it is ordered that the said report be, and the same hereby is, in all things ratified and confirmed.

V. Forms in Proceedings to Compel Specific Performance of Contract of Ancestor.

No. 271.

PETITION TO COMPEL SPECIFIC PERFORMANCE OF CONTRACT OF ANCESTOR.

See ante, Vol. I., p. 464.

To the Supreme Court of the State of New York [*or*, to the County Court of the County of ——, *or*, to the Court of Common Pleas of the City and County of New York]:

The petition of A. B., of, *&c.*, respectfully shows: That on the —— day of ——, 18—, J. K., of, *&c.*, now deceased, duly entered into a written contract with L. M., of the same place, by which the said J. K., for a good and valuable consideration, covenanted and agreed to convey to the said L. M., on the —— day of ——, 18—, the following described premises, situated in the town of ——, in the county of ——, and State of New York, viz.: [*describe premises*]. That the said L. M., in consideration of the promises and agreements on the part of the said J. K., covenanted and agreed to pay to the said J. K., on the said —— day of ——, 18—, the sum of —— dollars, and also on that day to execute and deliver to said J. K. the bond of the said L. M., in the penalty of —— dollars, conditioned to pay to the said J. K., on the —— day of ——, 18—, the sum of —— dollars, with interest thereon annually, and also his mortgage, covering the premises aforesaid, and conditioned as aforesaid, a copy of which contract is hereto annexed, marked "A," and to which, for greater particularity, your petitioner refers.

Your petitioner further shows, that the said J. K. died on the —— day of ——, 18—, without performing the said contract, and leaving three adult and three infant children him surviving. That, as heirs of the said J. K., the said children are now seized of the said premises in fee. That the names of said adult children are L. K., R. K., and B. K., and that they reside in —— aforesaid. That the names of said infant children are A. K., who is now aged five years; C. K., who is now aged ten years; and E. K., who is now aged fifteen years. That said infant children reside in —— aforesaid, and have no general guardian.

Your petitioner further shows, that he was duly qualified and appointed, by the surrogate of the county of ——, as the executor of the last will and testament of the said J. K. [*or*, as the administrator of the estate of the said J. K. (*a*)], late of —— aforesaid, deceased, on the —— day of ——, 18—.

That your petitioner is desirous that a specific performance of the said contract, on the part of said infants, should be decreed by the court.

(*a*) The application may also be made by the surviving party to the contract, or any other person interested in it. 2 *Rev. Stat.* 194, *sec.* 169, *ante*, Vol. I., *p.* 463.

That the said L. M. is also willing that such performance should be decreed, as are also the said adult children, as will more fully appear by the written consent of said L. M. and said adult children, which is hereto annexed, marked "B."

Your petitioner therefore prays that an order may be entered, directing the said infant children to convey to the said L. M. all their right, title, and interest in and to the said premises, which they derived from the said J. K., as aforesaid, according to the terms of said contract, upon the performance, by the said L. M., of the covenants and agreements to be performed by him in and by said contract, or that the guardian *ad litem* of said infants execute such conveyance in the name of such infants, upon the performance by said L. M. aforesaid. And for such other or further order or relief in the premises as may be just. A. B.

[*Add verification as in No.* 258, *and annex schedules mentioned in the petition.*]

No. 272.

NOTICE OF MOTION TO COMPEL SPECIFIC PERFORMANCE BY INFANTS, ETC.

See ante, Vol. I., p. 464

IN SUPREME COURT [*or other court*].

In the matter of an application to compel a specific performance by infants of the contract of their ancestor to convey land.

SIR: Take notice, that I shall move this court, at the next special term thereof, to be held at the Court House in ——, on the —— day of —— next, at the opening of the court on that day, or as soon thereafter as counsel can be heard, for an order that [*follow, substantially, the prayer in the last form*]. And for such other or further relief in the premises as may be just.

Yours, &c., L. P. C., Att'y for Petitioner.

To L. M., *&c.*

No. 273.

ORDER DIRECTING SPECIFIC PERFORMANCE.

See ante, Vol. I, p. 464.

[*Title as in last form.*] At a Special Term, *&c.* [*as in No.* 6].

On reading and filing the petition of A. B., executor of the estate of J. K., deceased, dated the —— day of ——, 18—, showing that, *&c.* [*recite the substance of the petition*]; and on reading and filing due proof of the service of said petition, and notice of motion, on L. M. [*and other parties inter-*

ested]; and after hearing L. P. C., of counsel for the petitioner, W. I. B., of counsel for L. M., and others above mentioned; and J. L., the guardian *ad litem* of A. K., C. K., and E. K., infant children of said J. K., deceased. (*)

It is ordered that J. L., the guardian *ad litem* of said infants, in the name of said infants, execute, acknowledge, and deliver to L. M., above mentioned, a good and sufficient conveyance of all the estate, right, title, and interest of the said infants in and to the premises aforesaid, upon his complying with the terms and conditions to be performed on his part under the contract aforesaid.

It is further ordered, *&c.* [*add clause in reference to costs, following the direction of the court.*]

VI. Forms in Proceedings to compel Infant Trustees to convey.

No. 274.

PETITION TO COMPEL INFANT TRUSTEE TO CONVEY.

See ante, Vol. I., p. 470.

State of New York, }
In Supreme Court. }

To the Supreme Court of the State of New York.

The petition of A. B., of, *&c.*, respectfully shows: That he is the general guardian of C. D. (*a*), an infant residing at, *&c.;* that the said infant is seized and possessed of the following lands and premises, situated in the town of ——, in the county of ——, and State of New York, and described as follows: [*insert description*]; which said lands and premises are held by the said infant in trust only, for E. F. and G. H., of, *&c.* That, *&c.* [*here set forth the character of the trust, and the particular facts to show that the infant should convey the premises, &c., &c.*]

Your petitioner therefore prays, that an order may be entered, directing the said infant to execute a conveyance of the lands and premises aforesaid, with the appurtenances, to the said E. F. and G. H., and their heirs and assigns, forever, or that the guardian of such infant execute such conveyance in the name of such infant. And for such further or other relief as may be just.

A. B.

[*Add verification as in No.* 258.]

(*a*) The petition may also be presented by any person in any way interested in the trust property, or in its transfer or conveyance. 2 *Rev. Stat.* 194, *sec.* 167.

No. 275.

NOTICE OF MOTION TO COMPEL INFANT TRUSTEE TO CONVEY.

See ante, Vol. I., p. 470.

IN SUPREME COURT.

In the matter of an application to compel C. D., an infant trustee, to convey real estate.

SIR,—Take notice, that I shall move this court at the next special term thereof, to be held at the Court House in ——, on the —— day of —— next, at the opening of the court on that day, or as soon thereafter as counsel can be heard, for an order that [*follow substantially the prayer in the petition, ante, No.* 274]. And for such other and further relief as the court may think proper to grant, which motion will be founded upon the petition, with a copy whereof you are herewith served. Dated, *&c.*

Yours, &c., L. P. C., Att'y for A. B., Guardian, &c.

To [*names of parties interested*].

No. 276.

ORDER DIRECTING CONVEYANCE BY INFANT TRUSTEES.

See ante, Vol. I., p. 470.

[*Follow substantially No.* 273 *to the* (*) *and then proceed* :]

It is ordered, that J. L., the guardian *ad litem* of said infant, in the name of said infant, execute, acknowledge, and deliver to E. F. and G. H. above named, a good and sufficient conveyance of all the estate, right, title, and interest of the said infant, as trustee as aforesaid, in and to the following premises, described in said petition, viz.: [*insert description*].

It is further ordered that the said E. F. and G. H. pay to the said guardian *ad litem* —— dollars costs of this proceeding [*or other direction in reference to costs*].

CHAPTER XIV.

FORMS IN PROCEEDINGS BY AND AGAINST INSOLVENT DEBTORS.

No. 282.

APPLICATION TO APPOINT TRUSTEES OF ESTATE OF DEBTOR CONFINED FOR CRIME.

See ante, Vol. I., p. 496.

To D. P. I., Justice of the Supreme Court [*or other officer*].

The undersigned, A. B., of, *&c.*, a creditor [*or*, relative] of C. D. [*or*, a relative of E. D., wife of C. D.], hereby makes application for the appointment of trustees to take charge of the estate of said C. D., who is now imprisoned in the State prison at ——, in the State of New York; which application is made under and in pursuance of article second, of title first, of chapter fifth, of part second of the Revised Statutes. A. B.

No. 283.

AFFIDAVIT TO ACCOMPANY THE ABOVE APPLICATION.

See ante, Vol. I., p. 496.

State of New York, County of ——, } ss.

A. B., of said county, being duly sworn, deposes and says, that C. D., the person named in the annexed certified copy of sentence of conviction, is now actually imprisoned in the State prison at ——, in the State of New York, under and in pursuance of the said sentence of conviction. That this deponent is a creditor [*or*, relative] of the said C. D. [*or*, a relative of E. D., wife of said C. D.], and that the said C. D. is indebted to this deponent [*or*, to E. F., of, *&c.*] in the sum of ——— dollars, on account for goods, wares, and merchandise sold and delivered to the said C. D. by this deponent [*or*, by the said E. F.] A. B.

Sworn to, *&c.* [*as in No.* 286].

[*Annex a certified copy of the sentence of conviction.*]

No. 284.

APPOINTMENT OF TRUSTEES

See ante, Vol. I., p. 496.

Whereas, A. B., a creditor [*or as the case may be*] of C. D., a debtor confined for crime, did, on the —— day of ——, 18—, make application to me for the appointment of trustees to take charge of the estate of the said C. D., and did also produce a copy of the sentence of conviction of the said C. D., duly certified by H. S., clerk of the court of [*name of court before which the conviction was had*], under his seal of office, by which court the said sentence of conviction was passed, together with an affidavit of the said A. B., showing that he is a creditor [*or*, relative] of the said C. D. [*or*, a relative of E. D., wife of said C. D.], and that the said C. D. is actually imprisoned under the said sentence, and is indebted to the said A. B. [*or other person*] in the sum of —— dollars.

Now, therefore, I, A. C. H., justice of the Supreme Court [*or other officer*] do, in pursuance of the authority to me given by article two, of title one, of chapter five, of part second of the Revised Statutes, hereby appoint L. M. and O. P., two fit persons, to be trustees of the estate of the said C. D., with such powers concerning the estate of the said C. D. as are conferred by the said statute.

Given under my hand this —— day of ——, 18—.

A. C. H.

No. 285.

PETITION FOR DISCHARGE FROM DEBTS—TWO-THIRD ACT.

See ante, Vol. I., p. 500.

To the Honorable D. P. I., Justice of the Supreme Court [*or other officer having jurisdiction*].

The petition of G. L., an insolvent debtor and an inhabitant, now actually residing within the city and county of New York [*or, other place*], and others whose names are hereunto subscribed, creditors of the said insolvent, residing within the United States, respectfully shows: That the said G. L., by reason of many unforeseen circumstances, has become insolvent, and wholly unable to pay his debts; wherefore, he and your other petitioners are desirous that his estate should be distributed among his creditors in payment of their debts so far as the same will extend; and for that purpose pray that all his estate, real and personal, may be assigned and delivered to W. M., of, *&c.*, as assignee, appointed by the said creditors, having debts in good faith owing to them by the said insolvent, now due or hereafter to become due, and amounting to at least two-thirds of all the debts owing by the said insolvent to creditors residing within the United States; and, further, that the said G. L. may be discharged from his debts in the manner authorized by the statutes of this State concerning "Voluntary assignments made pursuant to the application of an insolvent and his creditors."

Dated, *&c.* G. L.

A. B. ....$	*[Insert opposite each signature the amount due to the creditor.]*
C. D. ....$	
E. F. & Co. ....$	

[If the creditor has, in his own name or in trust for him, any mortgage, judgment, or other security, or assignment by way of security, for securing the payment of his demand, then add to his signature the following: And the mortgage [*or*, judgment, *or other security, as the case may be, describing it*], held by me as security for the said debt, which mortgage is dated on, *&c.*, and was executed by —— to ——, is hereby relinquished to the assignee to be appointed in these proceedings, for the benefit of all the creditors of the said insolvent.]

No. 286.

AFFIDAVIT OF RESIDENCE OF INSOLVENT, TO BE ANNEXED TO PETITION.

See ante, Vol. I., p. 508.

City and County of New York, ss.: I, N. B. O., of said city and county, do swear that G. L., in the annexed petition named, is an inhabitant actually residing within the city and county and State of New York.

Sworn to before me, this N. B. O.
—— day of ——, 18—.
R. J. T., Notary Public
[*or other officer authorized to take affidavits*].

No. 287.

AFFIDAVIT OF CREDITOR TO BE ANNEXED TO PETITION.

See ante, Vol. I., p. 504.

State of New York,
City and County of New York, } ss.

A. B., of said city and county, one of the petitioning creditors of G. L., an insolvent debtor, being duly sworn, says: That the sum of —— dollars, lawful money of the United States, being the sum affixed to the name of this deponent subscribed to the petition annexed hereto, is justly due to him [*or*, will become due to him on the —— day of ——, 18—], from the said insolvent, for [*or*, on a promissory note given for] goods, wares, and merchandise sold and delivered by him to the said insolvent [*or as the fact may be, setting out the nature of the demand, and whether arising on any written security or otherwise, and the general ground and consideration of the indebtedness*], and that neither this deponent, nor any person to his use, has received from said insolvent, or from any other person, payment of any demand, or any part thereof, in money, or in any other way whatever, or any gift or reward whatsoever, upon any express or implied trust or confidence, that he should become a petitioner for the said insolvent. A. B.

Sworn to, *&c.* [*as in No.* 286].

No. 288.

LIKE AFFIDAVIT OF CREDITOR WHO IS A MEMBER OF A FIRM.

See ante, Vol. I., p. 504.

State of New York, } ss.
City and County of New York, }

D. E., of said city and county, one of the members of the firm or copartnership of E. F. & Co., and who as one of the copartners, and in their behalf, has subscribed to the petition the name or firm of their said copartnership, as petitioning creditors of G. L., an insolvent debtor, being duly sworn, doth depose and say, that the sum of —— dollars, lawful money of the United States, being the sum annexed to the name of the said copartnership subscribed to the petition annexed hereto, is justly due [*or*, will become due on the —— day of ——, 18—] to the said copartnership from the said insolvent, for [*or*, on a promissory note given for] goods, wares, and merchandise sold and delivered by them to the said insolvent [*or*, *as the fact may be, setting out the nature of the demand, and whether arising on any written security or otherwise, and the general ground and consideration of the indebtedness*], and that neither this deponent, nor any member of said firm, nor any person to his or their use, has received from the said insolvent, or any other person, payment of any demand, or any part thereof, in money or in any other way whatever, or any gift or reward whatsoever, upon any express or implied trust or confidence that he or they should become a petitioner or petitioners for the said insolvent. D. E.

Sworn, *&c.* [*as in No.* 286].

No. 289.

SCHEDULE OF CREDITORS.

See ante, Vol. I., p. 506.

A full and true account of all the creditors of G. L., an insolvent debtor, with the place of residence of each, the sum owing to each of them by the said insolvent, the nature of each debt or demand, with the true cause and consideration thereof, and the place where the same accrued.

Creditors.	Residence.	Amount.		Nature of debt, with the true cause and consideration thereof, and whether arising on written security, on account, or otherwise.	Accrued at	Statement of any existing judgment, mortgage, or collateral or other security for the payment of any such debt.
		Dollars.	Cents.			

No. 290.

INVENTORY OF PROPERTY [*being part of Schedule, and to be annexed to No.* 289].

See ante, Vol. I., p. 506.

A full and true inventory of all the estate, both real and personal, in law and equity, of G. L., an insolvent debtor, of the incumbrances existing thereon, and of all the books, vouchers, and securities relating thereto.

[*Insert them.*]

No. 291.

INSOLVENT'S AFFIDAVIT.

See ante, Vol. I., p. 505.

City and County of New York, ss.: I, G. L., do swear [*or*, affirm, *as the case may be*] that the account of my creditors, and the inventory of my estate, which are annexed to my petition, and herewith delivered, are in all respects just and true; and that I have not, at any time, or in any manner whatsoever, disposed of, or made over, any part of my estate, for the future benefit of myself or my family, or in order to defraud any of my creditors; and that I have in no instance created or acknowledged a debt for a greater sum than I honestly and truly owed; and that I have not paid, secured to be paid, or in any way compounded with any of my creditors, with a view fraudulently to obtain the prayer of my petition. G. L.

Sworn to before me, this
—— day of ——, 18—,

D. P. I., Justice of Supreme Court
[*or other officer before whom the proceedings are commenced*].

No. 292.

ORDER TO SHOW CAUSE.

See ante, Vol. I., p. 509.

Upon reading the petition of G. L., and creditors of G. L., an insolvent debtor, and the schedule and affidavits annexed thereto, it is ordered that all the creditors of the said G. L. show cause, if any they have, before me, (*a*) on the —— day of —— next, at —— o'clock in the ——noon, at the chambers of the Supreme Court, in the City Hall, New York [*or other place*], why an assignment of the said insolvent's estate should not be made, and he be discharged from his debts, pursuant to the provisions of the statute for the discharge of an insolvent from his debts. Notice of which is to be published for six weeks [*or*, ten weeks, *as the case may be*], in the State paper, and in the newspaper printed in the city [*or*, village] of ——, entitled the [*name the newspaper. Add, also, if necessary:* and also in the newspaper printed in the city of New York, entitled the ——].

And I do hereby further direct that notice of this order be served, either in person or by letter, on each of the creditors of the said insolvent, G. L., residing in the United States, and whose place of residence is known to the said G. L. And the service of the notice of this order shall be made on each of the said creditors in person, or by letter, addressed to him by mail, at his known and usual place of residence. If such service shall be personal, then it shall be at least twenty days, and if by mail, then forty days, before the said —— day of —— next.

Dated, *&c.* D. P. I., Justice of Supreme Court
[*or other officer*].

(*a*) If the officer making the order be a judge of a county court, and not of the degree of counselor at law, the order should require cause to be shown, at the term of the court to be held next after the expiration of the time of publication of the notice thereof; and the order should specify the time and place at which the term will be held. *Ante*, vol. I., *p.* 509.

No. 293.

NOTICE TO CREDITORS.

See ante, Vol. I., p. 510.

To A. K. [*name of creditor.*]

You will please take notice, that on the —— day of ——, 18—, an order was granted by the Honorable D. P. I., justice of the Supreme Court [*or*, county judge, *or as the case may be*], on the petition of G. L., of, *&c.*, an insolvent debtor, and so many of his creditors residing within the United States whose debts amounted to at least two-thirds of all the debts owing by the said G. L., to creditors residing within the United States, requiring all the creditors of the said G. L. to show cause before him at the chambers of the Supreme Court, in the City Hall, New York [*or other place*], on the —— day of ——, 18—, at — o'clock in the —— noon of that day, why an assignment of the estate of the said G. L. should not be made, and he be discharged from his debts [and from the debts of R. C. & Co., of which he was a member], pursuant to the provisions of the third article, of title first, of chapter fifth, of part second of the Revised Statutes.

Dated, *&c.* G. L., Insolvent.

No. 294.

NOTICE TO BE PUBLISHED.

See ante, Vol. I., p. 510.

Notice of application for the discharge of an insolvent from his debts pursuant to the provisions of article third, of title first, of chapter fifth, of the second part of the Revised Statutes. G. L., applicant. Notice first published on the —— day of ——, 18—, Creditors are required toappear before D. P. I., justice of the Supreme Court [*or other officer*] at the chambers, of the Supreme Court, in the City Hall, New York, on the —— day of ——, 18—, at — o'clock A. M.

Dated, *&c.*

No. 295.

AFFIDAVIT OF SERVICE OF NOTICE.

See ante, Vol. I., p. 510.

State of New York,
City and County of New York, } ss.

L. M., of said city and county, being duly sworn, says, that on the —— day of ——, 18—, he served upon A. B., C. D., and E. F., and each and every of them, a copy of the annexed notice to creditors, by delivering to the said persons, and each and every of them, personally, a true copy of the said notice.

[*If the service was by depositing in the post-office, say* :] That on the —— day of ——, 18—, he served upon A. B. a copy of the annexed notice to creditors, by depositing a true copy thereof in the United States post-office in the city of New York [*or other place*], properly folded and directed to the said A. B., at his place of residence, to wit, at ——, and paying the postage on the same.

Sworn, *&c.* [*as in No.* 286]. L. M.

No. 296.

AFFIDAVIT OF PUBLICATION OF NOTICE TO CREDITORS.

See ante, Vol. I., p. 511.

State of New York,
City and County of New York, } ss.

E. F., of said city, being duly sworn, says: That he is, and during the whole time hereinafter mentioned has been, the printer [*or*, foreman, *or*, principal clerk of the printer] of the ——, a newspaper printed in said city and county, and that the annexed printed notice to creditors was published in the said newspaper six [*or*, ten] weeks successively, at least once in each week; which publication commenced on the —— day of ——, 18—, and terminated on the —— day of ——, 18—.

Sworn, *&c.* [*as in No.* 286]. E. F.

No. 297.

DEMAND OF A JURY AND SPECIFICATIONS OF OBJECTIONS.

See ante, Vol. I., pp. 513, 514.

In the matter of the application of G. L. to be discharged from his debts. }

To D. P. I., Esq., Justice of the Supreme Court [*or other officer or court*]:

I, A. B., one of the creditors of the said G. L., do hereby object to the discharge of said G. L. as an insolvent debtor, and demand that the case of the said G. L., returnable before you this day, be heard and determined by a jury.

And I do hereby specify the following grounds of my objections to such discharge:

1. That the petition herein is not signed by so many of the creditors of the said G. L, residing within the United States, as have debts in good faith owing to them by such debtor, then due or thereafter to become due, and

amounting to at least two-thirds of all the debts owing by him to creditors residing within the United States.

2. That the said G. L., in order to obtain his discharge, has procured C. D., one of the persons signing his petition herein, to become a petitioning creditor for the sum of —— dollars and upward, not due to him from the said G. L.

3. That, &c. [*set out any other objections in detail which the creditor may have*].

Dated, &c. A. B.

No. 298.

ORDER THEREUPON.

See ante, Vol. I., p. 513.

[*Title as in last form.*]

A. B., one of the creditors of G. L., an insolvent debtor, having demanded that the case of the said insolvent be heard and determined by a jury, and having filed with me [*or*, the clerk of this court] a specification in writing of the grounds of his objections to the discharge of said G. L., as an insolvent debtor: It is ordered, that the case of the said insolvent be heard and determined by a jury. [*If the application is to a court, add:* and that the said jury be drawn, in the same manner as for the trial of civil causes, from the jurors summoned and attending this court.]

No. 299

SUMMONS FOR JURY.

See ante, Vol. I., p. 514.

The People of the State of New York, to the Sheriff of the County of —— [*or*, to any one of the Constables of the County of ——, *or*, Marshals of the City of ——, in the County of ——], greeting.

Whereas, on the —— day of ——, 18—, on the application of G. L., an insolvent debtor, I issued an order that the creditors of the said G. L. show cause before me, on the —— day of ——, 18—, why an assignment of the estate of the said G. L. should not be made, and he be discharged from his debts, pursuant to the provisions of chapter five, of part second of the Revised Statutes.

And whereas, on the return day of such order, A. B., one of the creditors of the said insolvent, objected to such discharge, setting forth in writing the grounds of his objections thereto, and demanded that the case of the said insolvent should be heard and determined by a jury.

I have therefore nominated eighteen reputable freeholders of the county of ——, to form a jury for the purpose of hearing and determining the case of the said insolvent, whose names are as follows: [*insert names of jurors*].

You are, therefore, hereby commanded to summon the persons so nominated by me, to appear before me at [*insert place for hearing*], on the —— day of ——, 18—, at —— o'clock –. M., for the purpose of hearing and determining the said case.

Witness my hand, this —— day of ——, 18—,

D. P. I., Justice of Supreme Court,
[*or other officer*].

No. 300.

ASSIGNMENT.

See ante, Vol. I., p. 518.

Know all men, by these presents: That I, G. L., an insolvent debtor, did, in conjunction with so many of my creditors residing within the United States whose debts in good faith amount to two-thirds of all the debts owing by me to creditors residing within the United States, present a petition to D. P. I., justice of the Supreme Court [*or other officer*], praying for relief, pursuant to the provisions of the statute authorizing an insolvent debtor to be discharged from his debts; whereupon the said justice ordered notice to be given to all my creditors to show cause, if any they had, before him, at a certain day and place, why the prayer of the said petition should not be granted; which notice was duly published and served as required by law; and no good cause appearing to the contrary; and the said justice, being satisfied that I have in all things conformed to those matters required by the said statute, has directed an assignment of all my estate to be made by me for the benefit of all my creditors.

Now, therefore, know ye: That, in conformity to the said direction, I have granted, released, assigned, and set over, and by these presents do grant, release, assign, and set over, unto W. M., of, *&c.*, assignee nominated to receive the same, all my estate, real and personal, both in law and equity, in possession, reversion, or remainder, and all books, vouchers, and securities relating thereto, to hold the same unto the said assignee to and for the use of all my creditors. [*If necessary, except from the assignment such articles of wearing apparel and bedding as in the opinion of the officer shall be reasonable and necessary for the insolvent and his family to retain. Also the arms and accouterments required by law.*]

In witness whereof, I have hereunto set my hand and seal, this —— day of ——, in the year one thousand eight hundred and ——.

Sealed and delivered in
the presence of

G. L. [L. S.]

[*Add acknowledgment or proof of execution, as in No. 44.*]

No. 301.

ASSIGNEE'S CERTIFICATE.

See ante, Vol. I., p. 519.

I, W. M., of, *&c.*, do hereby certify, that G. L., an insolvent debtor, has this day granted, conveyed, assigned, and delivered to me, for the use and benefit of all his creditors, all his estate, real and personal, both in law and equity, in possession, reversion, or remainder, and all books, vouchers, and securities relating to the same, except such articles of wearing apparel and bedding as are reasonable and necessary for the said insolvent and his family to retain, and also his arms and accouterments.

In witness whereof, I have hereunto set my hand and seal, this —— day of ——, in the year one thousand eight hundred and ——.

W. M.

Executed in the presence of [*two witnesses*].

[*Add proof of execution of certificate by one of the witnesses, as in No.* 44.].

No. 302.

CLERK'S CERTIFICATE OF RECORDING OF ASSIGNMENT.

See ante, Vol. I., p. 520.

I, H. W. G., clerk of the county of ——, do hereby certify that an assignment of all the estate, real and personal, both in law and equity, in possession, reversion, and remainder, and all books, vouchers, and securities relating thereto of G. L., an insolvent debtor, made by the said G. L. to W. M., to and for the use of the creditors of the said G. L., and dated the —— day of ——, 18—, was duly recorded in the clerk's office of said county, on the —— day of ——, 18—.

In witness whereof I have hereunto subscribed my name and affixed my official seal, this —— day of ——, 18—.

[SEAL.] H. W. G., Clerk.

No. 303.

ASSIGNEE'S OATH OF OFFICE.

See ante, Vol. I., p. 519.

I, W. M., having been appointed assignee of G. L., an insolvent debtor, do swear [*or*, affirm] that I will well and truly execute the trust by that appointment reposed in me, according to the best of my skill and understanding.

W. M.

Sworn to, *&c.* [*as in No.* 286].

No. 304.

DISCHARGE.

See ante, Vol. I., p. 521.

To all to whom these presents shall come or may concern:

I, D. P. I., justice of the Supreme Court of the State of New York [*or other officer*], send greeting: Whereas, G. L., an insolvent debtor, residing within the city and county of New York [*or other place*], did, in conjunction with so many of his creditors, residing within the United States, as have debts in good faith owing to them by the said insolvent, amounting to at least two-thirds of all the debts owing by him to creditors residing within the United States, present a petition to me, praying that the estate of the said insolvent might be assigned for the benefit of his creditors, and he be discharged from his debts, pursuant to the provisions of the statute authorizing an insolvent debtor to be discharged from his debts: whereupon I ordered notice to be given, as required by law, to all the creditors of the said insolvent, to show cause, if any they had, before me, at a certain time and place, why an assignment of the said insolvent's estate should not be made, and he be discharged from his debts, proof of the service whereof on such of the creditors of said insolvent, whose places of residence are known to the insolvent, as required by law, and of the publication whereof, hath been duly made. And, whereas, it satisfactorily appearing to me that the proceedings on the part of the creditors are just and fair, and that the said insolvent has conformed in all things to those matters required of him by the said statute, I directed an assignment to be made, by the said insolvent, of all his estate, real and personal, both in law and equity, in possession, reversion, or remainder, to W. M., assignee nominated by the creditors to receive the same; and the said insolvent having, on the —— day of ——, 18—, made such assignment, and produced to me a certificate thereof, executed by the said assignee, and duly proved, and also a certificate of the clerk of said county of ——, that such assignment is duly recorded in his office: Now, therefore, know ye, that, by virtue of the power and authority in me vested, I do hereby discharge the said insolvent from all his debts, and from imprisonment, pursuant to the provisions of the said statute.

In witness whereof, I have hereunto set my hand, the —— day of ——, in the year of our Lord one thousand eight hundred and ——.

D. P. I., Justice of the Supreme Court [*or other officer*].

No. 305.

CERTIORARI TO REMOVE PROCEEDINGS INTO SUPREME COURT.

See ante, Vol. I., p. 533.

[*Same, with necessary alterations, as in No.* 94. *See also No.* 92 *for form of affidavit on which to apply for certiorari.*]

No. 306.

PETITION FOR DISCHARGE FROM IMPRISONMENT ON EXECUTION.

See ante, Vol. I., p. 547.

To the Supreme Court of the State of New York [*or other court*]:

The petition of L. L., of, &c., shows to the court, that he is a prisoner, confined in the jail of the county of ——, on an execution against the person, issued out of this court, in a civil action wherein W. C. is plaintiff, and your petitioner is defendant; and in which action judgment was rendered against your petitioner for the sum of —— dollars, on the —— day of ——, 18—. That the said sum of —— dollars is now due and unpaid on said execution [*if the imprisonment is for a sum exceeding five hundred dollars, add:* and that your petitioner has been imprisoned on said execution for more than three months].

Your petitioner further shows, that annexed hereto, marked as schedules "*A*" and "*B*," is a just and true account of all his estate, real and personal, in law and equity, and of all charges affecting the same, both as such estate and charges existed at the time of his imprisonment, and as they exist at the time of preparing this petition, together with a just and true account of all deeds, securities, books, and writings whatsoever relating to the said estate, and the charges thereon, with the names and places of abode of the witnesses to such, deeds, securities, and writings.

Your petitioner, therefore, prays, that an order may be made directing the sheriff of said county to bring your petitioner into court on a day assigned for that purpose; and that your petitioner may be discharged from his said imprisonment on his compliance with the provisions of the statute; and that your petitioner may have such further or other relief as he may be entitled to under the provisions of the statute authorizing debtors, imprisoned in execution in civil causes, to be discharged from imprisonment.

Dated, &c. [*Signature of prisoner.*]

[*Annex schedules as follows:*]

SCHEDULE "*A*," *referred to in the petition annexed.*

A just and true account of all the estate, real and personal, in law and equity, and of all charges affecting the same, of L. L., an imprisoned debtor, as the same existed at the time of his imprisonment, as stated in said petition, together with a just and true account of all deeds, securities, books, and writings whatsoever relating to the said estate and the charges thereon, with the names and places of abode of the witnesses to such deeds, securities, and writings, according to the best of his knowledge, information, and belief.

Real estate, as follows: [*set it out*].

Personal estate, as follows: [*set it out*].

Charges affecting the said estate, as follows: [*state the charges in full*].

Account of all deeds, securities, books, and writings relating to the said estate, and the charges thereon, and the names and places of abode of the witnesses to the same, as follows: [*set out the account in full*].

SCHEDULE "*B*," *referred to in the petition annexed.*

[*Same form as schedule* "*A*," *except in the place of the words* "at the time of his imprisonment, as stated in said petition," *insert the words*, "at the time of preparing the said petition."]

No. 307.

NOTICE TO CREDITORS.

See ante, Vol. I., p. 549.

SUPREME COURT [*or other court*].

In the matter of L. L., an imprisoned debtor.

To W. C.

Sir,—Please to take notice that I shall present to the Supreme Court [*or other court*], at the next special term thereof, to be held at the Court House at ——, in the county of ——, on the —— day of ——, 18—, at ten o'clock in the forenoon, or as soon thereafter as counsel can be heard, the petition, together with the account annexed thereto, with copies whereof you are herewith served; and that I shall then and there apply to the said court that the prayer of the said petition be granted.

Dated, &c. Yours, &c., L. L.

No. 308.

AFFIDAVIT TO BE INDORSED ON PETITION.

See ante, Vol. I., p. 549.

County of ——, ss.

I, the within-named petitioner, do swear [*or*, affirm, *as the case may be*], that the within petition and account of my estate, and of the charges thereon, are in all respects just and true; and that I have not, at any time or in any manner, disposed of or made over any part of my property with a view to the future benefit of myself or my family, or with an intent to injure or defraud any of my creditors. L. L.

Sworn to before me this —— day of ——, 18—,

D. P. I., Justice of Supreme Court [*or other officer holding the court*].

No. 309.

AFFIDAVIT OF SERVICE OF PETITION, ACCOUNT, AND NOTICE.

See ante, Vol. I., p. 549.

[*Same as in No.* 295, *with necessary alterations.*]

No. 310.

ORDER TO BRING PRISONER BEFORE THE COURT.

See ante, Vol. I., p. 549.

[*Title as in No.* 307.] At a special term, *&c.* [*as in No.* 6].

The said L. L., having presented his petition to this court, praying for an order directing the sheriff of the county of —— to bring him, the said L. L., into this court on a day assigned for that purpose, and that the said L. L. be discharged from his imprisonment upon an execution issued out of this court in an action wherein W. C. is plaintiff and the said L. L. is defendant; (*) and due proof being made to the court of the service upon the said W. C. of a copy of said petition, and of the account annexed thereto, with the notice of the presentation of the same, It is ordered, that the sheriff of said county of —— bring the said L. L. before this court, at the present special term thereof, now sitting at the Court House in the village of ——, in said county, on the —— day of ——, 18—, at ten o'clock in the forenoon of that day.

No. 311.

ORDER DIRECTING ASSIGNMENT.

See ante, Vol. I., p. 550.

[*Same as in last form to the asterisk* (*), *and then as follows*]*:* and the said order having been duly issued, and the said L. L. brought before the court in pursuance thereof; and the court having heard and determined the proofs and allegations of the parties, and being satisfied that the petition and account of the said L. L. are correct, and that his proceedings are just and fair; It is therefore ordered, that an assignment be made by the said imprisoned debtor to A. B., of, *&c.*, who is hereby appointed assignee to receive the same, of all the said debtor's property, except such articles as are exempt by law from levy and sale on execution.

No. 312.

ASSIGNMENT TO BE INDORSED ON PETITION.

See ante, Vol. I., p. 550.

Whereas, I, L. L., did present the within petition to the Supreme Court [*or other court*], and an order having been duly made thereupon, requiring the sheriff of the county of —— to bring the said L. L. before the said court at the special term thereof, held at the Court House in the village of ——, in said county, on the —— day of ——, 18—, and the said sheriff having complied with the said order; and the court, thereupon, after hearing the proofs and allegations of the parties, having ordered the said L. L. to make an assignment of all his property, except such articles as are by law exempt from levy and sale on execution, to A. B., of, *&c.*, who was appointed assignee to receive the same.

Now, therefore, in consideration thereof, and in conformity to the order of said court, I have assigned and transferred, and hereby do assign and transfer, unto the said A. B., as such assignee, all the property owned by me, except such articles as are exempt by law from levy and sale on execution.

No. 313.

CERTIFICATE OF ASSIGNEE.

See ante, Vol. I., p. 551.

I, A. B., duly appointed assignee of the property of L. L., an imprisoned debtor, do hereby certify that the said L. L. has this day actually delivered to me all the property directed to be assigned to me by an order of the Supreme Court [*or other court*], dated the —— day of ——, 18—.

Dated, *&c.* A. B., Assignee.

Witness.

[*Add acknowledgment or proof of signature, as in No.* 44.]

No. 314.

ORDER DISCHARGING PRISONER.

See ante, Vol. I., p. 551.

[*Title as in No.* 307.] At a special term, *&c.* [*as in No.* 6].

The said L. L. having presented his petition to this court, praying for an order directing the sheriff of the county of —— to bring him, the said L. L., into this court on a day assigned for that purpose, and that the said L. L. be discharged from his imprisonment upon an execution issued out of the said court in an action wherein W. C. was plaintiff and the said L. L. was defendant; and the said order having been duly issued, and the said L. L. brought before the court in pursuance thereof; and the court having heard and determined the proofs and allegations of the parties; and being satisfied that the petition and account of the said L. L. are correct, and that his proceedings have been just and fair; and having thereupon made a further order directing an assignment to be made by the said L. L., of all his property, except such articles as are exempt from execution, to A. B., of, *&c.*, who was appointed assignee to receive the same; and the said assignment having been duly made; and satisfactory evidence having been furnished to the court that the said property has been actually delivered to the said assignee [*or*, and security, approved by the court, having been given by the said L. L. for the future delivery of said property to the said assignee]:

It is, therefore, hereby ordered, that the said L. L. be, and he is hereby, discharged from his imprisonment under and in pursuance of the execution aforesaid.

CHAPTER XV.

FORMS IN ACTIONS AND PROCEEDINGS AGAINST LEGATEES, HEIRS, JOINT DEBTORS, Etc.

I. Forms in Proceedings against Heirs, Joint Debtors, etc.

No. 315.

SUMMONS AGAINST HEIRS, DEVISEES, ETC.

See ante, Vol. I., pp. 589, 599

[*Title of the cause in which judgment was rendered.*]

To E. F., G. H., and J. K., heirs [*or as the case may be*] of R. F., defendant above named:

You are hereby summoned and required to show cause, within twenty days after the service of this summons upon you, why the judgment entered in the above-entitled action, on the —— day of ——, 18—, in the clerk's office of the county of ——, in favor of A. B., plaintiff above named, against R. F., defendant above named, for —— dollars, damages and costs, should not be enforced against the estate of the said R. F., in your hands, to wit: against that piece or parcel of land situated, *&c.* [*describe the estate*].

Dated, *&c.*

E. B., Att'y for Plaintiff,
[*adding his address*].

No. 316.

SUMMONS AGAINST JOINT DEBTORS.

See ante, Vol. I., p. 607.

[*Title of the cause in which judgment was rendered.*]

To E. F., defendant above named:

You are hereby summoned and required to show cause, within twenty days after the service of this summons upon you, why you should not be bound by the judgment entered in the above-entitled action, on the —— day of ——, 18—, in the clerk's office of the county of ——, in favor of A. B., plaintiff above named, against C. D. and E. F., for —— dollars, damages and costs, in the same manner as if you had been originally summoned therein.

E. B., Att'y for Plaintiff,
[*adding his address*].

Dated, *&c.*

No. 317.

AFFIDAVIT TO ACCOMPANY SUMMONS.

See ante, Vol. I., p. 607.

[*Title of the cause.*]

County of ——, ss.: E. B., attorney for the plaintiff above mentioned, being duly sworn, deposes and says: He is the person subscribing the above summons, as attorney for the plaintiff. That the judgment mentioned in said summons has not been satisfied, to deponent's knowledge or information and belief; and that the amount now due upon said judgment is the sum of —— dollars, with interest thereon from the —— day of ——, 18—.

Sworn, *&c.* E. B.

II. Forms in Actions against Next of Kin, Heirs, etc.

No. 318.

COMPLAINT—CREDITOR AGAINST NEXT OF KIN.

See ante, Vol. I., p. 584.

[*Title of the cause as in No.* 165,]

The complaint of the above-named plaintiff, by A. N. W., his attorney, shows to the court:

That, *&c.* [*set forth a cause of action against the ancestor of the defendant, showing, also, that the debt is due and unpaid; and then proceed:*]

The plaintiff further shows, upon information and belief,(*) that on the —— day of ——, 18—, at ——, in the county of ——, the said C. D. [*the decedent*] died intestate, and that afterward, and on or about the —— day of ——, 18—, letters of administration upon his estate were duly issued to R. D., by the surrogate of the county of ——, in this State, whereby the said R. D. was duly appointed administratrix of all and singular the goods, chattels, and credits of the said deceased [*or*, that on the —— day of ——, 18—, at the town of ——, in the county of ——, the said C. D. departed this life, leaving a last will and testament, by which R. D. was appointed sole executrix of the estate of the said deceased. That the said will was duly proved and admitted to probate by the surrogate of the county of ——, and letters testamentary thereupon were thereafter duly issued by him to the said R. D.]

The plaintiff further shows upon information and belief, that the defendant is one of the next of kin of the said intestate, and that the said administratrix, prior to the commencement of this action, paid over to said defendant assets of said estate, amounting to the sum of —— dollars.

Wherefore, the plaintiff demands judgment against the defendant for the amount of his aforesaid claim, with interest thereon from the —— day of ——, 18—, or so much of said amount as the moneys received by the defendant, as aforesaid, will pay of the same.

A. N. W., Att'y for Plaintiff.

[*Verification as in No.* 169.]

No. 319.

COMPLAINT—CREDITOR AGAINST LEGATEE.

See ante, Vol. I., p. 587.

[*Title, &c., as in last form to the asterisk* (*) *and then as follows:*] that on the —— day of ——, 18—, at the town of ——, in the county of ——, the said C. D. departed this life, leaving a last will and testament, by which R. D. was appointed sole executrix of the estate of the said deceased. That the said will was duly proved and admitted to probate by the surrogate of the county of ——, and letters testamentary thereupon were thereafter duly issued by him to the said R. D.

The plaintiff further shows, upon information and belief, that, in and by his said will, the said C. D. bequeathed a legacy of —— dollars to the defendant; and that, before the commencement of this action, the said executrix paid to the defendant, as such legatee, the sum of —— dollars, out of said estate, being the amount of such legacy.

The plaintiff further shows upon information and belief, that no assets have been delivered by the said executrix to the next of kin of the said deceased, or any of them.

Wherefore, the plaintiff demands judgment against the defendant for the amount of his said claim, with interest thereon from the —— day of ——, 18—, together with the costs of this action.

A. N. W., Attorney for Plaintiff.

[*Add verification as in No.* 169.]

No. 320.

COMPLAINT—CREDITOR AGAINST HEIR.

See ante, Vol. I., pp. 589, 595.

[*Title of the cause as in No.* 165,]

The complaint of the above-named plaintiff, by A. N. W., his attorney shows to the court:

That, *&c.* [*set forth a cause of action against the ancestor of the defendant, showing, also, that the debt is due and unpaid, and then proceed:*]

And the plaintiff further shows, upon information and belief, that on the —— day of ——, 18—, at the town of ——, in the county of ——, C. D. above named, departed this life, intestate; and that more than three years before the commencement of this action, to wit: on the —— day of ——, 18—, letters of administration were duly issued upon the estate of the said intestate, by the surrogate of the county of ——, in this State, whereby R. D. was duly appointed administratrix of the goods, chattels, and credits of the said deceased.

The plaintiff further shows, upon information and belief, that the defendant is the only heir of the said deceased; and that the following described premises descended from the said deceased to the said defendant, as such heir, viz.: [*insert description of real estate.*]

The plaintiff further shows, upon information and belief, that the personal assets of the said deceased were insufficient to pay the plaintiff's claim, as aforesaid.

Wherefore, the plaintiff demands judgment, that the premises above described be sold, and that the plaintiff's aforesaid claim, with the interest upon the same, be paid out of the proceeds of such sale, together with the plaintiff's costs of this action.

A. N. W., Attorney for Plaintiff.

[*Verification as in No.* 169.]

CHAPTER XVI.

FORMS UNDER LIEN LAWS IN FAVOR OF MECHANICS AND OTHERS.

I. FORMS UNDER LIEN LAW FOR THE CITY OF NEW YORK.

No. 321.

NOTICE OF LIEN BY CONTRACTOR.

See ante, Vol. I., pp. 625 to 628.

To W. C. C., Esq., Clerk of the City and County of New York:

SIR: Take notice that I, A. B., residing at No. —— Street, in the city of New York, have a claim against E. F., now due [*or*, which will be due on the —— day of ——, 18—], amounting to the sum of —— dollars, for three months' labor performed for the said E. F., as a carpenter and joiner [*or*, for large quantities of lumber furnished to the said E. F.], in pursuance of, or in conformity with, an agreement with him. That the said labor was performed [*or*, the said materials were furnished] in erecting the building and appurtenances [*or*, in altering, improving, and repairing the building and appurtenances] situated on —— Street, in said city, and known as No. —— on said street [*or*, situated on —— Street, in said city, on the northerly side thereof, and on a lot twenty-five feet front, commencing two hundred feet easterly from the Fifth Avenue, a diagram of which is annexed hereto, *or*, accompanying this notice]. That three months have not elapsed since the performance and completion of such labor [*or*, since the said materials were furnished]. That the said E. F. is the owner of the said building and appurtenances, and lot on which the same stand, and which lot and premises are situated on —— Street aforesaid, and are known and described as follows: [*insert brief description of the premises, by street, number, or a diagram or boundary, or by a reference to maps open to the public, so as to furnish information to persons examining titles*].

Also take notice (*) that I have and claim a lien on the building and appurtenances above mentioned, and upon the lot of land upon which the said building and appurtenances stand, pursuant to the provisions of an act of the Legislature of the State of New York, entitled, "An act to secure the payment of mechanics, laborers, and persons furnishing materials toward the erection, altering, or repairing of buildings in the city of New York," passed May 5th, 1863.

Dated, *&c.* A. B., Claimant.

A. N. W., Att'y for Claimant.

City and County of New York, ss.: A. B., being duly sworn, says: He is the claimant above named; that the foregoing notice of claim, and statement therein, is true to his own knowledge, except as to the matters therein stated on information and belief, and as to those matters he believes it to be true.

Sworn to, *&c.* A. B.

No. 322.

NOTICE OF LIEN BY OTHER PERSON THAN THE CONTRACTOR.

See ante, Vol. I., pp. 625 to 628.

To W. C. C., Esq., Clerk of the City and County of New York:

SIR: Take notice that I, C. D., residing at No. —— Street, in the city of New York, have a claim against A. B., now due [*or*, which will be due on the —— day of ——, 18—], amounting to the sum of —— dollars, for three months' labor performed for the said A. B., as a carpenter and joiner [*or*, for large quantities of lumber furnished to the said A. B.], in pursuance of an employment, or an agreement, between me and the said A. B. That the said A. B. is the contractor of E. F., hereinafter named; and the said labor was performed [*or*, the said materials were furnished] in erecting the building and appurtenances [*or*, in altering, improving, and repairing the building and appurtenances] situated in the —— ward, in said city, on the lot hereinafter more particularly described, and known as No. —— Street. That the said E. F. is the owner of the said building and appurtenances, and lot on which the same stand; and that the said labor was performed [*or*, the said materials were furnished] in erecting the building and appurtenances [*or*, in altering, improving, and repairing the building and appurtenances] aforesaid, and in pursuance of, or in conformity with, the terms of the contract between the said A. B. and the said E. F. [*or*, in pursuance of an employment by the said E. F. of the said A. B.; *or*, in accordance with the directions of the said E. F., owner, aforesaid; *or*, in accordance with the directions of S. F., the agent of the said E. F., owner, aforesaid].

That three months have not elapsed since the performance and completion of such labor [*or*, since the said materials were furnished].

That the said lot and premises are known and described as follows: [*insert brief description of the premises, as in last form*].

Also take notice, that, *&c.* [*conclude substantially as in last form from the asterisk* (*), *including the verification of the notice*].

No. 323.

CONTRACTOR'S NOTICE OF FORECLOSURE OF LIEN.

See ante, Vol. I., pp. 631 to 635.

IN SUPREME COURT [*or other court*]:

A. B.   *against*   E. F. and R. S.

To E. F. above named, the owner of the building and premises hereinafter mentioned, and R. S., having a lien or incumbrance thereon:

Take notice, that I, A. B. above named, residing at, *&c.*, have a claim against you, the said E. F., amounting to the sum of —— dollars, with interest thereon from the —— day of ——, 18—, for three months' labor performed for you as a carpenter and joiner [*or*, for large quantities of materials furnished to you], in pursuance of, or in conformity with, an agreement with you; and which labor was performed [*or*, materials were furnished] in erecting the building [*or*, in altering, improving, and repairing the building] No. — and appurtenances, owned by you, the lot upon which the same stand being bounded and described as follows: [*insert description as in notice of lien*].

Also take notice (*), that within three months after the performance and completion of such labor [*or*, the furnishing of such materials], to wit: on the —— day of ——, 18—, I duly filed with the clerk of the city and county of New York the notice required by law to effect a lien on the building and premises above mentioned, for the amount of the claim, as aforesaid.

You will also take notice, that you are required to appear before this court at, *&c.*, on the —— day of ——, 18—, at 10 o'clock A. M., then and there to answer this notice; and, in default thereof, the said claimant will apply to the court for judgment against you, the said E. F., for the amount claimed, as aforesaid, to wit, for the sum of —— dollars, and interest thereon from the —— day of ——, 18—, with the costs of the action; and that the said judgment be enforced against the said building and premises.

Dated, *&c.*

A. B., Claimant.

A. N. W., Att'y for Claimant.

No. 324.

NOTICE OF THE FORECLOSURE OF LIEN BY OTHER PERSON THAN A CONTRACTOR.

See ante, Vol. I., pp. 631 to 635.

IN SUPREME COURT [*or other court*]:

C. D. *against* E. F. and R. S.

To E. F. above named, owner of the building and premises hereinafter mentioned, and to R. S., having a lien or incumbrance thereon:

Take notice, that I, C. D. above named, residing at, *&c.*, have a claim against A. B., of ——, in said county, who was the contractor with you, the said E. F., for the erection of the building and appurtenances hereinafter mentioned, amounting to the sum of —— dollars, with interest thereon from the —— day of ——, 18—, for three months' labor performed for the said A B., as a carpenter and joiner [*or*, for large quantities of materials furnished to the said A. B.], in pursuance of an agreement with him; and which labor was performed [*or*, which materials were furnished] in erecting the building No. — and appurtenances, owned by you, the lot upon which the same stand being bounded and described as follows: [*insert description as in the notice of lien*].

Also, take notice, *&c.* [*as in last form from the asterisk*].

No. 325.

AFFIDAVIT OF THE SERVICE OF THE NOTICE.

See ante, Vol. I., p. 635.

[*Title.*]

City and County of New York, ss.:

H. S., of said city and county, being duly sworn, deposes and says: That on the —— day of ——, 18—, he personally served a copy of the annexed notice upon E. F., the owner mentioned therein, by delivering the same to, and leaving the same with, the said E. F., at his residence No. ——, in said city. And deponent further says, that he knew the person so served to be the person mentioned and described in said notice as owner and defendant therein.

H. S.

Sworn, *&c.*

No. 326.

COMPLAINT, OR STATEMENT OF CLAIM, OF CONTRACTOR AGAINST OWNER.

See ante, Vol. I, p. 639.

[*Title of the cause, as in No.* 323.]

The complaint of A. B., the plaintiff, shows to the court: That on the —— day of ——, 18—, at, *&c.*, the plaintiff, by virtue of a contract with the defendant, E. F., sold and delivered to the said defendant certain building materials, consisting of ——, of the value of —— dollars. That, by the terms of said contract of sale, the said sum of —— dollars became due to the plaintiff on the —— day of ——, 18—; but the defendant, E. F., has not paid the same, and is now justly indebted therefor to the plaintiff. That the said materials were used in erecting a building and appurtenances situated in the —— ward of the city and county of New York, on, *&c.* [*describe the situation of the premises*]: and which building and premises were, at the time of making the said contract, and until the filing of the notice of lien hereinafter mentioned, the property of the defendant, E. F.

The plaintiff further shows: That on the —— day of ——, 18—, the said plaintiff duly filed with the clerk of the city and county of New York a notice of lien claimed upon said premises for the indebtedness aforesaid; which notice was duly verified, and specified the amount of the claim, as above stated, and also specified the defendant, E. F., as the person against whom the claim was made, and as the owner of said building, and which building was therein described by the street and number, as aforesaid.

The plaintiff further shows, upon information and belief, that the defendant R. S. has, or claims to have, some interest in, or lien upon, the said building and premises, or some part thereof.

Wherefore, the plaintiff demands judgment directing a sale of the interest of the defendant in the building, appurtenances, and premises, aforesaid, to the extent of the right of the defendant at the time the notice of lien was filed, as aforesaid; and directing also, that the proceeds of such sale be applied to the payment of the costs of these proceedings, and the plaintiff's claim, as aforesaid, and that the residue of the proceeds, if any, be paid to the clerk of the city and county of New York, to abide the further order of the court.

The plaintiff also demands judgment against the defendant, E. F., for the sum of —— dollars, aforesaid, with interest thereon from the —— day of ——, 18—, besides the costs of this action.

A. N. W., Attorney for Plaintiff.

No. 327.

COMPLAINT, OR STATEMENT OF CLAIM, AGAINST BOTH OWNER AND CONTRACTOR.

See ante, Vol. I., p. 639.

IN SUPREME COURT [*or other court*] CITY AND COUNTY OF NEW YORK.

C. D.
against
A. B., E. F., and R. S.

The complaint of C. D., the plaintiff, shows to the court: That on the —— day of ——, 18—, the defendant, A. B., entered into a contract with the defendant, E. F., for the erection of [*or*, was employed by the defendant, E. F., to erect] a building and appurtenances upon the premises hereinafter described; by the terms of which contract [*or*, employment] it was agreed that, *&c.* [*state the terms of contract or employment*].

And the plaintiff further shows: That the said contract has been performed by the said defendant, A. B., and the defendant, E. F., is justly indebted to the said A. B., upon the same, in the sum of —— dollars.

That between the —— day of ——, 18—, and the —— day of ——, 18—, the said plaintiff, in pursuance of an agreement theretofore entered into by him with the defendant, A. B., and in conformity to the terms of the contract [*or*, employment] above mentioned, performed labor for the defendant, C. D., as a carpenter, to the value of —— dollars. That, by the terms of the agreement between the plaintiff and the defendant, A. B., the said sum of —— dollars became due on the —— day of ——, 18—; but the said defendant has not paid the same, or any part thereof, and is now justly indebted therefor to the plaintiff. That the said labor was performed in erecting [*or*, altering, *or*, repairing, *or*, improving] a building and appurtenances, situated in the —— ward of the city and county of New York, on, *&c.* [*describe the situation of the premises*]. That the said building and premises were at the time the said labor was performed, and until the filing the notice of lien hereinafter mentioned, the property of the defendant, E. F.

And the said plaintiff further shows: That on the —— day of ——, 18—, he duly filed with the clerk of the city and county of New York a notice of lien claimed upon said premises for the indebtedness aforesaid, which notice was duly verified, and specified the amount of the claim, as above stated, and also specified the defendant, A. B., as the person against whom the claim was made, and the defendant, E. F., as the owner of said building, and which building was therein described by the street and number, as aforesaid.

The plaintiff further shows, upon information and belief, that the defendant, R. S., has, or claims to have, some interest in, or lien upon, the said building and premises, or some part thereof.

Wherefore the plaintiff demands judgment, directing a sale of the interest of the defendant, E. F., in the building, appurtenances, and premises above described, to the extent of the right of the said defendant at the time the notice of lien was filed, as aforesaid; and directing, also, that the proceeds of such sale be applied to the payment of the costs of these proceedings, and to the payment of the plaintiff's claim, as aforesaid; and that the residue of such proceeds, if any, be paid to the clerk of the city and county of New York, to abide the further order of the court; and the said plaintiff also demands judgment against the defendants A. B. and E. F., for the sum of —— dollars aforesaid, with interest from the —— day of ——, 18—, together with the costs of these proceedings.

A. N. W., Attorney for Plaintiff.

No. 328.

JUDGMENT ON FAILURE OF OWNER TO APPEAR.

See ante, Vol. I., pp. 635, 649.

[*Title of the cause.*] At a special term, *&c.* [*as in No.* 6].

The above-named A. B., having acquired a lien against the defendant, E. F., as owner, on the —— day of ——, 18—, for the sum of —— dollars, in pursuance of the statute, upon the building and premises hereinafter described; and the said defendant having failed to appear on the —— day of ——, 18—, as required by the notice to enforce such lien, duly served on the defendant, on the —— day of ——, 18—. And the court having made an order on the said —— day of ——, 18—, that a writ of inquiry issue to the sheriff of the city and county of New York [*or*, that it be referred to M. F., of the city and county of New York], to assess the amount of the plaintiff's claim and damages therein; and the said sheriff having, on the —— day of ——, 18—, by the oaths of twelve good and lawful men, duly assessed the amount thereof, and having found the same to be the sum of —— dollars, as appears by the inquisition duly returned [*or*, and the said referee having, on the —— day of ——, 18—, made his report in writing, wherein it appears that he has assessed the amount thereof, and found the same to be the sum of —— dollars, as will more fully appear by the said report, on file with the clerk of this court].

Now, on motion of A. N. W., attorney for the said plaintiff, it is ordered, adjudged, and decreed that judgment be recovered by the plaintiff herein for the sum of —— dollars damages, and —— dollars costs, amounting, in all, to —— dollars.

And it is further ordered, adjudged, and decreed, that the right of the said defendant, E. F., in the building and premises upon which said lien exists, to wit: All that certain piece or lot of land, *&c.* [*describe the premises*], to the extent of the right of the defendant, at the time the notice of lien was filed as aforesaid, be sold at public auction, in the manner prescribed by law, and that the said sheriff be, and he hereby is, directed to apply the proceeds of such sale to the payment of the costs of these proceedings above mentioned, and to the payment of the amount of the plaintiff's claim, as assessed as aforesaid; and that the residue of said proceeds, if any, be paid to the clerk of the city and county of New York, to abide the further order of this court.

It is further ordered, that the said sheriff make a report of such sale, and file it with the said clerk, with all convenient speed; and that, if the proceeds of such sale be insufficient to pay the amount of this judgment, with the interest and costs, as aforesaid, the said sheriff specify the amount of such deficiency in his report of sale, and that the plaintiff have execution against the real and personal property of the defendant for such deficiency.

No. 329.

SATISFACTION OF LIEN.

See ante, Vol. I., p. 630.

I do hereby certify that a certain lien for labor performed [*or*, materials furnished], filed in the office of the clerk of the city and county of New York, on the —— day of ——, one thousand eight hundred and ——, at — o'clock in the —— noon, in favor of A. B., claimant, and against the building and lot situate in the —— ward of said city, on, *&c.* [*describe their situation*], owned by E. F., upon a claim against one C. D., contractor, is paid, satisfied, and discharged.

A. B.

[*Add acknowledgment or proof in the usual form. See No.* 44.]

II. Forms under the General Law in favor of Mechanics, etc.

No. 332.

CONTRACTOR'S NOTICE OF LIEN.

See ante, Vol. I., p. 661.

To J. W. M., Clerk of the County of ——.——,

Take notice, that I, A. B., a resident of the village of ——, in said county, have a claim against E. F., of said village, amounting to the sum of —— dollars, for three months' labor performed for the said E. F., as a carpenter and joiner [*or*, for large quantities of lumber furnished to the said E. F.], in pursuance of an agreement with him. That the said labor was performed [*or*, the said materials were furnished] in erecting the building, No. ——, and appurtenances, situated on Main Street, in said village; and thirty days have not elapsed since the performance and completion of such labor [*or*, since the said materials were furnished]. That the said E. F. is the owner (*) of the said building and appurtenances, and the lot and premises upon which the same stand, which said lot and premises are situated in the town of ——, aforesaid, and are known and described as follows: [*describe premises*].

Also take notice, that I have and claim a lien upon said building and appurtenances, and the lot upon which the same stand, as security for the amount due me, as aforesaid, in pursuance of the statute in such case made and provided. [*Claimant's signature.*]

No. 333.

NOTICE OF LIEN BY OTHER PERSON THAN CONTRACTOR.

See ante, Vol. I., p. 661.

To J. W. M., Clerk of the County of——.

Take notice, that I, C. D., a resident of the village of ——, in said county, have a claim against A. B., who was the contractor with E. F., of said village, for the erection of the building and appurtenances hereinafter mentioned, amounting to the sum of —— dollars, for three months' labor performed for the said A. B., as a carpenter and joiner [*or*, for large quantities of lumber furnished to the said A. B.], in pursuance of an agreement with him. That the said labor was performed [*or*, the said materials were furnished] in erecting the building No. —— and appurtenances situated on Main Street in said village; and thirty days have not elapsed since the performance of such labor [*or*, since the said materials were furnished]. That the said E. F. is the owner, &c. [*conclude as in the last form, from the asterisk*].

No. 334.

CONTRACTOR'S NOTICE TO ENFORCE LIEN.

See ante, Vol. I., p. 666.

IN SUPREME COURT [*or*, In the County Court, —— County].

A. B., Claimant,
against
E. F., Owner.

To E. F. above named, owner of the building and premises hereinafter mentioned:

Take notice, that I, A. B., above-named, residing within the county of ——, have a claim against you, amounting to the sum of —— dollars, with interest thereon from the —— day of —— last, for three months' labor performed for you as a carpenter and joiner [*or*, for large quantities of lumber furnished to you], in pursuance of an agreement with you, the same being fully set forth in the bill of particulars hereto annexed; and which labor was performed [*or*, which materials were furnished] in erecting the building No. ——, and appurtenances owned by you, situated on Main street (*) in the village of ——, in the town of ——, in said county, the lot upon which the same stand being bounded and described as follows: [*describe premises*].

Also take notice, that within thirty days after the performance and completion of such labor [*or*, the final furnishing of such materials], to wit, on the —— day of ——, 18—, I duly filed, with the Clerk of the County of ——, the notice required by law to effect a lien on the building and premises above mentioned, owned by you as aforesaid, for the amount of the claim above stated, to wit, for the sum of —— dollars, and interest as aforesaid.

You will also take notice, that you are required to appear in person, or by attorney, within thirty days after the service of this notice, and answer the same, and to serve upon me, or my attorney, a copy of your answer, together with a notice of any set-off that you may have; or, in default thereof, I will take judgment against you for the amount claimed as aforesaid, to wit, the sum of —— dollars, and interest thereon from the —— day of ——, 18—, together with the costs of this action.

L. P. C., Attorney for Claimant. A. B., Claimant.

Dated, &c.

[*Annex bill of particulars, see form in No.* 336, *post.*]

No. 335.

NOTICE TO ENFORCE LIEN BY OTHER PERSON THAN CONTRACTOR.

See ante, Vol. I., p. 666.

IN SUPREME COURT [*or other court, as in last form*].

C. D., Claimant,
against
E. F., Owner.

To E. F. above named, owner of the building and premises hereinafter mentioned:

Take notice, that I, C. D. above named, residing within the county of ——, have a claim against A. B., of the village of ——, in said county, who was the contractor with you for the erection of the building and appurtenances hereinafter mentioned, amounting to the sum of —— dollars, with interest thereon from the —— day of —— last, for three months' labor performed for the said A. B., as a carpenter and joiner [*or*, for large quantities of lumber furnished to the said A. B.], in pursuance of an agreement with him, the same being fully set out in the bill of particulars hereto annexed; and which labor was performed [*or*, which materials were furnished] in erecting the building No. — and appurtenances, owned by you, situated on Main street, *&c.* [*conclude as in the last form, from the asterisk*].

[*Signed,*] C. D., Claimant.

O. F. C., Attorney for Claimant.

[*Annex bill of particulars, see No.* 336.]

No. 336.

CLAIMANT'S BILL OF PARTICULARS.

See ante, Vol. I., p. 666.

Bill of particulars referred to in the annexed notice, being a bill of particulars of the amount claimed to be due from E. F., the owner mentioned in said notice [*or*, A. B., the contractor mentioned in said notice], for the work performed [*or*, the materials furnished], as therein mentioned, to wit:

E. F., owner [*or*, A. B., contractor].

To A. B., contractor, [*or*, C. D., laborer, *as the case may be*], Dr.

1858.

Aug. 1. To, *&c.* [*set out the length of time the claimant was in the employment of the owner, or contractor, the time when the labor was performed, and the price or value of the same; and if the claim is for materials furnished, set out the items in full, and the price of the same, &c*].

County of ——, ss.: A. B. [*or*, C. D.], the above-named claimant, being duly sworn, says, that the bill of particulars above mentioned is in all respects true.

Sworn, *&c.* A. B.

No. 337.

AFFIDAVIT OF SERVICE OF NOTICE AND BILL OF PARTICULARS.

See ante, Vol. I., pp. 666, 667.

[*Title.*] County of ——, ss. H. S., of ——, in said county, being duly sworn, says: That on the —— day of ——, 18—, he personally served a copy of the annexed notice and bill of particulars upon E. F., the owner mentioned therein, by delivering the same to, and leaving the same with, the said E. F., at his residence in the village of ——, in said county. And deponent further says, that he knew the person so served to be the person mentioned and described in said notice as owner and defendant therein.

Sworn, *&c.* H. S.

No. 338.

AFFIDAVIT OF FACTS JUSTIFYING SERVICE BY PUBLICATION.

See ante, Vol. I., pp. 666, 667.

[*Title.*] County of ——, ss.: H. S., of ——, in said county, being duly sworn, says: That he is acquainted with E. F., the owner mentioned in the annexed notice; that the said E. F. is now absent from this State, and has been so absent for —— days, or more, last past [*or*, that deponent has made diligent inquiry to find the said E. F., for the purpose of serving him with a copy of the notice and bill of particulars annexed, and has been several times to his house with a view of making such service, and has looked and inquired in other places for said E. F.; that said E. F. was well aware that deponent was looking for him to make such service, and kept out of the way purposely, as deponent believes, to avoid said service].

And deponent further says, that on the —— day of ——, 18—, he left a copy of said notice and bill of particulars annexed at the last place of residence of the said E. F., in the village of ——, with the wife of said E. F. [*or other person*].

Sworn, *&c.* H. S.

No. 339.

AFFIDAVIT OF PUBLICATION OF NOTICE.

See ante, Vol. I., pp. 666, 667.

[*Title.*] County of ——, ss.: E. D. B., of ——, in said county, being duly sworn, says: He is the publisher [*or*, printer, *or*, foreman] of the —— Herald, a newspaper printed in said county of ——, and that the annexed printed notice was published in the said newspaper three weeks successively, at least once in each week; which publication commenced on the —— day of ——, 18—, and terminated on the —— day of ——, 18—.

[*Attach here a printed copy of notice.*]

Sworn, *&c.* E. D. B.

No. 340.

AFFIDAVIT OF OWNER'S DEFAULT.

See ante, Vol. I., p. 667.

[*Title.*] County of ——, ss.: L. P. C., being duly sworn, says, He is the attorney for A. B., the plaintiff in the above action; that this action was commenced to enforce a lien against real property owned by the defendant above named, and the notice and bill of particulars herein were served on the defendant on the —— day of ——, as appears by the affidavit of H. S., hereto annexed.

And deponent further says, that no answer or copy of answer has been received herein by deponent, nor has the defendant appeared in this action.

Sworn, *&c.* L. P. C.

No. 341.

JUDGMENT ON FAILURE OF OWNER TO APPEAR.

See ante, Vol. I., p. 667.

[*Title as in No.* 334 *or* 335.] Judgment, August 1, 1866.

The notice and bill of particulars in the above action having been personally served on E. F., the owner and defendant above named, more than thirty days previous to this date, and no copy of an answer to the same having been served upon the plaintiff's attorney as required by said notice; and due proof of the service of such notice and bill of particulars, and of the defendant's failure to appear as aforesaid, having been made and filed; and the plaintiff having also given evidence showing that he has acquired a valid lien upon the building and premises of the defendant, situated in the village of ——, in the county of ——, and which premises are particularly described in said notice; and also evidence to establish the value of the labor performed [*or*, materials furnished] by the plaintiff, as stated in said notice, and that the same was performed for [*or*, were delivered to] the said defendant [*or*, A. B., the original contractor with said defendant, as stated in said notice], in the erection of the building above mentioned and the appurtenances thereto; and the plaintiff's claim having been assessed by the court [*or*, by the clerk of said county] at the sum of —— dollars;

Now, therefore, on motion of L. P. C., attorney for the plaintiff, it is ordered and adjudged, that the plaintiff recover of E. F., the owner and defendant above named, the sum of —— dollars and —— cents, with —— dollars and —— cents costs and disbursements, amounting in the whole to —— dollars and —— cents.

No. 342.

ANSWER OF OWNER AND BILL OF PARTICULARS.

See ante, Vol. I., p. 668.

[*Title as in No.* 334 *or* 335.]

The defendant, E. F., above named, in answer to the notice of the above-named C. D. [*or* A. B.], says: [*Set forth the defenses which the defendant has to the plaintiff's claim, as in an answer in an ordinary action*].

The said defendant, in further answering said notice, says: That the said plaintiff, C. D., is indebted to him in the sum of —— dollars, for moneys loaned and advanced to the plaintiff, from time to time, and which moneys are fully set out in the bill of particulars hereto annexed.

[The defendant also says, in further answering said notice, that A. B., the contractor mentioned therein, is also indebted to him in the sum of —— dollars, for moneys loaned and advanced to the said A. B. during the time the building mentioned in said notice was in the progress of erection,—the items of which are set forth in said bill of particulars annexed.]

And the defendant claims to set off the demands above mentioned, and set out in said bill of particulars, against the claim of said plaintiff, as stated in said notice. E. F., Owner.

E. H., Attorney for Owner.

County of ——, ss.: E. F., the owner above named, being duly sworn, says: That the foregoing answer is true to his own knowledge, except as to the matters therein stated on information and belief, and as to those matters he believes it to be true. E. F.

Sworn, *&c.*

BILL OF PARTICULARS.

Bill of Particulars of set-off claimed by E. F., owner, in the action commenced by ——, to enforce a lien under the statute, and mentioned in the answer of E. F., hereto annexed, viz.:

Moneys loaned by the said E. F. to C. D., at the times and to the amounts following:

1865.

June 1. To cash lent this day $200 00

" 6. To, *&c.* [*set out items*].

[Moneys advanced by E. F., above named, to A. B., the contractor mentioned in the notice, to enforce said lien, at the times and to the amounts following:

1865.

Aug. 1. To, *&c.* [*set out the items and amounts*].

E. F., Owner.

No. 343.

JUDGMENT ON ISSUE AND TRIAL.

See ante, Vol. I., p. 670.

[*Title as in No.* 334.] Judgment, August 1, 1866.

This action being at issue upon the claimant's notice and bill of particulars to enforce his lien, and the owner's answer and bill of particulars of set-off annexed thereto; and the issue being an issue of fact and triable by the court; and such issue being tried by the court on the —— day of ——, 18—, the Hon. C. R. I., justice [*or*, county judge], presiding, whose decision, in writing, has been filed with the clerk of this court, whereby judgment is ordered against the said E. F., owner, in favor of the above-named claimant, for —— dollars, with costs and disbursements against said owner to be taxed.

Now, on motion of L. P. C., attorney for A. B., the above plaintiff, it is ordered and adjudged that the said plaintiff recover of E. F., owner above named, the aforesaid sum of —— dollars, together with the sum of —— dollars costs and disbursements, amounting in the whole to the sum of —— dollars.

No. 344.

EXECUTION AGAINST THE PROPERTY COVERED BY LIEN.

See ante, Vol. I., p. 672.

The People of the State of New York, to the Sheriff of the County of ——, greeting:

Whereas, judgment was rendered on the —— day of ——, one thousand eight hundred and ——, for the sum of —— dollars, in favor of A. B., plaintiff, against E. F., defendant, in an action in the Supreme Court [*or*, county court of the county of ——], commenced against the said E. F., as owner, to enforce a lien under the statute existing in favor of the said A. B., as claimant, against the building No. ——, on Main Street, in the village of ——, in said county, and the lot of land and premises upon which the same stands, and which lot and premises are bounded and described as follows: [*describe premises*].

And whereas, the said E. F. was the owner of said building and premises at the time said lien was created, to wit: on the —— day of ——, 18—;

And whereas, the said lien was created to secure a claim for three months, labor performed by the said A. B., for the said E. F., as a carpenter and joiner [*or*, for large quantities of lumber which the said A. B. furnished to the said E. F.], in erecting the building aforesaid and the appurtenances thereto; which matters above recited will more fully appear by the judgment roll filed in the office of the clerk of the county of ——, reference being thereunto had;

And whereas, the said judgment was docketed in your county on the —— day of ——, 18—, and the sum of —— dollars, with interest thereon from the —— day of ——, 18—, is now actually due upon said judgment.(*)

Therefore, we command you, that you sell the right, title, and interest which the said E. F., owner as aforesaid, had in the building and premises above mentioned, at the time the notice creating said lien was filed, to wit: on the —— day of ——, 18—, and out of the avails of said sale, that you satisfy the amount of said judgment, and return this execution, within sixty days after its receipt by you, to the clerk of the county of —— .

Witness, C. R. I., Esq., Justice of the Supreme Court [*or*, county judge of said county], the —— day of ——, 18—.

L. P. C., Attorney for Plaintiff.

[*To be indorsed:*]

[*Title as in No.* 334.]

To the Sheriff of the County of ——: Levy, as within directed, the sum of —— dollars, with interest thereon from the —— day of ——, 18—, besides your fees.

L. P. C., Plaintiff's Attorney.

No. 345.

EXECUTION AGAINST REAL ESTATE GENERALLY.

See ante, Vol. I., p. 672, and notes.

[*As in the last form to the* (*), *and then continue:*]

Therefore, we command you, that you satisfy the said judgment out of the real property in your county belonging to said defendant on the day when the said judgment was so docketed in your county, or at any time thereafter, and return this execution, within sixty days after its receipt by you, to the clerk of the county of ——.

Witness, &c. [*as in last form.*]

[*Indorsement as in last form.*]

No. 346.

CONTRACTOR'S NOTICE TO ENFORCE LIEN IN JUSTICE'S COURT.

See ante, Vol. I., p. 673.

IN JUSTICE'S COURT, before W. B. B., Justice.

A. B., Claimant,
against
E. F., Owner.

To E. F. above named, owner of the building and premises hereinafter mentioned:

Take notice, that I, A. B. above named, residing within the county of ——, have a claim against you, amounting to the sum of —— dollars, with interest thereon from the —— day of —— last, for three months' labor performed for you as a carpenter and joiner [*or*, for large quantities of lumber furnished to you], in pursuance of an agreement with you, the same being fully set forth in the bill of particulars hereto annexed; and which labor was performed [*or*, which materials were furnished] in erecting the building No. ——, and appurtenances, owned by you, situated on Main Street (*), in the village of ——, in the town of ——, in said county; the lot upon which the same stand being bounded and described as follows: [*describe premises*].

Also take notice, that within thirty days after the performance and completion of such labor [*or*, the final furnishing of such materials], to wit: on the —— day of ——, 18—, I duly filed with the Clerk of the County of —— the notice required by law to effect a lien on the building and premises above mentioned, owned by you as aforesaid, for the amount of the claim above stated, to wit: for the sum of —— dollars, and interest as aforesaid.

You will, therefore, also take notice, that you are required to appear, in person or by attorney, before W. B. B., Esq., a justice of the peace in and for said town, at his office in said town, on the —— day of —— next, (*a*) at ten o'clock A. M., and answer this notice, or in default thereof, I, the said claimant, will take judgment against you for the amount claimed, as aforesaid, to wit: the sum of —— dollars, and interest thereon from the —— day of ——, 18—, with costs.

Dated, *&c.* A. B., Claimant.

L. P. C., Att'y for Claimant.

[*Annex bill of particulars, see form in No.* 336, *ante.*]

No. 347.

LIKE NOTICE IN JUSTICE'S COURT, BY OTHER PERSON THAN CONTRACTOR.

See ante, Vol. I., p. 673.

IN JUSTICE'S COURT, before W. B. B., Justice.

C. D., Claimant,
against
E. F., Owner.

To E. F. above named, owner of the building and premises hereinafter mentioned:

Take notice, that I, C. D. above named, residing within the county of ——, have a claim against A. B., of the village of ——, in said county, who was the contractor with you for the erection of the building and appurtenances hereinafter mentioned, amounting to the sum of —— dollars, with in-

(*a*) The time must be not less than thirty days after the service of the notice. See *ante*, Vol. I., *p.* 673.

terest thereon from the —— day of —— last, for three months' labor performed for the said A. B., as a carpenter and joiner [*or*, for large quantities of lumber furnished to the said A. B.], in pursuance of an agreement with him, the same being fully set out in the bill of particulars hereto annexed, and which labor was performed [*or*, which materials were furnished] in erecting the building No. ——, and appurtenances, owned by you, situated on Main Street, *&c.* [*conclude as in the last form from the asterisk*].

[*Signed*,] C. D., Claimant.

O. F. C., Att'y for Claimant.

[*Annex bill of particulars, as in No.* 336, *ante.*]

No. 348.

CLAIMANT'S BILL OF PARTICULARS IN JUSTICE'S COURT.

See ante, Vol. I., p. 673.

[*Same as in No.* 336, *ante.*

No. 349.

AFFIDAVITS OF SERVICE OF NOTICE, ETC., ON FAILURE TO APPEAR IN JUSTICE'S COURT.

See ante, Vol. I., p. 673.

[*For forms of affidavits of service of notice, personal and by publication, and of affidavit of facts justifying service by publication, see Nos.* 337, 338, 339, *ante.*]

No. 350.

AFFIDAVIT OF OWNER'S DEFAULT IN JUSTICE'S COURT.

See ante, Vol. I., p. 674.

[*Title.*]

County of ——, ss.: A. B. above named [*or*, L. P. C., attorney for A. B. above-named], being duly sworn, says: He is the plaintiff [*or*, attorney for the plaintiff] in the above action. That this action was commenced to enforce a lien against real property owned by the defendant above named; and the notice commencing the same is returnable before W. B. B., Esq., justice of the peace, at his office in the town of ——, on the —— day of ——, at ten o'clock A. M., as will more fully appear by said notice hereto annexed.

And deponent further says: That the said E. F. has not appeared before the said justice as required by said notice, and that one hour and over has elapsed since the time fixed in said notice for the appearance of said defendant. [*Signature of deponent.*]

Sworn, *&c.*

No. 351.

OWNER'S ANSWER, BEFORE JUSTICE.

See ante, Vol. I., p. 674.

[*Title as in suit before a justice; and then proceed the same as in No.* 342, *ante, including the verification and bill of particulars there given.*]

No. 352.

NOTICE REQUIRING CLAIMS TO BE PRESENTED.

See ante, Vol. I., p. 676.

To all persons having claims under any of the provisions of the act entitled "An act for the better security of mechanics and others erecting buildings in either of the counties of this State, except the counties of Erie, Kings, Queens, New York, and Onondaga, passed April 17, 1864, as amended by chapter 558, of the laws of 1869, against his building No. — and appurtenances, owned by the undersigned, and the land upon which the same stand, and which is situated in the town of ——, in the county of ——, and is described as follows: [*insert brief description of premises*] at the time of the first publication of this notice (to wit: the — day of ——, 18—).

Take notice, that you are required to present the said claims, with vouchers in support thereof, to W. B. B., Esq., a justice of the peace of said town, at his office, in said town, on or before the 17th day of November next [*or*, on or before 10 o'clock A. M., of the 17th day of November next].

Dated, *&c.* E. F., Owner.

No. 353.

NOTICE REQUIRING CLAIMANT TO COMMENCE AN ACTION.

See ante, Vol. I., pp. 654, 677.

To A. B. [*or*, C. D.], claimant: You will take notice, that you are required, within twenty days after the service of this notice, to commence an action to enforce a lien, created by you on the —— day of ——, 18—, against the building No. —— and appurtenances, and the lot upon which the same stand, owned by E. F., to secure an alleged claim for —— dollars, alleged to exist against the said E. F., as owner [*or*, against A. B., as contractor].

The building and premises above mentioned are described in the notice creating said lien, as follows: [*insert description*].

Dated, *&c.* E. F., Owner,
[*or*, T. C., Attorney for E. F., the owner above named;
or, A. B., Contractor; *or*, C. D., Sub-Contractor].

No. 354.

AFFIDAVITS OF SERVICE OF NO. 353, AND THAT ACTION IS NOT COMMENCED.

See ante, Vol. I., pp. 654, 677.

County of ——, ss.: H. S., of ——, in said county, being duly sworn, says: That, on the —— day of ——, 18—, he personally served a notice, of which the above is a copy, upon A. B. [*or*, C. D.], the claimant mentioned therein, by delivering the same to, and leaving the same with, the said A. B. [*or*, C. D.], at his residence, in the village of ——, in said county. And deponent further says, that he knew the person so served to be the person mentioned and described in said notice as claimant therein.

Sworn, *&c.* H. S.

County of ——, ss.: E. F., being duly sworn, says: That more than twenty days have elapsed since the service of the notice mentioned in the affidavit of H. S., hereto annexed; and that no action has been commenced against him to enforce the lien mentioned in said notice.

Sworn, *&c.* E. F.

No. 355.

SATISFACTION OF LIEN.

See ante, Vol. I., p. 678.

[*Same substantially as in No.* 329, *ante.*]

III. Forms in Proceedings to acquire Liens against Ships and Vessels.

No. 357.

SPECIFICATIONS OF LIEN.

See ante, Vol. I., p. 685.

City and County of ——, ss.: A. B., of said city, being duly sworn, deposes and says: He claims a lien upon the ship "Admiral," a sea-going and ocean-bound vessel [*or other description of the vessel*], her tackle, apparel, and furniture, for a debt amounting to —— dollars, contracted by C. D., master [*or*, owner, *&c.*, *as the case may be*] of said vessel, within the State of New York, for the following purposes: On account of work done [*or*, materials, or, other articles, furnished, in this State], for or toward the building [*or*, repairing, *or*, fitting, *or*, furnishing, *or*, equipping] such vessel [*or*, for such provisions and stores, furnished within this State, as were fit and proper for the use of such vessel at the time when the same were furnished; *or*, on account of the wharfage and expenses of keeping such vessel in port, including the expense incurred in employing persons to watch her; *or*, on account of loading, *or* unloading; *or*, for advances made for the purpose of procuring necessaries for such vessel; *or*, for the insurance of such vessel; *or* (*if the debt amounts to* $25 *or upward*), on account of the towing or piloting of such vessel; *or*, on account of the insurance, or premiums of insurance, of or on such vessel, *or*, of or on the freight of such vessel].

And deponent further says, that the following are specifications of the said lien, consisting of a bill of particulars of his aforesaid demand [*or*, consisting of a copy of the written contract under which the said work was done], and containing a statement of the amount claimed to be due from said vessel, viz. : [*set out the items, with amounts, &c., in full*].

And deponent further says, that the said specifications are correct, according to his best knowledge, information, and belief.

Sworn, *&c.* A. B.

E. L. S., Attorney for Applicant.

No. 358.

APPLICATION FOR WARRANT.

See ante, Vol. I., p. 687.

In the matter of the attachment of the ship "Admiral," her tackle apparel, and furniture.

To the Hon. W. H. L., Justice of the Supreme Court:

The application of A. B. shows, that he has due to him a debt amounting to —— dollars, contracted by C. D., master [*or*, owner, *&c.*, *as the case may be*] of the ship "Admiral," a sea-going and ocean-bound vessel [*or other description of the vessel*], her tackle, apparel, and furniture, within the State of New York, for the following purpose: On account of work done, in said State, for or toward the building of said vessel [*or for any other of the purposes stated in the last form*].

The said applicant further shows, that the said debt is a lien upon said vessel, her tackle, apparel, and furniture, and was contracted by C. D., the master [*or*, owner, *or as the case may be*] of said vessel, within the said State, to wit, at the city of New York, for the purpose aforesaid, on the —— day of ——, 18—; that the said debt amounted to the sum of —— dollars, and that the same is justly due to the said applicant, over and above all payments and just deductions; that the following are the items composing said debt, viz.: [*set out the items; or, if they are numerous, say:* that the items composing said debt are set forth in the account or schedule annexed hereto, and forming a part of this application].

And the said applicant further shows, that the said debt was, on the —— day of ——, 18—, by an assignment in writing, prepared and executed in due form of law, assigned and transferred to the said applicant, who is now the holder and owner of the same.

That six months have not expired since said debt was contracted [*or*, that the said debt was contracted on the —— day of ——, 18—, and, at the expiration of six months from that date, the said vessel was absent from the port at which such debt was contracted; and that ten days have not expired since said vessel next returned to the said port]; that the said vessel left the port at which such debt was contracted on the —— day of ——, 18—; and that the said applicant did, on the —— day of ——, 18—, and within twelve days after such departure, cause to be drawn up and filed, in the office of the clerk of the city and county of New York, specifications of such lien, consisting of a bill of particulars of his demand [*or*, consisting of a copy of the written contract under which the said work was done], and containing a statement of the amount claimed to be due from said vessel, the correctness of which was duly sworn to by said applicant.

[*If the lien is upon a vessel navigating the western or north-western lakes, instead of the last paragraph, insert the following:* That six months after the first day of January next succeeding the time such debt was contracted, have not expired [*or*, That the said debt was contracted on the —— day of ——, 18—, and, during the six months after the first day of January next succeeding the time such debt was contracted, the said vessel was absent from the port at which such debt was contracted, and that ten days have not expired since the said vessel next returned to the said port]; that the said applicant did, on the —— day of ——, 18—, and by the first Tuesday of February next succeeding the time such debt was contracted, cause to be drawn up and filed, in the office of the clerk of the county of Erie, specifications of such lien, consisting of a bill of particulars of his demand [*or*, consisting of a copy of the written contract under which the said work was done], and containing a statement of the amount claimed to be due from said vessel, the correctness of which was duly sworn to by said applicant.]

Wherefore, the said applicant prays for a warrant to enforce the said lien against the said vessel, her tackle, apparel, and furniture, and to collect the amount of his aforesaid demand, pursuant to the provisions of the statute providing for the collection of demands against ships and vessels, passed April 24, 1862, and the acts amendatory thereof.

Dated, *&c.* A. B.

E. L. S., Att'y for Applicant.

City and County of New York, ss.: A. B. being duly sworn, deposes and says: He is the applicant in the foregoing application named; that the said application is true, to his own knowledge, except as to the matters therein stated on information and belief, and as to those matters he believes it to be true.

Sworn, *&c.* A. B.

No. 359.

APPLICATION FOR WARRANT AGAINST PROCEEDS.

See ante, Vol. I., pp. 687, 695.

[*Same as in last form, except that before the prayer insert the following clause:*]

And the said applicant further shows, that the said vessel has been seized by the sheriff of the city and county of New York, under a warrant issued on the —— day of ——, 18—, by the Hon. W. H. L., justice of the Supreme Court, on the application of E. F.; that the said vessel, together with her tackle, apparel, and furniture, has been sold by the said sheriff, and that the proceeds of such sale amount to —— dollars, which now stand in place of said vessel, and have not been distributed.

No. 360.

UNDERTAKING BY APPLICANT.

See ante, Vol. I., p. 688.

[*Title as in No.* 358.]

A. B. having applied to W. H. L., one of the justices of the Supreme Court, for a warrant to enforce the lien of said applicant upon the ship "Admiral," and to collect the amount of his demand:

We, A. B., of No. 30 —— Street, in the city of New York, and S. D., of No. 32 —— Street, in the same city, merchants, do undertake, pursuant to the statute in such case made and provided, in the sum of —— dollars, that if the said applicant do not, within three months from the delivery hereof to the said officer, prosecute any bond which may be given upon the discharge of such warrant, or if the said applicant, in any action brought upon such bond, be finally adjudged not to have been entitled to such warrant, they will pay all costs that may be awarded against the said applicant, not exceeding the said sum of —— dollars, and any damages that may be sustained by reason of the seizure of such vessel under such warrant, not exceeding fifty dollars.

[*Add proof or acknowledgment, and affidavit of surety, as in No.* 44.]

APPROVAL [*to be indorsed*]:

I approve of the within undertaking. W. H. L., Justice, *&c.*

No. 361.

WARRANT OF ATTACHMENT.

See ante, Vol. I., p. 688.

To the Sheriff of the City and County of New York, greeting:

Whereas, A. B. has this day presented an application to me, duly verified, exhibiting an account of his demand against the ship "Admiral," now at the port of New York, within the State of New York, whereby it appears that a lien exists upon the said vessel, her tackle, apparel, and furniture, for the sum of —— dollars; and in which he prays for a warrant to enforce the said lien, and to collect the amount of his demand, pursuant to the provisions of the statute providing for the collection of demands against ships and vessels. And the said A. B. having delivered to me the undertaking required by law, to be filed by me.

You are commanded, therefore, to attach, seize, and safely keep the said vessel, her tackle, apparel, and furniture, to satisfy such claim, if established to be a lien upon such vessel according to law, and to make return of your proceedings under this warrant to me within ten days after you shall have made such seizure.

Witness my hand at the City Hall, in the city of New York, the —— day of ——, 18—.

W. H. L.,
Justice of the Supreme Court.

E. L. S.,
Attorney for Applicant.

No. 362.

NOTICE TO PARTIES INTERESTED—TO BE PUBLISHED.

See ante, Vol. I., p. 689.

[*Title as in No.* 358.]

Notice is hereby given, that on the —— day of ——, 18—, a warrant of attachment was issued by the Hon. W. H. L., justice of the Supreme Court in and for the city and county of New York, for the sum of —— dollars, on the application of A. B., directed to the sheriff of said city and county, commanding him to attach, seize, and safely keep the ship "Admiral," then at the port of New York, to satisfy the claim of the said A. B. specified therein at —— dollars; and that the said vessel, her tackle, apparel, and furniture will be sold for the payment of the claims against her, unless the master, owner, or consignee thereof, or some person interested therein, appear and discharge such warrant according to law, within thirty days from the first publication of this notice.

Dated, *&c.* Yours, &c.,

E. L. S.,

Attorney for Applicant.

No. 363.

NOTICE OF APPLICATION TO DISCHARGE WARRANT.

See ante, Vol. I., p. 689.

[*Title as in No.* 358.]

To A. B. [*or*, to E. L. S., Attorney for A. B.]

Take notice, that I shall apply to the Hon. W. H. L., justice of the Supreme Court, at chambers in the City Hall, New York, on the —— day of ——, 18—, at ten o'clock in the forenoon, for an order to discharge the warrant issued by him in this matter on the —— day of ——, 18—; and that the following are the names, places of residence, and places of business of the sureties in the bond proposed to be given by me to obtain such discharge, viz.: S. D., residing at No. 93 Livingston Street, Brooklyn, and doing business at No. 161 Broadway, New York, and L. P., residing at No. 13 Bond Street, and doing business at No. 44 Broad Street, New York.

Dated, *&c.* Yours, &c.,

C. D., Owner of said vessel.

No. 364.

BOND TO OBTAIN DISCHARGE OF WARRANT.

See ante, Vol. I., p. 690.

[*Title as in No.* 358.]

Know all men, by these presents, that we, C. D., residing at No. ——, in the city of New York, owner of the ship "Admiral," S. D., residing at No. 93 Livingston Street, in the city of Brooklyn, and L. P., residing at No. 13 Bond Street, in the city of New York, are held and firmly bound unto A. B., of said city, his executors, administrators, and assigns, in the sum of —— dollars, lawful money of the United States; for which payment well and truly to be made, we bind ourselves, our, and each of our, heirs, executors, and administrators, jointly and severally, firmly by these presents. Sealed with our seals, and dated the —— day of ——, 18—.

Whereas, the sheriff of the city and county of New York has seized the ship "Admiral," her tackle, apparel, and furniture, by virtue of a warrant issued on the application of A. B., claiming to have a lien thereon under the provisions of the act entitled "An act to provide for the collection of demands against ships and vessels," passed April 24, 1862.

Now, therefore, the condition of this obligation is such, that if the obligors above named will pay the amount of any and all claims and demands which shall be established to be due to the said A. B., and to have been a subsisting lien upon such vessel, pursuant to the provisions of the act aforesaid, then this obligation to be void, otherwise, to remain in full force and virtue.

Sealed and delivered in presence of O. P.

C. D., [L. S.]
S. D., [L. S.]
L. P., [L. S.]

[*Add proof or acknowledgment, and affidavit of sureties, as in No.* 44.]

No. 365.

ORDER DISCHARGING WARRANT.

See ante, Vol. I., p. 690.

[*Title as in No.* 358.]

A warrant of attachment having heretofore been issued by me to the sheriff of the city and county of New York, pursuant to the provisions of the act entitled "An act to provide for the collection of demands against ships and vessels," passed April 24, 1862, on the application of A. B. against the ship "Admiral," her tackle, apparel, and furniture; and the said vessel having been seized by the said sheriff, and C. D., the owner of said vessel, having applied to me to discharge the said vessel, and executed a bond according to law, which has been delivered by me to the said A. B., and the taxed fees of the sheriff having been paid:

Now, on motion of T. C., attorney for said owner, I do hereby order that the said warrant be, and the same is hereby, discharged.

W. H. L., Justice of the Supreme Court.

No. 366.

COMPLAINT ON BOND.

See ante, Vol. I., p. 691.

[*Title substantially as in No.* 165.]

The plaintiff complains of the defendant, and shows to the court:

That, as the plaintiff is informed and believes, the defendant, C. D., was the owner of the ship "Admiral," at the several times hereinafter named, and that the said ship was a sea-going and ocean-bound vessel. That the said C. D., on the —— day of ——, 18—, contracted a debt to the plaintiff, within this State, on account of work done and materials furnished in this State, for or toward the repairing, fitting, furnishing, or equipping said vessel [*or as the nature of the debt may be*], which said work and materials were of the value of —— dollars, and that there was justly due the plaintiff upon the said account, on the —— day of ——, 18—, the sum of —— dollars, over and above all payments and just deductions.

The plaintiff further shows, that on the —— day of ——, 18—, and within twelve days after the departure of said vessel from the port at which such debt was contracted, the said plaintiff caused to be drawn up specifications of his lien upon the said vessel (the correctness of which was duly sworn to by the plaintiff), and filed the same in the clerk's office of the city and county of New York, in which county the said lien was created; and that the said claim was a subsisting lien upon the said vessel at the time of the exhibition thereof, as hereinafter mentioned. That the said vessel left the port of New York on the —— day of ——, 18—, and did not return until the —— day of ——, 18—.

The plaintiff further shows, that on the —— day of ——, 18—, the said plaintiff, pursuant to an act entitled "An act to provide for the collection of demands against ships and vessels," passed April 24, 1862, duly applied to the Hon. W. H. L., one of the justices of the Supreme Court, in the city and county of New York (that being the county within which the said vessel then was), for a warrant to enforce the said lien, and to collect the amount thereof; that the said application was in writing, duly verified by the plaintiff, and exhibited by whom and when such debt was contracted, and for what vessel; the items composing such debt; the amount claimed, and that the same was justly due to the plaintiff over and above all payments and just deductions, and the time and place when and where the specifications of such debt were filed. That thereupon the said officer issued his warrant to the sheriff of the city and county of New York, commanding him to attach, seize, and safely keep such ship, her tackle, apparel, and furniture, to satisfy such claim, if established, to be a lien according to law, and to make return of his proceedings under such warrant to the said officer within ten days after such seizure. That the said sheriff did, in pursuance of such warrant, forthwith execute the same, and seized the said vessel as therein directed That, thereupon C. D., owner of the said vessel, on the —— day of ——

18—, and before any order for the sale of said vessel was made, applied to the said justice for an order to discharge the said warrant, and thereupon the said C. D. and the other defendants, S. D. and L. P., duly executed and delivered to the said justice a bond to the creditors prosecuting such warrant, a copy of which is annexed hereto, marked as "Schedule A," whereby they bound themselves, jointly and severally, to pay the plaintiff the sum of —— dollars, subject to the condition expressed in said bond; and that thereupon the said warrant was discharged.

And the plaintiff further shows, that the condition of said bond has been broken by the defendants, and assigns, as a breach of the condition of said bond, that the plaintiff's said claim has not been paid, nor any part thereof; and that the whole amount thereof is due to the plaintiff, with interest thereon from the —— day of ——, 18—.

Wherefore, the plaintiff demands judgment against the defendants for the said sum of —— dollars, with interest thereon from the —— day of ——, 18—, together with the costs of said attachment, and the costs and allowances of this action.

E. L. S., Attorney for Plaintiff.

[*Add verification, if desired, as in No.* 169.]

No. 367.

AFFIDAVIT TO OBTAIN ORDER OF SALE.

See ante, Vol. I., p. 692.

[*Title as in No.* 358.]

City and County of New York, ss.: A. B., being duly sworn, says: He is the applicant for the warrant of attachment in this proceeding; which warrant was issued against the ship "Admiral," by the Hon. W. H. L., one of the justices of the Supreme Court, on the —— day of ——, 18—, and directed to the sheriff of the city and county of New York; and that the said ship, together with her tackle, apparel, and furniture, was seized by the said sheriff on the same day. That thirty days have elápsed since the first publication of the notice required by the 9th section of the act entitled "An act to provide for the collection of demands against ships and vessels," passed April 24, 1862, under which the said proceeding was taken; that the amount of deponent's claim is —— dollars; that the same has not been satisfied, and that the said vessel has not been discharged.

And deponent further says, that, &c. [*set forth the other unsatisfied claims, if any, which have been exhibited against the vessel; and annex to the affidavit proof of the publication of the notice above mentioned. See form of affidavit of publication, Appendix, No.* 190, *with necessary alterations*].

Sworn, &c. A. B.

No. 368.

AFFIDAVIT, NOTICES, ETC.

See ante, Vol. I., p. 692.

[If the application for the order of sale is made upon proof of the *personal service* of the notice required by the 9th section of the statute, and of notice to the owner, &c., follow the affidavit in the last form, omitting the clause in reference to the expiration of thirty days; and, instead of annexing proof of the publication of notice, annex proof of the personal service of the notices required by the statute [*ante*, Vol. I., p. 692]. For forms, see *Appendix*, No. 337.]

The following form of notice of application for the order of sale may be used:

[*Title as in No.* 358.]

To C. D., owner, and to, *&c.* [*the other creditors*].

Take notice, that I shall apply to the Hon. W. H. L., justice of the Supreme Court, at chambers, in the City Hall, New York, on the —— day of ——, 18—, at ten o clock in the forenoon, for an order to the sheriff of the city and county of New York, directing him to sell the ship "Admiral," her tackle, apparel, and furniture, to satisfy the claims which I have against the said ship, &c., under the provisions of the act entitled "An act to provide for the collection of demands against ships and vessels," passed April 24, 1862. Yours, &c., A. B.

Dated, *&c.*

No. 369.

ORDER DIRECTING SALE.

See ante, Vol. I., p. 692.

[*Title as in No.* 358.]

A warrant of attachment against the ship "Admiral" having been issued by me on the —— day of ——, 18—, on the application of A. B., pursuant to an act entitled "An act to provide for the collection of demands against ships and vessels," passed April 24, 1862, directed to the sheriff of the city and county of New York; and the said vessel having on the same day been seized by the said sheriff; and more than thirty days having elapsed since the first publication of the notice required by the ninth section of said act; and the claim of the said A. B. not having been satisfied, and the said vessel not having been discharged; I do hereby direct the said sheriff to proceed and sell the said vessel, her tackle, apparel, and furniture.

And I do hereby declare that the amount deemed necessary to be raised, to satisfy all unsatisfied liens which have been exhibited against the said vessel, is the sum of —— dollars.

I do further order, that notice be published in the —— (that being the newspaper in which the notice of seizure was published), once a week for three weeks, requiring all persons who have any liens upon the said vessel by virtue of the provisions of the said statute, and the master, owner, agent, or consignee, and all other persons interested in the said vessel, to appear before me at the chambers of the Supreme Court, in the City Hall, New York, on the —— day of ——, 18—, at 10 o'clock in the forenoon [*or*, before L. F., Esq., referee, on the —— day of ——, 18—, at his office, No. 128 Broadway, New York], to attend a distribution of the proceeds arising from the sale of such vessel, her tackle, apparel, and furniture.

[And I do hereby further direct that the said distribution be made before the said L. F., who is hereby appointed referee for that purpose.]

W. H. L., Justice of the Supreme Court.

No. 370.

NOTICE OF DISTRIBUTION—TO BE PUBLISHED.

See ante, Vol. I., p. 695.

[*Title as in No.* 358.]

Notice is hereby given that the ship "Admiral," her tackle, apparel, and furniture, will be sold by the sheriff of the city and county of New York, on the —— day of ——, 18—, at 12 o'clock at noon, on board of said vessel, at Pier No. — East River, New York, by virtue of a warrant directed to the said sheriff on the —— day of ——, 18—, pursuant to the provisions of an act entitled "An act to provide for the collection of demands against ships and vessels," passed April 24, 1862; and that all persons having any liens upon the said vessel, by virtue of the provisions of the said act, and the master, owner, agent, or consignee, and all other persons interested in the said vessel, are required to appear before the Hon. W. H. L., justice of the Supreme Court, at chambers, in the City Hall, New York, on the —— day of ——, 18—, at 10 o'clock A. M. [*or*, before L. F., Esq., referee duly appointed for that purpose, on the —— day of ——, 18—, at his office, No. 128 Broadway, New York], to attend a distribution of the proceeds arising from the sale of such vessel, her tackle, apparel, and furniture.

Dated, *&c.* E. L. S., Attorney for Attaching Creditor.

No. 371.

SHERIFF'S RETURN.

See ante, Vol. I., p. 693.

[*Title as in No.* 358.]

To Hon. W. H. L., Justice of the Supreme Court:

I, J. K., sheriff of the city and county of New York, to whom, on the application of A. B., a warrant of attachment, against the ship "Admiral," was issued on the —— day of ——, 18—, under the provisions of the act entitled, "An act to provide for the collection of demands against ships and vessels," passed April 24, 1862, do return, that on the —— day of ——, 18—, I seized the said vessel, her tackle, apparel, and furniture.

I further return, that on the —— day of ——, 18—, I received an order, dated on that day, directing me to proceed and sell the said vessel, her tackle, apparel, and furniture; that I thereupon proceeded to sell, and did sell, the said vessel, her tackle, apparel, and furniture, upon the same notice, in the same manner, and in all respects subject to the provisions of law in case of the sale of personal property upon execution; which sale took place on board of said vessel, in the city of New York, on the —— day of ——, 18—; and that S. S. was the purchaser of said vessel, her tackle, apparel, and furniture, at the sum of —— dollars. That my fees and expenses in seizing, preserving, watching, and selling said vessel have been duly taxed, and amount to the sum of —— dollars; and that the proceeds of said sale, after deducting such fees and expenses, amount to —— dollars.

I further return, that I have not seized the said vessel by virtue of any other warrant than that above mentioned [*or, if there are other warrants, state in whose behalf, and for what sums respectively, and the time of his reception thereof*].

Dated, *&c.* J. K., Sheriff.

No. 372.

ANSWER CONTESTING APPLICANT'S CLAIM.

See ante, Vol. I., p. 694.

[*Title as in No.* 358.]

C. D., the owner [*or*, master, *&c.*; *or*, a person having an interest in the proceeds] of the ship "Admiral," contests the claim which has been exhibited by A. B. against the said vessel, and makes the following objections thereto:

1. He denies the allegations in the written application of the said A. B., that, *&c.* [*set out the matters intended to be controverted*].

2. He further shows, by way of defense to the said claim, that, *&c.* [*set up matters of defense; as, payment, &c.*] C. D.

City and County of New York, ss.: C. D., the owner named in the above answer, being duly sworn, says, that the said answer is true to the best of his knowledge and belief.

Sworn, *&c.* C. D.

No. 373.

ORDER OF REFERENCE.

See ante, Vol. I., p. 695.

[*Title as in No.* 358.]

The issue in this matter, between A. B., applicant, and C. D., owner and contestant, is hereby referred to L. F., Esq., to hear and determine the same.

Dated, *&c.* W. H. L., Justice, *&c.*

No. 374.

ORDER DIRECTING DISTRIBUTION.

See ante, Vol. I., p. 696

[*Title as in No.* 358.]

It appearing to me that due notice has been published requiring all persons who have any liens upon the ship "Admiral," under the provisions of the act entitled "An act to provide for the collection of demands against ships and vessels," passed April 24, 1862, and the master, owner, agent, or consignee, and all other persons interested in the said vessel, to appear before me on the —— day of ——, 18—, to attend a distribution of the proceeds arising from the sale of said vessel, her tackle, apparel, and furniture. And the said parties having appeared before me at the time stated in said notice; and the various claims found to be subsisting liens upon the said vessel, having been exhibited to me;

Now, therefore, it is ordered that the claims aforesaid, amounting, respectively, to the sums hereinafter mentioned, be paid by the sheriff of the city and county of New York, out of the proceeds of the sale of said vessel, in the following order:

1. To A. B., the sum of —— dollars, and interest thereon from the —— day of ——, 18—; and also the sum of —— dollars, being the costs, expenses, and allowances awarded to the said A. B. in this matter.

2. To E. F., the sum, *&c.* [*as before*].

Dated, *&c.* W. H. L., Justice.

No. 375.

LIKE ORDER, WHERE CLAIMS HAVE BEEN CONTESTED.

See ante, Vol. I., p. 696.

At a special term, *&c.* [*as in No.* 6].

[*Title as in No.* 358.]

It appearing to the court that the amount of all the claims which have been exhibited in this matter against the ship "Admiral," and which are found to have been subsisting liens upon the said vessel at the time of exhibiting the same, have been finally determined. Now, on motion of E. L. S., attorney for A. B., applicant, after hearing T. C., attorney for the owner, it is ordered, that the proceeds of the sale of said vessel be distributed and paid by the sheriff of the city and county of New York, as follows:

1. To A. B., the sum of —— dollars, and interest thereon from the —— day of ——, 18—.

2. To E. F., the sum, *&c.* [*as before*].

It is further ordered, that the said sheriff pay to the said A. B. the sum of —— dollars for his costs, expenses, and allowances in this matter [*or other provision as to costs*].

No. 376.

LIKE ORDER, IN RESPECT TO PRIOR UNCONTESTED CLAIMS.

See ante, Vol. I., p. 696.

[*Title, &c., as in last form.*]

It appearing to the court that the claim of A. B. in this matter, amounting to —— dollars, is a valid and subsisting lien upon the ship "Admiral," her tackle, apparel, and furniture; that the said claim is uncontested; and that the same is entitled to be paid out of the proceeds of the sale of said vessel prior to the claims of E. F. and G. H., both of which are contested.

It is now, on motion of E. L. S., attorney for the said A. B., after hearing T. C., attorney for the other parties interested, ordered that the sheriff of the city and county of New York pay the said A. B., out of said proceeds, the amount of his aforesaid claim, to wit: —— dollars, and interest thereon from the —— day of ——, 18—, together with —— dollars costs and expenses.

No. 377.

LIKE ORDER, IN RESPECT TO SUBSEQUENT UNCONTESTED CLAIMS.

See ante, Vol. I., p. 696.

[*Title, &c., as in last form.*]

It appearing to the court that the claim of A. B. against the ship "Admiral," amounting to —— dollars, has been contested by the owner of said vessel; and that the subsequent claim of E. F., amounting to —— dollars, has not been contested; and that those are the only claims against the said vessel; and it appearing also, that the proceeds of the sale of said vessel, now in the hands of the sheriff of the city and county of New York, amount to —— dollars, and that, after deducting an amount sufficient to pay the said contested claim, with the costs, there will remain a surplus of such proceeds applicable to the payment of such subsequent uncontested claim:

Now, on motion of T. C., attorney for E. F., after hearing E. L. S., at torney for A. B., and J. W. F., attorney for the other parties interested, it is ordered, that the said sheriff pay out of such surplus the claim of the said E. F., amounting to —— dollars, with the interest upon the same, from the —— day of ——, 18—, together with —— dollars, costs and expenses.

No. 378.

NOTICE OF APPLICATION FOR SURPLUS PROCEEDS.

See ante, Vol. I, pp. 696, 697.

[*Title as in No.* 358.]

Notice is hereby given, pursuant to an act entitled "An act to provide for the collection of demands against ships and vessels," passed April 24, 1862, that the ship "Admiral" was sold under and by virtue of a warrant issued in this matter, on the —— day of ——, 18—; that the proceeds of said sale amounted to —— dollars, and that a surplus thereof remains after paying all claims which have been exhibited and payable out of such proceeds; which surplus amounts to —— dollars; and that C. D., the late owner of said vessel, will apply to the Hon. W. H. L., one of the justices of the Supreme Court, at the chambers of the said court, in the City Hall, New York, on the —— day of ——, 18—, at 10 o'clock in the forenoon, for an order directing the said surplus proceeds to be paid over to him, as the person entitled thereto.

Dated, *&c.* A. N. W., Attorney for said C. D.

No. 379.

APPLICATION TO DISCHARGE LIEN—NO WARRANT ISSUED.

See ante, Vol. I., p. 697.

[*Title as in No.* 358.]

To Hon. W. H. L., Justice of the Supreme Court:

The application of C. D. shows that he is the owner of the ship "Admiral"; that A. B., on the —— day of ——, 18—, filed in the clerk's office of the city and county of New York specifications of his lien upon the said ship, and that no warrant has yet been issued to enforce the same; that the amount of the lien claimed by him to be subsisting against the said vessel is the sum of —— dollars, and interest thereon from the —— day of ——, 18—; that the said applicant has a defense to the said lien; and that the grounds of such defense are [*set out the grounds of defense*]. (*)

That the said applicant desires the discharge of said lien, and his proposed sureties for the same are S. D., residing at No. 93 Livingston Street, Brooklyn, whose place of business is at No. 161 Broadway, New York, and L. P., residing at No. 13 Bond Street, and whose place of business is at No. 44 Broad Street, New York.

Wherefore the said applicant prays for leave to discharge the said lien, upon giving bonds pursuant to the statute.

Dated, *&c.* C. D.

[*Add verification as in No.* 358, *and annex to the application the following notice*.]

[*Title as in No.* 358.]

To A. B: Take notice that an application, of which the annexed is a copy, will be presented to Hon. W. H. L., justice of the Supreme Court, at the City Hall, New York, on the —— day of ——, 18—, at ten o'clock A. M.

Yours, &c., A. N. W., Attorney for C. D.

Dated, *&c.*

No. 380.

ORDER GRANTING LEAVE TO BOND THE CLAIM.

See ante, Vol. I., p. 697.

[*Title as in No.* 358.]

It appearing by the application of C. D., that he is the owner of the ship "Admiral"; that, *&c.* [*recite the matters in the last form to the asterisk* (*), *and then as follows:*]

It appearing further, by due proof, that a copy of the said application, with notice of the time and place of presenting the same, was served on the said A. B. on the —— day of ——, 18—, and no just cause being shown in opposition thereto;

It is now, on motion of T. C., attorney for the said owner, ordered, that the said owner have leave to bond the said claim. It is further ordered that the said bond be made in the penal sum of —— dollars, and that the sureties therein justify before me on —— days' notice to A. B., the person having said lien. W. H. L., Justice of the Supreme Court.

Dated, *&c.*

No. 381.

ORDER DIRECTING DISCHARGE OF LIEN.

See ante, Vol. I., p. 697.

[*Title as in No.* 358.]

Leave having been given by me, by an order made herein on the —— day of ——, 18—, to bond the ship "Admiral"; and such bond, approved by me, having been duly executed and delivered to A. B., the person having the lien on said vessel, I do hereby direct that the said lien, amounting to —— dollars, of which specifications were filed in the clerk's office of the city and county of New York, on the —— day of ——, 18—, be marked by said clerk as discharged; and that the same shall cease to be a lien upon the said vessel. W. H. L., Justice, *&c.*

Dated, *&c.*

No. 382.

ASSIGNMENT OF LIEN.

See ante, Vol. I., p. 698.

In consideration of —— dollars, to me in hand paid by G. H., of the city of New York, I have assigned and transferred, and hereby do assign and transfer, unto the said G. H., his heirs and assigns, my debt and lien against the ship "Admiral" and her owners, whereof specifications were filed in the office of the clerk of the city and county of New York, on the —— day of ——, 18—. The said debt amounts to —— dollars, and interest thereon from the —— day of ——, 18—, and is for goods furnished, *&c.* [*describe the debt*].

In witness whereof, I have hereunto set my hand and seal this —— day of ——, 18—. A. B.

CHAPTER XVII.

FORMS IN LIMITED PARTNERSHIPS, AND COMPROMISES BY JOINT DEBTORS.

No. 383.

CERTIFICATE OF FORMATION OF LIMITED PARTNERSHIP.

See ante, Vol. I., p. 704.

This is to certify, that we, whose names are severally undersigned, are desirous of forming, and do hereby form, a limited partnership, pursuant to the laws of the State of New York.

1. The name or firm under which such partnership is to be conducted is "Smith and Jones" [*or*, "John J. Smith and Company"; *or*, "John J. Smith & Co."].

2. The general nature of the business intended to be transacted by such partnership is the general dry goods business, on commission or otherwise.

3. The names of all the general and special partners interested in said business are John J. Smith, Albert Jones, Seth Rogers, and William Brown. The said John J. Smith is a general partner, and his place of residence is in the city and county and State of New York; the said Albert Jones is also a general partner, and his place of residence is in the city of Brooklyn, in the county of Kings, and State of New York; the said Seth Rogers is a special

partner, and his place of residence is in Salem, in the county of Washington, and State of New York; and the said William Brown is also a special partner, and his place of residence is in North Adams, in the State of Massachusetts.

4. The amount of capital which each of the said special partners has contributed to the common stock of said partnership is as follows: The said Seth Rogers has contributed the sum of —— dollars, and the said William Brown has contributed the sum of —— dollars.

5. The period at which the said partnership is to commence, is the —— day of ——, 18—, and the period at which it will terminate is the —— day of ——, 18—.

Witness our hands this —— day of ——, 18—.

JOHN J. SMITH.
ALBERT JONES.
SETH ROGERS.
WILLIAM BROWN.

[*Attach U. S. Rev. Stamp.*]

City and County of New York, ss.: On this —— day of ——, 18—, before me personally came the above-named John J. Smith, Albert Jones, Seth Rogers, and William Brown, to me known to be the individuals described in and who executed the above certificate, and severally acknowledged that they executed the same.

[*Signature, &c., of Officer.*]

No. 384.

AFFIDAVIT OF A GENERAL PARTNER.

See ante, Vol I., p. 705.

State of New York,
City and County of New York, } ss.

John J. Smith, of said city and county, being duly sworn, deposes and says: He is one of the general partners named in the certificate hereto annexed, and that the sums specified in the said certificate to have been contributed, by each of the special partners therein named, to the common stock of the said partnership, have, and each and every of them has, been actually and in good faith paid in cash.

Sworn, *&c.*

JOHN J. SMITH.

[*Attach U. S. Rev. Stamp.*]

No. 385.

DESIGNATION, BY CLERK, OF NEWSPAPERS IN WHICH TO PUBLISH NOTICE.

See ante, Vol. I., p. 706.

Let the terms of the limited partnership between John J. Smith, Albert Jones, Seth Rogers, and William Brown, be published in the —— and ——, two newspapers published in the city and county of New York.

Dated, *&c.*

H. G., County Clerk.

No. 386.

NOTICE OF THE TERMS OF PARTNERSHIP—TO BE PUBLISHED.

See ante, Vol. I., p. 706.

LIMITED PARTNERSHIP.

Notice is hereby given, that a limited partnership has been formed by the undersigned, pursuant to the laws of the State of New York. That the name or firm under which such partnership is to be conducted is [*insert the firm name*]; that the general nature of the business intended to be transacted by such partnership is [*insert it*]; that the names of all the general and special partners interested in the said business are [*insert the names*]; that the said John J. Smith is a general partner, and his place of residence is in the city and county of New York; and that the said Albert Jones is also a general partner, and his place of residence is in the city of Brooklyn and county of Kings; that the said Seth Rogers is a special partner, and his place of residence is in Salem, in the county of Washington; and that the said William Brown is also a special partner, and his place of residence is in North Adams, in the State of Massachusetts; that the amount of capital which each of said special partners has contributed to the common stock is as follows: the said Seth Rogers has contributed the sum of —— dollars, and the said William Brown has contributed the sum of —— dollars; that the period at which the said partnership is to commence is the —— day of ——, 18—, and the period at which it will terminate is the —— day of —— 18—.

Dated, *&c.*

JOHN J. SMITH,
ALBERT JONES, } General Partners.

SETH ROGERS,
WILLIAM BROWN, } Special Partners.

[*For affidavit of publication of notice, see ante, No.* 190.]

No. 387.

CLAUSE IN PARTNERSHIP AGREEMENT, PROVIDING FOR CONTINUANCE OF BUSINESS BY SURVIVING PARTNERS.

See ante, Vol. I., p. 720.

[It is further agreed by and between the said partners, that in the event of the death of any of the partners, whether general or special, the partnership shall be continued by the survivors the same as if such partner had remained alive.]

No. 388.

NOTICE OF DISSOLUTION.

See ante, Vol. I., p. 717.

DISSOLUTION OF LIMITED PARTNERSHIP.

Notice is hereby given that the limited partnership of "Smith & Jones," composed of the undersigned as general and special partners, is dissolved by mutual consent.

Dated, *&c.* [*Signatures of partners, as in No.* 386.]

No. 389.

CERTIFICATE SHOWING ADDITIONAL SPECIAL PARTNERS ADDED TO THE FIRM.

See ante, Vol. I., p. 717.

This is to certify, that the limited partnership formed on the —— day of ——, 18—, under the name or firm of "Smith & Jones," has been altered or changed by adding to the firm one [*or*, two, *or as the case may be*] special partner, viz.: James Smith, who resides at ——, in the county of ——.

We further certify, that the amount of capital which has been contributed by the said James Smith to the common stock of said partnership is the sum of —— dollars. [*If there is more than one additional special partner, state the amount contributed by each ; and attach U. S. Rev. Stamp.*]

Dated, *&c.*

JOHN J. SMITH,
ALBERT JONES,
General Partners.

State of New York,
City and County of New York, } ss.

John J. Smith above named, being duly sworn, deposes and says: He is one of the general partners in the firm of "Smith & Jones," mentioned in the above certificate; and that the matters stated in the said certificate are true according to the best of his knowledge and belief.

Sworn, *&c.* JOHN J. SMITH.

No. 390.

NOTICE OF SALE BY SPECIAL PARTNER.

See ante, Vol. I., p. 718.

To whom it may concern: Take notice, that I have this day sold and transferred to E. F., of ——, in the county of ——, all my right, title, and interest in and to the limited partnership firm of "Smith & Jones," in which firm I was a special partner, having contributed to the common stock of said firm the sum of —— dollars. SETH ROGERS.

Dated, *&c.*

No. 391.

RELEASE OF ONE OF TWO OR MORE JOINT DEBTORS.

See ante, Vol. I., p. 720.

Whereas, John Jones and Henry Jones, of the city and county of New York, lately composing the firm of John Jones & Co., are indebted to me, the undersigned John J. Smith, of the same place, in the sum of —— dollars, upon a judgment duly recovered by me against them in the Supreme Court of the State of New York, which judgment was for —— dollars, and was docketed in the clerk's office of said city and county on the —— day of——, 18— [*or*, for goods, wares, and merchandise sold and delivered by me to the said firm, prior to the dissolution thereof]. And whereas, I have agreed with the said Henry Jones to release and discharge him from such indebtedness, under the authority of the act for the relief of partners and joint debtors, passed April 18, 1838.

Now, therefore, in consideration of the sum of —— dollars, to me in hand paid by the said Henry Jones, at or before the execution of this release, the receipt whereof is hereby acknowledged, I have exonerated, released, and discharged, and do, in pursuance and under the authority of the statute aforesaid, hereby exonerate, release, and discharge the said Henry Jones of and from all and every individual liability, claim, and demand whatsoever, arising from, or in respect to, the indebtedness aforesaid.

Dated, *&c.* JOHN J. SMITH.

CHAPTER XVIII.

FORMS IN RESPECT TO IDIOTS, LUNATICS, HABITUAL DRUNKARDS, ETC.

No. 393.

PETITION FOR A COMMISSION OF LUNACY.

See ante, p. 6.

IN SUPREME COURT [*or other court*]:

In the matter
of
A. T. R., a supposed lunatic.

To the Supreme Court of the State of New York [*or*, To the County Court of the County of ——; *or*, To the Court of Common Pleas of the City and County of New York].

The petition of H. R., of the town of ——, in the county of ——, respectfully shows: That A. T. R., who resides in said town of ——, farmer, and who is the father of your petitioner, now is, and, for the space of two or more years last past, has been, so far deprived of his reason and understanding, as to be altogether unfit and unable to govern himself, or to manage his affairs, as will more fully appear by the affidavits hereto annexed.

[*If the supposed lunatic is a non-resident, then proceed:* And your petitioner further shows, that the said A. T. R. is the owner of property situated within this State.]

Your petitioner, therefore, prays that a commission, in the nature of a writ *de lunatico inquirendo*, may issue out of, and under, the seal of this court, to inquire of the lunacy of the said A. T. R., and to be directed to such persons as to the court may seem proper.

L. P. C., Attorney. H. R.

State of New York, }
County of ——, } ss.

On this —— day of ——, 18—, before me personally appeared the above-named H. R., and made oath that he has read [*or*, heard read] the above petition subscribed by him, and knows the contents thereof, and that the same is true of his own knowledge, except as to the matters which are therein stated to be on his information or belief, and that, as to those matters, he believes it to be true. A. B. L., Justice of the Peace.

AFFIDAVITS ANNEXED.

[*Title as in No.* 393.]

County of ——, ss.: R. T., of ——, in said county, being duly sworn, says: That he is well acquainted with A. T. R., of said town of ——, and has been acquainted with him for ten years or more last past; that the said A. T. R., for the last six years, has at times been more or less affected by an alienation of mind, rendering him unfit, for the time being, to have the government of himself, or the management of his affairs.

And deponent further says, that he has seen the said A. T. R. frequently within the last two years; and that, according to the best of his judgment and belief, the said A. T. R. has been, during the whole of that time, of unsound mind and understanding.

And deponent further says, that the language and actions of the said A. T. R., during the past two years, have been those of an insane person. That, *&c.* [*set out the acts and language of the party indicating insanity or unsoundness of mind, &c.*] And deponent believes that the said A. T. R. is still of unsound mind and understanding, and unfit for the government of himself, or the management of his affairs.

Sworn, *&c.* R. T.

[*Title as in No.* 393.]

County of ——, ss.: G. A., being duly sworn, says: That he is a practicing physician, and resides in the town of ——, in said county; that he is acquainted with A. T. R., of said town of ——, and has attended him several times professionally within the last year, and has seen him frequently within the past two years.

And deponent further says: That the said A. T. R., in the opinion of deponent, is of unsoundmind and understanding, and wholly unfit for the government of himself, or the management of his property; and that he has been in that state or condition for two or more years last past. That the grounds of deponent's opinion and belief are as follows: [*set out reasons for the opinion, and the facts and circumstances showing insanity, or unsoundness of mind, in the party.*]

Sworn, *&c.* G. A.

No. 394.

PETITION FOR COMMISSION ON THE GROUND OF EXTREME OLD AGE.

See ante, p. 6.

[*Title, &c., as in No.* 393.]

The petition of H. R., of the town of ——, in the county of ——, shows: That he is the nephew and one of the next of kin of J. D., of the town of ——, in said county; that the said J. D. is of the age of ninety years and upward; that by reason of such extreme age, she is so far deprived of her reason and understanding as to be altogether unfit and unable to govern herself, or to manage her affairs, as will more fully appear by the affidavits hereto annexed.

Your petitioner, therefore, *&c.* [*conclude as in No.* 393].

No. 395.

PETITION FOR A COMMISSION OF IDIOCY.

See ante, p. 6.

[*Title as in No.* 393.]

The petition of H. M., of the town of ——, in said county, shows: That he is a brother of L. M., of the town of ——, in said county. That the said L. M. has been from the time of his birth, and still is, wholly deficient in reason and understanding, and to all intents and purposes an idiot; as, by the affidavits hereto annexed, will fully appear.

Your petitioner, therefore, prays that a commission, in the nature of a writ *de idiota inquirendo*, may issue to inquire of the idiocy of the said L. M., directed to such persons as to the court may seem proper.

[*Verification as in No.* 393.] H. M.

No. 396.

PETITION FOR A COMMISSION AGAINST AN HABITUAL DRUNKARD.

See ante, p. 6.

[*Title, &c., as in No.* 393.]

The petition of J. P., of the town of ——, in the county of ——, shows: That O. P., aged about thirty years, who resides in said town, and who is a brother of your petitioner, is an habitual drunkard, and has been such for six months, or more, last past.

And your petitioner further shows: That about one year ago, the said O. P. began the use of intoxicating drinks, and shortly thereafter became quite intemperate. That for the six months last past he has been an habitual drunkard, and in consequence thereof has, during the whole of that time, been incapable of conducting his own affairs, and is still in the same condition; as, by reference to the affidavits hereto annexed, will more fully appear.

Your petitioner therefore prays that a commission may issue, to inquire of the habitual drunkenness of the said O. P., to be directed to such persons as to the court may seem proper. J. P.

[*Verification as in No.* 393.]

No. 397.

PETITION BY OVERSEERS OF THE POOR FOR A COMMISSION AGAINST AN HABITUAL DRUNKARD.

See ante, p. 3.

[*Title, &c., as in No.* 393]

The petition of R. F. and C. A. respectfully shows: That they are overseers of the poor of the town of ——, in the county of ——. That O. P., who resides in said town of ——, farmer, is an habitual drunkard, and has been such for six months, or more, last past. That the said O. P. is aged about thirty years, and has a family, to wit: a wife and two children, who are dependent upon him and his property for support. That the said O. P. is the owner of real estate situated in —— aforesaid, consisting of a small farm of about 80 acres, with dwelling-house, &c., thereon; and also the owner of personal property, consisting of the usual stock, farming utensils, &c., necessary for the carrying on of said farm. That the said real estate is estimated to be worth about two thousand dollars; but the same is incumbered by mortgage amounting to eight hundred dollars, and interest thereon for about one year. That the said personal property is believed to be worth about two hundred dollars.

And your petitioners further show, that about one year ago the said O. P. began the use of intoxicating drinks, and shortly thereafter became quite intemperate; and for the six months last past has been an habitual drunkard, and wholly incapable of the transaction of business; and is still in the same condition.

And your petitioners further show, that in consequence of such habitual drunkenness, the said O. P. is rapidly spending his property, and is liable to be defrauded and plundered by others; and that, if he is allowed to have the control and management of his property much longer, he will, as your petitioners believe, soon squander and be stripped of what now remains, and he and his family will become burdens to the town in which they reside; which facts will more fully appear by the affidavits hereto annexed.

Your petitioners, therefore, pray that a commission may issue to inquire into the fact of the habitual drunkenness of the said O. P., directed to such persons as to the court may seem proper.

R. F. } Overseers of
[*Verification as in No.* 393.] C. A. } the Poor.

No. 398.

ORDER FOR A COMMISSION.

See ante, p. 7.

[*Title, as in No.* 393.] At a special term, *&c.* [*as in No.* 6].

On reading and filing the petition of H. R., of, *&c.*, dated the —— day of ——, 18—, and the affidavits of R. T., of, *&c.*, and G. A., of the same place, annexed to the said petition, and on motion of L. P. C., of counsel for the petitioner, it is ordered that a commission, in the nature of a writ *de lunatico inquirendo*, be issued out of and under the seal of this court, in the usual form, directed to L. F., counselor at law, J. M. F., physician, and J. A., gentleman, all of the county of ——, to inquire by a jury of the said county, and of the neighborhood where the said A. T. R. resides, of the lunacy of the said A. T. R.; and that the sheriff of said county be instructed in said commission to summon such jury.

And it is further ordered, that the said commission be executed at, or at some convenient place near to, the residence of the said A. T. R.; and that previous notice of the time and place of such execution be given to the said A. T. R., and to the person or persons having the care of him.

And it is further ordered, that upon the execution of the said commission, the person or persons having the care or custody of the said A. T. R. do produce him before the said commissioners and jury, to be inspected and examined by them, whenever required to do so by such commissioners.

No. 399.

COMMISSION TO INQUIRE OF LUNACY, ETC.

See ante, p. 7.

The People of the State of New York, to L. F., J. M. F., and J. A., of the County of ——, greeting:

[L. S.] Know ye, that we have assigned to you, or any two of you, to inquire, by the oaths of good and lawful men of the county of ——, by whom the truth of the matter may be the better known, whether A. T. R., of the town of ——, in said county, is a lunatic, or enjoys lucid intervals [*or*, is an idiot], so that he is not sufficient for the government of himself, or the management of his lands and tenements, goods and chattels [*or*, is incapable of conducting his own affairs in consequence of habitual drunkenness]; and if so, from what time, after what manner, and how. And if the said A. T. R., being in that condition, has alienated any lands and tenements or not, and if so, what lands and tenements, to what person or persons, when, where, after what manner, and how; and what lands and tenements, goods and chattels, as yet remain to him; and of what value the lands and tenements by him alienated, as well as those by him retained, are, and how much the issues and profits thereof are worth by the year, and what is the value of his goods, chattels, and personal estate; and who are the nearest heirs of the said A. T. R., who will be entitled to his estate in case of his death, and of what age. And therefore we command you, or any two of you, that at a certain day and place, or at certain days and places, which you for that purpose shall appoint, you diligently make inquisition in the premises; and that you cause reasonable notice of the time and place by you appointed for that purpose, to be given to the said A. T. R.; and that you send the inquisition which you shall thereupon make, under your seals, or the seals of any two of you, and the seals of those persons by whom it shall be made, distinctly and plainly, and without delay, to our Supreme Court [*or other court*], together with this writ.

And by the tenor of these presents, we command the sheriff of the county of ——, that at a certain day and place, or at certain days and places, which you shall make known to him, he cause to come before you, or any two of you, so many and such good and lawful men of his bailiwick as you shall direct, by whom the truth of the matters aforesaid may be the better inquired into.

Witness, E. H. R., one of the justices of said court, at ——, the —— day of ——, 18—.

L. P. C., Attorney. N. B. M., Clerk.

[*Indorsed.*] "By the Court," N. B. M., Clerk.

Return indorsed on Commission.

The execution of this commission appears in the schedule hereunto annexed. Dated, *&c.*

L. F. }
J. M. F. } Commissioners.
J. A. }

No. 400.

PRECEPT TO SHERIFF TO SUMMON A JURY.

See ante, p. 10.

To the Sheriff of the County of ——.

By virtue of a commission in the nature of a writ *de lunatico inquirendo*, issued out of and under the seal of the Supreme Court [*or other court*], bearing date the —— day of ——, 18—, to us whose names are subscribed hereto directed, to inquire if A. T. R., of the town of ——, in the county of ——, be a lunatic or not.

These are therefore to require you to cause to come and appear before us twenty-four honest and lawful men of the county aforesaid, and of the neighborhood where the said A. T. R. resides, on the —— day of —— next, by ten o'clock in the forenoon of the same day, at the hotel kept by ——, in the village of —— [*or*, at the school-house in School District No. ——, in the town of ——, aforesaid], then and there upon their oaths to inquire of the lunacy of the said A. T. R.; and of all such matters and things as shall be given them in charge by virtue of said commission. Hereof fail not at your peril.

Given under our hands and seals this —— day of ——, in the year of our Lord one thousand eight hundred and ——.

[*Signatures and seals of Commissioners.*]

SHERIFF'S RETURN [*to be indorsed on precept*].

The execution of this precept appears in the panel hereto annexed.

H. R. C., Sheriff.

SCHEDULE OF JURORS [*to be annexed to return*].

Names of the jurors summoned to inquire according to the tenor of the precept annexed. [*Names of Jurors.*]

No. 401.

NOTICE TO LUNATIC, ETC., OF EXECUTION OF COMMISSION.

See ante, p. 11.

[*Title as in No.* 393.]

To A. T. R. Sir: Take notice, that a commission to inquire as to your lunacy [*or*, idiocy, *or*, habitual drunkenness], issued out of and under the seal of the Supreme Court [*or other court*], and directed to the undersigned, as commissioners, will be executed at the hotel kept by ——, in the village of —— [*or*, at the school-house in School District No. ——, in the town of —— aforesaid], on the —— day of —— instant, at 10 o'clock A. M.

Dated, &c. [*Signatures of Commissioners.*]

No. 402.

AFFIDAVIT OF SERVICE OF NOTICE.

See ante, p. 11.

[*Title as in No.* 393.]

County of ——, ss.: H. S., of ——, in said county, being duly sworn, says: That on the —— day of ——, 18—, he served on A. T. R., of, &c., a copy of the annexed [*or*, above] notice, by delivering the same to, and leaving the same with, the said A. T. R., at the town of —— aforesaid. And he further says, that he knew the person so named to be the person mentioned and described in the said notice.

Sworn, &c. H. S.

No. 403.

NOTICE TO PRODUCE LUNATIC, ETC.

See ante, p. 11.

[*Title as in No.* 393.]

To S. R., and to all others having in their custody or power the above-named A. T. R.

The undersigned, by virtue of a commission issued out of the Supreme Court [*or other court*], to inquire as to the lunacy [*or*, idiocy, *or*, habitual drunkenness] of A. T. R., of, &c., dated the —— day of ——, 18—, do hereby require you to produce before us the said A. T. R., at the execution of said commission, at the hotel kept by ——, in the village of —— [*or*, at the school-house, in School District No. ——, in the town of —— aforesaid], on the —— day of ——, 18—, at ten o'clock in the forenoon, there to be examined and inspected by us; and you are to give him notice accordingly.

Given under our hands and seals, this —— day of ——, 18—.

[*Signed and sealed by Commissioners.*]

No. 404.

SUBPŒNA FOR WITNESSES.

See ante, p. 10.

By virtue of a commission issued out of and under the seal of the Supreme Court of the State of New York [*or other court*], dated the —— day of ——, 18—, and directed to the undersigned, to inquire whether A. T. R., of the town of ——, in the county of ——, be a lunatic [*or*, idiot, *or*, an habitual drunkard], or not; we, the undersigned, do hereby require you and each of you, personally, to be and appear before us at the execution of the said commission, at the hotel kept by ——, in the village of ——, in said county [*or*, at the school-house in School District No. ——, in said town], on the —— day of —— inst., at ten o'clock in the forenoon, then and there to testify those things which you, or either of you, know, touching the lunacy [*or*, idiocy, *or*, habitual drunkenness] of the said A. T. R.; and all such other matters as shall be demanded of you by virtue of the said commission. Hereof fail not at your peril.

Given under our hands and seals the —— day of ——, 18—.

[*Signatures and Seals of Commissioners.*]

To S. R., B. R., and O. P. G., *&c.*

No. 405.

OATH TO JURORS.

See ante, p. 11.

You do swear [*or*, affirm] well and truly to inquire touching the lunacy [*or*, idiocy, *or*, habitual drunkenness] of A. T. R., and of all such matters and things as shall be given you in charge by virtue of a commission issued out of and under the seal of the Supreme Court [*or other court*], and now here to be executed, and a true inquisition make according to evidence.

No. 406.

OATH OF WITNESSES.

See ante, p. 11.

You do swear [*or*, affirm], that the evidence you shall give touching the lunacy [*or*, idiocy, *or*, habitual drunkenness] of A. T. R., and as to who are his next of kin, and the nature, extent, and value of his real and personal estate, and all such other matters and things as shall be required of you, by virtue of a commission issued out of the Supreme Court [*or other court*], to inquire into the said lunacy [*or*, idiocy, *&c.*], and now here to be executed, shall be the truth, the whole truth, and nothing but the truth.

No. 407.

INQUISITION.

See ante, p. 12.

An inquisition, taken at the hotel kept by ——, in the village of ——, in the county of —— [*or*, at the school-house, in School District No. —, in the town of ——], on the —— day of ——, in the year one thousand eight hundred and ——, before L. F., J. A., and J. M. F., commissioners appointed by virtue of a commission in the nature of a writ *de lunatico* [*or*, *idiota*] *inquirendo*, issued out of and under the seal of the Supreme Court of the State of New York [*or other court*], dated on the —— day of ——, 18—, directed to the said commissioners, to inquire, among other things, of the lunacy of A. T. R., upon the oaths of J. S. M., *&c.* [*insert the names of the jurors*], good and lawful men of the said county, who, being summoned, sworn, and charged, upon their oaths, say, that the said A. T. R., at the time of taking this inquisition, is a lunatic, and of unsound mind, and does not enjoy lucid intervals, so that he is incapable of the government of himself, or of the management of his lands, tenements, goods and chattels; and that he has been in the same state of lunacy for the space of two years last past. That the said A. T. R. has occasionally, for many years past, been afflicted with mental alienation; but what occasioned such mental alienation, or his present lunacy, the jurors aforesaid have no information, and know not.

And the jurors aforesaid, upon their oaths aforesaid, further say, that whether the said A. T. R., being in that state, has alienated any lands and tenements, or not, the jurors aforesaid know not [*or*, that the said A. T. R., being in the condition aforesaid, did, on or about the —— day of ——, 18—, at the village of ——, in said county, convey, by warrantee deed, to one A. O. R., of, *&c.*, a certain lot owned by him in the village of ——, in said county, for the nominal consideration of —— dollars; and the money actually received by the said A. T. R., upon the sale of said lot, was only the sum of —— dollars, being not one-fifth of the actual value of said lot].

And the jurors aforesaid, upon their oaths aforesaid, do further say that the following lands and tenements, situated in the town of —— aforesaid, yet remain to him, the said A. T. R., to wit: [*describe real estate*]. That the said lands and tenements, above described, are worth about —— dollars; and the issues and profits thereof, by the year, are worth about the sum of —— dollars.

And the jurors aforesaid, upon their oaths aforesaid, do further say that the following goods and chattels yet remain to the said A. T. R., to wit: [*give general description of the personal property*]. That the value of the said goods and chattels, of the said A. T. R., is about the sum of —— dollars.

And the jurors aforesaid, upon their oaths aforesaid, do further say: That S. R. is the wife of the said A. T. R., and resides with him in —— aforesaid. That N. R., H. R., R. R., and J. R., are the children of the said A. T. R., all of whom, except the said N. R., reside with said lunatic in —— aforesaid. That the said N. R. resides in ——, in the State of ——, and is aged about

30 years. That the said H. R. is aged about 26 years; the said R. R. is aged about 24 years; and the said J. R. is aged about 21 years; and that the said children will be entitled to the estate of the said A. T. R. in equal proportions, in case of his death.

In witness whereof, as well the said commissioners, as the jurors aforesaid, have to this inquisition set their hands and seals, the day and year first above written.

[*Signatures and Seals of Commissioners.*]
[*Signatures and Seals of Jurors.*]

No. 408.

NOTICE OF MOTION TO CONFIRM FINDING OF JURY.

See ante, p. 15.

[*Title as in No.* 393.]

Sir:—Take notice, that I shall apply to the next term of this court, to be held at the Court House, in —— in and for the county of ——, on the —— day of —— next [*or*, instant], at the opening of the court on that day, or as soon thereafter as counsel can be heard, for a rule or order confirming the finding of the jury upon the commission heretofore issued in the above matter.

Also take notice, that I shall, at the same time and place, apply for the appointment of a committee of the person and estate of said A. T. R.; or for such other or further order or relief as the court may think proper to grant; which motions will be founded on the said commission and the return thereto, and the inquisition taken under such commission; together with the petition, with a copy of which you are herewith served.

Dated, *&c.* Yours, &c.,

L. P. C., Att'y for Petitioner.

To A. T. R. above named [*or*, to O. R. I., Att'y for said A. T. R.]

No. 409.

PETITION FOR APPOINTMENT OF COMMITTEE.

See ante, pp. 16, 17.

[*Title, &c., as in No.* 393.]

The petition of H. R., of the town of ——, in the county of ——, respectfully shows: That the commission heretofore issued out of this court, in pursuance of an order made on the —— day of ——, 18—, directed to L. F., J. A., and J. M. F., to inquire of the lunacy [*or*, idiocy, *or*, habitual drunkenness] of A. T. R., of the town of —— aforesaid, who is the father of your petitioner, has been duly executed and returned by the commissioners, and filed in the office of the clerk of this court. That from the inquisition annexed to the said commission, and returned therewith, it appears that the jury have found the said A. T. R. is a lunatic and of unsound mind [*or*, that the said A. T. R. is an idiot], so that he is incapable of the government of himself or the management of his lands, goods, and chattels, as by reference to said inquisition will more fully appear.

Your petitioner therefore prays: That he may be appointed the committee of the person and estate of the said A. T. R., upon his giving security for the faithful performance of his trust as such committee, according to the statute, and in conformity with the rules and practice of the court [*or*, That a referee may be appointed to inquire and report who is a suitable and proper person to be appointed committee of the person and estate of the said A. T. R., and to approve of the bond and sureties offered by him]. And for such other or further order as the court may think proper to grant.

[*Verification as in No.* 393.] H. R.

CONSENT ANNEXED.

[*Title as in No.* 393.]

We, S. R., wife of A. T. R. above named, and R. R. and J. R., of, *&c.*, children of the said A. T. R., do hereby consent that H. R., of, *&c.*, be appointed committee of the person and estate of said A. T. R. And we do hereby request the said court to appoint said H. R. as such committee.

Dated, *&c.*, [*Signatures.*]

[*Acknowledged or proved in usual form. See No.* 44.]

No. 410.

ORDER CONFIRMING FINDING OF JURY, APPOINTING COMMITTEE, ETC.

See ante, p. 17.

At a special term, *&c.* [*as in No.* 6].

IN SUPREME COURT [*or other court*]:

In the matter of A. T. R., a lunatic.

On reading and filing the inquisition in the above matter, taken under a commission issued out of the Supreme Court [*or other court*], from which it appears that the jury have found the said A. T. R. is a lunatic, and of unsound mind [*or*, that the said A. T. R. is an idiot], so that he is incapable of the government of himself, or of the management of his lands, tenements, goods, and chattels; and from which it also appears that the said A. T. R. is possessed of certain real and personal estate in the said inquisition described. Now, on motion of L. P. C., attorney for H. R., and on hearing C. R. I., in behalf of said A. T. R., it is ordered that the finding of the jury upon the execution of the said commission, as set forth in said inquisition, be, and the same is hereby, confirmed.

And on reading and filing the petition of H. R., a son of said lunatic, dated the —— day of ——, 18—, praying for the appointment of a committee of the person and estate of said A. T. R. [and the consent of S. R. and R. R. and J. R., the wife and two of the children of said A. T. R., that said H. R. be appointed such committee], it is, on like motion, ordered, (*) that the said H. R. be, and he is hereby, appointed the committee of the person and estate of the said A. T. R., upon his filing with the clerk of this court a bond with two sufficient sureties, to be approved of by a justice [*or*, judge] of this court, in the penalty of —— dollars, and conditioned for the faithful performance of his trust as such committee, according to the statute and the rules and practice of the court, and to account, whenever required, in conformity with such rules and practice.

[*If a reference is ordered to inquire as to the proper person to be appointed committee, &c., then from the* (*) *above, proceed as follows:* That it be referred to O. F. T., Esq., residing at ——, in the county of ——, to inquire and report who is a suitable and proper person to be appointed committee of the person and estate of the said A. T. R., and also to inquire and report as to the form and penalty of the bond to be given by such committee, and the sufficiency of the sureties offered by him. And it is further ordered, that the referee cause —— days' notice in writing to be served upon S. R. and R. R. and J. R., the wife and two of the children of the said A. T. R., residing in this State, of the time and place of executing the said reference; and that the said referee report hereon with all convenient speed.]

No. 411.

REFEREE'S REPORT AS TO COMMITTEE.

See ante, p. 17.

[*Title as in No.* 410.]

To the Supreme Court of the State of New York [*or*, To the County Court of the County of ——; *or*, To the Court of Common Pleas of the City and County of New York].

The undersigned, to whom it was referred, by an order of this court, dated the —— day of ——, 18—, to inquire and report who is a suitable and proper person to be appointed committee of the person and estate of A. T. R. above named; and as to the form and penalty of the bond to be given by such committee, and the sufficiency of the sureties offered by him, do respectfully report:

That before entering upon the execution of said order, I caused —— days' notice, in writing, to be given to S. R. and R. R. and J. R., the wife and two of the children of the said lunatic, of the time and place of executing the same, to wit: on the —— day of ——, 18—, at ten o'clock A. M., at my office in the village of ——. That, at the time and place last aforesaid, I proceeded to execute the said order of reference, in the presence of L. P. C., Esq., attorney for the petitioner, and R. R. and J. R. above named. That after hearing the parties present, and making the necessary inquiries, I am of opinion that H. R., of the town of —— aforesaid a son of said lunatic, is a suitable and proper person to be appointed the committee of the person and estate of the said lunatic.

And I further certify and report that, in the opinion of the undersigned, the said H. R. should, before entering upon the said trust, execute and file with the clerk of this court his bond, in the penalty of —— dollars, being double the value of the property of the said A. T. R., as found by the inquisition of the jury, conditioned for the faithful performance of his trust as such committee, according to the statute, and to account, whenever required, in conformity with the rules and practice of this court. That the said H. R. proposed as his sureties W. T. F. and J. G. R., of, *&c.;* and having taken from each of them an affidavit as to his sufficiency, and made inquiries relative thereto, I am satisfied that the sureties so proposed are sufficient; each being worth the sum of —— dollars, over and above all debts and responsibilities he owes or has incurred.

I further certify and report that I have indorsed upon the bond of the said H. R., signed by him and his sureties aforesaid, in the penalty aforesaid, and conditioned as aforesaid, my approval of its form and manner of execution.

All which is respectfully submitted.

Dated, *&c.* O. F. T., Referee.

No. 412.

ORDER CONFIRMING REFEREE'S REPORT.

See ante, p. 17.

[*Title as in No.* 410.] At a special term, *&c.* [*as in No.* 6].

On reading and filing the report of O. F. T., referee, dated the —— day of ——, 18—, made in pursuance of an order of this court, dated the —— day of ——, 18—; and on motion of L. P. C., attorney for the petitioner in this matter, no one appearing in opposition thereto, it is ordered, that the said report be, and the same is hereby, confirmed.

And it is further ordered, that H. R., of, *&c.*, be, and he is hereby, appointed the committee of the person and estate of the said A. T. R., upon his executing and filing with the clerk of this court the bond mentioned in said report, to wit, the bond of the said H. R., in the penalty of —— dollars, signed by W. T. F. and J. G. R., of, *&c.*, as sureties, duly acknowledged, &c., according to the rules of the court, and conditioned for the faithful performance, on the part of the said H. R., of the trust reposed in him as such committee, according to the statute, and that he will account, whenever required, in conformity with the rules and practice of this court.

And it is further ordered, that upon the filing of such bond, a commission may be issued to such committee, under the seal of this court.

No. 413.

BOND OF COMMITTEE.

See ante, p. 17.

Know all men by these presents, That we, H. R., of the town of ——, in the county of ——, and W. T. F. and J. G. R., of the same place, are held and firmly bound unto N. B. M., clerk of the county of ——, and to his successor or successors in office, in the penal sum of —— dollars, to be paid to the said clerk, or to his successors aforesaid, for which payment well and truly to be made, we bind ourselves, our heirs, executors, and administrators, jointly and severally, firmly by these presents. Sealed with our seals, and dated the —— day of ——, 18—. (*)

Whereas, by an order of the Supreme Court [*or other court*], dated the —— day of ——, 18—, the said H. R. was appointed committee of the person and estate of A. T. R., of, *&c.*, who, by an inquisition taken under a commission issued out of said court, had previously thereto been found to be a lunatic, upon his giving the bond required by the said order.

Now, therefore, the condition of this obligation is such, that if the above-bounden H. R. shall faithfully perform the trust reposed in him as such committee, according to the statute, and shall render an account whenever required, in conformity with the rules and practice of the said court, and shall observe the orders and directions of the said court in relation to such trust, then this obligation to be void, otherwise to remain in full force and virtue.

H. R. [L. S.]

Signed and sealed W. T. F. [L. S.]

in the presence of A. B. J. G. R. [L. S.]

[*Acknowledgment or proof, and Affidavit of Sureties, as in No.* 44.]

No. 414.

PETITION FOR LEAVE TO TRAVERSE, OR FOR AN ISSUE.

See ante, pp. 18 to 20.

IN SUPREME COURT [*or other court*]:

In the matter
of
E. H., an alleged lunatic.

To the Supreme Court of the State of New York [*or other court*]:

The petition of E. H., of, *&c.*, respectfully shows, That on the —— day of —— last, at the city of New York, a notice was delivered to him, setting forth that a commission, to inquire as to his lunacy, issued out of this court, and directed to J. B., H. B., and W. A., as commissioners, would be executed at the house kept by L. R., in the town of —— aforesaid, on the —— day of ——, 18—, at 10 o'clock A. M. That your petitioner was then residing with his friends and relatives at the city of New York, which is distant more than two hundred miles from the place where the said commission was to be executed. That he proceeded at once to make preparation to leave that city for the purpose of attending the execution of said commission. That although he used every effort to arrive in said town of ——, where said commission was to be executed, prior to the said —— day of ——, 18—, yet he did not arrive there until about 9 o'clock A. M. of that day; too late to enable him to procure the attendance of several witnesses residing in the vicinity of that place, and who were material and necessary witnesses for your petitioner on the execution of said commission, as he verily believes. That the execution of said commission was proceeded with, by said commissioners, at the time and place aforesaid. That immediately prior thereto, your petitioner applied to them for a postponement thereof, to enable your petitioner to obtain the testimony of the said witnesses; and made affidavit before said commissioners to the materiality of said witnesses, and that he could not safely proceed to the trial of the question of your petitioner's lunacy without the benefit of their testimony; but the said commissioners refused to postpone said trial. That the said trial then proceeded as follows:

D. H. was called as a witness for the prosecution, and testified as follows: [*state the evidence, and proceed in same form as to other witnesses*].

After the testimony was closed, the matter was submitted to the jury, under the charge of one of the commissioners, twelve of whom found an inquisition that your petitioner was a lunatic, and incapable of the government of himself, or the management of his affairs, as by reference to said inquisition will more fully appear. That four of said jurors dissented from the inquisition so found, and were in favor of finding your petitioner of sound mind and memory, as your petitioner is informed and believes.

And your petitioner further shows, that upon the execution of said commission before the jury and commissioners, and in and about the house when and where the said trial was had, one J. C. F., upon whose petition the said commission of lunacy was issued, pursued an insulting and irritating course toward your petitioner, telling your petitioner he lied, and using other unbecoming, provoking, and insulting expressions; and your petitioner says, that the anger exhibited by him under the influence of such conduct was contrasted with his usual ma er, and urged, and, as your petitioner believes, taken, as evidence of h s insanity.

And your petitioner further shows, that D. H., of, &c., who is a son of your petitioner, since the execution of the said commission, as your petitioner is informed and believes, has been appointed committee of the person and estate of your petitioner, and, as such, has taken possession and assumed the control of the whole real and personal estate of your petitioner. That the value of said property is about the sum of —— dollars.

And your petitioner further shows, that he is of sound mind, and entirely competent to manage his own affairs and business (as appears by the affidavits hereto annexed), and which your petitioner can fully establish by numerous individuals, physicians and others.

Your petitioner therefore prays that an order may be granted, allowing your petitioner to traverse the said inquisition, or that an issue may be awarded to try the fact of the lunacy of your petitioner, and whether he is incapable of the government of himself, or the management of his affairs; and also that your petitioner be allowed out of his estate a reasonable sum to defray the costs and expenses of trying said issue, and the costs of this application, and for such other or further relief as the court may think proper to grant.

M. F., Attorney for Petitioner. E. H.

[*Verification as in No.* 393, *to the end thereof, and then continue as follows:*]

And I further certify that I have examined the said E. H., for the purpose of ascertaining the state of his mind, and whether he is capable of understanding the nature or object of said petition; and that he is apparently of sound mind, and capable of understanding the same. [*If the alleged lunatic is blind, the officer should further certify as follows:* And I further certify that, before the said petition was sworn to by said E. H., the same was carefully and correctly read over to him in my presence.]

W. B. B., Justice of the Peace.

No. 416.

AFFIDAVITS ON APPLICATION FOR AN ISSUE.

See ante, pp. 19, 20.

[*Title as in No.* 414.]

City and County of New York, ss.: W. G., of said city, being duly sworn, says: That he is acquainted with E. H. above-named. That he saw said H. frequently during the two months next previous to the execution of the commission in the above matter, during the most of which time, said H. boarded with deponent. That deponent has never seen anything in the conduct or language of said H., that induced him to believe he was insane. And deponent believes said H. is not insane; but of sound mind and memory, and fully competent for the management of himself and his property.

Sworn, *&c.* W. G.

[*Title as in No.* 414.]

County of ——, ss.: T. W., of, *&c.*, being duly sworn, says: That he is a practicing physician and surgeon, and has been, for twenty-five years last past. That he is acquainted with E. H., of ——, in said county. That he has had a personal interview with the said E. H. this day; and that, in the judgment of this deponent, the said H. is not a lunatic or an insane person. That deponent has frequently seen the said H., when it was said he was a lunatic; but this deponent could never discover that said H. was a lunatic or an insane person, and believes he is not, and has not been.

Sworn, *&c.* T. W.

[*Title as in No.* 414.]

County of ——, ss.: J. B., being duly sworn, says: He is a practicing physician and surgeon, and resides at ——, in said county. That deponent has been acquainted with E. H., of, *&c.*, for more than twenty years last past, and for the last two years has been his family physician. That deponent has seen much of said H. within the last year or more, and has conversed with him frequently during that time. That deponent has always believed said H. was a man of sound mind and understanding. That deponent has seen and conversed with said H. within the last week, and deponent still believes said H. is of sound mind and memory, and fully competent to manage himself and his property.

Sworn, *&c.* J. B.

No. 417.

NOTICE OF MOTION FOR LEAVE TO TRAVERSE, ETC.

See ante, pp. 18 to 20.

[*Title as in No.* 414.]

Sir:—You will take notice that I intend to move this court, at the next special term thereof, to be held at the Court House in ——, in and for the county of ——, on the —— day of —— instant, at —— o'clock A. M., or as soon thereafter as counsel can be heard, for an order that [the commission and return thereon, and the inquisition, and all subsequent or other proceedings in this matter, be set aside for irregularity, with costs to be paid by J. C. F., on whose petition said proceedings were had, and in case the said proceedings shall not be set aside that] E. H. above named, have leave to traverse the inquisition in this matter, or that an issue be awarded to try the fact of the lunacy of said H. and whether he is capable of the government of himself or the management of his affairs, and that said H. be allowed, out of his estate, a reasonable sum to defray the costs and expenses of trying said issue, and the costs of this application. And for such other or further relief as the court may think proper to grant; which motion will be founded upon the inquisition in this matter, and upon the petition and affidavits, with copies of which you are herewith served.

Dated, *&c.* Yours, &c.

To D. H., Committee. M. F., Attorney for Petitioner.

No. 418.

ORDER DIRECTING AN ISSUE.

See ante, p. 20.

[*Title as in No.* 414.] At a special term, *&c.* [*as in No.* 6].

On reading and filing the petition of E. H. above named, dated the —— day of ——, 18—, praying for an order directing an issue to try the question whether the said E. H. is a lunatic, and incompetent for the government of himself or the management of his estate; and on reading and filing the affidavits of W. G. and others, in support of said petition; it is, on motion of M. F., attorney for said petitioner, after hearing J. C. B., in behalf of the committee of the said E. H., ordered, that an issue be made up and settled to try the question, whether E. H. above named be a lunatic, and mentally incapable of the government of himself, or the management of his affairs; and that the said issue be tried at the next circuit to be held in and for the county of—— [*or*, at the term of this court commencing on the —— day of —— next].

And it is further ordered, that the attorney for said E. H. in the first instance prepare the issue, and submit it to the attorney of the said committee and that if they cannot agree as to the form, &c., that application be made to the court; and that if the attorney for said E. H. shall omit to prepare such issue, and to serve the same on the attorney for the said committee, within twenty days after service of a copy of this order, then the order for an issue shall be deemed discharged.

And it is further ordered that the said committee pay to the attorney of said E. H. the sum of ——— dollars; and also pay to said E. H., or to his attorney, such further reasonable sums as shall be requisite to procure the attendance of witnesses upon the trial of said issue, and for the employment of proper counsel before the court and jury.

No. 419.

PETITION TO SUPERSEDE COMMISSION.

See ante, p. 23.

[*Title as in No.* 410.]

The petition of E. H., of, *&c.*, respectfully shows:

That your petitioner has been adjudged a lunatic and incompetent to manage his own affairs and property, by virtue of an inquisition of lunacy heretofore ordered by this court. That the property, real and personal, of your petitioner, has been placed in the care and custody of D. H., of, *&c.*, who was appointed the committee of the person and estate of your petitioner; and the said D. H. is still such committee.

And your petitioner further shows, that he is now of sound mind and understanding, and entirely competent to manage his own affairs and business, as appears by the affidavits hereto annexed, and which your petitioner can fully establish by numerous individuals, physicians and others.

Your petitioner therefore prays, that he may be at liberty to attend in open court, or before a referee, for the purpose of being examined as to his sanity of mind, and his competency to manage himself and his property; and that the said commission and inquisition, and proceedings therein, may be superseded forthwith; and that a *supersedeas* may issue for that purpose, and that a referee may be appointed to take and state the account of said committee; or for such other or further order as may be proper.

[*Verification as in No.* 414.] E. H.

AFFIDAVIT ANNEXED.

[*Title as in No.* 410.]

County of ——, ss.: O. P. G., of ——, in said county, being duly sworn, says: That he is now, and has been for the last twenty-five years, a practicing physician and surgeon; that he is well acquainted with E. H., of, *&c.*; and has been for the last few weeks in a situation to see him and converse with him almost daily; that deponent verily believes that the said H. is now perfectly sane and of sound mind, and competent in every respect to manage his own affairs and business. And deponent further says, that he believes the said H. has been of sound mind and competent to manage his own affairs for several weeks last past. O. P. G.

Sworn, *&c.*

No. 420.

NOTICE OF MOTION TO SUPERSEDE COMMISSION.

See ante, p. 23.

[*Title as in No.* 410.]

Sir: Take notice that a petition and affidavits, with copies whereof you are herewith served, will be presented to the Supreme Court [*or other court*] at the next special term thereof, to be held at the Court House, in ——, on the —— day of —— instant, at the opening of the court on that day, or as soon thereafter as counsel can be heard; and that, upon reading and filing the same, a motion will be made that the prayer of said petition be granted; or for such other or further order as the court may think proper to grant. Dated, *&c.* Yours, &c.,

B. F. A., Attorney for Petitioner.

To D. H., Committee, *&c.*

No. 421.

ORDER TO SUPERSEDE COMMISSION.

See ante, p. 23.

[*Title as in No.* 410.] At a special term, *&c.* [*as in No.* 6].

On reading and filing the petition of E. H. above named, dated the —— day of ——, 18—, praying that the commission, inquisition, &c., in the above matter, may be superseded; and also, on reading and filing the affidavits of O. P. G., R. D. S., and R. T. F., in support of said petition, and upon examining the said E. H., in open court, as to his sanity of mind and competency of understanding,—it is, on motion of Mr. A., attorney for said E. H., no one appearing in opposition thereto, ordered, that the commission of lunacy issued against the said E. H., and the inquisition taken thereon, be, and the same is hereby, superseded and determined. [*Or*, that the commission of lunacy issued against the said E. H. be, and the same is hereby, suspended until the further order of this court.]

No. 422.

ORDER OF REFERENCE ON MOTION TO SUPERSEDE COMMISSION.

See ante, p. 23.

[*Title as in No.* 410.] At a special term, *&c.* [*as in No.* 6].

On reading and filing the petition of E. H. above named, dated the —— day of ——, 18—, praying for an order that the commission in this matter be superseded, and on reading and filing sundry affidavits in support of said petition, and notice of motion; and on motion of Mr. A., attorney for the petitioner, after hearing Mr. W., of counsel for the committee, it is ordered that it be referred to J. M., Esq., residing in the county of ——, to inquire and report whether the said E. H. is of sound mind and memory, and capable of the government of himself and the management of his affairs; and whether the commission heretofore issued against the said E. H. as a lunatic, may with propriety be superseded, and the said E. H. be restored to his personal liberty and the management of his property; that the said referee cause notice to be given of the time and place for conducting his examination, to the said E. H., and to D. H., committee of the person and estate of the said E. H.; that the said referee be at liberty to examine witnesses under oath; and also personally to examine the said E. H., if he shall deem it advisable so to do; and that the said referee report his opinion, formed from the said testimony and personal interview, with all convenient speed.

No. 423.

REFEREE'S REPORT THEREON.

See ante, p. 23.

[*Title as in No.* 410.]

To the Supreme Court of the State of New York [*or other court*]:

In pursuance of an order of the Supreme Court [*or other court*], made in the above-entitled matter, dated the —— day of ——, 18—, by which it was referred to J. M., residing in the county of ——, to inquire and report whether, *&c.* [*set out the substance of the order*], I, the said referee, do report:

That I have been attended by the said E. H. and his attorney, and by D. H., the committee of the person and estate of the said E. H., after due service upon them of the notice required to be given to them, as aforesaid, for that purpose; and, after taking proofs by the examination of witnesses produced before me, and also after a personal examination of the said E. H., I, the said referee, am satisfied that the said E. H. is of sound mind and memory, and capable of the control of himself and the management of his affairs.

And I do further report, that the commission heretofore issued against the said E. H., as a lunatic, may with propriety be superseded, and the said E. H. restored to his personal liberty and the management of his property [*or*, may with propriety be suspended until the further order of the court].

All which is respectfully submitted.

Dated, *&c.* J. M., Referee.

No. 424.

ORDER SUPERSEDING COMMISSION ON REFEREE'S REPORT.

See ante, p. 23.

[*Title as in No.* 410.] At a special term, *&c.* [*as in No.* 6].

On reading and filing the report of J. M., Esq., referee, dated the —— day of——, 18—, made in pursuance of an order of this court, bearing date the —— day of —— last, and on motion of B. F. A., of counsel for the petitioner, it is ordered that the said report, and all things therein contained, do stand ratified and confirmed.

And it is further ordered, adjudged, and determined, and this court, by virtue of the power and authority therein vested, does order, adjudge, and determine, that the commission of lunacy issued against the said E. H., dated the —— day of——, 18—, and the subsequent proceedings thereon, be forthwith superseded and determined [*or*, suspended until the further order of this court].

No. 425.

CERTIFICATE OF OFFICER TO AFFIDAVIT OR PETITION OF LUNATIC, ETC.

See ante, p. 25.

[*Verification substantially as in No.* 393, *and then proceed as follows:*] And I further certify that I have examined the said E. H., for the purpose of ascertaining the state of his mind, and whether he is capable of understanding the nature or object of said affidavit [*or*, petition], and that he is apparently of sound mind and capable of understanding the same. [*If the party is blind, the officer should further certify as follows:* And I further certify that, before the said affidavit [*or*, petition] was sworn to by the said E. H., the same was carefully and correctly read over to him in my presence.]

H. F., Justice of the Peace.

No. 426.

PETITION FOR ORDER DIRECTING PAYMENT OF CLAIM OUT OF LUNATIC'S ESTATE.

See ante, p. 26.

IN SUPREME COURT [*or other court*]:

In the matter of the application of R. M. F.

To the Supreme Court of the State of New York [*or other court*]:

The petition of R. M. F., of, *&c.*, respectfully shows: That E. H., of, *&c.*, is justly indebted to your petitioner in the sum of —— dollars, with interest thereon from the —— day of ——, 18—, for goods, wares, and merchandise furnished to him at his request, during the years 1856 and 1857. That an account of the goods, &c., so furnished, as aforesaid, is hereto annexed, marked schedule "A." That the items mentioned in said account are in all respects correct; that the goods, wares, and merchandise there charged were in fact delivered to the said E. H. at the times stated in said account, and that no part of said account has been paid or satisfied [except the sum of —— dollars, which is credited therein].

And your petitioner further shows, that the said E. H. is also indebted to your petitioner in the further sum of —— dollars, with interest thereon from the —— day of ——, 18—, for the services and disbursements of your petitioner, mentioned in the account hereto annexed, marked schedule "B." That the items in said account, last aforesaid, are in all respects correct; that such services and disbursements have in fact been rendered or made, and that no part of said account has been paid or satisfied [except the sum of —— dollars, stated therein].

And your petitioner further shows, that he is informed and believes that the said E. H. has been declared a lunatic by the Supreme Court [*or other court*], and that D. H., residing at ——, in said county, is now the committee of his person and estate; and that he has been such committee for several months last past.

Your petitioner further shows, that he has duly presented the said accounts [*or*, has caused the said accounts to be duly presented] to the said committee, for payment; but the said committee declined [*or*, refused, *or*, has neglected] to pay the same, or any part thereof; and the sum of —— dollars, with interest as aforesaid, is now justly due thereon to your petitioner.

Your petitioner therefore prays, that an order may be entered directing the said committee to pay to your petitioner the amount of his accounts aforesaid [or the balance due thereon], to wit: the sum of —— dollars, with interest thereon from the —— day of ——, 18—; or that a reference may be ordered to pass upon the said accounts; or that your petitioner may have leave to bring an action against the said committee to establish and adjust the said accounts, and the amount due him upon the same; or for such other or further order as the court may think proper to make. R. M. F.

A. N. W., Att'y for Petitioner.

[*Verification as in No.* 393.]

Schedule "A," referred to in the annexed petition.

Schedule "B," referred to in the annexed petition.

No. 427.

NOTICE OF MOTION TO COMPEL PAYMENT OF CLAIM.

See ante, p. 26.

[*Title as in last form.*]

SIR: Take notice, that I shall apply to the next special term of the Supreme Court [*or other court*], to be held at the Court House in ——, on the —— day of —— next, at the opening of the court on that day, or as soon thereafter as counsel can be heard, for an order that the prayer of the petition hereto annexed be granted with costs, to be paid out of the estate of E. H., a lunatic, or for such other or further order as the court may think proper to grant; which motion will be founded upon the said petition, with a copy of which you are herewith served. Yours, &c.,

Dated, *&c.* A. N. W., Att'y for Petitioner.

To D. H., Committee of E. H., a lunatic.

No. 428.

ORDER THEREUPON

See ante, p. 26.

[*Title as in No.* 426.] At a special term, *&c.* [*as in No.* 6].

[*Title, also, as in No.* 410.]

On reading and filing the petition of R. M. F., of, *&c.*, dated the —— day of ——, 18—, praying for an order requiring D. H., committee of the person and estate of the above-named lunatic, to pay the accounts and demands stated in said petition, &c.; and, after hearing A. N. W., Esq., attorney for the petitioner, and U. G. P., Esq., counsel for the said committee, it is ordered, (*) that the committee of the estate of E. H. above named pay to the said petitioner, or to his attorney, within —— days from the service of a copy of this order upon him, the amount of the said petitioner's claims, mentioned in said petition, and which are here adjusted at the sum of —— dollars, and interest thereon from the —— day of ——, 18—. And it is further ordered, that the said committee pay to the attorney for the said petitioner ten dollars costs of this application. [*Or, from the asterisk,* (*) *proceed as follows:* that it be referred to L. F., Esq., residing in the county of ——, to pass upon and adjust the several accounts and demands of the said petitioner mentioned in the said petition, and to determine the amount justly due the said petitioner thereon; and that the said referee make his report to the court with all convenient speed. [*Or*, that R. M. F., above named, have leave to bring an action in the Supreme Court [*or other court*] against D. H., the committee of said lunatic, for the purpose of establishing and adjusting the claims and accounts mentioned in said petition, and the amount due thereon, if anything, to the said petitioner. And that the said petitioner, if he shall think proper so to do, may join the said E. H., as a party defendant in said action.]

No. 429.

ANNUAL INVENTORY AND ACCOUNT CURRENT, TO BE RENDERED BY COMMITTEE.

See ante, p. 30; and see, also, Ch. Court Rules, 1844, p. 169; and Rules of S. C. in Eq. 1847, p. 102.

[*Title as in No.* 410.] INVENTORY.

A just and true inventory of the real and personal estate and effects of the above-named lunatic [*or other person*], on the 31st December, 1865. (*a*)

1865, Dec. 31.

Balance of cash on hand this day	$16 74
Robert Gay's bond and mortgage on real estate, which is well secured, with interest at 7 per cent., from 31st December, 1865	350 00

[*Proceed in like manner in respect to other items.*]

D. H., Committee.

ACCOUNT CURRENT.

The estate of A. B., a lunatic.

To D. H., Committee.

1865.		Dr.
May 2.	To cash paid M. Low's bill for board and lodging, &c. . .	$27 33
June 4.	Dr. Jones's bill for medical attendance . . .	9 17

[*Proceed in like manner with other items.*]

CONTRA.

1865.		Cr.
Jan. 1.	Balance due as by last annual account . . .	$27 32
Feb. 2.	Cash received, one quarter's rent on dwelling-house in Utica	45 00

[*Continue with the items as before, and foot up the columns, so as to show balance due to the estate, if any.*]

Dated, *&c.* D. H., Committee.

(*a*) The original, or first, inventory filed should also contain a list of the debts existing against the lunatic, so far as the same can be ascertained by the committee, with the names of the creditors, and the nature of the indebtedness. See 2 *Rev. Stat.* 58, *sec.* 8; *ante, p.* 30.

County of ——, ss.: D. H., the committee of the above-named lunatic, being duly sworn, says: That the above is a just and true inventory of the whole real and personal estate and effects of the above-named lunatic, so far as the same have come to his knowledge, and a just and true account of all the receipts and disbursements on account of the said estate [since this deponent rendered his last account current in this matter to this court]. [*In the first account, the words between the brackets are to be omitted.*]

Sworn, *&c.* D. H.

No. 430.

PETITION FOR A SALE OF REAL ESTATE TO PAY DEBTS. (*a*)

See ante, pp. 37, 39.

[*Title as in No.* 410.]

To the Supreme Court of the State of New York [*or other court*]:

The petition of H. R., of, *&c.*, respectfully shows: That he is the committee of the person and estate of A. T. R. above named; and was appointed such committee by an order of this court, dated the —— day of ——, 18—. That, after his appointment as such committee, he duly made out and verified an inventory of the real and personal estate of the said A. T. R., and in such inventory stated the value thereof, and the amount of the rents and profits of the said real estate, and the debts owing by the said lunatic, and the credits and effects belonging to the said estate, a copy of which inventory is hereto annexed, marked Schedule "A."

And your petitioner further shows, that the said A. T. R. is the owner of the following real estate situated in the town of ——, in said county, and bounded and described as follows: [*insert description*]. That the said real estate is worth about the sum of —— dollars, and the issues and profits thereof by the year are worth about the sum of —— dollars; and the actual amount realized therefor by your petitioner, since his appointment as such committee, is the sum of —— dollars. That the value of the personal estate of said A. T. R., at the time of your petitioner's appointment as such committee, was the sum of —— dollars; but your petitioner has been obliged to sell and dispose of a considerable part thereof, to wit, the articles mentioned in Schedule "B.," hereto annexed, for the purpose of paying debts owing by the said lunatic, and the necessary expenses and disbursements attending said trust; and that the debts so paid, and the items of the expenses and disbursements aforesaid, are stated in the schedule hereto annexed, marked "C." That all the personal property in your petitioner's possession now belonging to the said lunatic is set forth in the schedule hereto annexed, marked "D."

And your petitioner further shows, that the debts yet existing against the said estate are set forth, with the amounts thereof, in the schedule hereto

(*a*) The proceedings for a sale, &c., for the maintenance of the lunatic, or his family, or for the education of his children, are similar to those on a sale for the payment of debts; and the forms Nos. 430 to 438 may be used, in such case, with the necessary alterations.

annexed, marked schedule "E." [*or*, that the following is an account of the debts now existing against the said estate, viz.: *set forth list of debts, with their amounts*]. That the aggregate amount of such debts is —— dollars, or thereabouts; for the payment of which, in addition to the expenses of supporting said lunatic, the income of said real and personal estate is wholly insufficient; and that the whole of said personal estate, if sold for that purpose, would not be sufficient to discharge the said debts.

Your petitioner therefore prays, that he may be authorized, by an order of this court, to mortgage or sell so much of the real estate of said lunatic as may be necessary for the payment of his debts. H. R.

[*Verification, as in No.* 393.]

[*Annex schedules mentioned in the petition.*]

No. 431.

ORDER OF REFERENCE THEREON.

See ante, p. 40.

[*Title as in No.* 410.] At a special term, *&c.* [*as in No.* 6].

On reading and filing the petition of H. R., committee of the person and estate of A. T. R., the above-named lunatic, dated the —— day of ——, 18—, praying for authority to mortgage or sell so much of the real estate of the said lunatic, as may be necessary for the payment of his debts; and on motion of L. P. C., of counsel for the petitioner, ordered, that it be referred to L. F., Esq., residing in the county of ——, to inquire into and report upon the matters in the said petition contained, and to inquire into the truth of the representations therein made, and to hear the parties interested in the said estate, and to report to this court with all convenient speed whether the personal estate of the said lunatic is insufficient for the payment of his debts; and whether a mortgage or sale of the real estate of the said lunatic, or any part thereof, is necessary for that purpose; and if so, which would be most advantageous to the said lunatic; and if a sale, his reasons therefor; and whether a sale or mortgage of the whole, or only a part, of said premises is necessary; and if only a part thereof is necessary to be mortgaged or sold, that he specify what particular part thereof can be disposed of, with the least injury to the interests of the said lunatic

---

No. 432.

NOTICE BY REFEREE OF PROCEEDINGS BEFORE HIM.

See ante, p. 40.

[*Title as in No.* 410.]

To R. R., and all others interested:

Whereas, by an order of this court, dated the —— day of ——, 18—, it was referred to the undersigned to inquire into and report upon the matters contained in the petition of H. R., committee, &c., praying for leave to sell or mortgage the real estate of A. T. R. above named, for the payment of his debts.

You will therefore take notice that I shall proceed to an examination into the said matters on the —— day of ——, 18—, at —— o'clock —. M. of that day, at my office in ——. L. F., Referee.

Dated, *&c.*

No. 433.

REFEREE'S REPORT AS TO THE NECESSITY OF A SALE, ETC.

See ante, p. 40.

[*Title as in No.* 410.]

To the Supreme Court of the State of New York [*or other court*]:

The undersigned, appointed referee by an order of this court, dated the —— day of ——, 18—, and therein directed to inquire and report as to the matters contained in the petition of H. R., committee of the estate of the above-named lunatic, do report:

That having caused —— days' notice in writing, to be given to R. R. and J. R., of, *&c.*, who are the children and next of kin of said lunatic, residing in this State, and having been attended by the attorney for the said committee, the said R. R. and J. R. failing to appear, I proceeded to make the inquiries directed by the said order.

That, from the evidence produced before me, I am satisfied that the facts stated in the said petition of H. R., committee aforesaid, are true. That I have ascertained that the personal estate now owned by the said lunatic is worth the sum of —— dollars. That a considerable part of the personal estate originally belonging to said lunatic has been sold and applied to his support and maintenance, and the payment of debts owing by him, and the necessary and proper expenses and disbursements attending said trust. That the personal property now owned by the said lunatic is insufficient for the payment of his debts; and that it is not advisable the same should be sold, for the reason that the most of it is necessary household furniture, and all of it is needed in the house and premises of said lunatic for the use of said lunatic and his family.

And I further report, that the debts owing by the said lunatic amount to the sum of —— dollars; and are due to the following persons: [*state names of creditors, and the amount and nature of the indebtedness*].

That a sale of a portion [*or*, the whole] of the real estate of said lunatic is necessary for the payment of those debts; and that such sale would be preferable to a mortgage, for the reason [*state reasons*]. That the part of said real estate which can be disposed of with the least injury to the interests of said lunatic is that piece or parcel of real estate situate, *&c.* [*describe it*], which is estimated to be worth about —— dollars.

All which is respectfully submitted.

Dated, *&c.* L. F., Referee.

No. 434.

ORDER TO CONFIRM REFEREE'S REPORT.

See ante, p. 40.

[*Title as in No.* 410.] At a special term, *&c.* [*as in No.* 6].

On reading and filing the report of L. F., Esq., referee, residing in the county of ——, dated the —— day of ——, 18—, and on motion of L. P. C., attorney for H. R., committee of the above-named lunatic, it is ordered that the said report be, and the same is hereby, confirmed.

And it appearing to the court from the said report, and an examination of the matter, that the personal estate of the said lunatic is insufficient for the payment of his debts, and that the same has been applied to that purpose as far as the circumstances of the case rendered proper; that the value of the personal estate now owned by him amounts to —— dollars, and that the debts now owing by the said lunatic amount to —— dollars, and that a sale of a portion [*or*, the whole] of the real estate of said lunatic is necessary for the payment of said debts; it is further ordered, that the said H. R., committee, aforesaid, be, and he is hereby, authorized and directed to sell, at public or private sale, subject to the approbation of this court, the piece or parcel of real estate owned by said lunatic, and described in said report, for the purpose of paying and discharging the debts of the said lunatic; which said real estate is described, as aforesaid, as follows: [*insert description*].

And it is further ordered, that before any conveyance in pursuance of such sale shall be executed, the terms of such sale shall be reported by the said committee, on oath, to the court, and confirmed by the said court.

No. 435.

REPORT OF SALE BY COMMITTEE.

See ante, p. 41.

[*Title as in No.* 410.]

To the Supreme Court of the State of New York [*or other court*]:

In pursuance of an order of this court in the above matter, dated the —— day of ——, 18—, authorizing and directing me to sell, at public or private sale, subject to the approbation of this court, the real estate mentioned in said order, for the purpose of paying and discharging the debts of the said lunatic, and directing me to report the terms of such sale to this court, upon oath, before any conveyance of said premises should be executed, I, the subscriber, the committee of the said lunatic, do report:

That I have sold, subject to the approbation of this court, to D. C., of, *&c.*, the piece or parcel of real estate specified in said order, at and for the price or sum of —— dollars, to be paid on the delivery of the deed therefor; which sum is the highest price that could be obtained for the said real estate. [*Or*, That pursuant to previous public notice given by me, for that purpose, for the space of —— weeks, I did, on the —— day of ——, 18—, at, *&c.*, sell at public auction, to D. C., of, *&c.*, the piece or parcel of real estate mentioned in said order, for the price or sum of —— dollars, the said D. C. being the highest bidder, and that being the highest sum bid therefor; and that by the terms of said sale the purchase-money is to be paid on the delivery of the deed, after the court shall have confirmed the said sale.]

All which is respectfully submitted.

Dated, *&c.* H. R., Committee.

County of ——, ss.: H. R., the committee of the estate of E. H., above named, being duly sworn, says, that he has read the above report, subscribed by him, and knows the contents thereof, and that the matters therein stated are true.

Sworn, *&c.* H. R.

No. 436.

ORDER CONFIRMING SALE AND DIRECTING CONVEYANCE.

See ante, p. 41.

[*Title as in No.* 410.] At a special term, *&c.* [*as in No.* 6].

On reading and filing the report of H. R., the committee of the estate of the above-named lunatic, made upon oath, dated the —— day of ——, 18—, stating, *&c.* [*set out the report*], it is, on motion of L. P. C., attorney for the said committee, ordered that the said report, and the sale therein mentioned, be, and the same are hereby, ratified and confirmed.

And it is further ordered that the said committee execute and deliver to D. C., the purchaser in the said report mentioned, a good and sufficient conveyance of the piece or parcel of land purchased by him, upon receiving the purchase-money agreed to be paid therefor. And that the said committee apply the net proceeds of the said sale, after deducting the costs of these proceedings, to be taxed, and the other necessary expenses of effecting said sale, to the payment and discharge of the debts of the said lunatic, specified in the report of L. F., Esq., bearing date the —— day of ——, 18—. (*a*)

[*If additional security is required to be given, add* :] And it is further ordered that the said committee, before receiving the said proceeds from the purchaser, shall give additional security, by a bond, with two sureties, to be approved of by a justice [*or*, a judge] of this court, and filed with the clerk, conditioned for the faithful application of, and accounting for, the proceeds of said sale.

(*a*) If a sale is ordered in cases where the personal estate is insufficient for the maintenance of the lunatic, &c., the order confirming the sale should direct the manner in which the proceeds of the sale shall be secured, and the income or produce thereof appropriated. 2 *Rev. Stat.* 54, *sec.* 17.

No. 437.

BOND OF COMMITTEE ON SALE OF REAL ESTATE.

See ante, p. 41.

[*The same as in No.* 413, *to the* (*), *and then as follows:*]

Whereas, by an order of the Supreme Court [*or other court*], dated the —— day of ——, 18—, H. R. above named, who is the committee of the person and estate of A. T. R., a lunatic, was authorized and directed to convey the real estate of said lunatic, situated in the town of —— aforesaid, mentioned in said order, to D. C., on his receiving the purchase-money agreed to be paid therefor.

Now, therefore, the condition of this obligation is such, that if the above-bounden H. R. shall faithfully apply the proceeds of such sale to the payment of the debts against said lunatic, and shall also faithfully account for the said proceeds, then the above obligation to be void, otherwise, to remain in full force and virtue.

[*Signed, acknowledged, &c., as in No.* 413.]

No. 438.

DEED OF COMMITTEE.

See ante, p. 41.

This indenture, made the —— day of ——, 18—, between H. R., of the town of ——, in the county of ——, and State of New York, committee of the person and estate of A. T. R., a lunatic, of the first part, and D. C., of the same place, of the second part.

Whereas, by an order of the Supreme Court [*or other court*], made on the —— day of ——, 18—, reciting that it appeared to the said court that the personal estate of the said A. T. R. was insufficient for the payment of his debts, and that a sale of a portion [*or*, the whole] of the real estate of the said lunatic was necessary for the payment thereof, the said party of the first part, as such committee, was, among other things, authorized and directed to sell, at public or private sale, subject to the approbation of the court, the piece or parcel of real estate owned by said lunatic and specified in said order, for the purpose of paying and discharging the debts of the said lunatic, and to report the terms of the sale made by him to the court on oath, before any conveyance of the said premises should be executed. And whereas, the said party of the first part, as such committee, having, in pursuance of the said order, on the —— day of ——, made his report to the court, stating, *&c.* [*state the substance of the report of sale*]. And whereas, by another order of the said court, dated the —— day of —— 18—, it was ordered that, *&c.* [*state order confirming sale, &c.*]

Now, therefore, this indenture witnesseth that the said party of the first part, committee as aforesaid, by virtue of the power and authority conferred upon him by the several orders above mentioned, and in pursuance of the statute in such case made and provided, for and in consideration of the sum of —— dollars, to him in hand paid at or before the ensealing and delivery of these presents, by the party of the second part, the receipt whereof is hereby confessed and acknowledged, has granted, bargained, sold, remised, released, and conveyed, and by these presents does grant, bargain, sell, remise, release, and convey unto the said party of the second part, his heirs and assigns forever, all the right, title, and interest of the said lunatic of, in, and to all that certain piece or parcel of land bounded and described as follows: [*insert description*]. To have and to hold the said premises, and every part and parcel thereof, with the appurtenances, to the said D. C., his heirs and assigns, to his and their only proper use, benefit, and behoof forever.

In witness whereof, the said party of the first part has hereunto set his hand and seal, the day and year first above written.

Sealed and delivered in the presence of L. F. H. R. [*Seal.*]

No. 439.

PETITION FOR SALE OF REAL ESTATE UNDER THE ACT OF 1864.

See ante, p. 42.

IN SUPREME COURT.

To the Supreme Court of the State of New York:

The petition of A. T. R., a lunatic, by H. R., his committee, respectfully shows:

That your petitioner has been adjudged a lunatic by virtue of an inquisition of lunacy heretofore ordered by this court. That the property, real and personal, of your petitioner, has been placed in the care and custody of H. R., of, *&c.*, who was appointed the committee of the person and estate of your petitioner; and that the said H. R. is still such committee.

That your petitioner is the owner in fee of the following piece or parcel of land, situated, lying, and being in the town of ——, in the county of ——, and bounded and described as follows: [*insert description*]. That the said piece or parcel of land is worth about —— dollars; but the same is wholly unproductive, being wild and unimproved [*or*, and produces an annual income of —— dollars].

Your petitioner further shows, that, *&c.* [*set out the facts to show that a disposition of the real estate is necessary and proper either for the support and maintenance of the lunatic or for his education, or because his interest requires or will be substantially promoted by such disposition, or has been contracted to be sold, and a conveyance thereof cannot be made by reason of such lunacy, or for any other peculiar reasons or circumstances*].

Your petitioner therefore prays that the said real estate may be sold by the said H. R., committee, as aforesaid, under the direction of the court, upon giving security as required by law. H. R., Committee.

[*Verification as in No.* 393.]

No. 440.

ORDER FOR SECURITY, AND DIRECTING REFERENCE—ACT OF 1864.

See ante, p. 42

At a special term of the Supreme Court, *&c.* [*as in No.* 6].

In the matter
of
A. T. R., a lunatic.

On reading and filing the petition of A. T. R., a lunatic, by H. R., the committee of his person and estate, dated the —— day of ——, 18—, praying for authority to sell the real estate of the said lunatic, and on motion of L. P. C., of counsel for the petitioner, it is ordered, that it be referred to A. W., Esq., residing in the county of ——, to inquire into and report upon the matters in the said petition contained, and to inquire into the truth of the representations made, and to hear the parties interested in the said estate, and to report to this court, with all convenient speed, whether the sale of said real estate, or any part thereof, is necessary and proper, and, if such sale is necessary or proper, his reasons therefor.

It is further ordered, that the said H. R. execute and file with the clerk of this court his bond, in the penal sum of —— dollars, with two sureties, conditioned for the faithful performance of the trust reposed in him, for the paying over, investing, and accounting for all moneys that shall be received by him, according to the order of any court having authority to give directions in the premises, and for the observance of the orders and directions of the court in relation to the trust.

And it is further ordered, that no proceedings be had before the said referee until the said H. R. produces a certificate of the clerk, in due form, that the security herein required has been duly proved or acknowledged, and filed, agreeably to this order.

No. 441.

BOND OF COMMITTEE, ON SALE, UNDER ACT OF 1864.

See ante, p. 43.

Know all men by these presents, that we, H. R., of the town of ——, in the county of ——, and W. T. F. and J. G. R., farmers, of the same place, are held and firmly bound unto A. T. R., a lunatic, of, *&c.*, in the sum of —— dollars, lawful money of the United States, to be paid to the said A. T. R., his executors, administrators, or assigns; for which payment, well and truly to be made, we bind ourselves, our, and each of our, heirs, executors, and administrators, firmly by these presents. Sealed with our seals, and dated the —— day of ——, 18—.

Whereas, the said A. T. R. has applied to the Supreme Court, by the said H. R., the committee of his person and estate, for authority to sell certain real estate owned by him, situated in the town of ——, in the county of ——.

Now, therefore, the condition of the above obligation is such that, if the above-bounden H. R. shall faithfully perform the trust reposed in him, and shall pay over, invest, and account for all moneys that shall be received by him, according to the order of any court having authority to give directions in the premises, and for the observance of the orders and directions of the court in relation to such trust; then this obligation to be void, otherwise to remain in full force and virtue. H. R. [L. S.]

Signed and sealed in the presence of A. B.

W. T. F. [L. S.]
J. G. R. [L. S.]

[*Acknowledgment or proof, and affidavit of sureties, as in No.* 44.]

No. 442.

CERTIFICATE OF CLERK; REFEREE'S REPORT, AND OTHER FORMS—ACT OF 1864.

See ante, pp. 42 to 45.

[*Same substantially as in Nos.* 262 *to* 267, *with the necessary alterations.*]

CHAPTER XIX.

FORMS IN MANDAMUS AND PROHIBITION.

No. 443.

AFFIDAVIT ON APPLICATION FOR MANDAMUS.

See ante, p. 62.

State of New York, County of ——, } ss.

A. B., of ——, in said county, being duly sworn, says: That, *&c.* [*set forth the facts to show that the relator is entitled to the writ, and to the relief demanded*].

Sworn, *&c.*

A. B.

No. 444.

NOTICE OF MOTION FOR A WRIT OF MANDAMUS.

See ante, pp. 63 to 65.

To C. D:

SIR,—You will take notice that I shall move the Supreme Court, at the next special term thereof, to be held at the Court House, in the village [*or*, city] of ——, on the —— day of —— instant, at the opening of the court on that day, or as soon thereafter as counsel can be heard, for an order (*) that a writ of mandamus issue out of the said court, directed to you, and commanding you that, *&c.* [*state the object of the writ*], or for such further or other relief as the court may be pleased to grant; which motion will be founded upon the affidavit, with a copy whereof you are herewith served.

Dated, *&c.* Yours, &c.,

L. P. C., Att'y for A. B.

No. 445.

ORDER THAT A MANDAMUS ISSUE, OR THAT THE DEFENDANT SHOW CAUSE.

See ante, p. 65.

At a special term of the Supreme Court held at the Court House in ——, in and for the county of ——, on the —— day of ——, 18—,

Present, Hon. A. B., Justice.

IN SUPREME COURT.

The People, *ex rel.* A. B.,
vs.
C. D.

On reading and filing the affidavit of A. B., the relator above-named, dated the —— day of ——, 18—, and on motion of L. P. C., Esq., of counsel for the relator, (*) [after hearing C. H., Esq., in opposition thereto], it is ordered, that a mandamus issue out of and under the seal of this court, directed to the said C. D., commanding him forthwith to, *&c.* [*state what is required to be done*], or that the said C. D. show cause to the contrary before this court at the next special term thereof, to be held at the Court House in ——, on the —— day of —— next.

No. 446.

ORDER TO SHOW CAUSE WHY MANDAMUS SHOULD NOT ISSUE.

See ante, pp. 63 to 65.

[*Same as in No.* 445 *to the asterisk,* (*) *and then continue*:] it is ordered that C. D. above named, show cause, at the next special term of this court, to be held [*or*, at the special term of this court now sitting], at the Court House in ——, on the —— day of —— instant, why the said C. D. should not be compelled forthwith, *&c.* [*state the matters required to be done*], or why an alternative mandamus should not issue, directed to the said C. D., in the usual form, and requiring him to do the acts above mentioned, or to show cause, &c.

And it is further ordered that a copy of this order, together with a copy of the affidavits on which the same is founded, be served on the said C. D., —— days before the time above mentioned.

No. 447.

ALTERNATIVE MANDAMUS—GENERAL FORM. (*a*)

See ante, p. 65.

The People of the State of New York, to C. D. [*or the court, commissioners, or other officers or persons to whom it is directed, naming them*], greeting:

[L. S.] Whereas [*here recite the facts or statements, briefly, which preceded the gravamen or injury*]. Nevertheless, you, the aforesaid C. D. [*or court, or officer*], have unjustly [*state briefly the order or proceeding complained of*], as we are informed by the complaint of the said A. B.

Now, therefore, we being willing that full and speedy justice be done in this behalf to him, the said A. B., do therefore command you that, immediately after the receipt of this writ, you, *&c.* [*insert the matter required to be done, or omitted, substantially according to the order of the court allowing the mandamus*], or that you show cause to the contrary thereof, before our Supreme Court, at the next special term thereof to be held at the Court House in ——, on the —— day of —— next, lest complaint shall again come to us by your default; and in what manner you shall have executed this our writ make known to our Supreme Court, at the next special term thereof, to be held at the time and place aforesaid.

Witness, A. B., Justice of the Supreme Court, at ——, the —— day of ——, 18—.

L. P. C., Attorney. N. B. M., Clerk.

[*Indorsed:*] "By the Court,"
N. B. M., Clerk.

(*a*) For a variety of forms of alternative mandamus, in particular cases, see 2 *Johns. Cas.*, 2d *ed.* 217—81 *to* 90, *notes.*

No. 448.

ANSWER OR RETURN TO ALTERNATIVE WRIT.

See ante, p. 70.

The answer or return of C. D. to the alternative writ of mandamus within mentioned.

I, the said C. D., do answer and return to the Supreme Court within mentioned, that, *&c.* [*deny the facts alleged in the writ, or set forth other facts in avoidance of the relator's claim*]. C. D.

ANOTHER FORM.

See Yates' Pl. 760.

The answer of the Mayor, Aldermen, and Commonalty of the City of ——, within mentioned.

We, the said Mayor, Aldermen, and Commonalty, do certify to the Supreme Court within mentioned, that the within-named A. B. was not elected an alderman, as by the within writ is within alleged; and, therefore, we could not cause him to be sworn nor admitted, as by that writ we were within commanded.

C. D., Mayor. [*Seal of Corporation.*]

No. 449.

NOTICE REQUIRING RELATOR TO DEMUR OR PLEAD.

See ante, p. 73.

[*Title as in No.* 445.]

To L. P. C., attorney for the relator [*or*, To A. B., the above-named relator].

Sir,—You will take notice that the defendant's return to the writ of mandamus in this cause has been duly filed with the clerk of ——— county; and that you are required to demur or plead to the said return within twenty days after the service of this notice. Yours, &c.,

Dated, *&c.* C. H., Att'y for the Defendant.

No. 450.

NOTICE OF HEARING, ON FAILURE OF RELATOR TO DEMUR OR PLEAD

See ante, p. 73.

[*Title as in No.* 445.]

To C. H., attorney for the defendant [*or*, To L. P. C., attorney for the relator]: (*a*)

(*a*) Either party may notice the matter for hearing. *See ante, p.* 73.

SIR,—You will please take notice that the above matter will be brought to a hearing on the return to the writ of mandamus in this matter, at the next special term of this court, to be held at the Court House in ——, on the —— day of —— instant, at the opening of the court on that day, or as soon thereafter as counsel can be heard.

Dated, the —— day of ——, A. D. 18—.

Yours, &c., L. P. C., Att'y for Relator
[*Or*, C. H., Att'y for Defendant.]

No. 451.

JUDGMENT RECORD ON MANDAMUS.

See ante, p. 78; and Yates' Pl. 760; 3 Burr. Pr. 523.

SUPREME COURT: Pleas before the Justices of the Supreme Court of Judicature of the People of the State of New York, at the City Hall in the City of ——, of the term of —— [*term of which judgment is entered*], in the year of our Lord one thousand eight hundred and ——.

Witness, W. M., Esq., Presiding Justice.
R. B. C., Clerk.

State of New York, ss.: The People of the State of New York (*) sent to [the Mayor, Aldermen, and Commonalty of the City of New York], their writ close in these words, to wit:

The People of the State of New York, &c. [*insert copy of mandamus in full*].

The answer of the Mayor, Aldermen, &c. [*insert copy of return in full*].

[*If an issue in fact is joined, the entries upon the record will be as follows:*]

And now, at this day, to wit, on, &c., before the justices aforesaid, at, &c., come as well the said A. B., by E. F., his attorney, as the said mayor, aldermen, and commonalty, by G. H., their attorney. And the said A. B., by his said attorney, says, that he was duly elected an alderman of the —— ward of the said city, as in the said writ is above alleged; and this the said A. B. prays may be inquired of by the country. And the said mayor, aldermen, and commonalty, by their said attorney, do the like, &c.

It is, therefore, ordered by the Supreme Court, that the issue above joined be tried at the circuit court, appointed to be held at the —— in the city of ——, on the —— day of ——, one thousand eight hundred and ——.

Afterward, to wit, on the day and at the place last mentioned, before H. E. D., Esq., one of the justices of the Supreme Court of the State of New York, according to the form of the statute in such case made and provided, come as well the above-named A. B., as the above-named mayor, aldermen, and commonalty, by their respective attorneys above mentioned; and the jurors of the jury, summoned to try the said issue, being called also come: who to speak the truth of the matters above contained, being chosen, tried, and sworn, say upon their oath that the said A. B. was duly elected an alderman, in manner and form as by the said writ of mandamus is within alleged; and they assess the damages which the said A. B. has sustained by reason of his not being sworn and admitted into the said office, as alleged in the said writ, over and above his costs and charges by him about his writ in this behalf expended, at —— dollars, and for those costs and charges to six cents. Whereupon the said A. B. prays judgment, and also, the people's writ of peremptory mandamus, to be directed to the said mayor, aldermen, and commonalty, commanding them to cause the said A. B. to be sworn and admitted into the said office of alderman, &c.

Judgment signed the —— day of ——, 18—. R. B. C., Clerk.

Therefore, it is considered that the said A. B. recover against the said mayor, aldermen, and commonalty his damages aforesaid by the jurors aforesaid, in form aforesaid found, and also —— dollars and —— cents, for his costs and charges by the court now here adjudged to the said A. B.; which said damages, costs, and charges, in the whole, amount to —— dollars and —— cents. And it is further considered that the people's writ of mandamus do forthwith issue, directed to the said mayor, aldermen, and commonalty, commanding them, upon pain and peril that shall fall thereon, to cause the said A. B. to be immediately sworn and admitted into the aforesaid office of alderman, according to the command of the said former writ of alternative mandamus, &c.

[*If the verdict was against the plaintiff, make the necessary alterations in the above, according to the fact, and then proceed as follows in respect to the judgment:*]

It is therefore considered that the said mayor, aldermen, and commonalty recover against the said A. B. —— dollars and —— cents, for their costs and charges by them laid out and expended in and about their defense to the said writ of mandamus, adjudged to the said mayor, aldermen, and commonalty, by their assent; and that they have execution therefor, &c.

No. 452.

PEREMPTORY MANDAMUS—GENERAL FORM.

See ante, pp. 63, 78.

The People of the State of New York to C. D. [*or the court, commissioners, or other officers, or persons to whom it is directed, naming them*], greeting:

[L. S.] Whereas, [*here recite the facts or statements, briefly, which preceded the gravamen or injury*]. Nevertheless, you, the aforesaid —— [*court, officer, or person*], have unjustly [*state briefly the order or proceeding complained of*], as we are informed by the complaint of A. B., and which complaint we have adjudged to be true as appears to us of record. Now, therefore, we being willing that full and speedy justice be done in this behalf to him the said A. B. as it is just, command you, firmly enjoining, that immediately after the receipt of this writ, you, *&c.* [*insert the thing or matter required to be done, substantially according to the order of the court allowing the mandamus*], lest complaint shall again come to us by your default; and in what manner this our command shall be executed, make appear to our said Supreme Court, on the —— day of ——, at the Court House in ——; then and there returning this our writ.

Witness, C. D. A., Justice of the Supreme Court, at ——, the —— day of ——, 18—. N. B. M., Clerk.

L. P. C., Attorney.

[*Indorsed:*] "By the Court,"

N. B. M., Clerk.

No. 453.

NOTICE OF MOTION FOR WRIT OF PROHIBITION.

See ante, p. 88.

[*Same substantially as in No.* 444 *to the asterisk, and then continue:*] That a writ of prohibition issue, directed to the county court, of the county of —— [*or other court to be restrained*], and to C. D., and commanding them to desist and refrain from any further proceedings in, *&c.* [*state the suit or matter sought to be prohibited*]; or for such further or other relief as the court may be pleased to grant; which motion will be founded upon the affidavits, copies of which are herewith served.

Yours, &c., L. H. N., Attorney for A. B.

Dated, *&c.*,

No. 454.

AFFIDAVIT ON APPLICATION FOR WRIT OF PROHIBITION.

See ante, p. 88.

[*Same form as in No.* 443, *ante.*]

No. 455.

ORDER THAT A WRIT OF PROHIBITION ISSUE.

See ante, p. 88.

[*Same substantially as in No.* 445 *to the asterisk, and then proceed:*] After hearing U. G. P., Esq., in opposition thereto, it is ordered that a writ of prohibition issue out of and under the seal of this court, directed to the county court of the county of ——, and to C. D., commanding them to desist and refrain from any further proceedings in, *&c.* [*state the suit or matter sought* *to be prohibited*], until the next term of this court, to be held at the Court House in ——, on the —— day of ——, 18—, and until the further order of the court thereon, and that they show cause, at the time and place last aforesaid, why they should not be absolutely restrained from any further proceedings in such suit or matter.

No. 456.

WRIT OF PROHIBITION.

See ante, p. 88.

[L. S.] The People of the State of New York, to the County Court, of the County of —— [*or other court to be restrained*], and to C. D., greeting:

Whereas, A. B., of, *&c.*, lately in our Supreme Court of judicature, at the Court House in ——, on the —— day of ——, 18—, represented to our said court that, *&c.* [*state the facts and proceedings complained of*]. (*)

Nevertheless, you, the said county court aforesaid [*or other court*], and the said C. D., well knowing the premises, yet contriving, as it is said, the said A. B. unjustly to aggrieve and oppress, have [*state the grievance*], in contempt of us, against the laws and customs of our said State, and to the manifest damage, prejudice, and grievance of him the said A. B.; wherefore the said A. B. has prayed relief, and our writ of prohibition in that behalf. We, therefore, being willing that the laws and customs of our said State should be observed, and that our citizens should in no wise be oppressed, do command you that you desist and refrain from any further proceedings, in, *&c.* [*state the matters to be prohibited*], until the next term of this court, to be held at the Court House in ——, on the —— day of ——, 18—, and until the further order of the court thereon; and that you show cause, before our said court, at the time and place last aforesaid, why you should not be absolutely restrained from any further proceedings in such suit or matter. And have you then there this writ.

Witness, C. R. I., Justice of the Supreme Court, at ——, the —— day of ——, 18—.

L. H. N., Attorney. N. B. M., Clerk.

[*Indorsed:*] "By the Court."

N. B. M., Clerk.

No. 457.

RETURN TO ALTERNATIVE WRIT OF PROHIBITION.

See ante, pp. 88, 89.

[*Same substantially as in cases of mandamus, see ante, No.* 448.]

[*If the party adopts the return of the court, then annex to the return the following:*]

[*Title.*] I, C. D., the party to whom the writ of prohibition hereto annexed is directed, do hereby adopt the return of the county court hereto annexed, and rely upon the matters contained in said return as sufficient cause why such court should not be restrained, as mentioned in said writ.

In witness whereof, I have hereunto subscribed my name, this —— day of ——, 18—. C. D.

No. 458.

NOTICE REQUIRING RELATOR TO DEMUR OR PLEAD.

See ante, p. 89.

[*Same as in No.* 449, *with necessary alterations.*]

No. 459.

NOTICE OF HEARING ON FAILURE OF RELATOR TO DEMUR OR PLEAD.

See ante, p. 89.

Same as in No. 450, *ante, with necessary alterations.*]

No. 460.

JUDGMENT RECORD ON PROHIBITION.

See ante, p. 89.

[*Same substantially as in No.* 451 *to the asterisk,* (*) *and then continue:*] Sent to the County Court of the county of —— [*or other court*], and to C. D., their writ of prohibition, close in these words, to wit: [*insert the writ of prohibition*].

At which day and place named in the return of said writ before the said Supreme Court, come as well the said A. B., by L. H. N., his attorney, as the said County Court, by U. G. P., their attorney. And the said County Court, now here, makes return to the said writ, and shows cause as follows, to wit: [*insert return*], and which return is, by an instrument in writing, signed by said C. D., adopted by him; which said writing is in the words following: [*insert the writing*].

And hereupon the said A. B. says, that he, by reason of anything in that return alleged and set forth, ought not to be barred or precluded from having a prohibition absolute, restraining the said County Court, and the said C. D., from [*state what*], because he says that, &c. [*insert the relator's plea*].

And the said C. D. says, that the said writ of prohibition absolute prayed for by said A. B. ought not to issue, because, &c. [*insert the other pleadings of the parties, if any, to issue, after which proceed with the record as in No.*

451. *If judgment is rendered for the relator, the further entry will be as follows:*]

Judgment signed this —— day of ——, 18—. N. B. M., Clerk.

Therefore, it is considered that the people's writ of prohibition absolute do issue, restraining [*state whom and what*]. And it is further considered, *&c.* [*add a judgment for costs, substantially as in No.* 451].

[*If judgment is rendered for the defendant, let the entry be thus:*]

Therefore, it is considered that the said C. D. go thereof without day, *&c.* And it is further considered, that the people's writ of consultation do issue, authorizing the said County Court, and the said C. D., to proceed in, *&c.* [*state what*]. And it is further considered, *&c.* [*judgment for costs, see No.* 451].

No. 461.

WRIT OF PROHIBITION—ABSOLUTE.

See ante, p. 89.

[*Same as in No.* 456, *to the* (*), *and then as follows:*]

Nevertheless, you, the said county court, aforesaid [*or other court*], and the said C. D., well knowing the premises, yet contriving the said A. B. unjustly to aggrieve and oppress, have [*state the grievance*], in contempt of us, against the laws and customs of our said State, and to the manifest damage, prejudice, and grievance of him, the said A. B. Wherefore the said A. B. has prayed relief, and our writ of prohibition in that behalf. We, therefore, having determined that the said A. B. is entitled to the said writ of prohibition, and to the said relief prayed for, do command you, that you absolutely desist and refrain from any further proceedings in, *&c.* [*state the matters to be prohibited*].

Witness, *&c.* [*as in No.* 456, *to the end*].

No. 462.

WRIT OF CONSULTATION.

See ante, p. 90.

[SEAL.] The People of the State of New York, to the County Court of the County of —— [*or other court*], and to C. D., greeting:

Whereas, A. B., of, *&c.*, lately prosecuted, and caused to be directed to you, our certain writ of prohibition, out of our Supreme Court, at a special term thereof, held at the Court House in ——, on the —— day of ——, 18—, that you should not, *&c.* [*state what the writ of prohibition commanded*], by pretense of which prohibition you have thence hitherto delayed, and yet do delay, further to proceed in [*state what*], as we have understood.

And our said Supreme Court having determined that the said A. B. was not entitled to the said writ of prohibition, and the said C. D. having prayed our aid and assistance in this behalf; and we, being willing that there should be no further delay in [*state the proceeding*]. Because in our said Supreme Court, at, *&c.*, it is in such manner provided that it is considered by the said court, that a writ of consultation may issue, our said writ of prohibition to the contrary thereof notwithstanding. We, therefore, being unwilling that the said C. D. should in any wise be injured in this behalf, do hereby authorize you to proceed in the said cause or matter, and further to do what you shall know to belong thereto, our said writ of prohibition to the contrary thereof in any wise notwithstanding.

Witness, *&c.* [*as in No.* 456, *to the end*].

CHAPTER XX.

FORMS IN THE PARTITION OF REAL ESTATE.

No. 466.

PETITION BY INFANT FOR LEAVE TO COMMENCE AN ACTION FOR PARTITION, AND FOR THE APPOINTMENT OF A GUARDIAN.

See ante, p. 109; 2 Van Sant. Eq. Pr. 447.

IN SUPREME COURT:

In the matter of the petition on behalf of C. D., an infant, by his general guardian, N. O.

To the Supreme Court of the State of New York:

The petition of C. D., an infant under the age of twenty-one years, and of the age of twelve years, by N. O., his general guardian, respectfully shows: That he was of the age of twelve years on the —— day of —— last, and resides in the town of ——, in the county of ——, with his mother, E. D., and is supported by her; and that the said N. O. has been appointed his general guardian by the surrogate of the county of ——. That said infant is one of the children and heirs-at-law of R. D., deceased, who died seized of certain real estate situated in said county, and bounded and described as follows: [*insert description*].

That the said infant, as such heir-at-law, is now a tenant in common, in fee-simple, of said premises, with the other children of said R. D., deceased, to wit: A. D., S. D., and P. D., subject to the dower right of their said mother.

That the said real estate is worth about the sum of —— dollars; that the said infant is not seized of any other real estate, and has personal property only to the amount of —— dollars, which is in the possession and under the control of his said guardian; and that the income of said personal property is insufficient for his support and maintenance.

That the said real estate consists of building lots, and is wholly unproductive [*or other facts to show that a sale of the premises is desirable*].

That the interests of said infant require a sale of said premises, the said infant being in need of the income of his proportional share for his maintenance and support.

That all the other tenants in common are infants under the age of twenty-one years [*or*, refuse to unite in a sale of said premises; *or other facts showing why the infant should be allowed to commence an action for partition.*]

Wherefore your petitioner prays that the court will allow proceedings to be instituted by action of partition, in behalf of said infant, for a division and partition of said real estate, and for a sale thereof, if it shall appear that partition cannot be made without great prejudice to the owners; and that the said N. O. be appointed the next friend or guardian of said infant, to conduct the proceedings in such action on his behalf.

And your petitioner will ever pray. N. O.

Dated, &c.

[*Add verification, substantially as in No.* 1.]

No. 467.

ORDER OF REFERENCE THEREON.

See ante, p. 109; 2 Van Sant. Pr. 449.

[*Title as in last form.*] At, &c. [*as in No.* 445].

On reading and filing the petition on behalf of C. D., an infant, by his general guardian, N. O., bearing date the —— day of ——, 18—, and duly verified, on motion of B. B. H., Esq., attorney for said guardian, it is ordered that it be referred to C. R. J., Esq., counselor-at-law, to inquire into the matters set forth in said petition, and report the facts to this court, with his opinion thereon.

No. 468.

REFEREE'S REPORT.

See ante, p. 109; 2 Van Sant. Pr. 449.

[*Title as in last form.*]

To the Supreme Court of the State of New York:

The undersigned, referee, to whom it was referred to inquire into the truth of the matters alleged in the petition in this matter. and to report the facts to this court, with his opinion thereon, respectfully reports:

That, after due examination and testimony taken therein, I find that the matters alleged in said petition are true; that the said infant is of the age of twelve years, and is tenant in common, *&c.* [*as stated in the petition, or as the case may be*].

That, *&c.* [*state other material facts found by the referee*].

From which facts so found by me, I am of the opinion that the interests of said infant require that an action should be brought for a partition and sale of said premises.

And I do further report that the person proposed as guardian to conduct the said action, is, in my opinion, a suitable and proper person for that purpose, and has no interest adverse to said infant.

All which is respectfully submitted.

Dated, *&c.* C. R. I., Referee.

No. 469.

ORDER CONFIRMING REPORT, AUTHORIZING ACTION, AND APPOINTING GUARDIAN AD LITEM.

See ante, p. 109.

[*Title as in No.* 466.] At a special term, *&c.* [*as in No.* 6].

On reading and filing the report of C. R. I., Esq., referee duly appointed in this matter, by an order dated the —— day of ——, 18—, said report bearing date the —— day of ——, 18—; and on motion of B. H. H., attorney for said guardian, it is ordered that the said report be, and the same is hereby, confirmed, and that the guardian *ad litem* hereinafter mentioned have leave to institute an action in this court on behalf of said infant, for a partition of the real estate mentioned in the petition in this matter, and for a sale thereof, if it shall appear that such partition cannot be made without great prejudice to the owners.

And it is further ordered that N. O., the general guardian of said infant, be, and he hereby is, appointed his next friend or guardian *ad litem*, to prosecute the said action, and conduct the proceedings on behalf of said infant, on his executing to the people of this State, duly acknowledged, a bond in the penalty of —— dollars, with two sufficient sureties, to be approved by a justice of this court, and filed with the clerk, as required by statute and the practice of the court.

No. 470.

SUMMONS.

See ante, p. 115.

SUPREME COURT [*or other court*], County of ——

A. B.
against
J. K., R. D., C. D., and all persons or owners unknown, having or claiming any interest in the premises sought to be partitioned in this action.

To the above-named defendants :

You are hereby summoned to answer the complaint of A. B. above named, a copy of which is hereto annexed [*or*, which will be filed in the office of the clerk of the county of ——], and to serve a copy of your answer on me at my office in the city [*or*, village] of ——, in said county, within twenty days after the service of this summons, exclusive of the day of service; and if said defendants fail to answer said complaint, as hereby required, the plaintiffs will apply to the Supreme Court [*or other court*], for the relief demanded in the complaint.

Dated, *&c.* L. P. C., Att'y for Plaintiff.

No. 471.

NOTICE OF OBJECT OF THE ACTION.

See ante, p. 115.

[*Title as in last form.*]

To the above-named defendants:

Take notice: That this action is commenced for the purpose of obtaining a partition and division, among the owners thereof, of certain real estate and premises, situated in the town of ——, in the county of ——, in which the above-named defendants have or claim some interest.

Also take notice that the said plaintiffs make no personal claim against you in this action.

The following is a brief description of the premises above mentioned: [*insert brief description.*] Yours, &c.,

Dated, *&c.* L. P. C., Att'y for Plaintiffs.

No. 472.

COMPLAINT FOR PARTITION.

See ante, p. 116.

[*Title as in No.* 470.]

The complaint of the plaintiff, by L. P. C., his attorney, shows to the court:

That the said plaintiff A. B., and J. K., of Chicago, in the State of Illinois, and C. D., of, &c., and R. D., of, &c., and some other person or persons to the plaintiff unknown, are seized in fee, as tenants in common, of the following pieces or parcels of land, with the appurtenances, situate, lying, and being in —— aforesaid, and bounded and described as follows: [*describe the premises particularly*].

The plaintiff further shows, that he is the owner of one undivided fifth part of the said premises, and obtained his title thereto by purchase from E. D., of, &c.

That the said J. K. is the owner of an undivided fifth part of said premises, and obtained title thereto by purchase from H. D., of, &c.

That the said R. D. and C. D. are each entitled to one undivided fifth part of said premises, and obtained title to the same by devise from their father, W. D., late of, &c., now deceased.

That one G. H. was formerly the owner of the remaining undivided fifth part of said premises, which he obtained by purchase from G. D., of, &c., and that the said G. H. died on the —— day of——, 18—, at——, as the plaintiff is informed and believes. But whether the said G. H. had sold his interest in the said premises, or left any will disposing of the same, or any heirs-at-law who would inherit the same, the plaintiff has been unable to ascertain, although he has made diligent inquiry for that purpose.

The plaintiff further shows, that the several pieces or parcels of land above described comprise the only real estate, within this State, owned in common by the plaintiff and the parties aforesaid.

And the plaintiff further shows, that he and the said J. K., and R. D., are all of full age. That the said C. D. is a minor under the age of twenty-one years, and having no general guardian, as the plaintiff is informed and believes.

The plaintiff further shows, upon information and belief, that there are no specific liens or incumbrances upon the several pieces of land above described, or any of them, against any of the owners thereof. [*Or*, that the one equal undivided fifth part of said several pieces of land is incumbered by mortgage executed by the said H. D. to the defendant S. T., of, &c., previous to the sale thereof to the said J. K., which mortgage was dated the —— day of ——, 18—, and was given to secure to the said S. T., his heirs and assigns, the sum of one thousand dollars, in five years from the date thereof, with interest annually; and the same has not been paid, and is still owned by the said S. T., as the plaintiff is informed and believes.]

The plaintiff further shows, that he is desirous of having a partition or sale of the above-mentioned premises, made under the direction, and with the sanction of this court.

Wherefore, the plaintiff demands judgment that partition and division of the several pieces or parcels of land above described may be made, by and under the direction of this court, between the plaintiff and the said J. K., and R. D., and C. D., and the person or persons unknown, as aforesaid, according to their respective rights and interests therein; and that commissioners may be appointed by the court for the purpose of making such partition; or, in case a partition of said premises, or of any part thereof, cannot be made without great prejudice to the owners, then that the said premises, or such part thereof as cannot be divided, may be sold by and under the direction of this court, and that the proceeds of the sale, after paying the costs and expenses of this action, may be divided among the owners thereof according to their respective rights and interests therein. And that the plaintiff may have such further or other relief as may be just.

L. P. C., Attorney for Plaintiff.

County of ——, ss.: A. B., the plaintiff named in the foregoing complaint, being duly sworn, deposes and says: The said complaint is true to his own knowledge, except as to the matters therein stated on information and belief, and as to those matters he believes it to be true.

Sworn, &c. A. B.

No. 473.

COMPLAINT FOR PARTITION (*a*)—(ANOTHER FORM).

See ante, p. 116.

[*Title substantially as in No.* 470.]

The complaint of the above-named plaintiffs, by H. & N., their attorneys, shows to the court:

That T. B., the grandfather of the said plaintiff, A. M. D., and late of the town of ——, county of ——, and State of New York, now deceased, was, at the time of making his last will and testament, hereinafter mentioned, and also at the time of his death, seized in fee-simple and possessed of all those certain farms, pieces or parcels of land, situated, lying, and being in the town of —— aforesaid, bounded and described as follows: [*insert description*].

And being so seized and possessed, as aforesaid, the said T. B. died on or about the —— day of ——, 18—.

The plaintiffs further show that the said T. B. in his lifetime, to wit: on or about the —— day of ——, 18—, made and published his last will and

(*a*) This complaint is from one drawn for actual use.

testament, in due form of law, and duly authenticated to pass real estate; a copy of which, together with a codicil thereto, is hereto annexed, and marked "Schedule A."

And that the said testator, in and by his said last will and testament, did, among other things, give, devise, and bequeath to the children of his daughters L. A. H., wife of S. H., and M. N., wife of J. N., the said above-described premises, to be equally divided between said children as they respectively arrived at the age of twenty-one years.

The said plaintiffs further show that at the time of the making of said last will and testament, and at the time of said testator's death, the said L. A. H., wife of S. H., and daughter of the said testator, had three children, to wit: L. B. H., now L. B. B., wife of E. B., M. H., and L. A. H., now L. A. P., wife of W. E. P. That the said M. N., wife of J. N., and daughter of the said testator, had three children, to wit: A. M. D., wife of C. B. D., one of said plaintiffs, and T. N., and J. H. N.

And the plaintiffs further show that the said L. B. B. and E. B. her husband, on or about the —— day of ——, 18—, by their certain deed, or instrument in writing, executed and acknowledged in due form of law to pass real estate, did remise, release, and quit-claim unto H. L. D., of ——, all their right, title, and interest in and to the aforesaid premises; and that the said H. L. D., and C., his wife, on or about the —— day of ——, 18—, by their certain deed, or instrument in writing, executed and acknowledged in due form of law to pass real estate, did remise, release, and quit-claim unto the said plaintiff, C. B. D., all their right, title, and interest, of, in, and to the aforesaid premises; as by reference to the said deeds and writings, when produced, will more fully appear.

The plaintiffs aver, that the said plaintiffs and the said defendants, W. E. P., and L. A. P., his wife, M. H., T. N., and J. H. N., are seized in fee simple, and entitled to the aforesaid farms, pieces or parcels of land, as tenants in common; and that their rights and interests therein are as follows: The said plaintiff, C. B. D., as grantee of the said H. L. D., is seized and entitled to an undivided one-sixth part thereof; that the said plaintiff, A. M. D., as one of the children of said M. N., is also seized of and entitled to an undivided one-sixth part thereof; that the said defendant, M. H., as one of the children of said L. A. H., is seized of and entitled to an undivided one-sixth part thereof; that the said defendants, W. E. P. and L. A. P., his wife, in right of the said L. A. P., as one of the children of the said L. A. H., are seized of and entitled to an undivided one-sixth part thereof; and that the said T. N. and J. H. N. are also each seized of and entitled to an undivided one-sixth part thereof.

The said plaintiffs further show that the above-described premises and lands are the only real estate owned in common by the parties to this action.

And the plaintiffs further show that there are no specific liens or incumbrances upon the said lands and premises, against any of the parties to this action, to the knowledge or belief of the said plaintiffs.

Wherefore, the plaintiffs demand judgment that the part or shares belonging to the said plaintiffs, and the other parties aforesaid, of, in, and to the aforesaid pieces or parcels of land, may be ascertained and determined by and under the direction of this court. And that a partition and division thereof may be made between the said plaintiffs and the other parties interested in the said premises, according to the respective rights and interests of each therein.

And that a commission of partition may be issued out of and under the seal of this court, and proper commissioners may be appointed for the purpose of making partition of said premises; or, in case a partition thereof, or any part thereof, cannot be made without great prejudice to the owners, that then the same, or such part thereof as cannot be divided, may be sold by and under the direction of this court, and that the proceeds of the sale, after paying the costs and charges of this action, may be divided among the owners thereof, according to their several rights and interests therein; and to that end, that the rights and interests of the parties interested in the said premises, or in the proceeds of the sale thereof, may be ascertained and declared by the judgment of this court.

H. & N., Plaintiffs' Attorneys.

[*Add verification as in last form*].

"SCHEDULE A," *referred to in the annexed complaint*, [*Insert copy will &c*]

No. 474 (A).

NOTICE OF LIS PENDENS.

See ante, p. 108.

[*Title as in No.* 470.]

Notice is hereby given to all whom it may concern, that the complaint in the above-entitled action is filed against the defendants, J. K., R. D., and C. D., therein named, and against all persons unknown having or claiming any interest in the premises described in said complaint, for the purpose of obtaining a partition and division of the said premises, among the owners thereof, by commissioners to be appointed for that purpose; and for a sale thereof under the direction of the Supreme Court [*or other court*], if a partition cannot be made, and for a division of the proceeds of such sale among such owners according to their several rights and interests therein; which premises are described in the said complaint as follows, to wit: [*describe the premises*].

Dated, *&c.* L. P. C., Att'y for Plaintiff.

No. 474 (B).

AFFIDAVIT OF FILING NOTICE OF LIS PENDENS.

See ante, p. 123.

[*Title of the cause.*]

County of ——, ss.: L. P. C., attorney for the plaintiff in the above-entitled action, being duly sworn, says, That this action was brought to obtain a partition or sale of the premises described in the complaint therein. That a notice of the pendency of the action and of the general object thereof, and containing a description of the land sought to be partitioned or sold, as the same is described in the complaint, was filed in the office of the clerk of —— county, in which the premises are situated, on the —— day of ——, 18—. That at the time of filing the said notice, the premises described therein were, and now are, situated in the town of ——, in the county of ——; and that since the filing of the said notice, the complaint in this cause has not been amended by making new parties to the action, or so as to affect other property not described in the said complaint.

Sworn, *&c.* L. P. C.

[*Or the following affidavit may be annexed to a copy of the notice:*]

County of ——, ss.: L. P. C., attorney for the plaintiff, being duly sworn, says, That a notice of *lis pendens*, of which the annexed is a copy, was, on the —— day of ——, 18—, filed in the office of the clerk of the county of ——, in which county the said premises are situated.

Sworn, *&c.* L. P. C.

No. 475.

PETITION BY RELATIVE OF INFANT DEFENDANT FOR APPOINTMENT OF GUARDIAN AD LITEM.

See ante, p. 109.

[*Title as in No.* 470.]

To the Supreme Court of the State of New York [*or other court*]: (*a*)

The petition of A. D., the mother of C. D., an infant under the age of fourteen years, respectfully shows:

That the said C. D. was ten years of age on the —— day of ——, 18—, and your petitioner is his mother, with whom he resides. That an action has been commenced in this court, against the said infant, by A. B., for a division and partition of certain real estate situated in the, *&c.*; and for a sale of said premises if it shall appear that a partition thereof cannot be made without great prejudice to the owners.

(*a*) Application for the appointment of a guardian may also be made to a judge of the court in which the action is prosecuted, or to a county judge. See *ante*, p. 111, note *a*.

That the summons in said action was served on said infant and on your petitioner on the —— day of ——, 18—; and no guardian *ad litem* has been appointed for said infant; and he has no general or testamentary guardian.

Wherefore your petitioner prays that the court may appoint a suitable and disinterested person to be a guardian for the said infant, for the special purpose of taking charge of the interests of the said infant in relation to the proceedings for a partition of the premises above mentioned.

Dated, *&c.* A. D.

L. P. C., Att'y for A. D.

County of ——, ss.: A. D., the petitioner above named, being duly sworn, deposes and says, that she has read [*or*, has heard read] the foregoing petition subscribed by her, and knows the contents thereof, and that the same is true of her own knowledge, except as to the matters therein stated on information and belief, and as to those matters she believes it to be true.

Sworn, *&c.* A. D.

No. 476.

PETITION OF PLAINTIFF OR OTHER PARTY TO APPOINT GUARDIAN FOR INFANT DEFENDANT ON HIS NEGLECT TO APPLY.

See ante, p. 109.

[*Title as in No.* 470.]

To the Supreme Court of the State of New York [*or other court*]:

The petition of A. B., of ——, *&c.*, respectfully shows:

That your petitioner has commenced an action in this court against C. D., and others, for a division and partition of certain premises situated in the, *&c.*; and for sale of said premises if it shall appear that a partition thereof cannot be made without great prejudice to the owners. That the said C. D. is an infant of the age of —— years, who resides with his mother, A. B., at ——, *&c.*, and has no general or testamentary guardian.

That the summons in said action was served on said C. D. more than twenty days since; and the said C. D. has not, nor has any relative, guardian, or friend for him, applied for the appointment of a guardian *ad litem* for the purpose of taking charge of his interests in said action.

Your petitioner, therefore, prays that the clerk of this court, residing in the county of ——, or some other suitable or proper person, be appointed guardian of the said C. D., for the purpose of taking charge of his interests in relation to the proceedings for a partition or sale of said premises.

Dated, *&c.* A. B.

[*Add verification substantially as in No.* 1.]

No. 477.

NOTICE OF APPLICATION FOR APPOINTMENT OF GUARDIAN.

See ante, p. 109.

[*Title as in No.* 470.]

To C. D., infant defendant [*or*, to A. D., guardian of C. D.]:

You will take notice, that upon the petition, with a copy whereof you are herewith served, and the summons and proceedings in this action, a motion will be made at the next special term of this court, to be held at the Court House in ——, on the —— day of ——, 18—, at the opening of the court on that day, or as soon thereafter as counsel can be heard, for an order appointing the clerk of this court, or some other suitable and proper person, to be the guardian *ad litem* of the said infant, for the purpose of taking charge of his interests in this action. Yours, &c.,

Dated, *&c.* L. P. C., Att'y for Plaintiff.

No. 478.

ORDER APPOINTING GUARDIAN.

See ante, p. 109.

[*Title of the cause.*] At a special term, *&c.* [*as in No.* 6].

On reading and filing the petition of A. B., the plaintiff in this action, with proof of the due service of a copy thereof, and of notice of this motion, on C. D., an infant defendant in this action, no one appearing in opposition thereto, it is, on motion of L. P. C., attorney for the plaintiff, ordered, that N. O., residing at ——, in the county of ——, be, and he is hereby, appointed guardian *ad litem* of said C. D., for the special purpose of taking charge of the interests of said infant in relation to the proceedings for partition in this action, on his executing to the people of this State, and duly acknowledging and filing, a bond in the penalty of —— dollars, with one sufficient surety [*or*, two sufficient sureties], to be approved by a justice of this court, and conditioned as required by the statute and the practice of this court

---

No. 479.

BOND OF GUARDIAN AD LITEM.

See ante, p. 113.

Know all men by these presents, that we, N. O., of, *&c.*, and R. W., of, *&c.*, and J. H., of, *&c.*, are held and firmly bound unto the people of the State of New York, in the penal sum of —— dollars, to be paid to the said people; to which payment well and truly to be made, we bind ourselves, our heirs, executors, and administrators, jointly and severally, firmly by these presents. Sealed with our seals, and dated the —— day of ——, 18—.

Whereas the above-bounden N. O. has been appointed by an order of the Supreme Court [*or other court*], made the —— day of ——, 18—, on the application of A. B., to be guardian for C. D., an infant, for the special purpose of taking charge of the interests of the said C. D., in relation to the proceedings for a partition in an action commenced in said court, wherein the said A. B. is plaintiff, and the said C. D. and others are defendants.

Now, therefore, the condition of the above obligation is such, that if the above-bounden N. O. shall faithfully discharge the said trust so committed to him, and shall render a just and true account of his guardianship in all courts and places when thereunto required, then the above obligation to be void, otherwise, to remain in full force and virtue.

Sealed and delivered in N. O. [L. S.]
the presence of R. W. [L. S.]
T. S. J. H. [L. S.]

[*Add acknowledgment and justification of sureties, and approval of the bond, as in No.* 261.]

No. 480.

AFFIDAVIT THAT NO ANSWER HAS BEEN RECEIVED, ETC.

See ante, pp. 118, 119.

[*Title of the cause.*]

County of ——, ss.: L. P. C., attorney for the plaintiff, being duly sworn, deposes and says: That this action is brought for the partition of real estate situated in the county of ——; that more than twenty days have elapsed since the service of the summons in the above-entitled action upon all the defendants, and of copy of the complaint upon the attorneys of such as have appeared therein, as appears by the sheriff's certificate and other proof of service thereof, and that no demurrer or answer has been received on behalf of any of the defendants [except that the defendant J. K. has put in an answer in which the rights and interests of the several parties, as stated in the complaint, are not contested or denied].

Sworn, *&c.* L. P. C.

No. 481.

LIKE AFFIDAVIT—ALL THE DEFENDANTS OF FULL AGE.

See ante, p. 118.

[*Same as in last form to the end, and then add:*] And that all the defendants are of full age, and have been personally served with the summons, and reside within this State, and that none have appeared therein, except, &c., who has made default as aforesaid.

Sworn. &c. L. P. C.

No. 482.

LIKE AFFIDAVIT—WHERE THERE ARE INFANT, ABSENT, AND UNKNOWN DEFENDANTS.

See ante, p. 118.

[*Same as in No.* 480 *to the end, and then as follows :*]

And deponent further says, that the defendant C. D. is an infant, and has put in the usual answer by N. O., his guardian *ad litem*, not controverting any material allegation of the complaint, and submitting his interests to the protection of the court; and that all the other defendants are of full age, and have been personally served with the summons, and reside within this State [*or*, and that the defendants J. K. and R. D. are non-residents of this State, and have been served by publication of the summons, pursuant to an order directing such service, in the form and manner prescribed by law; and that some of the defendants are unknown owners, and have been served by publication of the summons, pursuant to the order, and in the form and manner aforesaid].

Sworn, &c. L. P. C.

No. 483.

LIKE AFFIDAVIT—WHERE A SALE OF THE PREMISES IS DESIRED

See ante, p. 118.

[*Same as in last forms, and then as follows :*]

And deponent further says, that the whole premises of which partition is sought are so circumstanced [*or*, that a portion of the premises of which partition is sought, to wit, the house and lot in the village of ——, which will exceed in value the share to which any of the tenants in common will be entitled, is so circumstanced] that a partition thereof cannot be made without great prejudice to the owners, due regard being had to the power of the court to decree compensation to be made for equality of partition, and to the ability of the respective parties to pay a reasonable compensation to produce such equality.

Sworn, &c. L. P. C.

No. 484.

AFFIDAVIT THAT TWO OF THE PARTIES DESIRE THEIR SHARES SET OFF IN COMMON.

See ante, p. 129.

[*Title of the cause.*]

County of ——, ss.: A. B., the plaintiff above named, being duly sworn, deposes and says: That this action is brought for the partition of real estate situated in the town of ——, in said county, which is owned in fee simple by the plaintiff and defendants, as tenants in common [*or as the case may be*]. That this deponent and the defendant R. D. are each seized, in fee simple, of the equal undivided one-fifth part of said premises, and are desirous of having their shares and interests set off to them in common, without partition or allotment as between themselves, which, as deponent believes, can be done without injury to the interests of any of the parties.

Sworn, *&c.* A. B.

No. 485.

NOTICE OF MOTION FOR THE RELIEF DEMANDED IN THE COMPLAINT, AND FOR ORDER OF REFERENCE, ETC.

See ante, p. 138.

[*Title of the cause.*]

To J. L., Esq., Attorney for the defendant, J. K.:

SIR,—Take notice, that upon the pleadings and proceedings in this action, and the usual proof of the due service of the summons upon all the defendants, and the affidavit, with a copy of which you are herewith served, the plaintiff will apply, at the next special term of this court, to be held at the Court House in ——, in the county of ——, on the —— day of ——, 18—, at the opening of the court on that day, or as soon thereafter as counsel can be heard, for the relief demanded in the complaint, and for the usual order of reference under the 78th Rule of this court. [And that the referee to be appointed on said motion be directed to ascertain and report whether the shares of A. B. and R. D. are so situated that they may be set off in common to them without injury to the interests of the other parties.]

Dated, *&c.* Yours, &c.,

L. P. C., Att'y for Plaintiff.

No. 486.

PETITION BY A PERSON NOT NAMED AS A PARTY, FOR LEAVE TO APPEAR AND ANSWER.

See ante, p. 107.

To the Supreme Court of the State of New York [*or other court; or*, To Hon. C. L. A., Justice of the Supreme Court; *or*, To Hon. A. D. W., County Judge of the County of ——]:

The petition of A. N., of, *&c.*, respectfully shows:

That your petitioner has an interest [*or*, a claim by which he may become interested at some future time] in the premises described in a certain complaint in an action brought in the Supreme Court [*or other court*] by A. B., of, *&c.* That the said interest [*or*, claim] of your petitioner in the said premises is [*here state the interest or claim particularly, and then proceed*].

And your petitioner further shows that he is not named as a party in the said complaint; and he therefore prays that he may be permitted to appear and answer the said complaint as a defendant therein.

Dated, *&c.* A. N.

M. F., Attorney.

[*Add verification, substantially as in No.* 1.]

No. 487.

ORDER PERMITTING PETITIONER TO APPEAR AND ANSWER.

See ante, p. 107.

[*Title of the cause.*] At a special term, *&c.* [*as in No.* 6].

On reading and filing the petition of A. N., dated the —— day of ——, 18—, stating that he has an interest [*or*, claim] in the premises described in the complaint in this action, and that he is not named as a party in said complaint; and on reading and filing the affidavit of the said A. N., of his interest [*or* claim] as aforesaid; it is, on motion of M. F., attorney for the said A. N., ordered, that the said A. N. be, and he is hereby, admitted to appear and answer the said complaint as a defendant.

No. 488.

ORDER FOR JUDGMENT ON DEFAULT—PROOF TAKEN BY THE COURT.

See ante, p. 118.

[*Title as in No.* 470.] At a special term, *&c.* [*as in No.* 6].

On reading and filing proof of the personal service of the summons on all the defendants, more than twenty days since, and on affidavit showing that this action is brought for a partition of real estate situated in the county of ——, and described in the complaint herein, and that all the defendants are residents of this State, and are of full age; and that none of them have appeared in this action; (*) and the said plaintiff having exhibited to the court proof of his title, and an abstract of the conveyances by which the same is held; which proof and abstract have been duly filed with the clerk of this court; and the court having ascertained, from the proof so taken, the rights, titles, and interests of the parties herein;

Now, on motion of L. P. C., attorney for the plaintiff, it is ordered and declared by the court, that the rights, titles, and interests of said parties, so far as the same have appeared, are as follows, to wit: [*state the rights and interests of the parties respectively, and the shares to which they are entitled according to the facts*].

And it is hereby further ordered and adjudged, that partition be made between the said parties, according to the rights and interests of the parties, respectively, as above declared.

And it is further ordered, that W. M., J. F., and R. T., three reputable freeholders, be, and they are hereby, appointed commissioners to make the partition so adjudged, according to the respective rights and interests of the parties, as the same are herein ascertained and determined by the court.

And it is further ordered, that one-fifth of the said premises remain undivided for the owners, aforesaid, whose interests are unknown and not ascertained.

No. 489.

ORDER OF REFERENCE ON DEFAULT—NO INFANTS OR ABSENTEES.

See ante, p. 118.

[*Same as in last form to the* *, *and then proceed:*]

It is, on motion of L. P. C., attorney for the plaintiff, ordered, that it be referred to L. F., Esq., of the village of ——, as a referee, to take proof of the plaintiff's title and interest in the premises described in said complaint, and of the several matters set forth in the said complaint, and to ascertain and report the rights and interests of the several parties in the premises, and an abstract of the conveyances by which the same are held.

And it is further ordered, that the said referee ascertain whether the said premises are so situated that the shares of the said plaintiff, and of the defendant R. D., can be set off in common, without partition or allotment between them, and without injury to the interests of any of the parties, and that he report the facts with his opinion thereon, to the end that such further order may be made in the premises as may be proper.

[*If it is desired to have the reference in some other county than that in which the place of trial is laid, insert:* And it is further ordered, that the said referee be at liberty to proceed on such reference in the county of ——.]

No. 490.

LIKE ORDER, WHERE THERE ARE INFANTS, OR UNKNOWN OWNERS, OR ABSENTEES, UNDER RULE 78.

See ante, pp. 118, 138.

[*Title of the cause.*] At a special term, *&c.* [*as in No.* 6].

On reading and filing proof of the personal service of the summons on all the defendants, more than twenty days since, and an affidavit showing that this action is brought for a partition of real estate situated in the county of ——, and described in the complaint in this action, and that all the defendants are residents of this State, and of full age, except the defendant C. D., who is an infant under the age of twenty-one years [*or*, who is an absentee, and has been served with the summons herein by publication thereof, pursuant to an order directing such service in the form and manner prescribed by law, *or*, except the heirs or representatives of G. H., a former owner of one undivided fifth part of said premises, whose places of residence are unknown, and cannot be ascertained, and who have been served with the summons by publication thereof as required by an order of this court], and that no answer or demurrer has been received on behalf of any of the defendants [except the said infant, who has put in the usual general answer by his guardian *ad litem*];

It is now, on motion of L. P. C., *&c.* [*as in last form.*]

No. 491.

ORDER OF REFERENCE WHERE PARTIES DESIRE THEIR SHARES TO BE SET OFF IN COMMON.

See ante, pp. 129, 138.

[*Same as in foregoing, and then add:*]

And it is further ordered, that the said referee ascertain whether the said premises are so situated that the shares of the said plaintiff, and of the defendant R. D., can be set off in common, without partition or allotment between them, and without injury to the interests of any of the parties, and that he report the facts with his opinion thereon, to the end that such further order may be made in the premises as shall be just and proper.

No. 492.

ORDER, WHERE A SALE OF THE PREMISES IS DESIRED, UNDER THE 79TH RULE.

See ante, p. 138.

[*Same as in foregoing, and then add:*]

And it is further ordered, that the said referee also inquire and report whether the whole premises, or any lot or separate parcel thereof, is so circumstanced that an actual partition cannot be made. And if the said referee arrives at the conclusion that the sale of the whole premises, or of any lot or separate parcel thereof, will be necessary, it is further ordered that he specify the same in his report, together with the reasons which render a sale necessary; and in such a case, that he also ascertain and report whether any creditor, not a party to the action, has a specific lien, by mortgage, devise, or otherwise, upon the undivided share or interest of any of the parties in that portion of the premises which it is necessary to sell; and if the said referee finds that there is no such specific lien in favor of any person, not a party to the action, that he further inquire and report whether the undivided share or interest of any of the parties in the premises is subject to a general lien or incumbrance, by judgment or decree.

And it is further ordered, that the said referee also ascertain and report the amount due to any party to the action who has either a general or specific lien on the premises to be sold, or any part thereof, and the amount due to any creditor, not a party, who has a general lien on any undivided share or interest therein by judgment or decree, and who shall appear and establish his claim on such reference.

And it is further ordered, that the said referee, if requested by the parties who appear before him on such reference, ascertain and report the amount due to any creditor, not a party to the action, which is either a specific or general lien or incumbrance upon all the shares or interests of the parties in the premises to be sold, and which would remain as an incumbrance thereon in the hands of the purchaser.

No. 493.

ORDER DIRECTING JUDGMENT OF PARTITION, AND APPOINTING COMMISSIONERS, WHERE ONE OR MORE OF THE PARTIES HAVE ANSWERED, AND AN ISSUE HAS BEEN JOINED, AND A TRIAL HAD.

See ante, pp. 122 to 127.

[*Title substantially as in No.* 470.]

This action, being at issue upon the answer to the complaint, of the guardian *ad litem* of the infant defendants, all the other defendants having failed to answer the complaint, was brought to trial on the —— day of ——, 18—, before the Hon. ——, justice of the Supreme Court [*or*, county judge of the county of ——, *or as the case may be*], and a trial by jury having been waived by the oral consent of parties, in open court, and entered in the minutes of the court, and the decision of the said court having been given in writing, and filed with the clerk of this court, whereby it is found that the said plaintiffs, C. B. D. and A. M. D. and the said defendants, T. N., J. H. N., M. H., and L. A. P., are each severally seized in fee, as tenants in common, and each entitled in fee, to an equal undivided one-sixth part of the premises described in the complaint in this action;

Now, on motion of H. & N., attorneys for the said plaintiffs, it is hereby ordered and adjudged, that the rights and interests of the parties to this action are as follows:

The said plaintiff C. B. D., as the grantee of L. H., one of the devisees in said complaint named, is seized of and entitled in fee to an equal undivided sixth part of the premises described in the complaint in this action. That the said A. M. D. is, &c. [*set out the interests of all the parties*].

And it is further ordered and adjudged that partition be made of the lands and premises mentioned and set forth in the complaint in this action; which said lands and premises are described as follows: [*insert description*].

And it is further ordered and adjudged, that B. F., E. S., and W. W., three reputable freeholders of the county of ——, be, and they are hereby, appointed commissioners for the purpose of making such partition.

And it is further ordered, that the said commissioners, before proceeding with the execution of their duties as such commissioners, be severally sworn or affirmed before some officer authorized by law to administer oaths, honestly and impartially to execute the trust reposed in them, and to make partition, as directed by this court; and that such oath or affirmation be filed with the clerk of this court, at or before the time the said commissioners shall make report of their proceedings as required by law.

And that the said commissioners shall divide the said lands and premises into six equal parts, quantity and quality relatively considered, and that they allot to the plaintiff, C. B. D., one of the said equal sixth parts of said premises; to the said A. M. D., *&c.* [*proceed the same as to the rights of the other parties*], to be held and enjoyed by the said parties in severalty, according to their rights and interests therein so ascertained, determined, and declared as aforesaid.

And that the said commissioners shall designate the parts or portions so allotted to each of the said parties, and the boundaries thereof, by sufficient description and monuments.

And it is further ordered that the said commissioners make a full and ample report to this court of their proceedings in this behalf, under their hands, or under the hands of any two of them, specifying therein the manner in which they shall have executed this judgment, and describing the lands divided and the parts or shares allotted to each party, with the quantity, courses, and distances of each share and description of the parts, stones, or other monuments thereof, and the items of their charges and expenses.

And all the parties to this action are hereby required to produce to, and leave with, the said commissioners, for such time as the commissioners shall deem reasonable, all deeds, writings, surveys, or maps, relating to the said premises or any part thereof.

And it is further ordered and adjudged, that in case partition of said premises cannot be made with perfect equality between the said parties, according to their respective rights and interests therein, unless compensation be made by one or more of the said parties to the other of them for equality of partition, that then, and in that case, the said commissioners ascertain and report the proper compensation which ought to be made for equality of partition; and by which of the parties the same should be paid, and to which the same ought to be allowed.

But the said commissioners shall not report compensation to be paid by an infant for equality of partition, unless it satisfactorily appears to them that such infant has sufficient personal estate to pay the same, and his portion of the costs and expenses of the proceedings, and all other liens on his share of the premises; except where, from the situation of the property, and of the interests of the parties, it cannot be charged upon the share of an adult.

And it is further ordered and adjudged, that any of the parties to this action be at liberty to apply to the court, on the foot of this judgment, for further direction.

No. 494.

RETURN OF COMMISSIONERS THAT PARTITION CANNOT BE MADE.

See ante, p. 136.

[*Title as in No.* 470.]

To the Supreme Court of the State of New York [*or other court*]:

The undersigned, W. M., J. F., and R. T., commissioners appointed by an order of the Supreme Court [*or other court*], dated the —— day of ——, 18—, to make partition of the lands and premises described in the complaint in the above-entitled action, do hereby certify and return to the said court, that after our appointment as such commissioners, as aforesaid, we took and subscribed the oath directed by the statute in such case made and provided; and that we then proceeded to examine the said premises for the purpose of making division and partition thereof, agreeably to the order of the court to that effect.

And we further certify and report, that the said premises are so circumstanced that an actual partition thereof cannot be made without great prejudice to the owners thereof, for the following reasons: [*state the reasons particularly*]. And we are therefore of opinion, that a sale of the whole of the said premises is necessary and expedient.

Dated, *&c.* [*Signatures of Commissioners.*]

L. P. C., Attorney for Pl'ff.

No. 495 (A).

ORDER TO BRING IN CREDITORS, AND OF REFERENCE AS TO INCUMBRANCES, ON THE RETURN BY COMMISSIONERS THAT PARTITION CANNOT BE MADE.

See ante, p. 138.

[*Title as in No.* 470.] At a special term, *&c.* [*as in No.* 6].

The commissioners appointed to make partition of the premises described in the complaint in this cause, having reported to the court that such partition cannot be made without great prejudice to the owners of said premises, and that a sale thereof is necessary and expedient; and it appearing to the court that the creditors having specific liens on said premises have not been made parties to the proceedings;

It is, on motion of L. P. C., attorney for the plaintiff, ordered that the plaintiff amend his complaint, by making a party to the proceedings every creditor having a specific lien on the undivided interest or estate of any of the parties to this suit, by mortgage, devise, or otherwise.

And it is further ordered, that it be referred to L. F., Esq., of ——, to ascertain and report whether the shares or interests in the said premises, of the parties to this proceeding, or any of them, are subject to any general lien or incumbrance, by judgment or otherwise.

No. 495 (B).

NOTICE OF HEARING BEFORE REFEREE.

See ante, p. 138.

[*Title of the cause.*]

To J. H. R., Esq., Attorney for guardian *ad litem* of infant defendant, A. L.:

SIR,—Take notice, that the proceedings on the order of reference heretofore made in this action, whereby it was referred to C. R. I., Esq., referee, among other things, to take proof of title of the premises sought to be partitioned, and to ascertain and report whether the same are so situated that a sale thereof is necessary, under the provisions of the 79th rule of this court, will be had before the said referee, at his office in ——, on the —— day of ——, 18—, at ten o'clock A. M. Yours, &c.,

Dated. &c. L. P. C., Plaintiff's Attorney.

No. 495 (C).

NOTICE OF HEARING ON THE COMING IN OF THE REPORT.

See ante, p. 138.

[*Title of the cause.*]

To J. W. F., Attorney for the defendants:

SIR,—Take notice that this action will be brought on for hearing, and application will be made for judgment for the relief demanded in the complaint; that is to say, for a partition of the premises described in said complaint, at the next special term of this court appointed to be held at the Court House in ——, on the —— day of ——, 18—, at the opening of the court on that day, or as soon thereafter as counsel can be heard, and a motion will then and there be made for the appointment by the court of three reputable freeholders, commissioners to make partition of the premises described in the complaint, according to the respective rights and interests of the parties to be adjudged by the said court; which motion will be founded upon the order of reference, and the referee's report thereon, and upon the pleadings and proceedings in this action. Yours, &c.,

Dated, &c. L. P. C., Plaintiff's Attorney.

No. 496.

ADVERTISEMENT BY REFEREE AS TO LIENS AND INCUMBRANCES

See ante, p. 143.

[*Title as in No.* 470.]

The undersigned, duly appointed referee, by an order of this court made in the above cause, on the —— day of ——, 18—, hereby requires all persons having any general lien or incumbrance, by judgment or decree, or otherwise, on the undivided share or interest of any of the owners, in the premises hereinafter described, to produce to the undersigned, on or before the —— day of —— next, at his office in the village of ——, in the county of —— [*or*, No. 128 Broadway, in the city of New York], proof of their respective liens and incumbrances, together with satisfactory evidence of the amount due thereon; and to specify the nature of such incumbrances, and the dates thereof, respectively.

The premises are described in the complaint in the above cause as follows: [*insert description.*]

Dated, *&c.* L. F., Referee.

L. P. C., Attorney.

No. 497.

REFEREE'S REPORT AS TO INCUMBRANCES, ETC., UNDER THE ORDER, ANTE, NO. 495.

See ante, p. 142.

[*Title of the cause.*]

To the Supreme Court of the State of New York [*or other court*]:

In pursuance of an order of this court, dated the —— day of ——, 18—, by which it was referred to the undersigned to ascertain and report to the court whether the shares or interests in the premises described in the complaint in this cause, of the parties to this suit, or any of them, are subject to any general lien or incumbrance by judgment or otherwise, I, the said referee, do respectfully report:

That I caused a notice to be published, as required by law, for all persons, having any general lien, or incumbrance, by judgment or decree, on the undivided share or interest of any of the parties, to the premises described in said complaint, to produce to me proof of their respective liens and incumbrances, together with satisfactory evidence of the amount due thereon; and to specify the nature of such incumbrances, and the dates thereof respectively.

And I further report that I have caused the necessary searches to be made; and I find that there is no general lien or incumbrance, by judgment or otherwise, on the undivided share or interest of any of the parties, in the premises aforesaid [*or*, that the share of J. K., one of the defendants herein, is subject to a judgment recovered in this court against the said J. K., in favor of B. F., docketed on the —— day of ——, 18—, on which there appears to be due the sum of $——, and interest thereon from the said —— day of ——, 18—, and that there is no general lien or incumbrance, by judgment or otherwise, on the undivided share or interest of any of the other parties, in the premises aforesaid].

And I further report that no creditor or person, having a general lien on any undivided share or interest in the premises, by judgment or decree, or otherwise, appeared before me on the said reference, to establish his claim, in pursuance of the notice published as aforesaid.

All which is respectfully submitted.

Dated, *&c.* L. F., Referee.

No. 498.

REPORT OF REFEREE WHERE A PARTITION ONLY IS SOUGHT.

See ante, pp. 118, 127.

[*Title of the cause.*]

To the Supreme Court of the State of New York [*or other court*]:

In pursuance of an order of this court, made in the above cause on the —— day of ——, 18—, by which it was referred to me to take proof of the plaintiff's title and interest in and to the premises described in the plaintiff's complaint, and of the several matters set forth in the said complaint; and to ascertain and report the rights and interests of the several parties in the premises, and an abstract of the conveyances by which the same are held; I, the subscriber, referee aforesaid, do report:

That (*) having been attended by the attorneys for the several parties who appeared in the cause, I proceeded to a hearing of the matters so referred.

I further report that on such hearing I took proof of the several matters set forth in said complaint, and find that the material facts therein alleged are true.

And I further report that the following is an abstract of the conveyances by which the premises described in said complaint are held, that is to say:

E. D.
to
A. B.

Quit-claim deed conveying the equal undivided one-fifth part of said premises. Deed dated the —— day of ——, 18—; duly acknowledged, the —— day of ——, 18—; consideration, —— dollars. Recorded in the clerk's office of —— county, on the —— day of ——, 18—, at — M. [*And so on, giving an abstract of the conveyances of the several undivided shares or interests of the parties, back to the time they were united in one common source.*]

And I further report, that the rights and interests of the parties in the premises are as follows, viz.:

A. B., the plaintiff, as grantee of E. D., is entitled to one undivided fifth part thereof.

The defendants R. D. and C. D. are each entitled to one undivided fifth thereof, as the devisees of W. D., late of, *&c.*, deceased.

The defendant J. K. is also entitled to one undivided fifth part of said premises, as grantee of H. D.

The remaining undivided fifth part of said premises was formerly owned by one G. H., who derived title thereto by purchase from G. D. But the said G. H. died on or about the —— day of ——, 18—, and the share of said G. H. is now owned by some person or persons unknown. [§]

And I further report that A. B. and R. D., two of the parties to this action, are desirous of enjoying their several shares in common with each other, and that a partition of said premises can be made in such manner as to set off to the said A. B. and R. D. the two undivided fifth parts of said premises, to be enjoyed by them in common, without prejudice to the interests of the parties, or any of them.

All which is respectfully submitted.

Dated, *&c.* L. F., Referee.

No. 499.

REPORT OF REFEREE THAT PARTITION CAN BE MADE.

See ante, pp. 118, 127.

[*Title of the cause.*]

To the Supreme Court of the State of New York [*or other court*]:

In pursuance of an order of this court, made in the above cause, on the —— day of ——, 18—, by which it was referred to the undersigned to take proof of the plaintiff's title and interest in and to the premises described in the plaintiff's complaint, and of the several matters set forth in the said complaint; and to ascertain and report the rights and interests of the several parties in the premises, and an abstract of the conveyances by which the same are held; and also to inquire and report whether the said premises, or any lot or separate parcel thereof, is so circumstanced that an actual partition thereof cannot be made; I, the subscriber, referee aforesaid, do report:

That, *&c.* [*follow the last form from the* (*) *to the* [§], *and then proceed as follows :*]

I further report, that in the opinion of the undersigned, the premises described in said complaint are so circumstanced that a partition thereof can be made without prejudice to the owners thereof, and that a partition of such premises would be more advantageous to such owners than a sale thereof.

All which is respectfully submitted.

Dated, *&c.* L. F., Referee.

No. 500.

REPORT OF REFEREE, UNDER RULE 79, THAT A SALE IS NECESSARY.

See ante, p. 138.

[*Title of the cause.*]

To the Supreme Court of the State of New York [*or other court*]:

In pursuance of an order of this court, made in the above-entitled action, on the —— day of ——, 18—, by which it was referred to the undersigned to take proof of the plaintiff's title and interest in and to the premises described in the plaintiff's complaint, and of the several matters set forth in the said complaint; and to ascertain and report the rights and interests of the several parties in the premises, and an abstract of the conveyances by which the same are held; and also to inquire and report whether the said premises, or any lot or separate parcel thereof, is so circumstanced that an actual partition thereof cannot be made; and if the said referee arrived at the conclusion that the sale of the whole premises, or of any lot or separate parcel thereof, will be necessary, that he specify the same in his report, together with the reasons which render a sale necessary; and in such a case, that he also ascertain and report whether any creditor, not a party to the action, has a specific lien, by mortgage, devise, or otherwise, upon the undivided share or interest of any of the parties in that portion of the premises which it is necessary to sell; and if the said referee finds that there is no such specific lien, that he further inquire and report whether the undivided share or interest of any of the parties in the premises is subject to a general lien or incumbrance, by judgment or decree; and that he also ascertain and report the amount due to any party to the action who has either a general or specific lien on the premises to be sold, or any part thereof, and the amount due to any creditor, not a party, who has a general lien on any undivided share or interest therein by judgment or decree, and who shall appear before said referee, and establish his claim; and also that he ascertain and report, if requested to do so by the parties who appear before him, the amount due to any creditor, not a party to the action, which is either a general or specific lien or incumbrance upon all the shares or interests of the parties in the premises to be sold, and which would remain as an incumbrance thereon in the hands of the purchaser;

I, the subscriber, referee as aforesaid, do respectfully report:

That I caused a notice to be published, as required by law, for all persons having any general lien or incumbrance, by judgment or decree, on the undivided share or interest of any of the parties to the premises described in said complaint, to produce to me proof of their respective liens and incumbrances, together with satisfactory evidence of the amount due thereon; and to specify the nature of such incumbrances, and the dates thereof respectively.

That afterwards, having been attended by the attorneys for the several parties who appeared in the cause, I proceeded to a hearing of the matter so referred.

I further report that, on such hearing, I took proof of the several matters set forth in said complaint, and find that the material facts therein alleged are true.

And I further report, that the following is an abstract of the conveyances by which the premises described in said complaint are held, that is to say:

E. D. to A. B.

Quit-claim deed conveying the equal undivided one-fifth part of said premises. Deed dated the —— day of ——, 18—; duly acknowledged the —— day of ——, 18—; consideration, —— dollars. Recorded in the clerk's office of —— county, on the —— day of ——, 18—, at —— o'clock, —. M. [*And so on, giving an abstract of the conveyances of the several undivided shares or interests of the parties, back to the time they were united in one common source.*]

And I further report, that the rights and interests of the parties in the premises are as follows, viz.

A. B., the plaintiff, as grantee of E. D., is entitled to one undivided fifth part thereof.

The defendants R. D. and C. D. are each entitled to one undivided fifth part thereof, as the devisees of W. D., late of, &c., deceased.

The defendant J. K. is also entitled to one undivided fifth part of said premises, as grantee of H. D.

The remaining undivided fifth part of said premises was formerly owned by one G. H., who derived title thereto by purchase from G. D. But the said G. H. died on or about the —— day of ——, 18—, and the share of said G. H. is now owned by some person or persons unknown.

And I further report, that the premises described in said complaint are so circumstanced that an actual partition thereof cannot be made without great prejudice to the owners thereof, and for the following reasons: [*state the reasons*]. I am of opinion, therefore, that a sale of the whole of said premises is necessary and expedient.

I further report, that I have caused the necessary searches to be made, and I find that no creditor, not a party to the action, has any specific lien, by mortgage, devise, or otherwise, upon the undivided share or interest of any of the parties in the premises [*or*, that I have caused the necessary searches to be made, and I find that the undivided one-fifth part of said premises owned by J. K., aforesaid, is incumbered by mortgage, executed by H. D., aforesaid, to S. T., of, &c., previous to the sale thereof to said J. K., as aforesaid, which mortgage was dated the —— day of ——, 18—, and was given to secure to the said S. T., his heirs and assigns, the sum of one thousand dollars, in five years from the date thereof, with interest annually; and that the said sum of one thousand dollars, with interest thereon from the —— day of ——, 18—, is now unpaid on said mortgage; and that the said S. T., who is not a party to this action, is still the owner and holder of said mortgage.

I further report, that there is no general lien or incumbrance, by judgment or decree, upon the undivided share or interest of any of the parties in the premises.

And I further report, that no creditor, not a party to this action, having a general lien on any undivided share or interest in the premises, by judgment or decree, or otherwise, appeared before me, on the said reference, to establish his claim, in pursuance of the notice published by me as aforesaid.

I further report, that the sum of five hundred dollars, with interest thereon from the —— day of ——, 18—, is due to R. S., of, *&c.*, who is not a party to this action, upon a mortgage executed by W. D., of, *&c.*, to the said R. S.; which mortgage is a lien upon the whole premises aforesaid, and is dated the —— day of ——, 18— [*or*, that the sum of five hundred dollars, and interest thereon from the —— day of ——, 18—, is due to R. S., of, *&c.*, who is the owner of a judgment [*or*, decree], obtained by the said R. S. against W. D., of, *&c.;* which judgment [*or*, decree] was docketed in the clerk's office of the county of ——, on the —— day of ——, 18—, and is a lien upon the whole premises aforesaid].

[*If creditors are made parties to the action, having either general or specific liens on the premises, or any part thereof, state the nature thereof, and the amounts due upon such liens, respectively.*]

All which is respectfully submitted.

Dated, *&c.* L. F., Referee.

No. 501 (A).

REPORT OF REFEREE AS TO RIGHT OF DOWER.

See ante, pp. 138, 144.

[*Same as in foregoing, and then add:*]

And I do further report, that the defendant R. H., as widow of L. H., deceased, is entitled to her right of dower in all the lands and premises mentioned and described in the plaintiff's complaint [*or*, in the one undivided fifth part of all the lands and premises mentioned and described in the plaintiff's complaint], and that such interest or estate should not be excepted from such sale, but should be sold, for the reason that, *&c.* [*state the reasons*].

No. 501 (B).

NOTICE OF FILING REPORT UNDER THE THIRTY-SECOND RULE.

See ante, pp. 138, 144.

[*Title of the cause.*]

To N. F., Esq., Attorney for defendant, B. C.:

SIR,—Take notice that the report of the referee, to whom it was referred to take proof of title, &c., in this action, and report the same to the court, with an abstract of the conveyances by which the same was held, which report bears date the —— day of ——, was filed in the office of the clerk of —— county, on the —— day of ——, 18—.

Yours, &c.,

Dated, &c. L. P. C., Plaintiff's Attorney.

No. 501 (C).

EXCEPTIONS TO REFEREE'S REPORT.

See ante, p. 141; 2 Van Sant. Eq. Pr. 476

[*Title of the cause.*]

Exceptions taken by ——, the above-named plaintiff [*or*, ——, one of the defendants; *or*, by ——, claiming a lien by judgment on the premises, *&c., as the case may be*], to the report of J. K. P., Esq., referee, dated the, *&c.*

First exception. The said —— excepts to the report of the said referee, in that the said referee has disallowed the claim and judgment of said —— against B. C., for —— dollars damages and costs rendered by the Supreme Court, on the ——, *&c.*, which judgment was proved before said referee, and is a general lien on the undivided share and interest of said B. C., upon the premises sought to be partitioned; whereas the said judgment ought to have been allowed by said referee, and reported and declared by him to be a general lien upon said undivided share.

Second exception. The said —— further excepts to the finding and report of said referee, that the amount due upon a certain mortgage executed to him by said B. C., bearing date ——, *&c.*, proved before said referee, and which is a specific lien upon the said undivided share of said B. C., is the sum of —— dollars; whereas the said —— claims and insists that the amount proved to be due on said mortgage is the sum of —— dollars.

Third exception. [*Specify distinctly each objectionable finding, either of fact, or conclusion of law, set forth in the report.*]

Wherefore, the said —— excepts to the said report in the particulars above specified, and asks that the same may be reviewed, and may be altogether set aside, or modified in accordance with the above exceptions.

G. & A., Attorneys for A. B., *&c.*

No. 502.

ORDER DIRECTING A SALE OF THE PREMISES BY COMMISSIONERS.

See ante, p. 136.

[*Title of the cause.* At a special term, *&c.* [*as in No.* 6.]

On reading and filing the report of W. M., J. F., and R. T., commissioners appointed to make partition of the lands and premises described in the complaint in this action, wherein the said commissioners report that the said premises are so circumstanced that an actual partition thereof cannot be made without great prejudice to the owners of said premises; and the court being satisfied that such report is just and correct;

It is, on motion of L. P. C., attorney for the plaintiff, ordered that the said commissioners sell the said premises, with the appurtenances, at public auction, to the highest bidder, after giving due notice of the time and place of such sale, according to law.

And it is further ordered that a credit of —— months [*or*, years] be given for one-third [*or*, one-half, *or such other portion as the court may direct*], of the purchase-money of said premises, to be secured at interest, by a mortgage on the premises sold, and also by a bond of the purchaser, conditioned for the payment of the said one-third [*or*, one-half, *&c.*] of the said purchase-money, in —— months [*or*, years] from the date of said sale.

And it is further ordered that the said commissioners forthwith, after the said sale, make report to this court of their proceedings thereon; and that after the said report shall have been duly confirmed, then that they execute a deed or deeds of the said premises to the purchaser or purchasers at the said sale, on their complying with the conditions upon which the deeds were to be delivered; and that such sale be valid and effectual forever.

No. 503.

ORDER FOR PARTITION, ON THE REPORT OF A REFEREE, AND APPOINTING COMMISSIONERS.

See antè, pp. 127, 130.

[*Title of the cause.*] At a special term, *&c.* [*as in No.* 6].

The referee appointed in this cause having made his report, dated the —— day of ——, whereby it appears that the premises described in the complaint of A. B., the plaintiff, are so circumstanced, that a partition thereof can be made without prejudice to the owners thereof; and that such partition would be more advantageous to the owners of said premises than a sale thereof; and whereby it also appears that the plaintiff, as grantee of E. D., is entitled to one undivided fifth part of said premises; and the other parties to this action to the several rights and interests set forth in said report.

Now, on reading and filing the said report and notice of motion, and proof of due service of the same upon the defendants herein, who have appeared, and on motion of L. P. C., attorney for the plaintiff, A. B., no one appearing for the defendants, it is ordered and adjudged, and this court does hereby order and adjudge, that the report of the said referee be, and the same is hereby, approved and confirmed.

It is further ordered, that the rights, titles, and interests of the several parties to this action, so far as the same have appeared, are as follows: [*state the rights and interests of the parties respectively, and the shares to which they are entitled, according to the facts*].

And it is hereby further ordered and adjudged, that partition be made between the said parties according to the rights and interests of the parties respectively, as above declared.

It is further ordered, that W. M., J. F., and R. T., three reputable freeholders, be, and they are hereby, appointed commissioners, to make the partition so adjudged, according to the respective rights and interests of the parties, as the same are herein ascertained and determined by the court.

And it is further ordered, that one-fifth of the said premises remain undivided for the owners aforesaid, whose interests are unknown, and not ascertained.

And it is further ordered and adjudged, that in case partition of such premises cannot be made with perfect equality between the said parties, according to their respective rights and interests therein, unless compensation be made by one or more of the said parties to the other of them for equality of partition, that then, and in that case, the said commissioners ascertain and report the proper compensation which ought to be made for equality of partition; and by which of the parties the same should be paid, and to which the same ought to be allowed.

But the said commissioners shall not report compensation to be made by an infant for equality of partition, unless it satisfactorily appears to them that such infant has sufficient personal estate to pay the same, and his portion of the costs and expenses of the proceedings, and all other liens on his share of the premises; except where, from the situation of the property and of the interests of the parties, it cannot be charged upon the share of an adult.

And it is further ordered, that all the parties herein shall produce to, and leave with, the said commissioners, for such time as the said commissioners shall deem reasonable, all deeds, writings, surveys, or maps, relating to the said premises or any part thereof.

No. 504.

ORDER THAT SHARES MAY BE SET OFF TO PARTIES IN COMMON.

See ante, p. 129.

[*The order will be in the usual form as to the shares of the parties desiring a partition; and then say:*] And it appearing to the court that A. B. and R. D., two of the persons interested in said premises, are desirous of enjoying their several shares or interests in common with each other, and that the same can be set off to them without prejudice to the interest of the parties, it is ordered that the said commissioners make the partition aforesaid in such manner that the shares of the said A. B. and R. D., consisting of two undivided fifth parts of said premises, remain without partition, to be enjoyed by the said A. B. and R. D. in common.

No. 505.

ORDER DIRECTING A SALE OF THE PREMISES BY A REFEREE—MADE ON THE REPORT OF A REFEREE.

See ante, p. 138.

[*Title of the cause.*] At a special term, *&c.* [*as in No.* 6].

The defendants J. K., R. D., and owners unknown, having failed to appear in this cause, or to put in any answer to the complaint of A. B., the plaintiff herein; and the guardian *ad litem* of the defendant C. D., having put in the usual general answer submitting the rights of the said C. D. to the court; and the report of L. F., Esq., referee, duly appointed by an order of this court, dated the —— day of ——, 18—, having been made to the court, by which report it appears, among other things, that an actual partition of the premises described in said complaint cannot be made without great prejudice to the owners thereof; and that a sale of the whole of said premises is necessary and expedient; and after hearing L. P. C., of counsel for the plaintiff, and T. C., of counsel for the guardian *ad litem* of the infant defendant C. D., and due deliberation being thereupon had, it is ordered that the said report be, and the same is hereby, approved, ratified, and confirmed.

And it is further ordered and adjudged, and this court does further order, adjudge, and declare, that the rights, titles, and interests of the parties in the premises aforesaid, so far as the same have appeared, are such as are stated in the said report, and are as follows, viz.: [*state the rights and interests of the parties respectively, and the shares to which they are entitled; and if the shares of any of the parties are incumbered, by any general or specific lien, set it out with the name of the owner thereof, the nature of such lien, the amount due thereon, &c.*]

And it is further ordered and adjudged, that all and singular the premises mentioned in the said complaint, and particularly described therein, together with all and singular the hereditaments and appurtenances thereunto belonging, or in any wise appertaining, to wit: all, *&c.* [*describe premises*], be sold at public auction, in the county of ——, where the said premises are situated, by W. B. B., referee, residing in that county, and who is hereby appointed such referee for that purpose. That the said referee give six weeks' notice of the time and place of such sale, in one of the public newspapers printed in said county, and in such other manner as required by law.

And it is further ordered, that a credit of —— months [*or* years] be given for one-third [*or*, one-half, *or such other portion as the court may direct*] of the purchase-money of said premises, to be secured at interest by one or more mortgages on the premises sold, and also by the bond or bonds of the purchaser, conditioned for the payment of the said one-third [*or* one-half, *&c.*] of the said purchase-money in —— months [*or* years] from the date of said sale.

And it is further ordered, that the said referee bring into court and pay to the treasurer of said county of —— the portion of the purchase-money arising from the sale of the estate, or interest of J. K., one of said defendants in the premises aforesaid, after deducting the portion of the costs, charges, and expenses to which it shall be liable. [*If portion of any other of the parties is incumbered, add a like order as to that.*]

And it is further ordered, that the said referee forthwith, after the said sale, make report to this court of his proceedings thereon; and that after the said report shall have been duly confirmed, then that he execute a deed or deeds of the said premises to the purchaser or purchasers at the said sale, on their complying with the conditions upon which the deeds were to be delivered; and that such sale be valid and effectual forever.

And it is further ordered, that the costs and expenses of the proceedings in this suit, which are adjusted according to law, at the sum of —— dollars, be deducted from the proceeds of the said sale, and that the said referee pay the same to the said plaintiff, or to his attorney. That the said referee in like manner deduct from the said proceeds the fees and disbursements to which he is entitled on such sale.

And it is further ordered, that the said referee pay to the said plaintiff, or bring into court for his use, the one-fifth part of the residue of the proceeds arising from said sale.

And it is further ordered, that the said referee bring into court for the use of C. D., an infant defendant in this action, and pay to the treasurer of said county [*or*, that the said referee pay to the general guardian of C. D., an infant, and one of the defendants herein, for the use of such infant] the one-fifth part of such residue. And the said treasurer [*or*, general guardian] is hereby directed to invest the said moneys on bond and mortgage upon unincumbered real estate of at least double the value of the moneys so invested; which investment shall be made in the name of such infant [*or*, in the name of such guardian].

And it is further ordered, that the said referee bring into court and pay to the treasurer of said county the one-fifth part of said residue for the use of the owners unknown, mentioned in the complaint in this action. And the said treasurer is hereby directed to invest the said moneys in permanent securities at interest, for the benefit of such unknown owners. [*If any of the parties are absentees, without legal representatives in this State, add a like order as to their share.*]

And it is further ordered, that such title-deeds and writings as may be in the possession or under the control of any of the parties, and as appear to relate solely to the said premises, or any part thereof, be delivered up to any person or persons who may on such sale become the purchaser or purchasers thereof. And that all other title-deeds or writings may be deposited with the clerk of the county of ——, for safe custody, there to remain for the benefit of all parties interested therein.

And it is further ordered, that the purchaser or purchasers of said premises, or of any part thereof, at such sale, be let into possession thereof; and that any of the parties who may be in possession of said premises, or any part thereof, and any person, who, since the commencement of this action, has come into the possession of the said premises, or any part thereof, deliver possession thereof to such purchaser or purchasers, on production of the referee's deed for such premises.

And it is further ordered, that the said referee make a report of his proceedings, under this order, subsequent to the confirmation of his report of sale, to be made as above directed.

No. 506 (A).

ORDER IN RESPECT TO THE RIGHT OF DOWER OF A PARTY.

See ante, pp. 144, 151, 156.

[*Same as the foregoing, and then add:*]

And the court having duly considered and determined that the dower interest of the defendant, R. H., in the said premises, should not be excepted from said sale, but that the same should be sold, it is further ordered, that the said referee ascertain and report whether the said defendant, R. H., is willing to accept, in lieu and instead of her said dower interest, a sum in gross, in satisfaction thereof, out of the net proceeds of the said premises, according to her rights as ascertained in the report of said referee, dated the —— day of ——, 18—; and also what would be a reasonable satisfaction for her said interest, on the principles applicable to life annuities. And if the said R. H. consents to accept such gross sum, that said referee pay the same to her, upon her executing, acknowledging, and delivering to him a release, to be approved of by said referee, of all her right, title, and interest, of, in, and to the said premises, and every part thereof. But if the said R. H. shall refuse to accept a gross sum in lieu of her dower interest, then it is further ordered that the said referee do bring one-third of the net proceeds of the said sale into court, to be invested for her benefit, the interest or dividends thereon, or to accrue thereon, to be paid over to her during her natural life.

No. 506 (B).

SPECIAL CLAUSES THAT MAY BE INSERTED IN A JUDGMENT.

See ante, pp. 144, 151, 156.

NOTE.—The following are recommended as precedents of special clauses that may be inserted in a judgment of sale. See *Edw. on Referees*, pp. 470, 474; 2 *Van Sant. Eq. Pr.* 481.

Clause applicable to a Dowress or Tenant for Life refusing to take a sum in gross.

And the said defendant, ——, widow of ——, deceased, by her counsel, declining to accept a sum in gross in lieu of her dower right and estate in and to the equal —— part of such premises, it is thereupon ordered and decreed, that such referee do ascertain and report the amount of the one-third part of the one —— part of the proceeds of such premises, after deducting all expenses, which, it is declared, is a just and reasonable sum to be invested for the benefit of the said ——, entitled to such estate and right of dower as aforesaid; and that such referee do bring such amount into court and pay the same to the treasurer of the county of ——; and further, that such treasurer do invest the said amount in bond and mortgage, or other permanent securities, at interest, and do pay such interest to the said —— during her natural life.

Clause applicable to a Dowress or Tenant for Life agreeing to take a sum in gross.

And the said defendant, ——, widow of ——, deceased, having consented to accept, in lieu of her right of dower and estate in the one —— part of such premises, such sum in gross as shall be deemed a reasonable satisfaction for such right of dower and estate, which consent has been given and proven by an instrument under seal, duly acknowledged in the manner that deeds are required to be proved to entitle them to be recorded, and annexed to the referee's report filed in this cause [*or*, now filed with the clerk of this court] thereupon it is ordered and decreed that the said referee do ascertain what sum in gross of the proceeds of such sales, after deducting all expenses, will, on the principles of life annuities, be a reasonable satisfaction for such estate or right of dower in the one —— part of such premises, and the said referee shall pay over to the said ——, widow as aforesaid, the amount so ascertained by him.

Clause applicable to a Dowress or Tenant for Life, making provisions if consent be afterward given.

And it is further ordered and adjudged, that the said referee ascertain whether ——, the widow of ——, deceased, is willing to accept, in lieu of her estate in dower in such premises, a sum in gross in satisfaction thereof out of the net proceeds of such premises; and if she shall so agree to accept a compensation therefor, then that such referee ascertain how much, on the principle of annuities, would be reasonable compensation for such right and estate, and that the said referee pay to the said —— such amount, on receiving from her release, to be approved by such referee, of all her right and claim of and for an estate fo dower in the said premises and every part thereof.

Clause where a Married Woman is an Infant, and has an inchoate Right of Dower.

And it appearing that the defendant ——, wife of the said defendant ——, is an infant under the age of twenty-one years, and is entitled only to an inchoate right of dower in the one —— part of such premises, it is further ordered and adjudged, that the referee ascertain, on the principles of annuities, what is the probable value of her contingent right of dower; that such amount be deducted from the —— part of the proceeds of such sale, after deducting the proper proportion of the costs and expenses to be borne by such —— part, and be paid into the hands of the treasurer of the county of ——, to be by him invested so that the same may accumulate during the joint lives of the said —— and ——; and, upon the death of either, application may be made to this court for the same by any person or persons entitled thereto [*or*, it is further ordered and adjudged that the said —— part of such proceeds be paid over to the said ——, on his giving security to the satisfaction of a justice of this court, to be approved of by him, that the interest or income of the one-third of such proceeds shall be paid to the said ——, after his death, during the term of her natural life, in case she survives him, the said ——].

No. 507.

NOTICE OF SALE IN PARTITION.

See ante, p. 145.

[*Title of the cause.*]

In pursuance of an order of the Supreme Court [*or other court*], made in the above-entitled action, dated the —— day of ——, 18—, the undersigned, commissioners [*or*, referee] in partition, will sell at public auction to the highest bidder, at the front steps of the Court House in the village of ——, on the —— day of ——, 18—, at 10 o'clock A. M., all that certain piece or parcel of land situated in the town of ——, in the county of ——, and bounded and described as follows: [*insert description*].

Dated, &c. [*Names of Commissioners or Referee.*]

No. 508.

REPORT OF SALE BY COMMISSIONER.

See ante, p. 147.

[*Title of the cause.*]

To the Supreme Court of the State of New York [*or other court*]:

The undersigned, W. M., J. F., and R. T., appointed commissioners in partition, and directed by an order of this court, dated the —— day of ——, 18—, to sell the premises described in said order, at public auction, to the highest bidder, do report:

That having caused a notice of the time and place of sale of the said premises, containing an accurate description thereof, to be published once in each week for six weeks immediately previous to such sale, in one of the public newspapers printed in the county of ——, where such premises are situated, and having also caused a copy of such notice to be put up at three public places in the town where the said premises were sold [*and if sold in a town different from that where situated, say:* and also in the town where the said premises are situated], we did, on the —— day of ——, 18—, at 10 o'clock in the forenoon, that being the time specified in the said notice, attend at the front steps of the Court House, in the village of ——, the place therein mentioned, and exposed the said premises for sale, at public auction, to the highest bidder, as directed by the said order.

We do further report, that the said premises were sold together, and were struck off to S. P., of, *&c.*, for the sum of —— dollars, that sum being the highest sum bidden for the same, and the said S. P. being the highest bidder therefor [*or*, that the said premises were put up, separately, and were each and every of them struck off to S. P., of, *&c.*, for the following sums:—Lot No. 1, for the sum of —— dollars; lot No. 2, for the sum of —— dollars; and lot No. 3, for the sum of —— dollars, those sums being the highest sums bidden for the said lots respectively, and the said S. P. being the highest bidder therefor; which several sums amount in the whole to —— dollars].

And we further report, that the terms and conditions of such sale were reduced to writing, and made known to the persons attending such sale, previous to putting up the said lots, and were as follows: [*state terms of sale*].

We further report, that the said S. P. has signed the written conditions of sale above mentioned, together with an acknowledgment that he has purchased the premises upon those terms; and he has in all respects complied with the terms of sale above mentioned.

All which is respectfully submitted.

Dated, *&c.* [*Signatures of Commissioners.*]

County of ——, ss.: On this —— day of ——, 18—, before me personally appeared W. M., J. F., and R. T., above named, and being severally sworn, each for himself deposes and says, that he has read the above report subscribed by him, and knows the contents thereof, and that the same is true, according to the best of his knowledge, information, and belief.

A. M., Justice of the Peace.

No. 509.

REPORT OF SALE, BY REFEREE.

See ante, p. 147.

[*Title of the cause.*]

To the Supreme Court of the State of New York [*or other court*]:

In pursuance of an order of this court, made in the above-entitled action, dated the —— day of ——, 18—, I, the subscriber, referee, residing in the county of ——, to whom the execution of said order was confided, do report:

That having, *&c.* [*as in last form, with the necessary changes, so as to make it the report of a referee, &c., instead of commissioners*].

No. 510.

OATH OF COMMISSIONERS.

See ante, p. 130.

[*Title of the cause.*]

We, W. M., J. F., and R. T., commissioners appointed by the Supreme Court [*or other court*] to make partition of the premises described in the complaint in the above-entitled action, being duly sworn, do make oath, and each for himself makes oath and says, that he will honestly and impartially execute the trust reposed in him as such commissioner, and will make partition as directed by the court.

W. M.
Subscribed and sworn, *&c.* J. F.
R. T

No. 511.

REPORT OF PARTITION BY COMMISSIONERS.

See ante, pp. 130, 133.

[*Title of the cause.*]

To the Supreme Court of the State of New York [*or other court*]:

In pursuance of, and in obedience to, an order of this court, made in the above cause, dated the —— day of ——, 18—, the undersigned, commissioners in partition, do hereby respectfully report and return:

That having been first duly sworn, and having severally taken the oath that we would honestly and impartially execute the trust reposed in us, and make partition as directed by the court, we have carefully examined the premises described in the complaint in this action, and caused the said premises to be surveyed, and have made partition thereof, between the said parties, according to their respective rights and interests therein, as the same have been ascertained, determined, and declared by the court, as follows, viz.:

We have divided the whole of said premises into five equal parts, quality and quantity relatively considered, which are designated, on the map hereto annexed, by the letters, "A," "B," "C," "D," and "E." And the division thus made, in our judgment, is the most beneficial one, under all the circumstances, that could be made of such premises.

We further report, that we have set off in severalty to the plaintiff, A. B., all that certain piece or parcel of said premises designated on the said map by the letter "A," and which is bounded and described as follows: [*insert description, containing the quantity, courses, and distances, and a description of the posts, stones, or other monuments thereof*].

We have also set off in severalty to the defendant, J. K., all that certain piece or parcel of said premises designated on the said map by the letter "B," and which is bounded and described as follows: [*insert description as to quantity, courses, and distance, &c., same as above*].

We have also set off, *&c.* [*continue with respect to the other shares, the same as before*].

We further report, that we have set off all that certain piece or parcel of said premises, being the one-fifth part thereof, designated on the said map by the letter "E," to remain undivided, for the owner or owners whose interests are unknown, and not yet ascertained; which piece or parcel of land, last aforesaid, is bounded and described as follows: [*insert description, quantity, &c., as above*].

And we further certify and report, that the items of the expenses and charges, attending the said partition, including our fees as commissioners, are as follows:

Three days' services for each of the commissioners, at $2 per day for each	$18 00
Cash paid W. S. for one day's service as surveyor	2 50
Cash paid for two chain and flag bearers, $1 each	2 00
	$22 50

In witness whereof, we, the said commissioners, have hereunto set our hands, this —— day of ——, A. D. 18—.

[*Signatures of Commissioners.*]

[*Add acknowledgment in usual form. See No.* 44.]

No. 512.

REPORT IN RESPECT TO COMPENSATION FOR EQUALITY OF PARTITION.

See ante, p. 132.

The same as in the foregoing, and then add:]

And we further certify and report that, in making the said partition, as the same could not otherwise be made equal between the said parties without prejudice to their rights and interests, we have, for the purpose of equalizing the same, ascertained the compensation and sums to be made and paid the parties respectively to whom compensation ought to be made, in regard to the difference of the value of the several parts or allotments into which the said premises were so divided as aforesaid for equality of partition, according to the nature and equity of the case, and did allot, direct, and award the same to be paid as follows: that is to say, we did ascertain the compensation which ought to be made by T. N., the party to whom the said allotment, division No. 2 of the said premises, was so allotted as aforesaid for equality of partition in the premises, to be the sum of —— dollars; and we do allot and award the said sum of —— dollars to be paid by the said T. N. to the said M. H., to whom the said allotment, division No. 6 of the said premises, was allotted as aforesaid, in full of the compensation to be made in the premises to that share of the said premises.

No. 513.

NOTICE OF MOTION TO CONFIRM SALE OR PARTITION.

See ante, pp. 134, 147.

[*Title of the cause.*]

SIR,—Take notice, that I shall move this court at the next special term thereof, to be held at the Court House in ——, in the county of ——, on the —— day of —— next [*or*, instant], or as soon thereafter as counsel can be heard, for an order confirming the report of the commissioners [*or*, referee] appointed to make partition [*or*, sale] of the premises described in the complaint in this action, and for judgment thereon; and for such further or other order as may be just; which motion will be founded upon the said report, a copy of which is herewith served.

Dated, *&c.* L. P. C., Attorney for Plaintiff.

No. 514.

ORDER CONFIRMING SALE BY COMMISSIONERS.

See ante, p. 147.

[*Title of the cause.*]

On reading and filing the report of W. M., J. F., and R. T., commissioners appointed to make partition between the parties, of the lands and premises described in the complaint in this action, whereby it appears that, *&c.* [*insert their report in substance*].

Now, on motion of L. P. C., attorney for A. B., the plaintiff, it is ordered, that the said sale be and the same is hereby ratified, approved, and confirmed by the court; and that the said commissioners, or any two of them, execute a conveyance for the said premises to the said S. P., pursuant to such sale.

It is further ordered that the costs and expenses of the proceedings in this action, which are adjusted, according to law, at the sum of —— dollars, be deducted from the proceeds of the said sale so made by the said commissioners, and be by them paid to the said A. B., or his attorney; and that the said commissioners also pay to the said A. B., or bring into court for his use, the one-fifth part of the residue of the proceeds arising from said sale.

And it is further ordered that the said commissioners bring into court, and pay to the treasurer of the county of ——, the one-fifth part of the said residue of said proceeds, being the share arising from the sale of the interest of J. K. in said premises, after deducting the portion of the costs and expenses to which such share is liable. [*If the portion of any other of the parties is incumbered, add a like order as to that.*]

It is further ordered that the said commissioners bring into court, for the use of C. D., an infant defendant in this action, and pay to the said treasurer [*or*, that the said commissioners pay to the general guardian of C. D., an infant and one of the defendants herein, for the use of such infant], the one-fifth part of the said residue. And the said treasurer [*or*, general guardian] is hereby directed to invest the said moneys, on bond and mortgage, in the name of such infant [*or*, general guardian], upon unincumbered real estate of at least double the value of the moneys so invested.

And it is further ordered that the said commissioners bring into court, and pay to the treasurer of the county of ——, the one-fifth part of said residue, for the use of the owners unknown, mentioned in the complaint in this action. And the said treasurer is hereby directed to invest the said moneys in permanent securities at interest, for the benefit of such unknown owners. [*If any of the parties are absentees, without legal representatives in this State, add a like order as to their share.*]

No. 515.

ORDER CONFIRMING SALE BY REFEREE.

See ante, p. 147.

[*Title as in No.* 470.] At a special term, *&c.* [*as in No.* 6].

On reading and filing the report of W. B. B., appointed referee to sell the premises described in the complaint in this action, whereby it appears, *&c.* [*insert the substance of the report*].

Now, on the motion of L. P. C., attorney for the plaintiff, it is ordered that the said sale be, and the same is hereby, ratified, approved, and confirmed.

And it is further ordered, that the said referee execute a conveyance for the said premises to the said S. P., pursuant to such sale.

It is further ordered, that, *&c.* [*insert clauses in respect to the disposition of the proceeds, substantially as in last form*].

No. 516.

ORDER CONFIRMING PARTITION BY COMMISSIONERS, AND FOR JUDGMENT ON THEIR REPORT.

See ante, pp. 133, 134.

[*Title as in No.* 470.] At a special term, *&c.* [*as in No.* 6].

This cause coming on to be heard upon the report of W. M., J. F., and R. T., commissioners appointed therein, by an order of this court dated the —— day of ——, 18—; and on reading and filing said report, which is dated the —— day of ——, 18—, by which it appears that the said commissioners have made partition of the premises described in the complaint in this action, between the parties herein, according to their respective rights and interests therein, as the same have been ascertained, determined, and declared by the court; and by which partition the said commissioners have divided the whole of said premises into five equal parts, which are designated on the map annexed to said report by the letters "A," "B," "C," "D," and "E," and have set off in severalty to the plaintiff, A. B., all that certain piece or parcel of said premises bounded and described in said report as follows: [*insert description*]. And also by which partition the said commissioners have set off in severalty to the said defendant J. K., *&c.* [*set out the share, &c., the same as in report; and so on with the other shares*].

And on reading and filing notice of motion for the confirmation of said report, and for judgment thereon, with due proof of the service of such notice upon the attorney for the defendants;

It is, on motion of L. P. C., attorney for the plaintiff, no one appearing for the defendants, ordered and adjudged, and this court does hereby order and adjudge, that the said report, and all things therein contained, do stand ratified and confirmed; and that the partition, so made, be firm and effectual forever.

And it is further ordered and adjudged, that the defendants, J. K., R. D., C. D., and owners unknown, each pay to the plaintiff, or his attorney, the one-fifth part of the costs and charges of the proceedings in this cause; which costs and charges are adjusted, according to law, at the sum of —— dollars; and that the plaintiff have execution therefor. [*Or*, And it is further ordered and adjudged that each share of said premises be charged with one-fifth of the aggregate amount of the costs of all the parties to this suit. And that the plaintiff recover his costs and disbursements herein, which are adjusted, according to law, at the sum of —— dollars. That the guardian *ad litem* of the defendant C. D. recover his costs and disbursements herein, which are adjusted, according to law, at the sum of —— dollars; and that the defendant J. K., who has appeared in this proceeding, recover his costs and disbursements, which are adjusted, according to law, at the sum of —— dollars. *Or, follow the form given post, No.* 518, *in respect to the costs.*]

No. 517.

ORDER DIRECTING COMPENSATION FOR EQUALITY OF PARTITION.

See ante, pp. 132 to 134.

[*Same as the foregoing, and then add*:]

And it appearing, from the report of said commissioners, that the said shares of J. K. and R. D. are worth more in proportion than the respective shares of the other tenants in common, which are herein allotted to them, it is further adjudged that the said J. K. and R. D. do make compensation for equality of partition, to the other tenants in common, and do pay to each of them, that is to say, to the said A. B., C. D., and E. F., each the sum of —— dollars, and that the said A. B., C. D., and E. F., each have execution against the said J. K. and R. D., for the sum so adjudged against them, and that the same be, and hereby is, declared a lien upon said portion of said premises so apportioned and assigned.

No. 518.

ANOTHER ORDER AS TO COSTS, IN CASE OF ACTUAL PARTITION.

See ante, pp. 149, 158; 2 Barb. Ch. Pr. 738; 7 Paige, 204.

[*Same as in Nos.* 516, 517, *and then add:*]

And it is further ordered and adjudged, that the costs and charges of the several parties in this action, to be adjusted by the clerk, shall be borne and paid by the plaintiffs and defendants as follows: The said G. T., the one-third part thereof; the said G. G. and L. G. C., each one-sixth part thereof; the said H. T., the one-sixth part of one-third thereof; and the said E. W. T., M. M. C., J. M. T., and S. M. T., each five seventy-second parts thereof; and that the parties entitled to such costs have execution according to the course and practice of the court; that is to say, that the parties whose several bills of costs and expenses as taxed exceed the amount of their respective portions of the costs, as aforesaid, have execution for such excess against the other parties respectively for the amount which the respective taxed bills of such other parties are less than the amount of their respective portions of the whole costs of all the parties.

And it is further ordered, that the costs of the guardian *ad litem* of the infant defendants respectively, to the extent of their several shares or portions of the whole costs of the action, are declared to be liens upon their respective shares of the premises in favor of such guardian *ad litem*, which costs the general guardians of the infants are authorized and directed to pay out of the rents and profits of such shares, or out of any other moneys which may come to their hands belonging to the said infants respectively. And that the guardian *ad litem* be at liberty to apply to the court for further directions, if necessary, as to the payment of such costs.

No. 519.

COMMISSIONERS' DEED TO PURCHASER.

See ante, p. 147.

This indenture, made this —— day of ——, in the year of our Lord one thousand eight hundred and sixty ——, between W. M., J. F., and R. T., all of, &c., commissioners in partition, duly appointed as hereinafter mentioned, parties of the first part, and S. P., of, &c., party of the second part: Whereas, A. B., of, &c., did exhibit to the Supreme Court [*or other court*] a complaint in an action for a division and partition of certain premises therein mentioned, according to the respective rights of the parties interested therein, and for a sale of such premises, if it should appear that a partition thereof could not be made without great prejudice to the owners, pursuant to the statute relating to the partition of lands; in which complaint are set forth the names of the parties so interested, and the nature and extent of their respective interests, as by reference to said complaint, on file with the clerk of said court, at his office in the county of ——, will more fully appear. And whereas, such proceedings were thereupon had, in the said court, that judgment was duly rendered that partition of the said premises should be made according to the several rights and interests of the said parties; and the parties of the first part were appointed commissioners to make such partition. And whereas, such proceedings were afterward had, in the said court, that the parties of the first part, as such commissioners, were, by an order of said court, directed to sell the said premises with the appurtenances, at public auction to the highest bidder, after giving due notice of the time and place of such sale, according to law, as by the records of said court will more fully and at large appear. And whereas the said commissioners, pursuant to the said order and direction, after giving public notice of the time and place of such sale, did, on the —— day of ——, 18—, at the front steps of the Court House in the village of ——, in said county, expose to sale at public auction all and singular the said premises, with the appurtenances; at which sale the said premises were sold to the party of the second part, for the sum of —— dollars, that being the highest sum bid for the same; and which premises are bounded and described as follows: [*insert description*].

And whereas, the proceedings of the said commissioners were afterward duly reported to the court; and the said sale was approved and confirmed on the —— day of ——, 18—, as by the records of said court, reference being thereunto had, will more fully appear. And the said commissioners were thereupon directed by the said court to execute to the said party of the second part a conveyance of said premises, pursuant to the sale so made as aforesaid.

Now, this indenture witnesseth, that the said parties of the first part, commissioners as aforesaid, in order to carry into effect the sale so made by them as aforesaid, and also by virtue of the statute in such case made and provided, and in consideration of the sum of money so bid as aforesaid, to them in hand paid by the said party of the second part, the receipt whereof is hereby confessed and acknowledged, have granted, bargained, sold, aliened, released, conveyed, and confirmed, and by these presents do grant, bargain, sell, alien, release, convey, and confirm, unto the said party of the second part, and to his heirs and assigns forever, all the estate, right, title, interest, claim, and demand of the said parties of the first part, and also all the right, title, interest, claim, and demand of all and singular the several and respective parties to the aforesaid proceedings in partition, of, in, and to all and singular the said premises above particularly described; together with all and singular the rights, titles, privileges, hereditaments, and appurtenances thereunto belonging, or in any wise appertaining. To have and to hold all and singular the said premises unto the said party of the second part, his heirs and assigns; to the sole and only proper use, benefit, and behoof of the said party of the second part, his heirs and assigns, forever.

In witness whereof, the said parties of the first part have hereunto set their hands and seals, the day and year first above written.

Signed, sealed, and delivered in presence of

W. M. [L. S.]
J. F. [L. S.]
R. T. [L. S.]

[*To be acknowledged in the usual form. See No.* 44.]

No. 520

REFEREE'S DEED TO PURCHASER.

See ante, p. 147.

[*Same as in last form, with proper alterations.*]

No. 521.

REFEREE'S FINAL REPORT AFTER A SALE.

See ante, p. 147.

[*Title of the cause.*]

To the Supreme Court of the State of New York [*or other court*]:

In pursuance of an order of this court, made in the above cause, dated the —— day of ——, 18—, I, the subscriber, referee, do report:

That, in obedience to the said order, I have executed, acknowledged, and delivered to S. P., the purchaser of the premises ordered to be sold by me, a deed of the said premises, on receiving from him the sum of —— dollars, the price for which the said premises were sold to him, as mentioned in my former report of such sale, and upon his complying with all the conditions upon which the said deed was to be delivered.

I further report that I have paid to the attorney for the plaintiff in this suit the sum of —— dollars, for the costs and expenses of the proceedings in this action, and have taken a receipt therefor, which is hereunto annexed; that I have retained from the proceeds of said sale the sum of —— dollars, for my fees and disbursements upon said sale.

And I further report, that I have paid to A. B., the plaintiff in this action, the sum of —— dollars, being his share of the said proceeds, after the deductions aforesaid, and have taken a receipt therefor, which is hereto annexed.

I further report, that I have brought into court, and paid to the treasurer of the county of ——, the sum of —— dollars, being the share or interest of J. K. in the residue of the said proceeds, as aforesaid, and have taken a receipt for the same, which is hereto annexed. [*Add a similar order as to the shares of absentees and unknown owners.*]

That I have also brought into court for the use of C. D., an infant defendant in this action, and have paid to said treasurer [*or*, that I have paid to the general guardian of C. D., an infant, and one of the defendants herein, for the use of such infant], the sum of —— dollars, being the share or interest of said C. D. in the residue of said proceeds, and have taken a receipt therefor, which is hereto annexed.

[*If a credit was given for any portion of the purchase-money, on the security directed to be taken by the court, state the facts with reference thereto.*]

All which is respectfully submitted.

Dated, *&c.* W. B. B., Referee.

No. 522.

REPORT AS TO WIDOW'S RIGHT OF DOWER.

See ante, pp. 144, 151, 155.

[*Same as the foregoing, then add:*]

And I do further report, that the defendant R. H., being willing to accept, in lieu of her dower interest in the said premises, a sum in gross, in satisfaction thereof, out of the net proceeds of the said premises, I computed the value of the said dower interest upon the principles of law applicable to life-annuities, and ascertained the same to be —— dollars. And the said R. H. having consented to accept that sum, I have paid the same to her, and have taken a release from her, duly executed and acknowledged, and approved by me, of all her right, title, and interest of, in, and to the said premises, and every part thereof, which release is hereto annexed.

No. 523.

ORDER CONFIRMING FINAL REPORT.

[*Title of the cause.*] At a special term, *&c.* [*as in No.* 6].

On reading and filing the report of W. B. B., referee, duly appointed by an order of this court, dated the —— day of ——, 18—, by which report it appears that the said referee has executed, acknowledged, and delivered to S. P., the purchaser of the premises sold by the said referee, a deed thereof, and that he has distributed the net proceeds of the sale of the said premises in the manner directed by the order of the court, and that the said referee has annexed to his report the receipts of the several persons to whom the said net proceeds were directed to be paid: Now, on motion of L. P. C., attorney for the plaintiff, it is ordered that the said report be, and the same is hereby, approved and confirmed.

No. 524.

AFFIDAVIT ON APPLICATION TO COURT FOR MONEYS.

See ante, p. 153.

[*Title of the cause.*]

County of ——, ss.: J. K., of, *&c.*, being duly sworn, deposes, and says: That he is one of the defendants above named; that this action was commenced for the partition of real estate situated in the county of ——, which real estate was owned by the parties herein as tenants in common; that the share or interest of deponent in said real estate was the undivided one-fifth part thereof; that, as deponent is informed and believes, such proceedings were had in said cause that the said real estate was sold by and under the order of this court, and the share or portion of the purchase-money belonging to deponent, after deducting the costs and charges to which it was liable, and which amounted to —— dollars, was ordered to be brought into court, and paid to the treasurer of said county; and the same is now in the possession of said treasurer, as deponent is also informed and believes.

And deponent further says, that the share or interest of deponent, in said premises as aforesaid, was incumbered at the time of said sale, by a judgment in favor of B. F., of, *&c.*, against deponent, and which judgment was docketed in the clerk's office of said county, on the —— day of ——, 18—, as by reference to the papers on file in this cause will more fully appear; that the said judgment is now owned by the said B. F., who resides at —— aforesaid, and the true amount actually due thereon is the sum of —— dollars, with interest thereon from the —— day of ——, 18—; that there are no other incumbrances chargeable upon the share of deponent, as aforesaid, as he verily believes. J. K.

Sworn, *&c.*

No. 525.

NOTICE OF SUCH APPLICATION, ETC.

See ante, p. 153.

[*Title of the cause.*]

To B. F., of, *&c.:* Sir,—Take notice, that I shall apply to this court, at the next special term thereof, to be held at the Court House in the village of ——, on the —— day of —— next, or as soon thereafter as counsel can be heard, for an order, that the share or portion of moneys belonging to J. K., in the suit for partition of certain real estate situated in the county of ——, commenced by A. B., of, *&c.*, against the said J. K., and R. D., C. D., and owners unknown, and now deposited with the treasurer of said county, be paid to the said J. K., after deducting therefrom the amount actually due to you on the judgment mentioned in the affidavit, with a copy whereof you are herewith served. Yours, &c.,

Dated, *&c.* A. N. W., Attorney for J. K.

No. 525 (B).

ORDER TO SHOW CAUSE.

See ante, p. 153.

[*Title of the cause.*] At a special term, *&c.* [*as in No.* 6].

On reading the affidavit of J. K., dated the —— day of ——, 18—, annexed hereto, and on motion of A. N. W., Esq., attorney for said J. K., it is ordered that the plaintiff in this action show cause at the next special term of this court, to be held at the Court House in ——, on the —— day of ——, 18—, why the share or portion of moneys belonging to the said J. K. in this action, and now deposited with the treasurer of the county of ——, should not be paid over to the said J. K., after making all proper deductions therefrom; or why the said J. K. should not have such other relief as may be proper.

W. H. L., Justice of the, *&c.*

No. 526.

AFFIDAVIT OF SERVICE OF NOTICE, ETC.

See ante, p. 154.

[*Title of the cause.*]

County of ——, ss.: M. N., of, *&c.*, being duly sworn, deposes and says: That on the —— day of ——, 18—, he served upon B. F., of, *&c.*, a notice, of which the annexed notice marked "A." is a copy, by delivering such notice to the said B. F., personally, and leaving the same with him, at the village of ——, in said county.

[*If the service was by leaving at his residence, then say*: That on the —— day of ——, 18—, he served upon B. F., of, *&c.*, a copy of the notice hereto annexed, by leaving such copy at his residence in ——, in said county, in charge of the wife [*or*, daughter, aged eighteen years or thereabouts, *or other person of proper age*] of the said B. F., the said B. F. being absent from his residence at the time.]

And deponent further says, that at the time and place of serving said notice, as aforesaid, he also served upon the said B. F., in like manner as aforesaid, a copy of the affidavit hereto annexed.

Sworn, *&c.* M. N.

No. 527.

TABLE FOR COMPUTING THE VALUE OF A LIFE INTEREST.

A table corresponding with the Northampton tables referred to in the 84th rule of the Supreme Court, showing the value of an annuity of one dollar, at six per cent., on a single life, at any age from one year to ninety-four inclusive.

Age.	No. of years' purchase the annuity is worth.	Age.	No. of years' purchase the annuity is worth..	Age.	No. of years' purchase the annuity is worth.	Age.	No. of years' purchase the annuity is worth.
1	10.107	25	12.063	49	9.563	73	4.781
2	11.724	26	11.992	50	9.417	74	4.565
3	12.348	27	11.917	51	9.273	75	4.354
4	12.769	28	11.841	52	9.129	76	4.154
5	12.962	29	11.763	53	8.980	77	3.952
6	13.156	30	11.682	54	8.827	78	3.742
7	13.275	31	11.598	55	8.670	79	3.514
8	13.337	32	11.512	56	8.509	80	3.281
9	13.335	33	11.423	57	8.343	81	3.156
10	13.285	34	11.331	58	8.173	82	2.926
11	13.212	35	11.236	59	7.999	83	2.713
12	13.130	36	11.137	60	7.820	84	2.551
13	13.044	37	11.035	61	7.637	85	2.402
14	12.953	38	10.929	62	7.449	86	2.266
15	12.857	39	10.819	63	7.253	87	2.138
16	12.755	40	10.705	64	7.052	88	2.031
17	12.655	41	10.589	65	6.841	89	1.882
18	12.562	42	10.473	66	6.625	90	1.689
19	12.477	43	10.356	67	6.405	91	1.422
20	12.398	44	10.235	68	6.179	92	1.136
21	12.329	45	10.110	69	5.949	93	806
22	12.265	46	9.980	70	5.716	94	518
23	12.200	47	9.846	71	5.479		
24	12.132	48	9.707	72	5.241		

Rule for computing the value of a life estate or annuity.

Calculate the interest at six per cent. for one year, upon the sum to the income of which the person is entitled. Multiply this interest by the number of years' purchase set opposite the person's age in the table, and the product is the gross value of the life estate of such person in said sum.

Examples.

Suppose a widow's age is 37; and she is entitled to dower in real estate, worth $350.75. One-third of this is $116.91⅔. Interest on $116.91, one year at six per cent. (as fixed by 84th rule), is $7.01. The number of years' purchase which an annuity of one dollar is worth, at the age of 37, as appears by the table, is 11 years, and $\frac{35}{1000}$ part of a year, which multiplied by $7.01, the income for one year, gives $77.35, and a fraction, as the gross value of her right of dower.

Suppose a man, whose age is 50, is tenant by the courtesy in the whole of an estate worth $9,000. The annual interest on the sum, at six per cent., is $540.00. The number of years' purchase which an annuity of one dollar is worth, at the age of 50, as per table, is $9\frac{417}{1000}$ parts of a year, which multiplied by $540, the value of one year gives $5,085.18 as the gross value of his life estate in the premises, or the proceeds thereof.

NOTE.—The values in this table are calculated on the supposition that the annuities are payable yearly; if payable half yearly, one-fifth of a year's purchase should be added to those values.

For the rule to compute the present value of an inchoate or contingent right of dower, vide *Jackson* v. *Edwards*, 7 *Paige*, 408; *McKean's Pr. Int. Tables*, 25, § 4; *Hendry's Ann. Tables*, 87, prob. 4. And of an inchoate tenancy by the courtesy, 11 *How.* 177, 180.

No. 528.

AFFIDAVIT FOR MOTION TO COMPEL PURCHASER TO COMPLETE SALE.

See ante, p. 147; 2 Van Sant. Eq. Pr. 486.

[*Title of the cause.*]

County of ——, ss.: B. H. H., of, *&c.*, the plaintiff's attorney, being duly sworn, says: That on the —— day of —— he attended at the office of H. H., Esq., the referee mentioned in the annexed conditions of sale, with the conveyances therein mentioned, properly executed and acknowledged, and ready to be delivered to the purchaser, B. L. P., who signed the agreement thereunder written and hereto annexed; but said purchaser did not attend. That deponent left said conveyances at the office of said referee at 11 A. M. of that day, with instructions to him to deliver the same to said purchaser on his demand and payment of the residue of said purchase-money; that said referee, as deponent is informed by him, was in attendance at his office all that day; but said purchaser did not call to receive his said deed and pay the residue of said purchase-money; nor has he at any time done so, as deponent is also informed by said referee, but, on the contrary, refuses to complete his said purchase.

B. H. H.

Sworn, *&c.*

No. 529.

NOTICE OF MOTION TO COMPEL PURCHASER TO COMPLETE PURCHASE.

See ante, p. 147.

[*Title of the cause.*]

To B. L. P.:

Take notice that upon the foregoing affidavit [*or*, certificate], with conditions of sale and agreement thereto annexed, and the judgment heretofore rendered in this action, and referee's report of sale, and order confirming the same, a motion will be made at the next special term of this court, at, *&c.*,

on, *&c.*, for an order requiring you to complete your said purchase, on or before a day therein to be named, and in default thereof that an attachment issue against you; or for such further or other order as the court shall think proper to make, with the costs of the motion,

Yours, &c.,

Dated, *&c.* L. P. C., Attorney for Plaintiff.

No. 530.

ORDER REQUIRING A PURCHASER TO COMPLETE HIS PURCHASE.

See ante, p. 147.

[*Title of the cause.*] At a special term, *&c.* [*as in No.* 6].

It appearing that B. L. P. became a purchaser at a referee's sale herein, of, *&c.*, for —— dollars, paying ten per cent. deposit, in conformity with the conditions of sale; but that he has not completed such purchase in conformity therewith; and on reading and filing affidavits of, *&c.*, and after hearing counsel for the respective parties, and due deliberation having been had; it is ordered that the said B. L. P. complete his said purchase, by paying the remainder of the purchase-money, with interest thereon from the day he should have completed his purchase, and receive the referee's deed, at the referee's office, on or before the —— day of ——, with —— dollars costs to the plaintiff, to be paid by the said purchaser, and that, in default thereof, an *ex parte* application for an attachment against the said B. L. P. may be made to the court in the premises.

No. 531.

CERTIFICATE OF REFEREE THAT PURCHASER STILL REFUSES TO COMPLETE HIS PURCHASE.

See ante, p. 147.

[*Title of the cause.*]

The undersigned, referee appointed by the judgment in this action to sell the premises therein described, certifies and reports that B. L. P. neglects and refuses to complete his purchase of a portion of said premises, by paying the residue of the purchase-money and accepting a conveyance thereof, pursuant to his agreement, upon the conditions of sale annexed to the certificate heretofore made by me [*or*, affidavit of, *&c.*], bearing date the, *&c.* That on the —— day of ——, 18— [*the day specified in the order*], the undersigned tendered said conveyance, duly executed and acknowledged [*or*, had the same ready for delivery at the office, *&c.*], and demanded the residue of the purchase-money, but said B. L. P. refused to pay the same and accept said conveyance.

Dated, *&c.* H. H., Referee.

No. 532.

ORDER OF ATTACHMENT AGAINST DEFAULTING PURCHASER.

See ante, p. 147.

[*Title of the cause.*] At a special term, *&c.* [*as in No.* 6].

On reading and filing an affidavit, showing that B. L. P. had not complied with an order in this action, dated, *&c.*, whereby he was ordered, *&c.*; now, on motion of L. P. C., Esq., counsel for the plaintiff, it is ordered that a warrant of attachment and commitment, directed to the sheriff of the county of ——, issue against the said B. L. P., on account of the contempt aforesaid.

No. 533.

ORDER FOR RE-SALE, AND THAT FIRST PURCHASER MAKE GOOD THE DEFICIT.

See ante, p. 147; 2 Van Sant. Eq. Pr. 488.

[*Title of the cause.*] At a special term, *&c.* [*as in No.* 6].

On reading and filing the affidavit of, *&c.*, bearing date on, *&c.*, whereby it appears that the premises mentioned in the complaint and judgment in this action were sold, on the —— day of ——, 18—, by the referee therein, pursuant to said judgment, and that the purchaser at said sale, B. L. P., has failed to complete his purchase, by the payment of the sum of —— dollars, the residue of the purchase-money, and which remains unpaid; and on reading and filing due proof of notice of this motion; and on motion of L. P. C., of counsel for the plaintiff, no one appearing to oppose [*or*, on hearing J. L. F., Esq., of counsel for said purchaser], it is ordered that the said premises, so purchased by said B. L. P., be again exposed, by said referee, for sale at public auction, pursuant to the said judgment, and in all respects as though such previous sale had not taken place. And it is further ordered that said B. L. P. be liable for, and make good, any deficiency there may be between the amount bid by him, at the sale heretofore made, and the sum that may be obtained for said premises at the re-sale herein ordered; and that said referee apply so much of the moneys, paid by said B. L. P. on such previous sale, as may be necessary to make up such deficiency, together with the interest on the whole sum from the time when such purchase should have been completed, and the costs and expenses of such re-sale, with ten dollars costs of this motion, and pay back the residue thereof, if any, to the said B. L. P.; and, with his final report, that he also report to the court his proceedings under this order.

No. 534.

ORDER FOR RE-SALE AND DISCHARGE OF PURCHASER.

See ante, p. 147; 2 Van Sant. Eq. Pr. 488.

[*Title of the cause.*] At a special term, *&c.* [*as in No.* 6].

On reading and filing the affidavit of B. H. H., plaintiff's attorney, bearing date &c., and the consent of B. L. P., and of the attorneys for the plaintiff and the guardian *ad litem* of the infant defendants; it is ordered, that the said B. L. P., the purchaser of the premises known as No. —, —— Street, sold to him under the judgment in this action on the —— day of —— last, as stated in said affidavit, be discharged from the said purchase, and that the said sale be, and the same is hereby, annulled; and that H. H., Esq., the referee, under whose direction the said sale was made, refund and pay to the said B. L. P. the sum of —— dollars, being the ten per cent. paid by him to the said referee, on the purchase-money of said lot, and the sum of —— dollars for the expenses of said B. L. P. arising out of said purchase, in the examination of the title and the disbursements relating thereto.(*) And it is further ordered, that the said lot, situate on —— Street, as aforesaid, be re-sold by said referee, in all respects pursuant to the judgment in this action; and that, upon such re-sale, the proceeds arising from said sale be distributed among the parties, according to the provisions of the said judgment.

[And the said plaintiff is at liberty to make such application to the court, in regard to an amendment of the proceedings and judgment in this action, as he may be advised.]

No. 535.

AFFIDAVIT BY PURCHASER; MOTION TO BE RELIEVED FROM PURCHASE, ON THE GROUND OF A DEFECT OF TITLE.

See ante, p. 147; 2 Van Sant. Eq. Pr. 489.

[*Title of the cause.*]

County of ——, ss.: B. L. P., of, &c., being duly sworn, says: That he attended the public sale at auction of the premises described in the complaint and judgment in the above-entitled action, which sale was made under the direction of H. H., the referee named in such judgment, at the, &c., on the —— day of ——, and, at such sale, the whole of said premises were struck off to deponent, for the sum of —— dollars, he being the highest bidder for the same. That deponent thereupon signed an agreement, annexed to the terms and conditions of sale, and pursuant thereto, to the effect that he had become the purchaser of said premises, for the sum of —— dollars, and that he promised and agreed to comply with said terms and conditions; that is to say, to pay down ten per cent. of the purchase-money, and the residue, &c. [*stating the conditions*]; and the deponent thereupon deposited, with said referee, the said ten per cent., to wit: the sum of —— dollars, but has not completed the purchase by paying the residue thereof. That since said sale, deponent has discovered a defect in the proceedings and judgment, impairing the title of a purchaser thereunder, to wit: that B. C., one of the defendants, is an infant, and that no guardian *ad litem* has been appointed, or has appeared for him, in the action, but that judgment has been taken by default against him [*or state any other defect, either jurisdictional, or of mere irregularity; or, if it be a defect of title, point out the same specifically, and state that he caused search to be made for the same, and the amount of expenses attending such search*], which defect was wholly unknown to deponent at the time of said sale. That deponent is willing, and desires to complete his said purchase, if he can obtain a good and valid title to said premises [*or*, that deponent is desirous of being wholly relieved from such sale, and of having his deposit, with interest thereon, paid back to him, with the expenses of such search, and costs of this motion, *or as the case may be*].

Sworn, *&c.* B. L. P.

No. 536 (A).

ORDER GRANTING MOTION UNLESS PLAINTIFF AMEND AND SUPPLY DEFECT IN THE JUDGMENT.

[*Same as No.* 534 *to the* (*), *then add:*] Unless the said plaintiff shall, within —— days, procure, under the order of the court, the necessary and proper amendments to be made to said proceedings and judgment, by obtaining, *&c.* [*stating the requisite amendments*]; in which case, the said purchase and sale, and the agreement therefor, shall stand and be valid in all respects according to the said written terms and conditions; the time for the completion of the same being hereby extended to the —— day of ——, at the place mentioned in said conditions. And it is further ordered that the plaintiff pay to the said purchaser —— dollars costs of this motion.

No. 536 (B).

ASSENT BY A WIFE TO HAVE HER SHARE PAID TO HER HUSBAND.

See ante, pp. 151, 157.

[*Title of the action.*]

I, M. C., defendant in this action, and wife of the defendant, A. P. C. do hereby consent and request that the whole of the proceeds of the sale of the premises, under and by virtue of any judgment, decree, and order in this action, to which I am at present entitled, or which I may hereafter be entitled to receive, be paid over at once absolutely and unconditionally to my said husband the said A. P. C. [And that in the judgment to be rendered herein, directing the apportionment and disposition of the said proceeds, a provision to correspond with this consent and request be inserted.]

Witness my hand and seal, the —— day of ——, 18—.

In the presence of, M. C. [SEAL.]

L. F., Referee.

County of ——, ss.: On this —— day of ——, before me, the subscriber, L. F., referee in the above-entitled action, appeared the above-named M. C., and thereupon I fully explained to her the nature and extent of her rights and interests in the premises embraced by the above action; and the said M. C., on a private examination apart from her husband, then acknowledged that she executed the above instrument freely, without any fear or compulsion of her said husband.

L. F., Referee.

No. 536 (C).

CONSENT BY WIDOW TO ACCEPT SUM IN GROSS IN LIEU OF DOWER.

See ante, p. 156.

[*Title of the cause.*]

I, the undersigned, B. C. D., one of the defendants in the above-entitled action, do hereby consent to accept, in lieu of my dower interest in the premises of which partition and sale is sought in this action, and in satisfaction thereof, a sum in gross, out of the proceeds of said premises, according to my rights, ascertained [*or*, to be ascertained] by the report of the referee herein, which sum is to be computed according to the principles applicable to life annuities, pursuant to the Portsmouth or Northampton tables and the eighty-fourth rule of this court; and that in the judgment to be rendered herein, directing the apportionment and disposition of the proceeds of the sale of said premises, a provision to correspond with this consent be inserted.

Dated, *&c.* B. C. D.

[*Add the usual proof or acknowledgment, as in No.* 44.]

CHAPTER XXI.

FORMS IN PROCEEDINGS TO OBTAIN LEAVE TO SUE AS A POOR PERSON.

No. 537.

PETITION AFTER ACTION BROUGHT.

See ante, p. 166.

[*Title of the action substantially as in No.* 165.]

To the Supreme Court of the State of New York [*or other court*]:

The petition of A. B., of ——, in the county of——, shows to the court, that the above-entitled action was brought to recover the sum of —— dollars and interest thereon from the —— day of ——, 18—, for the work, labor, and services performed by your petitioner for the above-named defendant C. D., at his request, during the years 18— and 18—.

Your petitioner further shows,(*) that he is a poor person, and is not worth twenty dollars, excepting the wearing apparel and furniture necessary for himself and his family, and excepting the claim of —— dollars due to him as aforesaid.

Wherefore, your petitioner prays that he may be admitted to prosecute the said action as a poor person, and that counsel, attorneys, and all other officers requisite for prosecuting the said action, may be assigned to him; and that your petitioner may have such further or other relief as may be proper.

[*Add verification as in No.* 1.] A. B.

CERTIFICATE OF A COUNSELOR OF THE COURT, TO BE ANNEXED.

I, L. F., a counselor of the Supreme Court of the State of New York, residing at ——, in the county of ——, do hereby certify, that I have examined the claim of A. B. against C. D., mentioned in the petition hereto annexed, and am of opinion that the said A. B. has a good cause of action against the said C. D.

Dated, *&c.* L. F.

No. 538.

NOTICE OF MOTION.

See ante, p. 166.

[*Title substantially as in No.* 165.]

To C. D. [*or*, To J. W. F., attorney for C. D.] above named:

Take notice, that I shall apply to the Supreme Court [*or other court*], at the next special term thereof, to be held at the Court House in the city [*or*, village] of ——, in the county of —— , on the —— day of ——, 18—, at 10 o'clock in the forenoon of that day, or as soon thereafter as counsel can be heard, for an order granting the prayer of the petition, a copy of which is hereto annexed. Yours, &c.,

Dated, *&c.* E. B., Attorney for Plaintiff.

No. 539.

PETITION BEFORE ACTION BROUGHT.

See ante, p. 166.

In the matter of the application of A. B.

To the Supreme Court of the State of New York [*or other court*]:

The petition of A. B., of ——, in the county of ——, shows to the court, that C. D., of, *&c.*, is justly indebted to your petitioner in the sum of —— dollars, and interest thereon from the —— day of ——, 18—, for work, labor, and services performed by your petitioner for the said C. D. at his request, during the years 18— and 18—, no part of which has been paid.

Your petitioner further shows, that, *&c.* [*follow substantially No.* 537, *from the asterisk* (*) *to the end, including the certificate of a counselor of the court*].

No. 540.

ORDER ADMITTING PARTY TO PROSECUTE AS A POOR PERSON.

See ante, p. 166.

[*Title as in petition.*] At a special term, *&c.* [*as in No.* 6].

On reading and filing the petition of A. B. above named, dated the —— day of ——, 18—, and the certificate of L. F., a counselor of this court, annexed thereto; and the court being satisfied that the matters alleged in said petition are true, and that the said A B. has a meritorious cause of action against C. D. above named, it is, on motion of E. B., of counsel for said A. B. [after hearing J. W. F., counsel for C. D., in opposition thereto], ordered that the said A. B. be, and he is hereby, admitted to prosecute his said cause of action in the Supreme Court [*or other court*] as a poor person.

It is further ordered that C. H. S., Esq., an attorney and counselor of this court, be, and he is hereby, assigned as attorney and counsel for the said A. B., to prosecute the said action.

CHAPTER XXII.

FORMS IN PROCEEDINGS TO DISCOVER THE DEATH OF PERSONS.

No. 541.

PETITION.

See ante, p. 169.

IN SUPREME COURT.

In the matter of the application
of
A. B., to discover the death of C. D.

To the Supreme Court of the State of New York:

The petition of A. B., of, *&c.*, shows to the court: That he is the owner in fee, subject to the life estate therein of C. D., of all that piece or parcel of land, situated in the town of ——, in the county of ——, and bounded and described as follows: [*insert description*]. That, by the last will and testament of R. D., late of said town of ——, deceased, the said lands were devised to the said C. D., for and during his natural life, and at his decease, to your petitioner in fee.

Your petitioner further shows, that he has cause to believe, and does believe, that the said C. D. is dead; and that his death is concealed by L. D., his father, who resides at ——, in said county, and who is entitled to the custody of the said C. D., if living.

Your petitioner therefore prays that an order may be entered, requiring the said L. D. to produce and show the said C. D., at a time and place, and to a referee or commissioner to be designated by the court; and that your petitioner may have such further or other order or relief as may be proper.

[*Add verification substantially as in No.* 1.] A. B.

No. 542.

NOTICE OF PRESENTATION OF PETITION.

See ante, p. 170.

[*Title as in last form.*]

To L. D., of, *&c.:*

Take notice, that the petition, with a copy whereof you are herewith served, will be presented to the Supreme Court at the next special term thereof, to be held at the Court House in, *&c.*, on the —— day of ——, 18—, at 10 o'clock in the forenoon of that day, or as soon thereafter as counsel can be heard, and a motion will then and there be made that the prayer of the said petition be granted.

Yours, &c.,

Dated, *&c.* A. B.

No. 543.

ORDER THEREUPON.

See ante, p. 170.

[*Title as in No.* 541.] At a special term, *&c.* [*as in No.* 6].

On reading and filing the petition of A. B. above named, dated the —— day of ——, 18—, and notice of motion for an order requiring L. D. to produce and show C. D. to a referee or commissioner to be appointed for that purpose; and due proof of the service of said petition and notice on the said L. D. having been produced to the court; it is, on motion of E. L. S., of counsel for the petitioner, ordered that the said L. D. produce and show the said C. D. to L. F., Esq., who is hereby appointed referee for that purpose, at the office of the said L. F., No. 128 Broadway, New York, on the —— day of ——, 18—, at 10 o'clock A. M.

No. 544.

REFEREE'S RETURN.

See ante, p. 170.

[*Title as in No.* 541.]

To the Supreme Court of the State of New York:

I, the undersigned L. F., appointed referee by an order of the Supreme Court, dated the —— day of ——, 18—, and to whom L. D. was required to produce and show C. D., do hereby report:

That the said L. D. did, at the time and place designated in said order, to wit, on the —— day of ——, 18—, at my office, No. 128 Broadway, in the City of New York, produce and show to me the said C. D., pursuant to the order of said court.

I further report, that I was personally acquainted with the said C. D. [*or*, that I was not personally acquainted with the said C. D., and that his identity was proved to me by R. L. and S. S., witnesses examined by me; and that the proof taken upon such examination is annexed hereto, and forms a part of this my report].

All which is respectfully submitted.

Dated, *&c.* L. F., Referee.

[*Annex examinations, if any were taken.*]

No. 545.

ORDER ON FILING RETURN.

See ante, p. 169.

Title as in No. 541.] At a special term, *&c.* [*as in No.* 6].

The referee appointed on this application, by an order herein, dated the —— day of ——, 18—, having made his return to the court, which has been filed, and from which return it appears the said order has been complied with; it is now, on motion of R. S. R., of counsel for L. D., ordered that the proceedings herein be, and the same are hereby, discharged; and that the costs of the said proceedings, adjusted at the sum of —— dollars, be paid by the said A. B. to the said L. D.

CHAPTER XXIII.

FORMS IN PROCEEDINGS BY PERSONS TO CHANGE THEIR NAMES.

No. 546.

PETITION.

See ante, p. 175.

IN THE COURT OF COMMON PLEAS, City and County of New York [*or*, in the County Court of the County of ——].

In the matter of the application of A. B., to change his name to C. D.

To the Court of Common Pleas of the City and County of New York [*or*, County Court, *&c.*]

The petition of A. B. shows to the court: That he is aged —— years, and resides in the city and county of New York.

That, *&c.* [*set forth facts from which the court can see that there is no reasonable objection to the petitioner's assuming another name*].

Wherefore your petitioner prays that an order may be entered, authorizing him to assume the name of C. D. above mentioned. A. B.

[*Add verification substantially as in No.* 1.]

No. 547.

ORDER AUTHORIZING CHANGE OF NAME.

See ante, p. 175.

[*Title as in last form.*] At a special term, *&c.* [*in substance as in No.* 6].

On reading and filing the petition of A. B., dated the —— day of ——, 18—, praying that he may be authorized to assume the name of C. D.; and the court being satisfied that there is no reasonable objection to his assuming such name;

Now, on motion of A. N. W., of counsel for the said petitioner, it is ordered that the said A. B. be, and he hereby is, authorized to assume the name of C. D., from and after the —— day of ——, 18— [*not less than* 30 *days from the date of the order*].

CHAPTER XXIV.

FORMS IN PROCEEDINGS TO PROVE FOREIGN WILLS.

No. 548.

PETITION FOR A COMMISSION TO PROVE WILL.

See ante, p. 180; 2 Barb. Ch. Pr. 315, 742.

In the matter of proving the will of J. S., deceased.

To the Supreme Court of the State of New York:

The petition of A. B., of, *&c.*, respectfully shows:

That J. S., late of Charleston, in the State of South Carolina, was at the time of his decease a citizen of the State of South Carolina, and domiciled at Charleston aforesaid; and that he departed this life on or about the —— day of ——, having previously made his last will and testament in due form of law, to pass his personal property according to the laws of South Carolina, which has been duly proved and recorded at Charleston aforesaid, according to the laws of the State of South Carolina, and a copy thereof is hereto annexed: by which said last will and testament he constituted and appointed your petitioner the sole executor thereof.

That said will was duly proven before T. L., Esq., ordinary for Charleston district, on the —— day of ——, 18—, and recorded in the office of the court of probate in said Charleston, denominated the ordinary's office for said Charleston district. And that the original will is also deposited in the office of said ordinary, pursuant to the laws of the State of South Carolina, and cannot be withdrawn therefrom; the laws of said State prohibiting the withdrawal of a will which has been duly admitted to probate, and only authorizing copies to be taken.

Your petitioner further shows, that the names of the persons who would have been entitled to the property of the said J. S., in case he had died intestate, and of his heirs-at-law, are, and were at the time of his decease, E. S., his widow, and three children, viz.: [*insert their names and ages*]. All of whom reside at Charleston aforesaid.

Your petitioner further shows, that since the death of the said J. S., the said P. G. S., by virtue of a devise contained in the said will, has become seized of certain lots of land situate in the city of New York, which he now holds as such devisee.

And your petitioner further shows that the said J. S., at the time of his decease, was the holder of certain bonds and mortgages upon real estate situate within the city of New York, and other demands for considerable sums of money, which are now due and unpaid; whereby the surrogate of the city of New York has jurisdiction to grant letters testamentary on the estate of the decedent.

Your petitioner further shows, that he is advised that the aforesaid will of J. S., deceased, is a will duly executed according to the laws of the State of New York for passing real as well as personal estate, and that the subscribing witnesses to said will are H. W., S. R., and P. S., all resident without the jurisdiction of this State, to wit, at Charleston aforesaid; and that the said will cannot be obtained from the said ordinary court to be proved in this State.

Your petitioner therefore prays, that an order may be granted, directing that said will be proved in this court, as a will both of real and personal estate, upon a commission or *dedimus potestatem*, to be issued for that purpose. And that such commission issue out of and under the seal of this court, to be directed to the said T. L., Esq., the aforesaid ordinary for Charleston district, and, to B. H., Esq., of said Charleston, counselor-at-law, authorizing them, or either of them, to take proof of the due execution of the said will and of such other matters as may be necessary, by the testimony of such subscribing witnesses and such other witnesses as may be produced before them, upon written interrogatories, to be annexed to said petition; and for such further or such other relief in the premises as shall seem meet.

A. B

[*Add verification substantially as in No.* 1.]

No. 549.

ORDER TO HEIRS-AT-LAW, ETC., TO SHOW CAUSE.

See ante, p. 180.

[*Title as in last form.*] At a special term, *&c.* [*as in No.* 445].

On reading and filing the petition of P. G. S. and C. F. S., executors of the last will and testament of J. S., deceased, and praying that the last will and testament of the said J. S., therein mentioned, may be proved in this court on a commission to be issued for that purpose, and on motion of M. H., of counsel for said petitioner, ordered: that the heirs-at-law of the said J. S., and all other persons interested in contesting the validity of such will, or the codicils thereto, show cause before the Supreme Court, at a special term of said court, to be held at, *&c.*, on the —— day of —— next, why a commission should not issue out of and under the seal of said court, directed to T. L., ordinary for Charleston district, in the State of South Carolina, and to B. H., of the same place, counselor-at-law, authorizing and empowering them, or either of them, to take proof of the execution of the said will as a will of real and personal estate, and of the facts stated in such petition, by the testimony of the subscribing witnesses to said will, and such other witnesses as may be produced before them, to the end that such will may be recorded as a will of the real and personal estate of the testator. And it is further ordered, that a copy of this order be published in the State paper once in each week, for —— weeks previous to that time, and that a copy thereof be served upon such of the heirs-at-law and next of kin of the said J. S. as reside within this State, either personally, or, in case of their absence, by leaving the same at their respective places of residence, at least —— days before the time appointed for showing cause.

CHAPTER XXV.

FORMS IN PROCEEDINGS BY ACTION TO RECOVER POSSESSION OF LAND.

No. 550.

NOTICE OF RE-ENTRY FOR NON-PAYMENT OF RENT.

See ante, p. 190.

To A. B., of, *&c.:*

Take notice that I intend to re-enter on the premises known as lot No. ——, in the town of ——, county of ——, and State of New York, demised by —— to ——, and of which premises, or a portion thereof, you have possession, unless the arrears of rent now due thereon shall be paid within fifteen days after the service of this notice. Yours, &c.

Dated, *&c.* C. D.

CHAPTER XXVI

FORMS IN QUO WARRANTO, AND IN PROCEEDINGS TO OBTAIN DELIVERY OF BOOKS AND PAPERS.

No. 551.

COMPLAINT IN QUO WARRANTO—TO DETERMINE TITLE TO AN OFFICE.

See ante, p. 200.

SUPREME COURT, County of ——.

The People of the State of New York, and J. S.,
against
J. J.

The complaint of the plaintiffs shows to the court:

That, on the —— day of November, 18—, an election was duly held in the —— judicial district of this State, for the office of justice of the Supreme Court, for the term of eight years from the first day of January, 18—.

That, at the said election, the above-named J. S. received the greatest number of legal votes for the said office.

That, on the —— day of ——, 18—, the defendant usurped the said office, and has ever since withheld the same from the said J. S.

Wherefore, the plaintiffs demand judgment that the defendant is not entitled to the said office, and that he be ousted therefrom; and that the said J. S. is entitled to and be put in possession of the same.

J. C., Attorney for Plaintiffs.

No. 552.

COMPLAINT IN QUO WARRANTO [*another form*].

See ante, p. 200.

SUPREME COURT, County of ——.

The People of the State of New York, and N. C. P.,
against
A. V. S.

The complaint of the plaintiff shows to the court:

I. That on the [thirtieth day of December, 1859], the defendant was appointed chamberlain of the city of New York, by the mayor of the said city, with the advice and consent of the Board of Aldermen of the said city, and immediately thereafter entered upon the duties of the said office, and continued therein until his removal, as hereinafter stated.

II. That [in May, 1860], the said defendant was duly removed from the said office, by the mayor of the said city, by and with the consent of the Board of Aldermen of the said city.

III. That immediately after the removal of the said A. V. S., as aforesaid, the said N. C. P. was duly appointed chamberlain of the said city, by the mayor thereof, with the advice and consent of the Board of Aldermen of the said city, to fill the vacancy made by the removal of the said defendant, as aforesaid.

IV. That the said N. C. P. thereupon accepted the said office, and, in the form and within the time required by law and the ordinances of the said city, took and subscribed, before the mayor of the said city, and filed in his office, the oath of office of the said N. C. P., as such chamberlain, and also executed and filed, in the office of the comptroller of the said city, an official bond, with sufficient sureties, approved by the said comptroller, in the amount prescribed by the ordinances of the said city.

V. That the said N. C. P., after the filing of such official oath and bond, demanded of the said defendant the possession of the said office, which the said defendant refused, and he still continues to usurp, hold, and exercise the said office, to the exclusion of the said N. C. P.

Wherefore, the plaintiffs demand judgment:

1. That the said defendant is not entitled to the said office, and that he be ousted and excluded therefrom.

2. That the said N. C. P. is entitled to the said office, and that he be admitted into the same, and to all the rights and emoluments thereof.

No. 553.

AFFIDAVIT TO OBTAIN ORDER TO COMPEL DELIVERY OF BOOKS, ETC.

See ante, p. 207.

In the matter of the application of A. B., to compel delivery of books and papers.

To Hon. S. R., Justice of the Supreme Court [*or*, County Judge]:

The application of A. B. above named, respectfully shows:

That C. D., late of the, *&c.*, deceased, was elected to the office of —— on or about the —— day of ——, 18—, to serve for —— years from the —— day of ——, 18—. That the said C. D. took possession of said office, and kept the possession thereof, until his death, on the —— day of ——, 18—. That afterward, and on the —— day of ——, 18—, the said applicant was duly appointed and commissioned to fill the vacancy in the said office, caused by the death of the said C. D.; and thereupon duly qualified himself to fill such vacancy, and became and was the legal successor to the said office. That the books, papers, maps, and documents, belonging and appertaining to the said office, viz.: [*describe the property*], have come to the hands of E. F., of, *&c.*

The said applicant further shows, that on the —— day of ——, 18—, the said applicant duly demanded the said books, papers, maps, and documents of the said E. F., who thereupon refused to deliver the same, or any of them, to him.

Wherefore, the said A. B. demands that the said E. F. be ordered to show cause before the said justice [*or*, judge] why he, the said E. F., should not be compelled to deliver the said books, maps, papers, and documents to the said A. B., and why the said A. B. should not have such further or other relief as may be proper.

A. B.

County of ——, ss.:

A. B., the applicant above named, being duly sworn, deposes and says, that the matters alleged in the above application are true according to his best knowledge, information, and belief.

Sworn, *&c.* A. B.

No. 554.

ORDER ON APPLICATION TO COMPEL DELIVERY OF BOOKS AND PAPERS.

See ante, p. 207; 5 Abb. 193, note.

[*Title substantially as in last form.*]

Whereas, on the 18th day of June, 1857, at the City Hall, in the city of New York, complaint was made to C. A. P., one of the justices of the Supreme Court of the State of New York, by D. D. C., setting forth, among other things, that J. S. T., who was, in November, 1855, elected to the office of street commissioner of the city of New York, to serve for three years from January, 1856, went into his said office in said January, and continued in office till the 9th of June, 1857, when he died.

That the said D. D. C. was, on the 12th day of said June, duly appointed and commissioned to fill the vacancy in the said office, caused by the death of the said T., and had duly qualified himself, and was the successor to the said office; that the books, papers, maps, and documents, belonging and appertaining to the said office, viz.: [*describe the property particularly*] had come to the hands of C. D.; that the said D. D. C. had demanded the said books, maps, papers, and documents from the said C. D., and that the said C. D. had withheld the said books, maps, papers, and documents, and refused to deliver the same to the said D. D. C.; and asking that the said C. D. might be ordered to show cause before the said justice why he should not be compelled to deliver the said books, maps, papers, and documents to the said D. D. C.; and whereas, being satisfied by the oath of the said D. D. C. that the said books, maps, papers, and documents were withheld, the said justice granted an order, directing the said C. D. to show cause before him, on the 23d day of June last, at the chambers of the justices of the said court, why he should not be so compelled, and, at the time and place so appointed, the said D. D. C. and the said C. D. appeared before the said justice, and due proof having been made of the service of the said order, the said justice proceeded to inquire into the circumstances, which inquiry was continued before him from day to day until this day, the matter having been thus regularly adjourned, and the said C. D. not having made oath that he has truly delivered to the said D. D. C. the said books, maps, papers, and documents, and it appearing to the said justice that the said D. D. C. is the successor to the said office of street commissioner of the city of New York, and that the said books, maps, papers, and documents are still withheld, and that the said C. D. still omits and refuses to deliver up the same,(*) It is hereby ordered, that the said C. D. forthwith deliver to the said D. D. C. all the books, maps, papers, and documents belonging or appertaining to the office of street commissioner of the city of New York which have come to the hands of said C. D., or, in default thereof, that a warrant issue to the sheriff of the city and county of New York to commit the said C. D. to the jail of the said city and county, therein to remain until he deliver to the said D. D. C. the said books, maps, papers, and documents, or be otherwise discharged according to law. And the same being required by the said D. D. C., it is further ordered that, on such default being made by said C. D., a search-warrant issue to the said sheriff, or any constable of the city and county of New York, commanding him to search in the daytime the apartments and rooms occupied and set apart for the office of street commissioner of the city of New York, and wherein the said books and papers are kept, for the said books, papers, maps, and documents, and to seize them and bring them before the said justice.

C. A. P., Justice, *&c.*

No. 555.

WARRANT OF ARREST.

See ante, p. 207; 5 Abb. 194, note.

The People of the State of New York, to the Sheriff of the City and County of New York:

Whereas, *&c.* [*recite the proceedings as in the last form to the asterisk* (*), *and then proceed :*] These presents are therefore to command you, the sheriff of the city and county of New York, and you are hereby commanded, to take the body of the said C. D. and commit him to the jail of the city and county of New York, there to remain until he shall deliver such books, maps, papers, and documents, or be otherwise discharged according to law.

In witness whereof, I have hereto set my hand and seal, at the City Hall in the city of New York, this 9th day of July, in the year of our Lord one thousand eight hundred and fifty-seven.

C. A. P. [SEAL.]
Justice, &c.

No. 556.

WARRANT TO SEARCH FOR BOOKS AND PAPERS.

See ante, p. 207; 5 Abb. 195, note; Ib. 282.

The People of the State of New York, to the Sheriff, or any Constable, of the City and County of New York:

Whereas, &c. [*recite the proceedings as in No.* 554 *to the asterisk* (*); *also, the direction to the sheriff to take the body of the said C. D.*, &c., *and then proceed*.]

And the said D. D. C. having further required a search warrant to be issued, you, the said sheriff of the city and county of New York, and any constable of said city and county, are hereby further commanded to search in the daytime the apartments and rooms occupied and set apart for the street commissioner of the city of New York, and wherein the said books, maps, papers, and documents are kept in said city, and to seize the said books, maps, papers, and documents, viz.: [*describe the property particularly*], and to bring the same before the undersigned forthwith, there to be disposed of according to law.

In witness whereof, I have hereto set my hand and seal, at the City Hall of the city of New York, this 9th day of July, A. D. 1857.

C. A. P. [SEAL.]
Justice, &c.

CHAPTER XXVII.

FORMS IN PROCEEDINGS TO ACQUIRE TITLE TO REAL ESTATE FOR RAILROAD PURPOSES.

No. 560.

PETITION FOR APPOINTMENT OF COMMISSIONERS.

See ante, p. 213.

SUPREME COURT.

In the matter of the application of the —— Railroad Company.

To the Supreme Court of the State of New York:

The petition of the —— Railroad Company respectfully shows, that the said company is a corporation duly organized under and by virtue of an act of the legislature of this State, entitled "An act to authorize the formation of railroad corporations, and to regulate the same," passed April 2, 1850 [*or other act*]; that the articles of association of said company, in due form, were filed, and said company became a body corporate, pursuant to said act, on the —— day of ——, 18—; that the first board of directors of said company were chosen, by-laws were made, officers were elected, surveys and a map and profile of the intended route of said road were made, certified, and filed by said company, according to said act; that it is the intention of the said company, in good faith, to construct and finish a railroad from and to the places named for that purpose in said articles of association, to wit, from the town [*or*, city] of ——, in the county of ——, in the State of New York, commencing at a point near [*describe point of commencement*] to the [*describe the point of termination*], in the town [*or*, city] of ——, in the county of ——, and State of New York; that the whole capital stock of said company has been in good faith subscribed, as required by said act; (*a*) that the said company has surveyed the line or route of its proposed road, and has made a map or survey thereof, by which such route or line is designated, and that they have located their railroad according to such survey, and have filed certificates of such location, signed by a majority of said directors, in the clerks' offices of the counties of —— and ——, those being the counties, and the only counties in this State, through or into which the said railroad is to be constructed.

Your petitioners further show, that the real estate described in the SCHEDULE hereunto annexed, and forming a part of this petition, is required for the purposes of the incorporation of said company, to wit, for the purpose of constructing and operating the said proposed road, and that the said company have not been able to acquire title thereto, for the reason that the owners thereof refuse to sell the same for any reasonable compensation [*or other reason*]; that the said schedule contains the names and places of residence of the parties, so far as the same can by reasonable diligence be ascertained, who own or have, or claim to own or have, estates or interests in the said real estate.

Your petitioners further show, upon information and belief, that A. B. and C. D., named in the said schedule, are infants, having no general guardian; and that the said A. B. is aged—— years, and the said C. D. is aged —— years.

Your petitioners further show, that, *&c.* [*if any of the owners or parties interested are idiots or persons of unsound mind, or are unknown, set out the facts as they exist; also set forth such allegations of liens or incumbrances on the real estate as the company may think proper to make*].

Your petitioners, therefore, with a view of acquiring title to the said real estate for the purposes aforesaid, pray for the appointment of three disinterested and competent persons who reside in the said county of ——, where the said premises are situated, and who are freeholders, as commissioners, to as-

(*a*) It is sufficient now if at least ten thousand dollars for every mile of the road proposed to be constructed in this State shall be in good faith subscribed to the capital stock, and ten per cent. thereof paid in. See *ante, p.* 212, *and notes.*

certain and appraise the compensation to be made to the owners or persons interested in the said real estate, pursuant to the provisions of the said act; and for such further or other order as the court may deem proper to grant.

M. F., Attorney for Petitioners. B. B.

State of New York, }
County of ——, } ss.

B. B., of ——, in said county, being duly sworn, deposes and says, that he is one of the directors of the —— Railroad Company, the petitioners above named; that he has read the foregoing petition by him subscribed, and knows the contents thereof, and that the same is true of his own knowledge, except as to the matters therein stated on information or belief, and as to those matters he believes it to be true.

Sworn to, *&c.* B. B.

[*Annex to the petition a schedule, as follows:*]

SCHEDULE referred to in the annexed petition and forming a part thereof.

Real estate described as follows: [*insert description*].

Names and places of residence of persons who own or have, or claim to own or have, estates or interests in the real estate above described, viz.: [*insert names and places of residence*].

No. 561.

NOTICE TO ACCOMPANY THE ABOVE PETITION.

See ante, pp. 213, 214.

[*Title as in last form.*]

To, *&c.* [*names of parties in interest*]:

You will take notice, that the petition, with a copy whereof you are herewith served, will be presented to the Supreme Court at the next special [*or*, general] term thereof, appointed to be held at the Court House in the town [*or*, city] of ——, in the county of ——, on the —— day of ——, 18—, at the opening of the court on that day, or as soon thereafter as counsel can be heard; and that a motion will then and there be made that the prayer of the said petition be granted. Yours, &c.

Dated, *&c.* M. F., Att'y for Petitioners.

No. 562.

NOTICE TO NON-RESIDENT OR UNKNOWN OWNERS, TO BE PUBLISHED.

See ante, p. 215.

[*Title as in No.* 560.]

To O. P., R. S., and all others owning, or interested in, the real estate hereinafter described:

Take notice, that the petition of the —— Railroad Company, stating and setting forth the several matters required to be stated and set forth therein by the provisions of the act of the legislature of the State of New York, entitled "An act to authorize the formation of railroad corporations, and to regulate the same," passed April 2, 1850, will be presented to the Supreme Court of the State of New York, at the next special [*or*, general] term thereof, to be held at the Court House in ——, in the county of ——, in said State, on the —— day of ——, 18—, at the opening of the court on that day, or as soon thereafter as counsel can be heard; and that a motion will then and there be made that the prayer of the said petition be granted; the object of the said application being to obtain the appointment of three disinterested and competent persons, as commissioners, to ascertain and appraise the compensation to be made to the owners of, or persons interested in, the real estate hereinafter described; the said company desiring to acquire the title to the said real estate for the purposes of its incorporation.

The following is a description of the real estate referred to, viz.: [*insert description*].

Dated, *&c.* M. F., Att'y for Petitioners.

No. 563.

ORDER APPOINTING COMMISSIONERS.

See ante, p. 218.

At a special [*or* general] term of the Supreme Court, held at the Court House in ——, in the County of ——, on the —— day of ——, 18—:

Present, A. B., Justice.

[*Title as in No.* 560.]

On reading and filing the petition of the —— Railroad Company, dated the —— day of ——, 18—, praying for the appointment of three disinterested and competent persons as commissioners to ascertain and appraise the compensation to be made to, *&c.* [*names of parties*], owners or persons interested in the real estate hereinafter described, which is proposed to be taken by the said company for the purposes of its incorporation; and on reading and filing the notice accompanying the said petition; and also on reading and filing proof of the due service of a copy of the said petition and notice upon each of the said owners or persons interested; and after hearing M. F., of counsel for the said petitioners, and J. H. M., of counsel for said owners or persons interested;

It is ordered, that E. D., M. L., and G. C., three disinterested and competent freeholders, residing in the county of ——, be, and they are hereby, appointed commissioners for the purpose of ascertaining and appraising the compensation to be made to the said owners or persons interested, for the real estate so proposed to be taken; which said real estate is situated in said county of ——, and is described as follows: [*insert description*].

It is further ordered, that the first meeting of the said commissioners be held at the [*place of meeting*], on the —— day of ——, 18—, at—— o'clock — M.

It also appearing to the court, from the said petition, that A. B. and C. D., persons interested in the said real estáte, are infants, having no general guardian; It is further ordered, that J. W. F., of, *&c.*, a counśelor of this court, be, and he is hereby, appointed the special guardian for the said infants, for the purpose of representing them, and attending to their interests in this proceeding.

No. 564.

OATH OF COMMISSIONER.

See ante, p. 219.

I, E. D., one of the commissioners appointed by the Supreme Court to ascertain and appraise the compensation to be made by the —— Railroad Company, to O. P., R. S., and others, for lands to be taken by the said company for the purposes of its incorporation, do solemnly swear [*or*, affirm] that I will support the Constitution of the United States, and the Constitution of the State of New York, and that I will faithfully discharge the duties of commissioner as aforesaid, according to the best of my ability.

Subscribed and sworn to before me, this —— of ——, 18—, } E. D.

W. B. B., Justice of the Peace.

No. 565

COMMISSIONERS' REPORT.

See ante, p. 222.

[*Title as in No.* 560.]

To the Supreme Court of the State of New York:

The undersigned, E. D., M. L., and G. C., commissioners appointed by an order of the Supreme Court, dated the —— day of ——, 18—, to ascertain and appraise the compensation to be made by the said —— Railroad Company to O. P., R. S., *&c.* [*insert names of parties*], owners and persons interested, for lands to be taken by the said company for the purposes of its incorporation, do hereby report:

That, having first severally duly taken and subscribed an oath to support the Constitution of the United States, and the Constitution of the State of New York, and faithfully to discharge the duties of commissioners, as aforesaid, we met at the time and place designated in the said order, and thereupon proceeded carefully to examine the real estate described in the petition in this matter, and to hear the proofs and allegations of the parties.

That we first examined the real estate owned by O. P. above named, and heard the proofs and allegations of the parties in respect thereto, and, after the testimony in respect to said claim was closed, we did, without any unnecessary delay, and before proceeding to the examination of any other claim, ascertain and determine that the compensation which ought justly to be made by the said company to the said O. P., for the said real estate, was the sum of —— dollars.

That we then examined the real estate owned by R. S. above named, *&c.* [*proceed as in the last case, and in the same manner as to all the cases*].

We further report that the minutes of the testimony taken by us in respect to each of the said claims is hereto annexed, marked as "Schedule A."

We do also report that the sum of —— dollars ought to be paid to J. W. F., special guardian for A. B. and C. D., infants above named, for costs, expenses, and counsel fees in this proceeding.

In testimony whereof, we, the said commissioners, have hereunto set our hands, this —— day of ——, 18—.

[*Signatures of Commissioners.*]

[*Annex the minutes of the testimony.*]

No. 566.

NOTICE OF MOTION TO CONFIRM REPORT.

See ante, p. 223.

[*Title as in No.* 560.]

SIR,—Take notice that I shall move this court, at the next special [*or*, general] term thereof, to be held at the Court House in ——, in the county of ——, on the —— day of ——, 18—, or as soon thereafter as counsel can be heard, for an order confirming the report of the commissioners appointed to ascertain and appraise the compensation to be made by the said company to you, and the other owners and parties interested, for lands to be taken by the said company for the purposes of its incorporation; which motion will be founded upon the said report, a copy of which is herewith served.

Dated, *&c.* M. F., Attorney for said Company.

No. 567.

ORDER CONFIRMING REPORT.

See ante, p. 223.

[*Title as in No.* 560.] At, *&c.* [*as in No.* 563].

It appearing to the court that the —— Railroad Company above mentioned, upon due notice to the owners and persons interested, duly presented to the Supreme Court, at the special [*or*, general] term thereof, held at the Court House in ——, on the —— day of ——, 18—, a petition in due form of law, praying for the appointment of three disinterested and competent persons, who were freeholders, as commissioners, to ascertain and appraise the compensation to be made to the said owners and persons interested, for the real estate hereinafter described, proposed to be taken by the said company for the purposes of its incorporation, and that an order was thereupon duly made by the said court, bearing date the —— day of ——, 18—, appointing E. D., M. L., and G. C., freeholders residing in the county of ——, as such commissioners for the purposes aforesaid, and fixing upon the —— day of ——, 18—, at the ——, as the time and place for the first meeting of the said commissioners.

And it appearing also to the court that the said commissioners have duly made a report of their proceedings upon the said appraisal, by which report it appears that the said commissioners, after taking and subscribing the oath prescribed by law, met at the time and place appointed in said order, and thereupon proceeded carefully to examine the said real estate, and to hear the proofs and allegations of the parties; and that they first examined the real estate of O. P., one of the owners or persons interested, described as [*insert description*], and duly appraised the compensation to be made by the said company to the said O. P., for the said real estate, at the sum of —— dollars; and that the said commissioners then examined the real estate of R. S., another owner or person interested, described as [*insert description*], and duly appraised the compensation to be made by the said company to the said R. S., for the said real estate, at the sum of —— dollars [*proceed in the same form as to the other cases*]; and that the sum of —— dollars ought to be paid to J. W. F., special guardian for A. B. and C. D., infants above named, for costs, expenses, and counsel fees in this proceeding; as will more fully appear by reference to said report, on file with the clerk of the county of ——.

It also appearing to the court, that due notice has been given to the parties or their attorneys of a motion to confirm the said report at the present term of this court,

Now, on motion of M. F., of counsel for the said company, no one appearing in opposition thereto [*or*, and after hearing J. H. M., of counsel for O. P., and J. W. F., special guardian for A. B. and C. D.], it is ordered that the said report and appraisal be, and the same is, in all respects confirmed.

It is further ordered, that the compensation awarded to O. P. above named, amounting to —— dollars, be paid to the said O. P., or to his attorney in the said proceeding [*or otherwise, as shall be deemed proper; stating to whom the money is to be paid, or in what bank, and in what manner it shall be deposited by the company*].

No. 568.

NOTICE OF APPEAL FROM COMMISSIONERS' REPORT.

See ante, p. 227.

[*Title as in No.* 560.]

To M. F., Esq., attorney for said company: Take notice, that O. P., one of the owners of the real estate described in the petition in this matter, appeals to the Supreme Court from the appraisal and report of E. D., M. L., and G. C., commissioners, appointed by the said court, to ascertain and determine the compensation which ought to be made to the owners and parties interested, for the real estate taken by the said company for the purposes of its incorporation; or from so much of the said appraisal and report as affects the said O. P. J. H. M., Att'y. for O. P.

Dated, *&c.*

No. 569.

NOTICE OF ARGUMENT OF APPEAL.

See ante, p. 227.

[*Title as in No.* 560.]

Take notice, that the appeal of O. P. from the appraisal and report of the commissioners appointed in this matter, will be brought to hearing and argument at the next special [*or*, general] term of this court, to be held at the Court House in ——, on the —— day of ——, 18—, at the opening of the court on that day, or as soon thereafter as counsel can be heard.

Yours, &c., J. H. M., Att'y for O. P.

Dated, *&c.*

CHAPTER XXVIII.

FORMS ON THE REDEMPTION OF REAL ESTATE.

No. 570.

CERTIFICATE OF SALE ON EXECUTION.

See ante, p. 233.

I, J. R. G., sheriff of the county of ——, do hereby certify, that, by virtue of an execution issued out of the Supreme Court of the State of New York [*or other court*], against the property of E. F., in an action wherein J. D. was plaintiff, and the said E. F. was defendant, I did, on the —— day of ——, 18—, at the Court House in ——, in the county of ——, sell at public auction to C. D. all that certain piece or parcel of land, situate, lying, and being in the town of ——, in said county, and bounded, *&c.* [*give particular description of premises*], for the sum of —— dollars, that being the highest sum bid for the same [*if the premises were sold in parcels, give the price bid for each distinct lot*].

I do further certify, that the whole consideration money paid for said premises was the sum of —— dollars; and that the time when the said sale will become absolute, and the purchaser be entitled to a conveyance of said premises, pursuant to law, will be the —— day of ——, 18—, unless the said premises shall be, before that time, redeemed agreeably to the provisions of the statute in such case made and provided. J. R. G., Sheriff.

Dated, *&c.*

No. 571.

AFFIDAVIT VERIFYING COPY OF ASSIGNMENT OF JUDGMENT.

See ante, pp. 245 to 249.

[*Title of action in which judgment was rendered.*]

County of ——, ss.:

O. K., being duly sworn, says: He is the assignee of the plaintiff in the above-entitled action; that the foregoing is a true copy of the assignment of the judgment therein mentioned, executed by the plaintiff above named to this deponent, and of the whole of such assignment. O. K.

Sworn, *&c.*

No. 572.

AFFIDAVIT OF AMOUNT DUE ON JUDGMENT.

See ante, pp. 245 to 249.

County of ——, ss.:

A. B., being duly sworn, deposes and says: He is the owner and holder [*or*, the attorney, *or*, agent, of the owner and holder] of the judgment mentioned in the certified copy of docket of judgment annexed hereto, and that the true sum this day due upon the said judgment is —— dollars and —— cents. A. B.

Sworn, *&c.*

No. 573.

AFFIDAVIT OF AMOUNT DUE ON MORTGAGE.

See ante, pp. 245 to 249.

County of ——, ss.:

A. B., being duly sworn, deposes and says: He is the owner and holder of the mortgage, a certified copy of which is annexed hereto; that the true sum this day due upon the said mortgage is —— dollars, over and above all payments thereon. A. B.

Sworn, *&c.*

No. 574.

LIKE AFFIDAVIT OF AGENT OR ATTORNEY OF OWNER.

See ante, pp. 245 to 249.

County of ——, ss.:

G. H., being duly sworn, deposes and says: He is the agent [*or*, attorney] for A. B., who claims to redeem certain premises from sale under execution; that the said A. B. is the owner and holder of the mortgage, a certified copy of which is annexed hereto; and that, *&c.* [*conclude as in last form*].

No. 575.

CERTIFICATE ON REDEMPTION BY JUDGMENT DEBTOR.

See ante, p. 254.

County of ——, ss.: I, J. R. G., sheriff of said county, do hereby certify, that on the —— day of ——, 18—, E. F., in due form of law, tendered to me —— dollars, being the amount alleged by him to have been bid by the purchaser on the sale of the premises hereinafter mentioned, under and by virtue of an execution issued out of the Supreme Court of the State of New York [*or other court*], against the said E. F., in favor of J. D., on the —— day of ——, 18—, with the interest thereon; and that the said E. F. then and there claimed the right to redeem the said premises, and that I received the moneys so tendered, amounting, principal and interest, to —— dollars, and have granted to the said E. F. this my certificate, in conformity to the statute in such case made and provided.

The premises so redeemed, or intended to be redeemed, are described in the certificate of the sale thereof as follows: [*insert description*].

In witness whereof, I have hereunto set my hand the —— day of ——, 18—.

J. R. G., Sheriff.

[*Add acknowledgment, as in No.* 44.]

No. 576.

CERTIFICATE ON REDEMPTION BY JUDGMENT CREDITOR.

See ante, p. 254.

County of ——, ss.: I, J. R. G., sheriff of said county, do hereby certify that on the —— day of ——, 18—, O. K. tendered to me —— dollars; and also presented to me a certified copy of the docket of a judgment in his favor [*or*, in favor of R. D.], against E. F., rendered in the Supreme Court of the State of New York [*or other court*] on the —— day of ——, 18—; [*if the judgment was not in favor of the person redeeming, add:* also a copy of an assignment of said judgment, to O. K., verified by his affidavit;] also an affidavit of the said O. K., showing the true sum due upon the said judgment; and thereupon the said O. K. claimed to redeem, as a judgment creditor, certain premises sold by me under and by virtue of an execution issued upon a judgment in the Supreme Court of this State [*or other court*] in favor of E. F. against J. D., on the —— day of ——, 18 —, and which premises are described in the certificate of sale, as follows: [*insert description*].

Whereupon I received the moneys so tendered, and the papers so presented, and do now give to the said O. K. this my certificate, in conformity to the statute in such case made and provided.

In witness, *&c.* [*as in last form*].

No. 577.

STATEMENT OF REDEMPTION TO FILE IN CLERK'S OFFICE.

See ante, p. 254.

[*Title of the cause.*]

County of ——, ss.: I, J. R. G., sheriff of said county, do hereby certify that O. K. has this day redeemed the premises hereinafter described from the sale made by me on the —— day of ——, 18—, under and by virtue of an execution issued on a judgment in favor of E. F. against J. D.; that such redemption was made under a judgment rendered in the above-entitled cause, on the —— day of ——, 18—, for —— dollars; that the said O. K. is the assignee of said last-mentioned judgment; that the sum claimed to be due thereon at the time of such redemption was —— dollars; and that the amount paid to redeem said premises was —— dollars.

The following is a description of the premises redeemed: [*insert description*].

J. R. G., Sheriff.

Dated, *&c.*

No. 578.

SHERIFF'S DEED.

See ante, p. 257.

This indenture, made the —— day of ——, 18—, between J. R. G., sheriff [*or*, late sheriff] of the county of ——, of the first part, and O. K., of, *&c.* of the second part:

Whereas, by virtue of a certain execution issued out of the Supreme Court of the State of New York [*or other court*], in an action wherein J. D. was plaintiff and E. F. was defendant, directed and delivered to the said sheriff, and commanding him that, *&c.* [*as in execution*], the party of the first part did, on the —— day of ——, 18—, sell the premises hereinafter described, at public auction, at the front door of the Court House in the town of ——, in said county, having first given public notice of the time and place of such sale, by causing a notice thereof to be published in a public newspaper published in said county, once in each week, for six weeks successively next preceding said day, and by affixing up in three public places in said town where said premises are situated, and where the same were advertised to be sold, on the —— day of ——, 18—, printed copies of said notice. And whereas, at such sale the said premises were struck off to C. D. for the sum of —— dollars, he being the highest bidder therefor, and that being the highest sum bid for the same. And whereas, the said premises, after the expiration of one year from the time of such sale, remained unredeemed by any person entitled to make redemption, within that time, and whereas, the said O. K., a creditor of the said E. F., having, in his own name [*or*, as assignee], a judgment against the said E. F., rendered before the expiration of fifteen months from the time of such sale, and which was a lien and charge upon the premises sold, has, within the time, and in the manner and form prescribed by the statute in such case made and provided, acquired all the right of the said purchaser to said premises; and more than twenty-four hours having elapsed since the last-mentioned redemption, and no other creditor of the said E. F. having redeemed the said premises from the said O. K.

Now, this indenture witnesseth; that the said party of the first part, in pursuance of the statute in such case made and provided, and in consideration of the sum of money so bid, as aforesaid, to him duly paid, has sold, and by these presents, does grant and convey, unto the said party of the second part, all the estate, right, title, and interest which the said defendant had on the —— day of ——, 18—, or at any time afterward, of, in, and to that piece or parcel of land situated in the town of —— aforesaid, and described as follows: [*insert description*].

To have and to hold the said premises unto the said party of the second part, his heirs and assigns, forever, as fully and as absolutely as the party of the first part as sheriff [*or*, late sheriff], as aforesaid, can convey the same, under the statute aforesaid.

In witness whereof, the party of the first part has hereunto set his hand and seal the day and year first above written. J. R. G., Sheriff.

Signed, sealed, and delivered
in presence of
J. W. F.

[*Add acknowledgment or proof, in usual form. See No.* 44.]

No. 579.

COMPLAINT TO REDEEM MORTGAGED PREMISES.

See ante, p. 263.

[*Title in full, substantially as in No.* 165.]

The plaintiff, by A. N. W., his attorney, complaining, shows to the court:

That A. B., who was the plaintiff's father, was, at the date of the execution of the mortgage hereinafter mentioned, and continued to be to the time of his death, seized in fee simple of a certain piece or parcel of land situated, *&c.* [*describing the premises*].

The said A. B., being so seized, on or about the —— day of ——, 18—, executed to the above-named defendant a mortgage upon said premises, for securing the repayment of the sum of —— dollars, with interest, then advanced by the defendant to said A. B.

That, soon after the making of said security, the defendant entered into the possession of said mortgaged premises and into the receipt of the rents and profits thereof, and has ever since continued in such possession and receipt.

That said A. B. departed this life intestate on or about the —— day of ——, 18—, leaving the plaintiff his sole heir-at-law.

That the plaintiff has applied to said defendant, since the death of said A. B., to come to an account of the rents and profits of the said premises so received by him, and to pay over to the plaintiff what he should appear so to have received beyond the amount of the principal and interest due him, and to deliver up the possession of the said mortgaged premises, but the defendant refused and still continues to refuse so to do.

Wherefore, the plaintiff demands that an account may be taken of what, if any thing, is due to the said defendant, for principal and interest on said mortgage, and that an account may also be taken of the rents and profits of the said mortgaged premises which have been possessed or received by said defendant, or by his order, or for his use, or which, without his willful default or neglect, might have been received; and that, if it shall appear that the said rents and profits have been more than sufficient to satisfy the principal and interest of the said mortgage, then that the residue may be paid over to the plaintiff, and that the plaintiff may be permitted to redeem the said premises, he being ready and willing, and hereby offering to pay what, if anything, shall appear to remain due in respect to the principal and interest on the said mortgage; and that the defendant may be adjudged to deliver up the possession of the said mortgaged premises to the plaintiff, or to such person as he shall direct, free from all incumbrances made by him, or by any person claiming under him, and may also deliver over to the plaintiff all deeds and writings in his custody or power, relating to said mortgaged premises, or for such further or other relief as to the court shall seem just.

A. N. W., Att'y for Plaintiff.

[*Add verification, if desired, as in No.* 169.]

CHAPTER XXIX.

FORMS ON SALE OF THE REAL ESTATE OF RELIGIOUS CORPORATIONS.

No. 580.

PETITION FOR SALE.

See ante, p. 277.

To the Supreme Court of the State of New York [*or*, To the County Court of the County of ——, *or other court*] :

The petition of The First Presbyterian Congregation of ——, adhering to the Associate Reformed Synod, respectfully represents :

That they are a religious association, duly incorporated under the act entitled "An act to provide for the incorporation of Religious Societies," passed April 5, 1813; that as such incorporated association, they are the owners of the following described piece or parcel of land, situated in the town of ——, in the county of ——, viz.: All, *&c.* [*describe the real estate*].

The said petitioners further show, that they are desirous of disposing of the said real estate; and that A. B., of ——, in said county, has agreed to pay for the same, upon receiving title thereto, the sum of —— dollars, which sum is the fair market value of said real estate, as your petitioners verily believe.

That the following are the reasons why your petitioners wish to sell the said real estate, viz.: [*state the reasons why a sale is desired*].

Your petitioners further show, that they are indebted to various individuals, residing in said county, to an amount in the aggregate equal to, or exceeding, the whole price or consideration which they expect to receive for said real estate, as aforesaid; and that they have no property with which to pay the said indebtedness, except the said real estate. That your petitioners are desirous that the avails of said real estate, when received by them, should be applied in payment and discharge of said indebtedness.

[*If the application is made to the Supreme Court in the city of New York, add, also, a clause to the following effect :*] Your petitioners further show that no real estate, or interest in real estate, belonging to said corporation, has been sold under any order of the court, at any time within five years last past [*or*, that within five years last passed the following real estate owned by said corporation has been sold by the corporation under an order of the —— court, viz.: [*brief description of the real estate*]. That the object for which the said sale was ordered, was to enable the said corporation to obtain moneys to pay off an indebtedness existing against it, amounting to —— dollars [*or other object, stating it*], and that the following is the disposition actually made of the proceeds of said sale, viz.: One thousand dollars thereof was paid to S. T., in payment and satisfaction of a claim which he had against the said corporation for moneys lent to it [*or as the case may be, giving a statement showing the disposition actually made of the proceeds*].

Your petitioners therefore pray that an order may be entered, authorizing them to sell the real estate aforesaid, upon the terms aforesaid; and that the proceeds of such sale may be applied as above specified.

[*Signatures of majority of Trustees.*]

County of ——, ss.:

J. H. C., T. S. S., E. M., and J. G. G., being duly sworn, each for himself, deposes and says: He resides in ——, in said county, and is one of the trustees of the [*name of corporation*]. That the persons whose names are subscribed to the above petition compose a majority of said trustees. That he has read [*or*, heard read] the said petition, subscribed by him, and knows the contents thereof, and that the same is true to his own knowledge, except as to the matters therein stated on information or belief, and as to those matters he believes it to be true.

[And the said deponents, each for himself, further says: That at a meeting of the qualified members of said association, held at their meeting-house in ——, in said county, on the —— day of —— last, the trustees aforesaid were duly authorized by a majority of said members to make this application for the sale aforesaid, upon the terms aforesaid, and that the proceeds of said sale be applied as stated in said petition.] (*a*)

Sworn, *&c.* [*Signatures.*]

No. 581.

ORDER DIRECTING SALE, AND APPLICATION OF PROCEEDS.

See ante, p. 278.

At a special term, *&c.* [*as in No.* 6].

In the matter of the petition of The First Presbyterian Congregation of ——, adhering to the Associate Reformed Synod.

On reading and filing the petition of the above-named congregation, dated the —— day of ——, 18—, praying for leave to sell the real estate described in said petition, and for the direction of the court in respect to the application of the proceeds thereof; and the affidavit of J. H. C., T. S. S., E. M., and J. G. G., four of the trustees of said congregation, and composing a majority of said trustees, verifying said petition, *&c.*, and on motion of L. P. C., at-

(*a*) There is a conflict of authority in respect to the question of the necessity of stating the facts alleged in this clause. See *ante*, p. 276, and note.

torney for the petitioners, it is ordered, that the said trustees be, and they are hereby, authorized to sell the said real estate at and for the consideration named in said petition, to wit, for the sum of —— dollars; which said real estate is described in said petition as follows: [*describe the real estate*].

And it is hereby further ordered, that the proceeds of said sale, after paying the expenses of this application, be applied by said trustees as follows: [*state the manner in which the proceeds shall be applied*].

CHAPTER XXX.

FORMS IN SUMMARY PROCEEDINGS TO REMOVE TENANTS.

No. 583.

NOTICE TO PAY RENT OR TO SURRENDER POSSESSION.

See ante, p. 288.

To C. D.:

SIR,—You will take notice, that you are indebted to me in the sum of —— dollars, for rent of the house and premises, No. ——, in —— Street, in the village [*or*, city] of ——, now occupied by you; and that I require the payment of said rent, on or before the —— day of —— instant [*three days' notice*], or the possession of said premises. Yours, &c.,

Dated, *&c.* A. B., Landlord.

[*For form of affidavit of service of the above notice, see post, No.* 585, *with necessary alterations.*]

No. 584.

NOTICE TO QUIT THE PREMISES.

See ante, p. 290.

To C. D.:

SIR,—You will take notice, that you are required to surrender and deliver up possession of the house and premises, No. ——, in —— Street, in the village [*or*, city] of ——, which you now hold of me; and to remove therefrom, on or before the —— day of —— next [*one month's notice*], pursuant to the statute relating to the rights and duties of landlord and tenant.

Dated, *&c.* Yours, &c.,

A. B., Landlord.

No. 585.

AFFIDAVIT OF SERVICE OF NOTICE.

See ante, p. 290

State of New York, }
County of ——, } ss.

H. S., of ——, in said county, being duly sworn, says: That on the —— day of ——, 18—, he served upon C. D., of ——, in said county, a notice, of which the notice annexed is a copy, by delivering such notice to, and leaving the same with, the said C. D., at ——, in said county [*or*, by delivering such notice to, and leaving the same with, R. D., the wife of C. D. (*or*, with W. D., the son of said C. D., aged twenty years), residing on the premises mentioned in said notice]. Dated, *&c.* H. S.

Sworn, *&c.*

No. 586.

AFFIDAVIT OF DEMAND OF POSSESSION—HOLDING OVER AFTER SALE ON EXECUTION.

See ante, p. 290.

State of New York, }
County of ——, } ss.

H. S., being duly sworn, says: That he is acquainted with C. D., residing at No. ——, in the village [*or*, city] of ——. That A. B., of, *&c.*, on the —— day of —— instant, at the residence of said C. D., demanded the possession of the house and premises so occupied by said C. D., as aforesaid, and that the said C. D. refused to surrender the possession of the same.

Sworn, *&c.* H. S.

No. 587.

AFFIDAVIT OF LANDLORD TO REMOVE TENANT—EXPIRATION OF TERM.

See ante, p. 292.

A. B.
against
C. D.

County of ——, ss.: A. B., of ——, in said county, being duly sworn, says: That on the —— day of ——, 18—, he let and rented unto C. D., of ——, in said county, the house and premises situated in the —— of ——, in said county, and described as follows: [*describe the premises definitely*]; which said premises were so let and rented to the said C. D. for the term of one year from the —— day of —— then next, and that the said term has expired.

And deponent further says, that the said C. D. [*or*, that E. F., the assignee, *or*, under-tenant, of the said C. D.] holds over and continues in the possession of the said premises, without the permission of this deponent, his landlord.

Sworn, *&c.* A. B.

No. 588.

LIKE AFFIDAVIT IN CASE OF TENANCY AT WILL.

See ante, p. 292.

[*Title as in last form.*]

County of ——, ss.: A. B., of ——, in said county, being duly sworn, says That on or about the —— day of —— last, he let and rented unto C. D., of the same place, during the will and pleasure of deponent, the house and premises situated in the —— of ——, in said county, and described as follows: [*describe the premises definitely*].

And deponent further says: That the said C. D. has held and occupied the said building and premises, as the tenant at will of this deponent, from the —— day of —— aforesaid, until the expiration of such tenancy as hereinafter mentioned.

And deponent further says: That he caused a notice in writing to be served upon the said C. D., in due form of law, on the —— day of ——, 18—, requiring the said C. D. to remove from the said premises on or before the —— day of ——, 18—. That the time within which the said C. D. was so required to remove has expired; and that the said C. D. holds over and continues in possession of the said premises, after the expiration of such time, without permission of this deponent, his landlord.

Sworn, *&c.* A. B.

No. 589.

LIKE AFFIDAVIT, IN CASE OF NON-PAYMENT OF RENT.

See ante, p. 292.

[*Title as in No.* 587.]

County of ——, ss.: A. B., of ——, in said county, being duly sworn, says: That on the —— day of — , 18—, he let and rented unto C. D., of the same place, for the term of two years, from the —— day of —— last, at an annual rent of —— dollars, payable quarterly, the house and premises situated in the —— of ——, in said county, and described as follows: [*describe the premises definitely*]. That the said C. D. is now justly indebted to deponent in the sum of —— dollars, and interest thereon from the —— day of —— last, for the rent of said premises, pursuant to the agreement under which said premises are held, as aforesaid, to wit, for the quarter's rent due by the terms of said agreement, on the —— day of —— last.

And deponent further says: That he caused a notice, in writing, to be served upon the said C. D., in due form of law, on the —— day of ——, 18—, requiring payment of said rent, so due, as aforesaid, on or before the —— day of —— last, or the possession of said premises; but which rent has not been paid, nor any part thereof.

And deponent further says, That the said C. D. holds over and continues in possession of the said premises, after default in the payment of such rent, as aforesaid, and without the permission of this deponent, his landlord.

Sworn to, *&c.* A. B.

No. 590.

AFFIDAVIT BY AGENT OF LANDLORD.

See ante, pp. 292, 294.

[*Title as in No.* 587.]

County of ——, ss.: G. H., being duly sworn, says: He is the agent of A. B., hereinafter mentioned, and is authorized to institute proceedings for the removal of C. D. from the premises hereinafter described. That, *&c.* [*proceed substantially as in the previous forms*].

No. 591.

SUMMONS TO REMOVE OR SHOW CAUSE.

[A copy of section three of Ch. 828, of the laws of 1868, is required to be written or printed upon the outside of every copy of the summons left in the absence of the tenant with a person of mature age residing on the premises.—*Laws of* 1868, *p.* 1930, § 3, *post. p.* 756.]

See ante, p. 295.

To C. D., of ——, in the county of ——, and any other person in the possession or claiming the possession of the premises hereinafter described:

Whereas, A. B., of ——, in said county, has made oath in writing, and presented the same to me, that, *&c.* [*recite the facts contained in the affidavits presented*].

Therefore, you are hereby required forthwith to remove from the said premises, or to show cause before me, at my office, in the —— of ——, in said county, on the —— day of ——, 18—, at —— o'clock —. M., why possession of said premises should not be delivered to the landlord.

Witness my hand, this —— day of ——, 18—,

A. D. W., County Judge

[*or*, W. B. B., Justice of the Peace].

No. 592.

AFFIDAVIT OF SERVICE OF SUMMONS.

See ante, p. 296.

County of——, ss.: H. S., of——, in said county, being duly sworn, says: That on the——day of——, 18—, at——o'clock — M., he served personally upon C. D., within mentioned, at, &c., [*state the exact place of service,*] the within summons, by delivering a true copy thereof to him, and at the same time showing him the said original summons. [*Or*, That on the——day of ——, 18—, at——o'clock — M., he served upon C. D., within mentioned, the within summons, by leaving a copy thereof at the place of residence of said C. D., in the city, [*or*, town,] where the demised premises within mentioned are situated, with R. D., the wife of said C. D., [*or*, with M. D., the daughter of said C. D., aged — years,] there residing; and that at the time of leaving such copy, the said C. D. was absent from his place of residence aforesaid. *Or*, That on the —— day of ——, at —— o'clock,— M., he served upon C. D., within mentioned, the within summons, by leaving a copy thereof at the demised premises within mentioned, with O. F., a person of mature age, there residing; and that at the time of leaving such copy, the said C. D. was absent from his place of residence in the city, [*or*, town,] of, &c., and no person of mature age residing at such place of residence could be found there. [*Or otherwise as the manner of service may have been, as authorized by sub.* 3 *of* §. 32, *ante p.* 296, *and note.*]

No. 593.

WARRANT TO PUT LANDLORD IN POSSESSION, ON DEFAULT OF TENANT.

See ante, p. 297.

The People of the State of New York, to the Sheriff of the County of —— [*or*, to any one of the Constables of the Town of —— ; *or*, Marshals of the City of ——, in the County of ——], greeting:

Whereas, A. B., of ——, in said county, has made oath, in writing, and presented the same to me, that, *&c.* [*recite the facts contained in the landlord's affidavits in full*].

Whereupon I issued a summons, requiring the said C. D., and any other person in the possession, or claiming the possession of the premises above described, forthwith to remove from the said premises, or show cause before me at my office, in ——, on the —— day of —— instant, at —— o'clock —. M., why the possession of the said premises should not be delivered to the landlord; and no sufficient cause having been shown to the contrary, and I being satisfied, by due proof, of the service of said summons, do therefore command you to remove all persons from the said premises, and to put the landlord, the said A. B., into the full possession thereof.

Witness my hand, this —— day of ——, A. D. 18—,

A. D. W., County Judge.

[*or*, W. B. B., Justice of the Peace].

No. 594.

AFFIDAVIT OF TENANT DENYING LANDLORD'S ALLEGATIONS.

See ante, p. 297.

[*Title as in No.* 587.]

County of ——, ss.: C. D., of ——, in said county, being duly sworn, says: He is the defendant above named. That, *&c.* [*deny specifically the facts intended to be controverted*].

Sworn, *&c.* C. D.

No. 595.

VENIRE, OR PRECEPT FOR JURY.

See ante, pp. 299, 300.

The People of the State of New York to the Sheriff, *&c.* [*direction as in No.* 593].

Whereas, A. B., of, *&c.*, has made oath in writing, and presented the same to me, stating that, *&c.* [*recite briefly the facts stated by the landlord*]; whereupon I issued a summons requiring the said C. D., and others in possession or claiming possession of said premises, forthwith to remove therefrom, or show cause before me, at a time now past, why possession of the premises should not be delivered to the said A. B., the landlord.

And, whereas, the said C. D. has, by his affidavit, filed with me, denied the facts, or some of them, upon which the said summons was issued.

And, whereas, a jury having been demanded to try the issue so joined, I have nominated twelve reputable persons, competent to serve as jurors in courts of record, to form a jury for that purpose, whose names are as follows: [*insert names of jurors*].

You are therefore hereby commanded to summon the persons so nominated by me, to appear before me, at my office, in the —— of ——, in said county, on the —— day of ——, 18—, at —— o'clock, —. M., for the purpose of trying the said matters in difference.

Witness my hand, this —— day of ——, A. D., 18—,

A. D. W., County Judge
[*or*, W. B. B., Justice of the Peace].

No. 596.

WARRANT TO PUT LANDLORD IN POSSESSION AFTER TRIAL.

See ante, p. 302.

The People of the State of New York to the Sheriff [*or*, to any Constable] of the County of ——, greeting:

Whereas, A. B., of ——, in said county, made oath, in writing, and presented the same to me, stating that, *&c.* [*recite the facts stated by landlord*];

whereupon I issued a summons, requiring the said C. D., and others in possession or claiming possession of said premises, forthwith to remove therefrom, or show cause before me, at a time now past, why possession of the premises should not be delivered to the said A. B., the landlord.

And, whereas, the said C. D., by his affidavit, filed with me, denied the facts, or some of them, upon which the said summons was issued; and thereupon the issue so joined was tried before me; and after hearing the evidence of the parties, I rendered a verdict in favor of said A. B. [*or*, before a jury duly nominated by me, and summoned for that purpose, who, after hearing the evidence of the parties, rendered a verdict in favor of said A. B., to wit, that the possession of the said premises should be delivered to said A. B.]; whereupon judgment was rendered by me in favor of the said A. B., against the said C. D., in pursuance of such decision [*or*, verdict], that the possession of said premises be delivered to the said A. B

Now, therefore, you are hereby commanded to put the said A. B. into the full possession of the premises aforesaid.

Witness, *&c.* [*as in No.* 595].

OFFICER'S RETURN TO WARRANT.

In pursuance of the within command, I have this day put the landlord into the full possession of the premises within described.

Dated, *&c.* H. R. C., Sheriff [*or*, Constable].

No. 597.

SECURITY TO PAY RENT IN TEN DAYS.

See ante, p. 303.

In consideration of one dollar, to us in hand paid, we do hereby jointly and severally engage to pay to A. B., of ——, in the county of ——, the sum of —— dollars, in ten days from this date, for the rent due him for the occupation of, *&c.* [*describe the demised premises*]. And, also, for the like consideration, we jointly and severally agree to pay to the said A. B., in ten days from this date, the costs and charges of certain proceedings commenced to remove C. D., of, *&c.*, from the said premises, under the provisions of the statute authorizing summary proceedings to recover the possession of land in certain cases.

Dated, *&c.* [*Signatures of Sureties.*]

No. 598.

SECURITY TO PAY RENT, THE TENANT HAVING TAKEN THE BENEFIT OF THE INSOLVENT ACT.

See ante, p. 303.

Whereas, A. B. has commenced proceedings to remove C. D., of, *&c.*, from the building and premises occupied by said C. D., in ——, in said county, under the statute relating to summary proceedings to recover possession of land, on the ground that the said C. D. has taken the benefit of an insolvent act [*or*, been discharged under the statute for the relief of his person from imprisonment]. And whereas, the said C. D. desires a stay of the said proceedings, so commenced, as aforesaid.

Now, therefore, the undersigned, in consideration thereof, and of one dollar to us in hand paid, do hereby agree to pay to the said A. B. the rent of said premises, as the same shall become due, according to the agreement under which the said premises are held.

Dated, *&c.* [*Signatures of Sureties.*]

No. 599.

AFFIDAVIT OF TITLE IN TENANT SUBSEQUENTLY ACQUIRED, ETC.

See ante, p. 304.

[*Title as in No.* 587.]

County of ——, ss.: C. D., of ——, in said county, being duly sworn, says: He is the defendant above named. That he claims the possession of the premises described in the affidavit of A. B., the plaintiff, dated the —— day of ——, 18—, by virtue of a right or title acquired to the same after the sale of said premises as mentioned in the affidavit of said plaintiff, that is to say [*set forth particulars*]; [*or*, that he claims the possession of said premises as the guardian of R. S., a minor, under the age of twenty-one years; *or*, as the trustee for C. B., of ——, in said county]. C. D.

Sworn, *&c.*

No. 600.

BOND TO STAY THE PROCEEDINGS,—SALE OF PREMISES ON EXECUTION.

See ante, p. 304.

Know all men by these presents: That we, C. D., of ——, in the county of ——, and J. M., farmer, and M. M., merchant, of the same place, are held and firmly bound unto A. B., of ——, in said county, in the sum of —— dollars, to be paid to the said A. B., his executors, administrators, or assigns;

for which payment well and truly to be made, we bind ourselves, our heirs, executors, and administrators, firmly by these presents. Sealed with our seals, and dated the —— day of ——, 18—.

Whereas, the above-named A. B. has instituted proceedings under the provisions of the statute authorizing summary proceedings to recover the possession of land in certain cases, for the purpose of obtaining possession of the building and premises situated, *&c.* [*describe premises*]; and which proceedings are founded upon an alleged sale by execution of said premises. And whereas, the said C. D. has made affidavit that he claims the possession of the said premises by virtue of a right or title acquired to the same subsequent to such alleged sale [*or*, as the guardian of R. S., a minor under the age of twenty-one years; *or*, as the trustee for C. B., of——, in said county].

Now, therefore, the condition of this obligation is such, that if the above-bounden C. D. shall pay the costs which may be recovered against him in any action that may be brought by the said A. B., within six months, for the recovery of the possession of such premises; and shall pay the value of the use and occupation of such premises, from the date hereof to the time the said A. B. shall obtain possession of the same by virtue of a recovery in such action; and shall not, during his occupation of said premises, commit any waste or injury to the said premises, then the above obligation to be void, otherwise to remain in full force and virtue.

Signed, sealed, and delivered C. D. [SEAL.]
in presence of J. M. [SEAL.]
W. B. B. M. M. [SEAL.]

No. 601.

NOTICE OF APPEAL FROM JUSTICE'S COURT TO COUNTY COURT.

See ante, pp. 305 to 308.

IN JUSTICE'S COURT.

A. B., Respondent,
against
C. D., Appellant.
} Summary Proceedings.

To A. B., above named, and to W. B. B., Esq., Justice of the Peace:

Take notice, that the above-named C. D. appeals to the county court of the county of ——, from the judgment rendered on the —— day of ——, 18—, before W. B. B., Esq., in favor of the said A. B., against the said C. D., under the provisions of the statute authorizing summary proceedings to recover the possession of land in certain cases; and in which judgment costs were included, amounting to —— dollars.

Also take notice, that the grounds upon which the said appeal is founded are as follows: [*state all the grounds of the appeal particularly*].

Dated, *&c.* C. D., Appellant.

No. 602.

UNDERTAKING ON APPEAL, AND TO PAY RENT.

See ante, p. 307.

[*Title as in last form.*]

The above-named C. D., having appealed to the county court of the county of ——, from the judgment rendered against him on the —— day of ——, before W. B. B., Esq., in favor of the said A. B., under the provisions of the statute authorizing summary proceedings to recover the possession of land in certain cases, and in which judgment costs were included, amounting to —— dollars.

Now, therefore, in order to stay the execution of the said judgment, and in consideration thereof, we, J. M. and M. M., do undertake and promise to and with the said A. B., that if judgment be rendered against the said C. D., on the said appeal, and execution thereon be returned unsatisfied, in whole or in part, we will pay the amount unsatisfied.

[*If the appeal is by the tenant, then continue:*]

And we do further undertake and promise, to and with the said A. B., that the said C. D. shall pay all rent accruing, or to accrue, upon the premises, the possession of which is sought to be recovered by the said A. B., in the proceeding before the justice aforesaid, subsequent to the application to said justice, and that in default thereof we will pay the same.

In witness whereof, we have hereunto set our hands and seals this —— day of ——, A. D. 18—.

J. M. [SEAL.]
M. M. [SEAL.]

I approve of the above undertaking, and the sureties therein mentioned.

Dated, *&c.* J. P., County Judge
[*or*, A. B., Justice Sup. Court].

No. 603

CERTIORARI.

See ante, p. 308.

[SEAL.] The People of the State of New York, to J. P., Esq., County Judge of the County of —— [*or*, W. B. B., Justice of the Peace of the Town of ——, in the County of ——], greeting:

Whereas, we have been informed by the complaint of C. D., of, *&c.*, that certain proceedings were had before you on behalf of A. B., against the said C. D., under the statute relating to summary proceedings to recover the possession of land in certain cases, whereby [*state the order or proceeding complained of*]; and we being willing, for certain reasons, to be certified of such proceedings, if any such were had before you, do command and strictly enjoin you, that you do certify and return those proceedings, with all things appertaining thereto, unto our justices of our Supreme Court of Judicature, at the Court House in ——, on the —— day of —— next, under your hand, as fully and amply as the same remain before you, so that our said justices may further cause to be done thereupon what of right and according to law ought to be done; and have you then there this writ.

Witness, A. B., Justice of the Supreme Court, at ——, the —— day of ——, A. D. 18—.

O. F. D., Attorney. N. B. M., Clerk.

Indorsed:] "By the Court."

N. B. M., Clerk.

No. 604.

RETURN TO WRIT OF CERTIORARI.

See ante, p. 308.

[*Follow the form given in No.* 97, *altering it to conform to a return in summary proceedings.*]

No. 605.

JUDGMENT RECORD ON CERTIORARI.

See ante, p. 308.

[*For form of Judgment Record, see ante, No.* 100.]

No. 606.

WRIT OF RESTITUTION.

See ante, p. 311.

The People of the State of New York, to the Sheriff of the County of ——, greeting:

Whereas, C. D., of ——, in said county, by certain proceedings had before [*name of officer*], under the provisions of article second, title ten, of chapter eight, of part third of the Revised Statutes, entitled, "Summary proceedings to recover the possession of land in certain cases," was removed from the possession of, &c. [*describe premises*]; and which proceedings we caused to be removed into our Supreme Court of judicature, by our writ of certiorari; and whereupon it was considered in our said court, before our said justices, that the said C. D. should be restored to the possession of the said premises whereof the said C. D. is evicted, as appears to us of record.

Now, therefore, we command you forthwith to restore the said C. D. to the full possession of the aforesaid described premises; and how and in what manner you shall have executed this our writ, make appear to our Supreme Court, at, &c., on, &c., and have then and there this writ.

Witness, &c. [*as in No.* 603].

INDEX.

[The lines in italic correspond with the italic headings in the body of the work.]

INDEX TO FORMS.

Made in the USA
San Bernardino, CA
03 March 2020

65249685R20482